£19.95

D1356300

Taylor/Gottschalk

# A GERMAN-ENGLISH DICTIONARY OF IDIOMS

RONALD TAYLOR / WALTER GOTTSCHALK

# A German-English Dictionary
# of Idioms

*Idiomatic and Figurative German Expressions*
*with English Translations*

HUEBER

**4. Auflage** ⁶ ⁵
© 1960 Max Hueber Verlag · München
Umschlaggestaltung: Erich Hölle, Otterfing
Druck: Friedrich Pustet, Regensburg
Printed in Germany
ISBN 3-19-006216-1

1001470697

# VORWORT

Die Erlernung der englischen Sprache mag in ihren Anfangsgründen für den Deutschen verhältnismäßig leicht sein, weil das Deutsche und das Englische, die beide der germanischen Sprachenfamilie angehören, gewisse Übereinstimmungen und Ähnlichkeiten aufzuweisen haben. Ungleich schwieriger aber gestaltet sich auch für ihn das Eindringen in die Feinheiten der englischen Stilistik, Phraseologie und Parömiologie. Hier hat jedes Volk zumeist seine eigene Vorstellung und Betrachtungsweise und demzufolge seine eigene Ausdrucksform. Wer etwa glaubt, das deutsche Sprichwort „Kehre jeder vor seiner Tür" oder „In der Not frißt der Teufel Fliegen" unter Verwendung des gleichen Bildes ins Englische übertragen zu können, befindet sich in einem bedauerlichen Irrtum, dem selbst Wörterbücher und Sammlungen von Redensarten durchaus nicht immer entgangen sind.

Erschöpfend kann keine Sammlung dieser Art sein; die Verfasser haben sich jedoch in mehrjähriger Zusammenarbeit bemüht, aus der kaum übersehbaren Fülle des sprachlichen Materials die wichtigsten deutschen Redensarten, einschließlich Einzelwörter bildhaften und umgangssprachlichen Charakters, mit den englischen Entsprechungen zusammenzutragen. Ihre Anordnung ist nach dem deutschen Hauptstichwort erfolgt, bei gleichen deutschen Stichwörtern wurde die Einreihung nach dem zweitwichtigsten Wort der Redensarten getroffen. – Bei den englischen Entsprechungen ist möglichst nach Fülle und Variiertheit gestrebt worden. Englische Redensarten umgangssprachlichen Charakters werden jeweils als "colloquial" (abgekürzt: colloq.) bzw. "slang" (sl.) bezeichnet; denn es dürfen durch die Verwendung solcher Ausdrücke keine stilistischen Inkongruenzen entstehen. Je familiärer der Ausdruck, desto reicher und sicherer müssen die allgemeinen Sprachkenntnisse sein. Dabei soll nicht übersehen werden, daß bei der Bezeichnung sowie bei der Verwendung dieser und aller anderen Ausdrücke der persönliche Geschmack eine nicht zu unterschätzende Rolle spielen muß.

Da das umfangreiche Buch kein reines Nachschlagewerk sein soll, sondern auch – in Auszügen benutzt – zu praktischen Übungen Anregung geben möchte, wird den deutschen Ausdrücken und Redewendungen mit ihren englischen Entsprechungen stets ein deutscher Übungssatz mit englischer Übertragung beigefügt. Es sei ausdrücklich darauf hingewiesen, daß alle angeführten englischen Übersetzungen einer beliebigen deutschen Redensart auf den jeweiligen Beispielsatz passen. Die inhaltlichen und formellen Eigenschaften eines jeden solchen Satzes müssen daher genau beobachtet werden. Es ist nämlich keineswegs gesagt, daß einem erweiterten Gebrauch des deutschen Ausdrucks ein in demselben Sinne erweiterter englischer Ausdruck entsprechen muß. Ob und in wieweit dies der Fall ist, läßt sich aus keinem Wörterbuch, sondern nur aus der persönlichen Erfahrung feststellen.

April 1960

*Ronald Taylor, M. A.,*
University College of Swansea
Great Britain

*Prof. Dr. Walter Gottschalk*
Leverkusen

## VORWORT ZUR ZWEITEN, VERBESSERTEN AUFLAGE

Die überaus freundliche Aufnahme, die unsere Erstauflage in allen Fachkreisen gefunden hat, macht eine Neuausgabe erforderlich. Die Auswahl der gebotenen englischen Ausdrücke wurde bisweilen erweitert.

*Prof. Dr. Ronald Taylor*
University of Sussex
England

*Prof. Dr. Walter Gottschalk*
Leverkusen

# A

**Wer A sagt, muß auch B sagen** (Sprichwort): *In for a penny, in for a pound (prov.)*

Wenn du eine Aufgabe begonnen hast, mußt du sie auch zu Ende führen. Wer A sagt, muß auch B sagen!
*Once you have started a job, you must finish it. In for a penny, in for a pound.*

**das A und O:** *the Alpha and Omega; the be-all and end-all*

Das A und O seines Lebens ist, möglichst bald reich zu werden.
*The be-all and end-all (The Alpha and Omega) of his life is to get rich as quickly as possible.*

**von A bis Z:** *from A to Z; from beginning to end; from start to finish;* (bei Büchern außerdem) *from cover to cover*

Ich habe den Roman in drei Stunden von A bis Z gelesen.
*I read the novel from beginning to end (from A to Z; from start to finish; from cover to cover) in three hours.*

**glatt wie ein Aal (aalglatt) sein:** *to be as slippery as an eel (a snake)*

Dieser Jurist antwortet nie klar und eindeutig. Er ist glatt wie ein Aal (aalglatt).
*That lawyer never answers clearly and unequivocally. He is as slippery as an eel (a snake).*

**sich winden wie ein Aal:** *to wriggle (to squirm) like an eel (a snake); to twist and turn*

Bei dem Verhör versuchte der Mann, sich aus der heiklen Situation herauszureden. Er wand sich wie ein Aal (Wurm; Er krümmte und wand sich [drehte und wendete sich]), jedoch vergebens.
*At the interrogation the man tried to talk himself out of the awkward situation. He wriggled (squirmed) like an eel (a snake; twisted and turned), but in vain.*

**sich aalen (fam.):** *to take it easy; to bask; to lounge*

Heute habe ich mich ausgeruht und (mich) in der Sonne geaalt.
*I have been resting today and taking it easy (basking; lounging) in the sun.*

**ein freches Aas sein (fam.):** cf. **ein freches Stück sein**

**ein kleines Aas sein (fam.):** *to be a little Tartar; to be a little devil (colloq.)*

Mein Schwesterchen ist wirklich ein kleines Aas (Biest; Luder; ein kleiner Teufel); es ist sehr raffiniert, wenn es etwas erreichen will.
*My little sister is a proper little Tartar (devil); she is very cunning when she wants to get something.*

Wo ein **Aas** ist, da sammeln sich die Geier (Adler) (Sprichw.): *Everybody wants to be in at the kill; Everybody wants his pick*

> Die Firma hat bankrott gemacht, und die Gläubiger warten alle auf ihr Geld. Wo ein Aas ist, da sammeln sich die Geier (Adler).
> *The firm has gone bankrupt and the creditors are all waiting for their money. Everybody wants to be in at the kill (wants his pick).*

mit seinen Kräften **aasen:** *to burn the candle at both ends; to drive o. s. to death; to wear o. s. out*

> Seine Gesundheit ist nicht mehr (so) gut, und ich wünschte, er würde nicht so mit seinen Kräften aasen (Schindluder treiben).
> *His health is no longer (so) strong, and I wish he would not burn the candle at both ends (drive himself to death; wear himself out) like that.*

**ab** und zu (ab und an): *now and then; now and again; on and off (off and on)*

> Ab und zu (Ab und an; Dann und wann) gehe ich ins Theater.
> *I go to the theatre now and then (now and again; on and off; off and on).*

etwas **abbekommen** (fam.): *to catch it (colloq.); to cop it (sl.); to get it in the neck (sl.)*

> Du hast eins der neuen Wassergläser zerbrochen? Da wirst du was abbekommen!
> *You've broken one of the new tumblers? You'll catch (cop) it (get it in the neck).*

etwas **abblasen** (fig. u. fam.): *to call s. th. off; to drop s. th.*

> Wegen der schweren Erkrankung des Präsidenten wurden alle Festlichkeiten in letzter Minute abgeblasen.
> *Because of the President's serious illness all the festivities were called off (were dropped) at the last moment.*

j.en **abblitzen** lassen: *to snub s. o.; to turn a blind eye (a deaf ear) to s. b.; to turn one's back on s. b.; to give s. b. the brush-off (colloq.).* Cf. auch: j.en kalt (kühl) **abrutschen** lassen

> Der Angestellte wollte etwas sagen, aber sein Chef ließ ihn abblitzen.
> *The clerk wanted to say something, but his boss snubbed him (turned a blind eye [a deaf ear] to him; turned his back on him; gave him the brush-off).*

(einer Sache) keinen **Abbruch** tun: *to do no harm to s. th.; not to harm (damage; prejudice) s. th.; not to cause a breach (a rift) in s. th.*

> Dieses Mißgeschick soll unserer Freundschaft keinen Abbruch tun.
> *Do not let this mishap do any harm to (shall not harm [damage; prejudice]; cause a breach [rift] in) our friendship.*

seine Strafe (im Gefängnis) **abbrummen** (fam.): *to serve (to do) one's stretch (one's time) (colloq.)*

Der Dieb hat seine Strafe jetzt abgebrummt und will ein neues Leben anfangen.
*The thief has now served (done) his stretch (time) and wants to start a new life.*

ein **Abc-Schütze** sein: *to be a beginner (a nipper)*

Die Abc-Schützen sind meistens sechs Jahre alt.
*The beginners (nippers) are mostly six years old.*

ein bunter **Abend**: *a variety entertainment; variety*

Heute um 9 Uhr wird im Café ein bunter Abend veranstaltet.
*At nine o'clock tonight a variety entertainment (variety) is being put on at the café.*

ein feuchtfröhlicher **Abend**: *a drinking session; a boozing party (sl.)*

Wie hat dir unser feuchtfröhlicher Abend gestern gefallen?
*How did you like our drinking session (boozing party) yesterday?*

Es ist noch nicht aller Tage **Abend**: cf. Es ist noch nicht aller **Tage** Abend

Wenn das (Wenn und das) **Aber** nicht wär'!: *If there were (had been) no (ifs and) buts*

Wenn das (Wenn und das) Aber nicht wär', hätten wir uns schon längst ein eigenes Haus gebaut.
*If there had been no (ifs and) buts, we should have built our own house long ago.*

j.em eine **Abfuhr** erteilen (fig.): *to snub s. b.; to give s. b. the bird (the brush-off) (colloq.).* Cf. auch: j.en **abblitzen** lassen

Ich hatte schon von seinem unehrlichen Benehmen gehört und habe ihm daher eine Abfuhr erteilt.
*I had already heard of his dishonest behaviour, and therefore snubbed him (gave him the bird [brush-off]).*

völlig **abgebrannt** sein (fig.): *to be right out of cash (out of funds); to be stony broke (colloq.); not to have a bean (a sou) (colloq.).* Cf. auch: knapp bei **Kasse** sein

Ich habe gerade ein neues Auto gekauft und bin jetzt völlig abgebrannt (blank).
*I have just bought a new car and am now right out of cash (funds; am now stony broke; haven't a bean [sou] now).*

**abgebrüht** sein (fig.): *to be impervious; to be hardened; to be hard-boiled (colloq.).* Cf. auch: **dickfellig** sein

Dieser Junge ist durch nichts zu erschüttern. Er ist völlig abgebrüht.
*This boy is not to be shaken by anything. He is completely impervious (hardened; hard-boiled).*

eine **abgedroschene** Redensart: *a cliché; a worn-out (stale; hackneyed) expression*

Unser Lehrer forderte uns auf, in unsern Aufsätzen abgedroschene (abgeklapperte) Redensarten zu vermeiden.
*Our master told us to avoid clichés (worn-out [stale; hackneyed] expressions) in our essays.*

**abgefeimt** sein: cf. **durchtrieben** sein

ein **abgehackter** Stil: *a halting (disjointed; jerky) style*

Der abgehackte Stil dieses Romans macht keinen guten Eindruck.
*The halting (disjointed; jerky) style of this novel does not leave a good impression.*

**abgekämpft** sein (fig.): cf. **absein**

eine **abgekartete** Sache: cf. ein abgekartetes **Spiel** sein

eine **abgeklapperte** Redensart: cf. eine **abgedroschene** Redensart

nicht **abgemalt** sein mögen (fig.): *not to want to be seen dead (colloq.)*

In einem solchen minderwertigen Milieu möchte ich nicht abgemalt sein.
*I wouldn't be seen dead in such low-class company.*

**abgerissen** sein (fig.): *to be in (rags and) tatters; to be down at heel*

Sein Sohn muß in den letzten Jahren sehr heruntergekommen sein, denn er kehrte unlängst ganz abgerissen nach Hause zurück.
*His son must have come down in the world a lot in recent years, for he returned home recently in (rags and) tatters (completely down at heel).*

**abgestumpft** (fig.): *blunted; dull; deadened*

Leider ist mit den Jahren seine Intelligenz abgestumpft, so daß man jetzt von seiner Gesellschaft nicht mehr viel hat.
*Unfortunately his intelligence has become blunted (dull; deadened) with the years, so that now one does not get very much out of his company.*

an j.em **abgleiten** (fig.): *to slide off s. b.; It is like water off a duck's back; to roll off s. b.; to leave s. b. cold.* Cf. auch: an j.em kalt *(*kühl*)* **abrutschen;** j.en **kaltlassen**

Vorwürfe und Ermahnungen beeindrucken deinen Bruder nicht. An ihm gleitet alles ab.
*Reproaches and warnings do not impress your brother. They slide off him (leave him cold; It is like water off a duck's back; Everything rolls off him).*

j.es **Abgott** sein (j.en **abgöttisch** lieben): *to be s. b.'s idol; to idolise s. b.; to be the apple of s. b.'s eye*

Seine einzige Enkeltochter ist Großvaters Abgott (Großvater liebt seine einzige Enkeltochter abgöttisch).
*Grandfather's only granddaughter is his idol (is the apple of his eye; Grandfather idolises his only granddaughter).*

etwas **abgrasen** (fig.): *to work s. th. out; to work s. th. dry; to clean s. th. out (colloq.).* Cf. auch: etwas **beackern**

Das Thema, das Sie behandeln wollen, ist schon vor Jahren von einem anderen abgegrast worden.
*The subject that you want to deal with was worked out (worked dry; cleaned out) by someone else years ago.*

**abhauen** (fig. u. fam.): *to get moving (colloq.); to make o. s. scarce (colloq.); to shove (to push) off (colloq.); to beat (to hop) it (sl.); to scram (sl.).* Cf. auch: **Fersengeld** geben; Ab durch die **Mitte**!

Ich will dich in meinem Hause nicht mehr sehen. Jetzt hau ab! (Verdufte!)
*I don't want to see you in my house again. Now get moving (make yourself scarce; shove [push] off; beat [hop] it; scram)!*

j.en **abkanzeln**: *to haul s. b. over the coals (colloq.); to tick s. b. off (colloq.); to come down on s. b. (like a ton [a sack] of coals) (colloq.); to give s. b. a ticking-off (a talking-to; a wigging; a dressing-down (colloq.); to tear s. b. off a strip (sl.); to blow s. b. up (sl.); to give s. b. a rocket (sl.).* Cf. auch: j.em eine **Standpauke** halten; j.en **anschnauzen**

Als einer meiner Kameraden in der Klasse Unfug gemacht hatte, hat ihn der Lehrer (schwer) abgekanzelt (abkapitelt; heruntergeputzt; Mores gelehrt; zurechtgestaucht; zurechtgestutzt; hat der Lehrer hochdeutsch mit ihm geredet; ihm heimgeleuchtet; den Kopf gewaschen; den Kopf zurechtgesetzt; den Kümmel gerieben; eine Lektion erteilt; die Leviten gelesen; den Marsch geblasen; die Meinung gesagt; einen Rüffel erteilt; den Schwein[e]hund geblasen; ist ihm der Lehrer auf den Kopf gekommen; aufs Dach gestiegen).
*When one of my companions misbehaved himself in class, the teacher hauled him properly over the coals (ticked him off properly; came down heavily on him; came down on him like a ton [sack] of coals; gave him a proper ticking-off [talking-to; wigging; dressing-down]; really tore him off a strip; blew him up; gave him a proper rocket).*

j.en **abkapiteln**: cf. j.en **abkanzeln**

sich **abkapseln** (fig.): *to cut (to shut) o. s. off*

Dieser alte Gelehrte hat sich von der Außenwelt ganz abgekapselt und lebt jetzt allein.
*This old scholar has cut (shut) himself off completely from the outside world and now lives by himself.*

etwas **abklappern** (fam.): *to rake (to comb) s. th. (colloq.); to knock s. th. up (colloq.)*

Bei unserer Sammlung haben wir sämtliche Häuser in der Gegend abgeklappert.
*We raked (combed; knocked up) all the houses in the district for our collection.*

nur ein **Abklatsch** sein (fig.): *to be only a re-hash*

Originelle Schöpfungskraft wird man in diesem Theaterstück vergebens suchen. Es ist nur ein Abklatsch alter Ideen.

*One will search in vain in this play for original creative power. It is only a re-hash of old ideas.*

sich etwas **abknapsen** (fam.): *to squeeze s. th. out of s. th. (colloq.)*

Mutter hat sich dieses Geschenk am Haushaltsgeld abgeknapst (abgeknausert; abgezwackt).
*Mother squeezed this present out of the housekeeping money.*

sich etwas **abknausern** (fam.): cf. sich etwas **abknapsen**

j.em etwas **abknöpfen** (fam.): *to get (to wangle; to wheedle; to squeeze; to coax) s. th. out of s. b. (colloq.)*

Dieser Hausierer versucht, für seine schlechte Ware den Leuten viel Geld abzuknöpfen (abzuluchsen; abzuschwatzen; aus der Nase zu ziehen).
*This canvasser tries to get (wangle; wheedle; squeeze; coax) a lot of money out of people for his rotten goods.*

**abkratzen** (fig. u. fam.): cf. um die **Ecke** gehen

**Ablenkungsmanöver** betreiben: *to draw a red herring across the trail (track); to put people off the scent; to put up a smoke-screen*

Obwohl der Dieb schuldig war, versuchte er zuerst, Ablenkungsmanöver zu betreiben.
*Although the thief was guilty, he first tried to draw a red herring across the trail (the track; to put people off the scent; to put up a smoke-screen).*

j.em etwas **abluchsen** (fam.): cf. j.em etwas **abknöpfen**

j.en **abmurksen** (fam.): cf. j.en um die **Ecke** bringen

sich **abrackern** (fam.): a) cf. arbeiten wie ein **Pferd**; sich **totarbeiten**; b) *to wear o. s. out; to fag o. s. out (sl.)*

b) Wilhelm hatte vier Stunden lang Tennis gespielt und kam ganz abgerackert (flügellahm; kaputt; wie gerädert) nach Hause.
*b) William had been playing tennis for four hours and came home completely worn (fagged) out.*

sich wie in **Abrahams** Schoß fühlen: *to feel as though one is (were) in Abraham's bosom; to feel that one is in a safe haven*

Nach seinen langen Reisen kehrte der Forscher in seine Heimatstadt zurück und fühlte sich wieder wie in Abrahams Schoß.
*After his long travels the explorer returned to his home town and felt as though he was (were) in Abraham's bosom (that he was in a safe haven) again.*

eine **Abreibung** kriegen (fig. u. fam.): *to get a dressing-down (a ticking-off; a telling-off; a talking-to; a wigging) (colloq.); to get ticked off (blown up) (colloq.); to get a rocket (sl.).* Cf. auch: j.en **abkanzeln**

Walter kriegte von seinen Eltern eine ordentliche Abreibung (einen ordentlichen Anpfiff [Anschnauzer]; sein Fett; eine Zigarre; eins aufs Dach [auf den
Kopf; auf den Deckel]), weil er seine neue Geldbörse verloren hatte.
*Walter got a proper dressing-down (ticking-off; telling-off; talking-to; wigging; rocket)
from (got properly ticked off [blown up] by) his parents for losing his new purse.*

an j.em kalt (kühl) **abrutschen** (fig. u. fam.): cf. j.en **kaltlassen**

j.en kalt (kühl) **abrutschen** lassen (fig. u. fam.): *to cut s. b. (dead); to cold-
shoulder s. b.; to give s. b. the cold shoulder; to send s. b. to Coventry; to give s. b. a
wide berth; to give s. b. the bird (colloq.).* Cf. auch: j.en **abblitzen** lassen

Wegen seines unehrlichen Benehmens ließen wir Karl einfach kalt (kühl) abrutschen (links liegen; zeigten wir Karl die kalte Schulter; haben wir Karl
einfach geschnitten).
*Because of his dishonest behaviour we simply cut Charles ([dead]; cold-shouldered Charles;
gave Charles the cold shoulder [a wide berth; the bird]; sent Charles to Coventry).*

**absacken** (fam.): cf. es geht mit j.em **bergab**

j.en **absägen** (fig.): cf. j.en in die **Wüste** schicken

**abschalten** (fig.): cf. eine **Kunstpause** machen

der **Abschaum** der Menschheit: *the scum of the earth; the dregs of humanity*

In diesem Bierkeller trifft sich der Abschaum der Menschheit (die Hefe des
Volkes).
*The scum of the earth (dregs of humanity) meet in this beer-cellar.*

sich **abschinden**: cf. arbeiten wie ein **Pferd**; sich **totarbeiten**

**abschrammen** (fam.): cf. um die **Ecke** gehen

sich **abschuften** (fam.): cf. arbeiten wie ein **Pferd**; sich **totarbeiten**

**absein** (fam.): *to be worn out; to be all in (colloq.); to be dead beat (colloq.); to
be knocked up (done for) (colloq.); to be whacked (colloq.); to be fagged out (sl.).*
Cf. auch: **hundemüde** sein; sich **abrackern** b)

Du mußt manchmal eine Pause machen. Man sieht es dir an, daß du vollkommen
ab (erledigt; erschlagen; erschossen; wie eine Zitrone ausgepreßt) bist (auf dem
Zahnfleisch gehst).
*You must have a rest sometimes. One can see that you are worn (fagged) out (all in;
dead beat; knocked up; done for; completely whacked).*

j.en mit leeren Worten **abspeisen**: *to give s. b. more praise than pudding; to
fob s. b. off with mere words of praise*

Ich war sehr enttäuscht, denn trotz meiner vielen Jahre in seinem Dienst hat
er mich mit leeren Worten abgespeist.

*I was very disappointed, for in spite of my long years in his service he gave me more praise than pudding (fobbed me off with mere words of praise).*

etwas **abstauben** (fig. u. fam.): *to "borrow" s. th. (colloq.).* Cf. auch: **klauen**

Als der Arbeiter des wiederholten Diebstahls in der Fabrik bezichtigt wurde, erklärte er, er habe lediglich bisweilen etwas abgestaubt.
*When the worker was accused of stealing repeatedly from the factory, he declared that he had only "borrowed" something occasionally.*

etwas **abstottern** (fam.): *to buy s. th. on the never-never (colloq.)*

Wir hatten nicht genug Bargeld und mußten das Klavier abstottern.
*We did not have enough money and had to buy the piano on the never-never.*

es geht mit j.em **abwärts** (fig.): cf. es geht mit j.em **bergab**

éin **Abwaschen** sein (fig.): cf. éin **Aufwaschen** sein

auf **Abwege** geraten (fig.): *to go astray; to go off the rails; to leave the straight and narrow (path).* Cf. auch: auf die abschüssige **Bahn** geraten; es geht mit j.em **bergab;** vor die **Hunde** gehen

Seitdem er die Schule verlassen hat, ist Karl leider auf Abwege geraten.
*Since he has left school Charles has unfortunately gone astray (gone off the rails; left the straight and narrow [path]).*

**abwegig** sein: *to be wide of the mark; to be wrong-headed (ill-directed)*

Dieser Politiker hält die Kritik der Opposition für ganz abwegig.
*That politician considers the opposition's criticism very wide of the mark (wrong-headed; ill-directed).*

durch **Abwesenheit** glänzen: *to be conspicuous by one's absence*

Einer der berühmten Professoren glänzte durch Abwesenheit.
*One of the famous professors was conspicuous by his absence.*

j.en (etwas) **abwimmeln** (fam.): *to keep s. o. (s. th.) away; to steer clear of s. b. (s. th.); to give s. b. (s. th.) a wide berth; to keep out of range of s. b. (s. th.)*

Wenn du so viel Arbeit zu tun hast, mußt du jeden Besuch abwimmeln.
*If you have so much work to do, you must keep all visitors away (steer clear [keep out of range] of all visitors; give all visitors a wide berth).*

sich etwas **abzwacken** (fam.): cf. sich etwas **abknapsen**

mit **Ach** und Krach (Weh): *with a strain; with great difficulty; by the skin of one's teeth; only just;* (Prüfung u. dgl. bestehen: auch) *to scrape (to scramble) through*

Dein Bruder hat nur mit Ach und Krach (Weh; Weh und Ach; Mühe und Not; mit knapper Not; mit Hängen und Würgen) sein Examen bestanden.

14

*Your brother has only passed his examination with a strain (with great difficulty; by the skin of his teeth; has only just passed his examination; has only scraped [scrambled] through his examination).*

**ach** und weh schreien: *to cry "woe is me" (alackaday); to raise a lament (a cry of lamentation); to bemoan (to bewail) one's fate*

Anstatt jetzt ach und weh zu schreien, hätte sie besser auf ihre Kinder aufpassen sollen.
*Instead of now crying "woe is me" (alackaday; Instead of now raising a lament [ a cry of lamentation]; Instead of bemoaning [bewailing] her fate), she would have done better to look after her children.*

j. es **Achillesferse** sein: *to be s. b.' s Achilles' heel.* Cf. auch: ein wunder **Punkt** sein

Geschichtsdaten sind seine Achillesferse.
*Historical dates are his Achilles' heel.*

j.en über die **Achsel** ansehen (fig.): *to look askance at s. b.; to eye s. b. askance; to look down one's nose at s. b.; to look down on s. b.; to turn up one's nose at s. b.*

Du hast keinen Grund, ihn über die Achsel (Schulter; scheel [schief]; von der Seite) anzusehen.
*You have no cause to look askance at him (to eye him askance; to look down your nose at him; to look down on him; to turn up your nose at him).*

etwas auf die leichte **Achsel** nehmen (fig.): *to make light of s. th.; to play down the importance of s. th.; to treat s. th. lightly; to shrug s. th. off; to soft-pedal s. th.*

Solche Ereignisse sollte man nicht auf die leichte Achsel (Schulter) nehmen.
*One should not make light of (play down the importance of; soft-pedal) such events (treat such events lightly; shrug such events off).*

j.en in **Acht** und Bann erklären (fig.): *to boycott s. b.; to ostracise s. b.; to send s. b. to Coventry*

Nach seiner Verurteilung wurde Peter von allen ehemaligen Freunden in Acht und Bann erklärt.
*After his conviction Peter was boycotted (ostracised; sent to Coventry) by all his former friends.*

j.en **achtkantig** hinauswerfen: *to throw s. b. out neck and crop; to kick s. b. out unceremoniously; to throw s. b. out by the scruff of his neck.* Cf. auch: j.en vor die **Tür** setzen

Wir haben den unverschämten Bettler achtkantig (hochkantig; Hals über Kopf) hinausgeworfen.
*We threw the insolent beggar out neck and crop (by the scruff of his neck; kicked . . . out unceremoniously).*

etwas **ad acta** legen (fig.): *to shelve s. th.; to lay s. th. aside; to put s. th. by*

Legen wir doch diesen Streitfall ein für allemal ad acta (zu den Akten).
*Let us shelve this dispute (lay this dispute aside; put this dispute by) once and for all.*

den alten **Adam** ausziehen: *to renounce the old Adam*

Dieser Mann hat den alten Adam ausgezogen und hat sich sehr zum Guten verändert.
*This man has renounced the old Adam and greatly changed for the better.*

einen neuen **Adam** anziehen: cf. einen neuen **Menschen** anziehen

nach **Adam Riese:** *according to Cocker*

Nach Adam Riese beläuft sich die Rechnung für jeden von uns auf 12.50 Mark.
*According to Cocker the bill for each of us comes to 12.50 marks.*

im **Adamskostüm** sein: *to be in one's birthday suit.* Cf. auch **splitternackt** sein

In den meisten Seebädern ist es untersagt, im Adams- bzw. Evaskostüm zu baden.
*In most seaside resorts bathing in one's birthday suit is prohibited.*

j.em das Blut in den **Adern** erstarren lassen: cf. j.em das **Blut** in den Adern erstarren lassen

eine leichte **Ader** haben: *to be happy-go-lucky; to be of an easy-come-easy-go disposition*

Er muß eine leichte Ader haben, da er so viele Schulden hat.
*He must be happy-go-lucky (must be of an easy-come-easy-go disposition), because he has so many debts.*

eine noble **Ader** haben: *to be free-handed (open-handed); to spare no expense*

Dein Onkel hat uns immer sehr großzügig behandelt. Er hat entschieden eine noble Ader.
*Your uncle has always treated us very generously. He is certainly free-handed (open-handed; certainly spares no expense).*

ein **Adonis** sein: *to be an Adonis*

Die jungen Mädchen sind alle in den neuen Lehrer verliebt. Er soll ein wahrer Adonis (ein junger Gott) sein.
*The young girls are all in love with the new teacher. He is said to be a real Adonis.*

an die falsche **Adresse** kommen: *to come to the wrong house (person); to knock at the wrong door; to pick the wrong man*

Mit einer solchen Bitte kommen Sie bei mir an die falsche Adresse (an den Unrechten).
*In making such a request to me you have come to the wrong house (person; are knocking at the wrong door; have picked the wrong man).*

sich aus der **Affäre** ziehen: *to wriggle out of ( to extricate o. s. from) the situation*

Der Diplomat hat sich geschickt aus der Affäre gezogen.
*The diplomat has skilfully wriggled out of (extricated himself from) the situation.*

ein eingebildeter **Affe** sein (fig. u. fam.): *to be a conceited ass (pup) (colloq.); to be a stuck-up person (colloq.)*

Was ist dein Vetter bloß für ein eingebildeter Affe (Laffe)! Dabei ist er in Wirklichkeit nur ein sehr mittelmäßiger Mensch.
*What a conceited ass (pup; stuck-up person) your cousin is! In fact he is only a very mediocre man.*

einen **Affen** an j.em gefressen haben (fam.): cf. einen **Narren** an j.em gefressen haben

einen (schweren) **Affen** haben (fam.): cf. einen **Schwips** haben

Ich denke, mich laust der **Affe!** (fam.): *Just imagine (fancy) ! (colloq.); Would you believe it! (colloq.). Well I never! (colloq.).*

Ich denke, mich laust der Affe (ich kriege die Motten)! Plötzlich steht ein alter Schulkamerad, den ich längst tot geglaubt hatte, vor mir.
*Just imagine! ([fancy!]; Would you believe it!; Well I never!) Suddenly an old school-friend, whom I had believed to have been dead for a long time, was standing in front of me.*

vom (tollen) **Affen** gebissen sein (fam.): cf. nicht richtig im **Dachstübchen** sein

mit **affenartiger** Geschwindigkeit (fam.): *with bewildering rapidity; with phenomenal speed; like mad (colloq.); like smoke (colloq.)*

Jede Arbeit mit den Händen führt deine Frau mit affenartiger Geschwindigkeit aus.
*Your wife does all manual work with bewildering rapidity (phenomenal speed; like mad [smoke]).*

eine **Affenhitze** (fam.): cf. eine **Bullenhitze**

**Affenliebe** (fig.): *infatuation; dotage*

In ihrer Affenliebe verwöhnt sie ihren Sohn schrecklich.
*She spoils her son terribly in her infatuation (dotage).*

eine **Affenschande** sein (fam.): *to be a crying scandal; to be a beastly (a rotten) shame (colloq.)*

Die ungerechte Behandlung dieses Mannes ist eine Affenschande.
*The unjust treatment of this man is a crying scandal (a beastly [rotten] shame).*

stinken wie im **Affenstall** (fam.): *to stink like a pig-sty (sl.)*

Reißt die Fenster auf! Hier stinkt's wie im Affenstall.
*Open the windows. It stinks in here like a pig-sty.*

ein **Affentheater** (fam.): *nonsense; tomfoolery; a pantomime; a fuss; blah (sl.)*

Wozu dieses Affentheater ([reine] Theater) mit den Schönheitsköniginnen?
*Why this nonsense (tomfoolery; pantomime; fuss; blah) about beauty queens?*

Das sieht ihm **ähnlich!**: *That's typical of him!; That's just like him! That's him all over!*

Johann sollte Obst aus der Stadt mitbringen, hat es aber vergessen. Das sieht ihm ähnlich! (Das ist wieder mal echt Johann!)
*John was to bring fruit from town but forgot it. That's typical of him! (That's just like him!; That's him all over!)*

keine (blasse) **Ahnung** von etwas haben: *to have not the faintest (slightest) idea (notion) about s. th.; not to know the first thing about s. th.; not to have a clue about s. th. (colloq.)*

Von altenglischer Literatur hat dieser Student keine (blasse) Ahnung (keinen [blassen] Dunst; keinen Schimmer).
*This student has not the faintest (slightest) idea (notion; does not know the first thing; hasn't a clue) about Old English literature.*

(nur) eine dunkle **Ahnung** von etwas haben: *to have an inkling (a faint [hazy] idea [notion]; a glimmering) of s. th.*

Ich habe nur eine dunkle Ahnung (schwache Vorstellung) von seinen künftigen Plänen.
*I have only an inkling (a faint [hazy] idea [notion]; a glimmering) of his future plans.*

Du hast eine **Ahnung!**: *That's what you think! (colloq.); A (fat) lot you know about it! (colloq.); Sez you! (sl.)*

Die Stadt soll nur 10 Kilometer weit weg sein, meinst du? Du hast eine Ahnung!
*The town is supposed to be only 10 kilometres away, you reckon? That's what you think! (A [fat] lot you know about it!; Sez you!)*

etwas zu den **Akten** legen (fig.): cf. etwas **ad acta** legen

Wie stehen die **Aktien**? (fig.): *What are the chances?; What is the position?; How do things stand?; What's the score? (colloq.)*

Ich weiß, daß du dich um eine sichere Stellung bemühst. Wie stehen die Aktien?
*I know that you are trying to find a permanent job. What are the chances? (How do things stand?; What's the position [the score]?)*

j.es **Aktien** steigen (fig.): *s. b.'s stock is rising (has risen)*

Seine Aktien steigen bei seinem Chef, seitdem er fleißiger geworden ist.
*His stock is rising (has risen) with his boss now that he has become harder-working.*

in **Aktion** treten: a) (von Sachen) *to come in useful (handy); to come into its own;* b) (von Menschen) *to go into action; to step in*

    a) Bei dem gestrigen schönen Wetter sind unsere Liegestühle zum ersten Mal in Aktion getreten.
    b) Da die Zuschauer nicht auseinandergehen wollten, mußte die Polizei in Aktion treten.
    *a) In yesterday's beautiful weather our deck-chairs came in useful (handy; came into their own) for the first time.*
    *b) As the spectators would not disperse, the police had to go into action (to step in).*

den **Akzent** auf etwas legen (fig.): cf. den **Hauptakzent** auf etwas legen

blinden **Alarm** schlagen: *to cry wolf; to raise a false alarm*

    Der Junge hatte oft blinden Alarm (Lärm) geschlagen. Jetzt, da er wirklich in Not war, wollte ihm niemand glauben.
    *The boy had often cried wolf (raised false alarms). Now, when he was really in distress, nobody would believe him.*

(ein) blinder **Alarm** sein: *to be a false alarm*

    Die Feuerwehr konnte gleich wieder abrücken, denn es war nur (ein) blinder Alarm (Lärm).
    *The fire engine was able to drive off again immediately, for it was only a false alarm.*

**alle** werden (fam.): cf. zur **Neige** gehen

Das ist doch **allerhand**!: cf. Das ist doch die **Höhe** (der Höhepunkt)!

ein **Allerweltskerl** sein: *to be a devil (a deuce) of a fellow (colloq.); to be a fellow and a half (colloq.)*

    Wie ich höre, kannst du auch malen und Geige spielen. Du bist ja ein Allerweltskerl (Mordskerl; Tausendkünstler; Tausendsasa; pfundiger Mensch; Pfundskerl; Teufelskerl).
    *I hear that you can paint and play the violin as well. You're a devil (a deuce) of a fellow (a fellow and a half).*

**alles** in allem: *all in all; on the whole; by and large*

    Alles in allem ist Wilhelm ein guter Kerl.
    *All in all (On the whole; By and large) William is a good fellow.*

Da hört sich doch **alles** auf!: cf. Das ist doch die **Höhe** (der Höhepunkt)!

**Allotria** treiben: *to get (to be) up to one's tricks (pranks); to lark about (colloq.)*

    Die Kinder treiben wieder Allotria, anstatt an ihre Schularbeiten zu denken.
    *The children are getting up (are up) to their tricks (pranks; are larking about) again instead of thinking of their homework.*

der graue **Alltag** (des Lebens): *the workaday (the everyday) world; the common (the humdrum) round; the daily drudge*

Nach den Ferien hat für mich der graue Alltag wieder begonnen.
*The workaday (everyday) world (The common [humdrum] round; The daily drudge) has started again (for me) after the holidays.*

**Allzuviel** ist ungesund (Sprichw.): cf. Allzuviel ist **ungesund**

j.em wie ein **Alp** auf der Seele liegen: *to be a (real) nightmare to s. b.; to lie heavily on s. b.'s conscience; to prey on s. b.'s mind; to be a load (to be like a ton weight) on s. b.'s mind*

Meine vielen unbeantworteten Briefe liegen mir wie ein Alp (brennen mir schwer) auf der Seele (liegen mir schwer auf dem Herzen).
*My many unanswered letters are a (real) nightmare to me (lie heavily on my conscience; are preying on [are a load on; are like a ton weight on] my mind.*

(so) **alt** wie Methusalem: cf. (so) alt wie **Methusalem**

Wie die **Alten** sungen, so zwitschern die Jungen (Sprichw.): cf. **Art** läßt nicht von Art

alles beim **alten** lassen: *to leave everything as it is; to leave things as they are; to maintain the status quo*

Unsere Partei möchte lieber alles beim alten lassen.
*Our party prefers to leave everything as it is (to leave things as they are; to maintain the status quo).*

am **alten** rütteln: *to attack the established order (the status quo); to shake things up (colloq.).* Cf. auch: etwas aus den **Angeln** heben

Die Jugend ist oft geneigt, tüchtig am alten zu rütteln.
*Youth is often inclined to attack vigorously the established order (the status quo; to shake things up).*

sich aufs **Altenteil** setzen: *to hang up one's hat (one's gloves; one's boots); to pull out (colloq.)*

Ich habe mich aufs Altenteil gesetzt und meinen Kindern das Geschäft überlassen.
*I have hung up my hat (gloves; boots; have pulled out) and left the business to my children.*

**altfränkisch** sein: *to be antiquated; to be old-fashioned; to be out-of-date.* Cf. auch: **vorsintflutlich**

Die alte Dame zieht sich sehr altfränkisch an.
*The old lady wears very antiquated (old-fashioned; out-of-date) clothes.*

fleißig wie eine **Ameise** sein: cf. fleißig wie eine **Biene** sein sicher wie das **Amen** in der Kirche: cf. mit tödlicher **Sicherheit**

ein **Ammenmärchen** erzählen (fig.): *to tell a fairy-tale (nursery-rhyme; cock-and-bull story); to pitch a yarn (colloq.)*

> Erzähle mir doch keine Ammenmärchen (Räubergeschichten)! Ich weiß genau, daß du erst um Mitternacht nach Hause gekommen bist.
> *Don't tell me any fairy-tales (nursery-rhymes; cock-and-bull stories; Don't pitch me a yarn)! I know for certain that you didn't come home until midnight.*

in **Amt** und Würden sein: *to be in office (in the saddle); to hold office*

> Mit seinen 65 Jahren ist mein Vater noch in Amt und Würden.
> *At sixty-five my father is still in office (in the saddle; is still holding office).*

**Amtsschimmel:** *red tape*

> In diesem Ministerium wird viel der Amtsschimmel geritten.
> *There is a great deal of red tape in this ministry.*

mit einem Mädchen **anbändeln** (fam.): *to get off with a girl (colloq.); to pick a girl up (colloq.)*

> Jede Woche bändelt er mit einem neuen Mädchen an.
> *Every week he gets off with (picks up) a new girl.*

Sie ist zum **Anbeißen** (fig. u. fam.): *I could eat her (gobble her up) (colloq.)*

> Deine Freundin ist zum Anbeißen (Fressen) (hübsch; könnte man vor Liebe fressen).
> *Your girl friend is so pretty that I could eat her (gobble her up).*

**anbeißen** (fig.): *to bite (colloq.); to take (to swallow) the bait (colloq.); to fall for it (colloq.).* Cf. auch: auf etwas **hereinfallen**

> Georg betonte wiederholt, daß er beinahe sein ganzes Geld ausgegeben habe. Aber sein Vater kannte ihn und wollte nicht anbeißen (auf den Leim gehen [kriechen]; wollte sich nicht anführen lassen).
> *George repeatedly emphasised that he had spent almost all his money, but his father knew him and would not bite (take [swallow] the bait; fall for it).*

mit j.em **anbinden** (fam.): *to cross swords with s. b.; to cross s. b.'s path; to fall out with s. b.; to get on the wrong side of s. b. (colloq.)*

> Ich warne Sie, mit diesem Mann anzubinden. Er ist ein grober Kerl.
> *I am warning you not to cross swords with (fall out with; get on the wrong side of) that man (cross that man's path). He is a rough fellow.*

j.en **anblaffen** (fam.): cf. j.en **anschnauzen**

ein **Anblick** für Götter sein: *to be a sight for the gods; to be a sight for sore eyes*

> Es ist ein Anblick (Bild; Schauspiel) für Götter, wie Großvater mit seinen Enkelkindern spielt.
> *The way grandfather plays with his grandchildren is a sight for the gods (for sore eyes).*

j.em etwas **andrehen** (fig. u. fam.): *to foist s. th. on to s. b.; to palm (to fob) s. b. off with s. th.*

Er hat mir diesen billigen Schlips angedreht (aufgehängt).
*He foisted this cheap tie on to me (He palmed [fobbed] me off with this cheap tie).*

bei j.em **anecken:** *to rile s. b.; to get on the wrong side of s. b.; to rub s. b. up the wrong way (colloq.).* Cf. auch: j.en vor den **Kopf** stoßen

Wilhelm ist sehr taktlos und eckt durch sein Benehmen bei vielen Leuten an.
*William is very tactless and riles (gets on the wrong side of) many people (rubs many people up the wrong way) by his behaviour.*

j.en **anfahren** (fig.): cf. j.en **anschnauzen;** j.en **abkanzeln**

der **Anfang** vom Ende sein: *to be the beginning of the end; the writing is on the wall*

Wenn das Publikum nicht mehr in diese Konzerte geht, so ist das der Anfang vom Ende.
*When the public no longer goes to these concerts, it is the beginning of the end (the writing is on the wall).*

j.en **anfauchen** (fig.): cf. j.en **anschnauzen;** j.en **abkanzeln**

sich **anführen** lassen: cf. auf den **Leim** gehen (kriechen)

**angeben** (fig. u. fam.): *to brag; to put on airs; to show off; to swank (colloq.)*

Du brauchst nicht so anzugeben ([wie ein Sack Läuse]; dich nicht so dicke zu tun; dich nicht so aufzuplustern; nicht so den dicken Wilhelm zu spielen; nicht so große Bogen zu spucken), bloß (nur) weil du ein neues Fahrrad bekommen hast.
*You don't need to brag (to put on airs; to show off; to swank) like that just because you've got a new bicycle.*

wie **angeblasen** kommen: *to come overnight; to drop from the clouds.* Cf. auch: im **Handumdrehen**

Seine Grippe ist wie angeblasen (angeflogen) gekommen. Gestern traf ich ihn noch ganz gesund in einem Café.
*His influenza must have come overnight (must have dropped from the clouds). He was quite well when I met him yesterday in a café.*

kurz **angebunden** sein (fig.): *to be a person of few words; to be short-spoken; to be tight-lipped*

Unser Chef ist zumeist kurz angebunden und redet selten mit seinem Personal.
*Our boss is usually a person of few words (short-spoken; tight-lipped) and rarely talks to his staff.*

seligen **Angedenkens:** *of happy (of blessed) memory; late; God rest his soul*

Unser Lateinlehrer seligen Angedenkens zitierte bei jeder Gelegenheit ein passendes Sprichwort.

*Our Latin master of happy (blessed) memory (Our late Latin master; Our Latin master, God rest his soul) used to quote a suitable proverb on every occasion.*

wie **angeflogen** kommen: cf. wie **angeblasen** kommen

wie **angegossen** passen (sitzen): *to fit like a glove; to fit to a T*

Dein Kostüm paßt (sitzt) wie angegossen.
*Your costume fits like a glove (to a T).*

sich einen **angekümmelt** haben (fam.): *to booze (sl.); to be tight (sl.).* Cf. auch: einen **Schwips** haben; eine **Fahne** haben

Du riechst nach Alkohol. Hast du dir schon wieder einen angekümmelt (ange-zwitschert)?
*You smell of alcohol. Have you been boozing again? (Are you tight again?)*

sich j.en **angeln** (fig. u. fam.): cf. sich j.en an **Land** ziehen

aus den **Angeln** gehen (fig.): cf. aus den **Fugen** gehen

die Welt aus den **Angeln** heben (fig.): cf. die **Welt** aus den Angeln heben

das **Angenehme** mit dem Nützlichen verbinden: *to combine business with pleasure*

Auf Geschäftsreisen pflegte er, das Angenehme mit dem Nützlichen zu ver-binden.
*On official trips he used to combine business with pleasure.*

**angesäuselt** sein (fam.): cf. zu tief in den **Becher** geguckt haben; einen **Schwips** haben

bei j.em gut **angeschrieben** sein (fig.): *to be in s. b.'s good books; to stand high in s. b.'s esteem; to be highly thought-of by s. b.*

Mein Bruder ist bei seinem Lehrer gut angeschrieben (hat . . . eine gute Num-mer; einen Stein im Brett).
*My brother is in his teacher's good books (stands high in his teacher's esteem; is highly thought-of by his teacher).*

(bei j.em) schlecht **angeschrieben** sein (fig.): *to be in s. b.'s bad books; to have blotted one's copy-book; to have cooked one's goose*

Seit diesem unglücklichen Vorfall bist du bei deinem Onkel schlecht angeschrie-ben (hast du . . . einen Klecks in den Akten) und wirst nie mehr etwas von ihm bekommen.
*You have been in your uncle's bad books since (You blotted your copy-book [cooked your goose] through) that unfortunate incident and will never get anything from him again.*

es j.em **angetan** haben: *to bewitch s. b.; to fascinate s. b.; to take hold of s. b.; s. b. has fallen for s. b. (s. th.); to be gone on s. b. (s. th.)*

Die moderne Malerei hat es ihm wirklich angetan (Er ist von moderner Malerei wirklich angetan).

*Modern painting has really bewitched him (really fascinates him; has really taken hold of him; He has really fallen for [is really gone on] modern painting).*

wie **angewurzelt** dastehen: cf. (wie) zur **Salzsäule** erstarrt sein

sich einen **angezwitschert** haben (fam.): cf. sich einen **angekümmelt** haben

j.en (etwas) **anglotzen** (fam.): *to goggle (to gape) at s. b. (s. th.)*

Warum glotzt er mich so an? Habe ich etwas Besonderes an mir?
*Why is he goggling (gaping) at me like that? Is there anything particular about me?*

zum **Angriff** blasen (fig.): *to sound the (one's) battle-cry.* Cf. auch: zum **Angriff** vorgehen

Erst kurz vor den Wahlen hat Ihre Partei zum Angriff geblasen.
*Not until shortly before the election did your party sound its (the) battle-cry.*

zum **Angriff** vorgehen (fig.): *to mount an attack; to go over to the attack; to take up arms; to enter the lists*

Nach dem ersten Mißerfolg gab die Gegenpartei nicht auf. Sie ging vielmehr wieder zum Angriff vor (Sie ritt . . . eine Attacke).
*The opposing party did not give up after the first failure. Rather, it mounted an attack (went over to the attack; took up arms; entered the lists) again.*

eine **Angriffsfläche** bieten (fig.): *to lay s. b. open (to expose s. b.) to an attack*

Deine unkluge Äußerung wird deinen Gegnern eine große Angriffsfläche bieten.
*Your unwise remark will lay you open (expose you) to a heavy attack from your opponents.*

einem **angst** und bange werden: *to be as scared as a mouse; s. th. puts the fear of God into s. b.; to be scared stiff (colloq.); to get the wind up (sl.); to be in a blue funk (sl.).* Cf. auch: eine **Heidenangst** haben

Bei dem heftigen Gewitter wurde es ihr angst und bange (himmelangst).
*During the violent storm she was as scared as a mouse (scared stiff; in a blue funk; she got the wind up; The violent storm put the fear of God into her).*

ein **Angsthase (Angstmeier)** sein: *to be chicken-hearted; to be white-livered; to be a rabbit (colloq.); to be a funk (sl.); to be windy (sl.)*

Trotz seiner 14 Jahre ist Karl noch ein großer Angsthase (Angstmeier; eine große Bangbuxe [Bangbüxe]).
*In spite of his fourteen years Charles is still chicken-hearted (white-livered; a rabbit; a funk; still windy).*

eine **Angströhre** (fam.): *a topper; a top-hat*

Heute setzt man nur noch bei wenigen Gelegenheiten eine Angströhre (einen Zylinder) auf.
*Today one only wears a topper (a top-hat) on a few occasions.*

per **Anhalter** fahren (fam.): *to hitch-hike; to thumb a lift; to thumb one's way*

Ich bin von Köln nach München per Anhalter gefahren (nach München getrampt).
*I hitch-hiked (thumbed a lift; thumbed my way) from Cologne to Munich.*

j.en **anhauen** (fam.): *to accost s. b.; to make up to s. b. (colloq.); to make a pass at s. b. (colloq.)*

Es ist sehr unanständig, eine junge Dame so auf der Straße anzuhauen.
*It is very improper to accost (make up to; make a pass at) a young lady in the street like that.*

auf (den ersten) **Anhieb:** a) *on the spur of the moment; off-hand;* b) *at the first go (attempt; shot)*

a) Ich muß darüber nachdenken; auf (den ersten) Anhieb kann ich es Ihnen leider nicht sagen.
b) Dem Mechaniker gelang es, das Auto auf (den ersten) Anhieb in Gang zu bringen.
*a) I must think about it; I am afraid I cannot tell you on the spur of the moment (off-hand).*
*b) The mechanic succeeded in starting the car at the first go (attempt; shot).*

j.en **anhimmeln** (fam.): *to make sheep's eyes at s. b. (colloq.); to look starry-eyed at s. b. (colloq.); to make goo-goo eyes at s. b. (sl.)*

Es ist lächerlich (zu sehen), wie er dieses Mädchen anhimmelt.
*It is ridiculous to see him making sheep's eyes (goo-goo eyes; looking starry-eyed) at that girl.*

Nerven wie **Ankertaue** haben: *to have nerves of iron (steel)*

Ein Fallschirmspringer muß Nerven wie Ankertaue (wie ein Drahtseil) haben.
*A parachutist must have nerves of iron (steel).*

j.em etwas **ankreiden** (fig.): *to give s. b. a bad mark; to enter it on s. b.'s debit side*

Wir haben es unserem Nachbarn übel angekreidet, daß er uns voriges Jahr nicht zu Hilfe gekommen ist.
*We gave our neighbour a bad mark for not coming (We entered it on our neighbour's debit side that he did not come) to our assistance last year.*

etwas **ankurbeln** (fig.): cf. etwas in **Gang** setzen (bringen)

einen **Anlauf** nehmen (fig.): *to think of getting down to s. th.; to make a move towards doing s. th.*

Du hast noch nicht einmal einen Anlauf genommen, deine Hausaufgabe zu machen.
*You have not even thought of getting down to (made a move towards) doing your homework yet.*

es auf etwas **anlegen:** *to be set (bent; intent) on s. th.; to set one's mind on s. th.; to be spoiling for s. th. (colloq.)*

Deine Schwester hat es bestimmt auf einen Streit mit uns angelegt.
*Your sister is definitely set (bent; intent; has definitely set her mind) on (is definitely spoiling for) a quarrel with us.*

eine **Anleihe** machen (fig.): *to make a borrowing; to borrow*

Dieser junge Schriftsteller hat viele Anleihen bei Autoren des 19. Jahrhunderts gemacht.
*This young author has made many borrowings (has borrowed a great deal) from nineteenth-century writers.*

im **Anmarsch** sein (fig.): *to be on its (the) way; to be blowing up*

Weitere Verwicklungen sind im Anmarsch.
*Further complications are on their (the) way (are blowing up).*

**Anno Tobak** (fam.): *the year dot*

Sein Auto ist sehr alt. Es muß von Anno Tobak sein (aus Olims Zeiten stammen).
*His car is very old. It must belong to the year dot.*

j.en **anpetzen:** cf. j.en **verpetzen**

einen **Anpfiff** kriegen (fam.): cf. eine **Abreibung** kriegen

j.en **anpflaumen** (fam.): cf. j.en auf den **Arm** nehmen

j.en **anprangern:** cf. j.en an den **Pranger** stellen

j.en (um etwas) **anpumpen** (fam.): *to tap (to touch) s. b. for s. th. (colloq.)*

Gestern kam Theodor zu mir und wollte mich um 20 Mark anpumpen (anzapfen).
*Theodor came to me yesterday and wanted to tap (touch) me for 20 marks.*

j.en **anranzen** (fam.): cf. j.en **anschnauzen;** j.en **abkanzeln**

etwas in **Anschlag** bringen: *to take s. th. into account (into consideration); to take account of s. th.*

Man sollte diesen Menschen nicht immer nur tadeln, sondern auch seine guten Qualitäten in Anschlag bringen.
*One should not always just blame this man but also take his good qualities into account (consideration; take account of his good qualities).*

den **Anschluß** verpassen (fig.): *to miss one's chance; to miss the bus (colloq.)*

Seine Schwester hat den Anschluß verpaßt und wird wohl immer unverheiratet bleiben.
*His sister has missed her chance (missed the bus) and will probably stay unmarried for ever.*

j.en mit etwas **anschmieren** (fam.): *to carny (to bribe) s. b. with s. th.; to grease s. b. with s. th. (colloq.)*

Er hat mich mit dem Versprechen einer Beteiligung am Gewinn angeschmiert.
*He carnied (bribed; greased) me with the promise of participation in the profit.*

j.en **anschnauzen** (fam.): *to haul s. b. over the coals; to come down on s. b. like a sack of coals; to let fly at s. b. (colloq.); to tear s. b. off a strip (sl.).* Cf. auch: j.en **abkanzeln**; j.em aufs **Dach** steigen

Der Lehrer hat den Schüler ordentlich angeschnauzt (angeblafft; angefahren; angefaucht; angeranzt), weil er seine Hausaufgabe nicht gemacht hatte.
*The teacher hauled the pupil properly over the coals (came down on the pupil like a sack of coals; let fly at the pupil properly; tore the pupil off a strip) because he had not done his homework.*

einen **Anschnauzer** kriegen (fam.): cf. eine **Abreibung** kriegen

j.en **anschwärzen** (fig.): *to paint s. b. black; to blacken s. b.'s character*

Ich kann es wirklich nicht dulden, daß dieser Mann mich so anschwärzt.
*I really cannot tolerate this man painting me black (blackening my character) like this.*

ohne **Ansehen** der Person: *without respect of persons*

Ohne Ansehen der Person wurden alle Passagiere durchsucht.
*All the passengers were searched, without respect of persons.*

**ansein** (fam.): *to be on*

In diesem Restaurant ist das Radio den ganzen Tag an.
*The radio is on the whole day in this restaurant.*

j.en **anstacheln** (fig.): *to spur s. b.; to goad s. b.; to egg s. b. on (colloq.)*

Der Erfolg meines Bruders hat mich zu größeren Anstrengungen angestachelt.
*My brother's success has spurred (goaded) me (egged me on) to greater efforts.*

ein **Anstandswauwau** sein (fam.): *to be a watch-dog; to play gooseberry (colloq.)*

Die Mutter begleitet ihre Tochter überall hin. Die Leute nennen sie den Anstandswauwau.
*The mother accompanies her daughter everywhere. People call her the watch-dog (People say she is playing gooseberry).*

sich **anstellen** a) *to feign; to pretend; to sham (colloq.); to put s. th. on (colloq.); to kid (sl.);* b) *to make a fuss (colloq.)*

a) Georg stellt sich nicht an; er ist wirklich krank.
b) Stell' dich doch nicht so an! Du kannst ohne weiteres eine zweite Portion essen.
*a) George is not shamming (feigning; pretending; putting it on; kidding); he really is ill.*
*b) Don't make such a fuss! You can easily eat a second portion.*

sich den **Anstrich** geben: *to play the part; to give o. s. airs; to act*

Er ist noch kein erfahrener Arzt. Er gibt sich aber den Anstrich, ein solcher zu sein.
*He is not yet an experienced doctor but he plays the part of one (gives himself airs [acts] as though he were one).*

einer Sache einen anderen **Anstrich** geben (fig.): *to give s. th. a new look (a new slant); to strike a new note with s. th.*

Wir beschlossen, unserm Fest in diesem Jahr einen anderen Anstrich zu geben.
*We decided to give our celebration a new look (slant; to strike a new note with our celebration) this year.*

einer Sache ins **Antlitz** sehen: cf. einer Sache ins **Auge** sehen

j.em die **Antwort** nicht schuldig bleiben: *not to be at a loss for an answer; to give s. b. tit for tat; to give as good as one gets; to answer (s. b.) back.* Cf. auch: **Gleiches** mit Gleichem vergelten

Heinrich wurde frech, aber ich bin ihm die Antwort nicht schuldig geblieben.
*Henry became cheeky but I was not at a loss for an answer (gave him tit for tat; gave as good as I got; answered [him] back).*

j.en **anzapfen** (fam.): cf. j.en **anpumpen**

etwas **anzetteln:** *to set (to spark) s. th. off; to get s. th. going; to kindle s. th.; to stir s. th. up; to set s. th. alight*

Unverantwortliche Elemente haben diesen offenen Aufruhr angezettelt (in Szene gesetzt; inszeniert).
*Irresponsible elements set (sparked) off (kindled; stirred up) this open rebellion (got this open rebellion going; set this open rebellion alight).*

im **Anzug** sein: *to be in the offing; to be brewing; to be getting (coming; blowing) up*

Ich bin sicher, daß ein Gewitter im Anzug ist. Wir sollten lieber gleich nach Hause gehen.
*I am sure that there is a storm in the offing (that a storm is brewing [getting (coming; blowing) up]). We had better go home at once.*

in den sau(e)ren **Apfel** beißen (fig.): cf. die bittere **Pille** schlucken

etwas für einen **Apfel** (Appel) und ein Ei kaufen (verkaufen) (fig.): cf. für ein **Butterbrot** verkaufen

Kein **Apfel** konnte zur Erde fallen: cf. gedrängt wie die **Heringe** sitzen

j.em wie ein reifer **Apfel** in den Schoß fallen: cf. j.em (wie ein reifer Apfel [wie eine reife Frucht]) in den **Schoß** fallen

Der **Apfel** fällt nicht weit vom Stamm (Sprichw.): cf. **Art** läßt nicht von Art

ein **Apfel** der Zwietracht sein: cf. ein **Zankapfel** sein

**Apothekerpreise** nehmen: *to charge exorbitant prices; to make one pay through the nose*

In Luxusgeschäften nimmt man Apothekerpreise (Wucherpreise).
*In luxury shops they charge exorbitant prices (they make one pay through the nose).*

j.en in den **April** schicken: *to make an April fool of s. b.; to send s. b. on a fool's errand*

Es ist ein beliebter Scherz, am 1. April die Leute in den April zu schicken, indem man ihnen etwas Falsches sagt.
*It is a popular joke to make April fools of people (to send people on a fool's errand) on April 1 by telling them something wrong.*

die **Arbeit** nicht erfunden haben: cf. sich kein **Bein** ausreißen

**Arbeit** macht das Leben süß (Sprichw.): *Work is what makes life worth while; Life is nothing without work*

Mein Schwager Johann ist sehr fleißig. Er behauptet: Arbeit macht das Leben süß.
*My brother-in-law John is very hard-working. He maintains that work is what makes life worth while (that life is nothing without work).*

ein **Arbeitstier** sein (fig.): *to be a glutton (a whale; a beaver) for work*

Dein Professor ist ein richtiges Arbeitstier.
*Your professor is a real glutton (whale; beaver) for work.*

im **argen** liegen: *to be in a bad way (in a poor state); to be a shambles (sl.)*

Die Schulverhältnisse in unserm Dorf liegen noch sehr im argen.
*School conditions in our village are still in a very bad way (state; are still a shambles).*

seinen **Ärger** herunterschlucken (verbeißen): *to swallow one's rage (anger)*

Über seinen frechen Brief war ich zunächst wütend, dann aber habe ich meinen Ärger heruntergeschluckt (verbissen).
*At first I was furious at his impudent letter, but then I swallowed my rage (anger).*

**Argusaugen** haben: cf. **Augen** wie ein Luchs haben

**arm** dran sein: *to be badly-off; to be in a bad way (colloq.)*

Seit dem Tode seiner Eltern ist dieser Junge wirklich arm (übel) dran.
*Since his parent's death this boy has been really badly-off (been really in a bad way).*

**arm** wie eine Kirchenmaus sein: cf. arm wie eine **Kirchenmaus** sein

j.em (einer Sache) in den **Arm** fallen (fig.): a) (von Personen) *to put a spoke in s. b.'s wheel; to stand in s. b.'s way;* b) (von Sachen) *to stand in the way of s. th.; to hinder the course of s. th.*

> a) Ich hatte große Ferienpläne, aber mein Vater ist mir (dabei) in den Arm gefallen.
> b) Hüte dich, der Gerechtigkeit in den Arm zu fallen.
> *a) I had great holiday plans but my father put a spoke in my wheel (stood in my way).*
> *b) Beware of standing in the way (hindering the course) of justice.*

einen langen **Arm** haben (fig.): *to have a long reach; to have long tentacles.* Cf. auch: am **Drücker** sitzen

> Mein Bruder im Ministerium wird Ihnen sicherlich helfen können. Er hat einen langen Arm.
> *My brother in the Ministry is sure to be able to help you. He has a long reach (long tentacles).*

j.em in die **Arme** laufen: *to run (to bump) into s. b.; to run across s. b.; to knock into s. b. (colloq.)*

> Vor einigen Tagen bin ich meinem alten Freund Kurt in die Arme gelaufen.
> *A few days ago I ran (bumped; knocked) into (ran across) my old friend Curt.*

j.en auf den **Arm** nehmen (fig. u. fam.): *to pull s. b.'s leg; to poke fun at s. b.; to make fun of s. b.; to take s. b. for a ride (colloq.)*

> Ich mußte darüber lachen, wie du deinen Bruder auf den Arm (die Schippe [Schüppe] genommen; angepflaumt; aufgezogen; zum besten gehabt; gefoppt; gefrotzelt; gehänselt; geuzt; veräppelt) hast.
> *I had to laugh at the way you pulled your brother's leg (poked fun at your brother; made fun of your brother; you took your brother for a ride).*

sich nicht auf den **Arm** nehmen lassen (fig. u. fam.): *to stand no nonsense; not to let o. s. be put upon (be made fun of); not to let o. s. be kidded (be taken for a ride) (sl.)*

> Unterlasse solche (Sei ruhig mit solchen) Geschichten! Ich lasse mich von dir nicht auf den Arm nehmen.
> *Be quiet with such stories. I am not going to stand any nonsense from you (to let myself be put upon [be made fun of; be kidded; be taken for a ride] by you).*

j.en mit offenen **Armen** aufnehmen (fig.): *to receive (to welcome) s. b. with open arms*

> Wir haben unsern künftigen Schwiegersohn mit offenen Armen aufgenommen.
> *We received (welcomed) our future son-in-law with open arms.*

j.em unter die **Arme** greifen (fig.): cf. j.em auf die **Beine** helfen

mit verschränkten **Armen** dastehen: *to stand by with arms folded (arms akimbo)*

Während die Frauen sich zankten, standen ihre Ehemänner mit verschränkten Armen da(bei).
*While the women were quarrelling, their husbands stood by with arms folded (akimbo).*

sich j.em in die **Arme** werfen (fig.): cf. sich j.em an den **Hals** werfen

etwas aus dem **Ärmel** schütteln (fig.): *to do s. th. (straight) off the reel; to reel s. th. (straight) off; to toss s. th. off; to do s. th. off-hand*

Solche Gedichte kann ich noch jederzeit aus dem Ärmel schütteln (aus dem Handgelenk machen).
*I can recite (write etc) such poems (straight) off the reel (off-hand; can reel such poems [straight] off; can toss such poems off) at any time.*

sich nicht aus dem **Ärmel** schütteln lassen (fig.): *not to be able to be tossed off (to be done) like that*

Eine fremde Sprache zu sprechen ist schwer. Es (Das) läßt sich nicht einfach aus dem Ärmel schütteln.
*To speak a foreign language is hard. It cannot be tossed off (done) just like that.*

eine **Armesündermiene**: *a hang-dog look; a long face*

An seiner Armesündermiene erkannten wir sofort, daß unser Dienstmädchen etwas zerbrochen hatte.
*By her hang-dog look (her long face) we realised at once that our maid had smashed something.*

sich ein **Armutszeugnis** ausstellen (fig.): *to give o. s. away; to give the game away; to betray (to reveal) one's inefficiency (incapacity; insufficiency); to show o. s. up*

Beim Wettrennen kam er als Letzter ans Ziel und stellte sich damit ein Armutszeugnis aus.
*He finished last in the race and so gave himself (the game) away (and so betrayed [revealed] his inefficiency [incapacity; insufficiency]; showed himself up).*

**Art** läßt nicht von Art (Sprichw.): *Like father, like son (prov.); Like takes after like (prov.)*

Johann hat die Charaktereigenschaften seines Vaters geerbt. Art läßt nicht von Art (Wie die Alten sungen, so zwitschern die Jungen; Der Apfel fällt nicht weit vom Stamm).
*John has inherited his father's characteristics. Like father, like son (Like takes after like).*

aus der **Art** schlagen: a) *to be odd man out;* b) (im schlechten Sinne): cf. auf die abschüssige **Bahn** geraten

Während wir alle blond sind, ist mein Bruder Heini mit seinem schwarzen Haar (ganz) aus der Art geschlagen.
*Whereas we are all fair, my brother Henry, with his black hair, is odd man out.*

Das ist keine **Art** und Weise: *That is no way (not the way) to behave*

Kannst du nicht artig sein? Das ist doch wirklich keine Art und Weise.
*Can't you be good? That's really no way (not the way) to behave.*

(ein) **Aschenbrödel (Aschenputtel)** sein: *to be a Cinderella*

Sie mußte immer Aschenbrödel (Aschenputtel) sein und die schmutzige Arbeit machen.
*She always had to be a Cinderella and do the dirty work.*

den **Ast** absägen, auf dem man sitzt (fig.): *to kill the goose that lays the golden eggs; to cut off one's nose to spite one's face; to quarrel with one's bread and butter*

Wenn du das tust, sägst du dir den Ast ab, auf dem du sitzt.
*If you do that, you will be killing the goose that lays the golden eggs (cutting off your nose to spite your face; quarrelling with your bread and butter).*

sich auf dem absteigenden **Ast** befinden (fig.): cf. Es geht mit j.em **bergab**

sich einen **Ast** lachen (fam.): cf. sich **totlachen**

nicht **astrein** sein: cf. nicht **hasenrein** sein

nicht in éinem **Atem** nennen (fig.): *not to mention in the same breath; not to compare for a moment*

Man kann doch diese beiden Maler nicht in éinem Atem nennen.
*You cannot mention these two painters in the same breath (compare these two painters for a moment).*

j.en in **Atem** halten (fig.): *to keep s. b. on the qui vive (on the alert; on the move; on the go; on his toes)*

Mein Chef hält mich ständig in Atem.
*My boss always keeps me on the qui vive (on the alert; on the move; on the go; on my toes).*

nicht zu **Atem** kommen (fig.): *not to have time to breathe*

Vor lauter Arbeit bin ich nicht zu Atem gekommen.
*I have not had time to breathe for work.*

einen kurzen **Atem** haben (fig.): *to be short-winded; to be short of breath*

Dieser Schriftsteller schreibt nur Novellen, keine langen Romane. Er hat offenbar einen kurzen Atem.
*This author only writes short stories, not full-length novels. He is evidently short-winded (short of breath).*

j.em den **Atem** nehmen (rauben, verschlagen) (fig.): *to take s. b.'s breath away; to stun s. b.; to leave s. b. speechless*

Diese Unglücksnachricht hat jedem den Atem genommen (geraubt, verschlagen).
*The news of this accident took everybody's breath away (stunned everybody; left everybody speechless).*

seinen **Atem** sparen (fig.): cf. seine **Lunge** schonen

eine **Atempause** (fig.): *a breathing-space; a breather (colloq.).* Cf. auch. eine **Kunstpause** machen; **ausspannen**

Die jetzigen Verhandlungen sind nur eine kurze Atempause in der Fortentwicklung dieses Landes.
*The present negotiations are only a short breathing-space (breather) in the continued development of that country.*

den letzten **Atemzug** tun: *to breathe one's last; to draw one's last breath.* Cf. auch: j.es **Lebenslicht** erlischt

Vor zwei Tagen tat mein achtzigjähriger Großvater den letzten Atemzug.
*Two days ago my grandfather breathed his last (drew his last breath).*

eine **Attacke** reiten (fig.): cf. zum **Angriff** vorgehen

das **Auf** und Ab: *the ups and downs*

Mein Onkel Georg ist kränklich, und jedes Mal wenn ich ihn besuche, erzählt er mir ausführlich von dem Auf und Ab (von den Höhen und Tiefen) seiner Krankheit.
*My uncle George is in poor health, and every time I visit him, he tells me in detail of his ups and downs.*

etwas **aufbauschen** (fig.): *to blow s. th. up (colloq.); to make a set-out (a fuss) about s. th. (colloq.).* Cf. auch: viel **Wind** um (von) etwas machen

Die Zeitungen haben den leichten Unfall mächtig aufgebauscht.
*The papers blew the minor accident up tremendously (made a tremendous set-out [fuss] about the minor accident).*

j.em etwas **aufbinden** (fig.): cf. j.em einen **Bären** aufbinden

Das kannst du anderen **aufbinden** (fig.): cf. Das kannst du deiner **Großmutter** erzählen

j.em etwas **aufbrummen** (fam.): *to sting s. b. for s. th. (sl.)*

Dem Angeklagten wurde eine beträchtliche Geldstrafe aufgebrummt.
*The accused was stung for a considerable fine.*

**aufdrehen** (fig.): *to turn (to put) on the pressure; to open up; to turn on the heat*

Unsere Mannschaft drehte (spielte) in der zweiten Halbzeit stark auf.
*Our team turned (put) on great pressure (opened up a lot; turned on the heat) in the second half.*

**aufflackern** (fig.): *to flare up; to break out*

Die Aufstände in verschiedenen Teilen Afrikas sind wieder aufgeflackert.
*Revolts have been flaring up (breaking out) again in various parts of Africa.*

**auffliegen** (fig.): *to be exploded (blown up); to blow up (to explode)*

Der ganze Schwindel ist durch eine Anzeige aufgeflogen.
*The whole swindle was exploded (blown up) by (The whole swindle blew up [exploded] as a result of) being reported.*

etwas (j.en) **aufgabeln** (fig.): *to pick s. th. (s. b.) up; to get hold of s. th. (s. b.)*

Wo hast du dieses seltene Buch aufgegabelt?
*Where did you pick up (get hold of) this rare book?*

**aufgeblasen** sein (fig.): cf. sich spreizen (blähen) wie ein **Truthahn**

**aufgedonnert** sein (fam.): cf. **aufgetakelt** sein

in etwas ganz **aufgehen:** *to put one's heart (and soul) into s. th.; to put all one has into s. th.; to throw o. s. into something*

Dieser Pianist geht ganz in seiner Arbeit auf.
*This pianist puts his heart (and soul; puts all he has) into his work (throws himself into his work).*

**aufgekratzt** sein (fam.): *to be in high spirits; to be lively; to be frisky (colloq.)*

Wir freuen uns, daß sie heute so aufgekratzt (aufgeräumt) ist.
*We are glad that she is in such high spirits (is so lively [frisky]) today.*

**aufgeräumt** sein (fig.): cf. **aufgekratzt** sein

**aufgeschmissen** sein (fam.): *to be all at sea (colloq.); to be in a spot (in a hole) (colloq.); to be up the creek (sl.)*

Als der Schüler das Gedicht vortragen sollte, war er aufgeschmissen, denn er hatte es zu Hause nicht gelernt.
*When the pupil was supposed to recite the poem, he was all at sea (in a spot [hole]; up the creek), because he had not learnt it at home.*

**Aufgeschoben** ist nicht aufgehoben (Sprichw.): *To defer a problem is not to solve it*

Früher oder später muß eine Lösung dieser Frage gefunden werden. Aufgeschoben ist nicht aufgehoben.
*Sooner or later a solution must be found to this question. To defer a problem is not to solve it.*

**aufgetakelt** sein (fig. u. fam.): *to be (all) dressed up; to be (all) dolled up (colloq.).* Cf. auch: geputzt (geschmückt) wie ein **Pfingstochse** sein

Ich war erstaunt, die Dorfschönen so aufgetakelt (aufgedonnert) zu sehen.
*I was astonished to see the village beauties (all) dressed up (dolled up) like that.*

ein **aufgewecktes** Kind sein: cf. ein **gewecktes** Kind sein

j.em etwas **aufhalsen** (fig.): cf. j.em etwas auf den **Hals** laden

j.em etwas **aufhängen** (fig.): cf. j.em etwas **andrehen**

viel **Aufhebens** von etwas machen: cf. viel **Wind** um (von) etwas machen

Da hört sich doch alles **auf!**: cf. Das ist doch die **Höhe** (der Höhepunkt)!

j.en **aufmöbeln** (fam.): *to cheer s. b. up; to buck s. b. up (colloq.)*
Sei doch nicht so ernst; komm mit ins Theater und laß dich aufmöbeln.
*Don't be so serious. Come with me to the theatre and cheer (buck) up.*

**aufmucken** (fam.): *to jib*
Vater kann es nicht vertragen, wenn wir gegen seine Anordnungen protestieren.
Wer von uns aufmuckt (sich lausig macht), wird bestraft.
*Father cannot stand us protesting against his orders. Anyone who jibs is punished.*

sich **aufplustern** (fig.): cf. **angeben**

sich **aufrappeln** (fam.): *to set to; to buckle to; to buck up (colloq.); to look lively (colloq.)*
Komm, rappele dich auf und geh an deine Arbeit!
*Come on, set to (buckle to; buck up; look lively) and start your work!*

(gründlich) **aufräumen** (fig.): cf. reine **Bahn** machen

alles **aufschnappen** (fig.): *to have long ears; to have ears like a donkey; to pick everything up*
Sprecht leiser! Unser Töchterchen schnappt alles auf.
*Talk quietly. Our little daughter has long ears (ears like a donkey; picks everything up).*

**aufsein:** a) *to be open;* b) (von Personen) *to be up*
a) Die Geschäfte sind meistens ab 8 Uhr auf.
b) Wir sind morgens immer sehr früh auf.
*a) The shops are generally open from eight o'clock.*
*b) We are always up very early in the morning.*

**aufspielen:** cf. **aufdrehe n**

den **Auftakt** zu etwas bilden (fig.): *to be the prelude to s. th.*
Dieses Konzert bildet den Auftakt zu den Festspielen.
*This concert is the prelude to the festival.*

etwas **auftischen** (fig.): *to dish s. th. up (colloq.); to trot s. th. out (colloq.)*

Von all den Märchen, die du da auftischen willst, glaube ich dir kein Wort.
*I don't believe a word of all those stories you are dishing up (trotting out).*

dick (stark) **auftragen** (fig.): *to pile (to ladle) it on (colloq.); to put it on thick (colloq.)*

Seine Leistung war wirklich nichts Außerordentliches; er hat aber dick (stark) aufgetragen, um uns zu imponieren.
*His performance was really nothing extraordinary, but he piled (ladled) it on (put it on thick) in order to impress us.*

alte Geschichten **aufwärmen** (fig.): *to rake up (to dish up; to dig out; to resurrect) old stories (colloq.)*

Ich möchte wissen, was er für ein Interesse daran hat, solche alte(n) Geschichten aufzuwärmen.
*I should like to know what interest he has in raking (dishing) up (digging out; resurrecting) such old stories.*

é in **Aufwaschen** sein (fig.): *to dispose of two (three etc.) things with one blow; to be a single job.* Cf. auch: zwei **Fliegen** mit éiner Klappe schlagen

Wenn wir die jungen Bäumchen in unsern Garten pflanzen, wollen wir gleich auch das Gras neu einsäen. Das ist dann éin Aufwaschen (Abwaschen).
*When we plant the young saplings in our garden, let us also sow new grass-seed at the same time. In that way we shall dispose of two things with one blow (It will then be a single job).*

j.en **aufziehen** (fig. u. fam.): cf. j.en auf den **Arm** nehmen

j.es **Augapfel** sein (fig.): *to be the apple of s. b.'s eye; to be s. b.'s darling*

Das kleine Mädchen ist der Augapfel (Liebling) seiner Eltern.
*The little girl is the apple of her parents' eyes (is her parents' darling).*

j.em etwas an den **Augen** ablesen (absehen) (fig.): *to know s. th. from s. b.'s face (expression); to see (to read) s. th. in s. b.'s eyes*

Der junge Mann hat seinen Eltern stets jeden Wunsch an den Augen abgelesen (abgesehen).
*The young man has always been able to know his parents' wishes from their faces (expressions; to see [to read] his parents' wishes in their eyes).*

etwas mit anderen **Augen** ansehen: *to see s. th. in a different light (from a different standpoint [a different angle]); to take a different view*

Ich kann ihre Meinung nicht teilen, denn ich sehe die Sache mit ganz anderen Augen an.
*I cannot share your opinion, for I see the matter in quite a different light (from quite a different standpoint [angle]; I take quite a different view).*

die **Augen** gehen j.em auf (fig.): cf. j.em geht ein **Licht** auf

**Auge** um Auge, Zahn um Zahn: *An eye for an eye, a tooth for a tooth*

„Auge um Auge, Zahn um Zahn" ist sein Schlagwort, aber eine solche Vergeltungspolitik sollte man nicht verfolgen.
*"An eye for an eye, a tooth for a tooth" is his slogan, but one ought not to pursue such a policy of retaliation.*

sich die **Augen** ausgucken (fig.): a) *to stare (to look) until one's eyes nearly drop (pop) out;* b) *to strain one's eyes*

    a) Wegen meiner auffallenden Ähnlichkeit mit seinem Bruder hat sich der Mann vor Staunen die Augen ausgeguckt, als er mich sah.
    b) Vergeblich haben wir uns die Augen nach unserm Besuch ausgeguckt.
    *a) Because of my striking resemblance to his brother the man stared (looked) until his eyes nearly dropped (popped) out when he saw me.*
    *b) We strained our eyes in vain for our visitor(s).*

j.em die **Augen** auskratzen (fig.): *to scratch s. b.'s eyes out*

Die feindlichen Nachbarn hätten sich am liebsten gegenseitig die Augen ausgekratzt.
*The hostile neighbours would have liked to scratch each other's eyes out.*

sich die **Augen** ausweinen: *to cry one's eyes out.* Cf. auch: in **Tränen** schwimmen

Als sein Hund starb, hat er sich die Augen ausgeweint (die Augen aus dem Kopf geweint).
*When his dog died, he cried his eyes out.*

etwas im **Auge** behalten (fig.): *to bear (to keep) s. th. in mind*

Ich werde Ihren freundlichen Vorschlag im Auge behalten (werde mir . . . vor Augen halten).
*I shall bear (keep) your kind suggestion in mind.*

mit einem blauen **Auge** davonkommen (fig.): *to get off (to escape) lightly; to get off cheaply.* Cf. auch: leichten **Kaufes** davonkommen

Der nachlässige Autofahrer ist mit einem blauen Auge davongekommen. Er bekam lediglich eine kleine Geldstrafe.
*The careless driver got off (escaped) lightly (got off cheaply). He merely got a small fine.*

ins **Auge** (in die Augen) fallen (springen) (fig.): *to catch the eye; to catch (to strike) the attention*

Das schöne Gemälde in seinem Zimmer fiel (sprang) jedem ins Auge.
*The beautiful painting in his room caught everybody's eye (caught [struck] everybody's attention).*

j.en (etwas) ins **Auge** fassen (fig.): *to keep an eye on s. b. (s. th.); to keep (to have) s. b. (s. th.) in mind (in view)*

Wir hatten ihn schon für diesen Posten ins Auge gefaßt (im Auge gehabt; Wir hatten schon ein Auge auf ihn geworfen).
*We had already been keeping an eye on him (had him [had been keeping him] in mind [view]; had already had an eye on him) for this post.*

j.em etwas (klar) vor **Augen** führen: *to make s. th. clear to s. b.; to bring s. th. home to s. b.; to rub s. th. in (colloq.)*

Mein Vater hat mir klar vor Augen geführt, daß er mit meiner Arbeit gar nicht zufrieden sei.
*My father made it clear to me (brought home to me the fact; rubbed in the fact) that he was not at all satisfied with my work.*

ganz **Auge** sein: *to be all eyes.* Cf. auch: j.en **anglotzen**

Als meine Tochter den Elefanten sah, war sie ganz Auge.
*When my daughter saw the elephant, she was all eyes.*

j.em wie aus den **Augen** geschnitten sein (fig.): *to be a chip off the old block; to be the very image (the living [spitting] image) of s. b.; to be the very spit*

Mein Freund ist seinem Vater wie aus den Augen (aus dem Gesicht) geschnitten (ist gespuckt der Vater).
*My friend is a chip off the old block (the very image [spit; the living (spitting) image] of his father).*

das **Auge** des Gesetzes: *the arm of the law*

Früher oder später erkennt jeder Verbrecher, daß das Auge des Gesetzes scharf sieht (wacht).
*Sooner or later every criminal realises that the arm of the law is long.*

(große) **Augen** machen: *to gape; to look wide-eyed.* Cf. auch: j.en (etwas) **anglotzen**

Über unsere modernen Wolkenkratzer würden unsere Vorfahren große Augen machen.
*Our forefathers would gape (look wide-eyed) at our modern skyscrapers.*

j.en (etwas) im **Auge** haben (fig.): cf. j.en (etwas) ins **Auge** fassen

sich etwas vor **Augen** halten: cf. etwas im **Auge** behalten

sich die **Augen** aus dem Kopf weinen (fig.): cf. sich die **Augen** ausweinen

mit einem lachenden und einem weinenden **Auge** (fig.): *with mixed feelings*

Selbst wenn ich mich in Hamburg beruflich verbessern würde, so würde ich meine Heimatstadt nur mit einem lachenden und einem weinenden Auge (mit gemischten Gefühlen) verlassen.
*Even if I were to improve my professional position in Hamburg, it would be with mixed feelings that I would leave my home town.*

j.en nicht aus den **Augen** lassen: *not to let s. b. out of one's sight; to keep one's eye(s) on s. b.*

Ich weiß nie, was mein kleiner Sohn machen wird, und ich kann ihn nicht aus den Augen lassen.
*I never know what my small son is going to do, and I cannot let him out of my sight (must always keep my eye[s] on him).*

leicht ins **Auge** gehen können (fig. u. fam.): *to be no joke; to be no laughing matter; to be able well (easily) to have ended with broken bones*

Diesmal bist du glimpflich davongekommen; das hätte aber leicht ins Auge gehen können.
*This time you have escaped unscathed, but it could well (easily) have been no joke (no laughing matter; have ended with broken bones).*

mit dem linken **Auge** in die rechte Westentasche sehen (fig. u. fam.):

cf. **schielen** wie ein Brummer ('ne Brumme)

**Augen** wie ein Luchs haben: *to have eyes like a hawk (like a lynx)*

Meinem Freund entgeht nichts; er hat Augen wie ein Luchs (hat Argusaugen [Luchsaugen]).
*Nothing escapes my friend. He has eyes like a hawk (lynx).*

Seine **Augen** sind größer als sein Magen (fig.): *His eyes are bigger than his stomach (belly)*

Das Kind hatte (sich) zuviel auf den Teller gelegt (getan). Seine Augen waren größer als sein Magen.
*The child had put too much on its plate. Its eyes were bigger than its stomach (belly).*

mit offenen **Augen** schlafen: *to be day-dreaming; to be wool-gathering*

Unser Lehrer behauptete, wir schliefen mit offenen Augen.
*Our teacher maintained that we were day-dreaming (wool-gathering).*

j.em die **Augen** öffnen (fig.): *to open s. b.'s eyes; to be an eye-opener for s. b. (colloq.)*

Diese schwere Enttäuschung hat jedem die Augen geöffnet.
*This grave disappointment opened everybody's eyes (was an eye-opener for everybody).*

sich die **Augen** reiben (fig.): *to rub one's eyes; to throw up one's arms*

Als ich diese Notiz in der Zeitung las, rieb ich mir vor Staunen die Augen (schlug ich . . . die Hände über dem Kopf zusammen).
*When I read this notice in the paper, I rubbed my eyes (I threw up my arms) in astonishment.*

ein scharfes **Auge** auf j.en haben: *to keep a sharp (close) watch on s. b.; to keep a sharp (keen) eye on s. b.; to gun for s. b. (sl.)*

Die Polizei hat ein scharfes Auge auf dieses Individuum (sieht diesem I. auf die Finger; hat dieses I. [scharf] aufs Korn genommen).
*The police are keeping a sharp (close) watch (a sharp [keen] eye) on (are gunning for) this character.*

j.em schöne **Augen** machen: *to make eyes at s. b.; to give s. b. the glad eye (colloq.)*

Sie macht jedem gut aussehenden Jungen schöne Augen.
*She makes eyes at every good-looking boy (gives every good-looking boy the glad eye).*

j.em schwarz vor den **Augen** werden: *to go black (blank) (before s. b.'s eyes)*

Es wurde ihr plötzlich alles schwarz (plötzlich Nacht) vor den Augen, und sie fiel in Ohnmacht.
*Everything suddenly went black (blank) (before her eyes) and she fainted.*

j.em vor **Augen** schweben (fig.): *to be dangling before s. b.'s eyes*

Die Möglichkeit einer Ausdehnung meines Geschäftes schwebt mir schon lange vor Augen.
*The possibility of expanding my business has been dangling before my eyes for a long time.*

Mir schwimmt es vor den **Augen**: cf. Der **Kopf** brummt mir

einer Sache ins **Auge** sehen (fig.): *to look s. th. in the face; to face (to confront) s. th.*

Man muß den Tatsachen ruhig ins Auge (Antlitz) sehen.
*One must look the facts quietly in the face (One must face [confront] the facts quietly).*

sehenden **Auges** (mit offenen Augen) ins Verderben rennen: *to plunge into disaster with one's eyes open*

Karl rannte sehenden Auges (mit offenen Augen) in sein Verderben.
*Charles plunged into disaster with his eyes open.*

Aus den **Augen**, aus dem Sinn (Sprichw.): *Out of sight, out of mind (prov.)*

Ich war lange fort, aber mein Freund hat mir kein einziges Mal geschrieben. Aus den Augen, aus dem Sinn.
*I was away for a long while but my friend did not write to me once. Out of sight, out of mind.*

j.em ins **Auge** stechen (fig.): *to take s. b.'s fancy; to take s. b.'s eye*

Dieses blaue Kleid sticht mir schon seit langem ins Auge.
*This blue dress took my eye (my fancy) a long while ago.*

j.em unter die **Augen** treten (fig.): *to look s. b. in the face; to show one's face (to s. b.); to face (to confront) s. b.*

Nach diesem Vorfall wird er es nicht wagen, uns wieder unter die Augen (vors Gesicht) zu treten.

*After this incident he will not dare to look us in the face again (to show [us] his face again; to face [confront] us again).*

Es blieb kein **Auge** trocken: *There was not a dry-eyed person present (in the place [room etc.]); There were tears in every eye*

Bei der Rede des Pfarrers am Grabe blieb kein Auge trocken.
*During the vicar's address at the graveside there was not a dry-eyed person present (there were tears in every eye).*

j.en aus den **Augen** verlieren (fig.): cf. j.es **Spur** verlieren

die **Augen** vor etwas verschließen (fig.): *to shut (to blind) one's eyes to s. th.; to blind o. s. to s. th.* Cf. auch: den **Kopf** in den Sand stecken

Träumen Sie denn? Sie dürfen doch die Augen nicht vor der Wirklichkeit verschließen.
*Are you dreaming? You must not shut (blind) your eyes (blind yourself) to reality.*

unter vier **Augen:** *in confidence (privacy); in private*

Kann ich Sie mal unter vier Augen sprechen?
*Can I speak to you in confidence (privacy; in private)?*

Vier **Augen** sehen mehr als zwei (Sprichw.): *Two heads are better than one (prov.)*

Wenn ich mir einen neuen Teppich kaufe, geh' bitte mit. Vier Augen sehen mehr als zwei.
*If I buy a new carpet, please go with me. Two heads are better than one.*

ein **Auge** auf j.en werfen (haben) (fig.): a) cf. j.en (etwas) ins **Auge** fassen; b) *to have one's eye on s. b.; to cast one's eye at s. b.; to shoot a glance at s. b.*

Er warf ein Auge auf das schöne Mädchen, als es vorbeiging.
*He had his eye on (cast his eye [shot a glance] at) the beautiful girl as she went by.*

éin **Auge** zudrücken (fig.): *to turn a blind eye; to wink at s. th.; to let pass*

Wir wollen bei dieser kleinen Verfehlung éin Auge zudrücken.
*We are going to turn a blind eye to (wink at) this slight offence (let . . . pass).*

kein **Auge** zutun: *not to sleep a wink*

Vor lauter Sorgen konnte ich kein Auge zutun.
*I could not sleep a wink for worry.*

im letzten **Augenblick:** cf. in zwölfter **Stunde**

ein **Augendiener** sein: *to be a toady; to be a yes-man (colloq.); to be a crawler (sl.)*

Dieser Angestellte schmeichelt seinen Vorgesetzten. Er ist ein Augendiener (kratzt sich bei seinen V. ein; macht sich bei seinen V. Liebkind).
*That clerk flatters his superiors. He is a toady (yes-man; crawler).*

**Augendienerei:** *toadying; pandering; currying of favour; fawning*

Eine solche Augendienerei (Liebedienerei) wirkt abstoßend auf mich.
*Such toadying (pandering; currying of favour; fawning) has a repellent effect on me.*

das reine (reinste) **Augenpulver** sein: *to be agony for the eyes*

Deine winzige Schrift ist das reine (reinste) Augenpulver.
*Your tiny writing is agony for the eyes.*

eine **Augenweide** sein: *to be a sight for sore eyes; to be a feast for the eyes*

Das neue Ballett war die reinste Augenweide.
*The new ballet was a sight for sore eyes (a feast for the eyes).*

den **Augiasstall** reinigen: cf. den **Stall** ausmisten

nicht **aus** noch ein wissen: *not to know which way to turn; to be on the horns of a dilemma; to be in a cleft stick.* Cf. auch: in der **Klemme** sein; mit seiner **Kunst** zu (am) Ende sein

Ich habe den Eindruck, daß die Regierung nicht aus noch ein (nicht ein noch aus; sich nicht zu retten) weiß.
*I have the impression that the government does not know which way to turn (is on the horns of a dilemma; is in a cleft stick).*

etwas **ausbaden** müssen (fig.): *to take the rap (colloq.); to stand the racket (sl.); to carry the can (sl.).* Cf. auch: die **Zeche** bezahlen müssen

Er war an allem schuld, aber da er rechtzeitig fortging, mußte ich alles ausbaden.
*It was all his fault, but because he got away in time, I had to take the rap (carry the can; stand the racket).*

j.en **ausbooten** (fig.): *to throw s. b. overboard; to kick (to boot) s. b. out (colloq.).* Cf. auch: j.en in die **Wüste** schicken

Dieser Minister soll verabschiedet worden sein. Wissen Sie, warum man ihn ausgebootet hat?
*This minister is said to have been dismissed. Do you know why he has been thrown overboard (been kicked [booted] out)?*

etwas **ausbrüten** (fig.): a) *to be sickening for s. th.;* b) *to hatch s. th.; to cook s. th. up (colloq.)*

a) Mein Bruder hat etwas Temperatur; er brütet wohl irgendeine Krankheit aus.
b) Wir sind gespannt, welche Pläne die Opposition jetzt ausbrütet.
*a) My brother has a slight temperature. He is probably sickening for something.*
*b) We are wondering what plans the opposition are hatching (are cooking up) now.*

sich **ausbügeln** (fig.): *to iron itself out; to smooth over; to settle itself.* Cf. auch: etwas ins **Geleise** bringen

Die Mißverständnisse zwischen uns haben sich jetzt ausgebügelt (sind jetzt ausgebügelt; haben sich in Wohlgefallen aufgelöst).

*The misunderstandings between us have now been ironed out (have now been smoothed over [settled themselves]).*

ein **Ausbund** von Gelehrsamkeit sein: *to be a well of knowledge (a fount of learning)*

Man sieht es diesen Büchern an, daß der Verfasser ein Ausbund von Gelehrsamkeit sein muß.

*One can see from these books that the author must be a well of knowledge (a fount of learning).*

ein **Ausbund** von Schurke sein: *to be an arch-knave; to be the embodiment of trickery*

Dieser Mann ist ein Ausbund von Schurke. Lassen Sie sich auf keinen Fall mit ihm ein.

*That man is an arch-knave (the embodiment of trickery). On no account have anything to do with him.*

ein **Ausbund** von Tugend sein: *to be a paragon of virtue*

Mit diesem Mädchen will keiner spielen, weil es ein Ausbund von Tugend (ein Tugendbold) ist.

*Nobody wants to play with that girl, because she is a paragon of virtue.*

etwas **ausfressen** (fig. u. fam.): *to get (to be) up to s. th. (colloq.); to get (to be) up to mischief (colloq.); to get into a scrape (colloq.)*

Was hast du denn jetzt ausgefressen?

*What (mischief) have you got (been) up to now? (What scrape have you got into now?)*

Man muß **ausfressen**, was man sich eingebrockt hat (Sprichw.): cf. Was der Mensch **säet**, das wird er ernten

bei etwas leer **ausgehen**: cf. **leer** bei etwas ausgehen

**ausgekocht** sein (fig.): cf. **durchtrieben** sein

ein **ausgemergeltes** Gesicht haben: *to have a care-worn (care-lined) face*

Unser Kollege muß viele Sorgen haben. Sehen Sie nur sein ausgemergeltes Gesicht!

*Our colleague must have a lot of worries. Just look at his care-worn (care-lined) face.*

**ausgerechnet:** a) (von Personen) *of all people; it has to be . . .;* b) (von Sachen) *of all places (times etc.); it would have to be . . .*

a) Ausgerechnet ich mußte die Rechnung bezahlen.
b) Ausgerechnet in Paris mußte ich meinen Fotoapparat verlieren. – Ausgerechnet in diesem heißen Monat war die Badeanstalt geschlossen.

*a) Of all people, I had to pay (It had to be me who paid) the bill.*
*b) In Paris, of all places, I had to lose my camera (I would have to lose my camera in Paris). – In this hot month, of all times, the bathing-pool was shut (The bathing-pool would have to be shut in this hot month).*

etwas **aushecken**: cf. etwas im **Schilde** führen

**auskneifen** (fam.): cf. **durchbrennen; Fersengeld** geben

**ausknobeln** (fam.): cf. **austüfteln**

Es ist kein **Auskommen** mit ihm: *It is impossible to get on with him; There is no getting on with him*

> Ich habe es mehrmals schon versucht, aber es ist leider kein Auskommen mit ihm.
> *I have tried several times but I am afraid that it is impossible to get on with him (that there is no getting on with him).*

Man **lernt** nie **aus**: *One is never too old (It is never too late) to learn (prov.)*

> Es taucht immer etwas Neues auf. Man lernt nie aus.
> *Something new is always cropping up. One is never too old (It is never too late) to learn.*

Man muß **auslöffeln,** was man sich eingebrockt hat (Sprichw.): cf. Was der Mensch **säet,** das wird er ernten

**Ausnahme:** cf. **Regel**

tüchtig **auspacken** (fig.): cf. kein **Blatt** vor den Mund nehmen

etwas **ausposaunen** (fig.): *to shout s. th. from the housetops; to blaze s. th. abroad; to broadcast s. th.*

> Es ärgert mich, daß du das, was ich dir im Vertrauen erzählt habe, überall ausposaunt (an die große Glocke gehängt) hast.
> *It annoys me that you have shouted from the house tops (blazed abroad; broadcast everywhere) what I told you in confidence.*

nach etwas **Ausschau** halten: *to keep an eye (one's eyes) open for s. th.; to look (to cast) out (round) for s. th.*

> Bevor der Schriftsteller seinen Roman zu schreiben begann, hielt er nach neuen Gedanken Ausschau.
> *Before the author began to write his novel, he kept an eye (his eyes) open (looked [cast] out [round]) for new ideas.*

den **Ausschlag** geben (fig.): *to tip (to turn) the scales (the balance)*
> Sein energisches Handeln gab den Ausschlag.
> *His vigorous action tipped (turned) the scales (the balance).*

sich **ausschütten** vor Lachen: cf. sich **totlachen**

**aussein:** a) *to be over (finished);* b) *to be all over (all up) with s. b. (colloq.)*
> a) Wann wird das Kino heute aussein?
> b) Seitdem der Boxkämpfer den entscheidenden Kampf verlor, ist es aus mit ihm.

44

*a) When will the film be over (finished) today?*
*b) Since the boxer lost the decisive fight, it is all over (up) with him.*

**außer** sich sein: cf. aus dem **Häuschen** sein

etwas aufs **Äußerste** (zum Äußersten) treiben: cf. etwas auf die **Spitze** treiben

**ausspannen** (fig.): *to make a break; to break off.* Cf. auch: eine **Atempause;** eine **Kunstpause** machen

> Wenn man so schwer und so lange gearbeitet hat, muß man eine Zeitlang ausspannen.
> *When one has worked so hard and so long, one must make a break (break off) for a while.*

etwas lang (weit) **ausspinnen** (fig.): *to drag (to spin) s. th. out.* Cf. auch: etwas **lang** und breit erzählen

> Dieser alte Soldat liebt es, seine Geschichten lang (weit) auszuspinnen (breitspurig zu erzählen; breitzutreten).
> *This old soldier likes to drag (to spin) out his stories.*

j.en nicht **ausstehen** können: cf. j.en nicht **riechen** können

auf dem **Aussterbeetat** stehen: *to be on its (their etc.) last legs (on its [their etc.] way out)*

> Die Straßenbahn steht schon seit einiger Zeit auf dem Aussterbeetat.
> *Trams have been on their last legs (on their way out) for some time.*

etwas **austüfteln** (fam.): *to concoct (to brew; to hatch) s. th.; to cook s. th. up (colloq.)*

> Ich bin mal gespannt, was dieser Erfinder jetzt noch austüftelt (ausknobelt).
> *I wonder what that inventor is concocting (brewing; hatching; cooking up) now.*

sich einen **Ausweg** offenlassen (offenhalten) (fig.): cf. sich eine **Hintertür** offenlassen

j.em eins **auswischen** (fam.): *to take s. b. to task; to put s. b. on the mat (carpet); to blow s. b. up (sl.); to give s. b. a rocket (sl.).* Cf. auch: j.en **abkanzeln**

> Mein Chef hat mir eins ausgewischt (mir einen Wischer gegeben), weil ich nicht schnell genug gearbeitet hatte.
> *My boss took me to task (put me on the mat [carpet]; blew me up; gave me a rocket) for not working fast enough.*

sich **auszahlen** (fig.): cf. sich **rentieren**

sich benehmen wie die **Axt** im Walde: cf. sich benehmen wie der **Elefant** im Porzellanladen

die **Axt** an die Wurzel einer Sache legen (fig.): *to strike at the root of s. th.;*
*to tackle s. th. at the roots*

> Dies ist keine unwichtige Sache; daher muß man die Axt an die Wurzel des
> Problems legen (das Problem an [bei] der Wurzel packen).
> *This is not an unimportant matter, so one must strike at the root of the problem (tackle*
> *the problem at the roots).*


# B


eine **babylonische** Verwirrung: cf. eine babylonische **Verwirrung**

abgehen wie beim **Bäcker** die Semmeln: cf. abgehen wie warme **Semmeln**

ein **Backfisch** sein (fig.): *to be a teenager; to be a flapper (a bobby-soxer) (colloq.)*
> Sonntags sieht man viele Backfische im Park spazierengehen.
> *On Sundays one sees many teenagers (flappers; bobby-soxers) walking in the park.*

eine **Backofenhitze** sein: cf. eine **Bullenhitze** sein

j.em eine **Backpfeife** geben: cf. j.em eine **kleben**

schwimmen wie ein **Backstein**: cf. schwimmen wie eine bleierne **Ente**

**baff** sein (fam.): cf. wie vom **Blitz** getroffen sein

die ganze **Bagage** (fam.): cf. die ganze **Blase**

auf die abschüssige (schiefe) **Bahn** geraten (fig.): *to go off the rails; to go*
*crooked (downhill); to go to the dogs; to go to rack and ruin.* Cf. auch: es geht mit
j.em **bergab;** vor die **Hunde** gehen; auf **Abwege** geraten

> Es ist traurig, wenn ein Sohn achtbarer Eltern auf die abschüssige (schiefe) Bahn
> (Ebene) gerät (absackt; aus der Art schlägt; verlottert; verludert; versackt; ver-
> schlampt).
> *It is sad when a son of respectable parents goes off the rails (goes crooked [downhill; to the*
> *dogs; to rack and ruin]).*

sich **Bahn** brechen (fig.): *to find a way; to break through; to carve a path for o. s.;*
*s. th. will out*
> Die Wahrheit wird sich früher oder später Bahn brechen.
> *Truth will find a way (will break through; will carve a path for itself; will out) sooner*
> *or later.*

reine **Bahn** machen (fig.): *to make a clean sweep*

Nach diesem Streik machte die Werksleitung reine Bahn (reinen Tisch; räumte die W. gründlich auf) und kündigte allen faulen Arbeitern.
*After this strike the management made a clean sweep and dismissed all lazy workers.*

j.en (etwas) aus der **Bahn** werfen (fig.): *to upset s. b. (s. th.); to throw s. b. (s. th.) out of gear (out of step); to put s. b. (s. th.) out of joint*

Der Tod seines Vaters hat ihn völlig aus der Bahn geworfen (aus dem Geleise gebracht).
*His father's death upset him completely (threw him completely out of gear [step]; put him completely out of joint).*

lügen, daß sich die **Balken** biegen: *to tell a pack of lies (a tissue of falsehoods); to lie o. s. blue in the face (colloq.); to tell the most thumping (whopping) lies (colloq.)*

Mißtraue seinen Worten; denn er lügt, daß sich die Balken biegen (lügt das Blaue vom Himmel herunter; lügt wie gedruckt; lügt dir die Hucke voll).
*Distrust his words, for he tells you a pack of lies (a tissue of falsehoods; he lies himself blue in the face; tells the most thumping [whopping] lies).*

(Das) Wasser hat keine **Balken** (Sprichw.): cf. (Das) **Wasser** hat keine Balken

**Balsam** für j.es Herz (Seele) sein: *to be balm to s. b.'s sad heart; to be manna to s. b.'s soul*

Nach so vielen Enttäuschungen war diese Anerkennung Balsam für ihr Herz (ihre Seele).
*After so many disappointments this appreciation was balm to her sad heart (manna to her soul).*

(einen) **Bammel** haben (fam.): cf. (eine) **Heidenangst** haben

am laufenden **Band** (fig.): *in endless succession; in an uninterrupted flow*

Sie erzählten sich Geschichten am laufenden Band.
*They told each other stories in endless succession (in an uninterrupted flow).*

eine gemeine **Bande** sein (fam.): *to be a low crowd (colloq.); to be a dirty lot (sl.)*

Du solltest mit diesen Leuten nichts zu tun haben; sie sind eine gemeine Bande.
*You should not have anything to do with those people; they are a low crowd (a dirty lot).*

**Bände** sprechen: *to speak volumes; to reveal a great deal*

Dieser Brief spricht Bände über den Charakter des Verfassers.
*This letter speaks volumes (reveals a great deal) about the writer's character.*

so lang wie ein **Bandwurm** sein: *to be as long as an eel*

Vermeide Sätze, die so lang wie ein Bandwurm sind!
*Avoid sentences which are as long as an eel.*

eine **Bangbuxe** (Bangbüxe) sein (fam.): cf. ein **Angsthase** sein

**Bange** machen gilt nicht!: *You can't give me the creeps! (colloq.); You can't put the wind up me! (sl.)*

Deine Spukgeschichten ängstigen mich nicht. Bange machen gilt nicht!
*Your ghost stories don't frighten me. You can't give me the creeps (You can't put the wind up me)!*

durch die **Bank** (fig.): *all one price; one and all*

Die Bücher dieses Verlages kosten durch die Bank zwei Mark.
*This publisher's books cost all one price – two marks (cost two marks, one and all).*

etwas auf die lange **Bank** schieben (fig.): *to shelve s. th.; to put s. th. aside (on one side); to put s. th. into cold storage*

Was unbedingt zu tun nötig ist, sollte man nicht erst auf die lange Bank schieben (auf Eis legen).
*One should not shelve (put aside [on one side; into cold storage]) what it is absolutely necessary to do at once.*

auf der **Bank** der Spötter sitzen: *to scoff at everything; to pooh-pooh everything (colloq.); to sniff at everything (colloq.); to turn up one's nose at everything (colloq.).*
Cf. auch: über etwas die **Nase** rümpfen

Dieser Kritiker ist wegen seiner Ironie bekannt; er sitzt (einfach) auf der Bank der Spötter (er sitzt, wo die Spötter sitzen).
*This critic is known for his irony; he simply scoffs (pooh-poohs; sniffs at; turns up his nose at) everything.*

unter dem **Bann** von j.em (etwas) stehen (fig.): *to be under the spell of s. b. (s. th.); to be spellbound by s. b. (s. th.)*

Karl ist nicht mehr unabhängig in seinen Ansichten, sondern steht vollkommen unter dem Bann seines Bruders.
*Charles is no longer independent in his views but is completely under the spell of (is completely spellbound by) his brother.*

j.em einen **Bären** aufbinden (fig.): *to pull s. b.'s leg; to take a rise out of s. b.; to take s. b. for a ride (colloq.); to kid s. b. (colloq.)*

Der Fremde versuchte, mir mit seiner Erzählung einen (Bären) aufzubinden (mir etwas weiszumachen; mich zu verkohlen).
*The stranger tried to pull my leg (to take a rise out of me; to take me for a ride; to kid me) with his story.*

brummig wie ein **Bär** sein: cf. ein alter **Brummbär** sein

hungrig wie ein **Bär** sein: cf. einen **Mordshunger** haben zu etwas Lust haben wie der **Bär** zum Tanzen: *to feel as much like doing s. th. as an elephant feels like skipping*

> Meine Kinder möchten, daß ich mit ihnen ins Kino gehe. Ich habe aber dazu Lust (so wenig Lust) wie der Bär zum Tanzen.
> *My children want me to go to the cinema with them, but I feel as much like doing so as an elephant feels like skipping.*

Man soll das Fell des **Bären** nicht verkaufen (verteilen), bevor man ihn erlegt hat (Sprichw.): cf. Man soll das **Fell** des Bären nicht verkaufen (verteilen), bevor man ihn erlegt hat

**bärbeißig** sein: *to be ratty (snappy) (colloq.)*

> Ein Polizist sollte höflich und freundlich, nicht reizbar und bärbeißig sein.
> *A policeman should be polite and friendly, not irritable and ratty (snappy).*

auf der **Bärenhaut** liegen (fig.): cf. **herumlungern**

einen **Bärenhunger** haben: cf. einen **Mordshunger** haben

**Bärenkräfte** haben (besitzen): *to be as strong as a horse (as an ox)*

> Ihr Bruder muß Bärenkräfte haben ([besitzen]; baumstark [stark wie eine Eiche]; ein Kerl wie ein Baum sein), denn er trug den schweren Tisch allein von einem Ende des Zimmers bis zum anderen.
> *Your brother must be as strong as a horse (as an ox), for he carried the heavy table by himself from one end of the room to the other.*

eine **Bärennatur** haben: *to have the constitution of a horse*

> Dein Vater muß eine Bärennatur haben, da er sich von seiner schweren Krankheit so rasch erholt hat.
> *Your father must have the constitution of a horse to recover so quickly from his serious illness.*

Der **Bart** ist ab! (fig. u. fam.): *It's all up (over) (colloq.)*

> Durch meine unüberlegte Bemerkung habe ich ihn verärgert. Nun ist der Bart ab!
> *I have annoyed him by my unconsidered remark. Now it's all up (over).*

in den **Bart** brummen (fig.): cf. in den **Bart** murmeln

j.em um den **Bart** gehen (fig.): *to pander to s. b.; to make up to s. b.; to soft-soap s. b. (colloq.)*

> Fritz pflegt, seinem Vater um den Bart zu gehen, wenn er etwas von ihm haben will.
> *Fred is accustomed to pander to his father (to make up to [to soft-soap] his father) when he wants something from him.*

einen **Bart** haben (fig. u. fam.): *to be as old as the hills (as old as Adam); to have whiskers; to be a chestnut; to be corny (sl.)*

> Dieser Witz ist so alt, daß er einen Bart hat (eine alte Jacke ist).
> *This joke is as old as the hills (as Adam; has [got] whiskers; is a chestnut; is corny).*

in den **Bart** murmeln (fig.): *to swallow one's words; to mumble into one's beard*

> Sprich laut und deutlich; ich kann dich nicht verstehen, wenn du in deinen Bart murmelst (brummst).
> *Speak loudly and clearly. I cannot understand you if you swallow your words (if you mumble into your beard).*

sich den **Bart** raufen (fig.): cf. sich die **Haare** raufen

wissen, wo **Barthel** den Most holt: *to know on which side one's bread is buttered; to know where one's interests lie.* Cf. auch: nicht auf den **Kopf** gefallen sein

> Mein Vetter denkt immer nur an seine eigenen Interessen. Er weiß schon, wo Barthel den Most holt.
> *My cousin always thinks only of his own interests. He knows on which side his bread is buttered (where his interests lie).*

Und damit **basta**!: *And that's the end of it.!; So that's that!; So there!*

> Nach diesen Erfahrungen leihe ich ihm keinen Pfennig mehr. Und damit basta (Punktum; Schluß)!
> *After these experiences I am not going to lend him another penny, and that's the end of it (so that's that; so there)!*

einen schönen **Batzen** Geld kosten: cf. eine **Stange** Geld kosten

vom **Bau** sein (fig.): *to know the ropes; to be in the know; to be on the inside*

> In solchen Dingen kann ich mich auf sein Urteil verlassen, da er doch vom Bau (Fach) ist.
> *I can rely on his judgement in such things, because he knows the ropes (is in the know [on the inside]).*

sich den **Bauch** vor Lachen halten: cf. sich **totlachen**

j.em ein Loch (Löcher) in den **Bauch** fragen (fig. u. fam.): cf. j.em ein **Loch** (Löcher) in den Kopf fragen

vor j.em auf dem **Bauche** rutschen (fig.): *to grovel before s. b.; to lick s. b.'s boots; to toady to s. b.*

> Es ist unwürdig, vor einflußreichen Persönlichkeiten auf dem Bauche zu rutschen (. . . Persönlichkeiten zu kriechen).
> *It is undignified to grovel before (to lick the boots of [to toady to]) influential personalities.*

sich den **Bauch** vollschlagen (fam.): *to gorge o. s.; to stuff o. s. (sl.).* Cf. auch: ein **Freßsack** sein

Er hatte sich den Bauch (Wanst) so vollgeschlagen, daß ihm auf dem Nach-
hauseweg schlecht wurde.
*He had gorged (stuffed) himself so much that he felt sick on the way home.*

auf etwas **bauen** (fig.): cf. mit etwas **rechnen**

auf j.en **bauen**: *to rely (to depend; to count) on s. b.*

Auf ihn kannst du bauen; er wird dir immer beistehen.
*You can rely (depend; count) on him; he will always assist you.*

**Bauer** bleibt Bauer (Sprichw.): *Once a simpleton, always a simpleton*

Der dumme Junge wurde von seinen Eltern auf die Höhere Schule geschickt.
Er hatte keinen Erfolg. Bauer bleibt doch Bauer.
*The stupid boy was sent by his parents to the secondary school. He was not successful.*
*Once a simpleton, always a simpleton.*

Die dümmsten **Bauern** haben die dicksten Kartoffeln (Sprichw.): *Fortune
favours fools (prov.)*

Obwohl wir nichts von Obstzucht verstehen, haben wir alljährlich eine große
Ernte an Pfirsichen. Die dümmsten Bauern haben die dicksten Kartoffeln.
*Although we do not understand anything about fruit cultivation, we get a large crop of
peaches every year. Fortune favours fools.*

ein **Bauernfänger** sein: *to be a shark (welsher; trickster; sharper)*

Mit dem Kerl sollte man niemals Karten spielen; er ist ein richtiger Bauernfänger.
*You should never play cards with that fellow; he's a proper shark (welsher; trickster;
sharper).*

**Bauernschlauheit (Bauernschläue)**: *native cunning; canniness; artfulness*

Trotz seiner Beschränktheit besitzt dieser Mann eine gewisse Bauernschlauheit
(-schläue).
*In spite of his stupidity this man possesses a certain native cunning (a certain canniness
[artfulness]).*

**Bauklötze** staunen (fam.): cf. wie aus den **Wolken** (ge)fallen

Den **Baum** muß man biegen, dieweil er noch jung ist (Sprichw.): cf.
Was **Hänschen** nicht lernt, lernt Hans nimmermehr (Sprichw.)

zwischen **Baum** und Borke stecken (fig.): *to find o. s. in an awkward (ticklish)
position; to find o. s. in a jam (in a spot) (colloq.).* Cf. auch: in der **Klemme**
sein; zwischen zwei **Feuern** sitzen

Wer sich in einen Streit zwischen Verwandten einmischt, steckt leicht zwischen
Baum und Borke.
*A person who intervenes in a quarrel between relations can easily find himself in an awkward
(ticklish) position (in a jam [spot]).*

keine **Bäume** ausreißen können: cf. kein **Herkules** sein

um auf die **Bäume** zu klettern (fam.): *enough to drive one (you) crazy (drive one [you] up the wall; drive one [you] round the bend) (colloq.)*

> Nun habe ich den letzten Zug verpaßt. Es ist wirklich, um auf die Bäume zu klettern (die Wände [Wand] hochzugehen).
> *Now I've missed the last train. It's enough to drive one (you) crazy (mad; enough to drive one [you] up the wall [round the bend]).*

Die **Bäume** wachsen einem nicht in den Himmel (Sprichw.): *Not everything turns to gold in one's hand; Providence provides a place for all things*

> Kurz vor unserm Erfolg haben wir einen schweren Rückschlag erlitten; es ist schon dafür gesorgt, daß einem die Bäume nicht in den Himmel wachsen.
> *Shortly before our success we suffered a severe reverse. It is ordained that not everything shall turn to gold in one's hand (Providence provides a place for all things).*

**baumlang** sein: cf. lang wie eine **Bohnenstange** sein

**baumstark** sein: cf. **Bärenkräfte** haben

in **Bausch** und Bogen (fig.): *lock, stock and barrel; hook, line and sinker*

> Die Regierungsparteien haben den Antrag der Opposition in Bausch und Bogen abgelehnt.
> *The government parties defeated the opposition motion lock, stock and barrel (hook, line and sinker).*

etwas **beackern** (fig.): *to work (to plough) s. th. over.* Cf. auch: etwas **abgrasen**

> Eine neue Dissertation über dieses Thema ist nicht zu empfehlen, da es schon viel beackert worden ist.
> *A new dissertation on this subject is not advisable, because it has often been worked (ploughed) over before.*

j.en **bearbeiten** (fig.): *to work on s. b.; to get at s. b. (colloq.); to get to work on s. b. (colloq.)*

> Meine Mutter wollte es zuerst nicht haben, daß ich so weit wegfahre; ich habe sie aber bearbeitet, so daß sie jetzt doch zugestimmt hat.
> *At first my mother did not want me to go so far, but I worked on her (got at her; got to work on her) so that she has now agreed after all.*

den **Becher** bis zur Neige leeren (fig.): *to drain the cup; to drink deeply of the cup; to have one's fill (one's share)*

> Die Flüchtlinge haben den Becher des Leides (den Kelch) bis zur Neige geleert.
> *Refugees have drained (drunk deeply of) the cup of sorrow (have had their fill [share] of sorrow).*

zu tief in den **Becher** geguckt haben: *to have been at the bottle; to have had one over the eight (colloq.); to have had a drop too much (colloq.); to be half seas over (colloq.).* Cf. auch: einen **Schwips** haben; **sternhagelvoll** sein

Auf dem Heimweg schwankte er hin und her; er hatte zu tief in den Becher (ins Glas; in die Flasche) geguckt (hatte Schlagseite; war angesäuselt [benebelt]; hatte einen über den Durst getrunken [einen in der Krone]).
*He tottered from side to side on his way home; he had been at the bottle (had had one over the eight; had had a drop too much; was half seas over).*

**bechern:** cf. (sich) einen hinter die **Binde** gießen

sich nicht mit Ruhm **bedecken:** cf. sich nicht mit **Ruhm** bedecken (bekleckern)

**bedeppert** sein (fam.): *to be flabbergasted (stupefied; open-mouthed)*

Als Karl sah, daß er mit seinem Ball das Fenster eingeworfen hatte, stand er bedeppert da.
*When Charles saw that he had broken the window with his ball, he stood there flabbergasted (stupefied; open-mouthed).*

alle Hoffnungen **begraben** (fig.): *to abandon (to give up; to relinquish) all hope(s)*

Wegen meiner Krankheit mußten wir leider alle Hoffnungen, ins Ausland zu fahren, begraben.
*Because of my illness we unfortunately had to abandon (give up; relinquish) all hope(s) of going abroad.*

sich **begraben** lassen (fig. u. fam.): *to go and drown (hang) o. s. (colloq.)*

Mit deiner Erfindung, die sowieso nicht neuartig ist, kannst du dich begraben lassen.
*You can go and drown (hang) yourself and your invention, which isn't new anyway.*

schwer von **Begriff** sein: cf. schwer von **Kapee** sein

wie **behext** sein: cf. (wie) zur **Salzsäule** erstarrt sein

nicht alle **beieinander** haben: cf. nicht richtig im **Dachstübchen** sein

**beileibe** nicht: *on no account; not for the world; not for anything; not for the life of me.* Cf. auch: nicht um alles in der **Welt**

Ich möchte beileibe nicht so ein faules Leben führen.
*On no account (Not for the world [for anything; for the life of me]) would I lead such a lazy life.*

sich die **Beine** nach etwas ablaufen: cf. sich die **Füße** (nach etwas) ablaufen sich ein **Bein** ausreißen (fig. u. fam.): *to spare no pains; to do one's level best; to try with might and main; to fall over o. s. (colloq.)*

Mein Kollege hat sich ein Bein ausgerissen, um dem Chef zu gefallen.
*My colleague spared no pains (did his level best; tried with might and main; fell over himself) to please the boss.*

sich kein **Bein** ausreißen (fig. u. fam.): *to take one's time; not to get a move on (colloq.); not to believe in straining o. s. (in sweating; in working o. s. to death; in breaking one's neck; in overdoing it) (colloq.)*

Heinrich ist ziemlich faul; er reißt sich kein Bein aus (hat die Arbeit nicht erfunden).
*Henry is pretty lazy. He takes his time (does not get a move on; does not believe in straining himself [in sweating; in working himself to death; in breaking his neck; in overdoing it]).*

sich einen Verlust ans **Bein** binden (fig. u. fam.): cf. sich einen **Verlust** ans Bein binden

etwas auf die **Beine** bringen (fig.): *to get s. th. going; to get s. th. started; to start (to get) up s. th.; to bring s. th. into existence*

Die Stadtverwaltung bemüht sich, eine Theatergruppe auf die Beine zu bringen.
*The town council is making an effort to get a theatre company going (started; to start [to get] up a theatrical company; to bring a theatre company into existence).*

(immer wieder) auf die **Beine** fallen (fig.): cf. (immer wieder) auf die **Füße** fallen

die **Beine** in die Hand nehmen (fig.): *to get a move on; to look sharp (lively) (colloq.); to buck up (colloq.); to look slippy (sl.)*

Wenn wir noch rechtzeitig zum Bus kommen wollen, müssen wir die Beine in die Hand nehmen.
*If we want to catch the bus in time, we must get a move on (look sharp [lively]; buck up; look slippy).*

alles, was **Beine** hatte: *the whole world; everybody who could walk; everything on two legs (colloq.)*

Alles, was Beine hatte, rannte in das Kino, um den neuesten Farbfilm zu sehen.
*The whole world (Everybody who could walk; Everything on two legs) went to the cinema to see the latest colour-film.*

j.em auf die **Beine** helfen (fig.): *to set s. b. on his feet; to give s. b. a leg-up; to help (to set) s. b. up; to lend (to give) s. b. a helping hand; to help s. b. to find his feet*

Ich hoffe, daß dir jemand beruflich (wieder) auf die Beine (Sprünge) helfen (unter die Arme greifen) wird.

54

*I hope that someone will set you on your feet again (give you a leg-up; help [set] you up again; lend [give] you a helping hand; help you to find your feet again) in your profession.*

wieder auf die **Beine** kommen (fig.): *to gain a new lease of life; to get back on to one's feet*

> Vor fünf Jahren machte er bankrott, er ist aber inzwischen wieder auf die Beine gekommen.
> *Five years ago he went bankrupt, but he has gained a new lease of life (got back on to his feet) in the meantime.*

mit dem linken (falschen, verkehrten) **Bein** (zuerst) aufstehen (fig.): cf. mit dem linken (falschen, verkehrten) **Fuß** (zuerst) aufstehen

Lügen haben kurze **Beine** (Sprichw.): *You won't get far by lying; Lies soon catch up with one*

> Du hast deinen Vater belogen. Früher oder später wird er die Wahrheit doch erfahren, denn Lügen haben kurze Beine.
> *You have deceived your father. Sooner or later, however, he will still find out the truth; you won't get far by lying (lies soon catch up with one).*

j.em **Beine** machen (fig. u. fam.): *to make s. b. get a move on (colloq.); to make s. b. buck up (colloq.); to make s. b. look sharp (lively) (colloq.); to shake s. b. up (sl.)*

> Mach', daß du fortkommst, oder ich werde dir Beine machen (auf die Sprünge helfen)!
> *Go away, or I'll make you get a move on (buck up; look sharp [lively]; or I'll shake you up).*

sich auf die **Beine** machen: *to get (to be) on one's way; to make a move; to push off (colloq.)*

> Mein Zug fährt in einer halben Stunde. Ich muß mich auf die Beine machen.
> *My train goes in half-an-hour. I must get (be) on my way (make a move; push off).*

früh auf den **Beinen** sein: *to be on one's feet (on the go; on the move) early*

> Ich war heute schon sehr früh auf den Beinen.
> *I was on my feet (on the go; on the move) very early this morning.*

Auf éinem **Bein** kann man nicht stehen! (fig.): *That one will only quench half your thirst; You can't fly on one wing*

> Laß uns noch eins (einen) trinken! Auf éinem Bein kann man nicht stehen!
> *Let's have another. That one will only quench half your thirst (You can't fly on one wing).*

mit beiden **Beinen** auf der Erde (im Leben; in der Wirklichkeit) stehen (fig.): cf. mit beiden **Füßen** auf der Erde (im Leben; in der Wirklichkeit) stehen sich die **Beine** in den Leib (Bauch) stehen (fam.): *to stand until one is fit to drop (until one's legs drop off)*

Nach dem Kriege mußte man sich vor manchen Geschäften die Beine in den Leib (Bauch) stehen.
*After the war one had to stand in front of certain shops until one was fit to drop (until one's legs dropped off).*

auf eigenen **Beinen** stehen (fig.): *to stand on one's own feet; to paddle one's own canoe; to fend for o. s.*

Schon seit meinem 20. Geburtstag stehe ich auf eigenen Beinen (Füßen).
*I have stood on my own feet (paddled my own canoe; fended for myself) since my twentieth birthday.*

j.em ein **Bein** stellen (fig.): *to trip s. b. up; to put a spoke in s. b.'s wheel; to lay a mine for s. b.* Cf. auch: j.em einen **Knüppel** zwischen die Beine werfen

Mit dieser Frage wollte er mir ein Bein stellen (Steine in den Weg legen).
*He wanted to trip me up (to put a spoke in my wheel; to lay a mine for me) with this question.*

sich die **Beine** vertreten: cf. sich die **Füße** vertreten

etwas **beiseite** schaffen: cf. etwas auf die **Seite** schaffen

sich **beißen** (fig.): *to clash*

Diese beiden Farben passen nicht zusammen. Sie beißen sich.
*These two colours do not match. They clash.*

nichts zu **beißen** (und zu brechen) haben: cf. am **Hungertuche** nagen

j.en nicht mit der **Beißzange** anfassen (anpacken) (mögen): cf. j.en nicht mit der **Feuerzange** anfassen (anpacken) (mögen)

sich nicht mit Ruhm **bekleckern** (fam.): cf. sich nicht mit **Ruhm** bedecken (bekleckern)

**bekloppt** sein (fam.): cf. nicht richtig im **Dachstübchen** sein

sich **bekriegen** (fam.): *to get over it (colloq.)*

Als ihr Bräutigam unerwartet die Verlobung löste, war Anna sprachlos; inzwischen aber hat sie sich bekriegt (sich eingekriegt).
*When her fiancé unexpectedly broke off the engagement, Anna was speechless, but in the meantime she has got over it.*

etwas **bekritteln**: *to pick holes in s. th.; to pull (to pick) s. th. to pieces; to find fault with s. th.*

56

Es gibt Leute, die mit nichts zufrieden sind und alles bekritteln (bemäkeln) müssen.
*There are people who are never satisfied with anything and have to pick holes in (find fault with) everything (pull [pick] everything to pieces).*

**belemmert** (fam.): *rotten (colloq.); lousy (sl.)*

Wenn man kein Geld hat, ist das Leben belemmert.
*Life is rotten (lousy) if you haven't got any money.*

etwas **bemäkeln**: cf. etwas **bekritteln**

etwas **bemänteln**: *to cover s. th. up; to gloss over s. th.*

Sag' die absolute Wahrheit und such', nichts zu bemänteln.
*Tell the whole truth and don't try to cover anything up (gloss over anything).*

**benebelt** sein (fam.): a) cf. zu tief in den **Becher** geguckt haben; einen **Schwips** haben; b) *to be dazed; to be befuddled (colloq.)*

b) Unsere geschwätzige Nachbarin hat eine ganze Stunde pausenlos auf uns eingeredet. Wir sind noch ganz benebelt.
*b) Our neighbour's loquacious wife talked at us for a whole hour without a break. We are still quite dazed (befuddled).*

etwas **berappen** müssen (fam.): cf. etwas **blechen** müssen

j.em goldene **Berge** versprechen (fig.): *to promise s. b. the moon (the earth); to promise s. b. heaven on earth; to feed s. b. with golden promises*

Vor der Hochzeit versprach er seiner Verlobten goldene Berge (das Blaue vom Himmel; den Himmel auf Erden).
*Before the wedding he promised his fiancée the moon (earth; heaven on earth; fed his fiancée with golden promises).*

hinterm **Berge** halten (fig.): *to beat about the bush; to hum and haw*

Man sollte mit seiner Meinung nicht hinterm Berge halten.
*One ought not to beat about the bush with (to hum and haw about) one's opinion.*

überall **Berge** sehen (fig.): *to find snags in everything; to see objections to everything*

Meine Tante ist gesundheitlich sehr heruntergekommen und sieht überall Berge.
*My aunt is very run down and finds snags in (sees objections to) everything.*

j.em stehen die Haare zu **Berge**: cf. j.em stehen die **Haare** zu Berge

über den **Berg** sein (fig.): *to be out of the wood (over the worst); to have passed the critical point*

Der Patient scheint jetzt über den Berg zu sein.
*The patient seems to be out of the wood (over the worst; to have passed the critical point) now.*

**über alle Berge** sein (fig.): *to be over the hills and far away; to be miles away.* Cf. auch: Der **Vogel** ist ausgeflogen (ist fort)

Als die Polizei eintraf, war der Verbrecher (längst) über alle Berge.
*By the time the police arrived, the criminal was over the hills and far away (was miles away).*

**Berge** versetzen (fig.): *to move mountains; to do wonders*

Die Mutter hofft immer noch auf die Rückkehr ihres Sohnes. Der Glaube kann Berge versetzen (Wunder tun).
*The mother still hopes for her son's return. Faith can move mountains (can do wonders).*

es geht mit j.em (mit etwas) **bergab** (fig.): *s. b. (s. th.) is going downhill (going from bad to worse); to be on the downward grade (path).* Cf. auch: auf die abschüssige (schiefe) **Bahn** geraten; vor die **Hunde** gehen

Man hat den Eindruck, daß es mit dieser Firma bergab (abwärts) geht (daß diese Firma sich auf dem absteigenden Ast befindet; absackt).
*One has the impression that this firm is going downhill (from bad to worse; is on the downward grade [path]).*

es geht mit j.em (mit etwas) **bergauf** (fig.): *s. b. (s. th.) is on the up-grade (on the upward path; on the mend)*

Er war sechs Monate krank; jetzt aber geht es mit ihm bergauf.
*He was ill for six months but now he is on the up-grade (the upward path; the mend).*

kämpfen wie ein **Berserker**: *to fight like a madman (a savage)*

Um seine Ziele zu erreichen, hat er wie ein Berserker (Verrückter; Wahnsinniger; wie verrückt) gekämpft.
*He fought like a madman (a savage) to achieve his aims.*

eine **Beruhigungspille** (fig.): *a crumb of comfort; a sop; like soothing syrup*

Die letzte Regierungserklärung sollte eine Beruhigungspille für das empörte Volk sein.
*The latest government announcement was meant as a crumb of comfort (a sop) for (to act like soothing syrup on) the indignant nation.*

j.em gründlich **Bescheid** sagen: *to give s. b. a piece of one's mind; to tell s. b. what's what; to tell (to tick) s. b. off; to tell s. b. a few home truths.* Cf. auch: j.en **abkanzeln**

Endlich ist jemand erschienen, der diesem ewigen Prahler gründlich Bescheid gesagt (den Standpunkt klargemacht; der es diesem ... ordentlich gegeben) hat.

*At last someone has appeared who has given that eternal boaster a piece of his mind (has told [ticked] that eternal boaster off; has told . . . what's what [a few home truths]).*

eine schöne (nette) **Bescherung** sein (fig.): a) *to be a pretty kettle of fish (a fine set-out [business]; how-d'ye-do) (colloq.);* b) *to be a mess*

    a) Ich habe meine Aktentasche in der Straßenbahn liegen lassen. Das ist eine schöne (nette) Bescherung (Da haben wir's; haben wir die Pastete [den Salat])!

    b) Die Flasche zerbrach, und ich hatte die ganze Bescherung in der Hand.

    *a) I have left my brief-case in the tram. That's a pretty kettle of fish (a fine set-out [business; how-d'ye-do])!*

    *b) The bottle broke and I had the whole mess in my hand.*

gut **beschlagen** sein (fig.): cf. gut **bestellt** sein

jeder **Beschreibung** spotten: *to beggar (to defy) description; to be beyond description; There are no words to describe . . .*

    Die Unordnung in ihrem Kleiderschrank spottet jeder Beschreibung.

    *The untidiness of her wardrobe beggars (defies) description (is beyond description; There are no words to describe the untidiness of her wardrobe).*

j.en **beschummeln (beschuppen)** (fam.): cf. j.en auf den **Leim** führen

**beschwipst** sein (fam.): cf. einen **Schwips** haben

j.en nicht **besehen** können (fig.): cf. j.en nicht **riechen** können

etwas mit eisernem **Besen** auskehren (fig.): *to make a clean sweep of s. th.; to wipe s. th. out*

    Die neue Regierung beabsichtigt, alle solche Mißbräuche (Mißstände) mit eisernem Besen auszukehren.

    *The new government intends to make a clean sweep of (to wipe out) all such abuses.*

einen **Besen** fressen (fam.): cf. sich **hängen** lassen a)

Neue **Besen** kehren gut (Sprichw.): *New brooms sweep clean (prov.)*

    Unser Geschäft ist wirklich gediehen, seitdem der alte Prokurist gegangen und der neue eingetreten ist. Neue Besen kehren gut.

    *Our business has really flourished since the old head-clerk left and the new one arrived. New brooms sweep clean.*

laufen wie ein **Besenbinder:** *to run as fast as one's legs will carry one; to run like a cat on hot bricks (like a scalded cat).* Cf. auch: wie **verrückt** laufen; was das **Zeug** hält

    Der Junge lief wie ein Besenbinder (Bürstenbinder; Wiesel) in die Schule (lief in die Schule, als wenn der Leibhaftige hinter ihm her wäre).

*The boy ran to school as fast as his legs would carry him (like a cat on hot bricks [a scalded cat]).*

einen **Besenstiel** verschluckt haben (fig.): *to be as stiff as a poker*

> Dieser ehemalige Offizier benimmt sich so steif, als wenn er einen Besenstiel (Stock; ein Lineal; eine Elle) verschluckt hätte. (Der ehemalige O. ist stock-steif [steif wie ein Stock]).
> *This former officer is as stiff as a poker.*

wie **besessen** (wie ein **Besessener**) rennen (laufen): cf. wie ein **Besenbinder** laufen; wie **verrückt** laufen

j.en nicht **besichtigen** können (fig.): cf. j.en nicht **riechen** können

**besoffen** sein (fam.): cf. **sternhagelvoll** sein

Das wäre noch **besser**! :cf. Das wäre noch **schöner**!

sich eines **Besseren** besinnen: *to think better of it; to have second thoughts*

> Der Fahrer leugnete zunächst hartnäckig; dann aber besann er sich eines Besseren (hielt er innere Einkehr [bei sich]) und gab seine Schuld zu.
> *The driver at first denied obstinately but then thought better of it (had second thoughts) and admitted his guilt.*

ein freches **Besteck** sein (fig. u. fam.): cf. ein freches **Stück** sein

nichts zu **bestellen** haben (fig.): *to go away empty-handed; not to bring anything back; not to get anything out of s. th. (colloq.); not to win a sausage (sl.)*

> Die internationalen Tennis-Wettspiele waren äußerst schwer. Leider hatten die deutschen Repräsentanten bei ihnen nichts zu bestellen (kein Wort mitzureden).
> *The international tennis tournament was extremely hard. Unfortunately the German competitors went away empty-handed (did not bring anything back; did not get anything out of it; did not win a sausage).*

wie **bestellt** und nicht abgeholt (fam.): *all dressed up with nowhere to go (colloq.)*

> Was ist denn mit dir los? Kann ich dir helfen? Du siehst ja aus wie bestellt und nicht abgeholt.
> *What is the matter with you? Can I help you? You look all dressed up with nowhere to go.*

gut **bestellt** sein (fig.): *s. h. is well equipped (is up to the mark [up to scratch]).* Cf. auch: **kapitelfest** sein; **sattelfest** sein

> Mit seinen Kenntnissen in Mathematik ist es gut bestellt. (In Mathematik ist er gut beschlagen [hat er etwas los]).
> *He is well equipped (up to the mark; up to scratch) in mathematics.*

j.en zum **besten** haben: cf. j.en auf den **Arm** nehmen

j.en ans **Bett** fesseln: *to confine s. b. to his bed*

Die schwere Krankheit wird meine Nichte wochenlang ans Bett fesseln.
*The serious illness will confine my niece to bed for weeks.*

sich ins gemachte **Bett** legen (fig.): *to walk (to step) into s. th. ready-made; to find s. th. ready-made*

Heinrich hat die Fabrik seines Vaters geerbt und sich so ins gemachte Bett gelegt.
*Henry has inherited his father's factory and so walked (stepped) into a ready-made position (found his position ready-made).*

das **Bett** hüten: *to keep (to) one's bed; to be confined to bed*

Mein Bruder ist oft krank und muß dann zumeist das Bett hüten.
*My brother is often ill, and then he generally has to keep (to) his bed (then he is generally confined to bed).*

Frau Holle schüttelt die **Betten:** cf. Frau Holle schüttelt die **Federn**

die nötige **Bettschwere** haben (fam.): *to be ready for bed; to long for bed*

Nach dieser anstrengenden Arbeit hatten wir die nötige Bettschwere (lechzten wir nach dem Bettzipfel).
*After this strenuous work we were ready for bed (longing for bed).*

nach dem **Bettzipfel** lechzen (fam.): cf. die nötige **Bettschwere** haben

**bettelarm** sein: cf. arm wie eine **Kirchenmaus** sein

j.en an den **Bettelstab** bringen (fig.): *to drive (to reduce) s. b. to beggary; to drive s. b. into the workhouse*

Dieser Gauner hätte meinen Schwager beinahe an den Bettelstab gebracht.
*This rogue almost drove (reduced) my brother-in-law to beggary (drove my brother-in-law into the workhouse).*

an den **Bettelstab** kommen (fig.): cf. die Passivformen der Ausdrücke unter: j.en an den **Bettelstab** bringen. Cf. auch: am **Hungertuch** nagen

sich warm **betten** (fig.): *to feather one's nest; to look after No. 1 (colloq.)*

Mein Onkel hat sich warm gebettet und kann seine alten Tage in Ruhe verleben.
*My uncle has feathered his nest (nicely) (has looked after No. 1) and can live his old age in comfort.*

Wie man sich **bettet**, so schläft man (Sprichw.): *As you make your bed, so you must lie on it (prov.)*

Sein Freund hat in dieser Angelegenheit eine verkehrte Entscheidung getroffen, kann aber die Situation nicht ändern. Wie man sich bettet, so schläft man.

*His friend has made a wrong decision in this matter but cannot alter the situation. As you make your bed, so you must lie on it.*

ein **Beutelschneider** sein: cf. ein **Bauernfänger** sein

**Beutelschneiderei**: cf. **Halsabschneiderei**

I **bewahre!**: *Not a bit of it!; Good Heavens, no!*

Hast du wirklich geglaubt, daß er ehrlich ist? – I bewahre! (I wo!) Ganz im Gegenteil.
*Did you really believe that he was honest? – Not a bit of it! (Good Heavens, no!) Quite the reverse.*

**bewandert** sein: cf. gut **bestellt** sein

j.en **beweihräuchern** (fig.): cf. j.em **Weihrauch** streuen

im **biblischen** Alter stehen: cf. alt wie **Methusalem** sein; in **Ehren** ergraut

auf **Biegen** und Brechen (fig.): cf. auf **Gedeih** und Verderb

mag es **biegen** oder brechen (fig.): *come what may; by hook or by crook*

Mein Ziel will ich erreichen, mag es biegen oder brechen.
*I will reach my goal, come what may (by hook or by crook).*

sich **biegen** vor Lachen: cf. sich **totlachen**

fleißig wie eine **Biene** sein (**Bienenfleiß** besitzen): *to be as busy as a bee; to be a busy bee*

Der Gelehrte muß fleißig wie eine Biene (Ameise) sein ([einen wahren] Bienenfleiß besitzen), wenn er dieses umfangreiche Werk schreiben will.
*The scholar will have to be as busy as a bee (be a busy bee) if he is going to write this voluminous work.*

etwas wie sauer **Bier** ausbieten: *to offer s. th. for sale dirt-cheap (at a knock-down price).* Cf. auch: **spottbillig**

Wir kaufen nichts, was wie sauer Bier ausgeboten wird.
*We do not buy anything which is offered for sale dirt-cheap (at a knock-down price).*

ein **Bierbankpolitiker** sein: *to be an armchair politician*

Ich habe nie zu den Bierbankpolitikern gezählt.
*I have never been one of the armchair politicians.*

**Biereifer** (fam.): *craze (colloq.)*

Was bezweckst du nur mit diesem Biereifer?
*What do you want to achieve by this craze?*

dick wie ein **Bierfaß** (eine **Biertonne**) sein: cf. **kugelrund** sein

fluchen wie ein **Bierkutscher**: cf. fluchen wie ein **Landsknecht**

eine **Bierreise** machen: *to go on a pub crawl (colloq.)*
> Die lustigen alten Herren unternahmen eine Bierreise von einem Wirtshaus zum anderen.
> *The merry old gentlemen went on a pub crawl from one inn to another.*

eine **Biesterei** sein (fam.): cf. eine **Herkulesarbeit** sein

**biestig** werden (fig. u. fam.): cf. **krötig** werden

ein **Bild** für Götter: cf. ein **Anblick** für Götter

ein **Bild** des Jammers: cf. ein **Häufchen** Unglück

sich ein **Bild** von etwas machen (fig.): *to picture s. th. to o. s.; to get the hang of s. th.; to form a picture of s. th.*
> Ich kann mir wegen der Komplikationen kein Bild von der eigentlichen Lage machen.
> *I cannot picture (get the hang; form a picture of) the actual situation because of the complications.*

ein **Bild** von einem Mädchen sein: cf. **bildschön** sein

im **Bilde** sein (fig.): *to be in the picture (in the know); to be au fait*
> Über die vergangenen Ereignisse sind wir genau im Bilde.
> *We are completely in the picture (in the know) about (au fait with) past events.*

auf der **Bildfläche** erscheinen: *to come in sight; to appear on the scene; to put in an appearance; to turn up*
> Als mehrere Polizisten auf der Bildfläche erschienen, liefen die Jungens fort.
> *When several policemen came in sight (appeared on the scene; put in an appearance; turned up), the boys ran off.*

von der **Bildfläche** verschwinden (fig.): *to vanish from the scene; to vanish into thin air*
> Ich wollte meinen Bruder zu Hause abholen; er war aber von der Bildfläche verschwunden.
> *I wanted to pick up my brother at home, but he had vanished from the scene (into thin air).*

**bildschön** sein: *to be as pretty as a picture*
> Man sieht es meiner Großmutter heute noch an, daß sie einmal bildschön (ein Bild von einem Mädchen; zum Malen schön) gewesen sein muß.
> *One can still see today that my grandmother must once have been as pretty as a picture.*

j.em die **Binde** von den Augen nehmen (fig.): *to open s. b.'s eyes to s. b.*
*(s. th.); to disillusion s. b. about s. b. (s. th.); to lift the scales from s. b.'s eyes; to*
*take the blinkers from s. b.'s eyes*

> Da meine Schwester von diesem Jüngling begeistert war, sah ich mich ge-
> zwungen, ihr die Binde von den Augen zu nehmen.
> *As my sister was keen on that youth, I felt myself compelled to open her eyes ([to him];*
> *to disillusion her about him; to lift the scales [take the blinkers] from her eyes).*

sich einen hinter die **Binde** gießen (fam.): *to wet one's whistle; to lift the elbow*

> Studenten gießen sich gern einen hinter die Binde (heben [kippen; schmettern]
> gern einen; bechern gern; begießen sich gern die Nase; lassen sich gern voll-
> laufen).
> *Students like wetting their whistles (lifting the elbow).*

Da hört (sich) doch der **Bindfaden** auf! (fam.): cf. Das ist doch die **Höhe!**

**Bindfäden** regnen: *to rain cats and dogs; to pour in torrents; to come down in*
*sheets*

> Den ganzen Tag hat es Bindfäden (in Strömen) geregnet.
> *It has been raining cats and dogs (has been pouring in torrents [coming down in sheets])*
> *all day.*

in die **Binsen** gehen (fig.): a) cf. ins **Wasser** fallen; b) **kaputt** sein

eine **Binsenwahrheit (Binsenweisheit)** sein: *to be a commonplace (plati-*
*tude)*

> Daß unsere klassischen Schriftsteller in der ganzen Welt bekannt sind, ist doch
> eine Binsenwahrheit (Binsenweisheit; ein Gemeinplatz).
> *That our classical writers are famous the whole world over, is a commonplace (platitude).*

ein fetter **Bissen** sein (fig.): *to be a godsend (a windfall); to be a stroke (a slice)*
*of luck.* Cf. auch: ein **Geschenk** des Himmels sein

> Dieser Lotteriegewinn war ein fetter Bissen für die arme Familie.
> *This win in the lottery was a godsend (a windfall; a stroke [slice] of luck) for the poor*
> *family.*

Der **Bissen** bleibt einem im Halse stecken: *One's food sticks in one's throat*

> Beim Mittagessen erhielt er eine erschütternde Nachricht, und der Bissen blieb
> ihm im Halse stecken.
> *He received some shattering news at lunch-time, and his food stuck in his throat.*

Da muß ich aber doch sehr **bitten!**: *How dare you!; I really must protest;*
*What do you think you're doing?*

> Du liest den Roman, den ich mir gerade gekauft habe. Da muß ich aber doch
> sehr bitten! (Na, erlaube mal!)

*You are reading the novel that I have just bought. How dare you! (I really must protest; What do you think you're doing?)*

**bitterböse** werden: cf. **mordswütend** werden

eine **Blamage** sein: *to be a come-down (a let-down); to be a blot on s. b.'s (e)scutcheon)*

Diese Scheidungssache war für ihn eine richtige Blamage.
*This divorce case was a real come-down (let-down) for him (was a real blot on his (e)scutcheon)*

sich **blamieren:** *to blunder; to disgrace o. s.; to make a fool of o. s.; to let o. s. down; to put one's foot in it (colloq.)*

Heinrich hat sich im Examen schwer blamiert.
*Henry has blundered badly (disgraced him completely; let himself down badly; made a proper fool of himself; put his foot in it properly) in the examination.*

**blank** sein: cf. (völlig) **abgebrannt** sein

die ganze **Blase** (fam.): *the whole lot (shoot; crowd) (colloq.); the whole crew (caboodle; shower) (sl.)*

Um 7 Uhr kam Johannes mit dem Auto an, und die ganze Blase (Bagage; Corona) ging dann ins Kino.
*At seven o'clock John arrived with the car and the whole lot (shoot; crowd; crew; caboodle; shower) went to the cinema.*

j.em etwas **blasen** (fig. u. fam.): *to see s. b. to blazes first (colloq.); to be damned if one will (colloq.); to see s. b. in hell first (sl.)*

Du verlangst von mir, daß ich dich verteidige, obwohl du unrecht hast. Ich werde dir was blasen (pfeifen; pusten).
*You expect me to defend you although you are wrong. I'll see you to blazes (in hell) first (I'll be damned if I will).*

auf einem anderen **Blatt** stehen (fig.): *to be (quite) a different pair of shoes; to be (quite) another matter (story; chapter)*

Seine Leistungen in der Schule sind sehr mittelmäßig. Daß er gut Klavier und Geige spielen kann, steht auf einem anderen Blatt.
*His performance at school is very mediocre. That he can play the piano and the violin well is quite a different pair of shoes (quite another matter [story; chapter]).*

Das **Blatt** hat sich gewendet (fig.): *The tide has (the tables are) turned; The boot is on the other foot; The balance has swung the other way*

Früher war er mir immer überlegen, jetzt aber hat sich das Blatt gewendet.
*Formerly he was always superior to me, but now the tide has (the tables are) turned (the boot is on the other foot; the balance has swung the other way).*

65

kein **Blatt** vor den Mund nehmen (fig.): *not to mince one's words; not to mince matters; not to pull one's punches (colloq.)*. Cf. auch: **klipp** und klar sagen

> Wenn mein Vater nicht mit mir zufrieden ist, nimmt er kein Blatt vor den Mund (redet er frei [frisch] von der Leber [weg]; redet er ungeschminkt [unverblümt]; packt er tüchtig aus).
> *When my father is not pleased with me, he does not mince his words (mince matters; pull his punches).*

ein unbeschriebenes **Blatt** sein (fig.): *to be an unknown quantity; to be a dark horse*

> Der junge Schriftsteller war den meisten Leuten noch ein unbeschriebenes Blatt (eine unbekannte Größe).
> *The young author was still an unknown quantity (a dark horse) to most people.*

**blau** sein (fam.): cf. **sternhagelvoll** sein

j.en **blau** und grün schlagen: cf. j.en **grün** und blau schlagen

das **Blaue** vom Himmel (herunter)lügen (fig.): cf. lügen, daß sich die **Balken** biegen

das **Blaue** vom Himmel herunterreden (fig.): a) *to talk o. s. hoarse; to talk one's head off (colloq.); to talk o. s. stupid (colloq.); to talk a horse's hind leg off (colloq.); to talk the hind leg off a donkey (colloq.); to talk twenty to the dozen (colloq.); to talk until one is blue in the face (colloq.)*. Cf. auch: j.em ein **Loch** (Löcher) in den Bauch reden; b) *to talk through one's hat (through the back of one's neck) (colloq.)*

> a) Dieser Abgeordnete will einfach nicht aufhören; er redet (ja) das Blaue vom Himmel herunter (einen dumm und dämlich; wie ein Wasserfall).
> b) Alles, was er sagt, ist Unsinn; er redet das Blaue vom Himmel herunter.
> *a) That delegate simply will not stop. He talks himself hoarse (stupid; talks his head off [a horse's hind leg off; the hind leg off a donkey; twenty to the dozen; until he is blue in the face]).*
> *b) Everything he says is nonsense. He talks through his hat (through the back of his neck).*

j.em das **Blaue** vom Himmel versprechen (fig.): cf. j.em goldene **Berge** versprechen

ins **Blaue** hineinreden (fig.): *to talk at random; to air one's ignorance*

> Da du von den Naturwissenschaften nichts verstehst, solltest du lieber schweigen als ins Blaue (in den Tag) hineinzureden (als zu faseln).
> *Since you do not understand anything about the natural sciences, you would do better to keep quiet than talk at random (air your ignorance).*

**blaumachen** (fam.): *to stay away; to cut work; to take French leave;* (nur in der Schule) *to play truant*. Cf. auch: blauen **Montag** machen

66

Nach dem Fest machten alle Arbeiter blau.
*After the celebration all the workers stayed away (cut work; took French leave).*

ein **Blaustrumpf** sein (fig.): *to be a blue-stocking*

Molière hat sich gern über die Blaustrümpfe seiner Zeit lustig gemacht.
*Molière enjoyed making fun of the blue-stockings of his time.*

**Blech** (zusammen)reden (fam.): cf. **Quatsch** reden

etwas **blechen** müssen (fam.):*to foot the bill; to have to cough up (to brass up; to fork out) for s. th. (colloq.)*

Johann war der einzige, der Geld bei sich hatte, und mußte deshalb alles blechen (berappen).
*John was the only one who had any money on him, and so he had to cough up (brass up; fork out) for the lot (to foot the bill).*

Es liegt (steckt) einem wie **Blei** in den Gliedern: cf. j.em in den **Gliedern** liegen

**bleischwer** auf j.em lasten: *to weigh heavily upon s. b.; to be a weight on s. b.'s mind*

Eine so feindliche Kritik lastet natürlich bleischwer (zentnerschwer; wie eine Zentnerlast) auf uns.
*Such a hostile review naturally weighs heavily upon us (is naturally a weight on our minds).*

j.en mit **Blicken** durchbohren: cf. j.en mit Blicken **durchbohren**

einen **Blick** hinter die Kulissen tun (fig.): cf. hinter die **Kulissen** gucken

j.en keines Blickes würdigen: *without as much as looking (without deigning to look; without as much as a glance) at s. b.*

Der Direktor würdigte uns keines Blickes, als er vorbeiging.
*The director went by without as much as looking (deigning to look; without as much as a glance) at us.*

im **Blickpunkt** stehen: *to be in the public eye (at the centre [focus])*. Cf. auch: im **Rampenlicht** stehen

Dieser bekannte Architekt steht in unserer Stadt im Blickpunkt (Brennpunkt) des Interesses.
*This well-known architect is in the public eye (at the centre [focus] of interest) in our town.*

**Blinder** Eifer schadet nur (Sprichw.): *Zeal without discretion only does harm (prov.)*

Dein Ziel läßt sich nicht im Sturm erreichen. Blinder Eifer schadet nur.
*Your goal cannot be taken by storm. Zeal without discretion only does harm.*

Liebe macht **blind** (Sprichw.): *Love is blind (prov.)*

Die beiden jungen Leute passen eigentlich nicht zueinander, aber Liebe macht blind.
*The two young people are not really suited to each other, but love is blind.*

Niemand ist so **blind** wie der, welcher nicht sehen will (Sprichw.): *None so blind as those that will not see (prov.)*

Ich habe es ihm ausführlich erklärt, er will es aber nicht einsehen. Niemand ist so blind wie der, welcher nicht sehen will.
*I have explained it fully to him but he does not want to understand. None so blind as those that will not see.*

eine **blinde** Wut: cf. eine blinde **Wut**

Unter den **Blinden** ist der Einäugige König (Sprichw.): *Among the blind the one-eyed is king (prov.)*

Gerhard ist kein großer Tennisspieler, aber die anderen verstehen noch weniger von dem Spiel. Unter den Blinden ist der Einäugige König.
*Gerhard is no great tennis-player, but the others know even less about the game. Among the blind the one-eyed is king.*

wie der **Blinde** von der Farbe sprechen: *to be out of one's depth; to be (all) at sea (colloq.)*

Wenn die Rede auf die Politik kommt, spricht mein Freund wie der Blinde von der Farbe.
*When the conversation turns to politics, my friend is out of his depth ([all]) at sea).*

Das kann doch ein **Blinder** sehen (mit dem Krückstock fühlen): *You can see that with half an eye; Even a blind man can see that*

Das kann doch ein Blinder sehen (mit dem Krückstock fühlen), daß hier etwas nicht in Ordnung ist.
*You can see with half an eye (Even a blind man can see) that there is something wrong here.*

**blink** und blank sein: cf. **blitzblank** sein

wie vom **Blitz** getroffen sein: *to be thunderstruck (stunned; staggered; flabbergasted); to be left gasping; to be rocked on one's heels; to be struck dumb*

Der Vater war wie vom Blitz getroffen (vom Donner [Schlag] gerührt; war baff; Den Vater rührte [traf] der Schlag; Dem Vater blieb die Spucke weg [fuhr der Schreck in die Glieder]), als er erfuhr, daß sein Sohn im Examen durchgefallen war.
*The father was thunderstruck (stunned; staggered; flabbergasted; left gasping; rocked on his heels; struck dumb) when he learned that his son had failed his examination.*

wie ein **Blitz** aus heiterm Himmel: *like a bolt from the blue (like a thunderbolt; like a shot from a gun)*

Die Nachricht von dem furchtbaren Eisenbahnunglück traf uns alle wie ein Blitz aus heiterm Himmel.
*The news of the terrible railway accident came to us all like a bolt from the blue (thunderbolt; a shot from a gun).*

wie ein geölter **Blitz** laufen: *to run like greased lightning*

Als der Besitzer des Obstgartens erschien, lief der Junge wie ein geölter Blitz nach Hause.
*When the owner of the orchard appeared, the boy ran home like greased lightning.*

sich wie der **Blitz** verbreiten: *to spread like lightning (like wildfire)*

Das Gerücht von der Heimkehr der Kriegsgefangenen verbreitete sich wie der Blitz (blitzschnell; mit Blitzesschnelle; wie ein Lauffeuer).
*The rumour of the return of the prisoners of war spread like lightning (like wildfire).*

der **Blitzableiter** sein (fig.): *to be a butt (a target) for s. b.'s feelings.* Cf. auch: der **Sündenbock** sein; an j.em sein **Mütchen** kühlen

Mein Freund hatte sich über einen andern geärgert. Als ich ihn ansprach, benutzte er mich als Blitzableiter und fing an zu schimpfen.
*My friend was annoyed with somebody else. When I spoke to him, he took me as a butt (target) for his anger and began to curse.*

**blitzartig**: *like lightning; like a (in a) flash; like a shot*

Die anderen wußten nicht, was tun. Da durchfuhr mich blitzartig ein kluger Gedanke.
*The others did not know what to do. Then a clever idea came to me like lightning (a flash; a shot; in a flash).*

**blitzblank (blitzsauber)** sein: *to be as bright as a new penny (as neat as a new pin; in apple-pie order)*

In ihrer neuen Wohnung ist alles blitzblank (blitzsauber; blink und blank; sieht alles wie geleckt aus).
*In her new flat everything is as bright as a new penny (as neat as a new pin; in apple-pie order).*

ein **Blitzmädel** sein: *to be a capital (first-rate) girl*

Anna ist in der Schule fleißig und im Haushalt sehr gewissenhaft; sie ist ein wahres Blitzmädel.
*Anna is hard-working at school and very conscientious in the home; she is a really capital (first-rate) girl.*

eine **Blitzreise** antreten: *to pay a lightning visit*

Unser Außenminister hat eine Blitzreise nach den USA angetreten.
*Our foreign minister is paying a lightning visit to the U.S.A.*

**blitzschnell** (mit **Blitzesschnelle**): cf. sich wie der **Blitz** verbreiten

blühender (höherer) **Blödsinn** sein: *to be out-and-out rubbish; to be sheer (utter) balderdash (colloq.).* Cf. auch: **Quatsch** sein

> Höre nicht auf sein dummes Geːchwätz; es ist blühender (höherer) Blödsinn.
> *Don't listen to his stupid chatter; iː is out-and-out rubbish (sheer [utter] balderdash).*

sich eine **Blöße** geben (fig.): *to betray one's weak spot; to reveal one's weakness; to give o. s. away at a (this etc.) point*

> Bei der mündlichen Prüfung hat sich dieser Kandidat viele Blößen gegeben.
> *At the oral examination this candidate betrayed his many weak spots (revealed his many weaknesses; gave himself away at many points).*

'rangehen wie **Blücher**: *to go in (to charge in) like a tank (like a steamroller)*

> Ihr müßt 'rangehen wie Blücher, wenn Ihr dieses schwere Wettspiel gewinnen wollt.
> *You must go (charge) in like tanks (steamrollers) if you want to win this tough competition.*

j.em **blüht** etwas (fig. u. fam.): *s. th. is in store for s. b.; s. b. is in for s. th. (colloq.)*

> Der Verbrecher ahnt immer noch nicht, was ihm blüht.
> *The criminal has still no idea what is in store for him (what he is in for).*

im **blühendsten** Alter stehen: *to be in one's prime; to be in the prime of life*

> Sein Tod bedeutete einen großen Verlust für die Humaniora (Klassischen Studien), denn er stand im blühendsten Alter.
> *His death meant a great loss to Classical studies, for he was in his prime (in the prime of life).*

j.em etwas durch die **Blume** sagen (fig.): *to tell s. b. s. th. in veiled language (in a roundabout way; in metaphors); to hint at s. th.*

> Ich habe ihm durch die Blume gesagt, daß ich mit seinem Verhalten gar nicht einverstanden bin.
> *I told him in veiled language (in a roundabout way; in metaphors; I hinted at the fact) that I did not at all agree with his conduct.*

sich keinen **Blumentopf** für etwas kaufen können (fig. u. fam.): *not to get a fig (a sausage) out of s. th. (colloq.)*

> Für diese nichtssagende Besprechung seines Buches kann sich mein Schwager keinen Blumentopf kaufen.
> *My brother-in-law will not get a fig (sausage) out of that trivial review of his book.*

j.en (etwas) bis aufs **Blut** aussaugen: cf. sich bis zum **Weißbluten** verzehren

blaues **Blut** in den Adern haben: *to have blue blood in one's veins*

> Euer Professor hat blaues Blut in den Adern, denn er stammt aus einem alten Adelsgeschlecht.

*Your professor has blue blood in his veins, for he is descended from an old family of aristocrats.*

böses **Blut** machen (fig.): *to make (to cause) bad blood (bad feeling)*

Die neue Steuererhöhung wird viel böses Blut machen.
*The new tax increase will make (cause) a lot of bad blood (feeling).*

j.em das **Blut** in den Adern erstarren lassen: *to freeze the blood in s. b.'s veins; to petrify s. b.*

Mit seinen entsetzlichen Schreien ließ er mir das Blut in den Adern erstarren.
*He froze the blood in my veins (petrified me) with his terrible cries.*

**Blut** geleckt haben (fig.): *to have tasted blood; to have the scent in one's nostrils; to have whetted one's appetite*

Nachdem Wilhelm einmal auf einem Motorrad gefahren ist, hat er Blut geleckt und möchte nun gern ein eigenes haben.
*Having once ridden on a motor-cycle, William has tasted blood (has got the scent in his nostrils; William's appetite has been whetted), and he would now like to have one of his own.*

j.em im **Blute** liegen (fig.): *to be (to run) in s. b.'s blood; to be in s. b.'s. veins (bones)*

Karl will absolut Matrose werden; denn der Seemannsberuf liegt ihm im Blute.
*Charles wants to become a sailor at all costs, for the sea is (runs) in his blood (is in his veins [bones]).*

j.en bis aufs **Blut** peinigen: *to pester (to worry) the life out of s. b.; to pester (to worry) s. b. to death.* Cf. auch: j.em auf die **Nerven** gehen

Mit seinem ewigen Nörgeln hat er mich bis aufs Blut gepeinigt.
*He has pestered (worried) the life out of me (pestered [worried] me to death) with his eternal nagging.*

(Nur) ruhig **Blut!**: *Keep cool (calm)!; Don't panic!*

(Nur) ruhig Blut! Wir werden es schon schaffen.
*Keep cool (calm; Don't panic)! We'll make it.*

j.es **Blut** wallen machen (in Wallung bringen): *to make s. b.'s blood boil; to lash s. b. into a fury; to get s. b.'s goat (colloq.)*

Mein bissiger Ton machte sein Blut wallen (brachte sein Blut in Wallung; Durch meinen bissigen Ton kochte es in ihm), und er konnte sich kaum noch beherrschen.
*My biting tone made his blood boil (lashed him into a fury; got his goat), and he could hardly control himself.*

**Blut** ist dicker als Wasser (Sprichw.): *Blood is thicker than water (prov.)*

In der Not wendet man sich an seine Verwandten. Blut ist dicker als Wasser.
*In time of need one turns to one's relatives. Blood is thicker than water.*

**Blut** und Wasser schwitzen: *to be in a cold sweat; to sweat blood*

Das Examen war schwer, und die Studenten haben Blut und Wasser geschwitzt.
*The examination was hard, and the students were in a cold sweat (sweated blood).*

**bluten** wie ein Schwein (eine Sau) (fam.): cf. bluten wie ein **Schwein**

tüchtig für etwas **bluten** müssen (fig.): *to have to pay for s. th. through the nose (colloq.)*

Dieses Buch ist nicht viel wert, aber ich mußte (bei seinem Kauf) tüchtig dafür (für es) bluten.
*This book is not worth much but I had to pay through the nose for it.*

**Blütenträume:** *fond hopes; cherished dreams; pipe-dreams*

An seinem Lebensende mußte sich der Greis gestehen, daß nicht alle seine Blütenträume in Erfüllung gegangen waren.
*At the end of his life the old man had to confess to himself that not all his fond hopes (cherished dreams; pipe-dreams) had been fulfilled.*

**blütenweiß** sein: cf. **schneeweiß** sein

ein **blutiger** Laie (in etwas) sein: *to be the veriest tyro (layman)*

In technischen Dingen bin ich ein blutiger Laie.
*In technical matters I am the veriest tyro (layman).*

den **Bock** zum Gärtner machen (fig.): *to set the fox to keep the geese; to set a thief to catch a thief*

Wenn Sie diesen unzuverlässigen Mann als Kassierer einstellen, machen Sie den Bock zum Gärtner.
*If you engage this unreliable man as a cashier, you will be setting the fox to keep the geese (setting a thief to catch a thief).*

einen **Bock** haben **(bockig** sein; j.en stößt der Bock) (fig.): *to be in a huff; to be pig-headed; to have a pique*

Wenn Ihr Söhnchen einen Bock hat (bockig ist; der Bock stößt), sollten Sie ihn (es) einfach nicht beachten.
*Whenever your little son is in a huff (is pig-headed; has a pique), you ought just to ignore him (it).*

die **Böcke** von den Schafen sondern (fig.): *to separate the sheep from the goats; to separate (to sift) the wheat from the chaff*

Die Prüfungen sind dazu da, die Böcke von den Schafen (die Spreu vom Weizen) zu sondern (die Prüflinge zu sieben).
*Examinations are for separating the sheep from the goats (for separating [sifting] the wheat from the chaff).*

einen **Bock** schießen (fig.): *to put one's foot in it (colloq.); to drop a brick (colloq.); to make a howler (bloomer; gaffe) (colloq.); to drop a clanger (sl.)*

Bei meiner Übersetzung ins Englische habe ich mehrere Böcke geschossen (Schnitzer gemacht).
*In my translation into English I put my foot in it several times (I dropped several bricks [clangers]; I made several howlers [bloomers; gaffes]).*

j.en ins **Bockshorn** jagen: *to bully s. b.; to put the wind up s. b. (sl.)*
Ich habe keine Angst. Ihr könnt mich nicht ins Bockshorn jagen.
*I am not afraid. You can't put the wind up me (can't bully me).*

j.em **Boden** abgewinnen (fig.): *to gain on s. b.; to gain ground over s. b.*. Cf. auch: (an) **Boden** gewinnen
Früher hat Karl im Englischen immer bessere Noten bekommen als ich, aber in letzter Zeit habe ich ihm Boden abgewonnen.
*Formerly Charles always got better marks in English than I, but recently I have been gaining on him (gaining ground over him).*

den **Boden** ebnen (bereiten) (fig.): *to clear the path (way); to pave the way*
Alle Schwierigkeiten scheinen jetzt beseitigt und der Boden für weitere Verhandlungen geebnet (bereitet) zu sein.
*All difficulties now seem to have been removed, and the path (way) cleared (and the way paved) for further negotiations.*

auf fruchtbaren **Boden** fallen (fig.): *to fall on fertile soil*
Die Ermahnungen des Lehrers sind bei dir offenbar auf fruchtbaren Boden gefallen, denn dein jetziges Zeugnis sieht wesentlich besser aus.
*The teacher's warnings to you have apparently fallen on fertile soil, for your present report looks appreciably better.*

der **Boden** brennt j.em unter den Füßen (fig.): *things are getting too hot for s. b.; the place becomes too hot to hold s. b.*
Nachdem er eine beträchtliche Summe gestohlen hatte, brannte ihm der Boden unter den Füßen und er flüchtete ins Ausland.
*After he had stolen a considerable sum of money, things got too hot for him (the place became too hot to hold him) and he fled abroad.*

festen **Boden** unter den Füßen haben (fig.): cf. festen **Fuß** fassen

Der **Boden** schwankt j.em unter den Füßen (fig.): *the ground seems to give way (to rock) under s. b.'s feet*
Als er entlassen wurde und seine Frau zur gleichen Zeit starb, schwankte ihm der Boden unter den Füßen.
*When he was dismissed, and at the same time his wife died, the ground seemed to give way (to rock) under his feet.*

den **Boden** unter den Füßen verlieren (fig.): *to lose one's grip; to lose one's hold on things*

Nach diesem geschäftlichen Rückschlag hat mein Onkel den Boden unter den Füßen verloren.
*After this business reverse my uncle lost his grip (his hold on things).*

j.em den **Boden** unter den Füßen wegziehen (fig.): *to cut the ground from under s. b.'s feet; to kick the stool from under s. b.*

Ich hatte mich schon für einen Angriff bereitgemacht, aber mein Gegner zog mir den Boden unter den Füßen (den Stuhl unter dem Hinterteil) weg.
*I had already prepared for an attack but my rival cut the ground from under my feet (kicked the stool from under me).*

(an) **Boden** gewinnen (fig.): *to gain ground*

Die neue Lehre verbreitete sich rasch und gewann viel (an) Boden.
*The new doctrine spread rapidly and gained a great deal of ground.*

etwas aus dem **Boden** stampfen (können) (fig.): *to conjure s. th. up; to come by s. th.; to dig (to whistle) s. th. up (colloq.)*

Das ist ja unmöglich! Wie soll ich eine so große Geldsumme aus dem Boden (aus der Erde; aus dem Erdboden) stampfen können?
*That's impossible! How am I to conjure up (come by; dig up; whistle up) such a large sum of money?*

an **Boden** verlieren (fig.): *to lose ground; to lose one's grip.* Cf. auch: ins **Hintertreffen** geraten; **Nackenschläge** bekommen

Bei den letzten Wahlen hat unsere Partei beträchtlich an Boden verloren.
*In the last election our party lost a considerable amount of ground (lost its grip considerably).*

auf dem **Boden** der Wirklichkeit stehen: *to be (firmly) rooted in reality; to have one's feet firmly established in reality (firmly on the ground)*

Dieser Diplomat hat keine Illusionen. Er steht fest auf dem Boden der Wirklichkeit.
*This diplomat has no illusions. He is firmly rooted (has his feet firmly established) in reality (has his feet firmly on the ground).*

einen großen **Bogen** um j.en machen (fig.): *to give s. b. a wide berth.* Cf. auch: sich j.en vom **Leibe** halten

Da diese Familie keinen guten Ruf hat, machen wir einen großen Bogen um sie.
*We give that family a wide berth because they have not got a good reputation.*

große **Bogen** spucken (fig. u. fam.): cf. **angeben**

den **Bogen** heraushaben (fam.): cf. den **Kniff** heraushaben

den **Bogen** überspannen (fig.): *to aim too high; to shoot beyond (to overstep) the mark*

In manchen Fächern werden von den Schülern zuviel Kenntnisse erwartet. Man sollte den Bogen nicht überspannen.
*In certain subjects too much knowledge is expected of the pupils. One ought not to aim too high (to shoot beyond [overstep] the mark).*

ein **Bohèmeleben** führen: *to lead a Bohemian life*

Dieser junge Künstler weiß nichts von einer geordneten Existenz. Er führt ein wahres Bohèmeleben (Bummelleben).
*That young artist knows nothing of an ordered existence. He leads a real Bohemian life.*

für j.en **böhmische** Dörfer sein (fig.): cf. für j.en böhmische **Dörfer** sein

nicht die **Bohne** (fam.): *not a shred (a scrap; a grain; an iota; a jot)*

An dem ganzen Gerücht war nicht die Bohne wahr (war kein Körnchen Wahrheit).
*There was not a shred (a scrap; a grain; an iota; a jot) of truth in the whole rumour.*

sich nicht die **Bohne** aus etwas machen: cf. sich keinen **Deut** aus etwas machen

lang wie eine **Bohnenstange** sein: *to be as tall as a lamp-post; to be a spindle-shanks (colloq.)*

Eduard ist sehr gewachsen; er ist jetzt so lang wie eine Bohnenstange (Hopfenstange; jetzt ein langer Laban; eine lange Latte [Stange]; ein langer Lulatsch; ein baumlanger Kerl).
*Edward has grown a lot; he is as tall as a lamp-post (is a real spindle-shanks) now.*

dumm wie **Bohnenstroh** sein: *to have the brains of a mouse; to be thick-skulled (dim-witted); to be as dumb as they make them (sl.).* Cf. auch **polizeiwidrig** dumm sein

Unsere Firma hat den Laufjungen wieder entlassen, weil er so dumm wie Bohnenstroh (strohdumm; saudumm; stockdumm; übers Kreuz dumm) ist.
*Our firm has dismissed the errand-boy again, because he has the brains of a mouse (is so thick-skulled [dim-witted]; is as dumb as they make them).*

wie eine **Bombe** einschlagen: *to burst (to land) like a bombshell*

Die Nachricht von der Ermordung des Präsidenten schlug wie eine Bombe ein.
*The news of the president's assassination burst (landed) like a bombshell.*

die **Bombe** zum Platzen bringen (fig.): *to spark off (to set off) the explosion; to trigger off the explosion (colloq.)*

Die erneute Ablehnung der Lohnforderungen hat die Bombe zum Platzen gebracht.
*The renewed rejection of the wage demands sparked (set; triggered) off the explosion.*

Jetzt ist die **Bombe** geplatzt (fig.): *Now the bombshell has burst; Now the balloon has gone up*

Die Regierung duldete lange die Angriffe dieser Partei; nun aber ist die Bombe geplatzt, und es sind verschiedene Leute verhaftet worden.
*The government endured the attacks of this party for a long while, but now the bombshell has burst (the balloon has gone up) and various people have been arrested.*

einen **Bombenerfolg** haben: *to sweep the board; to come off with flying colours; to win a tremendous victory*

In seinem Wettlauf gegen die älteren Jungens hat Hans einen Bombenerfolg gehabt und kam mit einem Vorsprung von 20 Metern als Erster ans Ziel.
*In his race against the older boys Jack swept the board (came off with flying colours; won a tremendous victory) and reached the winning-post with a lead of twenty metres.*

ein **Bombenerfolg** sein: *to be a howling success (colloq.); to be a smash hit (sl.); to be bang-on (sl.)*

Mein Einfall, diese beiden Getränke zu (ver)mischen, war ein Bombenerfolg.
*My idea of mixing these two drinks together was a howling success (a smash hit; was bang-on).*

**bombenfest** (fig.): *cast-iron; hard and fast*

Er gab mir eine bombenfeste Garantie, daß das Auto in Ordnung sei.
*He gave me a cast-iron (hard and fast) guarantee that the car was in order.*

**Bombengeschäfte** machen: *to do a roaring trade; to sell s. th. like hot cakes.* Cf. auch: abgehen wie warme **Semmeln**

Der Mann hat eine sehr günstige Stelle am Strand gefunden und macht Bombengeschäfte (flotte Geschäfte) mit seiner Schokolade und seinen Süßigkeiten.
*The man has found a very profitable place on the beach and is doing a roaring trade with his chocolate and sweets (and is selling his chocolate and sweets like hot cakes).*

ein **Bombenkerl** sein (fam.): *to be a grand chap (a great fellow) (colloq.).* Cf. auch: ein **Allerweltskerl** sein

Mein Freund hat unzählige Qualitäten; er ist wirklich ein Bombenkerl.
*My friend has innumerable qualities; he is really a grand chap (great fellow).*

eine **Bombenrolle:** *a magnificent (a grand) part; a whale of a part (colloq.)*

Der junge Schauspieler hat wirklich eine Bombenrolle bekommen.
*The young actor has got a really magnificent (grand) part (a whale of a part).*

eine **bombensichere** Sache sein: cf. eine **todsichere** Sache sein

ein **Bonze** sein: *to be a party boss; to be a big shot (sl.)*

Es ist nicht gut für ein Land, wenn in ihm die Bonzen regieren.
*It is not good for a country to be ruled by party bosses (by big shots).*

in éinem **Boot** sitzen (fig.): *to be in the same boat*

Vom wirtschaftlichen Standpunkt aus sitzen wir alle in éinem Boot (sind wir in gleich übler Lage).
*From the economic point of view we are all in the same boat.*

etwas über **Bord** werfen (fig.): *to throw s. th. overboard; to throw s. th. to the winds; to jettison s. th.*

Der junge Mann warf alle guten Vorsätze über Bord und ergab sich wieder dem Trunk.
*The young man threw all his good intentions overboard (to the winds; jettisoned all his good intentions) and turned to drink again.*

**böse** mit j.em werden: cf. sich mit j.em in die **Haare** geraten

**Böses** kommt geritten, geht aber fort mit Schritten (Sprichw.): *Bad luck is quick to come but slow to leave (to go)*

Man kann sich eine Erkältung schnell holen, aber manchmal dauert es Wochen, bis sie wieder verschwunden ist. Böses kommt geritten, geht aber fort mit Schritten.
*One can quickly catch a chill, but it sometimes takes weeks before it has gone. Bad luck is quick to come but slow to leave (to go).*

einen **Brandbrief** schreiben: *to write a strong (stiff) letter*

Ich muß ihm wegen seines langen Schweigens einen Brandbrief schreiben.
*I must write him a strong (stiff) letter about his long silence.*

Da haben wir den **Braten!** (fig. u. fam.): cf. eine schöne (nette) **Bescherung**

den **Braten** riechen (fig.): *to smell a rat (colloq.)*

Du möchtest Geld von mir borgen? Ich rieche schon den Braten (den Speck; schon Lunte; wittere schon die Falle).
*You would like to borrow money from me? I smell a rat.*

die gekränkte **Bratwurst** spielen (fam.): cf. die gekränkte **Leberwurst** spielen

j.en **braun** und blau schlagen: cf. j.en **grün** und blau schlagen

ein **Brausekopf** sein: cf. ein **Heißsporn** sein

mit j.em **brechen**: *to break with s. b.; to have finished with s. b.; to have done with s. b.*

Früher waren wir gut miteinander befreundet, aber seit dieser unverzeihlichen Beleidigung habe ich mit ihm gebrochen.
*We used to be good friends, but since that unpardonable insult I have broken (finished; done) with him.*

nichts zu **brechen** und zu beißen haben: *not to have a scrap (a bite; a morsel) to eat; not to know where the next meal is coming from*

Dieser arme Bettler tut mir sehr leid, denn er hat nichts zu brechen und zu beißen.
*I am very sorry for that poor beggar, because he has not got a scrap (bite; morsel) to eat (does not know where the next meal is coming from).*

**brechend** voll sein: cf. **pfropfenvoll** sein

ein **Brechmittel** sein (fig. u. fam.): *(to be enough) to make one sick (colloq.)*

Dieser eitle Geck ist für uns alle das reine Brechmittel.
*This vain dandy is enough to make (makes) us all sick.*

j.en zu **Brei** schlagen (fam.): *to beat s. b. to a jelly (a pulp).* Cf. auch: **Hackfleisch** aus j.em machen

In seiner Wut drohte er, seinen Gegner zu Brei (in Klump[atsch]; windelweich) zu schlagen (wie einen Hund zu prügeln [verprügeln]).
*In his fury he threatened to beat his opponent to a jelly (pulp).*

in die **Breite** gehen: cf. **Fett** ansetzen

j.en **breitschlagen** (fig. u. fam.): *to win s. b. over; to talk s. b. down*

Vater hat sich breitschlagen lassen und ist mit uns in den Zirkus gegangen.
*Father allowed himself to be won over (to be talked down) and went with us to the circus.*

**breitspurig** auftreten: cf. **großspurig** auftreten

etwas **breitspurig** erzählen: cf. etwas lang (weit) **ausspinnen**

etwas **breittreten** (fig.): cf. etwas lang (weit) **ausspinnen**

**bremsen** (fig.): *to let up; to put on the brake; to take it easy.* Cf. auch: eine **Atempause; ausspannen;** eine **Kunstpause** machen

Du hast in den letzten Wochen zu viel gearbeitet und mußt jetzt mal bremsen (kurztreten; langsamtreten).
*You have been working too hard in the last few weeks and must now let up (put on the brake; take it easy).*

darauf **brennen,** etwas zu tun: *to be burning (dying; aching; itching) to do s. th.*

Ich brenne darauf, ein neues Auto zu kaufen; ich werde jedoch (immer) noch ein paar Monate warten müssen.
*I am burning (dying; aching; itching) to buy a new car, but I shall still have to wait a few months.*

Wo **brennt's** ? (fig.): *Where's the fire ?; What's up ?*

Der Mann kam aufgeregt in mein Büro gestürzt. „Wo brennt's?" fragte ich.
*The man rushed excitedly into my office. "Where's the fire? (What's up?)" I asked.*

im **Brennpunkt** stehen (fig.): cf. im **Blickpunkt** stehen

etwas in den **Brennpunkt** rücken (fig.): *to bring s. th. to the fore (the forefront); to focus attention on s. th.*

> Die neue Regierung will die soziale Fürsorge in den Brennpunkt der Reformen rücken.
> *The new government intends to bring social security to the fore (forefront; to focus attention on social security) in its reforms.*

eine **Bresche** schlagen (fig.): *to drive a wedge; to make a breach*

> Der Minister hat durch sein Buch eine Bresche in die Ideen der Oppositionspartei geschlagen.
> *By his book the minister has driven a wedge into (made a breach in) the ideas of the opposition party.*

in die **Bresche** springen (fig.): cf. in die **Lücke** springen

flach wie ein **Brett** sein: cf. platt wie 'ne **Flunder** sein

ein **Brett** vor dem Kopf haben (fig.): *to be a blockhead (dim-wit; dullard).* Cf. auch: schwer von **Kapee** sein

> Der neue Schüler hat wohl ein Brett vor dem Kopf, denn er faßt alles sehr langsam auf.
> *The new pupil must be a blockhead (dim-wit; dullard), because he picks everything up very slowly.*

die **Bretter,** die die Welt bedeuten: *the stage which is the world*

> In gehobener Sprache nennt man das Theater die Bretter, die die Welt bedeuten.
> *In elevated language the theatre is called the stage which is the world.*

(Das geht) wie's **Brezelbacken:** cf. im **Handumdrehen**

den blauen **Brief** bekommen: *to be cashiered; to get the sack (colloq.); to get one's cards (colloq.)*

> Heute haben mehrere Offiziere den blauen Brief bekommen.
> *Several officers were cashiered (got the sack; got their cards) today.*

einen geharnischten **Brief** schreiben: cf. j.em einen **geharnischten** Brief schreiben

j.em **Brief** und Siegel für etwas geben (fig.): *to assure s. b. on one's oath; to give (to pledge) s. b. one's word for s. th.*

> Ich kann Ihnen Brief und Siegel dafür geben, daß mein Schwager Sie bei dem geplanten Geschäft nicht ausnützen wird.
> *I can assure you on my oath (can give [pledge] you my word) that my brother-in-law will not take advantage of you in the deal that you are planning.*

platt wie 'ne **Briefmarke** sein (fam.): cf. platt wie 'ne **Flunder** sein

etwas durch eine fremde **Brille** sehen (betrachten) (fig.): *to see s. th. through other people's eyes*

> Man darf die Sachlage nicht immer nur vom eigenen Standpunkt aus betrachten, man muß sie auch einmal durch eine fremde Brille sehen.
> *One must not always regard the situation only from one's own standpoint; one must also see it through other people's eyes.*

alles durch die rosarote (rosige) **Brille** betrachten (fig.): *to see everything through rose-coloured spectacles.* Cf. auch: etwas in rosigem **Licht** betrachten; Der **Himmel** hängt einem voller Geigen

> Als Optimist betrachtet mein Vater alles durch die rosarote (rosige) Brille.
> *My father, being an optimist, sees everything through rose-coloured spectacles.*

(viel) **Brimborium** um etwas machen (fam.): *to make (to kick up) a fuss (a to-do; a schemozzle) about s. th. (colloq.).* Cf. auch: viel **Wind** um etwas machen

> Er machte viel Brimborium (Trara, ein großes Getue), als er erfuhr, daß sein Sohn die Aufnahmeprüfung nicht bestanden hatte.
> *He made (kicked up) a great fuss (to-do; schemozzle) when he learned that his son had not passed the entrance examination.*

seine **Brocken** (zusammen)packen (fam.): cf. seine **Siebensachen** (zusammen)packen

abgehen wie geschnitten **Brot:** cf. abgehen wie warme **Semmeln**

j.en um sein **Brot** bringen: *to deprive (to rob) s. b. of his livelihood; to cut s. b.'s lifeline; to do s. b. out of a job (colloq.)*

> Die Stelle des Pedells ist abgeschafft worden, was leider diesen alten Mann um sein Brot gebracht hat.
> *The post of caretaker has been abolished, which has unfortunately deprived (robbed) this old man of his livelihood (has cut this old man's lifeline; has done this old man out of a job).*

Wes **Brot** ich ess', des Lied ich sing' (Sprichw.): *I take my master's part; I play the tune I'm paid to*

> Dieser Angestellte lobt seinen Chef sehr. Wes Brot ich ess', des Lied ich sing'.
> *That clerk greatly praises his boss. He takes his master's part (He plays the tune he's paid to).*

sich das **Brot** am Munde absparen: *to starve o. s.; to pinch and scrape*

> Die arme Witwe sparte sich das Brot am Munde ab, um ihren Sohn studieren zu lassen.
> *The poor widow starved herself (pinched and scraped) in order to let her son study.*

j.em etwas aufs **Brot** schmieren (fig. u. fam.): cf. j. em etwas aufs **Butterbrot** schmieren

sein **Brot** verdienen: *to earn one's bread-and-butter (one's living)*

Da seine Eltern bereits gestorben waren, mußte sich Karl schon mit 14 Jahren sein Brot selbst verdienen.
*Since his parents were already dead, Charles had to earn his bread-and-butter (his living) at the early age of fourteen.*

j.em den **Brotkorb** höher hängen (fig.): *to make s. b. tighten his belt; to keep s. b. short*

Man sollte ihm den Brotkorb höher hängen (ihn kurzhalten), da er sehr verschwenderisch lebt.
*One ought to make him tighten his belt (keep him short), for he lives very wastefully.*

sich einen **Bruch** lachen (fam.): cf. sich **totlachen**

in die **Brüche** gehen (fig.): *to go to pieces; to break (to crack) up; to fall apart*

Durch unvorhergesehene Mißverständnisse ist unsere Freundschaft in die Brüche gegangen.
*Our friendship went to pieces (broke up; cracked up; fell apart) through unforeseen misunderstandings.*

alle **Brücken** hinter sich abbrechen (fig.): *to burn one's boats (one's bridges); to uproot o. s.; to break with the past*

Diese Familie hat alle Brücken hinter sich abgebrochen und ist nach Australien ausgewandert.
*This family has burned its boats (bridges; uprooted itself; broken with the past) and emigrated to Australia.*

j.em goldene **Brücken** (eine goldene Brücke) bauen (fig.): *to build s. b. a golden bridge to cross*

Als der Schüler seinen Lehrer versehentlich mit seinem Spitznamen anredete, wollte der Lehrer ihm goldene Brücken (eine goldene Brücke) bauen und sagte, er habe ihn nicht richtig verstanden.
*When the pupil addressed his teacher by his nickname by mistake, the teacher wanted to build him a golden bridge to cross, and said that he had not understood him properly.*

sich wie die feindlichen **Brüder** gegenüberstehen: *to be at daggers drawn.* Cf. auch: sich mit j.em in den **Haaren** liegen

Seit dem Rückgang ihres Geschäftes stehen sich die beiden Teilhaber wie die feindlichen Brüder gegenüber.
*Since their firm's decline the two partners have been at daggers drawn.*

Gleiche **Brüder,** gleiche Kappen (Sprichw.): cf. **Gleich** und Gleich gesellt sich gern unter **Brüdern** . . . wert sein: *to be a bargain at* . . .

Der Ring, den du von diesem Händler gekauft hast, ist unter Brüdern mindestens 300 Mark wert.
*The ring you bought from that dealer would be a bargain at 300 marks.*

etwas **brühwarm** weitererzählen: *to spread s. th. while it is still hot*

Ich bitte dich, diese Neuigkeit nicht gleich brühwarm weiterzuerzählen.
*I beg you not to spread this news while it is still hot.*

Das ist (ja) zum **Brüllen!** (fam.): cf. Das ist (ja) zum **Piepen!**

ein alter **Brummbär** sein **(brummig** sein): *to be like a bear with a sore tail; to be an old moaner (grumbler; growler) (colloq.)*

Ich kann diesen Onkel nicht leiden. Er versteht keinen Spaß und ist ein alter Brummbär (brummig wie ein Bär).
*I cannot stand this uncle. He cannot take a joke, and is like a bear with a sore tail (is an old moaner [grumbler; growler]).*

**brummen** müssen (fam.): cf. in den **Kasten** kommen; hinter **Schloß** und Riegel sitzen

vor Dummheit **brummen** (so dumm sein, daß man brummt) (fam.): cf. ein **Rindvieh** sein

Der Kopf (Schädel) **brummt** mir (Mir brummt der Kopf [Schädel]): cf. Der **Kopf** brummt mir

schielen wie ein **Brummer** ('ne **Brumme)** (fam.): cf. **schielen** wie ein Brummer

einen **Brummschädel** haben: *to have a splitting headache; s. b.'s head is going round and round.* Cf. auch: einen **Kater** haben; Der **Kopf** brummt mir

Nach den Festlichkeiten der Silvesternacht hatte ich einen ordentlichen Brummschädel.
*After the festivities of New Year's Eve I had an absolutely splitting headache (my head was going round and round).*

den **Brunnen** zudecken, wenn das Kind ertrunken ist (fig.): *to shut the stable-door when the horse is stolen (has bolted)*

Du bist mit deiner Warnung zu spät gekommen, denn das Geld ist bereits gestohlen worden. Es hat keinen Zweck, den Brunnen zuzudecken, wenn das Kind ertrunken ist.
*Your warning has come too late, because the money has already been stolen. It is no good shutting the stable-door when the horse is stolen (has bolted).*

**Brunnenvergiftung** (fig.): *scandalmongering*

Es ist nichts als üble Brunnenvergiftung, wenn behauptet wird, die führenden Männer dieses Staates hätten ihre Privatgelder im Ausland angelegt.
*It is nothing but wicked scandalmongering to maintain that the leaders of that country have invested their private capital abroad.*

sich an die **Brust** schlagen (fig.): *to beat one's breast*

Anstatt mir Vorwürfe zu machen, solltest du dich an die eigene Brust schlagen.
*Instead of blaming me, you ought to beat your own breast.*

aus voller **Brust** singen: cf. aus voller **Kehle** singen

etwas in seiner **Brust** verschließen (fig.): *to keep s. th. to o. s.; to keep s. th. quiet (dark); to keep s. th. in one's heart*

Fünf Jahre lang hatte er das Geheimnis in seiner Brust verschlossen (im Busen bewahrt).
*For five years he had kept the secret to himself (quiet [dark]; in his heart).*

sich in die **Brust** werfen (sich **brüsten**): *to puff (to blow) out one's chest.* Cf. auch: sich spreizen wie ein **Truthahn; angeben**

Du brauchst dich nicht so in die Brust zu werfen (zu brüsten), weil du das letzte Diktat fast fehlerlos geschrieben hast.
*You don't need to puff (blow) out your chest like that because you did the last dictation almost perfectly.*

etwas mit dem **Brustton** der Überzeugung erklären: *to pronounce s. th. with loud conviction (with brazen confidence)*

Mein Neffe erklärte mit dem Brustton der Überzeugung, daß er den Wettlauf leicht gewinnen werde.
*My nephew pronounced with loud conviction (brazen confidence) that he would win the race easily.*

eine **Bruthitze** sein: cf. eine **Bullenhitze** sein

ein gemeines **Bubenstück** sein: *to be a shabby (a low) trick (move); to be a dirty (a rotten) trick (colloq.)*

Die neugepflanzten Bäumchen abzubrechen, war ein gemeines Bubenstück (gemeiner Streich).
*It was a shabby (low) trick (move; a dirty [rotten] trick) to break down the newly-planted saplings.*

einen **Bubikopf** tragen: *to have one's hair bobbed; to wear a bob; to wear an urchin cut*

Es ist heutzutage Mode, einen Bubikopf (Herrenschnitt) zu tragen.
*It is the fashion today to have one's hair bobbed (to wear a bob; to wear an urchin cut).*

ein offenes **Buch** sein (fig.): *to be an open  book*

> Die Politik dieses Landes ist noch nie ein offenes Buch gewesen.
> *The politics of this country have never been an open book.*

reden wie ein **Buch**: *to talk like a book; to have the gift of the gab*

> Mein Freund sollte Politiker werden, denn er redet wie ein Buch ([Wasserfall]; hat Pappelwasser getrunken).
> *My friend ought to become a politician, because he has the gift of the gab (he talks like a book).*

ein **Buch** mit sieben Siegeln bleiben (fig.): *to remain a closed book*

> Die moderne Malerei bleibt für viele Menschen zeitlebens ein Buch mit sieben Siegeln.
> *Modern painting remains a closed book to many people all their lives.*

wie er im **Buche** steht: *out of the book (copy-book); of the first water (rank; order)*

> Dein Vetter ist ein Prahler, wie er im Buche steht (von reinstem Wasser; ersten Ranges).
> *Your cousin is a boaster out of the book (copy-book; a boaster of the first water [rank; order]).*

ein **Bücherwurm** sein: *to be a bookworm*

> Viele Gelehrte sind Bücherwürmer (Leseratten; Stubengelehrte); sie sitzen den ganzen Tag an ihrem Schreibtisch und lesen.
> *Many scholars are bookworms; they sit at their desks the whole day and read.*

ein munterer **Buchfink** sein (fig.): cf. **kreuzfidel** sein

sich an den **Buchstaben** halten: *to keep (to stick) to the letter*

> Der Polizist hat sich an den Buchstaben seiner Vorschriften gehalten und den Namen des Radfahrers aufgeschrieben.
> *The policeman kept (stuck) to the letter of his regulations and took the cyclist's name.*

den **Buckel** voll Arbeit haben: cf. alle **Hände** voll zu tun haben

einen breiten **Buckel** haben (fig.): *to have a broad back; to be like water off a duck's back; to be able to take it (colloq.).* Cf. auch: ein dickes **Fell** haben

> Die ungerechten Bezichtigungen meines Vorgesetzten stören mich nicht. Ich habe einen breiten Buckel (Rücken).
> *My boss's unjust accusations do not worry me. I have a broad back (It is like water off a duck's back; I can take them).*

j.en auf dem **Buckel** haben (fig.): cf. j.en auf dem **Halse** haben

j.em den **Buckel** herunterrutschen (heraufsteigen) können (fig. u. fam.):

*to see s. b. to blazes (in hell) first (sl.) ; to take a running jump at o. s. (sl.).* Cf. auch: Scher' dich zum **Henker!**

Ich denke nicht daran, dir meine Uhr zu verkaufen. Du kannst mir den Buckel herunterrutschen (heraufsteigen; gestohlen [gewogen] bleiben; den Hobel ausblasen; im Mondschein begegnen; kannst mich gernhaben [liebhaben]). *I've no intention of selling you my watch. I'll see you to blazes (in hell) first (Take a running jump at yourself)!*

j.en juckt der **Buckel** (fig.): cf. j.en juckt das **Fell**

den **Buckel** vollkriegen (fam.): cf. die **Jacke** vollkriegen

sich den **Buckel** voll lachen: cf. sich **totlachen**

die (ganze) **Bude** auf den Kopf stellen (fam.): cf. alles auf den **Kopf** stellen

j.em auf die **Bude** rücken (fam.): *to go and give s. b. a piece of one's mind; to go and shake s. b. up (colloq.)*

Man muß ihm auf die Bude rücken, wenn man bei ihm etwas erreichen will. *You must go and give him a piece of your mind (shake him up) if you want to get anywhere with him.*

einen **Budenzauber** veranstalten (fam.): *to have (to indulge in) high jinks*

Es herrschte die ganze Nacht über ein furchtbarer Krach. Der Künstler von nebenan hatte mal wieder einen Budenzauber veranstaltet. *There was a terrible row all night through. The artist next door was having (indulging in) high jinks again.*

**büffeln** (fam.): *to swot (colloq.); to mug up (colloq.); to cram (colloq.)*

Stört ihn jetzt nicht! Er büffelt (ochst) für sein Examen. *Don't disturb him now; he's swotting (mugging up; cramming) for his exam.*

j.em einen (Warnschuß) vor den **Bug** feuern (fig.): *to fire a (warning) shot across s. b.'s bows*

Als der Redner zu freisinnige Meinungen äußerte, hat ihm seine Parteileitung einen vor den Bug gefeuert (einen Schuß vor den Bug gesetzt) und ihn zum Schweigen gebracht. *When the speaker expressed too progressive opinions, the party leaders fired a warning shot across his bows and silenced him.*

platt wie ein **Bügelbrett** sein (fam.): cf. platt wie 'ne **Flunder** sein

sich **bügelhoch** zanken: *to bite each other's heads off; to snap at each other; to be at each other's throats; to snarl at each other*

Der Junge und seine Schwester zanken sich oft bügelhoch. *The boy and his sister often bite each other's heads off (snap [snarl] at each other; are often at each other's throats).*

von der **Bühne** abtreten (fig.): *to withdraw (to retire) from the scene (arena)*

Dieses Volk ist seit langem von der Bühne des Weltgeschehens abgetreten.
*That nation withdrew (retired) long ago from the scene (arena) of world events.*

über die **Bühne** gehen (fig.): *to go (to pass) off*

Wir hatten zunächst mit gewissen Schwierigkeiten gerechnet; es ist jedoch alles reibungslos über die Bühne gegangen.
*We had reckoned at first with certain difficulties, but everything went (passed) off smoothly.*

eine **Bullenhitze** (fam.): *a scorching (baking; tropical) heat; a scorcher (colloq.)*

Bei dieser Bullenhitze (Affen-, Backofen-, Brut-, Treibhaus-, Tropenhitze [tropischen Hitze]) kann ich unmöglich arbeiten.
*It is impossible for me to work in this scorching (baking; tropical) heat (this scorcher).*

auf den **Bummel** gehen: *to go for (to take) a stroll; to take a turn*

Es ist eine seiner Lieblingsbeschäftigungen, abends am Rhein auf den Bummel zu gehen (zu bummeln).
*It is one of his favourite occupations to go for (to take) a stroll (to take a turn) in the evenings along the Rhine.*

ein **Bummelfritze** sein (fam.): cf. ein **Trödelfritze** sein

ein **Bummelleben** führen: cf. ein **Bohèmeleben** führen

eine **Bummelliese** sein (fam.): *to be a slow-coach*

Unsere Zeitungsfrau ist eine furchtbare Bummelliese (ein Tränentier; eine Transuse; Tranlampe). Sie kommt immer erst, wenn ich gerade zur Schule muß.
*Our paper-woman is a terrible slow-coach. She only comes just as I have to go to school.*

**bummeln:** a) cf. auf den **Bummel** gehen; b) *to dawdle; to dilly-dally (colloq.)*

b) Du bist mit deiner Arbeit nicht fertig, weil du wieder einmal so gebummelt (gemärt; gezottelt) hast.
*b) You have not finished your work because you have been dawdling (dilly-dallying) again.*

den **Bund** fürs Leben schließen: *to enter into holy wedlock (holy matrimony)*

Meine Eltern haben vor bald 30 Jahren den Bund fürs Leben geschlossen.
*My parents entered into holy wedlock (matrimony) almost thirty years ago.*

sein **Bündel** schnüren: *to pack one's bags (one's things).* Cf. auch: seine **Siebensachen** (zusammen)packen

Da unser Dienstmädchen sehr unsauber war, muß es jetzt sein Bündel schnüren und sonstwo Arbeit suchen.
*As our maid was very dirty, she has now got to pack her bags (things) and look for work elsewhere.*

j.en sein **Bündel** schnüren lassen: cf. j.en auf die **Straße** setzen sein **Bündel** tragen (fig.): cf. sein **Kreuz** tragen

j.em zu **bunt** werden: *to become too much of a good thing; to go too far; to get fed up with s. th. (colloq.); to be a bit thick (colloq.).* Cf. auch: j.em auf die **Nerven** gehen

> Jeden Tag kommen die Nachbarn, um bei mir zu telefonieren. Das wird mir allmählich doch zu bunt (zu dumm).
> *Every day the neighbours come to telephone from my house. It's gradually becoming too much of a good thing (It's going too far; I'm gradually getting fed up with it; It's a bit thick).*

laufen wie ein **Bürstenbinder**: cf. laufen wie ein **Besenbinder**

bei j.em auf den **Busch** klopfen (fig.): cf. bei j.em einen **Fühler** ausstrecken

etwas im **Busen** bewahren: cf. etwas in seiner **Brust** verschließen

**Busenfreunde** sein: *to be bosom (close; firm) friends; to be as thick as thieves; to be chums (colloq.)*

> Karl und Heinrich sind seit langem Busenfreunde (dicke Freunde; halten seit langem wie Pech und Schwefel zusammen; Heinrich ist Karls Intimus); man sieht sie immer zusammen spielen.
> *Charles and Henry have been bosom (close; firm) friends (as thick as thieves; have been chums) for a long while; one always sees them playing together.*

sich die **Butter** vom Brot nehmen lassen (fig.): *to let o. s. be put upon; to let o. s. be taken advantage of*

> Ich lasse mir von ihm nichts gefallen; ich wäre dumm, wenn ich mir von ihm die Butter vom Brot nehmen ließe.
> *I'm not going to put up with anything from him; I should be stupid to let myself be put upon by him (to let myself be taken advantage of by him).*

in **Butter** sein (fam.): *to be on ice; to be plain sailing; to be in clover; to be in apple-pie order; to be going swimmingly (colloq.)*

> Nachdem wir zunächst viel Ärger hatten, ist nun alles in Butter.
> *After we had had a great deal of trouble at first, everything is now on ice (plain sailing; in clover; in apple-pie order; is going swimmingly).*

wie **Butter** an der Sonne zergehen (schmelzen): *to dwindle (to fade) into nothingness; to melt away; to shrink to nothing*

> Infolge solcher Spekulationen ist sein Kapital wie Butter (Schnee) an der Sonne zergangen (geschmolzen).
> *As a result of such speculations his capital has dwindled (faded) into nothingness (melted away; shrunk to nothing).*

j.em etwas aufs **Butterbrot** schmieren (fig. u. fam.): *to rub (to din) s. th. in to s. b.; to ram s. th. down s. b.'s throat (colloq.)*

> Man sollte Wilhelm nicht immer aufs (Butter)brot schmieren (unter die Nase reiben; unter die Weste schieben), daß er aus sehr einfachen Verhältnissen stammt.
> *One ought not always to rub (din) it in to William (to ram it down William's throat) that he comes from a very simple home.*

etwas für ein **Butterbrot** verkaufen (fig.): *to sell s. th. for a song (for next to nothing)*

> Diese törichten Leute haben ihr schönes Landhaus für ein Butterbrot (für einen Apfel und ein Ei; für einen Pappenstiel) verkauft.
> *These foolish people have sold their lovely country house for a song (for next to nothing).*

auf die **Butterseite** fallen (fig.): *to miss the target; to come unstuck (colloq.)*

> Mein Gesuch ist leider auf die Butterseite gefallen; ich habe den Posten nicht bekommen.
> *My application has unfortunately missed the target (come unstuck); I have not got the job.*

**butterweich** sein: *to be as soft as butter*

> Die Birnen aus euerm Garten sind schmackhaft und butterweich.
> *The pears in your garden have a delicious flavour and are as soft as butter.*

in **Buxtehude** wohnen (fig.): *to live in Timbuctu (in the back of beyond; in the backwoods)*

> Kommt uns doch mal besuchen! Ihr wohnt doch nicht in Buxtehude (Krähwinkel; Posemuckel; am Ende [aus] der Welt; wo sich die Füchse gute Nacht sagen).
> Come and visit us. You don't live in Timbuctu (in the back of beyond; in the backwoods).


# C

**Chic** haben: *to be (to look) smart*

> Deine junge Frau lenkt durch ihre elegante Kleidung große Aufmerksamkeit auf sich. Sie hat wirklich Chic.
> *Your young wife attracts great attention by her elegant clothes. She is (looks) really smart.*

aussehen wie das Leiden **Christi** (fam.): cf. aussehen wie eine **Wasserleiche**

(sich) etwas **christlich** teilen: *to share s. th. fairly; to share s. th. without respect of persons*

Die beiden Brüder haben sich alle Geschenke christlich geteilt. Jeder nahm sich genau die Hälfte.
*The two brothers shared all the presents fairly (without respect of persons). Each took exactly half.*

sich in einem **circulus vitiosus** bewegen: *to be (to be caught up) in a vicious circle; to be like a dog chasing its own tail*

Ich sehe keinen Ausweg aus dieser Situation. Wir bewegen uns einfach in einem circulus vitiosus (sind wie die [eine] Katze, die sich in den [eigenen] Schwanz beißt; Wir drehen uns im Kreise).
*I see no way out of this situation. We are simply (caught up) in a vicious circle (are like a dog chasing its own tail).*

den **Clown** spielen: cf. den **Hanswurst** spielen

die ganze **Corona** (Korona): cf. die ganze **Blase**

die **Cour** schneiden: cf. einer Frau den **Hof** machen

zur **Crème** der Gesellschaft gehören: cf. zur **Hautevolee** gehören


# D


**da capo** rufen: *to encore s. b.*

Die Zuhörer waren von der Arie der Sängerin so begeistert, daß sie da capo riefen.
*The listeners were so enthusiastic about the singer's aria that they encored her.*

eins aufs **Dach** bekommen (fam.): cf. eine **Abreibung** kriegen

etwas unter **Dach** und Fach bringen (fig.): *to round s. th. off; to get through s. th.; to wrap s. th. up (colloq.)*

Das Unterhaus will dieses Gesetz noch vor den Ferien unter Dach und Fach bringen.
*The lower house wants to round off (get through; wrap up) this bill before the recess.*

j.em das **Dach** überm Kopf anzünden: *to burn down the house over s. b.'s head*

Die Leute waren über den Verräter so wütend, daß sie ihm das Dach überm Kopf anzündeten.
*The people were so furious with the traitor that they burned the house down over his head.*

j.em aufs **Dach** steigen (fig. u. fam.): cf. j.en **abkanzeln**

einen **Dachschaden** haben (fig. u. fam.): cf. nicht richtig im **Dachstübchen** sein

nicht richtig im **Dachstübchen** sein (fam.): *to be out of one's mind; to have a screw loose (colloq.); to have bats in the belfry (colloq.); to be not quite right in the upper storey (colloq.); to be daft (dotty; balmy; bats; nuts; cracked; crazy) (colloq.); to be off one's rocker (colloq.); to be not (quite) all there (colloq.); to be round the bend (sl.)*

> Wie kannst du mir so etwas zumuten! Bei dir ist's wohl nicht richtig im Dachstübchen (Oberstübchen; Bei dir piepst es wohl; ist wohl eine Schraube [ein Rad] locker [los]; Du hast wohl einen Dachschaden [Fimmel; Hau; Klaps; Knall; Piepmatz; Raptus; Span; Sparren; Spleen; Vogel]; nicht alle Tassen im Schrank [nicht alle beieinander; wohl einen weg]; Du bist wohl vom [tollen] Affen [vom wilden Waz] gebissen [bekloppt; meschugge]; nicht [recht] gescheit [bei Groschen; klug; bei Trost]; Du siehst wohl weiße Mäuse; Du spinnst wohl).
> *How can you expect me to do such a thing? You must be out of your mind (must have a screw loose [bats in the belfry]; must be not quite right in the upper storey; must be daft [dotty; bats; nuts; balmy; cracked; crazy]; must be off your rocker [not (quite) all there; round the bend]).*

ein junger **Dachs** sein (fig.): cf. ein **Grünschnabel** sein

etwas bis **dahin** (stehen) haben (fam.): *to be sick ([and tired]; sick to death) of s. th. (colloq.); to be fed up (to the back teeth) with s. th. (colloq.); to be browned off (cheesed off) with s. th. (sl.)*

> Ich hab's bis dahin (bis zur Halskrause) ([stehen]; habe es satt [dick; knüppeldick]; hab' die Nase [gestrichen] voll; Es hängt [wächst] mir zum Hals heraus; Es wird mir zu dumm), jeden Tag dein dummes Geschwätz anzuhören.
> *I'm sick ([and tired]; sick to death) of (fed up [to the back teeth]; browned [cheesed] off with) listening to your stupid chatter every day.*

**dahinterkommen** (fig.): *to ferret out; to rumble (colloq.); to get wise (sl.)*

> Ich bin noch nicht dahintergekommen, ob mich mein Freund belogen hat oder nicht.
> *I have not yet ferreted out (rumbled; got wise to) whether my friend has swindled me or not.*

**dahinterstecken** (fig.): cf. seine **Finger** im Spiel haben

Es steckt nichts **dahinter** (fig.): *There is nothing to (behind) it (them)*

> Diese Zeitungsartikel werden viel gelesen, aber es steckt nichts dahinter.
> *These newspaper articles are widely read, but there is nothing to (behind) them.*

ein **Däm(e)lack** sein (fam.): cf. ein **Rindvieh** sein

90

j.en wieder auf den **Damm** bringen (fig.): *to set (to put) s. b. on his feet again;
to set s. b. up again.* Cf. auch: j.em wieder auf die **Beine** helfen

> Im vorigen Jahr war ich oft krank. Aber unser Hausarzt hat mich wieder auf
> den Damm gebracht.
> *Last year I was often ill, but our family doctor has set (put) me on my feet again (set
> me up again).*

einer Sache einen **Damm** entgegensetzen (fig.): cf. einer Sache **Halt** gebieten

auf dem **Damm** sein (fig.): cf. auf der **Höhe** sein

es **dämmert** j.em: cf. j.em geht ein **Licht** auf.

das **Damoklesschwert:** *the sword of Damocles*

> Ein neuer Krieg schwebt wie ein Damoklesschwert über den Völkern der Erde.
> *A new war hangs over the nations of the world like the sword of Damocles.*

**Dampf** dahinter machen (fig.): *to bring (some) pressure to bear; to make s. b. get
a move on (colloq.); to ginger (to hustle; to shake) s. b. up about s. th. (colloq.)*

> Mein Gesuch ist immer noch nicht beantwortet. Ich muß mal persönlich zum
> Ministerium gehen und Dampf (Feuer) dahinter machen (und den Leuten Feuer
> unter den Schwanz machen).
> *My application has still not been answered. I must go to the Ministry in person and bring
> (some) pressure to bear (make them get a move on; ginger [hustle; shake] them up
> about it).*

Hans **Dampf** in allen Gassen sein: cf. **Hans** Dampf in allen Gassen sein

**Dampf** vor etwas haben (fig.): cf. (eine) **Heidenangst** haben

einer Sache einen **Dämpfer** aufsetzen (fig.): *to put a damper (curb; mute) on
s. th.; to dampen (to curb; to mute) s. th.*

> Diese traurige Nachricht setzte seinem Enthusiasmus einen Dämpfer auf.
> *This sad news put a damper (curb; mute) on (dampened; curbed; muted) his enthusiasm.*

ein **Danaergeschenk** sein: *to be a Greek gift (a gift of doubtful value)*

> Die neue Erfindung wird von den meisten Menschen als ein Danaergeschenk
> betrachtet.
> *The new invention is considered by most people to be a Greek gift (a gift of doubtful value).*

ein **Danaidenfaß** sein: cf. ein bodenloses **Faß** sein

sich gründlich (schwer) **danebensetzen** (fig.): *to be very wide (well wide) of
the mark; to be well out; to be right off the target*

Wenn du glaubst, daß Lausanne in Frankreich liegt, so hast du dich gründlich (schwer) dànebengesetzt.
*If you think that Lausanne is in France, you are very (well) wide of the mark (well out; right off the target).*

Es ist etwas faul im Staate **Dänemark**: cf. Es ist etwas **faul** im Staate Dänemark

**dann** und wann: cf. **ab** und zu

Auch **das** noch!: *This is the last straw; This on top of it all; It never rains but it pours*

Mein Vater ist schon seit längerer Zeit krank, und nun muß sich auch meine Mutter zu Bett legen. Auch das noch!
*My father has been ill for some time, and now my mother has got to take to her bed. This is the last straw (This on top of it all; It never rains but it pours).*

die **Daumen (Däumchen)** drehen: *to twiddle one's thumbs; to count one's fingers*

Ich muß immer eine Beschäftigung haben. Untätig dasitzen und die Daumen ([die] Däumchen) drehen (in der Nase bohren), kann ich nicht.
*I must always have a job (something to do). I cannot sit idly twiddling my thumbs (counting my fingers).*

die **Daumen** für j.en drücken (halten): *to keep one's fingers crossed for s. b.*

Viel Glück bei Ihrer Prüfung! Ich werde für Sie die Daumen drücken (halten).
*Good luck for your examination! I'll keep my fingers crossed for you.*

den **Daumen** auf etwas halten (fig.): *to keep a tight hand (a firm hold) on s. th.*

Vater hält den Daumen darauf, daß wir nicht zuviel Geld ausgeben.
*Father keeps a tight hand (a firm hold) on us to see that we do not spend too much money.*

über den **Daumen** peilen (fig.): *to give a rough idea; to make a rough guess (a rough shot)*

Den genauen Preis dieses Buches kann ich Ihnen im Augenblick nicht sagen. Aber, über den Daumen gepeilt, wird es etwa 20 Mark kosten.
*I cannot tell you the exact price of this book at the moment. To give you a rough idea (At a rough guess [shot]), however, it will cost about 20 marks.*

j.em **Daumenschrauben** anlegen (fig.): *to put pressure on s. b.; to bring pressure to bear on s. b.; to employ third-degree methods on s. b. (colloq.); to put the screw on s. b. (colloq.)*

Ist es nicht eine Schande, diesen Leuten Daumenschrauben anzulegen (Druck auf diese Leute auszuüben; diese Leute unter Druck zu setzen), indem man sie zwingt, ihren Besitz zu verkaufen?

*Is it not a shame to put pressure (to bring pressure to bear; to employ third-degree methods; to put the screw) on these people by making them sell their possessions?*

ein **Däumling** sein: cf. ein **Knirps** sein

**dazwischenfahren** (fam.: **-funken**): *to step in; to intervene*

Sein Bruder wollte ein zweifelhaftes Mädchen heiraten, aber seine Eltern sind rechtzeitig dazwischengefahren (haben . . . dazwischengefunkt).
*His brother wanted to marry a girl of doubtful character but his parents stepped in (intervened) in time.*

vor Freude an die **Decke** springen (fig.): *to jump (to leap) for joy*

Als der Junge sein gutes Zeugnis bekam, wäre er am liebsten vor Freude an die Decke gesprungen.
*When the boy got his good report, he would have liked to jump (to leap) for joy.*

unter éiner **Decke** stecken (fig.): *to be hand in glove; to be in league*

Gauner pflegen oft, unter éiner Decke zu stecken.
*Rogues are often hand in glove (often in league) with each other.*

sich nach der **Decke** strecken (fig.): *to cut one's coat according to one's cloth; to suit one's requirements to one's situation; to make the best of it*

Bei den steigenden Preisen wird es mancher lernen müssen, sich nach der Decke zu strecken und seine Ausgaben zu vermindern.
*With rising prices many will have to learn to cut their coat according to their cloth (to suit their requirements to their situation; to make the best of it) and cut down their expenditure.*

eins auf den **Deckel** bekommen (fam.): cf. eine **Abreibung** kriegen

j.em eins auf den **Deckel** geben (fam.): cf. j.em eins auf den **Hut** geben

unter dem **Deckmantel**: *under the cloak (guise)*

Diese Spende wurde unter dem Deckmantel der christlichen Nächstenliebe erhoben; es war aber in Wirklichkeit eine bewußte Irreführung.
*This collection was made under the cloak (guise) of Christian charity, but in reality it was a deliberate fraud.*

mit j.em die **Degen** kreuzen (fig.): cf. mit j.em die **Klingen** kreuzen

etwas **deichseln** (fam.): cf. etwas zu **Wege** bringen

ein **Denkzettel**: *something to think about*

Für seine Ungezogenheit hat ihm sein Vater einen tüchtigen Denkzettel gegeben.
*His father really gave him something to think about for his rudeness.*

keinen **Deut**: *not a scrap (a whit; a jot; an iota; a bit)*. Cf. auch: nicht die **Bohne**

Er hat sich seit vorigem Jahr (um) keinen Deut gebessert.
*He has not improved a scrap (a whit; a jot; an iota; a bit) since last year.*

sich keinen **Deut** aus etwas machen: *not to care two hoots (two pins; a fig; a scrap; a whit; a jot; an iota; a bit) about s. th.; not to care a damn (a tinker's cuss) about s. th. (sl.); not to be able to care less (sl.)*

Von mir aus kann er ruhig nach Italien fahren, wenn er will; ich mache mir keinen Deut (nicht die Bohne; nicht einen Dreck) daraus (frage den Teufel danach; kümmere mich den Teufel darum).
*As far as I am concerned he can go to Italy if he likes; I don't care two hoots (two pins; a fig; a scrap; a whit; a jot; an iota; a bit; a damn; a tinker's cuss; I couldn't care less) about it.*

keinen **Deut** wert sein: cf. keinen (roten) **Heller** wert sein

auf gut **deutsch** (fig.): *in so many words; in plain language (plain English); The long and (the) short of it is . . .; The blunt (brute) fact is . . .*

Warum soviel unnütze Worte? Auf gut deutsch: Sie lehnen es ab, sich zu beteiligen.
*Why so much useless talk? In so many words (In plain language [English]; The long and the short of it is; The blunt [brute] fact is), you refuse to participate.*

**deutsch** mit j.em reden (fig.): *to call a spade a spade; to speak one's mind to s. b.; not to mince matters; not to pull one's punches (colloq.)*. Cf. auch: das **Kind** beim rechten Namen nennen

Mit zarten Anspielungen kommt man bei ihm nicht weit. Man muß klar seine Meinung sagen und deutsch (Fraktur) mit ihm reden.
*You won't get far with him with subtle allusions. You must give your opinion plainly and call a spade a spade (speak your mind to him; not mince matters; not pull your punches).*

**Dichten** und Trachten: *thoughts and dreams; hopes and ambitions*

All sein Dichten (Sinnen) und Trachten richtet sich darauf, einmal ein großer Pianist zu werden.
*All his thoughts and dreams (hopes and ambitions) are directed towards becoming a great pianist.*

**dichthalten** (fig.): *to keep one's mouth shut; to keep mum (colloq.)*

Sie hat tatsächlich dichtgehalten und mein Geheimnis nicht verraten.
*She really did keep her mouth shut (keep mum) and not give my secret away.*

für j.en durch **dick** und dünn gehen (fig.): *to go through thick and thin for s. b.* Cf. auch: für j.en durchs **Feuer** gehen

Unser Lehrer ist sehr beliebt. Wir würden für ihn durch dick und dünn gehen.
*Our teacher is very popular. We would go through thick and thin for him.*

94

**dicke** Freunde sein: cf. **Busenfreunde** sein

**dickfellig** sein: cf. ein dickes **Fell** haben

etwas **dickhaben** (fam.): cf. etwas bis **dahin** (stehen) haben

sich **dick(e)tun** (fam.): cf. **angeben**

ein **Dickkopf (Dickschädel) (dickköpfig)** sein: *to be a pig-headed (mule-headed) person; to be pig-headed (mule-headed; thick-skulled); to be a thick-head (a blockhead) (colloq.)*

> Obwohl ihm jeder sagt, daß er auf diese Weise nichts erreicht, bleibt er unbelehrbar. Er ist eben ein Dickkopf (Dickschädel) (eben dickköpfig).
> *Although everyone tells him that he won't get anywhere that way, he remains unteachable. He is just a pig-headed (mule-headed) person (a thick-head; a blockhead; pig-headed; mule-headed; thick-skulled).*

sich **diebisch** freuen (einen diebischen Spaß haben): *to be as pleased as Punch (as happy as a sandboy [as a king])*

> Ich habe mich diebisch (kindlich) gefreut (habe einen diebischen Spaß gehabt; mich gefreut wie ein Kind; Mops; Schneekönig; Stint), als ich zum Geburtstag ein neues Fahrrad bekam.
> *I was as pleased as Punch (as happy as a sandboy [king]) when I got a new bicycle for my birthday.*

Geld ist ein guter **Diener,** aber ein schlechter Herr (Sprichw.): *Money is a good servant but a bad master (prov.)*

> Der Neffe hätte die Erbschaft seines Onkels nützlich verwenden können; er hat das Geld jedoch in kurzer Zeit leichtsinnig ausgegeben. Geld ist ein guter Diener, aber ein schlechter Herr.
> *The nephew could have put his uncle's inheritance to good use; within a short time, however, he spent the money frivolously. Money is a good servant but a bad master.*

das arme **Dier** kriegen (fam.): *to get down in the dumps (colloq.); to get the mopes (sl.)*

> Als meine Tante so viel Trauriges erfuhr, bekam sie das arme Dier und fing an zu weinen.
> *When my aunt heard so much sad news, she got down in the dumps (got the mopes) and began to cry.*

Armes **Ding!** (fam.): cf. Armes **Wurm** (Würmchen)!

Gut **Ding** will Weile haben (Sprichw.): *A thing done well cannot be done quickly (prov.)*

> Du mußt dir zu deinem Aufsatz mehr Zeit nehmen. Gut Ding will Weile haben.
> *You must take more time over your essay. A thing done well cannot be done quickly.*

Aller guten **Dinge** sind drei (Sprichw.): *Good things always come in threes*

Zu meinem Geburtstag habe ich eine Armbanduhr, ein Fahrrad und einen Foto-apparat bekommen. Aller guten Dinge sind drei.
*For my birthday I got a wrist-watch, a bicycle and a camera. Good things always come in threes.*

guter **Dinge** sein: *to be in good spirits (in the best of spirits); to be in the pink (colloq.)*

Wir sind alle guter Dinge und hoffen, daß diese Zeilen auch Euch bei bester Gesundheit erreichen werden.
*We are all in good spirits (in the best of spirits; in the pink) and hope that these words find you in the best of health as well.*

nicht mit rechten **Dingen** zugehen: *Things are not all above board; There is something fishy (colloq.); There is something phoney (sl.)*

Dieser Arbeiter fährt plötzlich in einem kolossalen Auto. Hier geht etwas nicht mit rechten Dingen zu.
*This worker is suddenly driving a huge car. Things are not all above board (There is something fishy [phoney]) here.*

über den **Dingen** stehen: *to be above party; to stand above things*

Ein Philosoph steht über den Dingen und läßt sich durch persönliche Wünsche nicht beeinflussen.
*A philosopher is above party (stands above things) and does not allow himself to be influenced by personal wishes.*

unverrichteter **Dinge** abziehen: *to go away with empty hands (empty-handed)*

Wir wollten uns von unserm Nachbarn etwas ausleihen, kamen jedoch vor die verschlossene Tür und mußten unverrichteter Dinge (Sache) wieder abziehen.
*We wanted to borrow something from our neighbour's but we found the door shut and had to go away with empty hands (empty-handed).*

j.en **dingfest** machen: *to put s. b. behind bars (under lock and key)*

Der Mann, der meiner Schwester die Handtasche entrissen hatte, wurde bald darauf dingfest gemacht (eingebuchtet; hinter Schloß und Riegel gesetzt).
*The man who had snatched the handbag from my sister was put behind bars (under lock and key) soon afterwards.*

Herr **Dingsda (Dingskirchen)** (fam.): *Mr Thingamy (Thingumajig; Thing-umybob) (colloq.)*

Im Zuge habe ich Ihren Freund, Herrn Dingsda (Dingskirchen), getroffen.
*In the train I met your friend Mr Thingamy (Thingumajig; Thingumybob).*

**Distanz** von j.em halten: *to keep one's distance from s. b.; to keep s. b. at arm's length.* Cf. auch: sich j.en vom **Leib** halten

Solche Leute sind kein richtiger Verkehr für dich. Du solltest Distanz von ihnen halten.
*Such people are no fit company for you. You ought to keep your distance from them (to keep them at arm's length).*

j.em den **Dolch** auf die Brust setzen (fig.): cf. j.em die **Pistole** auf die Brust setzen

j.em einen **Dolchstoß** versetzen (fig.): *to cut (to pierce) s. b. to the quick*
Die Untreue ihres Verlobten hat meiner Kusine einen Dolchstoß (einen Stich [ins Herz]) versetzt.
*Her fiancé's unfaithfulness cut (pierced) my cousin to the quick.*

ein **Don Juan** sein: cf. ein **Herzensdieb** sein

wie vom **Donner** gerührt sein: cf. wie vom **Blitz** getroffen sein

sich auf ein **Donnerwetter** gefaßt machen (fig. u. fam.): cf. sich auf etwas **gefaßt** machen b)

ein **Donnerwetter** loslassen (wie ein heiliges Donnerwetter dreinfahren) (fig. u. fam.): *to raise merry hell (sl.); to kick up a stink (sl.)*
Unser Direktor ließ ein Donnerwetter los (fuhr wie ein heiliges Donnerwetter drein), als er feststellte, daß die Schüler ihn belogen hatten.
*Our headmaster raised merry hell (kicked up a stink) when he discovered that the pupils had deceived him.*

**Doppelt** genäht hält besser (Sprichw.): *Two for safety; It is better to be on the safe side*
Für den Fall, daß ich eins verlege oder verliere, habe ich mir gleich zwei Feuerzeuge gekauft. Doppelt genäht hält besser.
*I have bought two cigarette-lighters in case I mislay or lose one. Two for safety (It is better to be on the safe side).*

für j.en böhmische **Dörfer** sein (fig.): *to be (all) Greek (double-Dutch) to s. b.*
Physik und Chemie kann er nie richtig begreifen; sie bleiben für ihn böhmische Dörfer.
*He can never understand physics and chemistry properly; they are (all) Greek (double-Dutch) to him.*

j.em ein **Dorn** im Auge sein (fig.): *to be a thorn in s. b.'s side (flesh)*
Dieser Dieb ist der Polizei schon lange ein Dorn im Auge (ein Pfahl im Fleisch).
*This thief has been a thorn in the side (flesh) of the police for a long time.*

ein **Drache** sein (fig.): cf. ein **Hausdrache** sein

auf **Draht** sein (fam.): *to be at one's best; to be in form; to be on top line (sl.)*

Morgen habe ich ein wichtiges Interview, und ich muß auf Draht sein.
*I have an important interview tomorrow and must be at my best (in form; on top line).*

Nerven wie ein **Drahtseil** haben: cf. Nerven wie **Ankertaue** haben

ein **Drahtzieher**: *a wire-puller (string-puller); a man behind the scenes; a back-room boy*

Man sieht viele Funktionäre, aber die eigentlichen Drahtzieher treten niemals vor die Öffentlichkeit.
*One sees many officials but the real wire-pullers (string-pullers; the real men behind the scenes; the real back-room boys) never appear in public.*

eine **Dralltype** sein (fam.): cf. ein komischer (närrischer) **Kauz** sein

Es ist schon etwas (Wahres) **dran**: *There is something in it (something to be said for it)*

Es ist schon etwas (Wahres) dran, daß man andere Länder und Völker kennenlernen soll.
*There is something in (something to be said for) getting to know other countries and peoples.*

j.en **drangsalieren**: *to irk (to plague; to pester) s. b.; to make o. s. a nuisance to s. b.*

Meine kleine Schwester drangsaliert (piesackt; scheucht; schikaniert; schurigelt; striezt; zwiebelt) unsere ganze Familie (fährt mit unserer ganzen F. schlitten).
*My little sister irks (plagues; pesters; makes herself a nuisance to) our whole family.*

**drauf** und dran sein: *to be on the point of; to do s. th. for two pins (colloq.).*
Cf. auch: um ein **Haar**

Ich war drauf und dran, mein Geld zurückzuverlangen, weil die Schuhe so schlecht waren.
*I was on the point of asking (For two pins I would have asked) for my money back because the shoes were so bad.*

eins **draufkriegen** (fam.): *to get a slap in the face (a box on the ear); to get a clip on the ear (sl.)*

Sobald sich einer von uns ungebührlich benimmt, kriegt er von dem Lehrer eins drauf.
*As soon as any of us misbehaves himself, he gets a slap in the face (a clip [box] on the ear) from the master.*

seinen **Dreck** alleine machen (fam.): *to go one's own way; to do what one damned well likes (sl.).* Cf. auch: j.en in seinem eigenen **Saft** schmoren lassen

Was geht mich das an? Mach' doch deinen Dreck alleine.
*What's that got to do with me? You can go your own way (do what you damned well like).*

j.en wie **Dreck** behandeln (fam.): cf. j.en wie einen **Schuhputzer** behandeln

j.en mit **Dreck** bewerfen (fig.): cf. j.en durch den **Dreck** ziehen

Geld wie **Dreck** haben (fam.): cf. **Geld** wie Heu haben

sich um jeden **Dreck** kümmern (fam.): *to concern o. s. with every trifle; to worry about every flea-bite (sl.)*

Ich kann mich wirklich nicht um jeden Dreck kümmern; ich habe Wichtigeres zu tun.
*I really cannot concern myself with every trifle (worry about every flea-bite); I have more important things to do.*

sich einen **Dreck** aus etwas machen (fam.): cf. sich keinen **Deut** aus etwas machen

im **Dreck** sitzen (fam.): cf. in der **Klemme** sitzen

mit **Dreck** und Speck (fam.): cf. schwarz wie ein **Mohr(enkind)**

**Dreck** am Stecken haben (fig. u. fam.): cf. Dreck am **Stecken** haben

j.en (etwas) in den **Dreck** ziehen (fig. u. fam.): *to slang s. b. (s. th.); to run s. b. (s. th.) down; to drag s. b. through the mire (mud); to throw mud (dirt) at s. b. (s. th.) (colloq.)*

Es ist taktlos, in Gegenwart anderer Leute deren Ideale in den Dreck (Kot; Schmutz; Staub; durch den Kakao) zu ziehen (mit Dreck zu bewerfen).
*It is tactless to slang other people's ideals (to run ... down; to drag ... through the mire [mud]; to throw mud [dirt] at other ...) in their presence.*

ein **Dreckspatz** sein (fig. u. fam.): cf. ein **Schmierfink** sein

den **Dreh** kriegen (fam.): cf. die **Kurve** kriegen

ein **Dreh** sein: *to be a wangle (a fiddle) (colloq.)*

Es war nichts als ein Dreh, daß er diese Stellung bekam.
*It was nothing but a wangle (fiddle) that he got that job.*

den (richtigen) **Dreh** heraushaben: cf. den **Kniff** heraushaben

an etwas ist nicht zu **drehen** und zu deuteln (fig.): cf. an etwas ist nicht zu **rütteln** und zu schütteln

sich **drehen** und wenden (fig.): cf. sich winden wie ein **Aal** sich nicht **drehen** und wenden können: a) *There is not room to swing a cat (colloq.);* b) *There is not room to budge (an inch).* Cf. auch: gedrängt wie die **Heringe** sitzen

a) Das Zimmer ist so klein, daß man sich darin kaum drehen und wenden kann.
b) Der Laden war so gerammelt voll, daß wir uns nicht drehen und wenden konnten.

*a) The room is so small that there isn't room to swing a cat in it.*
*b) The shop was so packed that we couldn't budge (an inch).*

nicht wissen, worum es sich **dreht**: cf. nicht wissen, was **gespielt** wird

ehe man bis **drei** zählen kann: cf. im **Handumdrehen**

nicht bis **drei** zählen können (fig.): *not to know how many beans make five; not to be able to count up to three; not to be able to say boo to a goose (colloq.); butter will not melt in s. b.'s mouth (colloq.)*

Der Bursche stellt sich absichtlich dumm und tut, als ob er nicht bis drei (vier) zählen könnte.
*The lad is deliberately pretending to be stupid and behaving as though he did not know how many beans made five (as though he could not count up to three; as though he could not say boo to a goose; as though butter would not melt in his mouth).*

nicht für einen **Dreier** haben: cf. nicht für einen **Pfennig** haben

ein **Dreikäsehoch** sein (fam.): cf. ein **Knirps** sein

**dreist** und gottesfürchtig sein: *to have a ready tongue in one's head (a ready answer)*

Deine Schwester läßt sich durch nichts einschüchtern; sie ist immer dreist und gottesfürchtig.
*Your sister does not allow herself to be intimidated by anything; she has a ready tongue in her head (a ready answer).*

Nun schlägt's **dreizehn**! (fam.): *Well, I'm blowed (jiggered)! (colloq.); That beats the band! (colloq.); That takes the cake! (colloq.).* Cf. auch: Das ist doch die **Höhe**!

Nun schlägt's dreizehn! (Nun wird's Tag!) Jemand hat meinen Mantel gestohlen.
*Well, I'm blowed (jiggered; That beats the band [takes the cake])! Somebody has stolen my coat.*

der **Dritte** im Bunde sein: *to make a third*

Willst du bei unserm Spiel der Dritte im Bunde sein?
*Do you want to make a third in our game?*

der lachende **Dritte**: *the lucky outsider*

Wenn zwei sich streiten, ist man häufig der lachende Dritte.
*When two people quarrel, one often finds oneself the lucky outsider.*

eine **Drohne** sein (fig.): *to be a drone*

Während diese reiche Frau ihre Angestellten tüchtig arbeiten läßt, ist sie selbst eine Drohne.
*Whilst that rich woman makes her employees work busily, she herself is a drone.*

fluchen wie ein **Droschkenkutscher**: cf. fluchen wie ein **Landsknecht**

auf j.en (einen) **Druck** ausüben (fig.): cf. j.em **Daumenschrauben** anlegen

**Druck** hinter etwas machen (fig.): cf. **Dampf** dahinter machen

j.en unter **Druck** setzen (fig.): cf. j.em **Daumenschrauben** anlegen

im **Druck** sein (sitzen) (fig.): cf. in der **Klemme** sein

ein **Drückeberger** sein: *to be a shirker (slacker; skulker; dodger)*

Kein Wunder, daß hier nichts geleistet wird. Die Arbeiter sind lauter Drückeberger.
*No wonder that nothing gets done here. The workers are nothing but shirkers (slackers; skulkers; dodgers).*

sich vor etwas **drücken**: *to get (to wriggle) out of s. th. (colloq.)*

Wenn ich meinen Sohn bitte, den Rasen zu mähen, versucht er immer, sich davor zu drücken.
*Whenever I ask my son to mow the lawn, he tries to get (to wriggle) out of it.*

am **Drücker** sitzen (fig. u. fam.): *to hold the whip-hand; to sit at the source of things; to give the orders; to issue the passes (colloq.); to say the word go (colloq.)*

Mein Schwager wird mir leicht zu dieser Stellung verhelfen können, denn er sitzt am Drücker.
*My brother-in-law will easily be able to help me to get this job because he holds the whip-hand (sits at the source of things; gives the orders; issues the passes; says the word go).*

etwas auf den letzten **Drücker** tun (fam.): *to leave s. th. till the eleventh hour (till the last minute [moment])*

Erledige alles rechtzeitig. Du solltest nicht alles erst auf den letzten Drücker tun.
*Attend to everything punctually. You ought not to leave everything till the eleventh hour (the last minute [moment]).*

das **Drum** und Dran: *the extras; the incidentals; the fancy bits (colloq.)*. Cf. auch: mit allen **Schikanen**

Eine Mittelmeerreise wäre an sich möglich; aber das Drum und Dran kostet auch noch eine Menge Geld.

*A Mediterranean cruise would in fact be possible, but the extras (incidentals; fancy bits) cost a pile of money as well.*

**drunter** durch bei j.em sein: *to be dropped by s. b.; to be done (to be through) with s. b.*

Seitdem Georg einen Klassenkameraden betrogen hat, ist er bei seinen Freunden drunter (unten) durch.
*Since George deceived a class-mate, he has been dropped by his friends (his friends are done [are through] with him).*

**drunter** und drüber gehen (fig.): *to be at sixes and sevens; to be higgledy-piggledy (topsy-turvy; upside-down); to go haywire (colloq.)*

Als unsere Mutter für ein paar Wochen verreist war, ging bei uns zu Hause alles drunter und drüber.
*When our mother went away for a few weeks, everything in our house was at sixes and sevens (higgledy-piggledy; topsy-turvy; upside-down; went haywire).*

auf **du** und du mit j.em stehen: *to be on intimate terms; to call s. b. by his Christian name*

Er liebt es nicht, mit jedermann auf du und du (auf dem Duz-Fuße) zu stehen.
*He does not like being on intimate terms with everybody (calling everybody by his Christian name).*

ein **Duckmäuser** sein: cf. ein **Leisetreter** sein

j.en **dumm** und dämlich reden: cf. j.em ein **Loch** (Löcher) in den Bauch reden

**dumm** geboren und nichts hinzugelernt: *Born a fool, always a fool.* Cf. auch: **Bauer** bleibt Bauer

Trotz jahrelanger Bemühung begreift er die Grundsätze der Geometrie noch immer nicht. Dumm geboren und nichts hinzugelernt.
*In spite of years of effort he still does not understand the principles of geometry. Born a fool, always a fool.*

j.em **dumm** kommen (fam.): *to cheek s. b. (colloq.)*

Er weiß jetzt, daß er mir nicht dumm kommen kann.
*He knows now that he cannot cheek me.*

Mir ist ganz **dumm** im Kopf: *My head is in a whirl (is going round and round; is swimming); I am in a daze (am dizzy).* Cf. auch: Der **Kopf** brummt mir

Geht es Ihnen wie mir? Mir ist von dem Lärm noch ganz dumm im Kopf.
*Do you feel like me? My head is still in a whirl (is still going round and round; is still swimming; I am still in a daze [still dizzy]) from the noise.*

sich von j.em nicht **dumm** machen lassen: cf. sich nicht für **dumm** verkaufen lassen sich nicht für **dumm** verkaufen lassen (fam.): *not to let o. s. be led up the garden path (be taken in); not to let o. s. be taken for a ride (sl.)*

Du kannst nicht erwarten, daß ich solche Geschichten glaube. Ich lasse mich nicht für dumm verkaufen (nicht dumm machen).
*You can't expect me to believe such tales. I'm not going to let myself be led up the garden path (be taken in; be taken for a ride).*

j.em zu **dumm** werden: cf. etwas bis **dahin** (stehen) haben

nicht von **Dummbach** sein (fig. u. fam.): cf. nicht aus **Dummsdorf** sein

ein kleiner **Dummbatz** sein (fam.): *to be a little silly (colloq.)*

Mit einem so großen (So ein großes) Fahrrad kannst du doch nicht fahren, du kleiner Dummbatz (Dummerjan).
*You can't ride a big bicycle like that, you little silly.*

der **Dumme** sein: *to be the loser; to be the mug (the sucker) (sl.); to be Joe Soap (sl.)*

Ich war der Dumme und mußte alles bezahlen.
*I was the loser (the mug; the sucker; Joe Soap) and had to pay for everything.*

einen **Dummen** an j.em finden: *to make a fool out of s. b.; to put one across s. b. (colloq.); to make a mug out of s. b. (colloq.)*

Glaube nur nicht, an mir einen Dummen gefunden zu haben, der dir deine Arbeit abnimmt.
*Don't think that you can make a fool (mug) out of me (put one across me) and make me do your work for you.*

ein kleiner **Dummerjan** sein (fam.): cf. ein kleiner **Dummbatz** sein

ein **Dummkopf** sein: cf. ein **Rindvieh** sein

nicht aus **Dummsdorf** (Klein-**Dummersdorf**) sein (fig. u. fam.): *to be not so green (not such a greenhorn) as that; to be not such a mug as that (colloq.).* Cf. auch: nicht von **gestern** sein

Ich soll diese unmögliche Geschichte glauben? Ich bin doch nicht aus Dummsdorf (aus Klein-Dummersdorf; von Dummbach).
*You expect me to believe this impossible story? I'm not so green as that (not such a greenhorn [mug] as that).*

j.en im **dunkeln** lassen (fig.): *to leave s. b. in the dark*

Über seine Reisepläne hat mich mein Schwager völlig im dunkeln gelassen.
*My brother-in-law has left me completely in the dark about his travelling plans.*

im **dunkeln** tappen (fig.): *to be in the dark; to be at a loss*

Wir tappen noch völlig im dunkeln, wer uns diesen geheimnisvollen Brief geschrieben hat.
*We are still completely in the dark (at a loss) as to who wrote us this mysterious letter.*

**dünn** gesät sein (fig.): *to be few and far between*
Fachleute auf diesem Gebiet sind dünn gesät.
*Experts in this field are few and far between.*

sich **dünne** machen: cf. **Fersengeld** geben. Cf. auch: **abhauen**

keinen blassen **Dunst** von etwas haben: cf. keine blasse **Ahnung** von etwas haben

j.em blauen **Dunst** vormachen: cf. j.em **Wind** vormachen

**durch** und durch: a) *(adv.) through and through; to the core;* b) *(adj.) out-and-out*
  a) Die neuen Äpfel waren schon nach zwei Monaten durch und durch verfault.
  b) Er ist jetzt durch und durch ein Schwindler (ein völliger Schwindler) geworden.
  *a) The new apples were rotten through and through (to the core) after two months.*
  *b) He has now become an out-and-out swindler (a swindler through and through [to the core]).*

j.em **durch** und durch gehen: *to pluck at s. b.'s heart-strings; to move s. b. to the depths of his being; to strike at the roots of s. b.'s heart*
Wenn ich Beethovens Neunte Sinfonie höre, geht es mir immer durch und durch.
*Whenever I hear Beethoven's Ninth Symphony it plucks at my heart-strings (moves me to the depths of my being; strikes at the roots of my heart).*

etwas **durchackern** (fam.): *to plough (to plod) through s. th. (colloq.)*
Der Student hat das Lehrbuch von A bis Z durchgeackert.
*The student ploughed (plodded) through the text-book from A to Z.*

sich **durchbeißen** (fam.): *to fight one's way through; to stick it out (colloq.)*
In seiner Stellung hatte es mein Vater zunächst sehr schwer; er hat sich aber durchgebissen.
*At first my father found things very difficult in his job, but he fought his way through (stuck it out).*

j.en **durchbleuen**: cf. j.en **vermöbeln**

j.en mit (seinen) Blicken **durchbohren**: *to look daggers at s. b.*
Er traute dem Fremden nicht und durchbohrte ihn mit seinen Blicken.
*He did not trust the stranger and looked daggers at him.*

**durchbrennen** (fam.): *to get away; to hop it (colloq.); to buzz off (colloq.); to skedaddle (sl.).* Cf. auch: **Fersengeld** geben; **abhauen**
Ich hatte einmal einen Hasen gefangen, aber zwei Tage später ist er (mir) durchgebrannt (ausgekniffen).
*Once I caught a hare but two days later it got away (hopped it; buzzed off; skedaddled).*

**durchgedreht** sein (fam.): *not to know whether one is standing on one's head or one's heels; to be quite (all) cut up (colloq.); to be churned up (sl.)*

Nachdem sie den aufregenden Roman gelesen hatte, war sie völlig durchgedreht.
*She did not know whether she was standing on her head or her heels (was quite [all] cut up [churned up]) after reading the exciting novel.*

j.en **durchhecheln** (fig.): *to run s. b. down; to pull s. b. to pieces; to drag s. b. through the mire (mud).* Cf. auch: j.en (etwas) durch (in) den **Dreck** ziehen

Es ist geschmacklos, seine ehemaligen Freunde durchzuhecheln.
*It is in bad taste to run down one's former friends (to pull one's former friends to pieces; to drag one's former friends through the mire [mud]).*

etwas **durchpeitschen** (fig.): *to rush (to rattle) s. th. through; to rush (to rattle) s. th. off*

Das Parlament hat diese Gesetze noch rasch durchgepeitscht und ist dann in die Ferien gegangen.
*Parliament rushed (rattled) these bills through (off) and then adjourned for the recess.*

sich **durchschlagen**: *to fight (to battle) one's way through; to get along (colloq.).* Cf. auch: sich durchs **Leben** schlagen

Die arme Familie hat sich irgendwie durchgeschlagen und hat jetzt eine neue Wohnung gemietet.
*The poor family has fought (battled) its way through (has got along) somehow and has now rented a new flat.*

etwas **durchschnüffeln** (fam.): *to nose through s. th. (colloq.); to poke one's nose into s. th. (colloq.).* Cf. auch: sich in alles (ein)**mischen**

Kannst du mir sagen, wer meine privaten Briefe durchschnüffelt hat?
*Can you tell me who has been nosing through (poking his nose into) my private letters?*

**durchsickern** (fig.): *to leak out; to seep through*

Trotz der Bemühungen der königlichen Familie ist die Nachricht von der Verlobung der Prinzessin durchgesickert.
*In spite of the efforts of the royal family, the news of the princess' engagement has leaked out (seeped through).*

etwas **durchstöbern**: *to rummage through s. th.; to ransack s. th.; to turn s. th. upside-down.* Cf. auch: alles auf den **Kopf** stellen

Die Polizei hat alle Akten der verbotenen Partei durchstöbert.
*The police rummaged through (ransacked) all the files of the banned political party (turned all . . . upside-down).*

**durchtrieben** sein : *to be a cunning old fox (colloq.); to be a sly old bird (old dog) (colloq.); to be as artful as a cartload of monkeys (colloq.)*

Man sollte von diesem Hausierer nichts kaufen; er ist durchtrieben (abgefeimt; ein durchtriebener [abgefeimter; ausgekochter; geriebener; gerissener] Kerl; schlau wie ein Fuchs).
*You should not buy anything from that peddlar; he is a cunning old fox (sly old bird [old dog]; as artful as a cartload of monkeys).*

j.en **durchwichsen** (fam.): cf. j.en **vermöbeln**

einen über den **Durst** getrunken haben: cf. zu tief in den **Becher** geguckt haben

wie eine kalte **Dusche** wirken: *to be (to act) like a cold douche (shower).* Cf. auch: ein **Schlag** ins Gesicht sein

Dieser unerwartete Vorwurf wirkte wie eine kalte Dusche (auf uns).
*This unexpected reproach was (acted) like a cold douche (shower).*

**Dusel** haben (fam.): cf. **Schwein** haben

j.en **dusselig** reden: cf. j.em ein **Loch** (Löcher) in den Bauch reden

Von j.em gehen zwölf auf ein **Dutzend**: *to be ten a penny; to be able to be picked up in the gutter (colloq.)*

Diesen langweiligen Redner hören wir uns nicht wieder an. Von ihm gehen zwölf auf ein Dutzend.
*We shall not listen to this boring speaker again. Such men are ten a penny (can be picked up in the gutter).*

ein **Dutzendmensch** sein: *to be a bread-and-butter fellow; to be one of the crowd; to be a common-or-garden chap (colloq.)*

Er hält sich für eine bedeutende Persönlichkeit, ist aber in Wirklichkeit nur ein Dutzendmensch.
*He considers himself an important figure but in reality he is only a bread-and-butter fellow (one of the crowd; a common-or-garden chap).*

auf (dem) **Duz-Fuß(e)** mit j.em stehen: cf. auf **du** und du mit j.em stehen


# E

bei j.em ist **Ebbe** in der Kasse: cf. knapp bei **Kasse** sein

auf die schiefe **Ebene** geraten (fig.): cf. auf die abschüssige **Bahn** geraten

wütend wie ein **Eber** sein: cf. wütend wie ein **Stier** sein

**echt** (fig.): cf. Das sieht ihm **ähnlich**!

j.en um die **Ecke** bringen (fig. u. fam.): *to do s. b. in (sl.); to knock (to bump)*
*s. b. off (sl.).* Cf. auch: j.en ins **Jenseits** befördern; j.en **kaltmachen**

Vor ihrer Verhaftung hatten die Banditen zahlreiche Menschen beraubt, ja sogar
einige von ihnen um die Ecke gebracht (abgemurkst).
*Before being arrested the bandits had robbed numerous people – in fact, even done some*
*of them in (knocked [bumped] some of them off).*

an allen **Ecken** und Enden (Kanten) fehlen: *not to have got enough to go round*
*(to make ends meet); to be short of a lot of things*

Dem jungen Ehepaar fehlt es noch an allen Ecken und Enden (Kanten), aber
die Eltern helfen nach bestem Können.
*The young couple have not got enough to go round (to make ends meet; are short of a lot*
*of things) but their parents help to the best of their ability.*

an allen **Ecken** und Enden (Kanten) sparen: cf. **eisern** sparen

um die **Ecke** gehen (fig. u. fam.): *to pop off (colloq.); to peg out (colloq.); to*
*kick the bucket (sl.); to snuff the candle (sl.)*

Dieser alte Bursche ist jetzt neunzig Jahre alt; er wird wohl bald um die Ecke
gehen (ins Gras beißen; abkratzen; abschrammen).
*This old chap is now ninety years old. I suppose he will soon pop off (peg out; kick the*
*bucket; snuff the candle).*

in allen **Ecken** und Winkeln suchen: *to search high and low; to search in every*
*nook and cranny (in every hole and corner; all over the place).* Cf. auch: **händerin-**
**gend** nach etwas suchen

Wir suchten in allen Ecken und Winkeln nach den vermißten Kindern.
*We searched high and low (in every nook and cranny [hole and corner]; all over the place)*
*for the missing children.*

etwas aus dem **Effeff** verstehen: cf. etwas aus dem **FF** verstehen

ein **Ehekrüppel** sein: *to be a henpecked husband; to be under petticoat rule*

Meine Frau ist sehr großzügig, und ich komme mir keineswegs als Ehekrüppel
(Pantoffelheld) vor (und ich stehe keineswegs unter dem Pantoffel).
*My wife is very broad-minded, and I do not feel in the least like a henpecked husband (do*
*not feel in the least that I am under petticoat rule).*

**Ehre,** wem Ehre gebührt (Sprichw.): *Honour to whom honour is due (prov.)*

Seine Theorien haben sich als richtig erwiesen. Ehre, wem Ehre gebührt (Dem
Verdienste seine Krone).
*His theories have proved to be correct. Honour to whom honour is due.*

**Ehre** einlegen: *s. th. is a feather in one's cap; s. th. reflects credit on s. b.; to*
*write s. th. on one's shield; to inscribe s. th. on one's banner*

Mit einer solchen ausgezeichneten Leistung kannst du wirklich Ehre einlegen.
*Such an outstanding performance is a real feather in your cap (reflects great credit on you;*
*You can write such an outstanding performance on your shield [inscribe... on your banner]).*

in **Ehren** ergraut sein: *to have reached a venerable old age*

Nach einem erfüllten Leben ist mein Vater jetzt in Ehren ergraut (steht mein
Vater jetzt im biblischen Alter).
*After a full life my father has now reached a venerable old age.*

auf **Ehre** und Gewissen: *with my (your etc.) hand on my (your etc.) heart; on*
*my (your etc.) honour.* Cf. auch: **Hand** aufs Herz

Ich versichere Ihnen auf Ehre und Gewissen, daß ich unschuldig bin.
*I assure you with my hand on my heart (on my honour) that I am innocent.*

keine **Ehre** im Leibe haben: *to be devoid of all decent (honourable) feeling; to*
*have no sense of honour (decency).*

Wie kannst du so handeln? Hast du denn keine Ehre im Leibe?
*How can you act like that? Are you devoid of all decent (honourable) feeling (Have you*
*no sense of honour [decency])?*

j.em die letzte **Ehre** erweisen: *to pay one's final tribute (one's last respects*
*[honours]) to s. b.*

Natürlich werden wir alle unserm verstorbenen Kollegen die letzte Ehre
erweisen (das letzte Geleit geben).
*We shall of course all pay our final tribute (our last respects [honours]) to our departed*
*colleague.*

ein dunkler **Ehrenmann** sein: *to be a shady (shifty) character.* Cf. auch: ein
unsicherer **Kantonist** sein

Nehmt Euch vor diesem Geschäftsmann in acht! Jeder weiß, daß er ein dunkler
Ehrenmann ist.
*Beware of that business man. Everybody knows that he is a shady (shifty) character.*

**Ehrlich** währt am längsten (Sprichw.): *Honesty is the best policy (prov.)*

Es war schön von dir, daß du das gefundene Portemonnaie auf dem Fundbüro
abgegeben hast. Ehrlich währt am längsten.
*It was good of you to hand in the purse that you found to the lost property office. Honesty is*
*the best policy.*

wie auf **Eiern** gehen: *to walk like a cat on the tiles; to step gingerly*

Auf der Straße war Glatteis, daher mußte ich wie auf Eiern gehen.
*The road was icy, so I had to walk like a cat on the tiles (to step gingerly).*

wie aus dem **Ei** gepellt: cf. **geschniegelt** und gebügelt sein

Sie gleichen sich wie ein **Ei** dem anderen: *They are as like as two peas*

Ich kann die Zwillingsbrüder nie voneinander unterscheiden; sie gleichen sich wie ein Ei dem anderen.
*I can never distinguish the twin brothers from each other; they are as like as two peas.*

Das **Ei** will klüger sein als die Henne (fig.): *Go and teach your grandmother to suck eggs (colloq.)*

Emma weiß alles besser als ihre Mutter. Es heißt in solchen Fällen: Das Ei will klüger sein als die Henne.
*Emma always knows better than her mother. It is a case of go and teach your grandmother to suck eggs.*

das **Ei** des Kolumbus: *a Columbus' egg*

Diese einfache und schnelle Lösung der Schwierigkeit war wirklich das Ei des Kolumbus.
*This simple and quick solution of the difficulty really was a Columbus' egg.*

j.en wie ein rohes **Ei** behandeln: cf. j.en mit **Glacéhandschuhen** anfassen

sich um ungelegte **Eier** kümmern (fig. u. fam.): *to cross one's bridges before one comes to them; to meet trouble half-way*

Denken wir an die Gegenwart und überlassen wir alles andere der Zukunft. Warum sollen wir uns um ungelegte Eier kümmern?
*Let us think of the present and leave all the rest to the future. Why should we cross our bridges before we come to them (meet trouble half-way)?*

Auf éinen Streich fällt keine **Eich(e)** (Sprichw.): *No tree falls at one blow (prov.); There is no short cut to success.* Cf. auch: **Rom** ist nicht an éinem Tage erbaut worden

So etwas Großes läßt sich nicht durch eine einmalige Kraftanstrengung erlangen. Auf éinen Streich fällt keine Eich(e).
*Something as big as that cannot be achieved by a single effort. No tree falls at one blow (There is no short cut to success).*

ein Kerl wie eine **Eiche** sein: cf. **Bärenkräfte** haben

munter wie ein **Eichhörnchen**: cf. **kreuzfidel** sein

einen über den **Eichstrich** getrunken haben: cf. einen **Schwips** haben

im **Eifer** des Gefechtes: *in the heat of the fray (of the moment)*

Im Eifer (In der Hitze) des Gefechtes wurden Worte gesprochen, die besser unterblieben wären.
*In the heat of the fray (moment) words were spoken which would have been better left unsaid.*

**Eile** mit Weile (Sprichw.): *More haste, less speed (prov.)*

Man muß sich bei einer solchen Arbeit Zeit nehmen. Denke an das Sprichwort: Eile mit Weile.
*One must take one's time over such a job. Remember the proverb: More haste, less speed.*

im **Eimer** sein (fam.): cf. zu **Wasser** werden

**ein** für allemal: *once (and) for all; for all time*

Ich sage dir ein für allemal, daß du kein Geld mehr von mir bekommst.
*I am telling you once (and) for all (telling you for all time) that you will get no more money from me.*

j.es **ein** und alles sein: *to be the apple of s. b.'s eye; to be all the world to s. b.; to be s. b.'s be-all and end-all.* Cf. auch: das **A und O**; j.es **Augapfel** sein

Seitdem die Frau ihren Sohn verloren hat, ist ihr Hund ihr ein und alles.
*Since the woman lost her son, her dog has been the apple of her eye (has been all the world to her [has been her be-all and end-all]).*

nicht **ein** noch aus wissen: cf. nicht **aus** noch ein wissen

Unter den Blinden ist der **Einäugige** König (Sprichw.): cf. Unter den **Blinden** ist der Einäugige König

j.em etwas **einbleuen** (fam.): *to drive (to hammer) s. th. into s. b.; to din (to drub; to drum) s. th. into s. b. (colloq.)*

Wir haben unseren Kindern eingebleut (eingehämmert; eingepaukt; eingetrichtert; [vor]gepredigt), von fremden Personen keine Geschenke anzunehmen.
*We have driven (dinned; hammered; drubbed; drummed) it into our children not to accept presents from strangers.*

sich etwas **einbrocken** (fig. u. fam.): *to bring s. th. (down) on one's head; to let o. s. in for s. th. (colloq.)*

Durch Ihre unüberlegte Handlung haben Sie sich einen großen Geldverlust eingebrockt.
*By your ill-considered action you have brought (down) a big financial loss on your head (have let yourself in for a big financial loss).*

j.en **einbuchten** (fam.): cf. j.en **dingfest** machen

**Eindruck** schinden (fam.): *to create (to make) an impression; to make o. s. conspicuous; to draw attention to o. s.*

Man sieht ihn bei Versammlungen jeglicher Art. Er hat es wohl nötig, Eindruck zu schinden.
*He is seen at meetings of every kind. He probably needs to create (make) an impression (to make himself conspicuous; to draw attention to himself).*

Du bist mir **einer!** (fam.): *You're a fine one! (colloq.); You're a bright specimen!
(colloq.)*

Du hast die schöne, wertvolle Vase auf den Fußboden fallen lassen. Du bist mir
aber einer!
*You've dropped the fine, valuable vase on the floor. You're a fine one (a bright specimen)!*

die **Einfalt** vom Lande sein: cf. die **Unschuld** vom Lande sein

ein **Einfaltspinsel** sein: *to be a simpleton (dolt); to be a mug (sl.).* Cf.
auch: ein **Rindvieh** sein

Wenn du nicht so ein Einfaltspinsel (Gimpel) gewesen wärest, hättest du dein
Geld schon längst bekommen.
*If you had not been such a simpleton (dolt [mug]), you would have got your money long ago.*

Was man sich **eingebrockt** hat, muß man auch auslöffeln (Sprichw.): cf.
Man muß **auslöffeln,** was man sich eingebrockt hat

**eingepfercht** sitzen: *to be sandwiched (squashed).* Cf. auch: gedrängt wie
die **Heringe** sitzen

In meinem Abteil mußte ich zwischen zwei dicken Männern eingepfercht sitzen.
*In my compartment I had to sit sandwiched (squashed) between two fat men.*

j.em etwas **einhämmern:** cf. j.em etwas **einbleuen**

beim Essen **einhauen:** *to tuck (to dig) in (colloq.); to fill one's boots (sl.)*

Heute gab es unser Lieblingsgericht, und wir haben tüchtig eingehauen (eine
gute Klinge geschlagen; ihm wacker zugesprochen).
*We had our favourite dish today, and we tucked (dug) in (filled our boots) properly.*

(innere) **Einkehr** bei sich halten: *to commune (to hold counsel) with o. s.; to
reflect on things; to search one's heart.* Cf. auch: sich eines **Besseren** besinnen

Der Dieb hat (innere) Einkehr bei sich gehalten und will sich nun bessern.
*The thief has communed (held counsel) with himself (reflected on things; searched his
heart) and now intends to reform.*

sich bei j.em **einkratzen** (fam.): cf. ein **Augendiener** sein

**Einmal** ist keinmal (Sprichw.): *Once is nothing at all; Once is no good*

Laß mich doch noch einmal mit dem Karussell fahren, Vater! Einmal ist (doch)
keinmal.
*Let me go on the roundabout again, father. Once is nothing at all (is no good).*

j.em etwas **einpauken** (fam.): cf. j.em etwas **einbleuen**

wie eine Bombe **einschlagen:** *to burst (to land) like a bombshell*

Die Nachricht von der Ermordung des Präsidenten schlug wie eine Bombe ein.
*The news of the president's assassination burst (landed) like a bombshell.*

**einschnappen** (fig. u. fam.): *to sulk; to go (to fly) into a huff (colloq.)*

Warum ist er eingeschnappt? Ich habe doch nichts Böses gesagt.
*Why is he sulking (has he gone [flown] into a huff)? I didn't say anything unkind.*

ein **Einsehen** haben: *to come to see reason; to come to one's senses*

So kann es nicht weitergehen. Wir müssen hoffen, daß die Behörden bald ein Einsehen haben werden.
*Things cannot go on like this. We must hope that the authorities will soon come to see reason (come to their senses).*

j.en **einseifen** (fig.): cf. j.en auf den **Leim** führen

**einsilbig** sein (fig.): cf. **zugeknöpft** sein

sich gut **einspielen** (fig.): *to settle down well; to become well set; to be now running smoothly*

Unsere geschäftliche Zusammenarbeit hat sich gut eingespielt.
*Our business partnership has settled down well (has become well set; is now running smoothly).*

etwas **einstecken** müssen (fig.): *to have to put up with s. th.; to have to eat dirt; to have to eat humble-pie; to have to grin and bear it; to have to lump it (colloq.)*

Es hat keinen Zweck, dich so zu beklagen; du mußt es einfach einstecken (auf dir sitzen lassen).
*There is no point in your complaining like that; you must just put up with it (eat dirt [humble-pie; you must just grin and bear it; just lump it]).*

eine **Eintagsfliege** sein (fig.): *to be here today and gone tomorrow; to be short-lived; to be a nine days' wonder*

Sein neues Stück hat nur einen Scheinerfolg gehabt; es wird (nur) eine Eintagsfliege sein.
*His new play has only had a superficial success; it will be here today and gone tomorrow (will be short-lived; will only be a nine days' wonder).*

j.em etwas **eintrichtern** (fig. u. fam.): cf. j.em etwas **einbleuen**

j.en **einwickeln** (fig.): cf. j.en um den (kleinen) **Finger** wickeln

Das **Eis** ist gebrochen (fig.): *The ice is broken*

Als wir uns nach unserm Streit wiedersahen, wechselten wir ein paar Worte, und das Eis war gebrochen.
*When we saw each other again after our quarrel, we exchanged a few words, and the ice was broken.*

etwas auf **Eis** legen (fig.): cf. etwas auf die lange **Bank** schieben j.en (etwas) zum alten **Eisen** werfen (fig.): *to throw s. b. (s. th.) on the scrap-heap; to scrap s. th.; to put s. b. on the shelf*

> Trotz seiner 60 Jahre ist unser Lehrer noch tüchtig und will sich noch nicht zum alten Eisen werfen lassen.
> *In spite of his sixty years our teacher is still efficient and does not want to be thrown on the scrap-heap (put on the shelf) yet.*

noch ein **Eisen** im Feuer haben (fig.): *to have an arrow (shaft) left in one's quiver (a bullet left in one's gun)*

> Ich bin noch nicht fertig mit ihm, denn ich habe noch ein Eisen im Feuer.
> *I have not yet finished with him, for I still have an arrow (shaft) left in my quiver (a bullet left in my gun).*

zwei (mehrere) **Eisen** im Feuer haben (fig.): *to have more than one iron in the fire; to have two (several) strings to one's bow*

> Ich möchte dir raten, keines der beiden Fächer aufzugeben; denn es ist gut, wenn man zwei (mehrere) Eisen im Feuer hat.
> *I should advise you not to give up either of the two subjects, for it is a good thing to have more than one iron in the fire (to have two [several] strings to one's bow).*

Schmiede das **Eisen** (Man soll das Eisen schmieden), solange es heiß ist (Sprichw.): *Strike (One must strike) while the iron is hot (prov.); Make (One must make) hay while the sun shines (prov.)*. Cf. auch: Man soll die **Feste** feiern, wie sie fallen

> Es hat keinen Zweck zu warten. Schmiede das Eisen (Man soll das Eisen schmieden), solange es heiß ist.
> *There is no point in waiting. Strike (One must strike) while the iron is hot (Make [One must make] hay while the sun shines).*

ein heißes **Eisen** anfassen (anpacken) (fig.): cf. ein heißes **Eisen** sein
ein heißes **Eisen** sein (fig.): *to be a hazardous (risky) business; to be like touching a red-hot poker*. Cf. auch: mit dem **Feuer** spielen

> An deiner Stelle würde ich mich da nicht einmengen. Es ist ein heißes Eisen (Du würdest ein heißes Eisen anfassen [anpacken]).
> *In your place I would not meddle in that. It is a hazardous (risky) business (is like touching a red-hot poker).*

Not bricht **Eisen** (Sprichw.): cf. **Not** kennt kein Gebot

Es ist höchste **Eisenbahn** (fam.): *It is high time*

> Es ist höchste Eisenbahn, daß wir den Zoo verlassen, da er um 7 Uhr geschlossen wird.
> *It is high time for us to leave the zoo, because it closes at seven o'clock.*

**eisern** bleiben (fig.): *to stand one's ground; to stand firm; to be as firm as a rock; to be unflinching (unyielding; unbending)*

Wenn dein Neffe wieder einmal Geld von dir haben will, mußt du eisern bleiben und es ihm verweigern.
*If your nephew wants money from you again, you must stand your ground (stand firm; be as firm as a rock; be unflinching [unyielding; unbending]) and refuse to give it to him.*

eine **eiserne** Miene machen: cf. eine **eisige** Miene machen

**eisern** sparen: *to save resolutely; to make a point of saving; to make a determined effort to save*

Da wir uns nächstes Jahr ein Auto kaufen wollen, müssen wir in den kommenden Monaten eisern (an allen Ecken und Enden [Kanten]) sparen.
*As we want to buy a car next year, we shall have to save resolutely (to make a point of saving; to make a determined effort to save) in the coming months.*

eine **eisige** Miene machen: *to put on (to assume) an icy (a cold) expression (look)*

Als ich um Gehaltserhöhung bat, machte der Prokurist eine eisige (eiserne) Miene.
*When I asked for a rise in salary, the chief clerk put on (assumed) an icy (a cold) expression (look).*

**eiskalt** sein (fig.): *to be as cold as ice (as an iceberg; as marble)*

Seine Frau ist zwar schön, aber eiskalt (kalt wie eine Hundeschnauze [wie Marmor]; hat aber Fischblut).
*His wife is certainly beautiful, but as cold as ice (as an iceberg; as marble).*

eine **Eiterbeule** aufstechen (fig.): *to expose a nuisance; to remove the source of infection*

Lange bestand eine Verschwörung gegen die Regierung. Jetzt ist es gelungen, die Eiterbeule (Pestbeule) aufzustechen und die Schuldigen zur Rechenschaft zu ziehen.
*For a long time there had been a conspiracy against the government. Now they have succeeded in exposing the nuisance (removing the source of infection) and bringing the guilty persons to justice.*

**Elbkähne** (fig. u. fam.): *barges (colloq.); beetle-crushers (colloq.)*

Er trägt schrecklich große Schuhe. Es sind die reinsten Elbkähne (Quadratlatschen).
*He wears terribly big shoes. They are veritable barges (beetle-crushers).*

sich benehmen wie der **Elefant** im Porzellanladen: *to behave like a bull in a china-shop*

Dieser grobe Bauer benimmt sich wie der Elefant im Porzellanladen (wie die Axt im Walde).
*This rough farmer behaves like a bull in a china-shop.*

ein **Elefantenküken** sein (fam.): *to be a baby elephant*

Unser Freund war so dick und ungelenk, daß wir ihn das Elefantenküken nannten.
*Our friend was so fat and clumsy that we called him the baby elephant.*

in seinem **Element** sein: *to be in one's element.* Cf. auch: sich (wohl)fühlen wie die **Made** im Speck; in j.es **Fach** schlagen

Wenn ich mathematische Berechnungen zu machen habe, bin ich ganz in meinem Element (im richtigen Fahrwasser).
*When I have mathematical calculations to do, I am right in my element.*

sich nicht in seinem **Element** fühlen: *to feel like a fish out of water; not to be in one's element*

Bei einer politischen Kundgebung fühle ich mich nicht in meinem Element.
*At a political meeting I feel like a fish out of water (am not in my element).*

das heulende **Elend** haben: cf. einen **Kater** haben

seine **Ellbogen** gebrauchen (fig.): *to use one's elbows; to elbow one's way through*

Wenn man sich im Leben durchsetzen will, muß man oft seine Ellbogen gebrauchen.
*If you want to get on in life, you often have to use your elbows (have to elbow your way through).*

**Ellbogenfreiheit:** *elbow-room; rope; room to manoeuvre*

Um seine großen Pläne zu verwirklichen, gebraucht dieser Ingenieur viel Ellbogenfreiheit (freien Spielraum).
*In order to realise his great plans, this engineer needs a great deal of elbow-room (rope; room to manoeuvre).*

eine **Elle** verschluckt haben (fig.): cf. einen **Besenstiel** verschluckt haben

eine diebische **Elster** sein (fig.): *to be a thieving magpie*

Unsere Nachbarin hat wiederholt in Geschäften gestohlen. Sie ist eine diebische Elster (stiehlt wie ein Rabe).
*Our neighbour's wife has repeatedly stolen from shops. She is a thieving magpie.*

geschwätzig wie eine **Elster** sein: *to chatter like a magpie*

Unsere Waschfrau ist geschwätzig wie eine Elster.
*Our washerwoman chatters like a magpie.*

nicht von schlechten **Eltern** sein (fig. u. fam.): *to come from a good home; to be well-bred*

Dieser Wein ist wahrhaftig nicht von schlechten Eltern (Zu diesem Wein kann man „Sie" sagen).
*This wine certainly comes from a good home (is certainly well-bred).*

Es hat alles einmal ein **Ende** (Sprichw.): cf. Auch das Schlimmste hat ein **Ende**

Das dicke **Ende** kommt nach: *The sting is in the tail; The worst is yet to come*

Sei nur nicht so sicher, daß dir dein Versuch gelingen wird; oft kommt das dicke Ende nach.
*Don't be so sure that your attempt will succeed; the sting is often in the tail (The worst may yet be to come).*

kein **Ende** finden können: *not to be able to bring o. s. to stop*

Wenn mein Onkel von seinen Erlebnissen im Ausland erzählt, kann er kein Ende finden.
*Whenever my uncle tells of his experiences abroad, he cannot bring himself to stop.*

**Ende** gut, alles gut (Sprichw.): *All's well that ends well (prov.)*

Es sah zuerst aus, als würden wir das Spiel verlieren; aber in den letzten 10 Minuten schossen wir zwei Tore. Ende gut, alles gut!
*It first looked as if we were going to lose the match but in the last ten minutes we scored two goals. All's well that ends well.*

das **Ende** vom Lied sein (fig.): *to be the end of it (of the matter)*

Die Jungens schaukelten so lange mit ihrem Boot, bis es endlich umkippte. Und das war das Ende vom Lied.
*The boys rocked their boat until it finally overturned, and that was the end of it (of the matter).*

Auch das Schlimmste hat ein **Ende** (Sprichw.): *Every cloud has a silver lining (prov.); It's a long lane (road) that has no turning (prov.)*

Obwohl alles schwarz aussieht, darfst du nicht vergessen, daß auch das Schlimmste ein Ende hat.
*Although everything looks black, you must not forget that every cloud has a silver lining (that it's a long lane [road] that has no turning).*

ein **Ende** mit Schrecken nehmen: *to come to a terrible (tragic) end; to end in tragedy*

Die Kundgebung nahm ein Ende mit Schrecken. Eine Bombe explodierte und mehrere Leute wurden getötet.
*The meeting came to a terrible (tragic) end (ended in tragedy): a bomb exploded and several people were killed.*

aus allen **Enden** der Welt: cf. aus aller **Herren** Länder

am **Ende** der Welt wohnen: cf. in **Buxtehude** wohnen

j.en in die **Enge** treiben (fig.): *to drive (to force) s. b. into a corner (against the wall); to corner s. b.; to catch s. b. in a cleft stick*

Bei dem Verhör auf dem Polizeiamt wurde er in die Enge getrieben, und er gab seine Fahrlässigkeit zu.
*In the interrogation at the police station he was driven (forced) into a corner (against the wall; was cornered; was caught in a cleft stick), and admitted his negligence.*

ein **Engel** sein (fig.): cf. eine wahre **Perle** sein

die **Engel** im Himmel pfeifen (singen) hören (fig.): *to see stars*

Als er mit dem Kopf gegen die Mauer stieß, hörte er die Engel im Himmel pfeifen (singen; sah er Sternchen).
*When he knocked his head against the wall, he saw stars.*

(eine) **Engelsgeduld**: cf. eine **Lammsgeduld** entwickeln

ein **Engpaß** tritt ein (fig.): *there is a bottleneck; a bottleneck has been caused*

Wegen der mangelhaften Zufuhren ist in der Versorgung dieses Landes ein Engpaß eingetreten.
*Because of inadequate deliveries, there is a bottleneck (a bottleneck has been caused) in supplies to this country.*

**engstirnig** sein: *to be narrow-minded (strait-laced)*

Diese engstirnige Mutter läßt ihre Kinder niemals ins Kino gehen.
*That narrow-minded (strait-laced) mother never lets her children go to the cinema.*

lahm wie eine **Ente** (eine lahme Ente) sein: cf. **lahm** wie eine Ente sein

eine **Ente** sein (fig.): *to be trumped-up; to be a hoax; to be a sell (colloq.)*

Es war mir von vornherein klar, daß diese Zeitungsnachricht eine Ente war
*It was obvious to me from the beginning that that newspaper report was trumped-up (was a hoax [a sell]).*

schwimmen wie eine bleierne **Ente**: *to swim like a brick; not to be able to swim for nuts (for toffee) (colloq.)*

Ich reise nicht gern zu (mit dem) Schiff, denn ich schwimme wie eine bleierne Ente (wie ein Backstein).
*I don't like sea voyages, because I swim like a brick (I can't swim for nuts [toffee]).*

**entgleisen** (fig.): *to go off the rails; to come unstuck (colloq.)*

Überlege dir in Zukunft deine Worte, damit du nicht wieder so entgleist.
*Be careful of your words in future, so that you do not go off the rails (come unstuck) like that again.*

j.en **entlarven**: *to unmask s. b.*

Endlich ist es der Polizei gelungen, den Betrüger zu entlarven.
*The police have finally succeeded in unmasking the imposter.*

sich als . . . **entpuppen:** *to turn out to be* . . .

Der angebliche Versicherungsagent entpuppte sich als ein Schwindler.
*The supposed insurance agent turned out to be a swindler.*

j.en **entwaffnen** (fig.): *to disarm s. b.; to spike s. b.'s guns*

Mit einigen gut gewählten Bemerkungen hat der Politiker alle Gegner ent-
waffnet.
*With a few well-chosen remarks the politician disarmed all his opponents (spiked all his
opponents' guns).*

**entweder-oder:** cf. Friß, **Vogel,** oder stirb!

j.en unter die **Erde** bringen: *to see s. b. in his grave; to be the death of s. b.*
*(colloq.)*

Mein Vater raufte sich die Haare und schrie: „Mit deinen ewigen dummen
Streichen wirst du mich noch unter die Erde bringen".
*My father tore his hair and shouted: "You'll see me in my grave (You'll be the death of
me) with your eternal stupid pranks!"*

etwas aus der **Erde** stampfen (fig.): cf. etwas aus dem **Boden** stampfen

wünschen, daß einen die **Erde** (der **Erdboden**) verschlingt: cf. sich in
ein **Mauseloch** verkriechen (mögen)

als hätte der **Erdboden** (die **Erde**) ihn verschlungen: *as if the earth had
swallowed him up*

Der Skifahrer war verschwunden, als hätte ihn der Erdboden (die Erde) verschlungen.
*The skier had vanished as if the earth had swallowed him up.*

in den **Erdboden** versinken mögen: cf. sich in ein **Mauseloch** verkriechen
(mögen)

Kommende **Ereignisse** werfen ihre Schatten voraus (Sprichw.): Kommende Ereignisse werfen ihre **Schatten** voraus

etwas über sich **ergehen** lassen: *to put up with s. th.; to take s. th. lying down;
to lump s. th. (colloq.)*

Ein Geschäftsreisender muß bereit sein, solche Kränkungen über sich ergehen
zu lassen.
*A commercial traveller must be prepared to put up with (to lump) such snubs (to take
such snubs lying down).*

**Na, erlaube** mal!: cf. Da muß ich doch sehr **bitten!**

etwas **erleben** können (fig. u. fam.): *to see what happens; to get the shock (surprise) of one's life; not to forget s. th. in a hurry; to be (in) for it (colloq.)*

Wenn du mir den Ball abnimmst, dann kannst du was (dein blaues Wunder) erleben!
*If you take the ball away from me, you'll see what happens (get the shock [surprise] of your life; you won't forget it in a hurry; you'll be [in] for it).*

**erledigt (erschlagen, erschossen)** sein (fam.): cf. **absein**

auf etwas **erpicht** sein: *to be keen on s. th.; to be after s. th.* Cf. auch: mit etwas **liebäugeln**

Ich danke dir für die französische Briefmarke. Ich war schon lange erpicht (scharf) auf sie (Sie steckte mir . . . in der Nase).
*Thank you for the French stamp. I had been keen on it (after it) for a long time.*

**erstklassig** sein: *to be A 1 (first class; top notch; superb; out of the top drawer); to be smashing (sl.)*

Dein Prüfungsergebnis war wirklich erstklassig (famos; prima).
*Your examination result was really A 1 (first class [top notch; superb; out of the top drawer; smashing]).*

**erstunken** und erlogen (fam.): *a pack of lies; all my eye and Betty Martin (sl.).* Cf. auch: **Lug** und Trug sein; aus der **Luft** gegriffen sein

Das ganze Gerücht ist unwahr. Alles ist erstunken (gestunken) und erlogen (gelogen).
*The whole rumour is untrue. It is all a pack of lies (all my eye and Betty Martin).*

Der **Ertrinkende** klammert sich an einen Strohhalm (Sprichw.): cf. Der Ertrinkende klammert sich an einen **Strohhalm**

sich für etwas **erwärmen** (fig.): *to work up an enthusiasm (to develop an affection) for s. th.; to warm to s. th.* Cf. auch: mit j.em nicht **warm** werden können

Für die gegenstandslose (abstrakte) Malerei kann ich mich nicht erwärmen.
*I cannot work up an enthusiasm (develop an affection) for (warm to) abstract painting.*

sich **erwehren**: *to ward off; to keep at bay*

Der junge Schauspieler konnte sich der begeisterten Zuschauer nicht erwehren.
*The young actor could not ward off the enthusiastic audience (could not keep . . . at bay).*

ein **Esel** sein (fig. u. fam.): cf. ein **Rindvieh** sein

beladen wie ein **Esel** sein: cf. der **Packesel** sein

Der **Esel** geht (Den Esel führt man) nur einmal aufs Eis (Sprichw.): cf. (Ein) gebranntes **Kind** scheut das Feuer

Ein **Esel** schimpft den andern Langohr (Sprichw.): *The pot calls the kettle black (prov.)*

> Erich kritisiert seinen Vetter; dabei ist er selbst nicht ohne Tadel. Ein Esel schimpft den andern Langohr.
> *Eric criticises his cousin, yet he himself is not blameless. The pot calls the kettle black.*

Wenn man den **Esel** nennt, kommt er gerennt (Sprichw.): *Talk of the devil . . .*

> Als wir gerade von Georg sprachen, kam er plötzlich ins Zimmer. Wenn man den Esel nennt, kommt er gerennt.
> *Just as we were speaking of George, he suddenly came into the room. Talk of the devil . . .*

Den Sack schlägt man, den **Esel** meint man (Sprichw.): cf. Den **Sack** schlägt man, den Esel meint man

störrisch wie ein **Esel** sein: *to be as obstinate (stubborn) as a mule*

> Hans ist störrisch wie ein Esel und hört nie auf das, was ich sage.
> *Jack is as obstinate (stubborn) as a mule and never listens to what I say.*

eine **Eselsbrücke** (fig. u. fam.): *a crib*

> Der Lehrer merkte, daß ich eine Eselsbrücke benutzte.
> *The master noticed that I was using a crib.*

**Eselsohren** (fig.): *dog-ears*

> Ich verleihe meine Bücher nicht mehr, da man mir wiederholt Eselsohren in sie hineingemacht hat.
> *I am not going to lend my books any more, since people have continually made dog-ears in them.*

zittern wie **Espenlaub**: *to tremble like an aspen leaf; to tremble all over*

> Die beiden Frauen zitterten wie Espenlaub (am ganzen Körper [Leibe]), als der Blitz in eine nahe Eiche einschlug.
> *The two women trembled like an aspen leaf (trembled all over) when the lightning struck a nearby oak.*

j.em ins **Essen** fallen (fig. u. fam.): *to arrive just as s. b. is having a (his) meal*

> Der Omnibus hatte Verspätung, und ich fiel der Familie meines Freundes genau ins Essen (in die Suppe).
> *The coach was late, and I arrived just as my friend's family were having a (their) meal.*

Damit ist es **Essig** (fam.): *to be all up with s. th.; to come to naught (nothing); to be off (colloq.)*

> Der Vergaser meines Autos funktioniert nicht richtig; daher ist es mit unserer geplanten Fahrt ins Gebirge Essig.
> *The carburettor of my car is not working properly, so it's all up with the trip we planned*

*into the mountains (so the trip we planned into the mountains will come to naught [no-thing]; is off).*

(zu) **Essig** werden (fig. u. fam.): cf. ins **Wasser** fallen

**etepetete** sein (fam.): *to be fussy (finicky); to be pernickety (colloq.)*

Die Mutter war so etepetete, daß sie ihre Kinder niemals mit anderen Kindern spielen ließ.
*The mother was so fussy (finicky; pernickety) that she never let her children play with other children.*

eine alte **Eule** sein (fig. u. fam.): cf. eine alte **Ziege** sein

**Eulen** nach Athen tragen (fig.): *to carry coals to Newcastle; to take milk to the cow*

Du willst doch wohl nicht Bier mit nach München nehmen? Das hieße doch Eulen nach Athen tragen.
*Surely you're not going to take beer with you to Munich? That would be carrying coals to Newcastle (taking milk to the cow).*

aussehen wie eine **Eule:** cf. wie eine **Vogelscheuche** aussehen

etwas für's **Evangelium** nehmen (fam.): *to take s. th. as gospel (as gospel truth; as Holy Writ).* Cf. auch: etwas für bare **Münze** nehmen

Karl hat ein solches Vertrauen zu mir, daß er alles, was ich sage, für's Evangelium nimmt.
*Charles has such confidence in me that he takes everything I say as gospel (gospel truth; Holy Writ).*

auf etwas wie aufs **Evangelium** schwören: cf. **felsenfest** auf etwas schwören

für j.en das **Evangelium** sein (fam.): *to be gospel (Holy Writ) to s. b.*

Was sein Vater sagt, ist für Johann das Evangelium.
*What his father says is gospel (Holy Writ) to John.*

im **Evaskostüm:** cf. im **Adamskostüm**

eine **Evastochter** sein: *to be a daughter of Eve (a child of woman)*

Schmeicheln versteht sie gut; sie ist eine richtige Evastochter.
*She knows (well) how to flatter; she is a real daughter of Eve (child of woman).*

eine **Ewigkeit** dauern: *to last for ages (an eternity [age])*

Das Konzert dauerte eine Ewigkeit.
*The concert lasted for ages (an eternity [age]).*

an j.em ein **Exempel** statuieren: *to make an example of s. b.*

Das Gericht hat den Autofahrer, der abends ohne Licht fuhr, streng bestraft, um an ihm ein Exempel zu statuieren.
*The court severely punished the car-driver who drove at night with no lights, in order to make an example of him.*

j.em eine **Extrawurst** braten (fig. u. fam.): *to give s. b. preferential treatment; to treat s. b. like a lord (like a V.I.P. [ = Very Important Person]); to treat s. b. like a big-wig (colloq.)*

Ich sehe nicht ein, warum ich ihn bevorzugen und ihm eine Extrawurst braten soll.
*I do not see why I should favour him and give him preferential treatment (treat him like a lord [V.I.P.; big-wig]).*

eine **Extrawurst** verlangen (fig. u. fam.): *to expect preferential treatment; to expect to be treated like a lord (a V.I.P.); to expect to be treated like a big-wig (colloq.)*

Der junge Bursche verlangt eine Extrawurst und will sofort bedient werden.
*The young fellow expects preferential treatment (to be treated like a lord [V.I.P.; big-wig]) and wants to be served immediately.*

# F

in j.es **Fach** schlagen: *to be up s. b.'s street; to be s. b.'s line; to be in s. b.'s department; to be down s. b.' s alley (colloq.)*

Wenn du etwas von elektrischen Geräten wissen willst, gehst du am besten zu Braun. Das schlägt gerade (genau) in sein Fach.
*If you want to know anything about electrical appliances, you had best go to Brown. That's just up his street (his line; in his department; down his alley).*

vom **Fach** sein: cf. vom **Bau** sein

**fachsimpeln** (fam.): *to talk shop*

Ich hatte mich auf einen unterhaltsamen Abend gefreut, aber mein Freund wollte nichts als fachsimpeln.
*I had been looking forward to an entertaining evening but my friend wanted to do nothing but talk shop.*

nicht lange **fackeln** (fam.): *not to waste any time; not to let the grass grow under one's feet; not to dilly-dally (colloq.).* Cf. auch: nicht viel **Federlesen(s)** machen

Als er hörte, daß das Geschäft jetzt geöffnet sei, hat er nicht lange gefackelt, sondern ist gleich hingelaufen.

*When he heard that the shop was now open, he did not waste any time (did not let the grass grow under his feet; did not dilly-dally) and ran there at once.*

keinen guten **Faden** an j.em (etwas) lassen (fig.): *not to have a good word to say for s. b. (s. th.); to pull (to hack; to tear) s. b. (s. th.) to pieces (to shreds)*

> Die Kritiker haben an der neuen Oper keinen guten Faden (kein gutes Haar) gelassen (haben die neue Oper verrissen [zerpflückt]).
> *The critics did not have a good word to say for the new opera (pulled [hacked; tore] the new opera to pieces [shreds]).*

alle **Fäden** in der Hand haben (halten) (fig.): *to have everything under one's thumb (under control).* Cf. auch: das **Heft** in der Hand haben

> Nach den Unruhen hat (hält) die Regierung jetzt alle Fäden wieder in der Hand.
> *After the disturbances the government now has everything under its thumb (under control) again.*

sich wie ein roter **Faden** hindurchziehen: *to run (right) through; to be woven into the texture of*

> Dieses Motiv zieht sich wie ein roter Faden durch das ganze Theaterstück.
> *This motif runs (right) through the play (is woven into the texture of the play).*

an einem seidenen (dünnen) **Faden (Fädchen)** hängen (fig.): *to hang by a thread; to hang in the balance*

> Die Ärzte machten besorgte Gesichter, denn das Leben des Patienten hing an einem seidenen (dünnen) Faden (Fädchen; Haar; Seidenfaden; Zwirnsfaden).
> *The doctors wore a worried expression, for the patient's life hung by a thread (in the balance).*

keinen trockenen **Faden** am (auf dem) Leibe haben: *not to have a dry stitch on one.* Cf. auch: bis auf die **Haut** durchnäßt sein

> Leider kamen wir in ein Gewitter und hatten bald keinen trockenen Faden (mehr) am (auf dem) Leibe.
> *Unfortunately we got caught in a storm and soon did not have a dry stitch on us.*

den **Faden** verlieren (fig.): *to lose the thread; to lose one's train of thought*

> Die Zuhörer mußten lächeln, als der Redner den Faden verlor und nicht weiter wußte.
> *The audience had to smile when the speaker lost the thread (his train of thought) and could not go on.*

den **Faden** wiederaufnehmen (fig.): *to take (to pick) up the thread (argument) again*

Nach einer langen Abschweifung nahm der Politiker den Faden (seiner Rede) wieder auf.
*After a long digression the politician took (picked) up the thread (argument) again.*

ein dünnes **Fähnchen** (fig.): *a slip*

Wenn du erkältest bist, solltest du ein dickes Unterhemd anziehen und nicht so ein dünnes Fähnchen.
*If you have a chill, you ought to wear a thick vest and not a slip like that.*

zu den **Fahnen** eilen (unter die Fahnen treten): *to flock to the colours*

Die Jugend des Landes blieb dem König treu und eilte zu den Fahnen (trat unter die Fahnen).
*The youth of the country remained faithful to the king and flocked to the colours.*

mit fliegenden **Fahnen** (fig.): *with colours (banners) flying*

Diese früheren Anhänger der Regierung sind jetzt mit fliegenden Fahnen zur Opposition übergegangen.
*These former government supporters have now gone over to the opposition with colours (banners) flying.*

eine **Fahne** haben (fig. u. fam.): *to smell of the bottle (colloq.)*

Als Fritz gegen Mitternacht nach Hause kam, merkten wir, daß er schwer getrunken hatte, denn er hatte eine ordentliche Fahne.
*When Fred came home towards midnight, we saw that he had been drinking heavily, because he smelt strongly of the bottle.*

die **Fahne** hochhalten (fig.): *to keep the flag (banner) flying*

Laßt uns die Fahne des Idealismus hochhalten, trotz der Tatsache, daß wir in letzter Zeit viele Enttäuschungen erlebt haben!
*Let us keep the flag (banner) of idealism flying, in spite of the fact that we have experienced many disappointments recently.*

die **Fahne** nach dem Winde drehen (fig.): cf. den **Mantel** nach dem Winde hängen

nicht schlecht bei etwas **fahren** (fig.): *not to come off (to do) badly*

Bei diesem Tauschgeschäft bin ich nicht schlecht gefahren.
*I didn't come off (do) badly in that exchange.*

eine **Fahrt** ins Blaue machen: *to go on a mystery trip (tour)*

Mit dem neuen Omnibus haben wir eine schöne Fahrt ins Blaue gemacht.
*We went on a nice mystery trip (tour) in the new charabanc.*

in **Fahrt** kommen (fig.): cf. in **Fluß** kommen

auf der falschen **Fährte** sein (fig.): cf. auf dem **Holzwege** sein

in j.es **Fahrwasser** plätschern (fig.): *to follow in s. b.'s wake; to deck (to adorn)*
*o. s. with borrowed plumes; to tag (to tail) along behind s. b.*

Neue Gedanken entwickelt dieser Schriftsteller nicht. Er plätschert ganz im
Fahrwasser früherer Autoren (schmückt sich mit fremden Federn).
*This author does not develop new ideas; he just follows in the wake of earlier writers*
*(decks [adorns] himself with borrowed plumes; tags [tails] along behind earlier writers).*

im richtigen **Fahrwasser** sein (fig.): cf. in seinem **Element** sein

j.en zu **Fall** bringen (fig.): *to bring about (to cause) s. b.' s downfall (fall); to*
*bring s. b. down.* Cf. auch: j.em ein **Bein** stellen

Die Opposition hat diesen Minister zu Fall gebracht.
*The opposition brought about (caused) this minister's downfall (fall; brought this minister*
*down).*

ganz j.es **Fall** sein: *to be just s. b.' s line (mark); to be just the thing for s. b.*
*(colloq.); to be just up s. b.'s street (colloq.); to be just s. b.'s cup of tea (colloq.)*

Ich gehe selten ins Kino, aber dieser Film war ganz mein Fall.
*Rarely do I go to the cinema, but that film was just my line (mark; just the thing for me;*
*just up my street; just my cup of tea).*

ein klarer **Fall** sein: *to be a clear-cut case.* Cf. auch: **sonnenklar** sein

Es ist ein klarer Fall, daß Heinrich seine Wette verlieren wird.
*It is a clear-cut case that Henry will lose his bet.*

in die **Falle** gehen (fig.): a) *to put one's head into the noose; to walk into the*
*trap.* Cf. auch: **anbeißen;** auf den **Leim** gehen; b) (fam.) *to go to bye-byes*
*(colloq.); to get some shut-eye (colloq.); to hit the hay (sl.)*

a) Die Räuberbande ist jetzt endlich in die Falle (ins Netz; in die Schlinge)
gegangen und konnte verhaftet werden.
b) Gestern war ich bis Mitternacht auf. Heute abend gehe ich aber früh in die
Falle (in die Klappe [Flohkiste]; krieche ich früh in die Federn).
*a) At last the gang of thieves has put its head into the noose (walked into the trap) and*
*could be arrested.*
*b) Yesterday I was up till midnight but tonight I shall go to bye-byes (get some shut-eye;*
*hit the hay) early.*

eine **Falle** sein (fig.): *to be a pitfall (a trap)*

Mein Geschäftsgegner schrieb mir einen liebenswürdigen Brief; ich bin jedoch
überzeugt, daß es eine Falle ist.
*My business rival wrote me a friendly letter; however, I am convinced that it is a pitfall*
*(trap).*

j.em eine **Falle** stellen (fig.): *to lay (to set) a trap (snare) for s. b.*

Die Schüler waren verärgert, weil man ihnen bei dem Diktat mehrere Fallen
gestellt (Fallstricke [Fußangeln] gelegt) hatte.

*The pupils were annoyed because several traps (snares) had been laid (set) for them in the dictation.*

eine **Falle** wittern (fig.): cf. den **Braten** riechen

j.en **fallen lassen** (fig.): *to drop s. b.* Cf. auch: j.en kalt **abrutschen** lassen

Als ich erfuhr, was er für ein Mann war, habe ich ihn einfach fallen lassen.
*When I learned what sort of man he was, I just dropped him.*

j.em **Fallstricke** legen (fig.): cf. j.em eine **Falle** stellen

in den besten **Familien** vorkommen: *to happen in the best of families*

Arthur hat sich etwas unhöflich benommen; aber das kommt auch in den besten Familien vor.
*Arthur behaved rather impolitely, but that happens even in the best of families.*

**famos** sein: cf. **erstklassig** sein

ein **famoser** Kerl sein: *to be a grand fellow (chap); to be a brick (colloq.)*

Karl hat mich bei allen meinen Schwierigkeiten unterstützt; er war wirklich ein famoser Kerl.
*Charles supported me in all my difficulties; he really was a grand fellow (chap; a brick).*

**Farbe** bekennen (fig.): *to reveal (to show) one's true colours; to nail one's colours to the mast; to come into the open; to declare one's allegiance*

Bei den kommenden Wahlen muß jeder Farbe bekennen und sich für die eine oder die andere Partei entscheiden.
*At the coming election everyone must reveal (show) his true colours (nail his colours to the mast; come into the open; declare his allegiance) and decide on one party or the other.*

**Farbe** bekommen (fig.): *to become lively; to brighten up; to perk (to buck) up (colloq.)*

In der zweiten Halbzeit bekam das Fußballspiel mehr Farbe.
*In the second half the football match became more lively (brightened [perked; bucked] up [a bit]).*

etwas in dunklen **Farben** zeichnen (fig.): *to paint a black picture of s. th.; to couch s. th. in sombre terms*

Der Bericht des Innenministers war in dunklen Farben gezeichnet.
*In his report the Minister of the Interior painted a black picture (The Minister of the Interior's report was couched in sombre terms).*

ein **Faselhans** sein: *to be a scatterbrain*

Nimm doch endlich einmal deine Gedanken zusammen, du Faselhans (Wirrkopf)!
*Do collect your thoughts, you scatterbrain!*

**faseln** (fam.): *to babble (colloq.); to gas (sl.)*. Cf. auch: ins **Blaue** hineinreden

Warum faselst du denn von Sachen, die du nicht verstehst?
*Why are you babbling (gassing) about things you don't understand?*

**fasernackt** sein: cf. **splitternackt** sein

Das schlägt dem **Faß** den Boden aus! (fig.): cf. Das ist doch die **Höhe!**

ein bodenloses **Faß** (ein Faß ohne Boden) sein (fig.): *to be like trying to fill a leaky bucket; to be like trying to count the stars*

Jede weitere Hilfe ist bei diesem verschwenderischen Menschen sinnlos. Es wäre (nur) ein bodenloses Faß (ein Faß ohne Boden; ein Danaidenfaß).
*Any further financial assistance to that extravagant man is pointless. It is like trying to fill a leaky bucket (to count the stars).*

wie ein **Faß** saufen (fam.): cf. saufen wie ein **Loch**

j.en aus der **Fassung** bringen: *to upset s.b.; to disconcert s.b.; to disturb s.b.'s equilibrium; to make s.b. lose his head; to put s.b. out of joint (out of gear; out of countenance)*

Keine Kritik kann ihn aus der Fassung bringen.
*No criticism can upset (disconcert) him (can disturb his equilibrium; can make him lose his head; put him out of joint [gear; countenance]).*

seine **Fassung** verlieren (aus der Fassung kommen): *to lose one's head (self-control; composure); to be rattled (colloq.)*

Als er die schreckliche Nachricht bekam, verlor er einen Augenblick seine Fassung (kam er . . . aus der Fassung).
*When he received the terrible news, he lost his head (self-control; composure; he was rattled) for a moment.*

Es ist etwas **faul** im Staate Dänemark: *There is something rotten in the state of Denmark (Shakespeare)*

In diesem Lande gilt die Ehre als etwas Unbedeutendes, und jeder ist nur auf sein eigenes Wohl bedacht. Es ist etwas faul im Staate Dänemark.
*In this country honour counts as something unimportant, and everyone is only intent on his own well-being. There is something rotten in the state of Denmark.*

vor **Faulheit** stinken (fam.): *to be a real (proper) lazybones (loafer; slacker) (colloq.)*

Fritz ist ein sehr begabter Schüler, er stinkt aber vor Faulheit (ist aber ein richtiger Faulpelz [ein richtiges Faultier]).
*Fred is a very gifted pupil but he is a real (proper) lazybones (loafer; slacker).*

ein **Faulpelz (Faultier)** sein (fig. u. fam.): cf. vor **Faulheit** stinken

wie die **Faust** aufs Auge passen: *to be completely out of keeping (out of place); to be a complete misnomer; to be like trying to put a square peg in a round hole*

Diesen Mann als bedeutenden Schriftsteller zu bezeichnen, paßt wie die Faust aufs Auge.

*To claim this man as a significant writer is completely out of keeping (place; is a complete misnomer; is like trying to put a square peg in a round hole).*

etwas auf eigene **Faust** tun (fig.): *to do s. th. off one's own bat (on one's own [one's own initiative]).* Cf. auch: aus freien **Stücken** etwas tun

Niemand hat ihn geheißen, so zu handeln; er hat es auf eigene Faust getan.

*Nobody told him to act like that; he did so off his own bat (on his own [initiative]).*

j.es **Faust** im Nacken spüren (fig.): *to feel s. b. at one's elbow (shoulder); to feel s. b. breathing down one's neck*

Dieses kleine Volk hat keine Handlungsfreiheit. Es spürt die Faust des starken Nachbarn im Nacken.

*This small nation has no freedom of action. It feels its powerful neighbour at its elbow (shoulder; feels . . . breathing down its neck).*

die **Faust** in der Tasche machen (die **Fäuste** ballen ) (fig.): *to clench one's fist*

Der beleidigte Junge machte die Faust in der Tasche (ballte die Fäuste), wagte es aber nicht zu antworten.

*The offended boy clenched his fist but did not dare to answer.*

sich ins **Fäustchen** lachen: *to laugh up one's sleeve*

Die Jungens lachten sich ins Fäustchen, als der Lehrer sich versprach.

*The boys laughed up their sleeves when the teacher made a slip of the tongue.*

etwas **faustdick** auftragen: a) *to lay (to put; to pile; to ladle) it on thick (colloq.);* b) *to blow (to play) s. th. up (colloq.)*

a) Er wurde eigentlich gar nicht schwer verletzt, er hat (es) jedoch faustdick aufgetragen.

b) Die Zeitung hat den Streit der beiden Schauspieler faustdick aufgetragen.

*a) Actually he was not seriously injured at all, but he laid (put; piled; ladled) it on thick.*

*b) The paper blew (played) up the quarrel between the two actors.*

eine **faustdicke** Lüge sein: *to be a shameless lie; to be a whopping lie (a whopper) (colloq.)*

Er behauptet, er alleine habe zwei Tore geschossen, aber das ist sicherlich eine faustdicke Lüge.

*He claims to have scored two goals himself, but that is certainly a shameless (whopping) lie (a whopper).*

es **faustdick** hinter den Ohren haben: cf. mit allen **Hunden** gehetzt sein

**Faxen** machen: *to play the fool; to ass (to lark) about (colloq.)*

Der Lehrer hat uns bestraft, weil wir Faxen gemacht hatten.
*The teacher punished us for playing the fool (for assing [larking] about).*

**fechten** gehen (fig.): *to go cadging (colloq.)*

Der faule Arbeiter wurde vorige Woche entlassen. Jetzt geht er fechten und bettelt an jeder Haustür.
*The lazy worker was sacked last week. Now he goes cadging, and begs at every door.*

sich mit fremden **Federn** schmücken (fig.): cf. in j.es **Fahrwasser** plätschern

früh aus den **Federn** sein: cf. beim ersten **Hahnenschrei** aufstehen

Frau Holle schüttelt die **Federn** (Betten): *Mother Carey is plucking her geese*

Kinder, seht nur, wie es schneit! Frau Holle schüttelt die Federn (Betten).
*Children, look how it's snowing! Mother Carey is plucking her geese.*

in die **Federn** kriechen (fam.): cf. in die **Falle** gehen b)

**Federn** lassen (fig.): cf. **Haare** lassen

eine spitze **Feder** führen (fig.): *to wield a sharp (poisonous; venomous) pen*

Dieser Journalist führt eine spitze Feder.
*This journalist wields a sharp (poisonous; venomous) pen.*

ein **Federfuchser** sein: *to be an old fuss-pot (colloq.)*

Dieser Postbeamte ist ein richtiger Federfuchser.
*That post-office clerk is a proper old fuss-pot.*

**federleicht** sein: *to be as light as a feather; to be a featherweight*

Ein Jockei muß federleicht (leicht wie ein Schneider) sein.
*A jockey has to be as light as a feather (a featherweight).*

nicht viel **Federlesen(s)** machen: *not to beat about the bush; not to dilly-dally; to make short work of it.* Cf. auch: nicht lange **fackeln**

Unser Lehrer machte nicht viel Federlesen(s) (Umstände), sondern bestrafte die Schuldigen sofort.
*Our teacher did not beat about the bush (did not dilly-dally) but (made short work of it and) punished the offenders at once.*

mit éinem **Federstrich** (fig.): *with a (single) stroke of the pen*

Mit éinem Federstrich hat mein Chef alle meine Pläne zunichtegemacht.
*With a (single) stroke of the pen my boss ruined all my plans.*

in **Fehde** liegen (fig.): *to carry on a feud; to wage a vendetta*

Diese beiden Familien liegen seit längerer Zeit in Fehde miteinander.
*These two families have been carrying on a feud with (waging a vendetta against) each other for a considerable time.*

j.em den **Fehdehandschuh** hinwerfen (fig.): *to throw (to fling) down the gauntlet to s.b.; to issue a challenge to s.b.*

Unser aggressiver Nachbar hat uns den Fehdehandschuh hingeworfen (uns in die Schranken gefordert).
*Our pugnacious neighbour has thrown (flung) down the gauntlet (issued a challenge) to us.*

Das **fehlte** noch gerade!: cf. Das ist doch die **Höhe!**

einen **Fehltritt** tun (fig.): *to commit a misdeed (misdemeanour [indiscretion])*

Das Mädchen hatte einen Fehltritt getan und kam in eine Besserungsanstalt.
*The girl had committed a misdeed (misdemeanour [indiscretion]) and was put in a reformatory.*

**Feierabend** machen: *to call it a day; to knock off (colloq.); to down tools (colloq.)*

Wir arbeiten schon seit 8 Uhr. Laß uns Feierabend machen!
*We have been working since eight o'clock. Let's call it a day (knock off; down tools).*

nicht mehr **feierlich** sein (fam.): *to be beyond a joke; to be too much of a good thing (colloq.)*

Diese Julihitze läßt sich schwer ertragen. Sie ist nicht mehr feierlich.
*One can hardly stand this July heat. It's beyond a joke (too much of a good thing).*

die letzte **Feile** anlegen (fig.): *to put the finishing (final) touches (strokes) to s.th.*

Der Dichter sieht seine Gedichtsammlung noch einmal durch, um die letzte Feile (Hand) anzulegen (um ihr den letzten Schliff zu geben).
*The poet is looking through his collection of poems again in order to put the finishing (final) touches (strokes) to it.*

**fein** heraus sein: cf. fein **heraus** sein

**feixen** (fam.): *to snigger; to titter (colloq.)*

Als der Schüler diese Antwort gab, feixten seine Klassenkameraden.
*When the pupil made that reply, his classmates sniggered (tittered).*

das **Feld** behaupten (fig.): *to win (to carry) the day; to hold the field*

Bei der Diskussion habe ich schließlich doch gesiegt und das Feld behauptet.
*I was finally victorious in the discussion after all and won (carried) the day (held the field).*

etwas ins **Feld** führen (fig.): cf. etwas ins **Gefecht** führen

j.em das **Feld** räumen (fig.): *to hand over to s.b.; to make way for s.b.*

Wir wollen jetzt unsere Wohnung aufgeben und einem anderen das Feld räumen.
*We now want to give up our flat and hand over to (make way for) someone else.*

j.en aus dem **Feld** schlagen (fig.); *to rout s.b.; to knock spots off s.b. (colloq.);*
*to go one better than s.b. (colloq.).* Cf. auch: j.en in den **Schatten** stellen

Wegen seiner ausgedehnteren Kenntnisse konnte mein Vetter alle seine Mit-
bewerber aus dem Feld schlagen.
*On account of his wider knowledge my cousin was able to rout (to knock spots off [to*
*go one better than] all his competitors.*

sich das **Feld** streitig machen (fig.): *to fight for the same ground (prize)*

Die beiden Firmen sind auf diesem Gebiet starke Konkurrenten und machen
sich das Feld streitig.
*The two firms are fierce competitors in this field and are fighting for the same ground*
*(prize).*

gegen j.en (etwas) zu **Felde** ziehen (fig.): *to campaign against s.b. (s.th.);*
*to hit out at (against) s.b. (s.th.).* Cf. auch: einen **Kreuzzug** für etwas unternehmen

Der Abgeordnete zog in seiner Rede energisch gegen den Mißbrauch des
Alkohols zu Felde.
*In his speech the delegate campaigned (hit out) at (against) the abuse of alcohol.*

**Feld-,** Wald- und Wiesen-....: *common-or-garden...*

Dieser Arzt ist kein Spezialist, sondern ein Feld-, Wald- und Wiesendoktor.
*This doctor is not a specialist but a common-or-garden practitioner.*

Man soll das **Fell** des Bären nicht verkaufen (verteilen), bevor man ihn erlegt hat (Sprichw.): *First catch your hare, then cook it (prov.); Don't count your*
*chickens before they are hatched (prov.)*

Er tut, als ob er das versprochene Geld schon bekommen hätte; man soll aber
das Fell des Bären nicht verkaufen (verteilen), bevor man ihn erlegt hat.
*He is behaving as if he had already got the money he had been promised, but one must first*
*catch one's hare, then cook it (but one must not count one's chickens before they are*
*hatched).*

ein dickes **Fell** haben (fig.): *to be thick-skinned; to have a thick skin*

Trotz der Beleidigungen blieb er ruhig. Er muß ein dickes Fell (einen breiten
Buckel) haben (dickfellig sein).
*In spite of the insults he remained calm. He must be thick-skinned (must have a thick skin).*

j.em das **Fell** gerben (fig.): *to tan s.b.'s hide; to give s.b. a good hiding (thrashing).*
Cf. auch: j.en **vermöbeln**

Wenn du dich weiterhin mit den Nachbarskindern zankst, werde ich dir das
Fell (Leder) gerben (den Frack vollhauen; die Hosen strammziehen): merk'
dir das!
*If you go on quarelling with the children next door, I'll tan your hide (I'll give you a*
*good hiding [thrashing]), remember that.*

j.en juckt das **Fell** (fig. u. fam.): *to be itching (asking) for trouble*

Ich hatte es ihm verboten, aber ihn juckte das Fell, und er tat es doch.
*I had forbidden him to do it, but he was itching (asking) for trouble and did it all the same.*

j.em das **Fell** über die Ohren ziehen (fig. u. fam.): *to take s.b. in; to pull the wool over s.b.'s eyes; to diddle s.b. (sl.); to sell s. b. down the river (sl.).* Cf. auch: j.en auf den **Leim** führen

Man hat dir das Fell über die Ohren gezogen (dich geschröpft), denn dieses Auto ist keine hundert Mark wert.
*You have been taken in (Somebody has pulled the wool over your eyes [has diddled you; has sold you down the river]), for that car isn't worth a hundred marks.*

j.em schwimmen alle **Felle** weg (fig.): *s.b.'s prospects crumble (shrivel) away; s. b. sees everything go up in smoke*

Bei dieser enttäuschenden Nachricht sind ihm alle Felle weggeschwommen.
*At this disappointing news his prospects crumbled (shrivelled) away (he saw everything go up in smoke).*

**felsenfest** auf etwas schwören: *to swear by all the powers that be (by all that is holy)*

Wir schwören felsenfest darauf (wie aufs Evangelium), daß dieser Mann keinen Betrug begangen hat.
*We swear by all the powers that be (by all that is holy) that this man has not carried on any deception.*

**felsenfest** überzeugt sein: *to be dead certain (sure); to be as certain (sure) as can be*

Wir sind felsenfest (davon) überzeugt, daß wir die beste Mannschaft haben.
*We are dead certain (sure; as certain [sure] as can be) that we have the best team.*

das **felsenfeste** Vertrauen haben: *to have (a) cast-iron confidence (an unshakeable [unwavering] conviction)*

Ich habe das felsenfeste Vertrauen, daß die Preise stabil bleiben.
*I have (a) cast-iron confidence in prices remaining (an unshakeable [unwavering] conviction that prices will remain) stable.*

das Geld zum **Fenster** hinauswerfen (fig.): *to pour (one's) money down the drain; to throw money away; to splash one's money about (colloq.)*

Während Georg sparsam ist, wirft sein jüngerer Bruder das Geld zum Fenster hinaus.
*Whilst George is very thrifty, his younger brother pours (his) money down the drain (throws his money away; splashes his money about).*

Wozu in die **Ferne** schweifen?: *Why roam (go) so far afield?*

Wozu in die Ferne schweifen? Das Problem läßt sich viel einfacher lösen.
*Why roam (go) so far afield? The problem can be solved much more easily.*

j.em auf den **Fersen** folgen: *to be hard (close) on s.b.'s heels.* Cf. auch: j.em
(einer Sache) auf dem **Fuße** folgen; j.em auf **Schritt** und Tritt folgen

Ein Polizist folgt dem verdächtigen Individuum hart auf den Fersen.
*A policeman is following hard (close) on the heels of the suspicious character.*

**Fersengeld** geben: *to take to one's heels; to turn tail; to decamp; to make o.s.
scarce; to show a clean pair of heels; to make (to clear) off; to beat (to hop) it (sl.);
to skedaddle (sl.).* Cf. auch: **abhauen**

Sobald sie merkten, daß man sie gesehen hatte, gaben die Diebe Fersengeld
(machten sich . . . dünne; ergriffen . . . das Hasenpanier; nahmen . . . Reißaus;
machten sich . . . aus dem Staub; gingen . . . stiften; suchten . . . das Weite;
kniffen . . . aus; hauten . . . ab; brannten . . . durch; verdufteten . . .).
*As soon as they realised that they had been seen, the thieves took to their heels (turned
tail; decamped; made themselves scarce; showed a clean pair of heels; made [cleared] off;
beat it; hopped it; skedaddled).*

**fertigsein** (fig. u. fam.): cf. **absein**

etwas **fest** und steif behaupten: *to stick (obstinately) to one's assertion; to assert
(to claim) s.th. with hide-bound stubbornness; to swear until one is blue in the face*

Der Mann behauptete fest und steif (steif und fest), daß er nicht der gesuchte
Verbrecher sei.
*The man stuck (obstinately) to his assertion (asserted [claimed] with hide-bound stub-
bornness; swore until he was blue in the face) that he was not the criminal they were
looking for.*

Man soll die **Feste** feiern, wie sie fallen (Sprichw.): *One must take one's
opportunities as they come.* Cf. auch: Schmiede das **Eisen**, solange es heiß ist

So eine schöne Gelegenheit darfst du nicht verpassen; deine Arbeit kannst du
später nachholen. Man soll die Feste feiern, wie sie fallen.
*You must not miss such a fine opportunity; you can make up your work later. One must
take one's opportunities as they come.*

sich ein **Fest (Festessen)** aus etwas machen (ein Festessen für j.en sein)
(fig.): cf. sich ein **Fressen** aus etwas machen

ein **Festessen (Festschmaus):** *a feast; a tuck-in (colloq.); a blow-out (sl.)*

Was uns deine Mutter heute vorgesetzt hat, war ein richtiges Festessen (richtiger Festschmaus).
*That was a real feast (tuck-in; blow-out) that your mother gave us today.*

j.en auf etwas **festnageln** (fig.): *to pin (to nail) s.b. down (to hold s.b.) to s.th.*

Wilhelm wollte uns auf eine Meinung, die wir vor Jahren geäußert hatten, festnageln.
*William wanted to pin (nail) us down (to hold us) to an opinion which we had expressed years before.*

das **Fett** abschöpfen (fig.): cf. den **Rahm** abschöpfen

**Fett** ansetzen: *to put on weight; to fill out (colloq.)*. Cf. auch: aufgehen wie ein **Hefekloß**

Während meines Urlaubs habe ich ordentlich Fett angesetzt (bin ich ordentlich in die Breite gegangen).
*During my holidays I put on a good deal of weight (I filled out a lot).*

sein **Fett** bekommen (fig. u. fam.): cf. eine **Abreibung** kriegen

Da hast du dein **Fett**! (fam.): *That serves you right (Serve you right)! (colloq.)*

Du hast nicht auf mich gehört und jetzt hast du dein Geld verloren. Da hast du dein Fett!
*You did not listen to me and now you have lost your money. That serves you right (Serve you right)!*

j.en in seinem eigenen **Fett** schmoren lassen (fig.): cf. j.en in seinem eigenen **Saft** schmoren lassen

**Fettlebe** machen (fam.): *to have a tuck-in (a binge; a blow-out) (colloq.); to stuff o.s. (sl.)*. Cf. auch: **Festessen** (Festschmaus); beim Essen **einhauen**

Es war ein großartiges Fest. Wir haben ordentlich Fettlebe gemacht.
*It was a wonderful party. We had a real tuck-in (binge; blow-out; we stuffed ourselves properly).*

ins **Fettnäpfchen** treten (fig. u. fam.): cf. sich in die **Nesseln** setzen

Es geht **feuchtfröhlich** zu: *There is much fun and merrymaking (fun and games; jollification)*. Cf. auch: ein feuchtfröhlicher **Abend**

Bei der goldenen Hochzeit meiner Großeltern ging es feuchtfröhlich zu.
*At my grandparents' golden wedding there was much fun and merrymaking (fun and games; jollification).*

**Feuer** dahinter machen (fig.): cf. **Dampf** dahinter machen

**Feuer** fangen (fig.): *to become inflamed with love; s.b.'s heart is burning*

Man konnte es seinem Gesichtsausdruck ansehen, daß er Feuer gefangen hatte.
*One could see from the expression on his face that he had become inflamed with love (that his heart was burning).*

**Feuer** und Flamme für etwas sein (fig.): *to be heart and soul for s.th.; to be as keen as mustard on s.th.; to be madly keen on s.th. (colloq.)*

Wie zu erwarten, waren alle Schüler Feuer und Flamme für einen Ausflug.
*As was to be expected, all the pupils were heart and soul for (as keen as mustard [madly keen] on) an excursion.*

**Feuer** und Flammen speien (spucken) (fig.): cf. **Gift** und Galle speien (spucken)

für j.en durchs **Feuer** gehen (fig.): *to go through fire and water for s.b.* Cf. auch: für j.en durch **dick** und dünn gehen

Für meinen Freund Heinrich würde ich durchs Feuer gehen.
*I would go through fire and water for my friend Henry.*

in **Feuer** geraten (fig.): *to fly into a passion; to see red; to blaze up (colloq.)*

Wenn wir auf dieses Thema zu sprechen kommen, geraten wir regelmäßig in Feuer.
*When we come to talk about that subject, we regularly fly into a passion (we regularly see red [blaze up]).*

für j.en (etwas) die Hand ins **Feuer** legen (fig.): cf. die **Hand** ins Feuer legen

Kein Rauch ohne **Feuer** (Sprichw.): *There is no smoke without fire (prov.)*

An jedem Gerücht ist etwas Wahres (dran). Kein Rauch ohne Feuer.
*There is something true in every rumour. There is no smoke without fire.*

j.em **Feuer** unter den Schwanz machen (fam.): cf. **Dampf** dahinter machen

etwas mit **Feuer** und Schwert ausrotten: *to take the sword to s.th.; to destroy s.th. root and branch; to remove s.th. by the roots.* Cf. auch: mit **Stumpf** und Stiel ausrotten

Die neue Regierung hat versprochen, alle Mißstände mit Feuer und Schwert auszurotten.
*The new government has promised to take the sword to all iniquities (to destroy all iniquities root and branch; to remove all iniquities by the roots).*

mit dem **Feuer** spielen (fig.): *to play with fire; to play a dangerous (risky) game.* Cf. auch: ein heißes **Eisen** sein

Ich warne dich, mit diesem zweifelhaften Menschen schönzutun. Du spielst mit dem Feuer (treibst ein gefährliches Spiel; malst den Teufel an die Wand).
*I warn you not to flirt with that dubious person. You are playing with fire (playing a dangerous [risky] game).*

verschieden sein wie **Feuer** und Wasser: cf. **grundverschieden** sein zwischen zwei **Feuern** stehen (sitzen) (fig.): *to be between the devil and the deep blue sea.* Cf. auch: in der **Klemme** sein

> Wenn Reinhard zu spät zur Schule kommt, wird er bestraft werden; wenn er aber wieder nach Hause. geht, wird er auch ausgeschimpft werden. Er steht (sitzt) eben zwischen zwei Feuern.
> *If Reinhard arrives late at school, he will be punished, but if he goes home again, he will be scolded too. He is between the devil and the deep blue sea.*

mit **Feuereifer** etwas tun: *to do something with a will; to go full-tilt at s. th.*

> Dieses Aufsatzthema machte uns viel Spaß, und wir machten uns mit Feuereifer an die Arbeit.
> *This essay subject gave us a great deal of pleasure, and we set to work with a will (we went full-tilt at it).*

die **Feuerprobe** bestehen (fig.): *to pass the acid test; to stand the test; to withstand the ordeal*

> Der junge Schauspieler, der zum ersten Male die Bühne betrat, hat seine Feuerprobe glänzend bestanden.
> *The young actor who was going on to the stage for the first time passed his acid test (stood the test; withstood the ordeal) brilliantly.*

**feuerrot** werden: cf. **knallrot** werden

die **Feuertaufe** empfangen: *to undergo one's baptism of fire (ordeal by fire)*

> Der junge Offizier wurde nach China geschickt, wo er seine Feuertaufe empfing.
> *The young officer was sent to China, where he underwent his baptism of fire (ordeal by fire).*

wie die **Feuerwehr** fahren (fam.): cf. **flitzen**

j.en nicht mit einer **Feuerzange** anfassen (fig.): *not to touch s. b. with a barge-pole (with a pair of tongs)*

> Dein neues Dienstmädchen sieht ja furchtbar aus. Ich möchte es nicht mit einer (Feuer)zange (Beißzange) anfassen.
> *Your new maid looks terrible. I wouldn't touch her with a barge-pole (a pair of tongs).*

etwas aus dem **FF** verstehen (fam.): *to know (to understand) s. th. to perfection; to have learnt s. th. to a T; to know s. th. inside-out (colloq.); to do a first-rate job (colloq.); to have s. th. thoroughly taped (colloq.).* Cf. auch: etwas bis zum **Tz** kennen

> Wir können Ihnen diesen erfahrenen Tischler empfehlen. Er versteht seine Sache aus dem FF (Effeff).
> *We can recommend you to this experienced joiner. He knows (understands) his job to perfection (has got [learnt] his job to a T; does a first-rate job; has his job [thoroughly] taped).*

**Fiasko** machen: *to be a fiasco; to be a flop (colloq.)*. Cf. auch: ein **Schlag** ins Wasser sein

> Mit seinem neuen Theaterstück hat der junge Dramatiker Fiasko gemacht.
> *The young dramatist's new play was a fiasco (flop).*

sich zur lächerlichen **Figur** machen: *to make an exhibition (idiot; a fool) of o.s.; to make o.s. a laughing-stock*

> Jeder Politiker muß bemüht sein, sich nicht zur lächerlichen Figur zu machen.
> *Every politician must be careful not to make an exhibition (idiot; a fool) of himself (to make himself a laughing stock).*

eine traurige **Figur** machen (spielen): *to cut a sorry (sad; poor) figure (caper)*

> Bei dieser Auseinandersetzung mit seinen Kollegen hat Heinrich eine sehr traurige Figur gemacht (gespielt; eine armselige Rolle gespielt).
> *During that argument with his colleagues Henry cut a very sorry (sad; poor) figure (caper).*

einen **Fimmel** haben (fam.): cf. nicht richtig im **Dachstübchen** sein

Es wird sich alles **finden** (fig.): *Everything will turn (come; work) out all right*

> Im Augenblick stehen die Dinge schlecht, es wird sich aber (schon) alles finden.
> *At the moment things are bad, but everything will turn (come; turn) out all right.*

sich etwas an den (an allen) zehn **Fingern** abzählen können: cf. **sonnenklar** sein

etwas an den **Fingern** hersagen können: cf. etwas im **Schlaf** hersagen können

Es juckt j.en in den **Fingern** (fig.): *s.b. is itching (aching) to do s.th.*

> Es juckt mich in den Fingern, diesem Gauner eine Ohrfeige zu geben.
> *I am itching (aching) to give that rogue a box on the ears.*

Wenn man ihm nur den kleinen **Finger** reicht, will er gleich die ganze Hand (fig.): *Give him an inch and he'll take an ell*

> Einmal habe ich meinem Nachbarn ein Buch geliehen; jetzt kommt er jede Woche und will etwas von mir. Wenn man ihm nur den kleinen Finger reicht, will er gleich die ganze Hand.
> *Once I lent my neighbour a book; now he comes every week and wants something from me. Give him an inch and he'll take an ell.*

j.em auf die **Finger** klopfen (fig.): *to rap s.b. over the knuckles; to rap s.b.'s fingers*

> Wenn du dich nicht besser benehmen kannst, werden wir dir mal auf die Finger klopfen müssen.
> *If you can't behave better, we shall have to rap you over the knuckles (rap your fingers).*

lange **Finger** machen (fig.): *to belong to the light-fingered gentry*

Ich muß unsern Laufjungen entlassen, weil ich festgestellt habe, daß er lange Finger macht (ein Langfinger ist).
*I must dismiss our office-boy because I have found out that he belongs to the light-fingered gentry.*

die **Finger** von etwas lassen (fig.): *to keep one's fingers out of s. th.; to keep away from s. th.; not to meddle in s. th.*

Ich kann Ihnen nur raten, die Finger von der Politik zu lassen.
*I can only advise you to keep your fingers out of (to keep away from; not to meddle in) politics.*

sich alle **Finger** nach etwas lecken (fig.): *to lick one's lips at s. th.; to lick one's chops at s. th. (colloq.)*

Es ist ein großzügiges Angebot, und jeder würde sich alle Finger danach lecken.
*It is a generous offer, and everyone would lick his lips (chops) at it.*

keinen **Finger** rühren (fig.): *not to stir (to move; to lift) a finger; not to lift a hand*

In dieser Angelegenheit werde ich keinen Finger rühren, da ich kein Vertrauen zu Ihnen habe.
*I shall not stir (move) a finger (lift a finger [hand]) in this matter, for I have no confidence in you.*

sich etwas aus den **Fingern** saugen (fig.): *to concoct s. th.; to think (to make; to trump) s. th. up*

Die Geschichte ist unwahr; der Junge hat sich alles einfach aus den Fingern gesogen (gesaugt).
*The story is untrue; the boy simply concocted it (thought [made; trumped] it up).*

sich in den **Finger** schneiden (fig.): *to be wide of the mark; to be sadly mistaken; to have another think coming (sl.)*

Wenn du glaubst, ich würde dir gegen meine Überzeugung helfen, so schneidest du dich ordentlich in den Finger.
*If you believe that I would help you against my conviction, then you are well wide of the mark (are sadly mistaken; have got another think coming).*

sich die **Finger** wund schreiben: *to write until one's fingers ache; to wear one's fingers out writing*

Ich habe mir mit Briefen an meine Schuldner die Finger wund geschrieben.
*I have written letters to my debtors until my fingers ache (have worn my fingers out writing letters to my debtors).*

j.em auf die **Finger** sehen (fig.): cf. ein scharfes **Auge** auf j.en haben

138

seine **Finger** im Spiel haben (fig.): *to have a finger in the pie; to have a say (a hand) in the business*

Ich wußte, daß man meine Ernennung durchsetzen würde, denn mein Onkel hat seine Finger (Hand) im Spiel gehabt (hat dahintergesteckt).
*I knew that my appointment would be put through, because my uncle had a finger in the pie (a say [hand] in the business).*

überall seine **Finger** drin haben (fig.): *to have a finger in every pie; to dabble in everything*

Dieser Apotheker kümmert sich nicht nur um seinen eigenen Beruf, sondern hat überall seine Finger drin.
*This chemist does not only concern himself with his own occupation, but has a finger in every pie (dabbles in everything).*

sich die **Finger** verbrennen (fig.): *to burn one's fingers; to get one's fingers trodden on; to get into hot water (colloq.).* Cf. auch: sich den **Mund** verbrennen

Ich wollte ihm schon einmal helfen, verbrannte mir aber die Finger (die Flügel) dabei und tue es jetzt nicht mehr.
*I wanted to help him once before, but I burned my fingers (got my fingers trodden on; got into hot water) and I am not going to do it again.*

j.en um den (kleinen) **Finger** wickeln (fig.): *to twist (to wrap) s.b. round one's little finger*

Marie versteht es, ihre Mutter um den (kleinen) Finger zu wickeln (einzuwickeln); sie kriegt alles, was sie nur haben will.
*Mary knows how to twist (wrap) her mother round her little finger; she gets whatever she wants.*

um den (kleinen) **Finger** zu wickeln sein (fig.): *one can wrap s.b. round one's little finger; to be like clay in s.b.'s hands*

Nach dieser Bestrafung war mein jüngerer Bruder um den (kleinen) Finger zu wickeln (war ... wie ein Ohrwürmchen).
*After that punishment you could wrap my younger brother round your little finger (my younger brother was like clay in my hands).*

den **Finger** auf die Wunde legen (fig.): *to put one's finger on the sore (raw) spot; to put one's finger on it*

Der Pfarrer legte den Finger auf die Wunde, als er auf die beunruhigende Wirkung der Inflation hinwies.
*The clergyman put his finger on the sore (raw) spot (on it) when he referred to the disturbing effect of inflation.*

mit **Fingern** auf j.en zeigen: *to point the finger of scorn (to wag one's head) at s.b.* Cf. auch: j.en (etwas) an den **Pranger** stellen

Nach seiner Entlassung aus dem Gefängnis verließ er die Stadt, wo man mit Fingern auf ihn zeigte.
*After his release from prison he left the town where people pointed the finger of scorn (wagged their heads) at him.*

j.em zwischen den **Fingern** zerrinnen (fig.): *to melt (to dissolve) in one's hand*
So ein kleiner Geldschein zerrinnt einem heutzutage zwischen den Fingern.
*A small banknote like that melts (dissolves) in one's hand these days.*

keinen **Fingerbreit** von etwas abweichen: *not to deviate (to depart) one iota (inch) from s. th.; not to falter from s. th.*
Während seiner ganzen dreißig Jahre im Amt ist dieser Beamte keinen Fingerbreit vom rechten Wege abgewichen.
*During his whole thirty years in office this civil servant has not deviated (departed) one iota (inch; has never faltered) from the correct path.*

**Fingerspitzengefühl** besitzen: *to possess fine feeling (a sense of propriety; tact); to have a delicate touch*
Leider besitzt meine Tante kein Fingerspitzengefühl in (der) Gesellschaft und macht daher einen unhöflichen Eindruck.
*Unfortunately my aunt possesses no fine feeling (no sense of propriety; no tact; has not got a delicate touch) in society and thus makes an impression of rudeness.*

j.em **Fingerzeige** (einen Fingerzeig) geben: *to give s. b. hints (indications; clues)*
Das Probespiel hat dem Trainer wichtige Fingerzeige (einen wichtigen Fingerzeig) für die künftige Aufstellung der Mannschaft gegeben.
*The trial match gave the trainer important hints (indications; clues) as to the future composition of the team.*

etwas **fingern** (fam.): cf. etwas zu **Wege** bringen

weder **Fisch** noch Fleisch sein (fig.): *to be neither fish nor flesh nor good red herring (neither one thing nor the other)*
Er gehört keiner politischen Partei an und sagt selbst von sich, er sei in dieser Hinsicht weder Fisch noch Fleisch (weder heiß noch kalt).
*He belongs to no political party, and says of himself that in this respect he is neither fish nor flesh nor good red herring (neither one thing nor the other).*

**Fisch** will schwimmen (Sprichw.): *(The) fish must float*
Kellner, zu unserm Karpfen bitte eine Flasche guten Rheinwein. Fisch will schwimmen.
*Waiter, please bring us a good bottle of Hock with our carp. (The) fish must float.*

stumm wie ein **Fisch** sein: *to be as mute as a fish (as silent as the Sphinx); to be like a dumb animal*
Stumm wie ein Fisch hörte meine Schwester unserer lebhaften Unterhaltung zu.

*My sister listened to our lively conversation as mute as a fish (as silent as the Sphinx; like a dumb animal).*

**gesund wie der Fisch** im Wasser: cf. **kerngesund**

**sich (wohl)fühlen wie der Fisch** im Wasser: cf. sich (wohl)fühlen wie die **Made** im Speck

**Fischblut** haben (fig.): cf. **eiskalt** sein

die **Fisimatenten** lassen (fam.): *to stop making a fuss*
Laß die Fisimatenten und beendige deine Hausaufgabe!
*Stop making a fuss and finish your homework.*

j.en unter seine **Fittiche** nehmen (fig.): *to take s.b. under one's wing; to take s.b. in charge*
Während der Abwesenheit unserer Eltern nahmen uns Onkel und Tante unter ihre Fittiche.
*During our parents' absence Uncle and Auntie took us under their wing (took us in charge).*

**fitzen** (fam.): cf. **flitzen**

**fix** und fertig sein: a) (von Sachen) *to be all finished;* b) (von Ideen usw.) *to be all made out; to be cut and dried;* c) cf. **absein**
a) Nach sechs Monaten hatten die Arbeiter das Haus schon fix und fertig.
b) Die Pläne für unsere Sommerferien haben wir jetzt fix und fertig.
*a) After six months the workmen had the house all finished.*
*b) We have now got the plans for our summer holidays all made out (all cut and dried).*

**flachsblond** sein: *to be flaxen-haired; to have flaxen hair*
Meine Schwester hat dunkles Haar; ich aber bin flachsblond.
*My sister has dark hair but I am flaxen-haired (have flaxen hair).*

**flachsen** (fam.): *to lark about (colloq.)*
Wir waren richtig lustig und haben viel geflachst.
*We were really merry and larked about a lot.*

unter falscher **Flagge** segeln (fig.): *to sail under false colours*
Dieses sogenannte Kinderbuch segelt unter falscher Flagge. In Wirklichkeit richtet es sich an Erwachsene.
*This so-called children's book is sailing under false colours. In reality it is intended for adults.*

die **Flagge** streichen (fig.): cf. die **Waffen** strecken

j.es alte **Flamme** sein (fig.): *to be s.b.'s old flame*
Erich errötete, als er im Tanzsaal eine seiner alten Flammen bemerkte.
*Eric blushed when he noticed one of his old flames in the dance-hall.*

j.em in die **Flanke** fallen (fig.): *to attack s.b. in the flank (in the rear)*

> Mit diesem zweideutigen Zeitungsartikel ist der Abgeordnete seiner eigenen Partei in die Flanke gefallen.
> *By this equivocal newspaper article the delegate has attacked his own party in the flank (rear).*

eine **Flasche** sein (fig. u. fam.): cf. ein **Muttersöhnchen** sein

zu tief in die **Flasche** geguckt haben: cf. zu tief in den **Becher** geguckt haben

j.em **Flausen** in den Kopf setzen: *to put an idea (ideas) in s.b.'s head; to put a bee in s.b.'s bonnet; to give s.b. a kink (colloq.)*

> Du willst zur Bühne oder zum Film? Wer hat dir denn diese Flausen (Raupen) in den Kopf (dir diesen Floh ins Ohr) gesetzt?
> *You want to go on the stage or into films? Who put that idea (those ideas) into your head (Who put that bee in your bonnet; Who gave you that kink)?*

sich **fläzen** (fam.): *to loll (to lounge; to sprawl) about (colloq.)*

> Sitz' still; fläze (lümmele) dich nicht so auf dem Sofa herum!
> *Sit still. Don't loll (lounge; sprawl) about on the sofa like that!*

vom **Fleck** weg: cf. auf der **Stelle**

nicht vom **Fleck** kommen (fig.): *not to get anywhere; not to make any headway*

> Heute komme ich mit diesen Problemen nicht vom Fleck, denn ich bin viel zu müde.
> *I cannot get anywhere (make any headway) with these problems today, because I am much too tired.*

in den **Flegeljahren** sein: *to be in one's teens; to be a teenager*

> Wenn du mal erst aus den Flegeljahren heraus bist, wird man vernünftiger mit dir reden können.
> *When once you're out of your teens (When you're no longer a teenager), one will be able to talk to you more sensibly.*

sein eigen **Fleisch** und Blut: *one's own flesh and blood*

> Um sein eigen Fleisch und Blut vor Schande zu bewahren, bezahlte der Vater selbst die Spielschulden seines Sohnes.
> *In order to save his own flesh and blood from disgrace, the father paid his son's gambling debts himself.*

j.em in **Fleisch** und Blut übergehen: *to become second nature to s.b.; to become ingrained in s.b.; to become a matter of course to s.b.*

> Die unregelmäßigen Verben sollten Wilhelm doch nun endlich in Fleisch und Blut übergegangen sein.

*The irregular verbs ought by now to have become second nature (a matter of course) to (become ingrained in) William.*

**sich ins eigene Fleisch schneiden** (fig.): *to cut off one's nose to spite one's face; to do o.s. a bad turn; to cut one's own throat*

Wenn du dich so frech benimmst, schneidest du dich nur ins eigene Fleisch, denn solche Kinder bekommen keine Geschenke.
*If you behave so cheekily, you are only cutting off your nose to spite your face (doing yourself a bad turn; cutting your own throat), because such children do not get presents.*

**Ohne Fleiß kein Preis** (Sprichw.): *Success has to be worked for; There is no easy road (way) to success*

Du mußt fleißig arbeiten, wenn du die Prüfung bestehen willst. Ohne Fleiß kein Preis (Von nichts kommt nichts).
*You must work hard if you want to pass the examination. Success has to be worked for (There is no easy road [way] to success).*

**flennen** (fam.): *to blub (colloq.); to grizzle (colloq.)*

Alles ist jetzt wieder gut. Nun hör' auf zu flennen.
*Everything is all right again now. Now stop blubbing (grizzling).*

**eine leichte Fliege sein** (fig. u. fam.): *to be flighty; to be a (social) butterfly (colloq.)*

Dieser Student kümmert sich um die Damen mehr als um sein Studium. Er ist eine leichte Fliege (ein Flittchen [allegro]; ein Bruder Leichtfuß; ein Schmetterling; ein lockerer [loser] Vogel; ein Windhund; ein lockerer Zeisig).
*That student is more concerned with the ladies than with his studies. He is flighty (a [social] butterfly).*

**zwei Fliegen mit éiner Klappe schlagen** (fig.): *to kill two birds with one stone*
Cf. auch: **éin Aufwaschen sein**

Wenn wir Sonntag in die Kirche gehen, können wir nachher noch die Kunstausstellung besuchen. So schlagen wir zwei Fliegen mit éiner Klappe.
*If we go to church on Sunday, we can visit the art exhibition afterwards. In that way we shall kill two birds with one stone.*

**matt wie eine Fliege sein:** *to be like a limp rag*

Peter kann diese große Hitze nicht vertragen. Er ist matt wie eine Fliege.
*Peter cannot stand this great heat. He is like a limp rag.*

**sterben wie die Fliegen:** *to die like flies (like cattle)*

In früheren Jahrhunderten starben bei jeder Epidemie die Menschen wie die Fliegen.
*In earlier centuries men died like flies (cattle) in any epidemic.*

**sich über die Fliege an der Wand ärgern** (fig.): *to flare up at the merest trifle; to become peppery at the merest trifle (colloq.)*

Mein Onkel ist manchmal so gereizt, daß er sich über die Fliege an der Wand ärgert.
*My uncle is sometimes so irritable that he flares up (becomes peppery) at the merest trifle.*

keiner **Fliege** etwas zuleide tun (fig.): *not to hurt (to harm) a fly.* Cf. auch: j.em kein **Haar** krümmen

Mein Bruder sieht stark und kräftig aus, er würde aber keiner Fliege etwas zuleide tun.
*My brother looks strong and powerful but he would not hurt (harm) a fly.*

Ihm **fliegt** alles zu (an): *He picks things up like child's-play; Everything comes easily to him; Things just land in his lap*

Die anderen in der Klasse müssen schwer arbeiten, Karl aber fliegt alles zu (an) und er ist schnell mit der Arbeit fertig.
*The others in the class have to work hard, but Charles picks things up like child's-play (everything comes easily to Charles; everything just lands in Charles' lap) and he soon finishes his work.*

alle Herzen **fliegen** j.em zu (fig.): cf. alle **Herzen** fliegen j.em zu

die **Flinte** ins Korn werfen (fig.): cf. den **Kampf** aufgeben

ein **Flittchen** (allegro) sein (fam.): cf. eine leichte **Fliege** sein

gespannt wie ein **Flitzebogen** sein: cf. gespannt wie ein **Regenschirm** sein

**flitzen** (fam.): *to speed; to nip (colloq.); to whiz (colloq.); to drive like blazes (colloq.)*

Wenn er weiterhin mit seinem Motorrad so durch die Straßen flitzt (fitzt; wie die Feuerwehr fährt), wird er stürzen.
*If he goes on speeding (nipping; whizzing; driving like blazes) through the streets on his motor-cycle like that, he will crash.*

j.em einen **Floh** ins Ohr setzen (fig.): cf. j.em **Flausen** in den Kopf setzen

die **Flöhe** husten (niesen) hören (fig. u. fam.): cf. das **Gras** wachsen hören

lieber **Flöhe** hüten (fam.): cf. lieber einen **Sack** Flöhe hüten

in die **Flohkiste** kriechen (fam.): cf. in die **Falle** gehen b)

nach j.es **Flöte** tanzen (fig.): cf. nach j.es **Pfeife** tanzen

**flöten** gehen (fam.): *to slip through one's fingers; to go by the board; to be frittered away; to go phut (sl.).* Cf. auch: durch die **Lappen** gehen

Da Ihr so unschlüssig wart, ist uns schon manche günstige Gelegenheit flöten gegangen.
*As you were so undecided, many favourable opportunities have slipped through our fingers (gone by the board; gone phut; been frittered away).*

j.em (die) **Flötentöne** beibringen (fig. u. fam.): *to teach s. b. manners; to teach s. b. a thing or two; to teach s. b. a lesson; to show s. b. what's what (colloq.)*. Cf. auch: j.en **abkanzeln;** j.em gründlich **Bescheid** sagen; j.en ins **Gebet** nehmen

> Der Gast hatte sich über unser schlechtes Benehmen geärgert und sagte: „Na, wartet nur, ich werde Euch schon (die) Flötentöne beibringen (den Kopf zurechtsetzen; Mores lehren)".
> *The guest was annoyed at our bad behaviour and said: "Just you wait. I'll teach you manners (a thing or two; a lesson; show you what's what)."*

**flotte** Geschäfte machen: cf. **Bombengeschäfte** machen

im **Fluge**: cf. im **Handumdrehen**

j.em die **Flügel** beschneiden (stutzen) (fig.): *to clip s. b.'s wings; to rein s. b. in.* Cf. auch: j.em den **Brotkorb** höher hängen

> Man muß ihm einmal die Flügel beschneiden (stutzen), damit er nicht zu übermütig wird.
> *One must clip his wings (rein him in) so that he does not become too overbearing.*

die **Flügel** hängen lassen (fig.): *to hang one's head; to be (to look) down in the mouth (colloq.); to be (to look) blue (colloq.)*

> Wegen dieses kleinen Irrtums braucht er die Flügel nicht so hängen zu lassen.
> *He does not need to hang his head like that (to be [to look] so down in the mouth; so blue) because of this little mistake.*

sich die **Flügel** verbrennen (fig.): cf. sich die **Finger** verbrennen

**flügellahm** sein: cf. sich **abrackern** b)

platt wie 'ne **Flunder** sein (fam.): *to be as flat as a pancake (as a board)*

> Die Katze war von einem Auto überfahren worden und (war) platt wie 'ne Flunder (eine Briefmarke; ein Pfannkuchen; ein Pfennig; eine Wanze; flach wie ein Brett [Bügel-, Plättbrett]).
> *The cat had been run over by a car and was as flat as a pancake (board).*

**flunkern** (fam.): cf. **kohlen**

allein auf weiter **Flur** stehen (fig.): *to be far and away the best; to be in a class by o. s.*

> Niemand kann bestreiten, daß dieser italienische Rennfahrer (mit seinen Glanzleistungen) allein auf weiter Flur steht.
> *Nobody can contest that that Italian racing-driver is far and away the best (is in a class by himself).*

**Flurschaden** anrichten (fig.): *to do damage (harm); to cause bad blood.* Cf. auch: böses **Blut** machen

Mit seinen unüberlegten Bemerkungen hat mein Vetter schon viel Flurschaden angerichtet (Porzellan zerschlagen).
*My cousin has done a great deal of damage (harm; caused a great deal of bad blood) with his unconsidered remarks.*

etwas in **Fluß** bringen: cf. etwas in **Gang** setzen

in **Fluß** halten: cf. in **Gang** halten

in **Fluß** kommen: *to get going; to get into swing; to get into one's stride; to get cracking (colloq.)*

Nach einem trägen Anfang ist das Geschäft jetzt in Fluß (Fahrt; Gang; Schuß; Schwung; auf [hohe] Touren) gekommen.
*After a listless start the business has now got going (got into swing [its stride]; got cracking).*

noch im **Fluß** sein: *to be in a state of flux; to be in the melting-pot*

Es ist noch viel zu früh, um eine endgültige Antwort auf diese Frage zu geben, weil alles noch im Fluß ist.
*It is still much too early to give a final answer to this question, because everything is still in a state of flux (in the melting-pot).*

**flutschen** (fam.): *to whiz (to bowl) along (colloq.).* Cf. auch: wie am **Schnür-chen** gehen

Unser Schuster ist ein fleißiger und geschickter Handwerker. Bei ihm flutscht die Arbeit.
*Our cobbler is a hard-working and skilful craftsman. His work whizzes (bowls) along.*

j.en auf die **Folter** spannen (fig.): *to keep s.b. on tenterhooks (in suspense; keyed [worked] up)*

Spanne uns nicht länger auf die Folter, sondern sage uns sofort, wer dir diesen Brief geschrieben hat.
*Don't keep us on tenterhooks (in suspense; keyed [worked] up) any longer and tell us immediately who wrote you this letter.*

j.en **foppen** (fam.): cf. j.en auf den **Arm** nehmen

feste **Form** (Formen) annehmen: *to take (on definite) shape; to crystalise*

Die Pläne für mein neues Haus nehmen langsam feste Form(en) an.
*The plans for my new house are slowly taking (on definite) shape (crystalising).*

sich in **Form** fühlen: *to feel in form; to feel fit; to feel in the pink; to feel on top line (colloq.)*

Heute werde ich dich beim Tennisspiel bestimmt schlagen, weil ich mich in Form fühle.
*I shall certainly beat you at tennis today because I feel in form (fit; in the pink; on top line).*

146

sich nicht in (guter) **Form** fühlen: cf. keinen guten **Tag** haben

ein Mann von **Format** sein: *to be a man of (some) stature (distinction [quality]); to be a man to reckon (to be reckoned) with*

> Man kann aus seinen Reden leicht erkennen, daß er ein Mann von Format ist.
> *One can easily recognise from his speeches that he is a man of (some) stature (distinction [quality]; a man to reckon [to be reckoned] with).*

sich einen **Frack** lachen (fam.): cf. sich **totlachen**

den **Frack** vollbekommen (fam.): *to get a (good) hiding (colloq.)*

> Als der ungezogene Junge nach Hause kam, bekam er von seinen Eltern tüchtig den Frack voll.
> *When the rude boy got home, he got a good hiding from his parents.*

j.em den **Frack** vollhauen (fam.): cf. j.em das **Fell** gerben

das **Fracksausen** haben (fam.): cf. (eine) **Heidenangst** haben

(nicht) außer **Frage** stehen: cf. nicht aus der **Welt** sein

etwas in **Frage** stellen: *to question (to query) s.th.; to call s.th. in question*

> Erich hegt gewisse Vorurteile auf diesem Gebiet; deshalb habe ich sein strenges Urteil gleich in Frage gestellt.
> *Eric has certain prejudices on this subject, and I therefore at once questioned (queried) his severe judgement (called his severe judgement in question).*

**Fraktur** mit j.em reden (fig.): cf. **deutsch** mit j.em reden

**frank** und frei sagen: cf. **klipp** und klar sagen

sich **Fransen** an den Mund reden (fam.): cf. sich den **Mund** fusselig reden

sich auf **französisch** empfehlen: *to take French leave*

> Wir stellten fest, daß mein jüngerer Bruder die Gesellschaft verlassen hatte, ohne uns ein Wort zu sagen; er hatte sich einfach auf französisch empfohlen (einfach verdrückt; verduftet; verkrümelt; er war verschwunden wie Schmidt's Katze).
> *We found out that my younger brother had left the party without saying a word to us. He had simply taken French leave.*

**Fratzen** schneiden: cf. **Grimassen** schneiden

Die **Frau** hat die Hosen an (fig. u. fam.): cf. die **Hosen** anhaben

ein freches **Frauenzimmer** sein (fam.): cf. ein freches **Stück** sein

**frech** wie Oskar sein (fam.): cf. ein **Frechdachs** sein

ein **Frechdachs** sein (fam.): *to be a cheeky (saucy) fellow; to be a cheeky Charlie (colloq.)*

Ernst ist ein richtiger Frechdachs (frecher Patron; frech wie Oskar; stinkfrech). Er ärgert seine Eltern furchtbar.
*Ernest is a proper cheeky (saucy) fellow (a proper cheeky Charlie). He annoys his parents terribly.*

einen **Freibrief** für j.en darstellen (fig.): *to give s.b. carte blanche; to give s.b. free rein*

Die Verlängerung der Polizeistunde stellt einen Freibrief für Verbrecher dar.
*The extension of the licensing hours will give carte blanche (free rein) to criminals.*

auf **Freiersfüßen** gehen: *to be on the look-out for a wife; to go a-wooing (colloq.)*
Seit wann geht denn dieser Junggeselle auf Freiersfüßen?
*How long has this bachelor been on the look-out for a wife (been a-wooing)?*

**fremdgehen** (fam.): cf. **nebenbeigehen**

eine **Fresse** ziehen (fam.): cf. ein **Gesicht** machen wie sieben Tage Regenwetter; ein schiefes **Gesicht** machen

ein gefundenes **Fressen** sein (fig. u. fam.): cf. ein **Geschenk** des Himmels sein

Sie ist zum **Fressen** (fig. u. fam.): cf. Sie ist zum **Anbeißen**

sich ein **Fressen** aus etwas machen (fig. u. fam.): *to revel in s.th.; to take a delight in s.th.; to go to town when doing s.th. (colloq.)*

Dieser Kritiker macht sich ein Fressen (Fest; Festessen) daraus, schlechte Opernsänger herunterzumachen.
*This critic revels (takes a delight) in denigrating (goes to town when denigrating) bad opera-singers.*

ein **Freßsack** sein (fam.): *to be a glutton; to be a gannet, a greedy-guts (sl.)*
Bei allen Mahlzeiten verzehrt mein Neffe unheimliche Massen. Er ist ein richtiger Freßsack (Vielfraß).
*My nephew consumes incredible quantities at every meal. He is a real glutton (gannet, greedy-guts)*

**Fressalien** (fam.): *grub (colloq.)*

Ihr braucht uns nichts zu essen anzubieten; wir haben unsere eigenen Fressalien mitgebracht.
*You don't need to offer us anything to eat. We've brought our own grub.*

herrlich und in **Freuden** leben: cf. leben wie ein **Fürst**

ein **Freudengeschrei** erheben: *to set up (to raise) a shout of joy (a cry of delight [jubilation])*

Die gesamte Presse erhob ein Freudengeschrei, als das unbeliebte Gesetz abgeschafft wurde.
*The entire press set up (raised) a shout of joy (cry of delight [jubilation]) when the unpopular law was repealed.*

es mit **Freund** und Feind halten: *to run with the hare and hunt with the hounds; to make the best of both worlds; to keep in with everybody*

Mancher denkt an seinen eigenen Vorteil und will sich bei niemandem unbeliebt machen; er hält es (dann) mit Freund und Feind.
*Many people think of their own advantage and do not want to make themselves unpopular with anyone; they run with the hare and hunt with the hounds (they make the best of both worlds; they keep in with everybody).*

(mein) lieber **Freund** und Kupferstecher: *my dear old pal (colloq.); old chap (fellow [man; boy]); my old cock-sparrow (sl.)*

Wie geht's, mein lieber Freund und Kupferstecher? Ich habe dich lange nicht gesehen.
*How are you, my dear old pal (old chap [fellow; boy; my old cock-sparrow])? I haven't seen you for a long time.*

in **Frieden** und Freundschaft auseinandergehen: *to part (to part company) on friendly (amicable) terms; to part good friends*

Wir haben uns kein böses Wort mehr gesagt, sondern sind in Frieden und Freundschaft auseinandergegangen.
*We said no more angry things to each other and parted (parted company) on amicable (friendly) terms (parted good friends).*

j.en in **Frieden** lassen: cf. j.en in **Ruhe** lassen

dem (lieben) **Frieden** nicht trauen (fig.): *not to trust (to be suspicious of) the look of things (the situation)*

Früher mochte er mich nicht leiden, jetzt ist er sehr liebenswürdig zu mir; aber ich traue dem (lieben) Frieden nicht.
*Previously he did not like me, now he is very kind to me; but I do not trust (I am suspicious of) the look of things (the situation).*

die **Friedenspfeife** mit j.em rauchen (fig.): *to smoke the pipe of peace with s. b.*

Unser Streit ist jetzt vorbei. Lassen Sie uns die Friedenspfeife miteinander rauchen.
*Our quarrel is now over. Let us smoke the pipe of peace together.*

etwas **frisieren** (fig.): *to touch s. th. up; to paint s. th.; to fiddle s. th. (sl.)*

Die Bilanz der Firma war nicht gut, aber der Buchhalter hat sie für die Bank etwas frisiert.
*The firm's accounts were not good but the bookkeeper touched them up (painted them; fiddled them) a bit for the bank.*

**Friß,** Vogel, oder stirb!: cf. Friß, **Vogel,** oder stirb!

ein **frommer** Wunsch: *a pious hope*

> Ein eigenes Haus zu besitzen, wird für mich wohl immer ein frommer Wunsch bleiben.
> *I suppose that to own my own house will always remain a pious hope.*

gegen j.en (etwas) **Front** machen (fig.): *to stand up to (to stand out against) s.b. (s.th.); to stand one's ground against s.b. (s.th.); to show a bold front to s.b. (s.th.); to make a stand against s.b. (s.th.)*

> Gegen diesen Beamten und seine Behandlung des Publikums sollte energisch Front gemacht werden.
> *One ought to stand up to (to stand out against; to stand one's ground against; to show a bold front to; to make a stand against) this official and his treatment of the public.*

in vorderster **Front** stehen (fig.): cf. in vorderster **Linie** stehen

Sei kein **Frosch!** (fam.): *Don't be such a mollycoddle! (colloq.); Don't be (so) soft! (sl.)*

> Daß es schneit, ist doch kein Grund, zu Hause zu bleiben. Sei kein Frosch und komm mit!
> *There's no reason to stay at home because it's snowing. Don't be such a mollycoddle (Don't be [so] soft) and come with me!*

j.en **frotzeln** (fam.): cf. j.en auf den **Arm** nehmen

j.em (wie ein reifer Apfel [wie eine reife **Frucht**]) in den Schoß fallen (fig.): cf. j.em (wie ein reifer Apfel [eine reife Frucht]) in den **Schoß** fallen

die verbotene **Frucht** (fig.): *forbidden fruit*

> Die verbotene Frucht lockt immer die Jugend.
> *Forbidden fruit always entices youth.*

Verbotene **Frucht** schmeckt am besten (Sprichw.): *Forbidden fruit is sweetest (prov.)*

> Er weiß, daß er das nicht nehmen darf, aber verbotene Frucht schmeckt am besten.
> *He knows that he is not allowed to take that, but forbidden fruit is sweetest.*

An ihren **Früchten** sollt ihr sie erkennen (Sprichw.): *By their fruits ye shall know them (prov.); Handsome is as handsome does (prov.)*

> Nach dem Aussehen allein kann man nicht urteilen. An ihren Früchten sollt ihr sie erkennen.
> *One cannot judge by appearances alone. By their fruits ye shall know them (Handsome is as handsome does).*

ein nettes (sauberes) **Früchtchen** sein (fam.): *to be a tough nut (colloq.); to be a proper handful (colloq.)*

> Schon mit seinen zehn Jahren begeht er allerlei Unehrlichkeiten. Er kann ein nettes (sauberes) Früchtchen werden.
> *Already at ten he does all kinds of dishonest things. He may become a tough nut (a proper handful).*

wo sich die **Füchse** gute Nacht sagen: cf. in **Buxtehude** wohnen

ein schlauer **Fuchs** sein (fig.): cf. **durchtrieben** sein

es **fuchst** j.en (fam.): *it peeves (riles) s.b.; it gets s.b.'s goat (colloq.)*

> Es fuchst ihn, daß er ein kleineres Gehalt bezieht als sein Bruder.
> *It peeves (riles) him (gets his goat) that he draws a smaller salary than his brother.*

**fuchsteufelswild** werden: cf. in **Harnisch** geraten; aus der **Haut** fahren. Cf. auch: **Gift** und Galle speien (spucken)

unter j.es **Fuchtel** stehen (fig.): *to be under s.b.'s thumb (in s.b.'s grip); to be tied to s.b.'s apron-strings (colloq.).* Cf. auch: j.en am **Gängelband** führen

> Georgs Mutter ist eine richtige Tyrannin, und der arme Kerl steht ganz unter ihrer Fuchtel (Knute).
> *George's mother is a real tyrant, and the poor fellow is completely under her thumb (in her grip; tied to her apron-strings).*

mit **Fug** und Recht: *with every justification; with good cause (reason); properly; rightly*

> Die Fabrikarbeiter haben mit Fug und Recht gegen die zu kurze Mittagspause protestiert.
> *The factory workers have with every justification (with good cause [reason]; properly [rightly]) protested against the excessive shortness of the lunch-break.*

aus den **Fugen** gehen (fig.): *to go to rack and ruin; to go to pieces*

> Wenn dieser Abteilungsleiter nicht entlassen wird, wird das Geschäft völlig aus den Fugen (Angeln) gehen.
> *If the head of this department is not dismissed, the business will go to rack and ruin (go utterly to pieces).*

in allen **Fugen** krachen (fig.): *to creak in every joint*

> Dieses veraltete System kracht jetzt in allen Fugen.
> *This out-of-date system is now creaking in every joint.*

bei j.em einen **Fühler** ausstrecken (fig.): *to throw (to stretch) out a feeler; to sound the situation; to find out the lie of the land*

> Du solltest (bei ihm) einen Fühler ausstrecken (auf den Busch klopfen; die Lage peilen; ihm den Puls [auf den Zahn] fühlen; einen Versuchsballon steigen lassen), um zu sehen, ob sich die alte Feindschaft nicht begraben läßt.

*You ought to throw (to stretch) out a feeler (to sound the situation; to find out the lie of the land) to see whether the old enmity cannot be buried.*

fluchen wie ein **Fuhrknecht:** cf. fluchen wie ein **Landsknecht**

etwas **fummeln** (fam.): cf. etwas zu **Wege** bringen

an etwas **fummeln** (fam.): cf. an etwas **herumfummeln**

eine **Fundgrube** (fig.): *a gold-mine; a mine of information (knowledge); a find*
Dein Buch ist eine wahre Fundgrube für Kenner.
*Your book is a real gold-mine (mine of information [knowledge]; a real find) for connoisseurs.*

**fünf** gerade sein lassen: *to stretch a point; to wink at things; to let things slide*
Unsere Mutter ist normalerweise sehr gewissenhaft; manchmal aber läßt sie auch fünf gerade sein (manchmal macht sie aber auch husch, husch, die Waldfee).
*Our mother is normally very conscientious, but sometimes she stretches a point (winks at things; lets things slide).*

mit etwas kurze **fünfe** machen (fam.): *to cut s. th. short; to break s. th. off early*
Mit dieser Mahlzeit machen wir heute mal kurze fünfe, weil wir nachher spazierengehen wollen.
*We're cutting this meal short (breaking this meal off early) today because we want to go for a walk afterwards.*

ein falscher **Fünfziger** (Fufziger) sein (fig. u. fam.): cf. ein **Wolf** im Schafspelz sein

**funkelnagelneu** sein: *to be brand-new*
Ich habe meine funkelnagelneue Uhr hinfallen lassen, und jetzt geht sie nicht mehr.
*I dropped my brand-new watch and now it will not go any more.*

daß die **Funken** fliegen: *so that the sparks fly*
Er ging mit solchem Eifer ans Holzhacken, daß die Funken flogen.
*He set himself to chopping wood with such zeal that the sparks flew.*

ein **Funken** Verstand: *a modicum (grain; glimmer; an iota) of sense; the least bit of sense*
Mit nur einem Funken Verstand konnte man sehen, daß sein Versuch erfolglos bleiben würde.
*With only a modicum (grain; glimmer; an iota; only the least bit) of sense one could see that his attempt would be unsuccessful.*

sein **Für** und Wider haben: *to have its pros and cons*

Manchmal denken wir, wir möchten auf dem Lande wohnen, manchmal wollen wir aber in unserer Heimatstadt bleiben. Es hat alles sein Für und Wider.

*Sometimes we think we should like to live in the country, but at other times we want to stay in our home town. Everything has its pros and cons.*

**Furore** machen: *to create (to make) a sensation (a furore)*

Mit deinem neuen Mantel wirst du bei deinen Freundinnen Furore machen.

*You will create (make) a sensation (furore) among your friends with your new coat.*

leben wie ein **Fürst (fürstlich** leben): *to live like a lord; to live in the lap of luxury; to live on the fat of the land; to live in clover.* Cf. auch: auf großem **Fuße** leben

Mit seinem enormen Gehalt kann er wie ein Fürst (fürstlich; wie Gott in Frankreich; herrlich und in Freuden) leben.

*With his enormous salary he can live like a lord (in the lap of luxury; on the fat of the land; in clover).*

sich die **Füße** ablaufen (fig.): *to run one's legs off; to run o.s. off one's feet; to run o.s. into the ground*

Ich habe mir die Füße (Beine; Hacken; Schuhsohlen) abgelaufen, um dieses Geburtstagsgeschenk für meine Schwester zu bekommen.

*I have run my legs off (run myself off my feet [into the ground]) to get this birthday present for my sister.*

mit beiden **Füßen** auf der Erde (im Leben; in der Wirklichkeit) stehen (fig.): *to have both feet firmly on the ground; to be firmly based in reality*

Mein Vater läßt sich nicht durch solche Illusionen irreführen; er steht mit beiden Füßen (Beinen) auf der Erde (im Leben; in der Wirklichkeit).

*My father does not allow himself to be misled by such illusions; he has both feet firmly on the ground (is firmly based in reality).*

j.em den Boden unter den **Füßen** wegziehen (fig.): cf. j.em den **Boden** unter den Füßen wegziehen

auf eigenen **Füßen** stehen (fig.): cf. auf eigenen **Beinen** stehen

auf die **Füße** fallen (fig.): *to fall on one's feet; to fall the right way up (colloq.)*

Trotz seiner vielen Mißerfolge ist er immer wieder auf die Füße gefallen.

*In spite of his many failures he has always fallen on his feet (the right way up).*

festen **Fuß** fassen (fig.): *to find one's feet; to gain (to get) a (firm) footing (foothold)*

Die meisten Flüchtlinge haben in anderen Ländern festen Fuß gefaßt (wieder festen Boden unter den Füßen).

*Most refugees have found their feet (gained [got] a [firm] footing [foothold]) in other countries.*

j.em (einer Sache) auf dem **Fuße** folgen (fig.): *to follow (hard) on the heels of s.b. (s.th.).* Cf. auch: j.em auf den **Fersen** folgen

Die Absetzung des Generals folgte der verlorenen Schlacht auf dem Fuße.
*The general's discharge followed (hard) on the heels of the lost battle.*

auf freiem **Fuße** sein: *to be at liberty; to be out; to be back in circulation (colloq.)*

Der Gefangene ist schon seit acht Tagen wieder auf freiem Fuße.
*The prisoner has now been at liberty (out again; back in circulation) for a week.*

j.en auf freien **Fuß** setzen: *to give s.b. his freedom; to set s.b. at liberty*

Als die Gerichtsverhandlung die völlige Unschuld des Angeklagten ergab, wurde er sofort auf freien Fuß gesetzt.
*When the trial revealed the complete innocence of the accused, he was at once given his freedom (set at liberty).*

mit j.em auf gespanntem **Fuße** stehen (leben) (fig.): cf. sich mit j.em in den **Haaren** liegen

mit éinem **Fuß** im Grabe stehen: *to have one foot in the grave*

Der Greis sah aus, als ob er schon mit éinem Fuß im Grabe stünde.
*The old man looked as though he had one foot in the grave.*

auf großem **Fuße** leben (fig.): *to live in great style (in the grand manner; on a big scale).* Cf. auch: leben wie ein **Fürst**

Der Kassierer hatte sich verdächtig gemacht, weil er trotz seines kleinen Gehalts auf großem Fuße lebte (ein großes Haus führte; sein Geld auf den Kopf haute [schlug]; zum Schornstein hinausjagte).
*The cashier attracted suspicion because in spite of his small salary he lived in great style (in the grand manner; on a big scale).*

auf gutem **Fuße** mit j.em stehen (leben): *to be on good terms with s.b.; to get on well with s.b.; to be well in with s.b. (colloq.)*

Er ist ein beliebter Mensch, der mit jedermann auf gutem Fuße steht (lebt; sich mit jedermann gut steht).
*He is a popular person who is on good terms (gets on well; is well in) with everybody.*

kalte **Füße** bekommen (fig. u. fam.): *to get cold feet (colloq.); to get the wind up (sl.)*

Karl wagte nicht, von zwei Metern hinabzuspringen. Bei solchen Gelegenheiten bekommt er immer kalte Füße.
*Charles did not dare to jump from two metres. He always gets cold feet (gets the wind up) on such occasions.*

j.em etwas zu **Füßen** legen (fig.): *to lay s.th. at s.b.'s feet*

Er legte der Schauspielerin sein ganzes Vermögen zu Füßen.
*He laid his entire fortune at the actress's feet.*

mit dem linken (falschen) **Fuß** zuerst aufstehen (aus dem Bett steigen) (fig.):
*to get out of bed the wrong side*

> Warum ist sie heute so schlecht gelaunt? Ist sie mit dem linken (falschen) Fuß
> (Bein) zuerst aufgestanden (aus dem Bett gestiegen)?
> *Why is she in such a bad mood today? Did she get out of bed the wrong side?*

j.em den **Fuß** auf den Nacken setzen (fig.): *to have one's foot on s.b.'s neck;*
*to pin s. b. down; to get one's hands on s. b.*

> Nach monatelangem Suchen nach dem Schmuggler hat ihm die Polizei nun
> endlich den Fuß auf den Nacken gesetzt.
> *After months of searching for the smuggler the police now have their foot on his neck*
> *(have now pinned him down; have now got their hands on him) at last.*

auf schwachen (tönernen) **Füßen** stehen (fig.): *to rest on a weak (shaky)*
*foundation; to be built on sand.* Cf. auch: auf **Sand** gebaut sein

> Seine ganze Beweisführung steht auf schwachen (tönernen) Füßen.
> *His whole argument rests on a weak (shaky) foundation (is built on sand).*

stehenden **Fußes:** cf. auf der **Stelle**

sich auf den **Fuß** getreten fühlen (fig.): *to take s.th. amiss; to feel as though*
*s.b. has trodden on one's pet corn; to fly into a huff (colloq.)*

> Bei dieser vollkommen harmlosen Bemerkung fühlte er sich infolge seiner Emp-
> findlichkeit auf den Fuß (die Hühneraugen) getreten.
> *Because of his sensitiveness he took that completely harmless remark amiss (felt at*
> *that . . . as though s.b. had trodden on his pet corn; flew into a huff at that . . .).*

j.em auf den **Fuß** treten (fig.): *to tread on s.b.'s corns (pet corns; toes); to put*
*s.b.'s back up; to put s.b.'s nose out of joint (colloq.)*

> Durch eine taktlose Bemerkung bin ich meinem Freund (habe ich meinen
> Freund) auf den Fuß (die Hühneraugen; die Zehen) getreten.
> *By a tactless remark I trod on my friend's corns (pet corns; toes; put my friend's back*
> *up; put my friend's nose out of joint).*

j.en (etwas) mit **Füßen** treten (fig.): *to trample s.b. (s.th.) underfoot.* Cf. auch:
über **Leichen** gehen; j.en zur **Schnecke** machen

> Ein Diktator hat kein Gewissen; alles, was ihm nicht paßt, tritt er mit Füßen.
> *A dictator has no conscience; he tramples underfoot everything that does not suit him.*

das Glück mit **Füßen** treten (fig.): *to be blind to one's own fortune; to cut one's*
*own throat.* Cf. auch: das **Huhn** schlachten, das die goldenen Eier legt

> Er hat einen guten Posten bekommen, aber jetzt fängt er an, mit dem Chef zu
> streiten, der ihn eingestellt hat. Er tritt (ja) das Glück mit Füßen.
> *He has got a good post but now he is starting to quarrel with the boss who engaged him.*
> *He is blind to his own good fortune (is cutting his own throat).*

sich die **Füße** vertreten: *to stretch one's legs*

> Im Unterricht müßt Ihr stillsitzen. Während der Pause könnt Ihr Euch auf dem Schulhof die Füße (Beine) vertreten.
> *During lessons you must sit still. At break you can stretch your legs in the playground.*

j.em etwas vor die **Füße** werfen: *to throw s. th. down; to throw s. th. on the ground*

> In ihrem Zorn warf sie dem jungen Mann den Ring vor die Füße.
> *In her anger she threw the young man's ring down (on the ground).*

j.em **Fußangeln** legen (fig.): cf. j.em eine **Falle** stellen

einen **Fußfall** tun: *to bend the knee; to prostrate o. s.*

> Der König weigerte sich, vor dem Eroberer einen Fußfall zu tun, und dankte lieber ab.
> *The king refused to bend the knee (to prostrate himself) before the conqueror and preferred to abdicate.*

in j.es **Fußstapfen** treten (fig.): *to follow in s. b.'s footsteps*

> Leider will der Sohn nicht in die Fußstapfen seines Vaters treten (nicht in den Spuren seines Vaters wandeln) und die Apotheke übernehmen. Er will Bildhauer werden.
> *Unfortunately the son does not want to follow in his father's footsteps and take over the chemist's. He wants to become a sculptor.*

sich (den Mund) **fusselig** reden: cf. sich den **Mund** fusselig reden

**futsch** sein (fam.): a) *to have vanished (disappeared);* b) cf. **hinsein;** c) cf. **kaputt** sein

> a) Ich kann meinen Füllfederhalter nicht finden. Er ist einfach futsch.
> *a) I cannot find my fountain-pen. It has just vanished (disappeared).*

gut im **Futter** sein (fam.): cf. gut bei **Leibe** sein

an der **Futterkrippe** sitzen (fig.): *to sit pretty (colloq.); to have a soft job (number) (colloq.); to have a cushy job (number) (sl.)*

> Viele behaupten von den Staatsbeamten, daß sie an der Futterkrippe sitzen, obwohl ihre Gehälter nicht besonders hoch sind.
> *Many say of civil servants that they are sitting pretty (have a soft [cushy] job [number]), though their salaries are not particularly high.*

Aus ihm spricht der **Futterneid** (fig.): *He is green with (bursting with) envy; He is eaten up with jealousy*

> Du sagst, der neue Abteilungsleiter sei nicht tüchtig, aber aus dir spricht ja nur der Futterneid, weil du selbst gern Abteilungsleiter geworden wärest.
> *You say that the new head of the department is not efficient, but you are only green (bursting) with envy (eaten up with jealousy) because you would have liked to become head of the department yourself.*

sich in **Gala** werfen: cf. sich in seine gute **Kluft** werfen

j.en an den **Galgen** bringen: *to bring s.b. to the gallows*

Der Polizei ist es endlich gelungen, den Verbrecher an den Galgen zu bringen.
*The police have finally succeeded in bringing the criminal to the gallows.*

eine **Galgenfrist** gewähren (fig.): *to give (to grant) s.b. breathing-space (a reprieve)*

Wenn die Galgenfrist, die ich meinem Schuldner gewährt habe, abgelaufen ist, werde ich ihn verklagen.
*When the breathing-space (reprieve) which I have granted (given) my debtor has expired, I shall sue him.*

falsch wie **Galgenholz** sein: *to be a snake in the grass; to be as deceitful as a snake.* Cf. auch: falsch wie eine **Katze** (eine falsche Katze) sein

Hüten Sie sich vor diesem Mann! Er ist falsch wie Galgenholz (wie eine Schlange).
*Beware of that man. He is a snake in the grass (as deceitful as a snake).*

**Galgenhumor:** *humour born of despair (grim humour; a grim jest)*

Es war nur Galgenhumor, wenn der Kranke sagte, es gehe ihm jetzt viel besser.
*It was only humour born of despair (grim humour; a grim jest) when the sick man said that he was much better now.*

j.em läuft die **Galle** über: cf. vor **Wut** kochen

**galle(n)bitter** sein: *to be as bitter as gall; to taste like bitter aloes*

Diese Arznei schmeckt galle(n)bitter, wirkt aber sehr.
*This medicine tastes as bitter as gall (like bitter aloes) but is very effective.*

**galliger** Laune sein: *to be in a foul (nasty; filthy) temper (colloq.)*

Er ist oft galliger Laune. Woher kommt diese Verbitterung?
*He is often in a foul (nasty; filthy) temper. Where does that bitterness come from?*

**gang** und gäbe sein: *to be a matter of course (the usual thing)*

Im Rheinland und in einem Teil von Westfalen ist es gang und gäbe, wochenlang Karneval zu feiern.
*In the Rhineland and in part of Westphalia it is a matter of course (the usual thing) to celebrate the carnival for weeks.*

etwas in **Gang** halten: *to keep s.th. going (moving); to keep the ball rolling*

Der Außenminister war bemüht, die Verhandlungen in Gang zu halten.
*The foreign minister was concerned to keep the negotiations going (moving; to keep the ball rolling).*

den **Gang** nach Kanossa antreten (fig.): *to eat humble pie; to eat dirt*

Da er seinen Geschäftsteilhaber beleidigt hatte, mußte er den Gang nach Kanossa antreten und sich bei ihm entschuldigen.
*As he had insulted his partner, he had to eat humble pie (dirt) and apologise to him.*

in **Gang** kommen: cf. in **Fluß** kommen

etwas in **Gang** setzen (bringen): *to set the ball rolling; to set s. th. moving (in motion); to get s. th. going; to launch s. th.; to get s. th. under way*

Der Diplomat versuchte noch einmal, die Verhandlungen in Gang zu setzen ([zu bringen]; in Fluß zu bringen; anzukurbeln; bei den V. den Stein ins Rollen zu bringen).
*The diplomat tried again to set the ball rolling ( to set the negotiations moving [in motion]; to get the negotiations going [under way]; to launch the negotiations).*

j.en am **Gängelband** führen (fig.): *to lead s. b. by the nose; to have s. b. on a string.* Cf. auch: unter j.es **Fuchtel** stehen

Marie führt ihren Mann am Gängelband (hat ihren Mann an der Strippe).
*Mary leads her husband by the nose (has her husband on a string).*

eine dumme **Gans** sein (fig. u. fam.): *to be a silly goose (colloq.)*

Mit deiner Schwester kann man nicht vernünftig reden. Sie ist eine dumme Gans (Kuh; Pute; Trine; ein dummes Huhn [Schaf]).
*One cannot talk sensibly to your sister. She is a silly goose.*

eine **Gänsehaut** überläuft j.en (fig.): cf. j.en **kalt** überlaufen

im **Gänsemarsch** gehen (fig.): *to walk in single file (in Indian file)*

Die Brücke war so schmal, daß wir im Gänsemarsch über sie gehen mußten.
*The bridge was so narrow that we had to go over it in single file (in Indian file).*

**Gänsewein** (fam.): *Adam's ale*

Kinder bekommen nur Gänsewein, sagte meine Mutter, und stellte uns einen Krug Wasser auf den Tisch.
*Children can only have Adam's ale, said my mother, putting a jug of water on the table.*

aufs **Ganze** gehen: *to go the whole hog (way); to go all out (colloq.)*

Der Redner sagte: Begnügen wir uns nicht mit halben Maßnahmen, sondern gehen wir (gleich) aufs Ganze.
*The speaker said: Let us not content ourselves with half-measures but go the whole hog (way; go all out).*

nichts **Ganzes** und nichts Halbes sein: *to be neither one thing nor the other; to be neither fish nor flesh nor good red herring.* Cf. auch: nicht **Fisch** noch Fleisch sein

Für viele Leute ist ein geselliges Beisammensein ohne Musik nichts Ganzes und nichts Halbes.
*A convivial gathering without music is for many people neither one thing nor the other (neither fish nor flesh nor good red herring).*

j.em (einer Sache) den **Garaus** machen: *to give s.b. (s.th.) the coup de grâce; to wipe s.b. (s.th.) out; to finish (to polish) s.b. (s.th.) off (colloq.)*

In den meisten Gegenden hat man den Wölfen schon längst den Garaus gemacht.
*In most districts wolves were given the coup de grâce (were wiped out; finished [polished] off) long ago.*

hinter schwedische **Gardinen** kommen: cf. in den **Kasten** kommen

hinter schwedischen **Gardinen** sitzen: cf. hinter **Schloß** und Riegel sitzen

j.em eine **Gardinenpredigt** halten: *to give s.b. a lecture (a talking-to).* Cf. auch: j.en **abkanzeln**

Jedesmal, wenn ich zu spät nach Hause komme, hält mir meine Frau eine Gardinenpredigt.
*Every time I come home late, my wife gives me a lecture (talking-to).*

j.em ins **Garn** gehen (fig.): *to fall into (to get caught in) s.b.'s trap; to put one's head into s.b.'s noose; to fall for s.b.'s yarn (colloq.)*

Viele unschuldige Menschen sind bereits diesem Gauner ins Garn gegangen.
*Many innocent people have already fallen into that rogue's trap (put their heads into ... noose; fallen for ... yarn).*

j.en ins **Garn** locken (fig.): *to lead s.b. up the garden path (colloq.); to send s.b. on a wild goose chase (colloq.); to kid s.b. (sl.)*

Dieser Mann hat mehrmals versucht, unwissende Menschen ins Garn zu locken.
*That man has tried several times to lead ignorant people up the garden path (to send ... on a wild goose chase; to kid ignorant people).*

ein **Garn** spinnen (fig.): *to spin (to pitch) a yarn*

Matrosen lieben es, ein Garn (Seemannsgarn) zu spinnen.
*Sailors love to spin (to pitch) a yarn.*

ein **Gassenbube, -junge:** *a street urchin; a street arab; a guttersnipe (colloq.)*

Wir dürfen nicht mit Gassenbuben (-jungen) spielen.
*We are not allowed to play with street urchins (street arabs; guttersnipes).*

ein **Gassenhauer:** *a popular tune; a dance-tune*

Mein Vater hat mir verboten, Gassenhauer zu pfeifen.
*My father has forbidden me to whistle popular tunes (dance-tunes).*

ein **Gaukelspiel** mit j.em treiben (fig.): *to double-cross s.b.; to play s.b. false; to play a double game with s.b.*

Diese Partei treibt oft ein Gaukelspiel mit dem Volk.
*This party often double-crosses the people (plays the people false; plays a double game with the people).*

Einem geschenkten **Gaul** schaut man nicht ins Maul (Sprichw.): *Never look a gift horse in the mouth (prov.)*

Du solltest von deinem Vater das gebrauchte Fahrrad annehmen, ohne zu fragen, wieviel es wert ist. Einem geschenkten Gaul schaut man nicht ins Maul.
*You ought to accept the second-hand bicycle from your father without asking how much it is worth. Never look a gift horse in the mouth.*

Mach' die **Gäule** nicht scheu! (fig. u. fam.): *Don't get the wind up! (sl.); Keep your hair on! (sl.)*

Weshalb drängst du so zum Aufbrechen? Mach' die Gäule nicht scheu; wir haben bis zur Abfahrt unseres Zuges noch viel Zeit!
*Why are you so anxious to set out? Don't get the wind up! (Keep your hair on!) We've got plenty of time before our train leaves.*

einen feinen **Gaumen** haben (fig.): cf. eine feine **Zunge** haben

in Schweiß **gebadet** sein: *to be bathed in sweat (perspiration)*

Während des packenden Films saßen die Zuschauer in Schweiß gebadet da.
*During the thrilling film the audience sat there bathed in sweat (perspiration)*

Es knistert im **Gebälk** (fig.): cf. **wackelig** stehen

sich etwas nicht **geben** und nicht nehmen können: *not to be able to do anything about s.th.; not to be able to help s.th.*

Meine Nervosität kann ich mir nicht geben und nicht nehmen.
*I cannot do anything about (cannot help) my nervousness.*

**Geben** ist seliger denn Nehmen (Sprichw.): *It is better to give than to receive (prov.)*

Du solltest nicht immer an dich denken, sondern du solltest auch Anderen Geschenke machen. Denn Geben ist seliger denn Nehmen.
*You ought not to think of yourself all the time but also give presents to others. It is better to give than to receive.*

j.em es ordentlich **geben**: cf. j.em gründlich **Bescheid** sagen

j.en ins **Gebet** nehmen (fig.): *to take s.b. to task; to call s.b. to account; to lay down the law; to put s.b. on the carpet (mat) (colloq.).* Cf. auch: j.en **abkanzeln;** j.em gründlich **Bescheid** sagen; j.em eins auf den **Hut** geben

Nach diesem Vorfall nahm uns der Lehrer schwer ins Gebet (stellte uns ...
zur Rede; ging der Lehrer mit uns streng ins Gericht) und drohte uns für
die Zukunft eine strenge Bestrafung an.
*After this incident the master took us severely to task (called us properly to account; laid
down the law properly; put us properly on the carpet [mat]) and threatened us with a
severe punishment in future.*

das richtige **Gebetbuch** haben (fig.): *to belong to the right denomination (sect;
confession; communion)*

> Dieser Abgeordnete ist gewählt worden, weil er das richtige Gebetbuch (Ge-
> sangbuch) hatte.
> *That delegate was elected because he belonged to the right denomination (sect; confession;·
> communion).*

nicht auf Rosen **gebettet** sein (fig.): cf. nicht auf **Rosen** gebettet sein

eine schwere **Geburt** sein (fam.): cf. eine **Herkulesarbeit** sein

ein **Gedächtnis** wie ein Sieb haben: *to have a head like a sieve*

> Schon wieder hat mein Onkel meinen Geburtstag vergessen. Er hat ein Ge-
> dächtnis wie ein Sieb.
> *Again my uncle has forgotten my birthday. He has a head like a sieve.*

sich **Gedanken** machen: *to worry (to trouble) one's head; to turn over in one's
mind.* Cf. auch: sich den **Kopf** zerbrechen

> Den ganzen Tag macht sich mein Bruder Gedanken über die Verwertung seiner
> Erfindung.
> *The whole day my brother worries (troubles) his head about (turns over in his mind) the
> utilisation of his invention.*

schwarzen **Gedanken** nachhängen: *to brood; to mope (colloq.); to be down in
the dumps (colloq.)*

> Heinrich tut mir sehr leid. Er muß (offenbar) schwarzen Gedanken nachhängen,
> denn er sieht sehr unglücklich aus.
> *I am very sorry for Henry. He must be brooding (moping; must be down in the dumps),
> because he looks very unhappy.*

j.em schwebt der **Gedanke** vor: *s. b. is toying with the idea*

> Mir schwebt der Gedanke vor, im Sommer nach Italien zu fahren; ob es mir
> wirklich gelingt, wird von meiner finanziellen Lage abhängen.
> *I am toying with the idea of going to Italy in the summer, but whether I really succeed
> will depend on my financial situation.*

ein **Gedankenblitz**: cf. ein **Geistesblitz**

auf **Gedeih** und Verderb: *for better or for worse*

Wir alle sind auf Gedeih und Verderb (auf Biegen und Brechen) von den Entscheidungen unserer Staatsmänner abhängig.
*For better or for worse, we are all dependent on the decisions of our statesmen.*

ein **Gedicht** sein (fig.): *to be a picture*

Ihr Blumenstrauß ist wirklich ein Gedicht (wie gemalt).
*Your bunch of flowers is a real picture.*

lügen wie **gedruckt:** cf. lügen, daß sich die **Balken** biegen

Mit **Geduld** und Spucke fängt man eine (manche) Mucke (Sprichw.): *If you wait long enough, you'll catch something*

Du kannst doch nicht gleich den ersten Preis gewinnen. Aber: Mit Geduld und Spucke fängt man eine (manche) Mucke.
*You can't win the first prize at once, but if you wait long enough, you'll catch something.*

j.em reißt die **Geduld** (der **Geduldsfaden**): *s. b. loses his patience; s. b.'s patience breaks.* Cf. auch: aus der **Haut** fahren

Es ist kein Wunder, daß einem Lehrer manchmal die Geduld (der Geduldsfaden) reißt, wenn er immer wieder von vorne anfangen muß.
*It is no wonder that a teacher sometimes loses his patience (that a teacher's patience sometimes breaks) when he keeps having to start from the beginning again.*

auf etwas **geeicht** sein (fig.): *to be well up (well versed) in s.th.; to be familiar with s.th.* Cf. auch: gut **bestellt** sein

Auf solche Reparaturen bin ich mehr geeicht als du.
*I am better up (better versed) in (more familiar with) such repairs than you.*

Das lasse ich mir **gefallen!**: *Good for you!; That's the stuff! (colloq.)*

Ihr habt also weiter gelesen, als ich sagte? Das lasse ich mir gefallen!
*So you've read further than I said? Good for you (That's the stuff)!*

**Gefasel** (fam.): *drivel; rubbish; bosh (gibberish) (colloq.).* Cf. auch: **faseln**

Was soll dieses alberne Gefasel? Rede doch vernünftig mit uns.
*What's the meaning of this stupid drivel (rubbish; bosh; gibberish)? Talk to us sensibly.*

sich auf etwas **gefaßt** machen: a) *to count (to reckon) on s.th.; to resign o.s. to s.th.;* b) *to watch out (for s.th.); to look out (to stand by) for squalls (colloq.); to watch out for a rocket (colloq.)*

a) Ich mache mich darauf gefaßt, daß ich nichts in der Lotterie gewinnen werde.
b) Wenn du wieder Streit mit ihm anfängst, kannst du dich auf etwas (auf ein Donnerwetter) gefaßt machen.
*a) I am not counting (reckoning) on winning (I have resigned myself to not winning) anything in the sweepstake.*
*b) If you start a quarrel with him again, you can watch out ([for something]); look out [stand by] for squalls; watch out for a rocket).*

etwas ins **Gefecht** führen (fig.): *to bring s.th. to the attack; to bring s.th. up; to adduce s.th.*

Zur Stützung seiner Beweisführung konnte der Rechtsanwalt mehrere frühere Gerichtsurteile ins Gefecht (Feld; Treffen) führen.
*In support of his argument the lawyer was able to bring several earlier convictions to the attack ( to bring up [ to adduce] several earlier convictions ).*

klar zum **Gefecht** sein (fig.): *to be ready (to be stripped) for action*

Als der Boxer den Ring betrat, war er schon klar zum Gefecht.
*When the boxer entered the ring he was ready (stripped) for action.*

j.en außer **Gefecht** setzen (fig.): *to put s.b. out of action; to sweep s.b. aside; to dispose of s.b. (colloq.); to get rid of s.b. (colloq.); to wipe the floor with s.b. (sl.)*

Der bekannte Schachspieler konnte mühelos seine sämtlichen Gegenspieler außer Gefecht setzen.
*The famous chess player was able to put all his opponents out of action ( to sweep all . . . aside; to get rid [dispose] of [to wipe the floor with] all . . .) without effort.*

ein **geflügeltes** Wort: *a household word*

Dieses Zitat ist ein geflügeltes Wort geworden.
*This quotation has become a household word.*

j.en **gefressen** haben (fig. u. fam.): *not to be able to stomach s.b. (to stand the sight of s.b.) (colloq.)*

Diesen frechen Jungen habe ich gefressen.
*I can't stomach (stand the sight of) that cheeky boy.*

seinen **Gefühlen** freien Lauf lassen: cf. seinen Gefühlen freien **Lauf** lassen

sich in dem **Gefühl** wiegen: *to bask (to luxuriate) in the feeling*

Eduard wiegt sich in dem Gefühl, sein Examen mit Leichtigkeit zu bestehen.
*Edward is basking (luxuriating) in the feeling that he will pass his examination with ease.*

Es wird nichts so heiß **gegessen,** wie es gekocht wird (Sprichw.): *Things are not as black as they look.* Cf. auch: **Hunde,** die bellen, beißen nicht

Der Polizist hat dich wegen der schlechten Beleuchtung deines Fahrrades aufgeschrieben; mach' dir aber keine Sorgen. Es wird nichts so heiß gegessen, wie es gekocht wird.
*The policeman took your name because the lights on your bicycle were bad, but don't worry. Things are not as black as they look.*

j.em einen **geharnischten** Brief schreiben: *to write s.b. a strong (stiff) letter to write s.b. a stinking letter (a stinker) (sl.)*

Schließlich sah ich mich gezwungen, meinem Schuldner einen geharnischten Brief (eine geharnischte Sonette) zu schreiben.
*I finally found myself forced to write my debtor a strong (stiff; stinking) letter (a stinker).*

163

j.em ins **Gehege** kommen (fig.): *to get in s.b.'s way; to cross s.b.'s path; to cross swords with s.b.; to poach on s.b.'s preserves; to encroach on s.b.'s rights*

> Anna ist meine Verlobte. Der junge Bursche, der jetzt mit ihr redet, soll es nur nicht wagen, mir ins Gehege zu kommen.
> *Anne is my fiancée. The young fellow who is talking to her now had better not dare to get in my way (cross my path; cross swords with me; poach on my preserves; encroach on my rights).*

Das ist das ganze **Geheimnis**: *That's the whole story; That's the long and short of it; That's all there is to it*

> Das ist das ganze Geheimnis. Mehr gibt es nicht zu sagen.
> *That's the whole story (That's the long and short of it; That's all there is to it). There is nothing more to tell.*

ein offenes **Geheimnis** sein: *to be an open secret*

> Es ist ein offenes Geheimnis, daß der Ministerpräsident bald von seinem Amt zurücktreten wird.
> *It is an open secret that the Prime Minister is soon going to retire from office.*

den **Geheimniskrämer (-tuer; Geheimtuer)** spielen: *to play the mystery-monger*

> Anstatt offen zu sagen, was los ist, spielt er den Geheimniskrämer (-tuer; Geheimtuer).
> *Instead of saying openly what the matter is, he is playing the mystery-monger.*

wie **gehenkt** aussehen: *to look like a scarecrow (a tramp); to look scruffy (colloq.)*

> Du mußt dir deine Hosen aufbügeln lassen; du siehst ja wie gehenkt aus.
> *You must get your trousers ironed; you look like a scarecrow (tramp; look scruffy).*

nicht j.es **Gehirn** entsprungen sein: cf. nicht j.es **Hirn** entsprungen sein

der **Gehirnskasten** (fam.): *the brain-box (colloq.); the nut (block) (sl.)*

> Astronomie und Astrologie sind doch nicht dasselbe! Geht das nicht in deinen Gehirnskasten (Hirnkasten)?
> *Astronomy and astrology are not the same thing. Can't you get that into your brain-box (nut; block)?*

wie er **geht** und steht: *(just) as he is*

> Ich kann nicht warten. Heinrich muß mitkommen, wie er geht und steht.
> *I cannot wait. Henry must come with me (just) as he is.*

Wo **gehobelt** wird, (da) fallen Späne (Sprichw.): *You cannot make an omelette without breaking eggs (prov.)*

> Bei dem Regierungswechsel sind viele Beamte entlassen worden. Wo gehobelt wird, (da) fallen Späne.

*With the change of government many officials have been dismissed. You cannot make an omelette without breaking eggs.*

**gehupft** wie gesprungen (fam.): *as broad as it's long; all the same; to make no odds; six of one and half-a-dozen of the other*

Wir können nach Köln oder nach Düsseldorf fliegen. Es ist gehupft wie gesprungen (Jacke wie Hose).
*We can fly to Cologne or to Düsseldorf. It's as broad as it's long (It's all the same; It makes no odds; It's six of one and half-a-dozen of the other).*

die erste **Geige** spielen (fig.): *to play first fiddle; to lead the dance; to be the leader of the band*

Es hat sie sehr geärgert, daß sie in diesem Theaterstück die führende Rolle nicht bekam; denn sie will immer die erste Geige (Rolle) spielen.
*It annoyed her very much that she did not get the leading role in this play, for she always wants to play first fiddle (lead the dance; be the leader of the band).*

nach j.es **Geige** tanzen (fig.): cf. nach j.es **Pfeife** tanzen

den **Geist** aufgeben: *to breathe one's last; to give up the ghost; to draw one's last breath*

Nach einer langen Krankheit hat mein Großvater heute Nacht den Geist aufgegeben (seine Seele ausgehaucht).
*Last night, after a long illness, my grandfather breathed his last (gave up the ghost; drew his last breath).*

wes **Geistes** Kind: *what sort (kind) of person*

Zuerst will ich wissen, wes Geistes Kind er ist, bevor ich ihm Geld leihe.
*First I want to know what sort (kind) of person he is before I lend him money.*

modernen **Geist** atmen: *to breathe the spirit of the age*

Dieses Trauerspiel atmet modernen Geist.
*This tragedy breathes the spirit of the age.*

ein **Geistesblitz**: *a brain-wave; a bright idea; a flash of inspiration*. Cf. auch:
ein **Geniestreich**

Die beiden Parteien konnten nicht einig werden. Da hatte ich den Geistesblitz (Gedankenblitz), einen gerechten Kompromiß vorzuschlagen.
*The two parties could not agree. Then I had a brain-wave (bright idea; flash of inspiration) and suggested a fair compromise.*

kein **Geistesheld** sein: cf. das **Pulver** nicht erfunden haben

ein **Geizhals** (**Geizkragen**) sein: *to be a miser (skinflint; niggard)*.
Cf. auch: **knauserig** (ein **Knauser**) sein

Unser Onkel ist ein richtiger Geizhals (Geizkragen; Pfennigfuchser). Er schickt uns nichts zu Weihnachten, weil ihm das Porto zu teuer ist.
*Our uncle is a proper miser (skinflint; niggard). He does not send us anything for Christmas because the postage costs too much.*

**Gekeife** (fam.): *squabbling; wrangling; bickering*

Ist dieses Gekeife (Gekreische) der beiden Nachbarn nicht unerträglich?
*Isn't that squabbling (wrangling; bickering) between the two neighbours intolerable?*

**Geklimper** (fam.): *strumming; drumming*

Dieses ewige Geklimper auf dem Klavier bringt mich allmählich zur Verzweiflung.
*This eternal strumming (drumming) on the piano is gradually driving me to desperation.*

**Gekrakel** (fam.): *scrawl; scribble*

Du mußt deutlicher schreiben. Ich kann dein Gekrakel (Gekritzel) kaum lesen.
*You must write more clearly. I can hardly read your scrawl (scribble).*

**Gekreische:** cf. **Gekeife**

**Gekritzel** (fam.): cf. **Gekrakel**

sich zum **Gelächter** machen: *to make o. s. a laughing-stock (a butt of ridicule)*. Cf. auch: die **Zielscheibe** des Spottes sein

Mit seiner extravaganten Kleidung macht sich der junge Künstler zum Gelächter der ganzen Stadt.
*The young artist is making himself the laughing-stock of (a butt of ridicule to) the whole town with his extravagant clothes.*

**gelackmeiert** sein (fam.): *to be taken in; to be rooked (colloq.); to be diddled (colloq.)*

Bei Käufen an der Haustür ist man meistens gelackmeiert.
*One is usually taken in (rooked; diddled) when buying things at the door.*

**geladen** sein (fig. u. fam.): *to be up in arms; to be wild; to be ratty (sl.)*

Ich bin auf meinen Kohlenhändler geladen (bei meinem K. auf neunundneunzig), da er seine Säcke niemals vollfüllt.
*I am up in arms against (wild [ratty] with) my coal merchant, because he never fills his sacks up.*

schwer **geladen** haben (fig. u. fam.): cf. einen **Schwips** haben

sich **gelb** und grün ärgern: cf. sich **grün** und blau ärgern

ein **Gelbschnabel** sein (fig.): cf. ein **Grünschnabel** sein

**Geld** wie Dreck haben (fam.): cf. **Geld** wie Heu haben

**Geld** wie Heu haben: *to have money to burn; to swim (to roll; to wallow) in money*

Leute, die Geld wie Heu (Dreck) haben (im Reichtum [Geld] schwimmen [wühlen]; Krösusse [steinreich; stinkreich] sind; Moneten [Kies; Moos; Pinke-pinke; Zaster] haben), sind oft sehr geizig.
*People who have money to burn (are swimming [rolling; wallowing] in money) are often very mean.*

ins **Geld** laufen (gehen): *to mount up; to cost a pretty penny.* Cf. auch: sich **zusammenläppern**

Die Unterhaltungskosten für ein Auto laufen (gehen) ins Geld.
*The maintenance costs of a car mount up (cost a pretty penny).*

**Geld** regiert die Welt (Sprichw.): cf. **Gold** öffnet jede Tür

**Geld** scheffeln (fig.): *to rake in the (to amass) money; to make money hand over fist*

Da er keine Konkurrenz zu fürchten hat, scheffelt er Geld.
*Since he has no competition to fear, he is raking in the money (amassing money; making money hand over fist).*

im **Geld** schwimmen (wühlen) (fig.): cf. **Geld** wie Heu haben

bei **Geld** sein: cf. (gut) bei **Kasse** sein

nicht für **Geld** und gute Worte: *not for love or money*

Ich bin von Geschäft zu Geschäft gegangen, aber dieses Buch ist im Augenblick nicht für Geld und gute Worte zu haben.
*I have been from shop to shop but at the moment this book is not to be had for love or money.*

In **Geldsachen** hört die Gemütlichkeit auf (Sprichw.): *Friendship and business do not mix (do not go together)*

Ich würde dir nicht raten, mit deinem Vetter zusammenzuarbeiten, denn es könnte Schwierigkeiten mit sich bringen. In Geldsachen hört die Gemütlichkeit auf.
*I would not advise you to work together with your cousin, because it could lead to difficulties. Friendship and business do not mix (do not go together).*

auf seinem **Geldsack** sitzen (fig.): *to sit on one's money; to hold on to (to keep a firm hold on) one's purse-strings.* Cf. auch: ein **Geizhals** (Geizkragen) sein

Obwohl mir mein Onkel finanziell gut helfen könnte, sitzt er auf seinem Geldsack und rückt keinen Pfennig heraus.
*Although my uncle could easily help me financially, he sits on his money (holds on to [keeps a firm hold on] his purse-strings) and won't produce a penny.*

**Geldschneiderei** cf. **Halsabschneiderei**

wie **geleckt** aussehen: cf. **blitzblank** (blitzsauber) sein

die **Gelegenheit** beim Schopf ergreifen (fassen, packen) (fig.): *to take the bull by the horns; to jump at the chance; to seize (to take; to grasp) the opportunity with both hands; to seize (to take; to grasp) the opportunity while it is hot; to strike while the iron is hot*

> Zufällig erkannte ich den Filmstar auf dem Bahnhof. Da ergriff (faßte; packte) ich die Gelegenheit beim Schopfe (packte ich den Stier bei den Hörnern; griff ich mit beiden Händen zu) und bat ihn um sein Autogramm.
> *I happened to recognise the film-star at the station, so I took the bull by the horns (jumped at the chance; seized [took; grasped] the opportunity with both hands [while it was hot]; struck while the iron was hot) and asked him for his autograph.*

Darüber sind sich die **Gelehrten** noch nicht einig: *It is a moot point (a debatable question); There are two schools of thought about that*

> Ob es billiger ist, mit der Eisenbahn oder mit dem Auto nach Italien zu fahren, darüber sind sich die Gelehrten noch nicht einig.
> *It is a moot point (a debatable question) whether (There are two schools of thought about whether) it is cheaper to go to Italy by train or by car.*

j.en (etwas) aus dem **Geleise** bringen (fig.): cf. j.en (etwas) aus der **Bahn** werfen. Cf. auch (bei Personen) die Aktivform der Ausdrücke unter: sich aus dem **Konzept** bringen lassen

etwas ins **Geleise** bringen (fig.): *to put (to set) s.th. right (straight); to straighten s.th. out.* Cf. auch: sich **ausbügeln**

> Mit etwas Überlegung und Geschick läßt sich alles wieder ins Geleise bringen.
> *With a little reflection and ingenuity everything can be put (set) right (straight; straightened out) again.*

ins alte **Geleise** kommen (fig.): *to drop back (to fall) into its old groove (rut); to return to its old pattern (way)*

> Nach der gescheiterten Revolution kam alles bald wieder ins alte Geleise.
> *After the failure of the revolution everything soon dropped back (fell) into its old groove (rut; everything soon returned to its old pattern [way]).*

wieder im richtigen **Geleise** sein (fig.): *to be (back) in the saddle again; to be (back) in the groove again (colloq.); to be on the job again (colloq.)*

> Nach vielen unangenehmen Erlebnissen im Ausland ist Harald zurückgekehrt; jetzt ist er wieder im richtigen Geleise.
> *After many unpleasant experiences abroad Harold has returned; now he is (back) in the saddle (groove) again (on the job again).*

j.em das letzte **Geleit** geben: cf. j.em die letzte **Ehre** erweisen

**geliefert** sein (fam.): *to be done for (colloq.)*

Die neue Vase fiel vom Tisch und war geliefert.
*The new vase fell from the table and was done for.*

wie **gemalt** sein: cf. ein **Gedicht** sein

ein **Gemeinplatz** sein: cf. eine **Binsenwahrheit** sein

mit **gemischten** Gefühlen: cf. mit einem lachenden und einem weinenden **Auge**

auf j.en **gemünzt** sein: *to be aimed at (meant for) s.b.; to be a dig at s.b. (colloq.)*

Hast du nicht gemerkt, daß diese Anspielung auf dich und deine Verschwendungssucht gemünzt war?
*Didn't you notice that that allusion was aimed at (meant for; a dig at) you and your wastefulness?*

junges **Gemüse** sein (fig. u. fam.): *to be small fry (teenagers); to be rookies (sprogs) (colloq.)*

Mit diesem jungen Gemüse kann man sich nicht vernünftig unterhalten.
*One cannot have a sensible conversation with those small fry (those teenagers [rookies; sprogs]).*

j.em etwas zu **Gemüte** führen: *to impress s.th. on s.b.; to bring s.th. home to s.b.; to rub (to din; to hammer; to drub; to drum; to knock) s.th. into s.b. (colloq.).*
Cf. auch: j.em etwas **einbleuen**

Die Lehrer haben uns immer wieder zu Gemüte geführt (ans Herz gelegt; auf die Seele gebunden), daß wir noch viel lernen müssen.
*The teachers have always impressed on us (brought it home to us; rubbed [dinned; hammered; drubbed; drummed; knocked] it into us) that we still have a lot to learn.*

sich etwas zu **Gemüte** führen (fam.): *to treat (to help) o.s. to s.th.; to lash o.s. up to s.th. (sl.)*

Wenn Sie gestatten, würde ich mir gern noch ein Stück Kuchen zu Gemüte führen.
*If you will permit me, I should like to treat (help) myself (lash myself up) to another piece of cake.*

es sich **gemütlich** machen: *to make o.s. comfortable; to take it easy; to make o.s. at home*

Setzen wir uns doch und machen wir es uns gemütlich!
*Let's sit down and make ourselves comfortable (take it easy; make ourselves at home).*

j.em das **Genick** brechen (fig.): *to be s.b.'s ruin (downfall); to put paid to s.b.; to bring s.b. down*

Seine schlechten Noten in Deutsch und Englisch haben meinem Freund das Genick gebrochen.
*My friend's bad marks in German and English were his ruin (downfall; put paid to him; brought him down).*

ein **Geniestreich**: *a stroke of genius.* Cf. auch: ein **Geistesblitz**

Das war wirklich ein Geniestreich von dir, die Aufsatzhefte im Klassenschrank zu verstecken.
*That was really a stroke of genius on your part to hide the composition books in the classroom cupboard.*

wie **geölt** gehen (fam.): cf. wie am **Schnürchen** gehen

**gepfropft** voll sein: cf. **pfropfenvoll** sein

wie **gerädert** sein (fig.): cf. sich **abrackern** b)

für etwas **geradestehen** (fig.): cf. für j.en die **Hand** ins Feuer legen

**gerammelt** voll sein: cf. **pfropfenvoll** sein

aufs **Geratewohl**: *at random; haphazardly.* Cf. auch: etwas auf gut **Glück** tun

Franz hat beim Taubenschießen nie richtig gezielt, sondern aufs Geratewohl geschossen.
*Francis never aimed properly when pigeon-shooting but fired at random (haphazardly).*

ins **Gerede** kommen: cf. in aller (Leute) **Munde** sein a)

mit j.em ins **Gericht** gehen (fig.): cf. j.en ins **Gebet** nehmen

über j.en (etwas) zu **Gericht** sitzen (fig.): *to sit in judgement upon s.b. (s. th.)*

Die ganze Familie hat über dein Betragen zu Gericht gesessen.
*The whole family has been sitting in judg(e)ment upon your behaviour.*

**gerieben (gerissen)** sein (fam.): cf. **durchtrieben** sein

Du kannst mich **gernhaben** (fam.)!: cf. j.em den **Buckel** herunterrutschen können; Scher' dich zum **Henker!**

**gertenschlank** sein: cf. schlank wie eine **Tanne** sein

in keinem guten **Geruch** stehen (fig.): *not to have a good reputation*

Unser Stadtviertel steht in keinem guten Geruch.
*Our district has not got a good reputation.*

j.em wie **gerufen** kommen: *(to be) the very thing (person) one wanted; to come just at the right moment*

> Sie kommen mir wie gerufen! Würden Sie mir helfen, mein Auto in die Garage zu schieben?
> *(You're) The very person I wanted (You've come just at the right moment)! Would you help me push my car into the garage?*

**Gerümpel:** *lumber; junk (colloq.)*

> Die alten Leute hatten viel Gerümpel auf dem Dachboden.
> *The old people had a lot of lumber (junk) in the attic.*

**gerupft** werden (fig.): cf. **Federn** lassen

**Gesagt,** getan!: *No sooner said than done*

> Ich sagte zu meinem Freund, daß ich gern in die Oper gehen möchte.Gesagt, getan! Er rief gleich an und bestellte zwei Karten.
> *I told my friend that I should like to go to the opera. No sooner said than done: he rang up at once and booked two tickets.*

Laß dir das **gesagt** sein!: cf. Das kannst du dir hinter den **Spiegel** stecken!

unter uns **gesagt:** *between you and me and the gate-post; within these four walls*

> Unter uns gesagt, ich halte von einer solchen Außenpolitik nicht viel.
> *Between you and me and the gate-post (Within these four walls), I don't think much of that sort of foreign policy.*

**gesalzen** (fig.): cf. eine gesalzene **Rechnung**

**gesalzen** und gepfeffert (fig.): *caustic; pungent; biting; acrid*

> Seine Kritik über die neue Sinfonie war gesalzen und gepfeffert.
> *His criticism of the new symphony was caustic (pungent; biting; acrid).*

das richtige **Gesangbuch** haben (fig.): cf. das richtige **Gebetbuch** haben

dünn **gesät** sein (fig.): cf. **dünn** gesät sein

um j.en **geschehen** sein: *to be all up with s.b. (colloq.); to be the end of s.b. (colloq.)*

> Als er die Schwester meines Freundes zum ersten Mal sah, da war's um ihn geschehen.
> *The first time he saw my friend's sister, it was all up with him (the end of him).*

nicht (recht) **gescheit** sein: cf. nicht richtig im **Dachstübchen** sein

ein **Geschenk** des Himmels sein: *to be a godsend (windfall; gift from heaven)*

> Die 1000 Mark, die ich im Toto gewonnen habe, waren wie ein Geschenk des Himmels (waren ein gefundenes Fressen).

*The 1000 marks which I won in the football pools was a godsend (windfall; gift from heaven).*

geradezu **geschenkt** sein: cf. **spottbillig** sein

Mach' doch keine **Geschichten!** (fam.): *Don't be so silly! (colloq.); What are you up to now? (colloq.)*

Mach' doch keine Geschichten! Wenn ich dich zu einer Tasse Tee einlade, brauchst du doch nicht so ein üppiges Geschenk mitzubringen.
*Don't be so silly! (What are you up to now?) If I invite you to have a cup of tea, you don't need to bring me such an extravagant present.*

sich ins **Geschirr** legen (fig.): cf. sich ins **Zeug** legen

das schöne (schwache) **Geschlecht:** *the fair (weaker; gentle) sex*

Vieles, was über das schöne (schwache) Geschlecht geschrieben wird, ist lauter Humbug.
*Much that is written about the fair (weaker; gentle) sex is nothing but humbug.*

auf den **Geschmack** kommen: *to develop (to acquire; to get) a taste for s. th.; to get (to come) to like s. th.*

Zuerst wollte ich keinen Rotwein trinken, ich bin aber allmählich auf den Geschmack gekommen.
*At first I did not want to drink red wine, but I have gradually developed (acquired; got) a taste for it (got [come] to like it).*

Über **Geschmack** läßt sich nicht streiten (Die **Geschmäcker** sind verschieden) (Sprichw.): *There is no accounting for taste; Tastes differ*

Der eine fährt gern ans Meer, der andere ins Gebirge. Über Geschmack läßt sich nicht streiten (Die Geschmäcker sind eben verschieden).
*Some like to go to the seaside, some into the mountains. There is just no accounting for taste (Tastes just differ).*

wie **geschmiert** gehen: cf. wie am **Schnürchen** gehen

Nun hat's aber **geschnappt!** (fam.): cf. Das ist doch die **Höhe!**

**geschniegelt** und gebügelt (gestriegelt) sein: *to be as bright (neat) as a new pin; to be spick and span; to be as fresh as a daisy; to be as smart as a guardsman; to be dressed up to the nines (colloq.).* Cf. auch: seinen feinsten **Staat** tragen

Du siehst so unordentlich aus. Nimm dir ein Beispiel an deinem Vetter, der immer (so) geschniegelt und gebügelt (gestriegelt; pikfein angezogen; wie aus dem Ei gepellt) ist.
*You look so untidy. Take an example from your cousin, who is always as bright (neat) as a new pin (spick and span; as fresh as a daisy; as smart as a guardsman; dressed up to the nines).*

**geschraubt** (fig.): *forced; mannered; stilted; affected*

Der geschraubte Stil dieses Schriftstellers gefällt mir nicht.
*I do not like this author's forced (mannered) style.*

grobes (schweres) **Geschütz** auffahren (fig.): *to bring up one's heavy artillery; to bring one's heavy guns to bear*

Meine Kritik war doch nicht bösartig gemeint. Er braucht nicht gleich grobes (schweres) Geschütz aufzufahren.
*My criticism was not intended to be spiteful. He does not need to bring up his heavy artillery (to bring his heavy guns to bear).*

**Geschwätz**: cf. **Klatsch** und **Tratsch**

ein **Gesellschaftstier** sein: *to be a society man (woman etc.; a social animal)*

Dein Onkel ist nicht gern allein; er ist ein ausgesprochenes Gesellschaftstier.
*Your uncle does not like being alone; he is a real society man (social animal).*

j.en zu **Gesicht** bekommen: *to set eyes on s.b.; to see something of s.b.*

Ich habe deine Schwester seit Monaten nicht mehr zu Gesicht bekommen.
*I have not set eyes on (seen anything of) your sister for months.*

wie aus dem **Gesicht** geschnitten: cf. wie aus den **Augen** geschnitten

j.em im **Gesicht** geschrieben stehen (fig.): cf. j.em auf der **Stirn** geschrieben stehen

ein **Gesicht** machen (wie sieben [drei] Tage Regenwetter): *to pull (to make) a face as long as a wet Sunday; to put on a woe-begone expression; to pull (to make) a face like a yard of pump-water (sl.)*

Der Junge machte ein Gesicht (wie sieben [drei] Tage Regenwetter; machte eine Leichenbittermiene; setzte eine Totengräbermiene auf), weil ihm niemand etwas geschenkt hatte.
*The boy made (pulled) a face as long as a wet Sunday (like a yard of pump-water; put on a woe-begone expression) because nobody had given him any presents.*

j.em etwas ins **Gesicht** sagen: *to tell s.b. s.th. to his face.* Cf. auch: **klipp** und klar sagen

Ich habe dem Schuster ins Gesicht gesagt, daß ich mit seiner Arbeit gar nicht zufrieden sei.
*I told the cobbler to his face that I was not at all satisfied with his work.*

ein schiefes **Gesicht** machen: *to pull a sulky (long) face; to look grumpy (colloq.)*

Als er hörte, daß er zu Hause bleiben mußte, machte er ein schiefes Gesicht (Maul).
*When he heard that he had to stay at home, he pulled a sulky (long) face (looked grumpy).*

einer Sache ins **Gesicht** schlagen (fig.): *to fly in the face of s.th.; to be an affront (an insult) to s.th.; to offend against s.th.*

Ein solches Benehmen schlägt dem guten Ton ins Gesicht.
*Such behaviour flies in the face of good manners (is an affront [insult] to good manners; offends against good manners).*

j.em ins **Gesicht** springen (fig.): cf. j.em an die **Kehle** fahren

j.em zu **Gesicht** stehen: *to suit s.b.'s complexion*

Steht mir die Farbe meiner Bluse gut zu Gesicht, oder sehe ich zu blaß aus?
*Does the colour of my blouse suit my complexion, or do I look too pale?*

j.em wieder vors **Gesicht** treten: cf. j.em wieder unter die **Augen** treten

das **Gesicht** wahren (fig.): *to save (one's) face*

Er versuchte krampfhaft, das Gesicht zu wahren, konnte aber seine Scham nicht verheimlichen.
*He tried desperately to save (his) face but could not disguise his shame.*

sein wahres **Gesicht** zeigen (fig.): *to show (to reveal) o.s. in one's true colours; to show (to reveal) one's true nature; to show the cloven hoof.* Cf. auch: die **Karten** aufdecken

Nun hat dieser Mann, der immer so ehrlich tat, sein wahres Gesicht gezeigt.
*That man, who always pretended to be so honest, has now shown (revealed) himself in his true colours (shown [revealed] his true nature; shown the cloven hoof).*

**Gesichter** schneiden: cf. **Grimassen** schneiden

j.en aus dem **Gesichtskreis** verlieren: cf. j.es **Spur** verlieren

**Gesindel:** cf. **Pack**

**Gespenster** sehen (fig.): *to see ghosts; to imagine (to see) things*

Du siehst ja Gespenster, wenn du glaubst, daß die Kirche einen goldenen Wetterhahn hat. Sie hat nie einen gehabt.
*You are seeing ghosts (imagining [seeing] things) if you think that the church has a golden weather-cock. It has never had one.*

nicht wissen, was **gespielt** wird (fig.): *not to know what is going on (what it is all about); not to know what's up (colloq.)*

Ich bin gerade erst angekommen und weiß nicht, was hier gespielt wird (worum es sich hier dreht [handelt]).
*I have only just arrived and do not know what is going on (what's up) here (what it is all about).*

Es ist nichts so fein **gesponnen,** es kommt doch ans Licht der Sonnen (Sprichw.): *Murder will out (prov.); You cannot keep anything quiet for ever*

Mehrere Jahre hindurch war es der Polizei unmöglich, den Mörder ausfindig zu machen. Jetzt aber wurde der Täter entlarvt. Es ist nichts so fein gesponnen, es kommt doch ans Licht der Sonnen.
*For many years it was impossible for the police to discover the murderer. Now, however, the criminal has been unmasked. Murder will out (You cannot keep anything quiet for ever).*

**gespuckt** (der Vater usw.) sein (fam.): cf. wie aus den **Augen** geschnitten sein

nicht von **gestern** sein (fam.): *not to be born yesterday; not to be as green (as simple) as that.* Cf. auch: nicht aus **Dummsdorf** sein

Das können Sie unerfahrenen Leuten erzählen, aber nicht mir. Ich bin doch nicht von gestern.
*You can tell that to inexperienced people but not to me. I wasn't born yesterday (I'm not as green [simple] as that).*

**gestiefelt** und gespornt sein (fig.): *to be booted and spurred; to be all dressed up; to be in full dress; to be on top line (colloq.)*

Wir standen schon um halb zehn gestiefelt und gespornt vor der Haustür, aber das Auto kam erst um zehn Uhr.
*We were standing at the door at half-past nine, booted and spurred (all dressed up; in full dress; on top line), but the car did not come until ten o'clock.*

wie **gestochen** schreiben: *to write like copperplate*

Ich erkenne die schöne Schrift auf dem Umschlag. Es ist die meines Vaters; er schreibt wie gestochen.
*I recognise the beautiful writing on the envelope. It is my father's; he writes like copperplate.*

j.em **gestohlen** bleiben können (fig. u. fam.): cf. j.em den **Buckel** herunterrutschen können; Scher' dich zum **Henker!**

**gestunken** und gelogen sein: cf. **erstunken** und erlogen sein

Aber sonst bist du **gesund!** (fam.): cf. (Aber) sonst geht's dir **gut!**

sich **gesund** machen (fam.: sich gesund stoßen) (fig.): cf. sein **Schäfchen** ins trockene bringen

**gesund** und munter sein: cf. auf der **Höhe** sein

**Getratsch(e)** (fam.): cf. **Klatsch** und Tratsch

(ein) großes **Getue** machen (fam.): cf. (viel) **Brimborium** um etwas machen

**Gewäsch** (fam.): cf. **Klatsch** und Tratsch

sich **gewaschen** haben (fig. u. fam.): *to hit the mark; to strike home*

Seine heftige Kritik in der Zeitung hatte sich gewaschen (war nicht von Pappe) und war auch völlig berechtigt.
*His violent criticism in the paper hit the mark (struck home) and was entirely justified, too.*

ein **gewecktes** Kind sein: *to be a bright child*

Die Lehrer interessieren sich für diesen Jungen sehr, weil er ein besonders (auf)gewecktes Kind ist.
*The teachers are very interested in this boy because he is a particularly bright child.*

So haben wir nicht **gewettet!** (fig.): *Things have not turned out as we planned (expected); That was not what we expected; We did not reckon with that*

Infolge deines Vorschlages habe ich viel Geld verloren. So hatten wir nicht gewettet!
*As a result of your suggestion I have lost a lot of money. Things have not turned out as we planned (expected; That was not what we expected; We did not reckon with that).*

ins **Gewicht** fallen (fig.): *to carry weight; to affect the issue; to be of some account*

Es ist unvermeidlich, daß bei den Arbeitern solche Preisunterschiede ins Gewicht fallen.
*It is inevitable that such price-variations should carry weight with (affect the issue for; be of some account to) the workers.*

nicht ins **Gewicht** fallen (fig.): *to be of no consequence (no account; no relevance); to count for nothing*

Daß Sie mit der theoretischen Seite dieser Arbeit völlig vertraut sind, fällt nicht ins Gewicht; denn für diesen Posten müssen Sie praktische Erfahrung (gehabt) haben.
*It is of no consequence (account; relevance; It counts for nothing) that you are thoroughly familiar with the theoretical side of this work, because for this post you must have had practical experience.*

großes **Gewicht** auf etwas legen (fig.): *to attach great importance to s.th.; to lay great stress on s.th.* Cf. auch: **viel** auf j.en (etwas) geben

Wir legen großes Gewicht (großen Wert) darauf, daß unsere Kinder eine gediegene Schulbildung erhalten.
*We attach great importance to (We lay great stress on) seeing that our children get a sound education.*

schief **gewickelt** sein (fig. u. fam.): cf. auf dem **Holzwege** sein

**gewieft (gewiegt)** sein (fam.): cf. **durchtrieben** sein

j.em aufs **Gewissen** fallen: *to weigh ([heavily]; to be) on s. b.'s conscience.* Cf. auch: j.em wie ein **Alp** auf der Seele liegen; j.em schwer auf die **Seele** fallen

Es fällt mir schwer aufs Gewissen, daß ich die Verabredung versäumt habe.
*It weighs ([heavily]; It is) on my conscience that I missed the appointment.*

j.en auf dem **Gewissen** haben: *to have s.b. on one's conscience; to have s.b. to answer for*

Der Verbrecher, der gerade verhaftet wurde, hat eine ganze Reihe von Opfern auf dem Gewissen.
*The criminal who has just been arrested has a whole series of victims on his conscience (to answer for).*

sich kein **Gewissen** aus etwas machen: *to have no scruples (qualms) about s.th.*

Dieser Mann hat sich kein Gewissen daraus gemacht, das Finanzamt hinsichtlich seines wahren Einkommens irrezuführen.
*This man had no scruples (qualms) about misleading the tax office over his real income.*

j.em ins **Gewissen** reden: *to appeal to s.b.'s conscience*

Als seine Eltern ihm ins Gewissen redeten, gab Jakob zu, die Birnen gestohlen zu haben.
*When his parents appealed to his conscience, James admitted to having stolen the pears.*

ein **Gewitter** bricht los (fig. u. fam.): *the storm breaks.* Cf. auch: ein **Donnerwetter** loslassen

Einen Augenblick beherrschte sich Vater noch; dann aber brach ein Gewitter los, und er schimpfte uns tüchtig aus.
*For a moment father controlled himself, but then the storm broke, and he scolded us roundly.*

**gewogen** und zu leicht befunden werden (fig.): *to have been weighed in the balance and found wanting*

Der leichtsinnige Angestellte wurde aus der Firma entlassen. Er war gewogen und zu leicht befunden worden.
*The careless employee was dismissed from the firm. He had been weighed in the balance and found wanting.*

j.em **gewogen** bleiben können (fam.): cf. j.em den **Buckel** herunterrutschen können

j.em **gewogen** sein: *to be well (favourably) disposed towards s.b.; to be favourably inclined towards s.b.* Cf. auch die umgekehrte Konstruktion unter: bei j.em gut **angeschrieben** sein

Meine Vorgesetzten sind mir sehr gewogen.
*My superiors are very well (favourably) disposed (very favourably inclined) towards me.*

ein **Gewohnheitstier** sein: *to be a creature of habit*

Mein Vater schaltet jeden Tag die Mittagsnachrichten im Radio ein, obwohl er nicht immer zuhört. Der Mensch ist eben ein Gewohnheitstier.

*My father switches the radio on for the midday news every day, although he does not always listen. Man is simply a creature of habit.*

Jung **gewohnt,** alt getan (Sprichw.): cf. **Jung** gewohnt, alt getan

Wie **gewonnen,** so zerronnen (Sprichw.): *Lightly (Easy) come, lightly (easy) go (prov.)*

Er hat sein Geld leicht verdient und es leichtsinnig ausgegeben. Wie gewonnen, so zerronnen.
*He earned his money easily and spent it recklessly. Lightly (Easy) come, lightly (easy) go.*

**Gezeter** (fam.): cf. **Zeter** und Mordio

die **Gicht** kriegen (fam.): sich **grün** und blau ärgern

**Gift** und Galle speien (spucken) (fig.): *to give vent to one's spleen; to see red.* Cf. auch: aus der **Haut** fahren

Der Bäckermeister spie (spuckte) Gift und Galle (Feuer und Flammen), wenn einer seiner Gesellen zu spät zur Arbeit kam.
*The master-baker gave vent to his spleen (saw red) whenever one of his apprentices came late to work.*

**Gift** auf etwas nehmen können (fig.): *to stake one's life on s.th.; to take one's oath on s.th.; to bet one's (sweet) life on s.th. (colloq.)*

Solche unberechtigte(n) Vorwürfe lasse ich mir nicht gefallen; darauf können Sie Gift nehmen.
*I am not going to put up with such unjust reproaches; you can stake your life (take your oath; bet your [sweet] life) on that.*

**giftig** (fam.: eine **Giftnudel)** sein (fig.): *to be a viper; to be poisonous (venomous; vicious)*

Seine Frau kann manchmal recht giftig (eine richtige Giftnudel) sein.
*His wife can sometimes be a real viper (really poisonous [venomous; vicious]).*

(seine) **Giftpfeile** schleudern (fig.): *to launch one's poisonous darts*

Er ist ein unangenehmer Mensch. Gegen jedermann schleudert er (seine) Giftpfeile.
*He is an unpleasant person. He launches his poisonous darts at everybody.*

ein **Gimpel** sein (fig.): cf. ein **Einfaltspinsel** sein

j.en mit **Glacéhandschuhen** anfassen (fig.): *to handle s.b. with velvet gloves (kid gloves); to handle s.b. gingerly*

Wenn Sie keinen Streit mit diesem Schneider haben wollen, müssen Sie ihn mit Glacéhandschuhen (Samthandschuhen; seidenen Handschuhen) anfassen (wie ein rohes Ei behandeln).
*If you do not want to quarrel with that tailor, you must handle him with velvet gloves (kid gloves; gingerly).*

eine **Glanzleistung** vollbringen: *to perform (to accomplish) a brilliant (magnificent) feat; to do o. s. proud (colloq.)*

Mit euerm Sieg über diese sehr bekannte Handballmannschaft habt Ihr wirklich eine Glanzleistung vollbracht.
*By your victory over that very famous handball team you have performed (accomplished) a really brilliant (magnificent) feat (have done yourselves proud).*

der **Glanzpunkt** sein: cf. die **Krönung** sein

zu tief ins **Glas** geguckt haben: cf. zu tief in den **Becher** geguckt haben

Wer im **Glashaus** sitzt, soll nicht mit Steinen werfen (Sprichw.): *People who live in glass houses should not throw stones (prov.)*

Wer selbst in einer heiklen Lage ist, kann es sich nicht leisten, andere zu kritisieren. Wer im Glashaus sitzt, soll nicht mit Steinen werfen.
*A person who is himself in a delicate situation cannot afford to criticise others. People who live in glass houses should not throw stones.*

j.en (etwas) **glatt** ablehnen: cf. j.en (etwas) **rundweg** ablehnen

j.en aufs **Glatteis** führen (fig.): *to mislead s.b.; to lead s.b. up the garden path; to lead s.b. astray; to lead s.b. a wild-goose-chase*

Mit dieser Frage wollte unser Lehrer uns aufs Glatteis führen, wir haben aber richtig antworten können.
*Our master wanted to mislead us (to lead us up the garden path [astray; a wild-goose-chase]) with that question, but we were able to answer correctly.*

Wer's **glaubt,** wird selig! (fam.): cf. Das kannst du deiner **Großmutter** erzählen!

**Gleich** und Gleich gesellt sich gern (Sprichw.): *Birds of a feather flock together (prov.)*

Dieses Lokal ist immer voller Verbrecher. Gleich und Gleich gesellt sich gern.
*This café is always full of criminals. Birds of a feather flock together.*

**Gleiches** mit Gleichem vergelten: *to pay s.b. back (in his own coin); to return like for like; to give tit for tat*

Ich werde seinen unhöflichen Brief höflich und sachlich beantworten. Ich denke nicht daran, Gleiches mit Gleichem zu vergelten (es ihm mit gleicher Münze heimzuzahlen).
*I shall reply to his impolite letter politely and objectively. I have no intention of paying him back ([in his own coin]; of giving tit for tat; of returning like for like).*

j.en aus dem (seelischen) **Gleichgewicht** bringen: *to throw s.b. off his balance; to upset s.b.; to disturb s.b.'s equilibrium (equanimity)*

Diese Enttäuschung hat meine Kusine ganz aus dem (seelischen) Gleichgewicht gebracht.
*This disappointment has thrown my cousin completely off her balance (has upset my cousin completely; has completely disturbed my cousin's equilibrium [equanimity]).*

etwas ins **Gleichgewicht** bringen (fig.): *to balance (to equate) s.th.*

Die Stadtverwaltung versprach, Ausgaben und Einnahmen ins Gleichgewicht zu bringen.
*The town council undertook to balance expenditure and income (to equate expenditure with income).*

sich das **Gleichgewicht** halten (fig.): *to strike a balance; to balance each other*

(Die) Vorzüge und Mängel halten sich bei diesem Menschen das Gleichgewicht.
*This person's virtues and shortcomings strike a balance (balance each other).*

j.em in die **Glieder** fahren: *to strike s.b. to the core; to pierce s.b. to the quick (the core).* Cf. auch: einem durch **Mark** und Bein gehen

Diese traurige Nachricht fuhr uns allen (mächtig) in die Glieder (Knochen; ging ... an die Nieren).
*This sad news struck us all to the core (pierced us all to the quick [core]).*

j.em in den **Gliedern** liegen (stecken): *to feel s.th. in one's bones*

Liegt (Steckt) Ihnen auch das milde Frühlingswetter (wie Blei) in den Gliedern (Knochen)?
*Can you feel the mild spring weather in your bones as well?*

wissen (merken), was die **Glocke** geschlagen hat (fig.): cf. merken, woher der **Wind** weht

etwas an die große **Glocke** hängen (fig.): cf. etwas **ausposaunen**

über alles seine **Glossen** machen: *always to have some comment to make; always to find fault with s. th.; always to have a jibe ready*

Ich wünschte, mein Sohn hätte mehr Respekt vor meinen Ansichten. Wenn ich meine Meinung ausspreche, macht er über alles seine Glossen.
*I wish my son had more respect for my views. He always has some comment to make (finds fault with something; has a jibe ready) when I express my opinion.*

**Glotzaugen** machen (fam.): cf. **Stielaugen** machen

das **Glück** mit Füßen treten (fig.): cf. das Glück mit **Füßen** treten

etwas auf gut **Glück** tun: *to do s.th. on the off chance; to take pot luck (colloq.).* Cf. auch: aufs **Geratewohl**

Wenn man etwas auf gut Glück tut, kann man sich nicht wundern, wenn es nicht gelingt.

*If one does something on the off chance, one cannot be surprised if it does not succeed (If one takes pot luck, one cannot . . . if one does not succeed).*

j.em lächelt das **Glück**: cf. j.es **Weizen** blüht

von **Glück** sagen können: *to be able to thank one's lucky stars; to be able to consider o.s. lucky*

Unser Großonkel konnte von Glück sagen, daß er seine Grippe so rasch überstanden hat.
*Our great-uncle could thank his lucky stars (could consider himself lucky) that he got over his influenza so quickly.*

**Glück** im Unglück sein: *to be a blessing in disguise*

Infolge der Explosion in der Fabrik wurde der Arbeiter von seinem nervösen Stottern geheilt. Das war wirklich Glück im Unglück.
*As a result of the explosion in the factory the workman was cured of his nervous stutter. It was really a blessing in disguise.*

mehr **Glück** als Verstand haben: *to have more luck than sense*

Der leichtsinnige Knabe brach durch die dünne Eisdecke ein, wurde aber von einem beherzten Mann gerettet. Er hatte wirklich mehr Glück als Verstand.
*The reckless boy fell through the thin ice but was rescued by a courageous man. He certainly had more luck than sense.*

das **Glück** an allen Zipfeln erwischt haben: cf. ein **Glückspilz** sein

ein **Glückskind** sein: *tb be a child of Fortune; to be born under a lucky star; to be one of Fortune's favourites; to be born with a silver spoon in one's mouth*

Mein Neffe ist ein wahres Glückskind ([Sonntagskind]; ist unter einem günstigen Stern geboren [mit einem goldenen Löffel auf die Welt gekommen]). Alle seine Unternehmungen gelingen ihm.
*My nephew is a real child of Fortune (was really born under a lucky star [with a silver spoon in his mouth]; is one of Fortune's real favourites). He succeeds in all his enterprises.*

ein **Glückspilz** sein: *to be a lucky fellow; to be a lucky dog (beggar) (colloq.)*

In der letzten Ziehung der Lotterie bin ich ein Glückspilz gewesen (habe ich das Glück an allen Zipfeln erwischt); ich habe tausend Mark gewonnen.
*I was a lucky fellow (dog; beggar) in the last sweepstake draw: I have won a thousand marks*

in den **Glückstopf** greifen (fig.): cf. das große **Los** ziehen b)

**Gnade** für Recht ergehen lassen: *to temper justice with mercy*

Der Verteidiger schlug vor, bei dem jugendlichen Angeklagten noch einmal Gnade für Recht ergehen zu lassen.
*Defending counsel pleaded for justice to be tempered with mercy once more in the case of the youthful defendant.*

sein **Gnadenbrot** essen (bei Tieren: fressen): *to eat one's bread of charity*

> Unser alter Hund ist fast erblindet; er frißt jetzt sein Gnadenbrot.
> *Our old dog is nearly blind; he is now eating his bread of charity.*

j.em den **Gnadenstoß** geben: *to give s. b. the coup de grâce; to put s. b. out of his agony*

> Mein Pferd hat beide Vorderbeine gebrochen. Man muß ihm den Gnadenstoß geben.
> *My horse has broken both forelegs. He will have to be given the coup de grâce (put out of his agony).*

sich nicht mit **Gold** aufwiegen lassen: *to be worth its weight in gold*

> Die Fähigkeiten meines Stellvertreters sind von unschätzbarem Wert. Sie lassen sich nicht mit Gold aufwiegen.
> *My deputy's qualities are of incalculable value. They are worth their weight in gold.*

Es ist nicht alles **Gold,** was glänzt (Sprichw.): *All that glitters is not gold (prov.)*

> Man soll sich durch den (äußeren) Schein nicht täuschen lassen. Es ist nicht alles Gold, was glänzt.
> *One must not be deceived by appearances. All that glitters is not gold.*

Morgenstunde hat **Gold** im Munde (Sprichw.): a) *The early bird catches the worm (prov.);* b) *Early to bed and early to rise, Makes a man healthy, wealthy and wise (prov.)*

> a) Wir wollen morgen früh schon um 6 Uhr aufstehen, um zu sehen, ob wir im Sommerschlußverkauf etwas Billiges kaufen können. Morgenstunde hat Gold im Munde.
> b) Wenn ich morgens früh um 7 Uhr anfange, kann ich meine Arbeit immer erledigen. Morgenstunde hat Gold im Munde.
> *a) We want to get up at six o'clock tomorrow morning to see if we can buy something cheap in the summer sales. The early bird catches the worm.*
> *b) When I start at seven o'clock in the morning, I am always able to finish my work. Early to bed and early to rise, Makes a man healthy, wealthy and wise.*

treu wie **Gold** sein: *to be as true as steel (as faithful as a bloodhound)*

> Unser altes Kindermädchen, das schon seit zehn Jahren bei uns ist, hat sich als zuverlässig und treu wie Gold erwiesen.
> *Our old nursemaid, who has been with us for ten years, has proved to be reliable and as true as steel (as faithful as a bloodhound).*

**Gold** öffnet jede Tür (Sprichw.): *Money opens all doors (Money rules the world) (prov.)*

> Wenn du dem Portier ein paar Mark gibst, wird er dir sicher eine Karte für die Oper besorgen. Gold öffnet jede Tür (Geld regiert die Welt).

*If you give the porter a few marks, he will be sure to get you a ticket for the opera. Money opens all doors (rules the world).*

eine **Goldgrube** sein (fig.): cf. eine **Fundgrube** sein

**goldig** (fig.): *charming; delightful*

Der Vater hatte seinem Töchterchen ein wirklich goldiges Kleid gekauft.
*The father had bought his little daughter a really charming (delightful) dress.*

etwas auf die **Goldwaage** legen (fig.): *to weigh (to ponder) s.th.*

Man sollte jedes Wort dieses Philosophen auf die Goldwaage (Waage; Waag-schale) legen.
*One should weigh (ponder) this philosopher's every word.*

den **Gordischen** Knoten durchschlagen (zerhauen): cf. den Gordi-schen **Knoten** durchschlagen (zerhauen)

j.en (etwas) aus der **Gosse** auflesen (fig.): *to pick s.b. (s.th.) up in the gutter*

Der jetzt berühmt gewordene Schauspieler wurde gleichsam aus der Gosse (von der Straße) aufgelesen.
*The now famous actor was, so to speak, picked up in the gutter.*

aussehen wie ein junger **Gott**: cf. ein **Adonis** sein

**Gott** behüte (bewahre)!: *God (Heaven; The Lord) forbid!*

Gott bewahre (behüte)! (Da sei Gott vor!) Einen so unsinnigen Vorschlag hätten wir Ihnen nie gemacht!
*God (Heaven; The Lord) forbid! We would never have suggested anything so stupid to you.*

**Gott** sei Dank!: *Thank goodness!; Thank Heaven(s)!; Thank God!*

Gott sei Dank geht es mir seit zwei Jahren wieder besser.
*I have been better these last two years, thank goodness (Heaven[s]; God).*

in **Gott** entschlafen: *to pass away; to return (to go) to one's creator.* Cf. auch: j.es **Lebenslicht** erlischt

Nach einem frommen Leben ist die Nonne sanft in Gott entschlafen.
*After a pious life the nun quietly passed away (returned [went] to her creator).*

leben wie **Gott** in Frankreich: cf. leben wie ein **Fürst**

in **Gottes** Hand stehen: *to be in God's hand(s) (in God's charge)*

Der Pfarrer wies darauf hin, daß das Volk in Gottes Hand stehe.
*The clergyman pointed out that the nation was in God's hand(s) (charge).*

Hilf dir selbst, so hilft dir **Gott** (Sprichw.): *God helps those who help them-selves (prov.)*

Anstatt hilflos dazusitzen, solltest du deine Interessen verteidigen. Hilf dir selbst, so hilft dir Gott (Sich regen bringt Segen).
*Instead of sitting there helplessly you ought to defend your interests. God helps those who help themselves.*

leider **Gottes:** *I am (We are etc.) very much afraid that . . .; to my (our etc.) (very) great regret*

Leider Gottes ist vorerst mit einer Wetterbesserung nicht zu rechnen.
*I am (We are etc.) very much afraid that we cannot (To my [our etc.] [very] great regret we cannot) count on an improvement in the weather for the moment.*

den lieben **Gott** einen guten Mann sein lassen (fam.): *to let things take their course (take care of themselves); to let things go their own way; to leave things to themselves*

Wir wollen einmal eine Woche von unserer Arbeit ausspannen und den lieben Gott (den Herrgott) einen guten Mann sein lassen.
*We are going to take a week off from our work and let things take their course (take care of themselves; go their way; and leave things to themselves).*

in **Gottes** Namen: a) *for goodness' (pity's; Heaven's) sake;* b) (etwas tun): *to go on and do s. th.*

a) Sag' doch in Gottes (Kuckucks) Namen (zum Kuckuck nochmal; um Gottes [Himmels] willen; Mann Gottes, Menschenskind; Mensch Meier), warum du so lange geschwiegen hast.
b) Tu' es in Gottes Namen; du weißt aber, daß ich dich gewarnt habe.
*a) For goodness' (pity's; Heaven's) sake tell me why you kept quiet so long.*
*b) Go on and do it, then, but you know that I've warned you.*

wie **Gott** den Schaden besieht: *when one comes to look at it; when it comes to the point*

Die Stenotypistin war überraschend schnell mit ihrer Arbeit fertig, aber wie Gott den Schaden besah, war ihr Text voller Tippfehler.
*The shorthand-typist finished her work surprisingly quickly, but when one came to look at it (when it came to the point), her text was full of typing errors.*

ganz von **Gott** verlassen sein (fig. u. fam.): *to have (quite) taken leave of one's senses; to be out of one's mind.* Cf. auch: nicht richtig im **Dachstübchen** sein

Sind Sie denn ganz von Gott verlassen? Sie wollen fortfahren, ohne das Haus abzuschließen?
*Have you (quite) taken leave of your senses (Are you out of your mind)? You're going away without locking the house?*

Da sei **Gott** vor: cf. **Gott** behüte (bewahre)!

um **Gottes** willen!: a) cf. in **Gottes** Namen!; b) cf. (Ach) du liebe **Zeit!**

weiß **Gott**: *Heaven (goodness; God) knows*

Das haben wir dir weiß Gott oft genug gesagt.
*We've told you that often enough, Heaven (goodness; God) knows.*

**Gott** und die Welt (an)treffen (fig.): *to meet all and sundry (the whole world).*
Cf. auch: **Hinz** und Kunz

In Veranstaltungen dieser Art trifft man Gott und die Welt (an).
*In performances of this kind one meets all and sundry (the whole world).*

Das wissen die **Götter!**: *Heaven (Goodness; God) (only) knows*

Wann diese Straße endlich einmal gepflastert (werden) wird, das wissen die Götter (das weiß der Himmel [Kuckuck; Teufel])!
*Heaven (Goodness; God) (only) knows when this street will finally be made up.*

eine **Gottesgabe** (ein **Gottessegen**) sein: *to be a blessing (godsend)*

Für Krankenhäuser ist das Fernsehen eine wahre Gottesgabe (ein wahrer [Gottes]segen).
*For hospitals television is a real blessing (godsend).*

sich **gottserbärmlich** (zum **Gotterbarmen**) fühlen: cf. sich **hundeelend** fühlen

**gottverlassen** (fig.): *God-forsaken; dead-and-alive (colloq.)*

Heinrich wohnt 20 Kilometer weit weg in einer gottverlassenen Gegend.
*Henry lives twenty kilometres away in a God-forsaken (dead-and-alive) area.*

**gottvoll** (fig.): *priceless*

Du mußt unbedingt diese gottvolle Geschichte lesen.
*You really must read this priceless story.*

Er bringt mich noch ins **Grab**: *He'll be the death of me yet (colloq.)*

Ich kann mit meinem unbändigen Sohn einfach nichts anfangen und bin beinahe am Verzweifeln. Er bringt mich noch ins Grab.
*I simply cannot do anything with my unruly son, and am almost in despair. He'll be the death of me yet.*

sich sein eigenes **Grab** graben (fig.): *to dig one's own grave; to prepare one's own downfall; to seal one's own fate; to cut one's own throat; to make a rod for one's own back*

Mit dieser unüberlegten Handlung hat sich der Botschafter sein eigenes Grab gegraben (Waffen gegen sich geschmiedet).
*By this unconsidered action the ambassador has dug his own grave (prepared his own downfall; sealed his own fate; cut his own throat; made a rod for his own back).*

ein feuchtes (nasses) **Grab** finden: *to go to a watery grave*

Das Flugzeug stürzte ins Meer, und alle Insassen fanden ein feuchtes (nasses) Grab.
*The aeroplane crashed into the sea and all the occupants went to a watery grave.*

sich im **Grabe** umdrehen (fig.): *to turn in one's grave*

Der Gründer dieses Eisenwerkes würde sich im Grabe umdrehen, wenn er wüßte, wie verschwenderisch seine Nachfolger arbeiten.
*The founder of this iron-works would turn in his grave if he knew how wastefully his successors were working.*

verschwiegen wie das **Grab** sein: *to be as silent as the grave*

Ein Dolmetscher, der zu diplomatischen Verhandlungen zugezogen wird, muß vor der Öffentlichkeit verschwiegen wie das Grab sein.
*An interpreter who is called in to diplomatic negotiations must be as silent as the grave in public.*

auf **Granit** beißen (fig.): *to knock one's head against (to kick) a brick wall (colloq.)*

Wir baten Vater, uns ein Motorrad zu kaufen, bissen jedoch bei ihm auf Granit. Er lehnte es schroff ab.
*We asked father to buy us a motor-cycle, but we were knocking our heads against (kicking) a brick wall. He brusquely rejected it.*

etwas cum **grano salis** nehmen: *to take s.th. with a pinch (a grain) of salt*

Die Geschichte von seinen Abenteuern im Gebirge muß man cum grano salis nehmen.
*One must take the story of his adventures in the mountains with a pinch (grain) of salt.*

ins **Gras** beißen (fig. u. fam.): cf. um die **Ecke** gehen

das **Gras** wachsen hören (fig.): *to have (to keep) one's ear close to the ground; to get wind of everything; to be able to hear a fly clear its throat (colloq.)*

Woher hast du denn schon wieder diese neue Nachricht? Du hörst ja das Gras wachsen (die Flöhe husten [niesen]; du bist ja überschlau).
*Where did you get this further item of news? You have certainly got (You certainly keep) your ear close to the ground (You certainly get wind of everything; You can hear a fly clear its throat).*

**Gras** über etwas wachsen lassen (fig.): *to bury s.th.; to sink s.th. in oblivion; to let bygones be bygones*

Wir wollen endlich Gras über diese leidige Angelegenheit wachsen lassen und sie nicht mehr erwähnen.
*Let us now bury this disagreeable affair (sink this disagreeable affair in oblivion) and not mention it any more (Let us now let bygones be bygones and not mention this disagreeable affair any more).*

**grasgrün:** *grass-green*

Unser Nachbar hat seine Fensterläden grasgrün anstreichen lassen.
*Our neighbour has had his window-shutters painted grass-green.*

**grau** in grau (fig.): *sombre; gloomy*

Die Zeitungen schreiben über die politische Lage sehr pessimistisch und malen die Zukunft grau in grau.
*The papers report very pessimistically about the political situation and paint the future in sombre (gloomy) colours.*

Die **Grazien** haben nicht an ihrer Wiege gestanden: *The (three) Graces were not present at her birth*

Obwohl die Grazien nicht an Emmas Wiege gestanden haben, hat sie jetzt doch einen Mann gefunden.
*Although the (three) Graces were not present at Emma's birth, she has now found a husband after all.*

zum **Greifen** naheliegen (fig.): *to be within reach (within one's grasp); to be at hand; to be in sight*

Wir dürfen jetzt den Mut nicht verlieren, denn der Erfolg liegt zum Greifen nahe.
*We must not lose courage now, for success is within reach (within our grasp; at hand; in sight).*

sich in engen **Grenzen** halten (fig.): *to keep within narrow limits*

Die Preiserhöhungen haben sich im verflossenen Jahr in engen Grenzen gehalten.
*Price-increases have kept within narrow limits during the past year.*

eine **Grenze** ziehen (fig.): cf. einen **Trennungsstrich** ziehen

etwas im **Griff** haben: cf. den **Kniff** heraushaben

ein **Grillenfänger** sein (fam.): *to be a grumpy dog (an old misery) (colloq.)*

Karl ist zumeist schlechter Laune, ein richtiger Grillenfänger.
*Charles is generally in a bad mood – a real grumpy dog (real old misery).*

**Grimassen** schneiden: *to pull (to make) faces*

Es ist nicht schön von dir, daß du hinter seinem Rücken Grimassen (Fratzen; Gesichter) schneidest.
*It is not nice of you to pull (make) faces behind his back.*

aus dem **Gröbsten** heraus sein : *to be (to have got) over the worst; to be almost out of the wood*

Wir haben schon vorige Woche angefangen, das Haus zu putzen. Jetzt sind wir glücklicherweise aus dem Gröbsten heraus.
*We started to clean the house last week. Fortunately we are now over (we have now got over) the worst (are almost out of the wood now).*

Der **Groschen** ist gefallen (fig. u. fam.): *s.th. has sunk in; The penny has dropped (colloq.)*. Cf. auch: j.em geht ein **Licht** auf

Er hat lange gebraucht, um meine Einwände gegen seinen Plan einzusehen, aber jetzt ist (bei ihm) der Groschen endlich gefallen.
*He took a long time to realise my objections to his plan, but now they have sunk in (the penny has dropped) at last.*

nicht (recht) bei **Groschen** sein (fam.): cf. nicht richtig im **Dachstübchen** sein

seine paar **Groschen** zusammenhalten: *to keep hold of (to keep a grip on) one's purse-strings; to hold on to one's coppers (one's cash)*

Wenn man nicht sehr vermögend ist, sollte man bescheiden leben und seine paar Groschen zusammenhalten.
*If one is not very wealthy, one should live modestly and keep hold of (keep a grip on) one's purse-strings (hold on to one's coppers [cash]).*

etwas **groß** und breit erzählen: cf. etwas **lang** und breit erzählen

**groß** und klein: *great and small (alike)*

Auf diesem Fest hat sich groß und klein königlich amüsiert.
*Great and small (alike) enjoyed themselves royally at that party.*

eine unbekannte **Größe** sein (fig.): cf. ein unbeschriebenes **Blatt** sein

im **großen** und ganzen: *on the whole; in the main; by and large*

Im großen und ganzen können wir mit unserer Fußballmannschaft zufrieden sein.
*On the whole (In the main; By and large) we can be content with our football team.*

**Großmannssucht:** *megalomania; swollen-headedness (colloq.)*

Dieser Geschäftsreisende leidet an wahrer Großmannssucht.
*This commercial traveller suffers from real megalomania (swollen-headedness).*

Das kannst du deiner **Großmutter** erzählen (fam.): *(You can) tell that to the marines (to your grandmother) (colloq.)*

Du sagst, du seiest schon zweimal über den Rhein geschwommen? Das kannst du deiner Großmutter erzählen (anderen aufbinden; Wer's glaubt, wird selig!).
*You say that you swam across the Rhine twice? (You can) tell that to the marines (to your grandmother).*

**großspurig** auftreten: *to behave bombastically; to shoot a line (colloq.)*. Cf. auch: **angeben**; den **Mund** vollnehmen

Der Sohn des Fabrikanten tritt überall großspurig (breitspurig) auf.
*The manufacturer's son behaves bombastically (shoots a line) everywhere.*

Wer andern eine **Grube** gräbt, fällt selbst hinein (Sprichw.): *He who digs a pit for others will fall in it himself (prov.)*

Erich bildet sich ein, sehr schlau gehandelt zu haben. Er wird aber bald einsehen, daß das Ergebnis seiner Handlung ein ganz anderes sein kann. Wer andern eine Grube gräbt, fällt selbst hinein.
*Eric imagines that he has acted very cunningly, but he will soon realise that the result of his action may be quite different. He who digs a pit for others will fall in it himself.*

sich **grün** und blau (schwarz) ärgern (fam.): *to be wild (furious); to go (to be) red with annoyance; to be hopping mad (sl.)*

Über den ungezogenen Nachbarsjungen hat sich der Gärtner grün und blau (gelb und grün; [grün und] schwarz; die Kränke [Schwindsucht] an den Hals; zu Tode) geärgert (hat der Gärtner die Kränke gekriegt; sich den Hals vollgeärgert).
*The gardener was wild (furious) with (went [was] red with annoyance [hopping mad] at) the rude boy next door.*

j.en **grün** und blau schlagen (fam.): *to beat s.b. black and blue.* Cf. auch: j.en zu **Brei** schlagen

Ihr Sohn hat, wie ich höre, diesen Jungen grün und blau (blau und grün; braun und blau; krumm und lahm) geschlagen.
*I hear that your son has beaten this boy black and blue.*

dasselbe in **Grün** (fig.): *the same thing over again*

Was sie jetzt sagt, hat ihr Mann bereits gestern gesagt. Es ist dasselbe in Grün.
*What she says now, her husband already said yesterday. It is the same thing over again.*

**grün** vor Neid werden: *to turn (to go) green with envy*

Als meine Schwester erfuhr, daß ich ein neues Fahrrad bekommen hatte, wurde sie grün vor Neid.
*When my sister learned that I had got a new bicycle, she turned (went) green with envy*

j.em nicht **grün** sein: *not to be on good terms with s.b.; to bear (to have) a grudge against s.b.*

Seitdem ich diesen Streit mit deinem Bruder hatte, ist er mir nicht mehr grün.
*Since I had that quarrel with your brother he has not been on good terms with me any more (has borne [had] a grudge against me).*

ein **Grünschnabel** sein (fig.): *to be a greenhorn*

So ein Grünschnabel (junger Dachs; grüner Junge; Gelbschnabel; Milchgesicht; Naseweis; So einer, der noch nicht trocken hinter den Ohren ist) kann doch kein ordentliches Gespräch mit Erwachsenen führen.
*A greenhorn like that cannot carry on a proper conversation with adults.*

nicht auf j.es **Grund** und Boden gewachsen sein (fig.): cf. nicht j.es **Hirn** entsprungen sein

einer Sache auf den **Grund** gehen (fig.): *to go (to get) to the root (bottom; core) of a matter*

> Wir müssen zunächst einmal die Tatsachen feststellen und der Sache auf den Grund gehen.
> *We must first ascertain the facts and go (get) to the root (bottom; core) of the matter.*

j.en in **Grund** und Boden verdammen: *to condemn s.b. down to the ground (outright; out of hand); to condemn s.b. left, right and centre (colloq.)*

> Sie dürfen ihn nicht in Grund und Boden verdammen, bevor seine Schuld feststeht.
> *You must not condemn him down to the ground (outright; out of hand; left, right and centre) before his guilt is proved.*

etwas in den **Grundfesten** erschüttern (fig.): *to shake s.th. to its (very) foundations (to the core; to the roots)*

> Durch diese tragischen Erfahrungen wurde mein politischer Glauben in den Grundfesten erschüttert.
> *As a result of these tragic experiences my political faith was shaken to its (very) foundations (to the core [roots]).*

**grundhäßlich** sein: cf. **mordshäßlich** sein

**grundschlecht** sein (einen grundschlechten Charakter haben): *to be rotten to the core (through and through)*

> Dieser Verbrecher ist grundschlecht (hat einen grundschlechten Charakter).
> *This criminal is rotten to the core (through and through).*

den **Grundstein** legen (fig.): *to lay the foundation(s); to form the basis*

> Ein gemeinsames Erlebnis hat den Grundstein zu unserer Freundschaft gelegt.
> *An experience which we shared laid the foundation(s) (formed the basis) of our friendship.*

**grundverschieden** sein: *to be as different as chalk and cheese; to be poles apart; There is a world of difference (all the difference in the world) between . . .; It is a far cry from s.th. to s.th.*

> In ihrem Charakter sind die beiden Brüder grundverschieden (verschieden wie Feuer und Wasser [Tag und Nacht]; himmelweit voneinander entfernt; Zwischen den beiden Brüdern ist im Charakter ein himmelweiter Unterschied).
> *The characters of the two brothers are as different as chalk and cheese (are poles apart; There is a world of difference [all the difference in the world] between the characters of the two brothers; It is a far cry from the character of the one brother to that of the other).*

auf **Grußfuß** mit j.em stehen: *to have a nodding acquaintance with s.b.; to pass the time of day with s.b.*

> Wir kennen uns nicht näher, sondern stehen nur auf Grußfuß miteinander.
> *We do not know each other well but only have a nodding acquaintance (with each other) (only pass the time of day with each other).*

**Grütze** im Kopf haben (fam.): *to have plenty of gumption (nous) (colloq.); to have one's head screwed on the right way (colloq.)*

Dieser Student hat entschieden Grütze im Kopf. Ich bin überzeugt, daß er ein glänzendes Examen machen wird.
*This student has certainly got plenty of gumption (nous; has certainly got his head screwed on the right way). I am sure that he will pass his examination brilliantly.*

Haus und Hof (Herd) durch die **Gurgel** jagen (fig.): *to drink o.s. and one's family into the workhouse (colloq.)*

Dieser Landwirt ist leider dem Trunk ergeben; er hat Haus und Hof (Herd) durch die Gurgel gejagt.
*This landlord has unfortunately given himself over to drink; he has drunk himself and his family into the workhouse.*

j.em an die **Gurgel** wollen: cf. j.em an die **Kehle** fahren

seinen **Gürtel** enger schnallen (fig.): cf. seinen **Riemen** enger schnallen

aus éinem **Guß** sein (fig.): *to be (all) of a piece*

Ihr Roman ist flott geschrieben und logisch aufgebaut. Er ist aus éinem Guß (Wurf).
*Your novel is stylishly written and logically constructed. It is (all) of a piece.*

**Gut** und Blut opfern: *to sacrifice health and wealth (life and property)*

Im zweiten Weltkrieg mußte auch die Zivilbevölkerung Gut und Blut opfern.
*In the Second World War civilians, too, had to sacrifice health and wealth (life and property).*

(Aber) sonst geht's dir **gut**? (fam.): *You're sure you're feeling all right? (colloq.); Are you all right in the head? (colloq.).* Cf. auch: nicht richtig im **Dachstübchen** sein

Du willst, wie ich höre, mit dem Fahrrad nach Indien fahren. (Aber) sonst geht's dir gut (bist du gesund; Dich haben sie wohl zu heiß gebadet; Du bist wohl nicht von hier; Du hast wohl Tinte getrunken [gesoffen])?
*I hear you want to cycle to India. You're sure you're feeling all right (Are you all right in the head)?*

sich **gut** mit j.em stehen: cf. auf gutem **Fuß** mit j.em stehen

Wer weiß, wozu es **gut** ist: *who knows – it may be all to the good (all for the best)*

Meine Bemühungen um einen Posten bei der Stadtverwaltung sind gescheitert, aber wer weiß, wozu es gut ist; vielleicht finde ich in der Industrie eine weit besser bezahlte Stellung.
*My efforts to get a job in local government have failed, but who knows – it may be all to the good (for the best); maybe I shall find a far better-paid position in industry.*

(Ach) du liebe (meine) **Güte!**: *Good Heavens!; Good Lord!; Heavens above!; Good gracious!; My goodness!*

> (Ach) du liebe (meine) Güte (du liebe Zeit; du lieber Himmel)! Dieses Fenster ist zerbrochen.
> *Good Heavens! (Good Lord!; Heavens above!; Good gracious!; My goodness!) This window is broken.*

des **Guten** zuviel sein: *to be too much of a good thing*

> Für eine Woche kann ich fortfahren, aber zwei Wochen wären des Guten zuviel.
> *I can go away for a week, but two weeks would be too much of a good thing.*

des **Guten** zuviel tun: *to overstep (to overshoot) the mark; to overdo things; to go too far*

> Dieser gutherzige Mann hilft jedem, der sich an ihn wendet, ohne seine Rechtschaffenheit zu prüfen. Man kann des Guten auch zuviel tun.
> *This good-natured man helps everybody who turns to him, without testing his honesty. One can overstep (overshoot) the mark (overdo things; go too far).*

sich **gütlich** an etwas tun: *to revel in s. th.; to do o. s. proud with s. th. (colloq.); to dig into s. th. (sl.).* Cf. auch: sich etwas zu **Gemüte** führen

> Bei der Geburtstagsfeier haben wir uns an den vielen Speisen gütlich getan.
> *At the birthday party we revelled in (did ourselves proud with; dug into) the many dishes.*

# H

j.em stehen die **Haare** zu Berge (fig.): *s. b.'s hair stands on end*

> Mir standen die Haare zu Berge, als ich die vielen unbezahlten Rechnungen meines Sohnes sah.
> *My hair stood on end when I saw my son's many unpaid bills.*

ein **Haar** in etwas finden (fig.): *to find a snag (drawback; stumbling-block) to s. th.* Cf. auch: Die Sache hat einen **Haken**

> Nachdem Sie uns so enttäuscht haben, haben wir ein Haar darin (in der Suppe) gefunden, Sie nochmals zu empfehlen.
> *Since you have disappointed us like this, we have found it a snag (drawback; stumbling-block) to recommending you again.*

sich mit j.em in die **Haare** geraten (fig.): *to have a row with s. b.; to fall out with s. b.; to fall foul of s. b.; to get on the wrong side of s. b.*

> Ihr Vater gerät sich immer mit seinem Schwiegersohn in die Haare (Wolle;

kriegt sich immer ... an die Köpfe; wird mit ... immer böse), wenn sie sich über Politik unterhalten.

*Her father always has a row (falls out) with (falls foul [gets on the wrong side] of) his son-in-law when they talk politics.*

j.em aufs **Haar** gleichen: (nur plur.) *to be as like as two peas.* Cf. auch: j.em wie aus den **Augen** geschnitten sein

Die Tochter gleicht ihrer Mutter aufs Haar.
*The daughter and the mother are as like as two peas.*

sich keine grauen **Haare** wachsen lassen (fig.): *not to get grey hairs; not to lose any sleep; not to worry one's head*

Laß dir wegen der Prüfungen keine grauen Haare wachsen.
*Don't get grey hairs (lose any sleep; worry your head) about the examinations.*

Es ist kein gutes **Haar** an ihm (fig.): *There is not a single good point about him (He has not a single good point); There is not a thing to be said in his favour*

Man behauptet, dieser Geschäftsmann habe einen schlechten Charakter und es sei kein gutes Haar an ihm.
*People say that that salesman has a bad character and that there is not a single good point about him (that he has not a single good point; that there is not a thing to be said in his favour).*

kein gutes **Haar** an j.em lassen (fig.): cf. keinen guten **Faden** an j.em lassen

an einem **Haar** hängen (fig.): cf. an einem seidenen **Faden** hängen

an den **Haaren** herbeigezogen sein (fig.): *to be far-fetched; to be stretching things too far*

Ein Vergleich zwischen diesen beiden Theaterstücken scheint uns an den Haaren herbeigezogen.
*A comparison between these two plays seems to us far-fetched (to be stretching things too far).*

etwas an den **Haaren** herbeiziehen (fig.): *to drag (to bring) s.th. in; to lug s.th. in (colloq.)*

Wenn von Abenteuern die Rede ist, versucht mein Bruder immer, seine Kriegserlebnisse an den Haaren herbeizuziehen.
*When the conversation is about adventures, my brother always tries to drag (bring; lug) in his war experiences.*

j.em die **Haare** vom Kopf fressen (fig. u. fam.): *to eat s.b. out of house and home; to eat the crumbs out of s.b.'s pocket (colloq.).* Cf. auch: einen **Mordshunger** haben

Seine Kinder haben einen solchen Appetit, daß sie ihm die Haare vom Kopf fressen.
*His children have such an appetite that they would eat him out of house and home (eat the crumbs out of his pocket).*

j.em kein **Haar** krümmen (fig.): *not to hurt (to harm) a hair of s.b.'s head.* Cf. auch: keiner **Fliege** etwas zuleide tun

Der Führer der Rebellen erklärte, daß er den Gefangenen kein Haar krümmen werde.
*The leader of the rebels declared that he would not hurt (harm) a hair of the prisoners' heads.*

**Haare** lassen (fig.): *to be in a bad way; to be seriously hit*

Infolge des Zusammenbruchs der Versicherungsgesellschaft mußten viele Leute Haare (Federn) lassen.
*As a result of the insurance company's going bankrupt, many people were in a bad way (were seriously hit).*

sich mit j.em in den **Haaren** liegen (fig.): *to be at loggerheads (at daggers drawn; at sixes and sevens; in a state of war; on bad terms; at odds) with s.b.*

Seit Jahren liege ich mich mit meinem Schwager in den Haaren (stehe [lebe] ich mit . . . auf gespanntem Fuße [auf Hauen und Stechen; auf Kriegsfuß]).
*I have been at loggerheads (at daggers drawn; at sixes and sevens; in a state of war; on bad terms; at odds) with my brother-in-law for years.*

sich die **Haare** (aus)raufen (fig.): *to tear one's hair*

Als ich erfuhr, daß ich die Prüfung nicht bestanden hatte, hätte ich mir die Haare (den Bart) (aus)raufen können.
*When I learned that I had not passed the examination, I could have torn my hair.*

aufs **Haar** (genau) stimmen (fig.): *to be correct to a T (to the letter); to be dead right (right [dead] on the mark); to be correct down to the last detail*

Ich weiß, daß der Bericht in unserer Zeitung über dieses Unglück aufs Haar (genau) (haargenau; [bis] aufs i-Tüpfelchen) stimmt, denn ich habe es selbst miterlebt.
*I know that the report in our paper about that accident is correct to a T ([to the letter; down to the last detail]; is dead right; is right on the mark; is dead on the mark), because I witnessed the accident myself.*

ein **Haar** in der Suppe finden (fig.): cf. ein **Haar** in etwas finden

um ein **Haar** (fig.): a) *all but; within a hair's breadth; it is a near thing (a close shave; touch-and-go); to come within an ace;* b) (als Ausruf) *That was touch-and-go! (That was a close shave! That was a near thing!)*

a) Um ein Haar (Um Haaresbreite) wäre ich ins Wasser gefallen.
b) „Um ein Haar! (Um Haaresbreite!)", sagte der Mann, der von einem Auto, das schnell um die Ecke fuhr, beinahe überfahren wurde.
*a) I all but fell (I was within a hair's breadth of falling; It was a near thing [a close shave; touch-and-go] whether I fell; I came within an ace of falling) into the water.*
*b) "That was touch-and-go (a close shave; a near thing)!" said the man, as he was almost run over by a car that drove quickly round the corner.*

um kein **Haar** (fig.): *not a jot (a whit; a scrap; a bit; an iota)*

Die Änderung deiner Jacke hat nichts genutzt. Sie sitzt um kein Haar (Jota) besser als vorher.

*The alteration to your jacket has not done any good. It does not fit a jot (whit; scrap; bit; an iota) better than before.*

**Haare** auf den Zähnen haben (fig. u. fam.): *to be a tough (a formidable) proposition; to have plenty of fight (in one); to be a Tartar; to be a tough (rough) customer (colloq.)*

Lassen Sie sich mit diesem Juristen nur nicht ein; er hat bekanntlich Haare auf den Zähnen.

*Don't have any dealings with that lawyer; he is known to be a tough (formidable) proposition (to have plenty of fight [in him]; to be a Tartar [a tough (rough) customer]).*

um **Haaresbreite**: cf. um ein **Haar**

**haargenau** stimmen: cf. aufs **Haar** stimmen

etwas **haarklein** erzählen: *to tell s. th. down to the last (smallest; minutest) detail*

Meine Freundin hat mir haarklein wiedererzählt, was du zu ihr gesagt hast.

*My friend told me down to the last (smallest; minutest) detail what you said to her.*

ein **Haarspalter** sein (fig.): cf. ein **Kleinigkeitskrämer** sein

**Haarspalterei(en)** treiben (fig.): *to split hairs; to indulge in hair-splitting (in quibbling)*

Manche Gelehrte sind pedantisch genau und treiben Haarspalterei(en).

*Many scholars are pedantically precise and split hairs (indulge in hair-splitting [quibbling]).*

bis in die **Haarspitzen (-wurzeln)** erröten: cf. **knallrot** werden

**haarsträubend** (fig.): *hair-raising; enough to make one tear one's hair (to turn one's hair grey)*

Sein Benehmen gegenüber den Gästen war einfach haarsträubend (hanebüchen).

*His behaviour in front of the guests was simply hair-raising (enough to make one tear one's hair (enough to turn one's hair grey).*

**Hab** und Gut verlieren: *to lose (all) one's goods and chattels (bag and baggage; [all] one's worldly wealth [possessions])*

Eine Bombe traf unser Haus, und wir verloren Hab und Gut (unsere Siebensachen).

*A bomb fell on our house and we lost (all) our goods and chattels (bag and baggage; [all] our worldly wealth [possessions]).*

für alles zu **haben** sein: *to be ready for anything; to be game for anything (colloq.)*

Er wird sicher bereit sein, diese abenteuerliche Tour mitzumachen; denn er ist für alles zu haben.
*He will certainly be prepared to go on this adventurous trip, for he is ready (game) for anything.*

Da **haben** wir's: cf. eine schöne *(nette)* **Bescherung**

nicht alle beieinander **haben** (fam.): cf. nicht richtig im **Dachstübchen** sein

ein **Habenichts** sein: *to be a penniless fellow (a have-not)*

Wir begreifen nicht, warum dieses reiche Mädchen so einen Habenichts geheiratet hat.
*We cannot understand why that rich girl has married such a penniless fellow (have-not).*

sich die **Hacken** nach etwas ablaufen (fig.): cf. sich die **Füße** ablaufen

**Hackfleisch** aus j.em machen (fig. u. fam.): *to make mincemeat out of s.b. (colloq.); to knock s.b. for six (sl.).* Cf. auch: j.en zu **Brei** schlagen

Vor diesem Menschen habe ich keine Angst. Wenn er mich bedroht, werde ich Hackfleisch (Kleinholz) aus ihm machen (ihn ins Mus [in die Wurst] hacken).
*I am not afraid of that person. If he threatens me, I shall make mincemeat of him (knock him for six).*

j.en sticht der **Hafer** (fig.): cf. j.en reitet der **Teufel**

**hageldicht:** *like hailstones*

Die Gewehrkugeln kamen hageldicht geflogen.
*The bullets flew past like hailstones.*

**hageln** (fig.): *to rain down*

Es hagelte Schläge auf den unehrlichen Jungen, der seine Klassenkameraden betrogen hatte.
*Blows rained down on the dishonest boy who had swindled his classmates.*

**Hahn** im Korb sein (fig.): *to be cock of the roost (of the walk); to rule the roost.* Cf. auch: das **Heft** in der Hand haben

Meine Schwester gab ein Teekränzchen, und als einziger Herr dabei war ich natürlich Hahn im Korb.
*My sister gave a tea-party, and as the only gentleman there, I was naturally cock of the roost (walk; I naturally ruled the roost).*

Kein **Hahn** kräht danach (fig.): *Nobody cares (gives) a brass farthing (cares tuppence [two hoots; a straw; a jot; a rap; a scrap])*

Unser Arzt ist sehr tüchtig. Kein Hahn kräht danach, daß er auf der Schule nur ein sehr mittelmäßiger Schüler gewesen ist.
*Our doctor is very efficient. Nobody cares (gives) a brass farthing (tuppence; two hoots; a straw; a jot; a rap; a scrap; Nobody worries a scrap [jot]) that he was only a very mediocre pupil at school.*

beim ersten **Hahnenschrei** aufstehen: *to get up at cock-crow; to rise with the lark.* Cf. auch: in aller **Herrgottsfrühe**

Beim ersten Hahnenschrei standen wir auf (Wir waren früh aus den Federn) und machten uns auf den Weg.
*At cock-crow we got up ( We rose with the lark) and set out.*

Die Sache hat einen **Haken** (fig.): *There is a snag (stumbling-block; drawback) to s. th.* Cf. auch: Da liegt der **Hase** im Pfeffer!

Wir möchten gern umziehen, aber die Sache hat einen Haken: Wohnungen sind heutzutage sehr teuer.
*We should like to move, but there is a snag (stumbling-block; drawback) to it: flats are very expensive nowadays.*

etwas **halb** und halb tun: *to half-do s. th.; as good as to do s. th.; more-or-less to do s. th.*

Da ich mich nicht wohlfühle, bin ich halb und halb entschlossen, an dem Ausflug nicht teilzunehmen.
*Since I do not feel well, I have half-decided (as good as decided; more-or-less decided) not to go on the excursion.*

j.es bessere **Hälfte**: *s. b.'s better half*

Er ist ein sehr angenehmer Mensch, aber seine bessere Hälfte kann ich nicht ausstehen.
*He is a very pleasant person but I cannot stand his better half.*

j.em den **Hals** abschneiden (fig. u. fam.): *to rook s. b. (left and right) (colloq.); to clean s. b. out (colloq.); to see s. b. off (sl.).* Cf. auch: j.en **rupfen**

Wir betreten dieses Luxusrestaurant nicht mehr, weil man einem dort den Hals abschneidet.
*We do not go to that luxury restaurant any more, because they rook you ( [left and right]; clean you out; see you off) there.*

sich den **Hals** ausrenken (verrenken; den Hals recken): *to crane (to crick) one's neck*

Als die Königin vorüberfuhr, renkten sich alle Zuschauer den Hals nach ihr aus (reckten [verrenkten sich] alle Zuschauer den Hals nach ihr).
*As the Queen drove by, all the onlookers craned (cricked) their necks to see her.*

bis an den **Hals** in Schulden stecken: cf. bis an (über) die **Ohren** in Schulden stecken

j.em vom **Halse** bleiben (fig.): cf. j.em vom **Leibe** bleiben

j.em den **Hals** brechen (j.en den Hals kosten) (fig.): *to cost s. b. his neck*

'Ein solches Wagnis würde Ihnen den Hals brechen (Sie den Hals kosten).
*Such a risk would cost you your neck.*

sich **Hals** und Bein brechen (sich den Hals brechen): *to break one's neck;*
*to come a cropper (colloq.)*

> Bei diesem Glatteis auf dem Bürgersteig kann man sich Hals und Bein brechen
> (sich den Hals brechen).
> *With this ice on the pavement one can break one's neck (can come a cropper).*

j.em um den **Hals** fallen: *to fly (to rush) into s.b.'s arms; to fall on s.b.'s neck*

> Als meine Schwester die schönen Geschenke sah, fiel sie der Mutter um den Hals.
> *When my sister saw the lovely presents, she flew (rushed) into her mother's arms (fell on*
> *her mother's neck).*

etwas in den falschen **Hals** bekommen (kriegen) (fig.): cf. etwas in die
falsche **Kehle** bekommen (kriegen)

es geht um j.es **Hals**: *s.b.'s life is at stake; It is a matter of life and death*

> Bei der Gerichtsverhandlung wußte der Verbrecher, daß es um seinen Hals
> (um Kopf und Kragen; ihm an den Kragen) ging.
> *During the trial the criminal knew that his life was at stake (that it was a matter*
> *of life and death).*

j.en (etwas) auf dem **Halse** haben (fig.): *to have s.b. (s.th.) on one's hands; to*
*be burdened (saddled) with s.b. (s.th.); to have s.b. (s.th.) on one's back (colloq.);*
*to be lumbered with s.b. (s.th.) (colloq.)*

> Sein Onkel und seine Tante haben noch immer die ganze Verwandtschaft auf
> dem Halse (Buckel; Nacken), da sie keine andere Unterkunft finden kann.
> *His uncle and aunt still have all their relatives on their hands (on their backs; are still*
> *burdened [saddled; lumbered] with all their relatives), because they cannot find any other*
> *accommodation.*

j.em eine Person (Sache) vom **Halse** halten (fig.): *to keep s.b. (s.th.) away*
*from s.b.*

> Der Schuldiener wurde angewiesen, den Lehrern Bettler und Hausierer vom
> Halse zu halten.
> *The school caretaker was instructed to keep beggars and hawkers away from the teachers.*

j.em zum **Halse** heraushängen (herauswachsen) (fig. u. fam.): cf. etwas
bis **dahin** (stehen) haben

j.en **Hals** über Kopf hinauswerfen: cf. j.en **achtkantig** hinauswerfen

etwas **Hals** über Kopf tun: *to do s.th. at breakneck speed (in double-quick time;*
*at the double; post-haste)*

> Plötzlich bekam ich ein Telegramm von zu Hause, und ich mußte Hals über
> Kopf zurückfahren.
> *I suddenly got a telegram from home and had to return at breakneck speed (in double*
> *quick time; at the double; post-haste).*

aus vollem **Halse** lachen: *to laugh at the top of one's voice*. Cf. auch: sich **totlachen**

Bei dieser witzigen Bemerkung unseres Lehrers lachten wir aus vollem Halse (aus Leibeskräften).
*At this witty remark of our teacher's we laughed at the top of our voices.*

sich etwas (j.en) auf den **Hals** laden (fig.): *to saddle (to burden) o.s. with s.th. (s.b.); to lumber o.s. with s.th. (s.b.) (colloq.)*

Warum hat er sich nun auch noch diese mühsame Arbeit auf den Hals geladen (Arbeit aufgehalst)?
*Why has he saddled (burdened; lumbered) himself with this laborious work as well?*

j.en einer Person vom **Halse** schaffen (fig.): *to get rid of s.b.; to send s.b. on his way; to send s.b. packing (colloq.)*

Ein Polizist erschien und schaffte mir den lästigen Bettler vom Halse (jagte . . . zum Teufel).
*A policeman appeared and got rid of the beggar (sent the beggar on his way [packing]) who was pestering me.*

j.em eine Person auf den **Hals** schicken (fig.): *to set s.b. on to s.b. (on s.b.'s track)*

Da der Fischhändler mit seinen Zahlungen im Rückstand war, schickte ihm sein Lieferant gleich den Gerichtsvollzieher auf den Hals.
*As the fishmonger was behind with his payments, his supplier immediately set the bailiff on to him (on his track).*

sich den **Hals** verrenken: cf. sich den **Hals** ausrenken

sich den **Hals** vollärgern (fam.): cf. sich **grün** und blau ärgern

den **Hals** nicht voll genug kriegen können (fig. u. fam.): *never to be able to get enough; never to have had one's fill*

Mein Bruder will immer mehr Geld verdienen. Er kann den Hals nicht voll genug kriegen.
*My brother wants to earn more and more money. He has never been able to get enough (has never had his fill).*

sich j.em an den **Hals** werfen: *to throw (to cast) o.s. at s.b.; to force o.s. on s.b.* Cf. auch: sich an j.en **wegwerfen**

Ein Mädchen, das sich den Männern an den Hals (in die Arme) wirft, wird allgemein verachtet.
*A girl who throws (casts) herself at (forces herself on) men is universally despised.*

ein **Halsabschneider** sein (fig.): *to be a shark (sharper; pirate; robber) (colloq.)*

Dieser Geschäftsmann steht in dem Rufe, ein Halsabschneider zu sein.
*This shopkeeper has the reputation of being a shark (sharper; pirate; robber).*

**Halsabschneiderei** sein (fig.): *to be daylight (absolute; sheer) robbery; to be extortion(ate)*

Solche Preise zu verlangen, ist Halsabschneiderei (Beutelschneiderei; Geldschneiderei; Nepperei).
*It is daylight (absolute; sheer) robbery (It is extortion[ate]) to ask such prices.*

j.em **Hals- und Beinbruch** wünschen (fig. u. fam.): *to wish s.b. good luck (all the best); Look after yourself!*

Sie wollen morgen nach Amerika fliegen? Da wünsche ich Ihnen Hals- und Beinbruch.
*So you're flying to America tomorrow? Well, I wish you good luck (all the best) (Look after yourself!).*

etwas bis zur **Halskrause** (stehen) haben (fam.): cf. etwas bis **dahin** (stehen) haben

einer Sache **Halt** gebieten: *to put a stop to s.th.; to call a halt to s.th.*

Man sollte solchen gefährlichen Versuchen Halt gebieten (einen Damm entgegensetzen).
*One ought to put a stop (call a halt) to such dangerous experiments.*

Es gibt kein **Halten** mehr: *There is no end to it; There is no more stopping me (you etc.) (colloq.)*

Als der Metzger einmal der Spielleidenschaft verfallen war, da gab es kein Halten mehr.
*Once the butcher had developed a passion for gambling, there was no end to it (no more stopping him).*

(sehr) auf etwas **halten**: *to be (greatly) concerned about s.th.; to be (greatly) exercised over the question of s. th.*

Meine Mutter hält (sehr) auf Ordnung und Sauberkeit in unserm Haus.
*My mother is (greatly) concerned about (is [greatly] exercised over the question of) tidiness and cleanliness in our house.*

viel von j.em (etwas) **halten**: *to think a lot (a great deal) of s.b. (s.th.)*

Ich halte viel von meinem Sohn und bin überzeugt, daß er eine erfolgreiche Zukunft vor sich hat.
*I think a lot (a great deal) of my son and am convinced that he has a successful future in front of him.*

um auf besagten **Hammel** zurückzukommen (fig.): *to get back (to return) to the point (at issue); to resume; to return to our muttons (colloq.)*

Wir sind von unserem Thema, der modernen Malerei, abgeschweift. Um auf besagten Hammel zurückzukommen: Waren Sie schon in der neuen Kunstausstellung?

*We have strayed from our subject, modern painting. To get back (To return) to the point ([at issue]; To resume; To return to our muttons), have you been to the new art exhibition?*

j.en bei (an) den **Hammelbeinen** kriegen (fig. u. fam.): *to lick (to knock) s.b. into shape (colloq.).* Cf. auch: j.en in die **Kur** nehmen

„Ich werde Euch bei (an) den Hammelbeinen kriegen", sagte der Trainer zu den jungen Fußballspielern.
*"I'll lick (knock) you into shape", said the trainer to the young footballers.*

unter den **Hammer** kommen: *to be sold by auction; to come under the hammer*

Nach dem Tode des Juweliers ist sein ganzer Besitz unter den Hammer gekommen.
*After the jeweller's death all his property was sold by auction (came under the hammer).*

die **Hand** von j.em abziehen (fig.): *to withdraw one's support from s.b.;* (finanz.) *to cut s.b. off with a shilling*

Mit Recht hat der Onkel jetzt die Hand von seinem leichtsinnigen Neffen abgezogen und ihm keinen Pfennig mehr gegeben.
*The uncle rightly withdrew his support from his reckless nephew and did not give him another penny (The uncle rightly cut his nephew off with a shilling).*

j.en (etwas) an (der) **Hand** haben (fig.): *to have s.b. (s.th.) on hand; to have s.b. (s.th.) on tap (colloq.); to have s.b. (s.th.) lined up (colloq.)*

In kalten Wintern ist es ratsam, mehrere Kohlenhändler an (der) Hand zu haben.
*In cold winters it is advisable to have several coal merchants on hand (on tap; lined up).*

an **Hand** von: *on the strength (basis) of*

Ich kann dieses Ergebnis an Hand meiner eigenen Erfahrung voraussagen.
*I can foretell this result on the strength (basis) of my own experience.*

um j.es **Hand** anhalten: *to ask for s.b.'s hand (in marriage)*

Harald hat bei seinem ehemaligen Lehrer um die Hand seiner Tochter angehalten.
*Harold has asked his former teacher for his daughter's hand (in marriage).*

**Hand** anlegen: *to lend (to give) a (helping) hand*

Bei dem Transport des Klaviers mußten wir alle Hand anlegen.
*We all had to lend (give) a (helping) hand with moving the piano.*

j.em in die **Hände** arbeiten (fig.): *to play into s.b.'s hands*

Wir dürfen der Abstimmung nicht fernbleiben, denn sonst arbeiten wir der Gegenpartei in die Hände.
*We must not stay away from the plebiscite, for otherwise we shall play into the hands of the opposition.*

auf der **Hand** liegen (fig.): cf. **sonnenklar** sein

rasch bei der **Hand** sein (fig.): *to be quickly off the mark; to be on the spot; to jump in quickly*

Die Geschäftsleute sind mit Preiserhöhungen immer rasch bei der Hand.
*Shopkeepers are always quickly off the mark (always on the spot; Shopkeepers always jump in quickly) with price-increases.*

mit beiden **Händen** zugreifen (fig.): cf. die **Gelegenheit** beim Schopfe fassen

die Beine in die **Hand** nehmen (fig.): cf. die **Beine** in die Hand nehmen

sich die **Hände** binden lassen (fig.): *to allow one's hands to be tied; to allow o. s. to be hobbled (shackled)*

Der Minister hat es abgelehnt, sich durch einzelne Interessengruppen die Hände binden zu lassen.
*The minister refused to allow his hands to be tied (to allow himself to be hobbled [shackled]) by individual group interests.*

aus dritter **Hand** (fig.): *from a third party; by a roundabout way*

Daß mein Schwager eine bedeutende Erfindung gemacht hat, habe ich nicht direkt, sondern erst aus dritter Hand erfahren.
*I did not learn directly that my brother-in-law had made an important discovery, but only from a third party (by a roundabout way).*

etwas aus erster **Hand** haben (fig.): cf. etwas aus erster **Quelle** haben

j.em in die **Hände** fallen (fig.): *to fall into s. b.'s hands (clutches)*

Der lange gesuchte Schwindler ist jetzt endlich der Polizei in die Hände gefallen.
*The long sought-after swindler has now fallen into the hands (clutches) of the police at last.*

für j.en (etwas) die **Hand** ins Feuer legen (fig.): *to stake one's life (reputation) on s. th.; to swear to s. th.*

Von der Ehrlichkeit und Zuverlässigkeit meiner Angestellten bin ich so fest überzeugt, daß ich jederzeit meine Hand für sie ins Feuer legen (für sie geradestehen) würde.
*So firmly convinced am I of the honesty and reliability of my employees that I would stake my life (reputation) on it (swear to it) at any time.*

freie **Hand** haben (fig.): *to have a free hand; to be a free agent*

Wenn er in seiner Tätigkeit freie Hand hat, leistet er entschieden mehr.
*If he has a free hand (is a free agent) in his activity, he will definitely achieve more.*

j.em freie **Hand** lassen (fig.): *to give s.b. a free hand (carte blanche; the fullest scope)*

Wir lassen Ihnen völlig freie Hand (freies Spiel), wie Sie die Neuorganisation durchführen wollen.
*We are giving you a completely free hand (carte blanche; the fullest scope) to carry out the reorganisation.*

j.em aus der **Hand** fressen (fig. u. fam.): *to eat out of s.b.'s hand*

Früher war dieser Gefangene mürrisch und eigensinnig, aber jetzt frißt er den Aufsehern aus der Hand.
*Previously this prisoner was sulky and obstinate but now he eats out of the warders' hands.*

**Hand** und Fuß haben (fig.): *to make sense; to hang together; to add up (colloq.)*

Dieser Reporter ist sehr zuverlässig, und alles, was er schreibt, hat Hand und Fuß.
*This reporter is very reliable, and everything he writes makes sense (hangs together; adds up).*

weder **Hand** noch Fuß haben: cf. **ungereimtes** Zeug sein

sich mit **Händen** und Füßen gegen etwas sträuben (wehren): *to fight tooth and nail against s.th.; to fight with might and main against s.th.; to fight for all one is worth against s.th.; to kick and fight against s.th.*

Der Angestellte sträubte (wehrte) sich mit Händen und Füßen gegen das ungerechte Verhalten seines Chefs, aber vergebens.
*The clerk fought tooth and nail (with might and main; for all he was worth; kicked and fought) against his boss's unjust conduct, but with no avail.*

mit gebundenen **Händen** (fig.): *tied hand and foot; unable to move a finger*

Mit gebundenen Händen mußten wir zusehen, wie über unser Schicksal entschieden wurde.
*Tied hand and foot (Unable to move a finger), we had to watch our fate being decided.*

j.em zur **Hand** (an die Hand) gehen: *to give (to lend) s.b. a hand (a helping hand)*. Cf. auch: **Hand** anlegen

Gute Kinder gehen ihren Eltern im Haus und im Garten gern zur (an die) Hand.
*Good children willingly give (lend) their parents a (helping) hand in the house and in the garden.*

j.en den **Händen** der Gerechtigkeit ausliefern: *to bring s.b. to justice; to hand s.b. over to the law*

Der Mann, der den Straßenraub verübt hatte, wurde den Händen der Gerechtigkeit ausgeliefert.
*The man who had committed the street robbery was brought to justice (handed over to the law).*

eine glückliche **Hand** haben (fig.): *to have a lucky touch*

Bei der Wahl seiner Mitarbeiter hatte der Außenminister eine glückliche Hand.
*The foreign minister had a lucky touch in his choice of collaborators.*

in guten **Händen** sein (fig.): *to be in good hands*

Bei diesem Vormund ist die arme Waise in guten Händen.
*The poor orphan is in good hands with this guardian.*

**Hand** in Hand (fig.): *hand in hand; hand in glove*

Dieser Architekt arbeitet Hand in Hand mit dem Stadtrat.
*That architect works hand in hand (hand in glove) with the town council.*

von **Hand** zu Hand gehen: *to go (to pass) from hand to hand; to change hands
many times.* Cf. auch: durch viele **Hände** gehen

Die Briefmarkensammlung ging lange von Hand zu Hand, bevor ihr richtiger
Wert erkannt wurde.
*The stamp collection went (passed) from hand to hand (changed hands many times) before
its real value was recognised.*

**Hand** aufs Herz: *on one's honour; cross one's heart; honour bright; on the level
(colloq.)*

Hand aufs Herz (Auf Ehre und Gewissen; Ehrenwort), hast du als Kind nie
gelogen?
*On your honour (Cross your heart; Honour bright; On the level), did you never tell a lie
as a child?*

etwas fest in der **Hand** haben (fig.): *to have a firm grip on s. th.; to have s. th.
well under control (well in hand)*

Trotz der vielen Gerüchte hat der Ministerpräsident die Situation fest in der
Hand.
*In spite of the many rumours the prime minister has a firm grip on the situation (has the
situation well under control [in hand]).*

etwas in die **Hand** nehmen (fig.): *to take s. th. in hand; to take s. th. up*

Am besten werde ich diese Angelegenheit selbst in die Hand nehmen (in dieser . . . selbst das Heft ergreifen).
*I had better take this matter in hand (take this matter up) myself.*

j.em etwas in die **Hand** spielen (fig.): *to put s. th. into s. b.'s hands*

Der Zufall hat der Polizei einen weiteren Beweis für die Schuld des Angeklagten
in die Hand gespielt.
*Chance has put further proof of the accused's guilt into the hands of the police.*

keine **Hand** rühren (fig.): cf. keinen **Schlag** tun

die **Hände** über dem Kopf zusammenschlagen (fig.): cf. sich die **Augen** reiben etwas kurzer **Hand** ablehnen: *to reject s. th. out of hand (outright); to turn s. th. down flat*

> Die Delegation lehnte die neuen Bedingungen kurzer Hand ab.
> *The delegation rejected the new conditions out of hand (outright; turned the . . . down flat).*

kurzer **Hand**: cf. auf der **Stelle**

von langer **Hand** vorbereitet sein: *to have been prepared long beforehand (in advance)*

> Dieser Überfall war offensichtlich von langer Hand vorbereitet.
> *This attack was obviously prepared long beforehand (in advance).*

j.em die **Hand** fürs Leben reichen: *to give s. b. one's hand (in marriage)*

> Wem hat deine ältere Schwester die Hand fürs Leben gereicht?
> *To whom has your elder sister given her hand (in marriage)?*

mit leeren **Händen**: *empty-handed; with empty hands*

> Zu meiner Überraschung und Enttäuschung erschienen einige Gäste mit leeren Händen.
> *To my astonishment and disappointment a few guests appeared empty-handed (with empty hands).*

**Hand** an sich legen: cf. sich das **Leben** nehmen

die **Hand** auf etwas legen (fig.): *to commandeer s. th.; to put one's mark on s. th.*

> Der Stadtrat hat die Hand auf diese baufälligen Häuser gelegt und will sie abreißen lassen.
> *The town council has commandeered (put its mark on) these decrepit houses and wants to have them pulled down.*

j.em leicht von der **Hand** gehen: *s. th. comes easily to s. b.; to toss s. th. off.* Cf. auch: **kinderleicht** sein

> Es geht meinem Bruder leicht von der Hand, Gedichte zu verfassen.
> *Writing poems comes easily to my brother (My brother just tosses off poems).*

die letzte **Hand** anlegen (fig.): cf. die letzte **Feile** anlegen

zwei linke **Hände** haben (fig. u. fam.): *to be all thumbs*

> Karl stellt sich beim Paketpacken sehr ungeschickt an. Er scheint, zwei linke Hände zu haben.
> *Charles goes very clumsily about packing parcels. He seems to be all thumbs.*

eine lockere (lose) **Hand** haben (fam.): cf. ein loses **Handgelenk** haben

seine milde **Hand** auftun: *to put one's hand in one's pocket; to feel for one's purse*

Jeder tat seine milde Hand auf, als er den unglücklichen Krüppel sah.
*Everyone put his hand in his pocket (felt for his purse) when he saw the unhappy cripple.*

von der **Hand** in den Mund leben (fig.): *to live from hand to mouth (from day to day; from one day to the next)*

Nach dem Kriege mußten die meisten von uns längere Zeit von der Hand in den Mund leben.

*After the war most of us had to live from hand to mouth (from day to day; from one day to the next) for a considerable time.*

eine offene **Hand** haben (fig.): *to be open-handed (free-handed)*

Unsere Familie hat eine offene Hand für alle Bettler.

*Our family are open-handed (free-handed) to all beggars.*

j.es rechte **Hand** sein (fig.): *to be s.b.'s right-hand man (right arm)*

Durch seine Tüchtigkeit ist Wilhelm bereits nach fünf Jahren die rechte Hand des Chefs geworden.

*By dint of his efficiency William has become his boss's right-hand man (right arm) after only five years.*

sich die **Hände** reiben (fig.): *to rub one's hands (with glee)*

Wegen seines großen Erfolges wird er sich sicherlich die Hände gerieben haben.

*He is sure to have rubbed his hands (with glee) at his great success.*

sich die **Hand** reichen können (fig.): cf. vom gleichen **Schlage** sein

die **Hände** in den Schoß legen: *to twiddle one's thumbs*

Meine Mutter ist immer beschäftigt; sie kann nicht einfach dasitzen und die Hände in den Schoß legen.

*My mother is always busy; she cannot just sit and twiddle her thumbs.*

seine **Hand** im Spiel haben (fig.): cf. seine **Finger** im Spiel haben

j.en auf **Händen** tragen (fig.): *to wait on s.b. hand and foot; to dote on s.b.*

Das junge Ehepaar trägt sich gegenseitig auf Händen.

*The young couple wait on each other hand and foot (dote on each other).*

etwas zu treuen **Händen** übergeben: *to hand s.th. over for safe keeping (safe custody)*

Ich habe dem Bibliothekar dieses alte, seltene Buch zu treuen Händen übergeben.

*I have handed over that old and rare book to the librarian for safe keeping (custody).*

in (die) unrechte(n) **Hände** fallen (fig.): *to fall into the wrong hands; to get into the wrong company*

Der unschuldige Junge ist leider in (die) unrechte(n) Hände gefallen.
*The innocent boy has unfortunately fallen into the wrong hands (got into the wrong company).*

seine **Hände** in Unschuld waschen (fig.): *to wash one's hands of s. th. (of the whole thing)*

Mit diesem unehrlichen Plan will ich nichts zu tun haben. Ich wasche meine Hände in Unschuld.
*I will have nothing to do with this dishonest plan. I wash my hands of it (of the whole thing).*

etwas unter der **Hand** erfahren (fig.): *to hear s. th. sub rosa; to hear s. th. under the counter (colloq.); A little bird told me (colloq.)*

Ich habe unter der Hand erfahren, daß er sein Haus verkaufen will.
*I have heard sub rosa (under the counter; A little bird told me) that he wants to sell his house.*

unter der **Hand** etwas kaufen (fig.): *to buy s. th. under the counter (at the back door)*

Im Geschäft ist diese Art (von) Teppich sehr teuer, ich habe aber einen unter der Hand (hintenherum) durch einen Bekannten viel billiger gekauft.
*In the shops this kind of carpet is very expensive but I bought one under the counter (at the back door) much cheaper through a friend.*

unter der **Hand** etwas sagen (fig.): *to say s. th. off the record (on the Q. T.)*

Mein Freund hatte mir schon unter der Hand gesagt, daß ich die Stellung bekommen würde.
*My friend had already told me off the record (on the Q. T.) that I would get the job.*

durch viele **Hände** gehen: *to pass through many hands.* Cf. auch: von **Hand** zu Hand gehen

Dieses alte Buch ist schon durch viele Hände gegangen.
*This old book has passed through many hands.*

Viele **Hände** machen (der Arbeit) bald ein Ende (Sprichw.): *Many hands make light work (prov.)*

Wir sollten ihm alle dabei helfen, in seine neue Wohnung umzuziehen. Viele Hände machen (der Arbeit) bald ein Ende.
*We all ought to help him move into his new flat. Many hands make light work.*

mit vollen **Händen** geben (schenken): *to give with both hands*

Meine Eltern sind glücklich, wenn sie mit vollen Händen geben (schenken) können.
*My parents are happy when they are able to give with both hands.*

alle **Hände** voll zu tun haben (fig.): *to have one's hands full; to have one's work cut out.* Cf. auch: sein gerüttelt **Maß** haben; viel um die **Ohren** haben

> Mit der Vorbereitung des Lustspiels haben wir alle Hände voll zu tun (den Buckel voll Arbeit; unsere liebe Not).
> *We have got our hands full (got our work cut out) rehearsing the comedy.*

vor der **Hand** (fig.): *for the time being; for the moment (for the present)*

> Es ist kaum zu erwarten, daß vor der Hand die Vorschriften in dieser Hinsicht geändert werden.
> *It is hardly to be expected that the regulations will be altered in this respect for the time being (for the moment [the present]).*

Eine **Hand** wäscht die andere (Sprichw.): *You scratch my back and I'll scratch yours (colloq.)*

> Wir sollten uns gegenseitig in diesen Dingen unterstützen. Eine Hand wäscht die andere.
> *We ought to support each other in these matters. You scratch my back and I'll scratch yours.*

nicht von der **Hand** zu weisen sein (fig.): *s. th. is not to be denied (gainsaid); s. th. is not to be shrugged off; there is no getting away from s. th. (colloq.)*

> Die Schwäche der deutschen Fußballmannschaft ist nicht von der Hand zu weisen.
> *The weakness of the German football team is not to be denied (gainsaid; shrugged off; There is no getting away from the weakness of . . .).*

etwas zur **Hand** haben: *to have s. th. at hand (at one's elbow; handy)*

> Wenn man viel unterwegs ist, muß man immer einen Fahrplan zur Hand haben.
> *If one travels a lot, one must always have a timetable at hand (at one's elbow; handy).*

eine **Handbreit**: *an inch; a step; a shade*

> Wäre er eine Handbreit weitergegangen, so wäre er in den Abgrund gestürzt.
> *If he had gone an inch (a step; a shade) further, he would have fallen into the ravine.*

nicht wissen, worum es sich **handelt**: cf. nicht wissen, was **gespielt** wird

**händeringend** nach etwas suchen (fig.): *to hunt (to search) for s. th. high and low.* Cf. auch: in allen **Ecken** und Winkeln suchen

> Seit einer Stunde suche ich händeringend nach meinem Wörterbuch.
> *For an hour I have been hunting (searching) high and low for my dictionary.*

ein loses **Handgelenk** haben (fam.): *to have a ready hand (a good arm)*

> Seine Mutter hat ein loses Handgelenk (eine lockere [lose] Hand) und teilt oft Ohrfeigen aus.
> *His mother has a ready hand (a good arm) and often deals out slaps.*

etwas aus dem **Handgelenk** machen (fig.): cf. etwas aus dem **Ärmel** schütteln

**handgreiflich** werden: *to come to blows.* Cf. auch: **Mord** und Totschlag geben
Die beiden Männer wurden bald handgreiflich, und wir mußten sie voneinander trennen.
*The two men soon came to blows and we had to separate them.*

eine **Handhabe** gegen j.en besitzen: *to have a hold on s.b.; to have s.th. on s.b.*
*(colloq.)*
Jetzt hat die Polizei endlich eine feste Handhabe gegen diesen Betrüger.
*Now the police have at last got a definite hold on (got something definite on) this swindler.*

mit seidenen **Handschuhen** anfassen (fig.): cf. mit **Glacéhandschuhen** anfassen

etwas im **Handstreich** nehmen: *to take s.th. by storm (by shock tactics)*
Die Festung wurde im Handstreich genommen.
*The fortress was taken by storm (shock tactics).*

im **Handumdrehen** (fig.): *in (less than) no time; in next to no time; in less time than it takes to tell; in a flash (trice; jiffy; split second); before you can say Jack Robinson; in the twinkling of an eye; before you know where you are; in two shakes of a lamb's tail (colloq.)*
Als der Vater vorschlug, eine kleine Dampferfahrt zu machen, waren wir im Handumdrehen (im Nu; wie's Brezelbacken; im Fluge; im Hui; ehe man bis drei zählen konnte; ehe man sich's versah) mit unserer Schularbeit fertig.
*When father suggested that we should go on a little steamer trip, we finished our home-work in (less than) no time (in next to no time; in less time than it takes to tell; in a flash [trice; jiffy; split second]; before you could say Jack Robinson; in the twinkling of an eye; before you knew where you were; in two shakes of a lamb's tail).*

j.em das **Handwerk** legen (fig.): *to put an end (a stop) to s.b.'s game (to s.b.'s nonsense); to shut s.b. up (sl.)*
Ich muß einmal meinem leichtsinnigen Vetter das Handwerk legen.
*I must put an end (a stop) to my reckless cousin's game (nonsense; I must shut my reckless cousin up).*

j.em ins **Handwerk** pfuschen (fig.): *to poach on s.b.'s preserves; to queer s.b.'s pitch (colloq.)*
Der Klempner war darüber verärgert, daß mein Bruder den Wasserhahn selbst repariert und ihm so ins Handwerk gepfuscht hatte.
*The plumber was annoyed that my brother had mended the water-tap himself and thus poached on his preserves (queered his pitch).*

Ein schlechter **Handwerker** schimpft (immer) auf sein Werkzeug: *A bad workman always blames his tools (prov.)*

> Wenn Gustav etwas verkehrt gemacht hat, findet er immer eine Ausrede. Ein schlechter Handwerker schimpft (immer) auf sein Werkzeug.
> *When Gustave has done something wrong, he always finds an excuse. A bad workman always blames his tools.*

**Handel** und Wandel: *business*

> Handel und Wandel gedeihen bei uns schon seit zehn Jahren.
> *Business has been flourishing here for ten years.*

mit j.em **Händel** haben: *to have words with s.b.; to cross swords with s.b.* Cf. auch: mit j.em die **Klingen** kreuzen

> Wegen der ungerechten Verteilung der Freikarten für das Konzert habe ich mit der Geschäftsleitung der Musikhalle Händel gehabt.
> *I had words (crossed swords) with the business manager of the concert hall about the unfair distribution of free tickets for the concert.*

**Händel** suchen: cf. einen **Streit** vom Zaun brechen

**hanebüchen** sein (fam.): cf. **haarsträubend** sein

ein kleiner (schwacher) **Hänfling** sein (fig.): cf. ein (wahrer; magerer) **Hering** sein

mit **Hangen** und Bangen: *on tenterhooks; with bated breath; with butterflies in one's stomach (colloq.)*

> Mit Hangen und Bangen warteten wir die Ergebnisse des Preisausschreibens ab.
> *We waited on tenterhooks (with bated breath; with butterflies in our stomachs) for the results of the competition.*

Etwas bleibt immer **hängen** (Sprichw.): *Something always sticks (prov.)*

> Mangels Beweisen ist der Angeklagte vor Gericht freigesprochen worden. Aber etwas bleibt immer hängen.
> *Because of lack of proof the accused was acquitted in court, but something always sticks.*

sich **hängen** lassen (fam.): a) *to eat one's hat (colloq.);* b) *to hang back*

> a) Ich will mich hängen lassen (einen Besen fressen; Hans [Meier] heißen; des Teufels [Todes] sein), wenn das nicht mit Streit endigt.
> b) Reiß dich zusammen und laß dich nicht so hängen! Du bist doch ein Mann.
> *a) I'll eat my hat if that doesn't end in a quarrel.*
> *b) Pull yourself together and don't hang back like that! You're a man, aren't you?*

mit **Hängen** und Würgen: cf. mit **Ach** und Krach

**Hans** und Franz: cf. **Hinz** und Kunz

**Hans** (Dampf) in allen Gassen sein: *to be (a) Jack of all trades.* Cf. auch: in allen **Sätteln** gerecht sein

Unser Hausmeister ist Hans (Dampf) in allen Gassen. Er macht alle Reparaturen selbst.
*Our caretaker is (a) Jack of all trades. He does all the repairs himself.*

**Hans** im Glück sein: *to be a lucky devil (beggar) (colloq.).* Cf. auch: ein **Glückspilz** sein

Albert ist Hans im Glück, denn er hat soeben tausend Mark im Fußball-Toto gewonnen.
*Albert is a lucky devil (beggar), for he has just won a thousand marks in the football pools.*

**Hans** Guckindieluft sein: *to be (a) Johnny Head-in-the-air*

Wer heutzutage als Hans Guckindieluft eine belebte Straße überquert, läuft Gefahr, überfahren zu werden.
*Anybody who crosses a busy street nowadays like (a) Johnny Head-in-the-air runs the risk of being run over.*

**Hans** heißen wollen, wenn . . . (fam.): cf. sich **hängen** lassen a)

ein **Hans** Tappinsmus sein (fam.): cf. ein **Tolpatsch** sein

Was **Hänschen** nicht lernt, lernt Hans nimmermehr (Sprichw.): *You can't teach an old dog new tricks (prov.); One must break a horse in young (prov.)*

Wenn du das jetzt noch nicht weißt, wirst du es niemals wissen. Was Hänschen nicht lernt, lernt Hans nimmermehr (Den Baum muß man biegen, dieweil er noch jung ist).
*If you don't know that now, you never will. You can't teach an old dog new tricks (One must break a horse in young).*

j.en **hänseln:** cf. j.en auf den **Arm** nehmen

den **Hanswurst** spielen: *to play (to act) the fool (the clown); to lark (to fool) about (colloq.).* Cf. auch: **Possen** reißen

Mein junger Bruder spielt gern den Hanswurst (Clown), aber mich ärgert es furchtbar.
*My young brother likes playing (acting) the fool (clown; likes larking [fooling] about), but it annoys me terribly.*

**happig** sein (von Preisen) (fam.): cf. ein gepfefferter **Preis**

j.em zeigen, was eine **Harke** ist (fig. u. fam.): *to show s.b. what's what (colloq.); to teach s.b. a lesson.* Cf. auch: j.em gründlich **Bescheid** sagen

Wenn dieser Mann nicht bald aufhört, so einen Krach zu machen, werde ich ihm zeigen, was eine Harke ist, und ihn bei der Polizei anzeigen.

*If that man does not stop making such a noise soon, I'll show him what's what (I'll teach him a lesson) and report him to the police.*

j.en in **Harnisch** bringen (fig.): cf. j.en in die **Wolle** bringen

in **Harnisch** geraten (fig.): *to fly into a rage; to cut up rough (colloq.).* Cf. auch: aus der **Haut** fahren; **mordswütend** werden

Mein Onkel ist sehr nervös und gerät oft in Harnisch (in die Wolle; aus dem Häuschen; wird oft fuchsteufelswild).
*My uncle is very nervous and often flies into a rage (often cuts up rough).*

**hart** auf hart gehen: a) *to go hammer and tongs;* b) *to be touch and go; to be a close (near) thing (a close shave)*

a) Im Unterhaus ging es hart auf hart um die fraglichen Maßnahmen der Regierung.
b) Bei dieser Operation wird es hart auf hart gehen, denn der Patient ist sehr schwach.
*a) In the lower house they were going hammer and tongs over the government's debatable measures.*
*b) This operation will be touch and go (a close [near] thing; a close shave), for the patient is very weak.*

**hartgesotten** sein (fig.): *to be hard-boiled*

Unser hartgesottener Chef hat für die Nöte seiner Angestellten kein Verständnis.
*Our hard-boiled boss has no sympathy for the sufferings of his employees.*

ein alter **Hase** sein (fig. u. fam.): cf. ein alter **Praktikus** sein

sehen, wie (wohin) der **Hase** läuft (fig.): cf. merken, woher der **Wind** weht

Mein Name ist **Hase**: cf. Mein **Name** ist Hase

Da liegt der **Hase** im Pfeffer (fig.): *That's the fly in the ointment; There's the rub; That's (just) the snag.* Cf. auch: Die Sache hat einen **Haken**

Wenn wir an dieser Stelle ein Haus bauen, müssen wir mit feuchten Wänden rechnen. Da liegt der Hase im Pfeffer (Da liegt der Hund begraben).
*If we build a house on this spot we shall have to reckon with damp walls. That's the fly in the ointment (That's [just] the snag; There's the rub).*

ein **Hasenfuß** sein (fig.): *to be as scared as a rabbit; to be chicken-hearted; to be lily-livered (yellow) (sl.)*

Mein Bruder ist ein solcher Hasenfuß (hat ein solches Hasenherz), daß er nicht einmal über diese Mauer klettern will.
*My brother is as scared as a rabbit and won't even climb (is so chicken-hearted [lily-livered; yellow] that he won't even climb) over that wall.*

ein **Hasenherz** haben (fig.): cf. ein **Hasenfuß** sein

das **Hasenpanier** ergreifen (fig. u. fam.): cf. **Fersengeld** geben

nicht **hasenrein** sein: *not to be above-board; not to be on the level (colloq.)*

An diesem geschäftlichen Unternehmen wollen wir uns nicht beteiligen, da es nicht hasenrein (astrein) ist.
*We will not take part in this business venture, because it is not above-board (on the level).*

Er **hat**'s ja (dazu)! (fam.): *He's got the necessary (the wherewithal); He's got the dough (sl.); He's got what it takes (sl.)*

Der reiche Fabrikant hat sich schon wieder ein neues Auto gekauft. Er hat's ja (dazu).
*The rich manufacturer has bought himself yet another new car. He's got the necessary (the wherewithal; the dough; what it takes).*

**Hat** sich was! (fam.): cf. Keine (Nicht die) **Spur!**

einen **Hau** haben (fam.): cf. nicht richtig im **Dachstübchen** sein

j.en unter die **Haube** bringen (fig.): *to marry s.b. off; to find a match for s.b.; to get s.b. spliced (colloq.)*

Die arme Witwe bemüht sich offensichtlich, ihre Töchter unter die Haube (an den Mann) zu bringen.
*The poor widow is obviously striving to marry her daughters off (find a match for her daughters; get her daughters spliced).*

unter die **Haube** kommen (fig.): *to get spliced (colloq.)*

Vorige Woche ist meine dreißigjährige Schwester endlich unter die Haube gekommen.
*Last week my thirty-year-old sister finally got spliced.*

auf **Hauen** und Stechen mit j.em stehen (fig.): cf. sich mit j.em in den **Haaren** liegen

ein **Häufchen** Unglück: *a picture of misery*

Was ist denn mit dir passiert? Du sitzt ja wie ein Häufchen Unglück (Elend; Bild des Jammers) da.
*What has happened to you? You are sitting there like a picture of misery.*

ein armer **Haufen** sein (fig. u. fam.): *to be a poor devil (wretch)*

Er ist ein armer Haufen (Schlucker; Teufel; ein armes Schwein [Würstchen]); er liegt schon seit zwei Jahren im Krankenhaus.
*He is a poor devil (wretch); he has been lying in hospital for two years.*

in hellen **Haufen**: *in (their) hundreds (thousands); in masses; like ants*

Als das Feuer in dem Sägewerk ausgebrochen war, kamen die Neugierigen in hellen Haufen herbeigerannt.

*When fire broke out in the saw-mill, inquisitive people came running up in (their) hundreds (thousands; in masses; like ants).*

j.en über den **Haufen** rennen: *to knock s.b. flying; to send s.b. cartwheeling; to knock s.b. for six (colloq.)*

Der wilde Stier rannte die Bäuerin über den Haufen.
*The wild bull knocked the farmer's wife flying (sent the farmer's wife cartwheeling; knocked the farmer's wife for six).*

etwas über den **Haufen** werfen (fig.): *to throw (to cast) s.th. overboard (aside; to the [four] winds).* Cf. auch: etwas über **Bord** werfen; etwas in den **Wind** schlagen

Der alte Holzfäller hat alle seine guten Vorsätze über den Haufen geworfen und trinkt bereits wieder.
*The old woodchopper has thrown (cast) all his good intentions overboard (aside; to the [four] winds) and is drinking again.*

etwas an **Haupt** und Gliedern reformieren: *to reform s.th. root and branch (lock, stock and barrel; from the bottom)*

Wenn bessere Verhältnisse eintreten sollen, müßte die Leitung den Betrieb an Haupt und Gliedern reformieren.
*If better conditions are to be brought about, the management will have to reform the works root and branch (lock, stock and barrel; from the bottom).*

j.en aufs **Haupt** schlagen: *to rout s.b.; to deal (to strike) s.b. a crippling (mortal) blow; to cripple s.b.*

Nachdem die Regierungstruppen den Feind aufs Haupt geschlagen hatten, kam es zum Frieden.
*After the government troops had routed the enemy (had dealt [struck] the enemy a crippling [mortal] blow; had crippled the enemy), peace was made.*

den **Hauptakzent** auf etwas legen (fig.): *to lay the greatest stress on s.th.; to put the accent (emphasis) on s.th.* Cf. auch: großes **Gewicht** auf etwas legen

Bei der mündlichen Prüfung wird der (Haupt)akzent (Schwerpunkt) auf eine tadellose Aussprache gelegt.
*In the oral examination the greatest stress is laid (the accent [emphasis] is [put]) on perfect pronunciation.*

sich einen **Hauptspaß** leisten: cf. sich einen **Mordsspaß** leisten

eine **Haupt- und Staatsaktion** aus etwas machen (fig.): *to make s.th. a matter of life and death; to make a great to-do (set-out; fuss) about s.th. (colloq.)*

Aus diesem bloßen Mißverständnis wurde eine Haupt- und Staatsaktion gemacht.
*This mere misunderstanding was made a matter of life and death (A great to-do [set-out; fuss] was made about this mere misunderstanding).*

**Häuser** auf j.en bauen (fig.): *to bank on s.b.; to put one's trust in s.b.; s.b. is as safe as houses (colloq.)*

Ich kenne diesen Mann schon seit Jahren. Man kann Häuser auf ihn bauen.
*I have known that man for years. You can bank on him (put your trust in him; He is as safe as houses).*

sein **Haus** bestellen (fig.): *to put one's house (affairs) in order*

Als Vater älter und schwächer wurde, hielt er es für an der Zeit, sein Haus zu bestellen, und machte sein Testament.
*As father got older and weaker, he considered it time to put his house (affairs) in order, and he made his will.*

j.em das **Haus** einrennen: *to overrun (to besiege) the house*

Seitdem unsere Söhne wieder zu Hause sind, rennen uns die Nachbarskinder das Haus ein.
*Since our sons have been home again, the neighbours' children have been overrunning (besieging) the house.*

ein fideles **Haus** sein (fig.): *to be a jolly (a cheerful) chap (fellow).* Cf. auch: **kreuzfidel** sein

Unser Onkel Fritz ist ein fideles Haus, und wir sind gern bei ihm.
*Our uncle Fred is a jolly (cheerful) chap (fellow), and we like being with him.*

ein gelehrtes **Haus** sein (fig.): *to be a pillar (a storehouse) of wisdom; to be a pundit*

Aus den Romanen dieses Schriftstellers merkt man, daß er ein gelehrtes Haus ist.
*One can see from this author's novels that he is a pillar (storehouse) of wisdom (a pundit).*

ein großes **Haus** führen (fig.): cf. auf großem **Fuße** leben

von **Haus** zu Haus (fig.): *from all of us to all of you; from our family to yours*

Im Namen meiner Frau und meiner Kinder beendigte ich meinen Brief an die Familie meines Freundes mit besten Grüßen von Haus zu Haus.
*On behalf of my wife and my children I ended my letter to my friend's family with best wishes from all of us to all of them (from our family to theirs).*

**Haus** und Hof verlassen: *to leave hearth and home*

Der Gauner hat Haus und Hof verlassen und ist nach Kanada ausgewandert.
*The rogue has left hearth and home and emigrated to Canada.*

in etwas zu **Hause** sein (fig.): *to be at home (at one's ease) in s.th.* Cf. auch: gut **bestellt** sein; **kapitelfest** sein

Ich bin in allen Zweigen der Physik zu Hause.
*I am at home (at my ease) in all branches of physics.*

das **Haus** auf den Kopf stellen (fig.): cf. alles auf den **Kopf** stellen

ein offenes **Haus** haben: *to keep open house*

> Sie sind jederzeit bei mir willkommen. Ich habe ein offenes Haus.
> *You are welcome in my home at any time. I keep open house.*

**hausbacken** sein (fig.): *to be homespun (homely)*

> Die Bauerstochter ist ein einfaches, hausbackenes Mädchen.
> *The farmer's daughter is a simple, homespun (homely) girl.*

j.en aus dem **Häuschen** bringen (fig.): cf. j.en in die **Wolle** bringen

aus dem **Häuschen** geraten (fig.): cf. in **Harnisch** geraten; aus der **Haut** fahren

aus dem **Häuschen** sein (fig.): *to be beside o.s.; to be in a state of . . .*

> Wir sind vor Freude ganz aus dem Häuschen (ganz außer uns; außer Rand und Band), weil wir in den Ferien in die Schweiz fahren dürfen.
> *We are quite beside ourselves with delight (in a state of delight [of ecstasy]) because we are going to be allowed to go to Switzerland in the holidays.*

ein **Hausdrache** sein (fig.): *to be an old battle-axe (colloq.).* Cf. auch: die **Hosen** anhaben

> Nach allem, was man hört, ist seine Frau ein wahrer (Haus)drache.
> *According to all one hears, his wife is a real old battle-axe.*

ein **Häusermeer**: *a sea of houses*

> Das Häusermeer unserer Hauptstadt bedrückt mich.
> *The sea of houses in our capital depresses me.*

mit seinen Kräften **haushalten**: *to conserve one's energy (strength); to watch one's step; not to overdo things*

> Da Vater jetzt älter geworden ist, muß er langsamer tun und mit seinen Kräften haushalten.
> *As father has now grown older, he has to go more slowly and conserve his energy (strength; has to watch his step; must not overdo things).*

j.em **haushoch** überlegen sein: *to be head and shoulders above s.b.; to be streets (miles) ahead of s.b. (colloq.); to knock s.b. into a cocked hat (colloq.); to beat s.b. hollow (all ends up) (colloq.).* Cf. auch: j.en (etwas) in den **Schatten** stellen; j.en in die **Tasche** stecken

> Was moderne Sprachen (an)betrifft, bin ich meinem Bruder haushoch (turmhoch) überlegen (überrage ich meinen Bruder turmhoch).
> *As concerns modern languages, I am head and shoulders above my brother (streets [miles] ahead of my brother; can knock my brother into a cocked hat; can beat my brother hollow [all ends up]).*

**haushoch** verschuldet sein: cf. bis über die **Ohren** in Schulden stecken mit etwas **hausieren** gehen (fig.): *to advertise s. th.; to play s. th. up; to go to town on s. th. (colloq.).* Cf. auch: etwas **ausposaunen**

> Wir wollen mit diesem Erfolg nicht hausieren gehen, denn unsere Gegner waren schwach.
> *We do not want to advertise that success (to play that success up; to go to town on that success) because our opponents were weak.*

bis auf die **Haut** durchnäßt sein: *to be soaked (drenched) to the skin (to the bone); to be soaking wet; to be dripping (sopping) wet (colloq.); to be like a drowned rat (colloq.).* Cf. auch: keinen trockenen **Faden** am (auf dem) Leibe haben

> Der Regen überraschte uns, und wir kamen bis auf die Haut (Knochen) durchnäßt (naß bis auf die Haut; naß wie eine Katze; klatschnaß; klitschnaß; patschnaß; pitschnaß; pudelnaß) zu Hause an.
> *The rain caught us by surprise, and we arrived home soaked (drenched) to the skin (bone; arrived home soaking [dripping; sopping] wet; like drowned rats).*

eine ehrliche **Haut** sein: *to be an honest soul; to be the soul of honesty*

> Du kannst dich fest auf ihn verlassen. Er ist eine ehrliche Haut.
> *You can rely on him completely. He is an honest soul (the soul of honesty).*

aus der **Haut** fahren (fig.): *to go off the deep end (colloq.); to fly off the handle (colloq.).* Cf. auch: in **Harnisch** geraten; **mordswütend** werden

> Immer wenn ich ruhig lesen will, stellt mein Nachbar das Radio an. Es ist, um aus der Haut zu fahren (um hochzugehen; in die Luft zu gehen; einen Koller zu bekommen; fuchsteufelswild zu werden; aus dem Häuschen [in die Wolle] zu geraten).
> *When I want to read quietly, my neighbour always switches the radio on. It's enough to make one go off the deep end (fly off the handle).*

sich auf die faule **Haut** legen (auf der faulen Haut liegen) (fig.): cf. **herum-lungern**

etwas mit **Haut** und Haar auffressen: *to eat s. th. down to the last morsel (scrap); to eat s. th. skin and bone*

> Unsere Katze hat die Maus mit Haut und Haar aufgefressen.
> *Our cat ate the mouse down to the last morsel (scrap; ate the mouse skin and bone).*

sich mit **Haut** und Haaren einer Sache verschreiben (fig.): *to devote o. s. (to give o. s. over) body (heart) and soul to a thing; to throw o. s. body (heart) and soul into s. th.*

> Der junge Gelehrte hatte sich mit Haut und Haaren seiner Forschung verschrieben.
> *The young scholar had devoted himself (given himself over) body (heart) and soul to (had thrown himself body [heart] and soul into) his research.*

mit heiler **Haut** davonkommen (fam.): *to save one's skin; to escape without a scratch; to get away with it (sl.)*

> Bei dem Autounfall ist meine ganze Familie glücklicherweise mit heiler Haut davongekommen.
> *Fortunately my whole family saved their skins (escaped without a scratch; got away with it) in the car crash.*

Man kann nicht aus seiner **Haut** heraus (Keiner kann aus seiner Haut) (fig.): *The leopard cannot change his spots (prov.)*

> Schon als Junge war er geizig, und heute ist er es immer noch. Man kann nicht aus seiner Haut heraus ([Keiner kann aus seiner Haut]; über seinen Schatten springen).
> *He was miserly as a boy, and he still is today. The leopard cannot change his spots.*

nur noch **Haut** und Knochen sein: *to be nothing but (to be all) skin and bone (nothing but a bag of bones); to be as thin (lean) as a rake.* Cf. auch: ein (wahrer; magerer) **Hering** sein

> Infolge einer langen und schweren Krankheit ist Onkel Friedrich jetzt nur noch Haut und Knochen (bis auf die Knochen abgemagert; klapperdürr; knochendürr; spindeldürr; nur noch ein Strich; hat . . . nichts Ordentliches mehr in den Rippen).
> *As the result of a long and serious illness Uncle Frederick is now nothing but (is all) skin and bone (is nothing but a bag of bones; is as thin [lean] as a rake).*

seine **Haut** zu Markte tragen (fig.): *to take one's life in one's hands; to risk one's life*

> Warum wollen Sie Ihre Haut zu Markte tragen, indem Sie sich mit solchen zweifelhaften Menschen abgeben?
> *Why are you taking your life in your hands (risking your life) by associating with such doubtful people?*

naß bis auf die **Haut** sein: cf. bis auf die **Haut** durchnäßt sein

seine **Haut** in Sicherheit bringen (fig.): *to save one's bacon (one's skin)*

> Heinrich fürchtete, daß man ihn erwischen würde, aber im letzten Augenblick konnte er seine Haut in Sicherheit bringen.
> *Henry feared that he would be caught, but at the last minute he was able to save his bacon (skin).*

nicht in j.es **Haut** stecken mögen (fig.): *not to like to be in s.b.'s shoes*

> Dieser Chirurg trägt eine riesige Verantwortung. Ich möchte nicht in seiner Haut stecken.
> *This surgeon bears an enormous responsibility. I shouldn't like to be in his shoes.*

in keiner gesunden (guten) **Haut** stecken (fig.): *to be in a bad way*

> Unser Bäcker sieht sehr blaß aus. Er steckt offenbar in keiner gesunden (guten) Haut.
> *Our baker looks very pale. He is obviously in a bad way.*

sich seiner **Haut** wehren (fig.): *to stand one's ground; to stick up for o.s. (colloq.).* Cf. auch: sich zur **Wehr** setzen

Wir müssen uns unserer Haut wehren, wenn man uns unlautere Geschäfte zumutet.
*We must stand our ground (stick up for ourselves) when we are suspected of underhand actions.*

sich in seiner **Haut** wohlfühlen (fig.); *to feel satisfied (pleased) with o. s.; to feel pleased with life.* Cf. auch: sich wohlfühlen wie die **Made** im Speck

Mein Vetter hat viel Geld und ist glücklich verheiratet. Er fühlt sich in seiner Haut sehr wohl.
*My cousin has a lot of money and is happily married. He feels very satisfied (pleased) with himself; very pleased with life).*

zur **Hautevolee** gehören: *to belong to the cream (the upper crust; the top flight) of society; to be one of the bigwigs (colloq.); to be out of the top drawer (colloq.)*

Frau Wenzel bildet sich ein, sie gehöre zur Hautevolee (zur Crème der Gesellschaft), in Wirklichkeit aber stammt sie aus armen Verhältnissen.
*Mrs Wenzel imagines that she belongs to the cream (upper crust; top flight) of society (that she is one of the bigwigs; that she is out of the top drawer) but in fact she comes from poor circumstances.*

(einen) **Hautgout** haben (Hautgout schmecken): *to smell high (ripe); to stink (to high heaven) (colloq.); to pong (sl.)*

Dieses Fleisch ist schon ein paar Wochen alt und hat jetzt einen ziemlichen Hautgout (und schmeckt ziemlich Hautgout).
*This meat is a few weeks old and now smells pretty high (ripe; now stinks [to high heaven]; now pongs a bit).*

den **Hebel** an der richtigen Stelle ansetzen (fig.): *to start (the job) in the proper place (at the right end); to tackle the job properly*

Bei dem Wiederaufbau unserer Stadt sollte die Verwaltung den Hebel an der richtigen Stelle ansetzen und sich zuerst mit der Stadtmitte befassen.
*In the reconstruction of our town the council ought to start (the job) in the proper place (at the right end; to tackle the job properly) and concern itself first with the town-centre.*

alle **Hebel** in Bewegung setzen (fig.): *to pull all the available strings; to move heaven and earth; to move mountains; to leave no stone unturned*

Der Arzt setzte alle Hebel (Himmel und Erde [Hölle]) in Bewegung (ließ alle Minen springen), um eine Vergrößerung des Krankenhauses zu erreichen.
*The doctor pulled all the available strings (moved heaven and earth [mountains]; left no stone unturned) to secure an expansion of the hospital.*

einen **heben** (fam.): cf. sich einen hinter die **Binde** gießen

sich wie der **Hecht** im Karpfenteich benehmen: *to behave like a cat among the pigeons*. Cf. auch: sich benehmen wie der **Elefant** im Porzellanladen

Du solltest dich deiner Umgₑbung anpassen und dich nicht wie der Hecht im Karpfenteich benehmen.
*You should adapt yourself to your surroundings and not behave like a cat among the pigeons.*

die **Hefe** des Volkes (fig.): cf. der **Abschaum** der Menschheit
aufgehen wie ein **Hefekloß** (fam.): *to become like a plum-pudding (dumpling; balloon); to split at the seams (colloq.)*. Cf. auch: **Fett** ansetzen

Früher war Erika schlank, aber jetzt ist sie aufgegangen wie ein Hefekloß (Pfannkuchen; ist sie aus dem Leim gegangen).
*Formerly Erica was slim, but now she has become like a plum-pudding (dumpling; balloon; she has split at the seams).*

das **Heft** ergreifen (fig.): cf. etwas in die **Hand** nehmen; ans **Ruder** kommen
das **Heft** in der Hand (in den Händen) haben (fig.): *to hold (to have) the reins in one's hands; to rule (to be cock of) the roost; to hold (to have) the whip-hand; to lay down the law; to be at the helm*. Cf. auch: fest im **Sattel** sitzen; **Hahn** im Korb sein

In unserm Klub hat Otto das Heft (das Ruder [die Zügel] fest) in der Hand (in den Händen; führt Otto das Steuer) und richtet alles nach seinem Willen ein.
*In our club Otto holds (has) the reins in his hand (rules [is cock of] the roost; holds [has] the whip-hand; lays down the law; is at the helm) and arranges everything according to his own will.*

j.en **hegen** und pflegen: *to cherish and watch over (look after) s.b.*

Während Ihrer langen Auslandsreise werden wir Ihre beiden Kinder hegen und pflegen wie unsere eigenen.
*During your long journey abroad we will cherish and watch over (look after) your two children as though they were our own.*

(eine) **Heidenangst** haben: *to be scared to death (scared out of one's wits); to be scared stiff (colloq.); to be in a blue funk (sl.); to get the wind up (sl.)*

Mein Bruder hatte (eine) Heidenangst (Höllenangst; hündische Angst; Mordsangst; hatte [großen] Bammel; hatte Dampf [davor]; das Fracksausen; die Hosen voll), daß er nicht mehr rechtzeitig zur Schule käme.
*My brother was scared to death (out of his wits [stiff]; was in a blue funk; had got the wind up) that he would not get to school in time.*

ein **Heidengeld** kosten: *to cost a mint of money (the earth; a fortune); to cost a pretty penny; to cost pots (no end) of money (colloq.)*

Niemand kann dieses Schloß kaufen, weil es ein Heidengeld kostet.
*Nobody can buy this palace because it costs a mint (no end) of money (the earth; a fortune; a pretty penny; pots of money).*

einen **Heidenlärm** machen: *to make (to kick up) a devil of a noise (row; an infernal [unholy] noise [row; din; shindy]) (colloq.)*

Ihr sollt auf dem Schulhof nicht einen solchen Heidenlärm (Teufelslärm; Höllenlärm; Krawall) machen (nicht so johlen)!
*You should not make (kick up) such a devil of a noise (row; infernal [unholy] noise [row; din; shindy]) in the playground.*

ein **heikles** Thema berühren: *to skate on thin ice; to tread (on) dangerous ground; to touch on a delicate (ticklish) subject*

Wenn Sie von der gegenwärtigen Sittlichkeit reden wollen, (dann) müssen Sie wissen, daß Sie ein heikles Thema berühren.
*If you want to talk about contemporary morality, you must know that you are skating on thin ice (treading [on] dangerous ground; touching on a delicate [ticklish] subject.*

sein **Heil** in der Flucht suchen: *to seek safety in flight; to make a dash (a bolt) for it; to flee for one's life.* Cf. auch: **Fersengeld** geben

Der geschlagene Feind suchte sein Heil in der Flucht.
*The defeated enemy sought safety in flight (made a dash [bolt] for it; fled for their lives).*

sein **Heil** versuchen (fig.): *to try one's luck (one's hand); to have a go (a shot) (colloq.); to have a bash (sl.)*

Bis jetzt habe ich noch kein Ölbild gemalt. Ich kann aber mal mein Heil versuchen.
*I've never painted an oil picture before, but I can try my hand (luck; I can have a go [a shot; a bash]).*

Es ist mein **heiliger** Ernst: *I am dead serious (in deadly earnest) (about it)*

Du darfst nicht denken, daß ich spaße. Es ist mein heiliger Ernst.
*You must not think that I am joking. I am dead serious (in deadly earnest) (about it).*

ein **heiliger** Zorn: cf. eine blinde **Wut**

**heilsfroh** sein: *to be jolly glad; to be mighty glad (pleased) (colloq.)*

Wir waren heilsfroh, als die stürmische Überfahrt vorüber war.
*We were jolly (mighty) glad (pleased) when the stormy crossing was over.*

sich einen **Heiligenschein** umhängen (fig.): *to put on (to wear) a halo*

Dieser Geschäftsmann liebt es, sich einen Heiligenschein umzuhängen, obwohl man weiß, daß er nicht besonders ehrlich ist.
*This shopkeeper likes to put on (to wear) a halo, although it is known that he is not particularly honest.*

ein wunderlicher (sonderbarer) **Heiliger** sein (fig.): cf. ein komischer (närrischer) **Kauz** sein

Der Zweck **heiligt** die Mittel: cf. Der **Zweck** heiligt die Mittel

etwas wie ein **Heiligtum** aufbewahren: *to preserve s.th. like a sacred (holy) relic*

> Die Witwe bewahrte die kleine Bibliothek ihres verstorbenen Mannes wie ein Heiligtum auf.
> *The widow preserved her dead husband's small library like a sacred (holy) relic.*

ein **Heimchen** sein (fig.): *to be as weak as a kitten*

> Mein Enkelkind ist sehr zart; es ist ein wahres Heimchen (zartes Vögelchen).
> *My grandchild is very delicate; he really is as weak as a kitten.*

j.em **heimleuchten** (fig. u. fam.): cf. j.en **abkanzeln;** j.em (die) **Flötentöne** beibringen

**heimlich,** still und leise: *in secret; on the quiet*

> Heimlich, still und leise hatte die fleißige Mutter für ihre Tochter einen wunderbaren Pullover gestrickt.
> *The busy mother had knitted a wonderful pullover for her daughter in secret (on the quiet).*

j.em etwas **heimzahlen:** *to pay s.b. out (back) for s.th.; to make s.b. pay for s.th.*

> Ich habe sein schlechtes Benehmen nicht vergessen und werde es ihm auch heimzahlen.
> *I haven't forgotten his bad behaviour, and I'll pay him out (back; make him pay) for it.*

j.en zu **heiß** gebadet haben (fig. u. fam.): cf. (Aber) sonst geht's dir **gut?**

Es wird nichts so **heiß** gegessen, wie es gekocht wird (Sprichw.): cf. Es wird nichts so heiß **gegessen,** wie es gekocht wird

weder **heiß** noch kalt sein (fig.): cf. weder **Fisch** noch Fleisch sein

j.en **heiß** und kalt überlaufen: *to go hot and cold all over.* Cf. auch: j.en **kalt** überlaufen

> Es überlief Karl heiß und kalt (Es lief . . . über den Rücken), als er merkte, daß er zu wenig Geld mit auf die Reise genommen hatte.
> *Charles went hot and cold all over when he realised that he had taken too little money with him for the journey.*

Was ich nicht weiß, macht mich nicht **heiß** (Sprichw.): cf. Was ich nicht **weiß,** macht mich nicht heiß

einen **Heißhunger** haben: cf. einen **Mordshunger** haben

ein **Heißsporn** sein: *to be a hothead (a madcap) (colloq.)*

Dieser Heißsporn (Brausekopf; Hitzkopf) übt einen gefährlichen Einfluß auf
die Jugend aus.
*This hothead (madcap) exercises a dangerous influence on young people.*

der **Held** des Tages sein: *to be the hero of the hour (the man of the moment)*

Wider Erwarten hatte ich den besten Aufsatz in der Klasse geschrieben und
war der Held (Mann) des Tages.
*Contrary to expectations I had written the best essay in the class and was the hero of the
hour (the man of the moment).*

kein **Heldenstück** sein (fig.): *not to be a decent thing to do; to be a dirty trick
(colloq.)*

Du hattest deinem Freund das Geld versprochen, und dann wolltest du es ihm
nicht geben. Das war kein Heldenstück von dir!
*You had promised your friend the money and then you did not want to give it to him.
That was not a decent thing to do (That was a dirty trick).*

**helle** sein: cf. ein heller **Kopf** sein

auf **Heller** und Pfennig: *to the last farthing*

Mein Schwager hat die ihm geliehene Summe pünktlich und auf Heller und
Pfennig zurückgezahlt.
*My brother-in-law paid back punctually and to the last farthing the sum lent to him.*

keinen roten **Heller** besitzen: *not to have a penny to one's name (to bless o.s.
with); not to have a shirt to one's back*

Als er das Spielkasino verließ, besaß er keinen roten Heller mehr (hatte er
kein Hemd mehr auf dem Leibe).
*When he left the casino he had not got a penny to his name (to bless himself with; he
had not got a shirt to his back).*

keinen roten **Heller** wert sein: *not to be worth a (brass) farthing (a penny; two
pins; a scrap; twopence [tuppence]).* Cf. auch: keinen **Schuß** Pulver wert sein

Diese Briefmarken sind alle beschädigt und daher keinen roten Heller (keinen
Pappenstiel; Pfifferling; Deut) wert.
*These stamps are all damaged and therefore not worth a (brass) farthing (a penny; two
pins; a scrap; twopence [tuppence]).*

j.en bis aufs **Hemd** ausziehen (fig.): *to squeeze s.b. dry; to bleed s.b. white;
to fleece s.b. (colloq.); to suck s.b. dry (sl.)*

Seine Verwandten haben ihn bis aufs Hemd ausgezogen, so daß er jetzt selbst
verarmt ist.
*His relations have squeezed (sucked) him dry (have bled him white; have fleeced him),
so that he is now poverty-stricken himself.*

kein **Hemd** auf dem Leibe haben (fig.): cf. keinen roten **Heller** besitzen

Das **Hemd** ist einem näher als der Rock (Sprichw.): *Charity begins at home (prov.); Near is my shirt but nearer is my skin (prov.)*

Es ist nicht gut, anderen imponieren zu wollen und (dabei) seine eigene Familie zu vernachlässigen. Das Hemd ist einem näher als der Rock.
*It is no good wanting to impress others and neglecting one's own family. Charity begins at home (Near is my shirt but nearer is my skin).*

**hemdsärmelig** mit j.em verfahren (fig. u. fam.): *to ride rough-shod over s.b.; to deal with s.b. in a cavalier manner (in a rough-and-ready way); to deal out rough justice to s.b.*

Feine Gefühle kann man von ihm nicht erwarten; mit jedem verfährt er hemdsärmelig.
*One cannot expect fine feelings from him. He rides rough-shod over everybody (deals with everybody in a cavalier manner [in a rough-and-ready way]; deals out rough justice to everybody).*

der **Hemmschuh** sein (fig.): cf. (ein) **Spielverderber** sein

Hol's der **Henker**!: cf. Hol's der **Teufel**!

Scher' dich zum **Henker**!: *Make yourself scarce!; Get out of my sight!; Go to the devil (to hell)! (colloq.); Clear off! (colloq.); Hop (Beat) it! (sl.); Buzz off! (sl.); Scram! (sl.); Take a running jump at yourself! (sl.)*

Scher' dich zum Henker (Kuckuck; Teufel; Hol' dich der Teufel [Kuckuck]; Du kannst mich gernhaben [liebhaben]; mir gestohlen bleiben; mir im Mondschein begegnen; mir den Buckel herunterrutschen). Ich will dich nicht mehr sehen.
*Make yourself scarce (Get out of my sight; Go to the devil [to hell]; Hop [Beat] it; Clear [Buzz] off; Scram; Take a running jump at yourself)! I don't want to see you again.*

die **Henkersmahlzeit** (fig.): *the farewell-party*

Da Onkel und Tante morgen früh wieder abreisen, gibt es heute abend zur Henkersmahlzeit eine gute Flasche Wein.
*As aunt and uncle are leaving again tomorrow morning, there will be a bottle of good wine at the farewell-party tonight.*

seine Forderungen **herabschrauben** (fig.): *to modify (to scale down; to cut down; to moderate) one's demands*

Jeder(mann) muß lernen, daß er nicht immer auf seinem Recht bestehen kann, sondern von Zeit zu Zeit seine Forderungen herabschrauben muß.
*Everyone has to learn that he cannot always insist on his right but must modify (scale down; cut down; moderate) his demands from time to time.*

fein **heraus** sein: *to be well off (all right); Things are all right for you (him, etc.); to be well away (colloq.)*

Wenn wir doppelt so viel Kundschaft hätten, wären wir fein heraus.
*If we had twice as many customers, we should be well off (all right; well away; things would be all right for us).*

sich etwas **herausnehmen** (fig.): *to presume; to take liberties; to make free.* Cf. auch: sich **mausig** machen

Heinrich ist gar nicht bescheiden. Im Gegenteil, er nimmt sich bei jeder Gelegenheit viel heraus (wird bei . . . üppig).
*Henry is far from modest. On the contrary, he presumes a great deal (takes many liberties; makes very free) on every occasion.*

j.en **herauspauken** (fig. u. fam.): cf. j.en **'rauspauken**

etwas aus j.em **herausquetschen** (fig.): *to worm (to ferret; to nose; to prise) s.th. out of s.b.*

Zuerst wollte er mir nichts sagen, aber es gelang mir schließlich, alles aus ihm herauszuquetschen.
*At first he would not tell me anything, but I finally succeeded in worming (ferreting; nosing; prising) everything out of him.*

etwas **herausstreichen** (fig.): *to show off s.th.; to play on s.th.*

Der junge Mann versteht es, seine Talente herauszustreichen.
*The young man knows how to show off (to play on) his talents.*

Eig'ner **Herd** ist Goldes wert (Sprichw.): *There's no place like home (prov.)*

Das junge Ehepaar ist viel glücklicher, seitdem es eine eigene Wohnung hat. Eig'ner Herd ist Goldes wert.
*The young couple are much happier since they have their own flat. There's no place like home.*

ein **Herdentier (Herdenmensch)** sein: *to belong to (to be one of) the (common) herd (the hoi polloi)*

Mein Bruder behauptet, er sei unabhängig und kein Herdentier (-mensch).
*My brother maintains that he is independent and not one of the (common) herd (of the hoi polloi; and does not belong to the [common] herd [the hoi polloi]).*

auf etwas **hereinfallen** (fig.): *to fall for s.th.; to swallow the bait.* Cf. auch: **anbeißen**

Der Vertreter war ein Betrüger. Sind Sie auch auf seinen Schwindel hereingefallen?
*The salesman was a swindler. Did you fall for his ruse (swallow the bait) as well?*

**hereinschneien** (fig. u. fam.): *to drop in; to blow (to pop) in (colloq.).* Cf. auch: eine **Stippvisite** machen

Entschuldige, wenn ich so hereinschneie.
*Excuse my dropping (popping; blowing) in like this.*

über j.en **herfallen** (fig.): *to descend (to come down) on s.b. like a ton of bricks (coals)*

Seine Freunde sind über ihn hergefallen und haben ihm sein schlechtes Benehmen vorgeworfen.
*His friends descended (came down) on him like a ton of bricks (coals) and blamed him for his bad behaviour.*

gedrängt wie die **Heringe** sitzen: *to sit packed (jammed) like sardines.* Cf. auch: **pfropfenvoll** sein

Für acht Personen war das Auto zu klein; wir saßen gedrängt wie die Heringe (Pökelheringe; wir saßen Kopf an Kopf [zusammengepfercht]; keine Nadel [kein Apfel; keine Stecknadel] konnte zur Erde fallen).
*The car was too small for eight people; we sat packed (jammed) like sardines.*

ein (wahrer; magerer) **Hering** sein (fig. u. fam.): *to be as thin (lean) as a rake (as thin as a lath; as a wafer).* Cf. auch: nur noch **Haut** und Knochen sein

Der Arzt hat dem Jungen, der ein (wahrer; magerer) Hering (ein kleiner [schwacher] Hänfling) ist, Lebertran verordnet, damit er kräftiger wird.
*The doctor has prescribed cod-liver oil for the boy, who is as thin (lean) as a rake (as thin as a lath; as a wafer), so that he will get stronger.*

kein **Herkules** sein: *to be no Hercules*

Obwohl es ihm nach seiner Operation schon viel besser geht, ist er doch noch kein Herkules (kann er doch noch keine Bäume ausreißen).
*Although he is much better since his operation, he is still no Hercules.*

eine **Herkulesarbeit** sein (fig.): *to be a Herculean task; to be a tough job (colloq.)*

Ich habe unzählige Stunden an diesem Aufsatz gearbeitet. Es war wirklich eine Herkulesarbeit (eine Schwergeburt; eine schwere Geburt; eine Biesterei [Viecherei]).
*I spent countless hours on this essay. It really was a Herculean task (a tough job).*

sein eigener **Herr** sein: *to be one's own master (boss)*

Früher oder später möchte jeder unabhängig und sein eigener Herr sein (frei schalten und walten).
*Sooner or later everyone would like to be independent and his own master (boss).*

den großen **Herrn** spielen: *to act like the lord of the manor; to play the fine gentleman; to act big (colloq.)*

Bei deinem kleinen Gehalt kannst du es dir nicht leisten, den großen Herrn zu spielen.

*With your small salary you cannot afford to act like the lord of the manor (to play the fine gentleman; to act big).*

**Herr** im Hause sein: *to be master of the house*
„Ich will euch zeigen", rief der zornige Vater, „wer hier Herr im Hause ist."
*I'll show you who's master of this house! „cried the angry father".*

**Herr** der Lage sein: cf. fest im **Sattel** sitzen

aus aller **Herren** Länder: *from every country under the sun; from all corners of the earth*
Die Konferenzteilnehmer kamen aus aller Herren Länder (aus allen Enden der Welt).
*The members of the conference came from every country under the sun (from all corners of the earth).*

nicht mehr **Herr** über sich selbst sein (fig.): *to lose control of o.s.; to lose one's head*
Der Müller, dem man zwei Säcke Mehl gestohlen hatte, geriet so in Zorn, daß er nicht mehr Herr über sich selbst war und seine schuldlosen Gesellen schlug.
*The miller, who had been robbed of two sacks of flour, became so enraged that he lost control of himself (lost his head) and struck his innocent apprentices.*

einer Sache **Herr** werden (fig.): *to master s.th.; to get to grips with (to get on top of) s.th.; to get s.th. under control*
Zuerst war mir die Arbeit fremd, aber jetzt bin ich ihrer Herr geworden.
*At first the work was strange to me but now I have mastered it (got to grips with it; got on top of it; got it under control).*

Niemand kann zweien **Herren** dienen (Sprichw.): *No man can serve two masters (prov.)*
Vater wünscht, daß ich meine Schulaufgabe zu Ende führe, und Mutter will, daß ich für sie Einkäufe mache. Niemand kann aber zweien Herren dienen.
*Father wishes me to finish my homework and mother wants me to do some shopping for her. But no man can serve two masters.*

**Herrenschnitt** tragen: cf. einen **Bubikopf** tragen

den **Herrgott** einen guten Mann sein lassen: cf. den lieben **Gott** einen guten Mann sein lassen

dem (lieben) **Herrgott** den Tag stehlen: cf. **herumlungern;** die **Zeit** totschlagen

in aller **Herrgottsfrühe:** *at an unearthly hour; at the crack of dawn.* Cf. auch: beim ersten **Hahnenschrei** aufstehen; mit den **Hühnern** aufstehen

In einem Hotel müssen die Angestellten in aller Herrgottsfrühe (vor Tau und Tag) aufstehen.

*In an hotel the employees have to get up at an unearthly hour (at the crack of dawn).*

**die ganze Herrlichkeit:** *the whole set-out (colloq.); the whole box (bag) of tricks (colloq.); the whole shoot (sl.)*

Die Veranstaltung hat nicht lange gedauert; um 10 Uhr war die ganze Herrlichkeit bereits zu Ende.

*The performance did not last long; at ten o'clock the whole set-out (the whole box [bag] of tricks; the whole shoot) was over.*

**an etwas herumdoktern** (fig. u. fam.): *to fiddle (to mess; to tinker) about with s.th. (colloq.)*

Wir haben seit Monaten vergebens an der Reparatur unseres Radios herumgedoktert. Jetzt lasse ich einen Fachmann kommen.

*We have been fiddling (messing; tinkering) about for months in vain trying to repair our radio. Now I'm going to send for an expert.*

**herumdrucksen** (fam.): *to hum and haw*

Lange druckste er herum (rückte er mit der Sprache nicht heraus), bis er endlich zu sprechen begann.

*He hummed and hawed for a long while before finally starting to talk.*

**an etwas herumfingern (herumfummeln)** (fam.): *to tamper with s.th.; to fiddle (to monkey) about with s.th. (colloq.); to finger s.th. about (colloq.)*

Ich habe meinen Kindern streng verboten, an meiner Schreibmaschine herumzufingern (herumzufummeln).

*I have strictly forbidden my children to tamper (to fiddle [to monkey] about) with my typewriter (to finger my typewriter about).*

**mit etwas herumfuchteln (herumfuhrwerken, herumfummeln)** (fam.): *to fiddle (to monkey) about with s.th.; to finger s.th. about (colloq.)*

Hör' doch auf, mit diesem Messer herumzufuchteln (herumzufuhrwerken; herumzufummeln; zu fummeln). Sonst verletzt du dich oder einen von uns.

*Do stop fiddling (monkeying) with that knife (Do stop fingering that knife about)! Otherwise you will hurt yourself or one of us.*

**herumkalbern** (fam.): cf. **kalbern**

**herumkrebsen** (fam.): *to crawl (to totter) around (colloq.)*

Ich habe Angst, daß Karl krank wird. Er fühlt sich nicht wohl und krebst schon seit einigen Tagen (nur) herum.

*I am afraid that Charles is going to be ill. He does not feel well, and has been crawling (tottering) around for some days.*

**herumlungern** (fam.): *to loaf (to hang; to moon; to loll; to laze) about (colloq.)*

Dieser Kerl scheint gar nichts zu tun zu haben. Er lungert den ganzen Tag herum (Er liegt den ganzen Tag auf der faulen Haut [auf der Bärenhaut; legt sich . . . auf die faule Haut]; Er stiehlt dem [lieben] Herrgott den Tag).
*That fellow seems to have nothing at all to do. He loafs (hangs; moons; lolls; lazes) about the whole day.*

**herummurksen** (fam.): cf. **murksen**

(ständig; immer) auf éinem Thema **herumreiten** (fig.): *to produce the same old story (yarn); to trot out (to harp on) the same old story (yarn) (colloq.); to sing the same old tune (colloq.)*

Wenn man den alten Flüchtling trifft, reitet er ständig (immer) auf éinem Thema herum (stimmt er immer die alte Leier an; singt er immer das gleiche [alte] Lied). Er klagt über den Verlust seines früheren Besitztums.
*Whenever one meets the old refugee, he produces (trots out; harps on) the same (old) story (yarn; sings the same old tune). He laments the loss of his former possessions.*

um j.en **herumscharwenzeln** (fam.): *to dance attendance on s.b.; to hover around s.b.; to hang around s.b. (sl.)*

Schon seit Monaten scharwenzelt Thomas um dieses junge Mädchen herum.
*For months Thomas has been dancing attendance on (hovering [hanging] around) that young girl.*

in etwas **herumschnüffeln** (fam.): *to ferret about; to poke one's nose into s.th.; to sniff (to nose; to snoop) around (about)*

Alma schnüffelt immer in meinen Angelegenheiten herum.
*Alma is always ferreting about in (poking her nose into; sniffing [nosing; snooping] about [around] in) my affairs.*

j.en **herunterputzen** (fam.): cf. j.en **abkanzeln**; j.en **anschnauzen**

etwas auf dem **Herzen** haben (fig.): *to have s.th. on one's mind (conscience); s.th. is on s.b.'s mind (conscience)*

Was führt Sie zu mir? Was haben Sie auf dem Herzen?
*What brings you to me? What have you got on your mind ([conscience]; What is on your mind [conscience])?*

sein **Herz** ausschütten (fig.): *to pour out (to open; to unburden) one's heart*

Meine Schwiegertochter war deprimiert und wollte mir ihr Herz ausschütten.
*My daughter-in-law was depressed and wanted to pour out (open; unburden) her heart to me.*

blutenden **Herzens** (fig.): *with a heavy heart; heavy of heart*

Blutenden (Schweren) Herzens (Mit schwerem Herzen) sah ich meinen Sohn nach Südafrika auswandern.
*With a heavy heart (Heavy of heart) I saw my son emigrate to South Africa.*

Mir blutet das **Herz** (fig.): *My heart bleeds*

> Mir blutet das Herz, wenn ich solche Tierquälerei sehe.
> *My heart bleeds when I see such cruelty to animals.*

Es bricht einem das **Herz**: *It breaks one's heart.* Cf. auch: einem durch **Mark** und Bein gehen

> Es bricht einem das Herz (schneidet einem [trifft einen] ins Herz), wenn man daran denkt, wieviele unschuldige Menschen in einem Kriege umkommen.
> *It breaks one's heart to think how many innocent people die in a war.*

etwas nicht übers **Herz** bringen können (nicht das Herz zu etwas haben) (fig.): *not to have (to find) the heart to do s.th.; not to have it in one's heart to do s.th.*

> Ich konnte es nicht übers Herz bringen (Ich hatte nicht das Herz), seiner Familie die volle Wahrheit zu sagen.
> *I had not (got) the heart (did [could] not find the heart; had not got it in my heart) to tell his family the whole truth.*

mit dem **Herzen** dabei sein: *to have (to put) one's heart in s.th.; to be heart and soul in s.th.; to be absorbed in s.th.*

> Man merkte es den Schülern an, daß sie bei den Proben für das Konzert mit dem Herzen dabei (bei der Sache) waren.
> *One saw that the pupils had their hearts (were putting their hearts; were heart and soul; were absorbed) in the rehearsals for the concert.*

Das **Herz** dreht sich einem (im Leibe) um (fig.): *One's heart turns over*

> Es dreht sich einem das Herz (im Leibe) um, wenn man soviel Elend sieht.
> *One's heart turns over when one sees so much misery.*

einem eng (schwach) ums **Herz** werden (fig.): *to feel (to be) sick at (of) heart*

> Als er seinen alten Hund töten lassen mußte, wurde es ihm eng (schwach) ums Herz.
> *He felt (was) sick at (of) heart when he had to have his old dog killed.*

des Menschen **Herz** erfreuen: *to warm the cockles of s.b.'s heart*

> Es erfreut des Menschen Herz, solche Großmut zu sehen.
> *It warms the cockles of one's heart to see such generosity.*

alle **Herzen** erobern (fig.): cf. alle **Herzen** fliegen j.em zu

j.em schwer aufs **Herz** fallen (fig.): cf. j.em schwer auf die **Seele** fallen

sich ein **Herz** fassen (fig.): *to pluck (to summon) up courage; to pluck up heart; to take the bit between one's teeth; to take one's courage in both hands*

Endlich faßte er sich ein Herz (nahm er sein Herz in die Hand) und forderte sein Geld zurück.
*At last he plucked (summoned) up courage (plucked up heart; took the bit between his teeth; took his courage in both hands) and asked for his money back.*

das **Herz** auf dem rechten Fleck haben (fig.): *to have one's heart in the right place; s.b.'s heart is in the right place*

Unser Bürgermeister ist sehr beliebt, denn er hat das Herz auf dem rechten Fleck.
*Our burgomaster is very popular, because he has his heart in the right place (his heart is in the right place).*

Alle **Herzen** fliegen j.em zu (fig.): *Everybody loses his heart to s.b.; to conquer all hearts; Everybody falls for s.b. (colloq.)*

Der neuen Lehrerin flogen sogleich alle Herzen ihrer Schülerinnen zu (Die neue Lehrerin eroberte sogleich alle H. ihrer Schülerinnen).
*All the pupils lost their hearts to (fell for) the new mistress at once (The new mistress conquered all the pupils' hearts at once).*

j.em zu **Herzen** gehen: cf. sich etwas zu **Herzen** nehmen

von **Herzen** gern: *with the greatest (of) pleasure; with pleasure; delighted*

Kannst du mir für ein paar Tage 50 Mark leihen? – Von Herzen gern.
*Can you lend me fifty marks for a few days? – With the greatest (of) pleasure (With pleasure; Delighted).*

j.em ans **Herz** gewachsen sein (fig.): *to be near (dear) to s.b.'s heart*

Die kleine Nichte ist deinen Eltern besonders ans Herz gewachsen.
*Their little niece is particularly near (dear) to your parents' hearts.*

j.em klopft das **Herz** bis an (in) den Hals: *s.b.'s heart leaps into his mouth*

Mir klopfte das Herz bis an (in) den Hals, als ich das Wildschwein vor mir stehen sah.
*My heart leapt into my mouth when I saw the wild boar standing in front of me.*

mit **Herz** und Hand: *heart and soul.* Cf. auch: mit **Leib** und Seele

Der junge Offizier hat sich mit Herz und Hand dem Vaterland verschrieben.
*The young officer has pledged himself heart and soul to his country.*

sein **Herz** in die Hand nehmen (fig.): cf. sich ein **Herz** fassen

j.es **Herz** hängt an etwas (fig.): *to be attached to s. th. (fond of s. th.); s. th. is dear to one's heart*

Obwohl diese Bücher alt sind, will ich sie nicht verkaufen; denn mein Herz hängt an ihnen.
*Although these books are old, I do not want to sell them, because I am greatly attached to (fond of) them (they are very dear to my heart).*

sein **Herz** an etwas hängen (fig.): *to set one's heart on s. th.*

Man sollte sein Herz nicht zu sehr an irdische Dinge hängen.
*One ought not to set one's heart too much on earthly things.*

Das **Herz** fällt einem in die Hose (fig. u. fam.): *One's heart drops; One's heart sinks into one's boots; to get cold feet (colloq.).* Cf. auch: kalte **Füße** bekommen

Das Herz fiel dem Studenten in die Hose (Schuhe), als er die Examensbedingungen las.
*The student's heart dropped (sank into his boots; The student got cold feet) when he read the examination requirements.*

Das **Herz** lacht einem im Leibe (fig.): *One's heart jumps (leaps) for joy; One's heart rejoices*

Das Herz lacht mir im Leibe (schlägt mir höher), wenn ich von meinen Kindern selbstgearbeitete Geschenke bekomme.
*My heart jumps (leaps) for joy (rejoices) when I get home-made presents from my children.*

j.em etwas ans **Herz** legen (fig.): cf. j.em etwas zu **Gemüte** führen

j.em sehr am **Herzen** liegen (fig.): a) *to set one's heart on s. th.;* b) *to have s. th. at heart*

a) Es liegt unsern Eltern sehr am Herzen, daß wir gute Schulnoten bekommen.
b) Sie wissen, daß mir Ihre Interessen sehr am Herzen liegen.
*a) Our parents have set their hearts on our getting good marks at school.*
*b) You know that I have your interests very much at heart.*

j.em schwer auf dem **Herzen** liegen (fig.): cf. j.em wie ein **Alp** auf der Seele liegen. Cf. auch: j.em (schwer) im **Magen** liegen

seinem **Herzen** Luft machen (fig.): *to give vent to one's feelings; to get it off one's chest (colloq.); to blow off steam (sl.).* Cf. auch: seinen Gefühlen freien **Lauf** lassen

Vater machte seinem Herzen Luft, indem er meinen frechen Bruder tüchtig ausschimpfte.
*Father gave vent to his feelings (got it off his chest; blew off steam) by scolding my impudent brother sharply.*

aus seinem **Herzen** keine Mördergrube machen (fig.): *not to play the hypocrite; not to garble (to dissemble) one's true feelings*

Ich will aus meinem Herzen keine Mördergrube machen, sondern offen bekennen, daß mir Ihr Neffe äußerst unsympathisch ist.
*I will not play the hypocrite (not garble [dissemble] my true feelings) but confess openly that I find your nephew extremely objectionable.*

Wes (Wovon) das **Herz** voll ist, des (davon) geht der Mund über (Sprichw.):
*What is in one's heart is on one's lips*

Wilhelm erzählte mir immer wieder von dem schönen Mädchen, das er kennengelernt hatte. Wes das Herz voll ist, des geht der Mund über.
*William told me again and again about the beautiful girl he had met. What is in one's*
*heart is on one's lips.*

sich etwas zu **Herzen** nehmen: *to take s.th. to heart; to be deeply touched by*
*s.th.; to take (to carry) on about s.th. (colloq.)*

Meine Freundin nahm sich den Tod (Meiner Freundin ging der Tod) ihrer
Eltern so zu Herzen (Meine Freundin nahm den Tod ... so tragisch), daß sie
schließlich ins Kloster ging.
*My friend took her parents' death so much to heart (took [carried] on so much about*
*[was so deeply touched by] her parents' death) that she finally went into a convent.*

j.en auf **Herz** und Nieren prüfen (fig.): *to put s.b. through his paces*

Die Examinatoren prüften uns mehrere Stunden auf Herz und Nieren.
*The examiners put us through our paces for several hours.*

sich etwas vom **Herzen** reißen (fig.:) *it is a wrench for s.b.*

Wenn ich Ihnen diese Erstausgabe schenke, so reiße ich sie mir wirklich vom
Herzen.
*It is a real wrench for me to give you this first edition.*

seinem **Herzen** einen Ruck geben (fig.): cf. sich einen **Ruck** geben

j.em sein **Herz** schenken: *to give (to pledge) s.b. one's heart*

Ernst hat Elisabeth sein Herz geschenkt und ihr ewige Treue geschworen.
*Ernest has given (pledged) Elizabeth his heart and sworn eternal faithfulness to her.*

Das **Herz** schlägt einem höher (fig.): Das **Herz** lacht einem im Leibe

j.en in sein **Herz** schließen (fig.): *to take s.b. to one's heart; to have a soft spot*
*for s.b.*

Wir Kinder hatten unsern Opa ganz besonders in unser Herz geschlossen.
*We children had particularly taken our grandpa to our hearts (had a specially soft spot*
*for our grandpa).*

Es schneidet einem ins **Herz** (fig.): cf. Es bricht einem das **Herz**

Das **Herz** fällt einem in die Schuhe (fig. u. fam.): cf. Das **Herz** fällt einem
in die Hose

mit schwerem **Herzen** (schweren Herzens): cf. blutenden **Herzens**

éin **Herz** und éine Seele sein (fig.): *to be of one heart and mind; to be as thick*
*as thieves (colloq.); to be all over each other (colloq.).* Cf. auch: **Busenfreunde** sein

233

Die beiden Brüder, die früher immer Streit miteinander hatten, sind jetzt éin Herz und éine Seele.

*The two brothers, who always used to be quarrelling, are now of one heart and mind (as thick as thieves; all over each other).*

j.em ins **Herz** sehen (schauen) (fig.): *to look into s.b.'s heart*

Ich habe meinem Freund ins Herz gesehen (geschaut) und festgestellt, welches seine wahren Gefühle sind.

*I have looked into my friend's heart and found out what his true feelings are.*

j.em aus dem **Herzen** sprechen: cf. j.em aus der **Seele** sprechen

j.es **Herz** steht danach (fig.): *s.b.'s heart is set on it*

Wenn dir dein Herz danach steht, dann kaufe ich dir diesen neuen Füller.

*If your heart is set on it, I will buy you that new fountain-pen.*

j.em das **Herz** stehlen (fig.): *to steal s.b.'s heart*

Mein Vetter kann diesem Mädchen nicht widerstehen; es hat ihm das Herz gestohlen.

*My cousin cannot resist that girl; she has stolen his heart.*

ein **Herz** von Stein haben (fig.): cf. ein Herz von **Stein** haben

seinem **Herzen** einen Stoß geben (fig.): cf. sich einen **Ruck** geben

j.en ins **Herz** treffen (fig.): cf. Es bricht einem das **Herz**

sein **Herz** verlieren (fig.): *to lose one's heart*

Als er das hübsche Mädchen sah, verlor er gleich sein Herz.

*When he saw the pretty girl, he lost his heart at once.*

Es zerreißt einem das **Herz** (fig.): *It wrings one's heart; It tears at one's heartstrings.* Cf. auch: Es bricht einem das **Herz**

Es zerreißt uns das Herz, soviel Armut und Elend zu sehen.

*It wrings our hearts (tears at our heartstrings) to see so much poverty and misery.*

dem Zuge des **Herzens** folgen (fig.): *to follow the dictates of one's heart*

Mein Freund will dem Zuge des Herzens folgen und dieses Mädchen heiraten, obwohl es sehr arm ist.

*My friend is going to follow the dictates of his heart and marry that girl, in spite of the fact that she is very poor.*

das **Herz** auf der Zunge haben (fig.): *to wear one's heart on one's sleeve*

Jeder weiß, was dein Bruder von diesem Mädchen hält, da er das Herz auf der Zunge hat.

*Everyone knows what your brother thinks of that girl, because he wears his heart on his sleeve.*

ein **Herzensbrecher** sein: cf. ein **Herzensdieb** sein

ein **Herzensdieb** sein: *to be a charmer (a Don Juan; a Casanova; a lady-killer)*

Dieser junge Künstler ist ein richtiger Herzensdieb (Herzensbrecher; Don Juan; Schürzenjäger; Schwerenöter).
*That young artist is a regular charmer (Don Juan; Casanova; lady-killer).*

nach **Herzenslust** etwas tun: *to do s. th. to one's heart's content*

Es war alles im Überfluß vorhanden. Wir konnten nach Herzenslust essen und trinken.
*Everything was available in abundance. We were able to eat and drink to our heart's content.*

Geld wie **Heu** haben: cf. **Geld** wie Heu haben

mit (unter) **Heulen** und Zähneklappern (fam.): *with weeping and gnashing of teeth; in fear and trembling; trembling (shivering) in one's shoes; in a blue funk (sl.).*
Cf. auch: eine **Heidenangst** haben

Er gestand mit (unter) (Heulen und) Zähneklappern (mit Zittern und Zagen), daß er die Äpfel gestohlen habe.
*He confessed with weeping and gnashing of teeth (in fear and trembling; trembling [shivering] in his shoes; in a blue funk) that he had stolen the apples.*

ein **Heulfritze** (eine **Heulsuse**) sein (fam.): *to be a cry-baby (colloq.); to be a blubber (sl.)*

Wein' doch nicht so, du dummer Heulfritze (du dumme Heulsuse)!
*Don't cry like that, you silly cry-baby (blubber)!*

eine alte **Hexe** sein (fig.): *to be an old witch (a fire-eater; a tartar; an old shrew) (colloq.)*

In dem Hause drüben wohnt eine alte Hexe (Xanthippe; böse Sieben), mit der niemand etwas zu tun haben will.
*In the house over there lives an old witch (fire-eater; tartar; old shrew) with whom no-one wants to have anything to do.*

Ich kann doch nicht **hexen**!: *I'm not a magician (a wizard)*

Wie kann ich in 10 Minuten das Mittagessen fertig haben? Ich kann doch nicht hexen!
*How can I get lunch ready in 10 minutes? I'm not a magician (wizard).*

Das ist doch keine **Hexerei**: *There's nothing (wonderful; marvellous) in that; There's nothing to it.* Cf. auch: **kinderleicht** sein

Dein Fahrrad werde ich bald repariert haben. Das ist doch keine Hexerei.
*I shall soon have mended your bicycle. There's nothing (wonderful; marvellous) in that (nothing to it).*

j.es **Hieb** parieren (fig.): *to parry (to counter) s.b.'s blow*

Der Minister wurde während der Debatte im Unterhaus scharf angegriffen, er hat jedoch den Hieb seines Gegners sofort pariert.
*The minister was violently attacked during the debate in the lower house but he parried (countered) his opponent's blow immediately.*

j.em einen **Hieb** versetzen (fig.): *to stop (to halt) s.b. in his tracks; to deal s.b. a blow*

Mit deiner Bemerkung über seine zweifelhafte Vergangenheit hast du ihm einen tüchtigen Hieb (Stich) versetzt.
*You stopped (halted) him in his tracks (dealt him a heavy blow) with your remark about his doubtful past.*

**hieb- und stichfest** sein (fig.): *to be watertight; to be fool-proof; to hold water*

Der Anwalt argumentierte sehr schlau, aber seine Beweisgründe waren nicht hieb- und stichfest (stichhaltig).
*The lawyer argued very cunningly, but his arguments were not watertight (fool-proof; did not hold water).*

Du bist wohl nicht von **hier!** (fam.): cf. Aber sonst geht's dir **gut?**

bis **hierher** und nicht weiter: *thus far and no further*

Ich habe Ihnen viele Konzessionen gemacht, aber jetzt ist Schluß. Bis hierher und nicht weiter.
*I have made many concessions to you but this is the end. Thus far and no further.*

das Blaue vom **Himmel** herunterreden (-schwatzen): cf. das **Blaue** vom Himmel herunterreden

das Blaue vom **Himmel** (herunter)lügen: cf. lügen, daß sich die **Balken** biegen

j.em das Blaue vom **Himmel** versprechen: cf. j.em goldene **Berge** versprechen

**Himmel** und Erde (Hölle) in Bewegung setzen (fig.): cf. alle **Hebel** in Bewegung setzen

j.em den **Himmel** auf Erden versprechen (fig.): cf. j.em goldene **Berge** versprechen

**Himmel** und Erde zu Zeugen anrufen (fig.): *to call heaven and earth to witness*

Der Angeklagte rief Himmel und Erde zu Zeugen an, um seine Unschuld zu beteuern.
*The accused called heaven and earth to witness and pleaded his innocence.*

aus allen **Himmeln** gefallen sein (fig.): cf. wie aus den **Wolken** gefallen

Gebe der **Himmel,** daß . . . : *I hope to goodness that* . . .

    Gebe der Himmel, daß wir während der Ferien gutes Wetter haben!
    *I hope to goodness that we have good weather during the holidays.*

Der **Himmel** hängt einem voller Geigen (fig.): *One sees the world through rose-coloured spectacles; One's hopes are high.* Cf. auch: alles durch die rosarote (rosige) **Brille** betrachten

    In der Jugend hängt einem meistens der Himmel voller Geigen.
    *In youth one generally sees the world through rose-coloured spectacles (one's hopes are generally high).*

j.en (etwas) in den **Himmel** (er)heben (fig.): *to praise (to laud; to extol) s.b. (s.th.) to the skies; to sing s.b.'s (s.th.'s) praises.* Cf. auch: j.em **Weihrauch** streuen

    Dieses Städtchen, das von den Ferienreisenden so in den Himmel gehoben (erhoben) wird (über den [grünen] Klee gelobt wird; auf das die F. so ein Loblied singen), möchte ich auch mal persönlich kennenlernen.
    *I should like to get to know for myself that little town which is praised (lauded; extolled) to the skies (whose praises are so much sung) by holidaymakers.*

Ach, du lieber **Himmel**!: cf. Ach, du liebe (meine) **Güte**!

im siebenten **Himmel** sein (fig.): *to be in the seventh heaven (of delight); to be walking (treading) on air*

    Seitdem der Künstler in Paris lebt, ist er im siebenten Himmel (ganz weg).
    *Since the artist has been living in Paris, he has been in the seventh heaven (of delight; he has been walking [treading] on air).*

zum **Himmel** schreien (stinken) (fig.): *to cry out; to cry to heaven*

    Diese grobe Ungerechtigkeit schreit (stinkt) zum Himmel.
    *This gross injustice cries out (cries to heaven).*

Weiß der **Himmel,** . . . (fam.): cf. Das wissen die **Götter**!

Um **Himmels** willen!: cf. In **Gottes** Namen! a)

einem **himmelangst** werden: cf. einem **angst** und bange werden. Cf. auch: (eine) **Heidenangst** haben

eine **Himmelfahrtsnase** haben (fam.): *to have a turned-up nose*

    Elisabeth wäre ein hübsches Mädchen, wenn sie nicht eine Himmelfahrtsnase hätte.
    *Elizabeth would be a pretty girl if she had not got a turned-up nose.*

ein **Himmelstürmer** sein (fig.): *to be a firebrand*

> Dieser junge Himmelstürmer will sein Ziel zu rasch erreichen.
> *This young firebrand wants to reach his goal too quickly.*

**himmelweit** von etwas entfernt sein (fig.): *to be far removed from s.th.; to be miles away from s.th. (colloq.)*

> Karl ist himmelweit davon entfernt, ein guter Pianist zu sein.
> *Charles is far removed (miles away) from being a good pianist.*

(charakterlich) **himmelweit** voneinander entfernt sein: cf. **grundverschieden** sein

ein **himmelweiter** Unterschied: cf. **grundverschieden** sein

nach vielem **Hin** und Her: cf. nach vielem **Wenn** und Aber

nicht **hin** und nicht her reichen: *not to be enough to make ends meet.* Cf. auch: nicht zum **Leben** und nicht zum Sterben reichen

> Unsere Lage wird ernst, denn mein Gehalt reicht nicht hin und nicht her.
> *Our situation is becoming serious, because my salary is not enough to make ends meet.*

**Hin** ist hin: *It's no good crying over spilt milk (prov.); What's done is done (What's past is past); It's (all) over and done with*

> Du hast die Gelegenheit verpaßt, und jetzt ist es zu spät. Hin ist hin.
> *You've missed the opportunity and now it's too late. It's no good crying over spilt milk (What's done [past] is done [past]; It's all over and done with).*

j.em **Hindernisse** in den Weg legen (fig.): *to put obstacles in s.b.'s way (path)*

> Anstatt mir zu helfen, hat er mir nur Hindernisse in den Weg gelegt.
> *Instead of helping me, he only put obstacles in my way (path).*

sich in etwas **hineinknien** (fig. u. fam.): *to get down to s.th.; to tackle s.th. properly*

> Man muß sich in diese Arbeit richtig hineinknien.
> *One must really get down to this work (really tackle this work properly).*

in etwas **hineinschlittern** (fig.): *to slide (to fall) into s.th.; to slither into s.th. (colloq.)*

> Wenn der Präsident die Gefahr nicht rechtzeitig erkannt hätte, so wäre das Land in eine schwierige Lage hineingeschlittert.
> *If the President had not recognised the danger in time, the country would have slid (fallen; slithered) into a difficult situation.*

**hingerissen** sein (fig.): cf. **hinsein** a)

**hin- und hergerissen** sein (fig.): *to be (caught) in two minds; to be torn between two (three etc.) things*

Ich war lange hin- und hergerissen, ob ich meinem neuen Kollegen Geld leihen oder ihm seine Bitte abschlagen sollte.
*For a long time I was (caught) in two minds as to whether to lend my new colleague money or to refuse (I was torn between lending . . . and refusing his request).*

**hinhauen** (fam.): a) *to scribble down; to rush (to bolt) through;* b) *to do (colloq.);* c) *to shake (colloq.); to knock sideways (colloq.); to shake rigid (sl.)*

a) Man sieht es deiner Schrift an, daß du deine schriftlichen Schulaufgaben rasch hingehauen (hingehudelt; hingesudelt) hast.
b) Wir haben jetzt 1000 Mark gespart. Das wird hinhauen, um ein gebrauchtes Auto zu kaufen.
c) Wenn ich Beethovens 5. Sinfonie höre, haut es mich jedesmal hin.
*a) One can see from your writing that you have (just) scribbled down (rushed [bolted] through) your homework.*
*b) We have now saved 1000 marks. That will do to buy a second-hand car.*
*c) Every time I hear Beethoven's Fifth Symphony I am shaken (knocked sideways; shaken rigid).*

**hinken** (fig.): *to miss the mark; not (quite) to click (colloq.)*

Die Vergleiche in deinem Aufsatz hinken.
*The similes in your essay miss the mark (don't [quite] click).*

**hinschlagen:** cf. Da **schlage** einer lang hin!

**hinsein** (fam.): a) *to be carried away (swept off one's feet);* b) *to be done for (colloq.); to have had it (sl.)*

a) Von diesem Roman bin ich einfach hin (hingerissen; futsch).
b) Meine Schwester ist in einen Regenguß geraten, und ihr neues Kleid ist hin (hinüber; hops).
*a) I am simply carried away (swept off my feet) by this novel.*
*b) My sister was caught in a downpour and her new dress is done for (has had it).*

j.en **hinten** und vorn bedienen: *to wait on s.b. hand and foot*

Diese treue Angestellte bedient ihre Herrin hinten und vorn.
*This faithful servant waits on her mistress hand and foot.*

j.en **hinten** und vorn betrügen: *to cheat s.b. left and right*

Ich habe erst jetzt gemerkt, daß mich mein Vertreter hinten und vorn (vorn und hinten) betrogen hat.
*I have only just noticed that my deputy has been cheating me left and right.*

es j.em vorn und **hinten** reinstecken (fig. u. fam.): *to spoon-feed s.b. (colloq.)*

Dein Vater verwöhnt dich zu sehr. Er steckt es dir vorn und hinten rein.
*Your father spoils you too much; he spoon-feeds you.*

etwas **hintenherum** kaufen: cf. unter der **Hand** etwas kaufen

**hinter** j.em hersein (fig. u. fam.): cf. j.em im **Nacken** sitzen

sich auf die **Hinterbeine** stellen (fig.): *to get up on one's hind legs (colloq.)*

Du solltest dich auf die Hinterbeine stellen und gegen diese ungerechten Maßnahmen protestieren.
*You ought to get up on your hind legs and protest against these unjust measures.*

**hinterdreinzotteln** (fam.): cf. **nachzotteln**

in den **Hintergrund** drängen: cf. in den **Schatten** stellen

sich im **Hintergrund** halten: *to keep in the background; to remain behind the scenes*

Dieser Minister ist selten an die Öffentlichkeit getreten, sondern hat sich meistens im Hintergrund gehalten.
*This minister has seldom appeared in public but generally kept in the background (remained behind the scenes).*

in den **Hintergrund** treten (fig.): *to pale into insignificance; to take a back seat (colloq.)*

Gegenüber diesem furchtbaren Eisenbahnunglück traten alle kleineren Unfälle in den Hintergrund.
*In the face of this terrible railway crash all smaller accidents paled into insignificance (took a back seat).*

ins **Hintertreffen** geraten (fig.): *to get behindhand; to get left behind.* Cf. auch: an **Boden** verlieren

Ein Forscher muß sich mit allen neuen Entdeckungen auf seinem Gebiet vertraut machen, sonst gerät er ins Hintertreffen.
*A research-worker has to make himself familiar with all new discoveries in his field, otherwise he will get behindhand (get left behind).*

**Hintertreppenliteratur:** *cheap (trashy) literature; trash*

Durch solche Hintertreppenliteratur sind viele Autoren reich geworden.
*Many authors have become rich through such cheap (trashy) literature (such trash).*

sich eine **Hintertür** offenlassen (fig.): *to leave o.s. a loop-hole (a way-out)*

Er hat uns nicht die volle Wahrheit gesagt. Offenbar will er sich eine Hintertür (einen Ausweg) offenlassen.
*He has not told us the whole truth. Obviously he wants to leave himself a loop-hole (way-out).*

ein **Hinterwäldler** sein: *to be a country bumpkin (a yokel; a Hottentot)*

Als der Bauer zum ersten Mal in die Großstadt kam, benahm er sich wie ein Hinterwäldler.

*When the farmer went up to town for the first time, he behaved like a country bumpkin (yokel; Hottentot).*

**hinüber** sein (fam.): cf. **hinsein** b)

**Hinz** und Kunz: *every Tom, Dick and Harry; all and sundry; the hoi polloi*
Ich wünschte, mein Sohn würde nicht mit Hinz und Kunz (Hans und Franz; Krethi und Plethi) verkehren.
*I wish my son would not mix with every Tom, Dick and Harry (with all and sundry; with the hoi polloi).*

arm wie **Hiob** sein: cf. arm wie eine **Kirchenmaus** sein

**Hiobsbotschaft (Hiobspost)**: *ill (bad) tidings; fateful news*
Ich erhielt die Hiobsbotschaft (Hiobspost), daß mein Schwager bei einem Unfall schwer verletzt worden sei.
*I received the ill (bad) tidings (fateful news) that my brother-in-law had been seriously injured in an accident.*

nicht j.es **Hirn** entsprungen sein: *not to spring from (not to come out of) s.b.'s mind (head); not to be s.b.'s brainwave (colloq.)*
Eine so unsinnige Idee kann doch wohl nicht deinem Hirn (Gehirn; Kopf) entsprungen (nicht auf deinem Grund und Boden [deinem Mist] gewachsen) sein?
*Such a senseless idea surely cannot have sprung from (come out of) your mind (head; surely cannot have been your brainwave)?*

sich das **Hirn** zermartern: cf. sich den **Kopf** zerbrechen

der **Hirnkasten** (fam.): cf. der **Gehirnskasten**

**hirnverbrannt**: *crazy (lunatic); cracked (bats; scatterbrained) (colloq.)*
Es wäre hirnverbrannt, sich an dieser Afrikareise zu beteiligen.
*It would be crazy (lunatic; cracked; bats; scatterbrained) to take part in this trip to Africa.*

in der **Hitze** des Gefechts (fig.): cf. im **Eifer** des Gefechts

ein **Hitzkopf** sein: cf. ein **Heißsporn** sein

j.em den **Hobel** ausblasen können (fig. u. fam.): cf. j.em den **Buckel** herunterrutschen (heraufsteigen) können. Cf. auch: Scher' dich zum **Henker!**

**hoch** und heilig versprechen: cf. j.em sein (Ehren)**wort** geben

**hoch** hergehen: *to go off (to be done) in grand (great) style (with great gusto [élan])*

Bei meiner Geburtstagsfeier ging es hoch her.
*My birthday party went off (was done) in grand (great) style (with great gusto [élan]).*

**hoch** hinauswollen: *to aim for the stars; to aim high; to take sights on the moon (colloq.)*

Unser Arzt will hoch hinaus. Er beabsichtigt, ein eigenes Sanatorium zu gründen.
*Our doctor is aiming for the stars (aiming high; has taken sights on the moon). He intends to found his own sanatorium.*

j.em zu **hoch** sein (hängen) (fig.): *to be above s.b.'s head (beyond s.b.); to be out of s.b.'s range; s.b. is out of his depth*

Die Philosophie dieses Denkers verstehe ich nicht. Sie ist (hängt) mir zu hoch (geht über [übersteigt] meinen Horizont).
*I do not understand this thinker's philosophy. It is above my head (beyond me; out of my range; I am out of my depth).*

eine **Hochburg**: *a bastion (a bulwark)*

Ihr Land ist eine Hochburg der Demokratie.
*Your country is a bastion (bulwark) of democracy.*

**hochdeutsch** mit j.em reden (fig.): cf. j.en **abkanzeln**

mit **Hochdruck** arbeiten: *to work at high pressure (under great strain; flat out)*

Wir arbeiten jetzt mit Hochdruck, damit die vielen Bestellungen rechtzeitig erledigt werden können.
*We are now working at high pressure (under great strain; flat out) so that the many orders can be attended to in time.*

ein **Hochflieger** sein (fig.): *to be a high-flyer*

Dieser Student sieht sich bereits als einen bedeutenden Gelehrten. Er ist ein wahrer Hochflieger.
*This student already sees himself as an important scholar. He is a real high-flyer.*

**hochgehen** (fig.): cf. aus der **Haut** fahren

**hochgestochen** sein: cf. **hochnäsig** sein

j.en **hochkantig** hinauswerfen: cf. j.en **achtkantig** hinauswerfen

wenn es **hochkommt**: *at the (very) most; at best; The most (best) I (you, etc.) can expect is . . .*

Wenn es hochkommt, fahre ich viermal im Jahr nach London.
*At the (very)most (At best) I go (The most I can expect is to go) to London four times a year.*

j.en **hochleben** lassen: *to give three cheers for s.b.*

Wir haben unsern Chef (dreimal) hochleben lassen.
*We gave three cheers for our boss.*

**Hochmut** kommt vor dem Fall (Sprichw.): *Pride goes before a fall (prov.)*

Heinrich hat für seinen Aufsatz eine gute Note bekommen und tut, als sei er uns überlegen. Aber Hochmut kommt vor dem Fall.
*Henry got a good mark for his essay and is behaving as though he were superior to us, but pride goes before a fall.*

vor **Hochmut** platzen: *to be eaten up (to be consumed) with pride*

Diese Gräfin ist eine unerträgliche Person. Sie platzt vor Hochmut.
*This countess is an unbearable person. She is eaten up (consumed) with pride.*

**hochnäsig** sein: *to give o.s. airs; to be stuck-up (puffed-up; snooty) (colloq.)*

Er stammt aus einfachen Verhältnissen und hat gar keine Veranlassung, so hochnäsig (hochgestochen) zu sein.
*He comes from humble circumstances and has no cause at all to give himself airs like that (to be so stuck-up [puffed up; snooty]).*

das **höchste** der Gefühle: *the limit; the most one can manage*

Ich kann nicht viel Alkohol vertragen; 2–3 Glas Bier sind für mich das höchste der Gefühle.
*I cannot take a great deal of alcohol; two or three glasses of beer are my limit (is the most I can manage).*

**hochtönend (hochtrabend):** *high-flown; inflated*

Dein Freund Wilhelm führt immer hochtönende (hochtrabende) Reden.
*Your friend William always makes high-flown (inflated) speeches.*

**Hochwasser** haben (fig. u. fam.): *s.b.'s trousers are at half-mast (colloq.)*

Fritz hat Hochwasser. Seine Hosen sind (ihm) viel zu kurz.
*Fred's trousers are at half-mast. They are far too short for him.*

einer Frau den **Hof** machen: *to court a woman*

Zwei Jahre lang machte ich meiner Frau den Hof (schnitt ich meiner Frau die Cour), bevor ich sie heiratete.
*I courted my wife for two years before I married her.*

guter **Hoffnung** sein : *to be in the family way (colloq.)*

Die Frau gegenüber ist guter Hoffnung (in anderen [gesegneten] Umständen). Sie erwartet ihr erstes Baby.
*The woman opposite is in the family way. She is expecting her first baby.*

j.en **hofieren:** *to woo s.b.; to curry favour with s.b.; to toady to s.b.; to dance attendance on s.b.; to crawl round s.b.; to soft-soap s.b. (colloq.)*

Erich ist bei seinen Kollegen nicht beliebt, weil er seinen Vorgesetzten immer hofiert (seinem V. Honig um den Bart [Mund] schmiert).
*Eric is not popular with his colleagues because he is always wooing (currying favour with; toadying to; dancing attendance on; crawling round; soft-soaping) his boss.*

auf der **Höhe** sein: *to be up to the mark (up to scratch); to be o.s.; to be as fit as a fiddle; to be in fine fettle (fine shape; fine form); to be as right as rain; to be in the pink (colloq.); to be on top line (colloq.)*

Ich war eine Zeitlang krank, aber jetzt bin ich wieder auf der Höhe (auf dem Damm [Posten]; im Lot; in [im] Schuß; gesund und munter; taktfest).
*I have been ill for a while but now I am up to the mark (up to scratch; myself; as fit as a fiddle; in fine fettle [shape; form]; as right as rain; in the pink; on top line) again.*

nicht auf der **Höhe** sein (sich nicht auf der Höhe fühlen): *to be out of sorts; to be off colour; not to be o.s.; not to be up to the mark (up to scratch); not to be on top line (colloq.); to feel seedy (sl.)*

Ich möchte heute lieber zu Hause bleiben. Denn ich bin (fühle mich) nicht auf der Höhe (in [im] Schuß).
*I should prefer to stay at home today because I am out of sorts (not up to the mark; off colour; not myself; not up to scratch; not on top line; I feel seedy)*

Das ist doch die **Höhe** (der **Höhepunkt**)!: *That's the limit!; That's the last straw!; That's more than flesh and blood can bear; That puts the lid on it! (colloq.); That takes the cake! (colloq.); That beats (caps) the lot! (colloq.); That's the (giddy) limit! (colloq.)*

Ich habe dir erst vorige Woche Geld geliehen, und jetzt willst du wieder 100 Mark von mir. Das ist doch die Höhe (der Höhepunkt; allerhand; ein dicker Hund; das Tüpfelchen auf dem i; ein starkes Stück; Da hört [sich] doch alles [der Bindfaden; die Hutschnur; die Weltgeschichte] auf; Das geht auf keine Kuhhaut; Das Maß ist voll; Das hat mir gerade noch gefehlt; Das schlägt dem Faß den Boden aus; Das setzt allem die Krone auf; Nun hat's aber geschnappt)!
*I lent you some money only last week and now you want another 100 marks from me. That's the (giddy) limit (the last straw; more than flesh and blood can bear; That puts the lid on it [takes the cake; beats (caps) the lot]).*

auf der **Höhe** des Lebens stehen: *to be in the prime of life*

Mein Vater ist jetzt vierzig Jahre alt und steht auf der Höhe des Lebens.
*My father is now forty years old and in the prime of life.*

die **Höhen** und Tiefen (fig.): cf. das **Auf** und Ab

sich in die **Höhle** des Löwen begeben (fig.): *to enter the lion's den (cage)*

Da er außer der Reihe Urlaub haben wollte, mußte er sich in die Höhle des Löwen begeben und den Chef selbst um Genehmigung bitten.

*As he wanted leave out of turn, he had to enter the lion's den (cage) and ask the boss himself for permission.*

ein **Hohlkopf** sein (fig.): *to be a dull-wit; to be a bone-head (a blockhead; a dunderhead) (colloq.); to be a moron (a cretin; a clot) (sl.).* Cf. auch: ein **Rindvieh** sein

Irmgard versteht die einfachsten Sachen nicht. Sie ist ein richtiger Hohlkopf.
*Irmgard does not understand the simplest things. She is a proper dull-wit (bone-head; blockhead; dunderhead; moron; cretin; clot).*

Frau **Holle** schüttelt die Federn (Betten): cf. Frau Holle schüttelt die **Federn** (Betten)

die **Hölle** auf Erden haben (fig.): *life is hell on earth for s.b.; to have a hell of a time (colloq.)*

Marie tut mir leid. Ihr Mann ist ein Säufer, und sie hat die Hölle auf Erden.
*I am sorry for Mary. Her husband is a drunkard, and life is hell on earth for her (and she has a hell of a time).*

j.em die **Hölle** heiß machen (fig.): *to worry the life out of s.b.; to make things hot for s.b. (colloq.); to lead s.b. a dog's life (colloq.); to give s.b. hell (sl.)*

Der Sohn hat seinem Vater die Hölle heiß (den Kopf warm) gemacht, bis er ihm endlich ein neues Fahrrad gekauft hat.
*The son worried the life out of his father (made things hot for his father; led his father a dog's life; gave his father hell) until he finally bought him a new bicycle.*

Die **Hölle** ist los (fig.): cf. Der **Teufel** ist los

eine **Höllenangst** haben: cf. (eine) **Heidenangst** haben

einen **Höllenlärm** machen: cf. einen **Heidenlärm** machen

**höllisch** aufpassen: *to keep one's eyes skinned; to keep a sharp look-out*

Man muß höllisch aufpassen, wenn man diesen seltenen Vogel sehen will.
*One must keep one's eyes skinned (keep a sharp look-out) if one wants to see this rare bird.*

**höllisch** teuer sein: cf. (nicht) die **Welt** kosten

**holterdiepolter** (fam.): *helter-skelter*

Die Tür des Klassenzimmers ging auf, und die Schüler liefen holterdiepolter hinaus.
*The classroom door opened and the pupils ran out helter-skelter.*

aus dem gleichen **Holze** geschnitzt (geschnitten) sein (fig.): *to be made of the same stuff; to be cast in the same mould; (nur im schlechten Sinne auch:) to be tarred with the same brush*

Heinrichs Vater war ein Dieb, und der Sohn scheint leider aus demselben Holze geschnitzt (geschnitten) zu sein.
*Henry's father was a thief, and the son seems unfortunately to be made of the same stuff (to be cast in the same mould; to be tarred with the same brush).*

an **Holz** klopfen: *to touch wood*

Warum klopfst du an Holz? – Damit mir alles weiterhin gut geht.
*Why do you touch wood? – So that everything will continue to go well with me.*

dastehen wie ein **Holzklotz**: *to stand there like a block of wood (like a statue)*

Los, mach' dich an die Arbeit! Du stehst ja da wie ein Holzklotz.
*Come on, get to work! You're standing there like a block of wood (like a statue).*

auf dem **Holzwege** sein (fig.): *to be barking up the wrong tree; to be on the wrong track (scent; tack); to have got hold of the wrong end of the stick*

Sie sind auf dem Holzwege (auf der falschen Fährte; auf dem falschen Wege; schief gewickelt), wenn Sie glauben, daß ich für diese Unruhen verantwortlich sei.
*You are barking up the wrong tree (You are on the wrong track [scent; tack]; have got hold of the wrong end of the stick) if you think that I am responsible for these disturbances.*

j.em **Honig** um den Bart (Mund) schmieren (fig.): cf. j.en **hofieren**

strahlen wie ein **Honigkuchenpferd** (fam.): *to beam from ear to ear; s.b.'s face is radiant with delight; s.b.'s face shines like a beacon (colloq.)*

Als ich dem Boten 3 Mark Trinkgeld gab, strahlte er wie ein Honigkuchenpferd.
*When I gave the messenger a 3 marks' tip, he beamed from ear to ear (his face was radiant with delight; shone like a beacon).*

**honigsüße** Worte: *honeyed words; soft soap (colloq.)*

Mit honigsüßen Worten versuchte er, das Mädchen für sich zu gewinnen.
*He tried to win over the girl with honeyed words (soft soap).*

an j.em ist **Hopfen** und Malz verloren (fig.): *It is a waste of effort (time) with s.b.; All effort is wasted on s.b.; S.b. is a hopeless case; It's a mug's game (sl.)*

Mein Vetter bekommt jetzt Nachhilfestunden, aber an ihm ist Hopfen und Malz verloren.
*My cousin now has extra coaching, but it is a waste of effort (time) with (all effort is wasted on) him (but he is a hopeless case; but it's a mug's game).*

lang wie eine **Hopfenstange** sein: cf. lang wie eine **Bohnenstange** sein

**hops** sein (gehen) (fam.): cf. **hinsein** b)

Wer nicht **hören** will, muß fühlen (Sprichw.): *If you (he etc.) won't hear (listen), you (he etc.) must be made to feel*

Ich muß Karl bestrafen, da er sehr ungehorsam ist. Wer nicht hören will, muß fühlen.
*I must punish Charles, because he is very disobedient. If he won't hear (listen), he must be made to feel.*

j.em vergeht **Hören** und Sehen: *to take s.b.'s breath away; s.b.'s head swims (goes round and round)*

Das Flugzeug flog so knapp über unser Dach, daß mir Hören und Sehen verging.
*The aeroplane flew so low over our roof that it took my breath away (that my head swam [went round and round]).*

sich nicht aufs **Hörensagen** verlassen: *not to rely on (to go by) hearsay*

Ich will selbst zu ihr hingehen und sie fragen. In solchen Fällen darf man sich nicht aufs Hörensagen verlassen.
*I will go and ask her myself. In such cases one must not rely on (go by) hearsay.*

über j.es **Horizont** gehen (j.es Horizont übersteigen) (fig.): cf. j.em zu **hoch** sein

ins gleiche **Horn** blasen (stoßen; tuten) (fig.): *to sing the same tune; to take the same line (attitude); to tell the same story; to plug the same line (colloq.); to trot out the same story (colloq.)*

Vater hält (den) Fußball(sport) für töricht, und Mutter bläst (stößt; tutet) leider ins gleiche Horn.
*Father considers football stupid, and mother unfortunately sings the same tune (takes the same line [attitude]; tells [trots out] the same story; plugs the same line).*

sich die **Hörner** ablaufen (fig.): a) *to sow one's wild oats; to have one's fling (colloq.);* b) *to be taken down a peg; to bite off more than one can chew*

a) Nachdem sich mein Schwager in der Studentenzeit die Hörner abgelaufen hatte, ist er jetzt ein solider Ehemann geworden.
b) Mein Bruder war immer selbstsicher, aber bei diesem Gegner hat er sich die Hörner abgelaufen.
*a) Having sown his wild oats (Having had his fling) during his student days, my brother-in-law has now become a respectable married man.*
*b) My brother was always self-confident, but that opponent took him down a peg (with that opponent he bit off more than he could chew).*

die **Hörner** einziehen (fig.): *to draw in one's horns; to pipe down (a bit) (colloq.); to soft-pedal (a bit) (colloq.).* Cf. auch: den **Schwanz** einziehen

Nach diesem leichtsinnigen Streich solltest du die Hörner einziehen und ein anständigeres Leben führen.

*After that reckless trick you ought to draw in your horns (pipe down [a bit]; soft-pedal [a bit]) and lead a more respectable life.*

die **Hörner** zeigen (fig.): cf. die **Zähne** zeigen

ausgehen wie das **Hornberger** Schießen: *to end (to go up) in smoke; to fall through; to lead (to get) nowhere; to fizzle (to peter) out; to come to nothing (naught); to be a flop (colloq.)*

Die langen Verhandlungen sind leider wie das Hornberger Schießen ausgegangen (im Sande verlaufen; in Rauch aufgegangen).
*The long negotiations unfortunately ended (went up) in smoke (fell through; led [got] nowhere; fizzled [petered] out; came to nothing [naught]; were a flop).*

ein **Hornochse (Hornvieh)** sein (fig. u. fam.): cf. ein **Rindvieh** sein

Da **hört** (sich) doch alles auf!: cf. Das ist doch die **Höhe!**

die **Hosen** anhaben (fig. u. fam.): *to rule the roost; to wear the breeches (the pants; the trousers) (colloq.).* Cf. auch: allein das **Wort** führen

In dieser Familie hat die Frau die Hosen an (schwingt die Frau den Pantoffel; führt die Frau das Regiment).
*The wife rules the roost (wears the breeches [pants; trousers]) in that family.*

sich auf die **Hosen** (den **Hosenboden**) setzen (fam.): *to get down to it; to buckle to; to buck up; to sit down on one's backside (sl.)*

Wenn du in die nächste Klasse versetzt werden willst, mußt du dich tüchtig auf die Hosen (den Hosenboden) setzen.
*If you want to be moved into the next class, you will really have to get down to it (to buckle to; to buck up; to sit down on your backside).*

j.em die **Hosen** strammziehen (fam.): cf. j.em das **Fell** gerben

die **Hosen** vollhaben (fam.): cf. (eine) **Heidenangst** haben

aussehen wie bei den **Hottentotten** (fam.): cf. ein **Schweinestall** sein

Der eine sagt **hü**, der andere sagt hott (fig.): *One says one thing, the other says another; One says this, the other says that; One takes one line, the other takes another*

In diesem Punkte sind wir uns leider nicht einig. Der eine sagt hü, der andere sagt hott.
*On this point I am afraid we do not agree. I say one thing (take one line), you say (take) another (I say this, you say that).*

j.em die **Hucke** vollügen (fam.): cf. lügen, daß sich die **Balken** biegen j.en **huckepack** tragen (fam.): *to give s.b. a pick-a-back (colloq.)*

Der Vater trug seinen kleinen Sohn huckepack durch das Zimmer.
*The father gave his small son a pick-a-back round the room.*

**hud(e)lig** (fam.): *slapdash (sloppy) (colloq.)*

Du bist bei deiner schriftlichen Arbeit wieder mal sehr hud(e)lig gewesen.
*You have been very slapdash (sloppy) again in your written work.*

mit den **Hühnern** aufstehen: *to rise with the lark.* Cf. auch: in aller **Herrgottsfrühe**

Morgen müssen wir mit den Hühnern aufstehen, weil unser Zug sehr früh abfährt.
*Tomorrow we shall have to rise with the lark because our train leaves very early.*

mit den **Hühnern** zu Bett gehen: *to go to bed in good time*

Heute werde ich mit den Hühnern zu Bett gehen, da ich morgen früh aufstehen muß.
*I shall go to bed in good time tonight because I have to get up early tomorrow.*

Ein blindes **Huhn** findet auch ein Korn (Sprichw.): *Every dog has its (his) day (prov.).* Cf. auch: Jeder hat einmal seinen guten **Tag**

Endlich habe ich auch einmal eine Schachpartie gewonnen. Ein blindes Huhn findet auch ein Korn.
*At last I, too, have won a game of chess. Every dog has its (his) day.*

ein dummes **Huhn** sein (fig.): cf. eine dumme **Gans** sein

das **Huhn** schlachten, das die goldenen Eier legt (fig.): *to kill the hen that lays the golden eggs; to bite the hand that feeds one*

Du darfst deinen reichen Onkel nicht kränken und so das Huhn schlachten, das die goldenen Eier legt.
*You must not offend your rich uncle and so kill the hen that lays the golden eggs (bite the hand that feeds you).*

Da lachen ja die **Hühner!** (fam.): *That's enough to make a horse laugh (colloq.); Don't make me laugh! (colloq.)*

Ihr behauptet, keine Zeit für eure Schulaufgaben zu haben? Da lachen ja die Hühner!
*You say that you haven't time to do your homework? That's enough to make a horse laugh (Don't make me laugh!).*

ein lahmes (krankes) **Huhn** sein (fig.): cf. **lahm** wie eine Ente sein

ein **Hühnchen** mit j.em zu rupfen haben (fig.): *to have a bone to pick with s.b.*

Der Apotheker sagte zu meinem Sohn, daß er ein Hühnchen mit ihm zu rupfen (daß er bei ihm noch etwas im Salz liegen) habe, obwohl der Junge doch nichts getan hatte.
*The chemist told my son that he had a bone to pick with him, although the boy had not done anything.*

### j.em auf die **Hühneraugen** treten (fig.): cf. j.em auf den **Fuß** treten

### im **Hui**: cf. im **Handumdrehen**

### in **Hülle** und Fülle: *heaps (stacks; masses; pots) of . . . (colloq.); . . . in plenty (in abundance); . . . galore (colloq.)*

Dieses Jahr haben wir in unserm Garten Erdbeeren in Hülle und Fülle gehabt.
*This year we had heaps (stacks; masses; pots) of strawberries (strawberries in plenty [abundance]; strawberries galore) in our garden.*

### die sterbliche **Hülle**: *the mortal remains*

Die sterbliche Hülle vieler großer Männer Frankreichs ruht im Pantheon.
*The mortal remains of many great men of France lie in the Pantheon.*

### eine wilde **Hummel** sein (fig.): *to be a tomboy (colloq.)*

Dieses Mädchen spielt immer mit (den) Jungens zusammen. Sie ist eine richtige wilde Hummel.
*This girl is always playing with the boys. She is a real tomboy.*

### auf dem **Hund** sein (fig.): a) *to be in a bad way (in poor shape); to be very shaky;* b) *to be down and out; to be down on one's uppers; to be on the rocks*

a) Vaters Krankheit war so schwer, daß er noch jetzt ganz auf dem Hund ist.
b) Der Juwelier hat sein ganzes Geld verloren und ist jetzt vollkommen auf dem Hund.
*a) Father's illness was so serious that he is still in a very poor way (in very poor shape; very shaky).*
*b) The jeweller has lost all his money and is now completely down and out (is now right down on his uppers; is now well and truly on the rocks).*

### Da liegt der **Hund** begraben (fig.): cf. Da liegt der **Hase** im Pfeffer

### j.en wie einen **Hund** begraben: *to bury s.b. like a dog (like a cur)*

Der Verbrecher wurde hingerichtet und wie ein Hund begraben.
*The criminal was executed and buried like a dog (cur).*

### Den Letzten beißen die **Hunde** (Sprichw.): *He who hesitates is lost (prov.)*

Als die Polizei erschien, sind die Diebe schleunigst davongelaufen. Denn den Letzten beißen die Hunde.
*When the police appeared, the thieves ran off as fast as they could, for he who hesitates is lost.*

**Hunde,** die bellen, beißen nicht (Sprichw.): *Barking dogs do not (or: seldom) bite (prov.); S.b.'s bark is worse than his bite (prov.).* Cf. auch: Es wird nichts so heiß **gegessen,** wie es gekocht wird

> Unser Pedell schimpft oft, aber in Wirklichkeit ist er nicht so unfreundlich. Hunde, die bellen, beißen nicht.
> *Our caretaker often grumbles, but in fact he is not so unfriendly. Barking dogs do not (seldom) bite (His bark is worse than his bite).*

Getroffener **Hund** bellt (Sprichw.): *Touché; The remark struck (went) home*

> Ich hatte meine abfällige Bemerkung nur ganz allgemein gemeint, aber Wilhelm fühlte sich durch sie beleidigt. Getroffener Hund bellt.
> *I had only intended my disparaging remark to be quite general, but William felt offended by it. Touché (The remark had struck [gone] home).*

bekannt sein wie ein bunter **Hund**: cf. **stadtbekannt** sein

ein dicker **Hund** sein (fig. u. fam.): cf. Das ist doch die **Höhe!**

j.em treu wie ein **Hund** folgen: *to follow s.b. like a dog*

> Obwohl er sie oft mißhandelt, folgt sie ihm treu wie ein Hund.
> *Although he often maltreats her, she follows him like a dog.*

vor die **Hunde** gehen (fig.): *to go to the dogs; to come down in the world; to go to pot (sl.).* Cf. auch: auf die abschüssige (schiefe) **Bahn** geraten; auf **Abwege** geraten; es geht mit j.em **bergab**

> Seit seiner Entlassung aus der Fabrik ist mein Bruder leider vor die Hunde gegangen (auf den Hund gekommen).
> *Since his dismissal from the factory I am afraid my brother has gone to the dogs (come down in the world; gone to pot).*

mit allen **Hunden** gehetzt sein (fig.): *to be as cunning (sly) as a fox; to be up to all the tricks (of the trade); to be up to scratch (snuff) (colloq.); to be as cunning (as sly) as they make them (colloq.); There are no flies on s.b. (sl.)*

> Ein guter Detektiv muß mit allen Hunden gehetzt (mit allen Wassern gewaschen) sein (muß es faustdick hinter den Ohren haben).
> *A good detective has to be as cunning (sly) as a fox (has to be up to all the tricks [of the trade]; has to be up to scratch [snuff]; has to be as cunning [sly] as they make them; There are no flies on a good detective).*

Viele **Hunde** sind des Hasen Tod (Sprichw.): *A lot of dogs, and the hare is dead*

> Unser Mittelstürmer sah sich plötzlich vier gegnerischen Spielern gegenüber und verlor den Ball. Viele Hunde sind des Hasen Tod.
> *Our centre-forward suddenly found himself confronted by four opponents and lost the ball. A lot of dogs, and the hare is dead.*

Es kann einen (alten) **Hund** jammern: *It's enough to make anybody (you) (sit down and) weep (sl.)*

Es kann einen (alten) Hund jammern, wenn man hört, wie er Klavier spielt.
*It's enough to make anybody (you) (sit down and) weep to hear him play the piano.*

wie **Hund** und Katze miteinander leben: *to live like cat and dog; to live a cat-and-dog life*

Die beiden Kinder zanken sich ständig. Sie leben wie Hund und Katze miteinander.
*The two children are always wrangling. They live like cat and dog (a cat-and-dog life).*

bei j.em liegt der Knüppel beim **Hund** (fig.): cf. bei j.em liegt der **Knüppel** beim Hund

auf den **Hund** kommen (fig.): cf. vor die **Hunde** gehen

Damit kann man keinen **Hund** hinter dem Ofen hervorlocken: *You won't catch (fool) anybody with that; That won't catch (fool) anybody*

Mit solchen zweifelhaften Angeboten kann man keinen Hund hinter dem Ofen hervorlocken.
*You won't catch (fool) anybody with such dubious offers (Such dubious offers won't catch [fool] anybody).*

j.en wie einen **Hund** (ver)prügeln: cf. j.en zu **Brei** schlagen

unterm **Hund** (unter allem Hund) sein (fig.): cf. unter aller **Kritik** sein

eine **Hundearbeit** sein: *to be back-breaking (crippling) work*

Diesen Baum zu fällen, ist eine richtige Hundearbeit (Pferdearbeit).
*It's back-breaking (crippling) work felling this tree.*

sich **hundeelend** fühlen: *to feel as sick as a dog; to feel rotten (awful) (colloq.)*

Während der stürmischen Überfahrt fühlte ich mich hundeelend (gottserbärmlich [zum Gotterbarmen]; hundsmiserabel).
*During the stormy crossing I felt as sick as a dog (felt rotten [awful]).*

eine **Hundekälte**: *bitterly (infernally) cold weather; brass-monkey weather (colloq.)*

Bei dieser Hundekälte muß man sich dickere Kleidung anziehen.
*In this bitterly (infernally) cold weather (brass-monkey weather) one must put on thicker clothes.*

Das ist ja zum Junge-**Hunde**-Kriegen (fam.): *It's enough to make anybody (you) have a baby (sl.); It's enough to drive anybody (you) round the bend (sl.)*

Ist der Klempner denn noch immer nicht gekommen? Das ist ja zum Junge-Hunde-Kriegen.

*Has the plumber still not come? It's enough to make anybody (you) have a baby (to drive anybody [you] round the bend).*

ein **Hundeleben** führen (fig.): *to lead a dog's life*

Die alten Männer in diesem Armenhaus führten früher ein Hundeleben.
*The old men in this workhouse used to lead a dog's life.*

**hundemüde** sein: *to be dog-tired (dead tired); to be all in (colloq.); to be dead beat (done up) (colloq.).* Cf. auch: **absein**

Nach meinem langen Spaziergang war ich hundemüde (todmüde; zum Umfallen müde; ging ich auf dem Zahnfleisch).
*After my long walk I was dog-tired (dead tired; all in; dead beat; done up).*

kalt wie eine **Hundeschnauze** sein (fam.): cf. **eiskalt** sein

**Hundewetter:** *shocking (terrible; awful) weather*

Laßt uns bei diesem Hundewetter (Sauwetter; Schweinewetter) lieber zu Hause bleiben!
*Let's stay at home in this shocking (terrible; awful) weather.*

eine **hündische** Angst haben: cf. (eine) **Heidenangst** haben

sich **hundsmiserabel** fühlen: cf. sich **hundeelend** fühlen

Nicht der **Hunderste** weiß das: *Not one in a hundred (a thousand) knows that*

Er hat Tatsachen im Kopf, die nicht der Hundertste (Zehnte) weiß.
*He has facts in his head which not one in a hundred (thousand) knows.*

vom **Hundertsten** ins Tausendste kommen: *to pass (to move; to jump) from one thing (subject) to another; to chop and change (about)*

Bei unserer Unterredung blieben wir nicht bei éiner Sache, sondern kamen bald vom Hundertsten ins Tausendste.
*During our discussion we did not keep to one subject but passed (moved; jumped) from one thing (subject) to another (chopped and changed [about]).*

**Hunger** ist der beste Koch (Sprichw.): *Hunger is the best sauce (prov.)*

Der kleine Fritz will nichts essen, aber ich zwänge (zwinge) ihm nichts auf. Hunger ist der beste Koch.
*Little Fred won't eat anything, but I shan't force anything on him. Hunger is the best sauce.*

am **Hungertuch** nagen (fig.): *not to have a bite to eat; not to be able to keep the wolf from the door*

Der Mann ist erst vor einem Jahr gestorben, aber seine Witwe nagt schon jetzt am Hungertuch (hat schon jetzt nichts mehr zu beißen [und zu brechen]; zu knabbern).

*The husband only died a year ago but already his widow has not a bite left to eat (is unable to keep the wolf from the door).*

eine **Hürde** nehmen (überspringen) (fig.): *to clear (to take) a hurdle*

Er hat eine glänzende Laufbahn vor sich, denn er nimmt (überspringt) alle Hürden mit Leichtigkeit.
*He has a brilliant career in front of him, for he clears (takes) all his hurdles with ease.*

**husch,** husch, die Waldfee machen (fam.): cf. **fünf** gerade sein lassen

den **Hut** vor j.em abnehmen (fig.): *to take off one's hat to s.b.; to salute s.b.*

Vor diesem mutigen Schwimmer nehme ich den Hut ab (ziehe ich den Hut).
*I take off my hat to (I salute) this courageous swimmer.*

auf der **Hut** sein: *to be on one's guard (on the qui vive; on the alert; on the look-out); to keep one's eyes skinned*

Vor Taschendieben muß man stets auf der Hut sein.
*One must be continually on one's guard (the qui vive; the alert; the look-out; continually keep one's eyes skinned) for pickpockets.*

unter éinen **Hut** bringen (fig.): *to bring into harmony with each other; to get into line; to bring under one roof*

Es ist natürlich ausgeschlossen, alle politischen Ansichten unter éinen Hut zu bringen.
*It is of course out of the question to bring all political views into harmony with each other (to get . . . into line; to bring . . . under one roof).*

j.em eins auf den **Hut** geben (fig. u. fam.): *to take s.b. down a peg; to rap s.b. over the knuckles; to cut s.b. down to size (colloq.).* Cf. auch: j.en **abkanzeln;** j.en ins **Gebet** nehmen

Es ist Zeit, daß du deinem frechen Sohn eins auf den Hut (Deckel) gibst.
*It is time that you took your impudent son down a peg (rapped . . . over the knuckles; cut . . . down to size).*

Da geht einem doch der **Hut** hoch! (fam.): *It makes one wild (colloq.); It gets one's goat (colloq.); It puts one's back up (colloq.)*

Die Geschäfte in diesem Stadtteil verlangen viel zu viel für ihre Waren. Da geht mir doch der Hut hoch!
*The shops in this part of the town charge much too much for their goods. It makes me wild (gets my goat; puts my back up).*

Das kannst du dir an den **Hut** stecken! (fam.): *You can keep it! (colloq.); You can stick it on the wall (stick it up your jumper)! (sl.)*

Dein Gedicht ist nichts wert. Das kannst du dir an den Hut stecken.
*Your poem is no use. You can keep it (can stick it on the wall [up your jumper])!*

vor j.em den **Hut** ziehen (fig.): cf. vor j.em den **Hut** abnehmen über die **Hutschnur** gehen (fig. u. fam.): *to overstep the mark; to go too far; to be past (beyond) a joke; to be too much of a good thing (colloq.)*

Ich kann viel vertragen, aber das geht doch über die Hutschnur (den Spaß).
*I can stand a lot, but that oversteps the mark (goes too far; is past [beyond] a joke; is too much of a good thing).*

Da hört (sich) doch die **Hutschnur** auf! (fig. u. fam.): cf. Das ist doch die **Höhe!**

# I

**i** bewahre!: cf. i **bewahre!**

**i** wo!: cf. i **bewahre!**

(bis) aufs **i-Tüpfelchen** stimmen: cf. aufs **Haar** stimmen

j.en als sein zweites **Ich** betrachten: *to regard s. b. as one's second self (one's alter ego)*

Der Chef verläßt sich immer auf seinen Prokuristen, den er als sein zweites Ich betrachtet.
*The boss always relies on his deputy, whom he regards as his second self (alter ego).*

eine fixe **Idee** sein: *to have a bee in one's bonnet; to have a fixed idea (an idée fixe); to be a fixed idea (an idée fixe); to be a fad (a kink) (colloq.)*

Es ist eine fixe Idee meines Freundes, die Fortschritte der modernen Physik zu verspotten.
*My friend has a bee in his bonnet (a fixed idea [an idée fixe]) about scoffing at (It is a fixed idea [an idée fixe; a fad; a kink] of my friend's to scoff at) the progress of modern physics.*

Sie haben eine **Idee!** (fam.): *That's what you think! (colloq.); Not on your life! (colloq.)*

Sie halten mich für reicher als sich selbst? Sie haben eine Idee! Ich kann mir keinen Luxus leisten.
*You reckon that I am richer than you? That's what you think (Not on your life)! I can't afford to live in luxury.*

**in** sich gehen: *to acknowledge the error of one's ways; to cry peccavi*

Der Betrüger ist in sich gegangen und hat Besserung versprochen.
*The swindler acknowledged the error of his ways (cried peccavi) and promised to reform.*

es **in** sich haben (fam.): a) *to have a kick in it (colloq.); to be the real thing (the genuine article) (colloq.); to be the real McCoy (sl.);* b) *to be s. b. (to be a force) to be reckoned with; to know one's stuff (to know what's what) (colloq.)*

a) Dieser Rotwein hat's wirklich in sich!
b) Der neue Innenminister ist ein kluger Diplomat. Er hat's in sich.
*a) This red wine really has a kick in it (is the real thing [the genuine article; the real McCoy]).*
*b) The new Minister of the Interior is a wise diplomat. He is somebody (a force) to be reckoned with (He knows his stuff [what's what])*

etwas **in-** und auswendig kennen: cf. etwas bis zum **Tz** kennen

j.en **in-** und auswendig kennen: *to know s.b. inside out; to know s.b. backwards; to know s.b. from A to Z; to be able to read s.b. like a book*

Durch den jahrelangen Kontakt mit diesem Manne kenne ich ihn in- und auswendig (wie meine Westentasche).
*Through years of contact with this man I know him inside out (from A to Z; backwards; I can read him like a book.*

ein **Industrieritter** sein: *to be a captain of industry; to be an industrial boss (magnate)*

In einem Kriege pflegen die Industrieritter viel Geld zu verdienen.
*In a war the captains of industry (industrial bosses [magnates] usually earn a lot of money.*

etwas **inszenieren** (fig.): cf. etwas **anzetteln**

j.es **Intimus** sein: cf. **Busenfreunde** sein

wie ein **Irrer (Irrsinniger; irrsinnig)** laufen: cf. wie **verrückt** (wie ein **Verrückter)** laufen

Was (noch) nicht **ist,** kann (ja) noch werden: *It will come in time; There is still time; All in good time*

Leider haben wir noch keinen Fernsehapparat. Aber was (noch) nicht ist, kann (ja) noch werden.
*Unfortunately we have not got a television set yet, but it will come in time (there is still time; all in good time).*

j.en **itterig** machen (fam.): cf. j.en **rappelig** machen

# J

**ja** und amen zu etwas sagen (fig.): *to say yea and amen to s.th.; to give one's blessing to s.th.*

Sagt deine Mutter ja und amen zu allem, was dein Vater bestimmt?
*Does your mother say yea and amen (give her blessing) to everything that your father decides?*

eine alte **Jacke** sein (fig. u. fam.): cf. einen **Bart** haben

Das ist **Jacke** wie Hose (fam.): cf. **gehupft** wie gesprungen

die **Jacke** vollkriegen (fam.): *to get a good hiding (colloq.); to get one's skin (hide) tanned (colloq.); to catch (to cop) a packet (sl.)*
Wenn du nicht gehorchst, kriegst du die Jacke (den Buckel) voll.
*If you don't obey, you'll get a good hiding (get your skin [hide] tanned; catch [cop] a packet).*

erfolglos **Jagd** auf etwas machen (fig.): *to hunt for s. th. in vain; it is a vain hunt*
Vater will diesen italienischen Satz für seine Briefmarkensammlung erwerben. Bisher aber hat er erfolglos Jagd auf ihn gemacht.
*Father wants to acquire this Italian set for his stamp-collection, but up to now he has been hunting for it in vain (it has been a vain hunt).*

**Jägerlatein:** *travellers' tales; tall stories*
Die drei Förster saßen im Wirtshaus und erzählten viel Jägerlatein.
*The three gamekeepers were sitting in the inn, telling a great number of travellers' tales (tall stories).*

hoch an **Jahren:** *at a ripe old age*
Vergangene Woche ist unsere Urgroßmutter hoch an Jahren gestorben.
*Last week our great-grandmother died at a ripe old age.*

in die **Jahre** kommen: *to be getting on (in years)*
Mein Vater ist nun schon in die Jahre gekommen und muß sich schonen.
*My father is now getting on (in years) and has to take care of himself.*

ein mageres **Jahr** sein: *to be a lean year*
1956 war für den Touristenverkehr ein mageres Jahr.
*1956 was a lean year for tourist traffic.*

**Jahr** und Tag: *for a year and a day*
In diesem Hotel möchte ich Jahr und Tag bleiben.
*I should like to stay in this hotel for a year and a day.*

auf **Jahr** und Tag: *to the day*
Wir sind am 1. April 1951 in unser Haus eingezogen. Ich weiß es noch auf Jahr und Tag.
*We moved into our house on April 1, 1951. I remember it to the day.*

seit **Jahr** und Tag: *for ages; since Domesday; since time immemorial*
Seit Jahr und Tag kämpft diese Partei für eine Besserung der sozialen Verhältnisse.
*For ages (Since Domesday; Since time immemorial) this party has been fighting for an improvement in social conditions.*

über **Jahr** und Tag: *some time or other; sooner or later*

Der Autor arbeitet an der Verbesserung seines Werkes, da er über Jahr und Tag mit einer Neuauflage rechnet.
*The author is engaged in improving his book, because he is counting on a new edition some time or other (sooner or later).*

**jahraus,** jahrein: *year in, year out*

Jahraus, jahrein machen wir zu Pfingsten einen Ausflug aufs Land.
*Year in, year out we go on an excursion into the country at Whitsun.*

der wahre **Jakob** sein (fam.): *to be just what one wants (needs); to be just the thing (the ticket; the job) (colloq.); to be the very thing (colloq.)*

Dieses neue Gerät wird dir die Arbeit wesentlich erleichtern. Es ist der wahre Jakob.
*This new gadget will considerably ease your work. It is just what you want (need; just the thing [ticket; job; the very thing]).*

ein **Jammerlappen** sein (fam.): *to be a cry-baby (a namby-pamby) (colloq.)*

Wie kannst du so ein Jammerlappen sein und vor dem Zahnarzt Angst haben?
*How can you be such a cry-baby (namby-pamby) to be afraid of the dentist?*

**jammerschade** sein: *to be a thousand pities (a great shame)*

Es ist jammerschade, daß Ernst wegen seiner Mandelentzündung nicht mit uns ins Theater gehen kann.
*It is a thousand pities (a great shame) that Ernest cannot come to the theatre with us because of his tonsilitis.*

das irdische **Jammertal:** *the Vale of Sorrows*

Seine kranke Frau wird bald von diesem irdischen Jammertal erlöst sein.
*His invalid wife will soon be freed from this Vale of Sorrows.*

ein **Jasager** sein: *to be a yes-man; to be a stooge (colloq.)*

Dieser Fabrikarbeiter hat keine eigene Meinung; er ist nichts als ein Jasager.
*This factory hand has no opinions of his own; he is nothing but a yes-man (a stooge).*

j.en ins **Jenseits** befördern (fam.): *to despatch s.b. to (to launch s.b. into) the next world (the nether regions; eternity)*

Wenn wir alle Fliegen in unserer Küche ins Jenseits befördern wollen, müssen wir eine Spritze oder einen Fliegenfänger kaufen.
*If we want to despatch all the flies in our kitchen to (to launch all . . . into) the next world (the nether regions; eternity), we must buy a spray or a fly-catcher.*

sich ein **Joch** auferlegen (fig.): *to take a burden (an onus) upon o.s.; to shoulder a burden (load)*

Meine alten Eltern haben sich ein schweres Joch auferlegt, indem sie die beiden verwaisten Kinder bei sich aufgenommen haben.

*My old parents have taken a heavy burden (onus) upon themselves (have shouldered a heavy burden [load] by accepting the two orphaned children into their home.*

**sich dem Joch beugen** (fig.): *to bow (to submit) to the yoke; to knuckle under (colloq.)*

Die besiegte Nation mußte sich dem Joch der Sieger beugen.
*The conquered nation had to bow (submit) to the victors' yoke (had to knuckle under to the victors).*

**johlen:** cf. einen **Heidenlärm** machen

**j.es Johann sein** (fam.): *to be s.b.'s stooge (colloq.)*

Der Einbrecher hatte einen Begleiter bei sich, der sein Johann war.
*The burglar had a companion with him who was his stooge.*

**ein keuscher Joseph sein** (fam.): *to be a flower of the field.* Cf. auch: unschuldig wie ein neugeborenes **Kind** sein

Mein Freund ist ein (wahrer) keuscher Joseph. Man hat ihn noch nie mit einem Mädchen zusammen gesehen.
*My friend is a real flower of the field. He has never been seen with a girl.*

**(um) kein Jota** (fig.): cf. um kein **Haar**

**(nur) alle Jubeljahre** (einmal): *once in a blue moon; once in a month of Sundays*

Meine ehemaligen Schulkameraden sehe ich jetzt leider nur noch alle Jubeljahre (einmal) wieder.
*Unfortunately I now only see my former school-friends once in a blue moon (once in a month of Sundays).*

**j.en juckt das Fell** (fig.): cf. j.en juckt das **Fell**

**es juckt j.en in den Fingern** (fig.): cf. es juckt j.en in den **Fingern**

**Wen es juckt, der kratze sich** (Sprichw.): *If the cap fits, wear it (prov.)*

Wenn du dich für diese Arbeit geeignet fühlst, mußt du dich melden. Wen es juckt, der kratze sich.
*If you feel yourself suited to this work, you must register for it. If the cap fits, wear it.*

**Was dich nicht juckt, das kratze nicht** (Sprichw.): *Let (Leave) well alone (prov.); Let sleeping dogs lie (prov.)*

An deiner Stelle würde ich mich um diese Angelegenheit, die dich nichts angeht, gar nicht kümmern. Was dich nicht juckt, das kratze nicht.
*If I were you, I would not worry about that matter which does not concern you. Let (Leave) well alone (Let sleeping dogs lie).*

**Jugend hat keine Tugend** (Sprichw.): *Boys will be boys (prov.)*

„Jugend hat keine Tugend", sagte mein Vater, als er sah, daß die Jungens die Äpfel von seinem Apfelbaum abgepflückt hatten.
*"Boys will be boys", said my father, when he saw that the boys had picked the apples from his apple-tree.*

**Jung** gewohnt, alt getan (Sprichw.): *Once learnt, never forgotten (prov.); The habits of youth remain*

Man behält als reifer Mensch das bei, wozu man in seiner Jugend erzogen worden ist. Jung gewohnt, alt getan.
*As a mature person one retains what one has been trained to do in one's youth. Once learnt, never forgotten (The habits of youth remain).*

ein grüner **Junge** sein (fig. u. fam.): cf. ein **Grünschnabel** sein

Das ist zum **Junge**-Hunde-Kriegen (fam.): cf. Das ist zum Junge-**Hunde**-Kriegen

ein schwerer **Junge** sein (fig. u. fam.): *to be a hardened criminal (a professional crook); to be an old lag (colloq.)*

Es stellte sich heraus, daß der Bettler eigentlich ein schwerer Junge war, der schon mehrmals im Gefängnis gesessen hatte.
*It turned out that the beggar was really a hardened criminal (professional crook; old lag) who had already been in prison several times.*

eine **Jungfernfahrt**: *a maiden voyage*

Im August 1958 machte die „Hanseatic" ihre Jungfernfahrt über den Atlantik.
*In August 1958 the "Hanseatic" made her maiden voyage across the Atlantic.*

eine **Jungfernrede**: *a maiden speech*

Bei seiner Jungfernrede im Unterhaus war der neue Abgeordnete sichtlich nervös.
*The new deputy was obviously nervous during his maiden speech in the lower house.*

# K

sich **kabbeln** (fam.): *to squabble (to brawl) (with each other)*

Mutter kann es nicht leiden, wenn wir Kinder uns kabbeln (katzbalgen; zerren).
*Mother cannot stand it when we children squabble (brawl [with each other]).*

**Kadavergehorsam**: *blind obedience (slavish obedience)*

Jedem freiheitliebenden Menschen ist Kadavergehorsam zuwider.
*Every freedom-loving person has an aversion to blind (slavish) obedience.*

ein reizender **Käfer** sein (fig. u. fam.): *to be a cute little thing (a [little] cutie; a cute little popsy) (colloq.)*

Ernsts Freundin ist wirklich ein reizender Käfer.
*Ernest's girl friend really is a cute little thing (a [little] cutie; a cute little popsy).*

ein **Kaff** (fam.): *a dump (a hole; a one-horse place) (sl.)*

Warum wohnst du denn in diesem Kaff (Kuhdorf)?
*Why do you live in this dump (hole; one-horse place)?*

**kaffeebraun** aussehen: *to look as brown as a berry (nut-brown)*

Er muß in Griechenland schöne Ferien verlebt haben, denn er sieht jetzt kaffee-braun aus.
*He must have had a fine holiday in Greece, for he looks as brown as a berry (nut-brown) now.*

ein **Kaffeekränzchen (Kaffeeklatsch;** eine **Kaffeeschlacht):** *a tea-party; a hen-party (colloq.); a gossip-session (colloq.)*

Bei den Kaffeekränzchen (Kaffeeklatschen; Kaffeeschlachten) unserer Mutter lassen wir Kinder uns nicht blicken.
*We children do not show ourselves at our mother's tea-parties (hen-parties; gossip-sessions).*

in einem goldenen **Käfig** sitzen (fig.): *to be only a bird in a gilded cage*

Meine Kusine hat zwar einen reichen Industriellen zum Mann, in Wirklichkeit aber sitzt sie in einem goldenen Käfig.
*My cousin admittedly has a husband who is a rich industrialist, but in fact she is only a bird in a gilded cage.*

das **Kainszeichen** tragen (fig.): *to bear the badge (mark; brand; stigma)*

Trotz seines Freispruchs wird dieser Geldverleiher weiterhin das Kainszeichen eines ruchlosen Menschen tragen.
*In spite of his acquittal this moneylender will still bear the badge (mark; brand; stigma) of a ruthless man.*

(sich) um des **Kaisers** Bart streiten (fig.): *to argue (to quarrel) about nothing*

Ihr streitet (euch) um des Kaisers Bart (um Lappalien), da dieses Haus vorige Woche bereits verkauft worden ist.
*You are arguing (quarrelling) about nothing, because that house was sold last week.*

Gebet dem **Kaiser,** was des Kaisers, und Gott, was Gottes ist (Sprichw.): *Render unto Caesar the things that are Caesar's, and unto God the things that are God's (prov.)*

Man muß die Ansprüche des Irdischen und des Überirdischen streng ausein-anderhalten. Gebet dem Kaiser, was des Kaisers, und Gott, was Gottes ist.
*One must keep the claims of the world and of the spirit strictly apart. Render unto Caesar the things that are Caesar's, and unto God the things that are God's.*

Wo nichts ist, hat (selbst) der **Kaiser** sein Recht verloren (Sprichw.): *You cannot get water out of a stone (prov.)*

> Ich kann dich nicht bezahlen, da ich alles verloren habe. Wo nichts ist, hat (selbst) der Kaiser sein Recht verloren.
> *I cannot pay you, because I have lost everything. You cannot get water out of a stone.*

j.en durch den **Kakao** ziehen (fig. u. fam.): cf. j.en durch den **Dreck** ziehen

ein **Kalauer:** *a feeble (weak) pun*

> Seine guten Witze hören wir gern, aber seine Kalauer sind entsetzlich.
> *We like to listen to his good jokes, but his feeble (weak) puns are terrible.*

das Goldene **Kalb** anbeten (fig.): *to worship the Golden Calf; to worship mammon*

> Heutzutage wollen die meisten Menschen zu Reichtum kommen und beten das Goldene Kalb an (führen einen Tanz ums Goldene Kalb auf).
> *Most people nowadays want to acquire wealth, and they worship the Golden Calf (worship mammon).*

**kalbern (kalbrig** sein) (fam.): *to ass (to fool; to lark) about (colloq.); to play the fool (colloq.); to indulge in horse-play (colloq.)*

> Ihr wißt doch, daß Ihr nicht kalbern (kalbrig sein) und nicht soviel Lärm machen sollt.
> *You know that you mustn't ass (fool; lark) about (play the fool; indulge in horse-play) and make so much noise.*

etwas rot im **Kalender** anstreichen (fig.): *to make it a red-letter day*

> Den heutigen Tag muß ich rot (im Kalender) anstreichen, da du endlich einmal pünktlich zum Essen gekommen bist.
> *I must make today a red-letter day, because at last you've arrived punctually for lunch.*

vom gleichen **Kaliber** sein (fig.): *to be of the same calibre (quality).* Cf. auch: vom gleichen **Schlage** sein

> Der Sohn ist vom gleichen Kaliber wie sein Vater.
> *The son is of the same calibre (quality) as his father.*

j.en **kalt** überlaufen: *to send a shiver (shivers) down s.b.'s back; to make s.b.'s skin creep; to give s.b. the shivers (the creeps) (colloq.)*

> Es überläuft uns kalt (eine Gänsehaut), wenn wir an die Möglichkeit eines neuen Krieges denken.
> *It sends a shiver (shivers) down our backs (makes our skin creep; gives us the shivers [creeps]) to think of the possibility of another war.*

**kaltblütig** sein: *to be cool, calm and collected; to be as cool as a cucumber.* Cf. auch: **eiskalt** sein

Die Gefahr war groß, aber Karl blieb vollkommen kaltblütig.
*The danger was great, but Charles remained cool, calm and collected (as cool as a cucumber).*

j.en **kaltlassen** (fig.): *to leave s.b. cold; to be like water on a duck's back; to cut no ice with s.b. (colloq.).* Cf. auch: an j.em kalt (kühl) **abrutschen;** an j.em **abgleiten**

Ihre Drohungen regen mich nicht auf; sie lassen mich völlig kalt (kühl; ziehen bei mir nicht).
*Your threats do not worry me; they leave me completely cold (cut no ice with me; are like water on a duck's back).*

j.en **kaltmachen** (fam.): *to knock (to bump) s.b. off (sl.); to do s.b. in (colloq.).* Cf. auch: j.en ins **Jenseits** befördern; j.en um die **Ecke** bringen

Die Banditen haben den armen Bankkassierer einfach kaltgemacht.
*The bandits simply knocked (bumped) the poor bank cashier off (did the poor bank cashier in).*

**kaltschnäuzig** sein (fam.): *to be testy (snappish; peevish)*

Die Leute waren über die kaltschnäuzige Art des Arztes mit Recht empört.
*The people were justifiably indignant at the doctor's testy (snappish; peevish) manner.*

j.en (etwas) **kaltstellen** (fig.): *to put s.b. (s.th.) into cold storage; to put s.b. (s.th.) on the shelf.* Cf. auch: j.en in die **Wüste** schicken

Infolge der Revolution wurden viele höhere Beamten kaltgestellt.
*As a result of the revolution many high officials were put into cold storage (on the shelf).*

olle **Kamellen:** *ancient history; old lumber (colloq.)*

Was du mir als sogenannte Neuigkeiten erzählst, sind doch in Wirklichkeit olle Kamellen.
*The things you are telling me which are supposed to be news are in fact ancient history (old lumber).*

etwas in den **Kamin** schreiben (fig.): cf. etwas in den **Schornstein** schreiben

Der **Kamm** ist j.em geschwollen (fig.): *s.b. has become very cocky; s.b. has a swollen head.* Cf. auch: sich spreizen wie ein **Truthahn**

Dem jungen Bildhauer ist anscheinend der Kamm geschwollen, seitdem er sein erstes Werk verkauft hat.
*The young sculptor has apparently become very cocky (has apparently had a swollen head) since he sold his first work.*

alles über éinen **Kamm** scheren (fig.): cf. alles über éinen **Leisten** schlagen

im stillen **Kämmerlein:** *in one's heart of hearts; deep down*

Der Politiker versuchte, seinen Standpunkt zu rechtfertigen, aber im stillen Kämmerlein gestand er sich, daß er vielleicht doch unrecht habe.
*The politician tried to justify his point of view, but in his heart of hearts (deep down) he admitted to himself that he might be wrong.*

den **Kampf** aufgeben: *to throw in (up) the sponge; to throw in the towel; to throw in one's hand; to give in; to give up (the fight); to give up the game as lost*

Viele Jahre lang hat die Opposition versucht, die Regierung zu stürzen, aber jetzt hat sie endlich den Kampf (die Partie; das Rennen) aufgegeben (die Flinte ins Korn geworfen; das Spiel verloren gegeben).
*For many years the opposition has tried to overthrow the government but now it has finally thrown in (up) the sponge (thrown in the towel; thrown in its hand; given in; given up [the fight]; given up the game as lost).*

den **Kampf** mit j.em aufnehmen: *to join battle (to join issue) with s.b.; to take up cudgels against s.b.; to come to grips with s.b.*

Ich habe jahrelang solche Beleidigungen geduldet, aber jetzt will ich endlich den Kampf mit meinem Gegner aufnehmen.
*I have endured such insults for years, but now I am going to join battle (issue; to come to grips) with (take up cudgels against) my opponent at last.*

ein **Kampfhahn** sein (fig.): *to be a fighting cock (a turkey-cock; a terrier)*

Mein Bruder kämpft energisch für seine Ansichten; er ist ein wahrer Kampfhahn.
*My brother fights strenuously for his views; he is a real fighting-cock (turkey-cock; terrier).*

j.en an die **Kandare** nehmen (fig.): *to break s.b. in; to take s.b. in hand*

Ich wünschte, mein Nachbar würde seinen ungezogenen Sohn endlich einmal tüchtig an die Kandare nehmen.
*I wish my neighbour would break his rude son in (take . . . in hand).*

sich vermehren wie die **Kaninchen** (fam.): *to multiply (to breed) like rabbits*

Diese arme Familie hat sich vermehrt wie die Kaninchen (Karnickel).
*This poor family has multiplied (has bred) like rabbits.*

eine große **Kanone** sein (fig.): *to be a big gun; to be a big bug (big shot; big noise; big pot; big-wig) (colloq.)*

Dieser Mathematiker gilt in Fachkreisen als eine große Kanone (Nummer; ein großes Tier).
*This mathematician is reckoned in expert circles to be a big gun (bug; shot; noise; pot; a big-wig).*

mit **Kanonen** nach Spatzen schießen (fig.): *to break a butterfly on the wheel; to take a steam-roller to crack a nut*

Dieser Mann ist so unbedeutend, daß die vielen heftigen Angriffe auf ihn über-
trieben erscheinen. Das nennt man mit Kanonen nach Spatzen schießen.
*This man is so insignificant that the many violent attacks on him appear exaggerated.*
*That is what one calls breaking a butterfly on the wheel (taking a steam-roller to crack*
*a nut).*

unter aller **Kanone** sein: cf. unter jeder **Kritik** sein

voll wie eine **Kanone** sein: cf. **sternhagelvoll** sein

**Kanonenfutter:** *cannon-fodder*

Niemand will in einem Kriege sein Leben vergebens opfern und lediglich
Kanonenfutter sein.
*Nobody wants to sacrifice his life vainly in a war and be just cannon-fodder.*

den Gang nach **Kanossa** antreten (fig.): cf. den **Gang** nach Kanossa antreten

etwas auf die hohe **Kante** legen: *to put (to lay) s.th. by (for a rainy day); to
put s.th. aside; to put s.th. in one's stocking; to put s.th. in the kitty (colloq.)*

Ich möchte dir raten, für den Notfall etwas Geld auf die hohe Kante (auf die
Seite) zu legen (in den Strumpf zu stecken; einen Notpfennig zurückzulegen).
*I should advise you to put (to lay) some money by ([for a rainy day]; to put s.th. aside
[in your stocking; in the kitty] for emergencies).*

j.en beim **Kanthaken** fassen (packen) (fig. u. fam.): *to grab s.b. by the scruff
of his neck (by his collar); to collar s.b. (colloq.)*

Der Einbrecher hatte kein Glück. Ein Polizist faßte (packte) ihn beim Kanthaken (Kragen; nahm ihn am [beim] Schlafittchen).
*The burglar was unlucky. A policeman grabbed him by the scruff of his neck (by the
collar; collared him).*

ein unsicherer **Kantonist** sein: *to be a nigger in the wood-pile; to be a shaky
fellow (a shaky [doubtful] proposition); to be a slippery customer (colloq.)*

Unser Buchhalter hat sich als ein unsicherer Kantonist erwiesen, und wir haben
ihn entlassen.
*Our book-keeper proved to be a nigger in the wood-pile (a shaky fellow; shaky [doubtful]
proposition; a slippery customer), and we dismissed him.*

schwer von **Kapee** sein (fam.): *to be slow on the uptake; to be dim-witted (dull-
witted); to be slow to cotton (to catch) on (colloq.).* Cf. auch: ein **Brett** vor dem
Kopf haben

Heinrich hat die Frage immer noch nicht begriffen; er ist sehr schwer von Kapee
(Begriff; hat eine lange Leitung).
*Henry has still not understood the question. He is very slow on the uptake (very dim-
witted [dull-witted]; very slow to cotton [catch] on).*

**Kapital** aus etwas schlagen (fig.): *to make capital out of s.th.; to cash in on s.th. (colloq.)*

> Nach seiner Rückkehr schlug der Geograph aus seiner Asienreise Kapital und schrieb ein Werk über China.
> *After his return the geographer made capital out of (cashed in on) his Asiatic tour and wrote a book on China.*

ein **Kapitel** für sich sein (fig.): *to be a story in itself; to be another story*

> Von meinen Erlebnissen in Rußland will ich dir ein anderes Mal erzählen. Das ist ein Kapitel für sich.
> *I'll tell you about my experiences in Russia another time. That is a story in itself (another story).*

**kapitelfest** sein: *to be on safe (firm) ground; to be sure of o.s.; to know one's onions (one's stuff) (colloq.); to be able to talk turkey (sl.).* Cf. auch: **sattelfest** sein; gut **bestellt** sein

> Über moderne Sprachen weiß er nichts, aber in Physik ist er kapitelfest.
> *He knows nothing about modern languages, but in physics he is on safe (firm) ground (sure of himself; he knows his onions [stuff]; he can talk turkey).*

etwas auf seine eigene **Kappe** nehmen (fig.): *to take s.th. on o.s. (on one's own shoulders [back]); to answer for s.th.*

> Du kannst dir diese Bücher meines Bruders ruhig borgen. Das nehme ich auf meine eigene Kappe.
> *It's all right – you can borrow these books of my brother's. I'll take it on myself (on my own shoulders [back]; I'll answer for it).*

**Kappes** reden (fam.): cf. **Quatsch** reden

**kaputt** sein (fam.): a) *to be broken; to be bust (busted) (sl.);* b) cf. sich **abrackern**

> a) Diese beiden neuen Lampen sind schon wieder kaputt (in die Binsen gegangen; futsch).
> *a) These two new lamps are broken (bust; busted) again already.*

**kariert** reden (fam.): cf. **Quatsch** reden

das **Karnickel** sein (fig. u. fam.): cf. der **Sündenbock** sein

sich wie die **Karnickel** vermehren (fam.): cf. sich wie die **Kaninchen** vermehren

die **Karre** (den **Karren**) aus dem Dreck ziehen müssen (fig.): *to have to get (to pull) the ship off the rocks; to put things straight; to get the ship afloat again; to clear up (to clean up) the mess (colloq.)*

Er muß jetzt die Karre (den Karren) aus dem Dreck ziehen, weil sein Vorgänger schwere Fehler begangen hat.
*He has now got to get (pull) the ship off the rocks (put things straight; get the ship afloat again; clear [clean] up the mess) because his predecessor made serious errors.*

seine **Karten** aufdecken (fig.): *to lay (to put) one's cards on the table; to show one's hand; to come into the open; to come clean (sl.)*

Wir hoffen, daß unsere Gegner endlich ihre Karten aufdecken (mit offenen Karten spielen; ein offenes Spiel spielen) und sagen werden, was sie eigentlich von uns wollen.
*We hope that our rivals will lay (put) their cards on the table (show their hand; come into the open; come clean) at last and say what they really want from us.*

alles auf éine **Karte** setzen (fig.): *to put all one's eggs into one basket; to put (to stake) everything on one horse; to back only one horse; to put everything into (to stake everything on) s.th.*

Wenn man bei einer großen Unternehmung alles auf éine Karte (éin Pferd; éinen Wurf) setzt, besteht die Gefahr, daß man sich ruiniert.
*If one puts all one's eggs into one basket (puts [stakes] everything on one horse; only backs one horse; If one puts everything into [stakes everything on] a big undertaking), there is a danger that one may be ruined.*

auf die falsche **Karte** setzen (fig.): cf. aufs falsche **Pferd** setzen

j.em in die **Karten** gucken (sehen) (fig.): cf. j.es **Spiel** durchschauen

sich nicht in die **Karten** gucken lassen (fig.): *not to show one's hand; not to give anything away*

Ein routinierter Diplomat ist verschwiegen und läßt sich nicht in die Karten gucken (spielt mit verdeckten Karten; verbirgt sein Spiel gut).
*An experienced diplomat keeps quiet and does not show his hand (does not give anything away).*

alle **Karten** in der Hand behalten (fig.): *to keep one's grip (one's hold) on things; to keep all the cards in one's hand.* Cf. auch: das **Heft** in der Hand haben

Trotz seines hohen Alters zieht sich unser Chef nicht zurück. Er will noch alle Karten in der Hand behalten.
*In spite of his age our boss is not retiring. He still wants to keep all the cards in his hand (to keep his grip [hold] on things).*

alle **Karten** in der Hand haben (fig.): *to hold all the trumps (trump-cards); to hold (to know) all the answers*

Der Arbeitgeber konnte die Entscheidung allein nach seinem eigenen Gutdünken treffen, denn er hatte alle Karten (Trümpfe) in der Hand.
*The employer was able to make the decision according to his own discretion alone, because he held all the trumps (trump-cards; held [knew] all the answers).*

seine letzte **Karte** ausspielen (fig.): *to play one's last card; to make one's last bid*

Karl will noch einen Versuch machen, bei dieser Firma angestellt zu werden. Er spielt jetzt seine letzte Karte aus.
*Charles is going to make another attempt to get a job with this firm. He is now playing his last card (making his last bid).*

mit offenen **Karten** spielen (fig.): cf. seine **Karten** aufdecken

mit verdeckten **Karten** spielen (fig.): cf. sich nicht in die **Karten** gucken lassen

wie ein **Kartenhaus** zusammenstürzen: *to collapse like a pack of cards; to be pricked like a balloon; to vanish like castles in the air*

Alle seine Pläne und Hoffnungen sind wie ein Kartenhaus zusammengestürzt.
*All his plans and hopes have collapsed like a pack of cards (have been pricked like a balloon; have vanished like castles in the air).*

Rin in die **Kartoffeln,** raus aus die Kartoffeln (fig. u. fam.): *First one thing, then the other; It is like the Duke of York and his men*

Zuerst wurden die alten Gesetze aufgehoben und durch neue ersetzt. Jetzt wurden diese zurückgenommen und die alten wieder eingeführt. Rin in die Kartoffeln, raus aus die Kartoffeln.
*First the old laws were repealed and replaced by new ones. Now the latter have been withdrawn and the old ones reintroduced. First one thing, then the other (It is like the Duke of York and his men).*

ein **Käseblatt** (fam.): *a rag (colloq.)*

Dieses entsetzliche Käseblatt (Revolverblatt) lese ich niemals.
*I never read that terrible rag.*

**Kasernenhofblüte:** *barrack-square expression; sergeant-major's expression*

Ein ehemaliger Offizier hat eine köstliche Anthologie von Kasernenhofblüten veröffentlicht.
*A former officer has published a priceless anthology of barrack-square (sergeant-major's) expressions.*

**käseweiß** sein: cf. weiß wie die **Wand** sein

(gut) bei **Kasse** sein: *to be in funds; to be well-off; to be in the money (colloq.); to be flush (colloq.)*

Da ich (gut) bei Kasse (Geld) war (Kies; Moneten; Moos; Pinke[pinke]; Zaster hatte), habe ich meinen Eltern einen Perserteppich geschenkt.
*Since I was in funds (well-off; in the money; flush), I gave my parents a Persian carpet.*

knapp (schlecht) bei **Kasse** sein: *to be hard up; to be on the rocks; to be short of money (of funds); to be on one's beam-ends (colloq.); to be high and dry (colloq.)*

Leider bin ich jetzt knapp (schlecht) bei Kasse (ist bei mir jetzt Ebbe in der Kasse; sitze ich jetzt auf dem trockenen), sonst würde ich dieses Bild kaufen.
*Unfortunately I am hard up (on the rocks; short of money [funds]; on my beam-ends; high and dry) now, or I would buy that picture.*

für j.en die **Kastanien** aus dem Feuer holen (fig.): *to pick (to pull) s.b.'s chestnuts out of the fire; to be s.b.'s cat's-paw (colloq.); to do s.b.'s dirty work for him (colloq.); to carry the can back for s.b. (sl.)*

Ich werde jetzt (endlich) aufhören, für meinen Bruder die Kastanien aus dem Feuer zu holen.
*I am now going to stop picking (pulling) my brother's chestnuts out of the fire (being my brother's cat's-paw; doing my brother's dirty work for him; carrying the can back for my brother).*

in den **Kasten** kommen (fig. u. fam.): *to be sent to (to be put in) quod (jug; clink) (colloq.); to be sent to (to be put in) the cooler (sl.); to get . . . quod (sl.)*

Diebstahl wird mit Gefängnis bestraft. Der Dieb ist für zwei Monate in den Kasten (ins Kittchen [Loch]; hinter schwedische Gardinen) gekommen (muß zwei Monate brummen; sitzt . . . bei Wasser und Brot).
*Larceny is punishable with imprisonment. The thief was sent to (put in) quod (jug; clink; the cooler) for two months (got two months' quod).*

im **Kasten** sitzen (fig. u. fam.): cf. hinter **Schloß** und Riegel sitzen

einen **Kater** haben (fig. u. fam.): *to have a hangover; to suffer from the morning after the night before (colloq.); to feel seedy (colloq.).* Cf. auch: einen **Brummschädel** haben

Wir hatten eine schöne Feier, aber am nächsten Morgen hatte ich einen entsetzlichen Kater (Katzenjammer; das heulende Elend).
*We had a fine party, but the next morning I had a terrible hangover (suffered terribly from the morning after the night before; felt terribly seedy).*

eine **Kateridee** sein (fam.): *to be a crazy (crackpot) idea (colloq.); to be a daft (dotty) idea (sl.)*

Es ist eine Kateridee (Schnapsidee) von Ihnen, bei diesem Wetter fortgehen zu wollen.
*It's a crazy (crackpot; daft; dotty) idea of yours to want to go out in this weather.*

eine **Kathederblüte**: *a slip of the tongue; a bloomer*

Alle Studenten wiederholen gern die Kathederblüten ihrer Professoren.
*All students like to repeat their professors' slips of the tongue (bloomers).*

wie die **Katze** um den heißen Brei gehen: *to beat about the bush; to dither about (colloq.)*

Kommen Sie doch endlich zur Sache! Sie gehen ja wie die Katze um den heißen Brei (machen einen langen Senf; halten einen langen Salm [Sermon]; machen [ja] nur schöne Worte).
*Do come to the point! You're beating about the bush (dithering).*

falsch wie eine **Katze** (eine falsche Katze) sein: *to play false; to play a double game.* Cf. auch: falsch wie **Galgenholz** sein; ein falsches (doppeltes) **Spiel** mit j.em treiben

> Dieses Mädchen ist unehrlich und falsch wie eine Katze ([Schlange]; eine falsche Katze; katzenfreundlich).
> *That girl is dishonest and playing false (playing a double game).*

Das ist alles (nur) für die **Katz'**! (fam.): *It's all for nothing; It's not an earthly bit of use (bit of good) (colloq.)*

> Solange es·draußen noch schneit, hat es keinen Zweck, den Schnee zu kehren. Das ist ja doch nur alles für die Katz'!
> *As long as it's still snowing, there's no point in sweeping away the snow. It's all for nothing (not an earthly bit of use [of good]).*

mit j.em **Katze** und Maus spielen (fig.): *to play cat-and-mouse with s.b.; to lead s.b. on a string; to give s.b. the run-around (sl.)*

> Elisabeth weiß nicht, ob Georg sie heiraten will oder nicht. Sie denkt manchmal, er spiele nur Katze und Maus mit ihr.
> *Elizabeth does not know whether George wants to marry her or not. Sometimes she thinks he is only playing cat-and-mouse with her (leading her on a string; giving her the run-around).*

naß wie eine **Katze** sein: cf. bis auf die **Haut** durchnäßt sein

die **Katze** im Sack kaufen (fig.): *to buy a pig in a poke*

> Ich muß zuerst den Stoff sehen, bevor ich den Anzug bestelle. Ich will doch nicht die Katze im Sack kaufen.
> *I must first see the material before I order the suit. I don't want to buy a pig in a poke.*

die **Katze** aus dem Sack lassen (fig.): *to let the cat out of the bag; to give the game away; to tip s.b. the wink (colloq.); to spill the beans (sl.)*

> Zuerst wollte der Minister nichts sagen, aber die Berichterstatter bestanden darauf, und er hat doch schließlich die Katze aus dem Sack gelassen.
> *At first the minister would not say anything, but the reporters insisted, and he did finally let the cat out of the bag (give the game away; tip them the wink; spill the beans).*

der **Katze** die Schelle umhängen (fig.): *to bell the cat*

> Einer von uns Jungens muß Herrn Müller um Entschuldigung bitten, weil wir sein Fenster zerbrochen haben. Aber wer soll der Katze die Schelle umhängen?
> *One of us boys must apologise to Mr. Miller for breaking his window. But who's going to bell the cat?*

die **Katze** sein, die sich in den Schwanz beißt (fig.): cf. ein **circulus vitiosus** sein

Das trägt die **Katze** auf dem Schwanze weg (fam.): *That is a mere trifle (a mere nothing); That's nothing to write home about (colloq.); That's chicken-feed (sl.)*. Cf. auch: **kinderleicht** sein
> Was du da geleistet hast, ist ganz alltäglich. Das trägt die Katze (Maus) auf dem Schwanze weg.
> *What you have just done is quite everyday. It is a mere trifle (nothing; nothing to write home about; chicken-feed).*

verschwinden wie Schmidt's **Katze**: cf. sich auf **französisch** empfehlen

sich **katzbalgen** (fam.): cf. sich **kabbeln**

eine **Katzbalgerei** (fam.): *a scrap; a scrimmage; a skirmish*
> Während der Katzbalgerei haben zwei der Kinder eine blutige Nase gekriegt.
> *During the scrap (scrimmage; skirmish) two of the children got bleeding noses.*

**katzbuckeln** (einen **Katzenbuckel** machen) (fig. u. fam.): *to kotow; to bow and scrape; to toady*. Cf. auch: j.en **hofieren**
> Dein Stolz sollte es dir verbieten, vor anderen Menschen zu katzbuckeln (einen Katzenbuckel zu machen).
> *Your pride ought to forbid you to kotow (to bow and scrape; to toady) to other people.*

einen **Katzenbuckel** haben: *to have a hump; to have round shoulders*
> Du solltest viel turnen, da du schon einen richtigen Katzenbuckel hast.
> *You ought to do a lot of gymnastics, because you have already got a proper hump (got proper round shoulders).*

kein **Katzendreck** sein (fam.): cf. kein **Pappenstiel** sein

**katzenfreundlich** sein: cf. falsch wie eine **Katze** (eine falsche Katze) sein

einen **Katzenjammer** haben (fam.): cf. einen **Kater** haben

**Katzenmusik** machen: *to kick up (to make) a row (din) (colloq.)*
> Mein Nachbar macht eine furchtbare Katzenmusik mit seiner Trompete.
> *My neighbour kicks up (makes) a terrible row (din) with his trumpet.*

nur ein **Katzensprung** sein (fig.): *to be only a stone's throw*
> Von meinem Haus bis zur Schule ist es nur ein Katzensprung.
> *It is only a stone's throw from my house to school.*

**Katzenwäsche** machen (fig. u. fam.): *to have a cat's lick (colloq.)*

Da die Kinder so müde sind, dürfen sie heute abend einmal Katzenwäsche machen, ehe sie zu Bett gehen.
*Since the children are so tired they can just have a cat's lick this evening before they go to bed.*

**Kauderwelsch** reden (fam.): *to talk double-Dutch (gibberish) (colloq.)*

Ich kann kein Wort verstehen von dem, was er sagt. Er redet (ja) so ein Kauderwelsch.
*I can't understand a word he says. He talks such double-Dutch (such gibberish).*

an etwas zu **kauen** haben (fig.): *s. th. gives s. b. something to think about; s. th. gives s. b. something to chew on (colloq.)*

An diesem Tadel durch seinen Lehrer wird Heinrich noch lange zu kauen (knacken) haben.
*That telling-off from his master will give Henry something to think about (to chew on) for a long time.*

leichten **Kaufes** davonkommen (fig.): *to get off (to be let off; to escape) lightly (cheaply)*

Diesmal ist der Dieb leichten Kaufes (mit einem blauen Auge) davongekommen, denn er wurde zu nur einem Monat Gefängnis verurteilt.
*This time the thief got off (was let off; escaped) lightly (cheaply), for he was only sentenced to a month's imprisonment.*

etwas (mit) in **Kauf** nehmen (fig.): *to put up with s. th.; to accept s. th. as part of the situation; to lump it (sl.).* Cf. auch: etwas **einstecken**

Der Vortrag war ausgezeichnet, aber die Luft in dem überfüllten Saal war furchtbar. Das mußte man jedoch (mit) in Kauf nehmen.
*The talk was excellent but the air in the crowded hall was terrible. However, we had to put up with that (we had to accept that as part of the situation; we had to lump that).*

Was kann ich mir dafür (schon) **kaufen**! (fam.): *What's the use (the good) of that? What use (What good) is that to me? What can I do (can I buy) with that?* Cf. auch: Schöne Worte machen den **Kohl** nicht fett

In meiner geldlichen Notlage helfen schöne Worte nichts. Was kann ich mir dafür (schon) kaufen!
*In my financial trouble fine words don't help. What's the use (the good) of them? (What good are they to me? What can I do [buy] with them?)*

j.en **kaufen** (fig.): *to bribe s. b.; to buy s. b. up (colloq.)*

Es hat sich herausgestellt, daß der Beschuldigte von einer fremden Macht gekauft worden war.
*It turned out that the accused had been bribed (bought up) by a foreign power.*

sich j.en **kaufen** (fig. u. fam.): *to put s. b. on the mat (carpet) (colloq.); to have s. b. up (colloq.)*

Den Jungen, der meine Unterschrift gefälscht hat, werde ich mir kaufen und aus der Firma entlassen.
*I'm going to put that boy on the mat ([carpet]; have that boy up) for forging my signature, and sack him from the firm.*

### ein **Kautschukparagraph**: *a flexible (an elastic) clause*

Gewisse Kautschukparagraphen dieses neuen Gesetzes geben Anlaß zu Meinungsverschiedenheiten.
*Certain flexible (elastic) clauses in this new law are giving rise to differences of opinion.*

### ein komischer (närrischer) **Kauz** sein (fig.): *to be a queer bird (card; customer; fish; an odd [strange] character [customer]); to be a rum 'un (colloq.)*

Der Schornsteinfeger macht immer seine Späße mit uns Kindern. Er ist ein komischer (närrischer) Kauz (wunderlicher [sonderbarer] Heiliger; ein Sonderling; eine komische Marke [Nudel; Type]; eine Dralltype).
*The sweep always jokes with us children. He is a queer bird (card; customer; fish; an odd [strange] character [customer]; a rum 'un).*

### Es muß auch solche **Käuze** geben! (fig.): *It takes all sorts to make a world*

Unser Nachbar ist Abstinenzler und Vegetarier. Es muß auch solche Käuze geben!
*Our neighbour is a teetotaller and a vegetarian. It takes all sorts to make a world!*

### sich die **Kehle** anfeuchten (schmieren): *to wet one's whistle*

Laßt uns in einen Gasthof gehen und uns die Kehle anfeuchten (schmieren).
*Let's go into a pub and wet our whistles.*

### j.em an die **Kehle** fahren: *to fly (to jump) at s. b.'s throat*

Der Mann wollte mir in seiner Wut an die Kehle fahren (an die Gurgel; an den Kragen gehen; ins Gesicht springen), und ich hatte Schwierigkeiten, ihn zu beruhigen.
*In his rage the man wanted to fly (jump) at my throat, and I had difficulty in calming him.*

### etwas in die falsche **Kehle** bekommen ((kriegen); j.em in die falsche Kehle kommen [geraten]) (fig.): *to take s. th. the wrong way*

Ich war wütend, weil Karl meine Bemerkung in die falsche Kehle (in die Sonntagskehle; in den falschen Hals) bekommen hatte (weil Karl meine ... gekommen [geraten] war).
*I was furious because Charles had taken my remark the wrong way.*

### sich die **Kehle** aus dem Hals schreien: cf. sich die **Lunge** aus dem Leibe schreien

### aus voller **Kehle** singen: *to sing at the top of one's voice*

Die Studenten sangen lange aus voller Kehle (Brust).
*The students sang for a long while at the top of their voices.*

Die **Kehle** ist einem wie zugeschnürt: *One feels a lump in one's throat*

Als ich von seinem Tod erfuhr, war mir die Kehle wie zugeschnürt, und ich konnte kein Wort sagen.
*When I heard of his death I felt a lump in my throat and could not say a word.*

die **Kehrseite** des Lebens: *the seamy (dark) side of life*

Diese Stadt ist wegen ihrer schönen Straßen sehr bekannt, aber im Hafengebiet sieht man die Kehrseite des Lebens.
*This town is famous for its fine streets but in the dock-area one sees the seamy (dark) side of life.*

die **Kehrseite** der Medaille (fig.): *the other (the reverse) side of the penny (of the picture; of the coin); the reverse of the medal*

Dieser Gelehrte arbeitet bis sehr spät abends. Die Kehrseite der Medaille (Die Schattenseite) ist aber, daß er sehr unruhig schläft.
*This scholar works very late in the evening. The other (reverse) side of the penny ([picture; coin]; the reverse of the medal) is, however, that he sleeps very restlessly.*

einen **Keil** zwischen zwei Menschen treiben (fig.): *to drive a wedge (to open a gulf) between two people*

Ein boshafter Mensch versuchte, einen Keil zwischen mich und meine Verlobte zu treiben.
*A malicious person tried to drive a wedge (to open a gulf) between me and my fiancée.*

Ein **Keil** treibt den anderen (Sprichw.): *One nail (One fire; One love) drives out another (prov.)*

Durch die Fülle neuer Erlebnisse habe ich die Reise nach Amerika, die ich vor zwei Jahren machte, beinahe vergessen. Ein Keil treibt den anderen.
*As a result of a mass of new experiences I have almost forgotten the journey to America which I made two years ago. One nail (fire; love) drives out another.*

j.en **keilen** (fam.): *to press-gang s.b. (colloq.); to dragoon s.b. (colloq.)*

Wir haben versucht, neue Mitglieder für unsern Verein zu keilen.
*We have been trying to press-gang (dragoon) new members into our club.*

etwas im **Keime** ersticken (fig.): *to nip s.th. in the bud; to quell s.th. at the source*

Es gelang der Polizei, den Aufruhr im Keime zu ersticken, so daß keine große Gefahr entstand.
*The police succeeded in nipping the revolt in the bud (in quelling the revolt at the source), so that no great danger arose.*

in einen goldenen **Kelch** blicken (fig.): *to see s.b. (s. th.) through rose-coloured glasses.* Cf. auch: alles durch die rosarote (rosige) **Brille** betrachten

Vater sieht die Schwächen und Fehler meiner Schwester einfach nicht. Er blickt (bei ihr) in einen goldenen Kelch.
*Father just does not see my sister's weaknesses and failings. He sees her through rose-coloured glasses.*

den **Kelch** bis zur Neige leeren (fig.): cf. den **Becher** bis zur Neige leeren

mit **Kennermiene**: *with an expert eye (a professional eye); with the eye of a connoisseur*

Der Kunstkritiker betrachtete die Werke in der Ausstellung mit Kennermiene.
*The art-critic regarded the works in the exhibition with an expert eye (a professional eye; with the eye of a connoisseur).*

in die gleiche **Kerbe** hauen (fig.): *to have the same aim; to have the same end in view; to have the same thought in mind; to aim at the same target*

Mein Bruder und ich hauen in die gleiche Kerbe. Wir wollen beide Mediziner werden.
*My brother and I have the same aim (the same end in view; the same thought in mind; are aiming at the same target): we both want to be doctors.*

etwas auf dem **Kerbholz** haben (fig.): *to have a black mark against one's name (a bad mark on one's slate).* Cf. auch: bei j.em schlecht **angeschrieben** sein

Paß nur auf, sagte der Lehrer zu mir, du hast schon viel(es) auf dem Kerbholz.
*You just watch out, said the teacher to me; you've already got a lot of black marks against your name (a lot of bad marks on your slate).*

ein ganzer **Kerl** sein: *to be a stout fellow (a real man [woman etc.])*

Ein Nachtwächter muß ein ganzer Kerl sein, da sein Beruf manchmal gefährlich ist.
*A night-watchman has to be a stout fellow (a real man), since his occupation is sometimes dangerous.*

einen guten **Kern** in einer rauhen Schale haben (fig.): *s.b.'s bark is worse than his bite; to be a rough diamond; s.b.'s rough exterior conceals a heart of gold*

Man muß meinem Vetter seine Grobheit verzeihen; er hat einen guten Kern in einer rauhen Schale.
*One must forgive my cousin his coarseness; his bark is worse than his bite (he is a rough diamond; his rough exterior conceals a heart of gold).*

der **Kern(punkt)** einer Sache: *the core (heart; root; crux) of a matter*

Jetzt kommen wir auf den Kern(punkt) der Sache zu sprechen.
*Now we are getting to the core (heart; root; crux) of the matter.*

**kerndeutsch** sein: *to be German through and through; to be German to the core (to the backbone; to the roots); to be an out-and-out German.* Cf. auch ein **Stockengländer** (Stockpreuße) sein

Dieser alte Soldat ist kerndeutsch (deutsch bis in die Knochen).
*This old soldier is German through and through (to the core [backbone; roots]; an out-and-out German).*

**kerngesund** sein: *to be as fit as a fiddle (fighting fit; as sound as a bell; in fine fettle);* (nur von älteren Menschen) *to be hale and hearty*

Mein Großvater ist trotz seines Alters immer noch kerngesund (gesund wie ein Fisch im Wasser).
*In spite of his age my grandfather is still as fit as a fiddle (fighting fit; as sound as a bell; in fine fettle; hale and hearty).*

**kerzengerade** sitzen: *to sit bolt upright; to sit as straight as a ramrod*

Schon mit anderthalb Jahren mußte das Kind kerzengerade am Tisch sitzen.
*Already at eighteen months the child was made to sit bolt upright (as straight as a ramrod) at the table.*

sich prügeln wie die **Kesselflicker**: *to fight like cocks; to fight like mad (colloq.); really to mix it (sl.)*

Die beiden Hafenarbeiter waren betrunken und prügelten sich wie die Kesselflicker.
*The two dockers were drunk and fighting like cocks (like mad; and really mixing it).*

ein **Kesseltreiben** veranstalten: *to hem (to hedge; to pen) s.b. in*

Der Mörder versuchte, das bereitstehende Auto zu erreichen, aber die Polizei veranstaltete ein Kesseltreiben, so daß er unmöglich entkommen konnte.
*The murderer tried to reach the car which was standing ready, but the police hemmed (hedged; penned) him in so that he could not possibly escape.*

heulen wie ein **Kettenhund**: cf. heulen wie ein **Schloßhund**

ein **Keulenschlag** für j.en sein (fig.): cf. wie ein **Schlag** ins Gesicht sein

j.en (etwas) auf dem **Kieker** haben (fam.): *to have one's eye on s.b. (s.th.); to set one's sights on s.b. (s.th.) (colloq.).* Cf. auch: ein scharfes **Auge** auf j.en haben

Schon seit Monaten habe ich diese Armbanduhr auf dem Kieker.
*For months I've had my eye (set my sights) on that wrist-watch.*

ein **Kiekindiewelt**: *a whippersnapper*

Dieser kleine Kiekindiewelt sollte schweigen, wenn wir uns unterhalten.
*That little whippersnapper ought to be quiet when we are talking.*

**Kies** haben (fam.): cf. (gut) bei **Kasse** sein; **Geld** wie Heu haben

ein **Kilometerfresser**: *a road-hog; a speed-merchant (colloq.)*

Ihr Bruder will die schöne Landschaft nicht genießen, sondern nur als Kilometerfresser in seinem neuen Auto herumrasen.
*Your brother does not want to enjoy the beautiful scenery but only to tear around like a road-hog (speed-merchant) in his new car.*

das **Kind** mit dem Bade ausschütten (fig.): *to throw out the baby with the bathwater; to throw away the wheat with the chaff*

Weil es ein paar Unglücksfälle gegeben hat, muß man doch nicht (gleich) das Kind mit dem Bade ausschütten und alle Schulausflüge verbieten.
*Because there have been a few accidents one does not have to throw out the baby with the bath-water (throw away the wheat with the chaff) and prohibit all school outings.*

(Ein) gebranntes **Kind** scheut das Feuer (Sprichw.): *Once bitten, twice shy (prov.)*

Wilhelm weigert sich, in den Kirschbaum zu klettern. Er ist früher einmal heruntergestürzt. (Ein) gebranntes Kind scheut das Feuer (Der Esel geht nur einmal aufs Eis; Der Ochse stößt sich nur einmal am Scheunentor).
*William refuses to climb up the cherry-tree; he fell down once before. Once bitten, twice shy.*

sich wie ein **Kind (kindlich)** freuen: cf. sich **diebisch** freuen

wes Geistes **Kind**: cf. wes **Geistes** Kind

wie (das) **Kind** im Hause sein: *to be (like) one of the family (of the household)*

Zuerst fühlte sie sich bei ihrer neuen Wirtin etwas schüchtern (scheu), aber bald war sie wie (das) Kind im Hause.
*At first she felt rather shy with her new landlady, but soon she was (like) one of the family (household).*

mit **Kind** und Kegel: *with bag and baggage; with all one's traps; with all one's chattels; lock, stock and barrel*

Unser Nachbar ist mit Kind und Kegel (Sack und Pack; seiner ganzen Sippe) nach Amerika ausgewandert.
*Our neighbour has emigrated to America with bag and baggage (with all his traps; with all his chattels; lock, stock and barrel).*

sich lieb **Kind** machen: *to curry favour with s.b.; to pander (to truckle) to s.b.; to soft-soap s.b. (sl.)*

Meine jüngere Schwester versteht es, sich überall lieb Kind zu machen (ein rotes Röckelchen zu verdienen).
*My younger sister knows how to curry favour with everybody (to pander [truckle] to everybody; to soft-soap everybody).*

das **Kind** beim rechten Namen nennen (fig.): *to call a spade a spade; not to beat about the bush; to be blunt (plain-spoken)*

Nennen wir doch das Kind (die Sache) beim rechten Namen: der Autor dieses Romans hat keine Ahnung von Literatur.
*Let's call a spade a spade ( Let's not beat about the bush; Let's be blunt [plain-spoken]): the author of this novel has no idea of literature.*

ein **Kind** des Todes sein: cf. ein **Mann** des Todes sein

ein totgeborenes **Kind** sein (fig.): *to be a still-born child; to be a doomed enterprise*

Die neue Partei hat wenig Anhänger gefunden. Sie war von Anfang an ein totgeborenes Kind.
*The new party has found few supporters. It was from the beginning a still-born child ( a doomed enterprise).*

unschuldig wie ein neugeborenes **Kind** sein: *to be as innocent as a new-born babe ( as a babe in the womb); to be as pure as the driven snow*

Seine Schwester ist völlig unverdorben. Sie ist unschuldig wie ein neugeborenes Kind.
*His sister is completely unspoilt. She is as innocent as a new-born babe ( a babe in the womb; is as pure as the driven snow).*

**Kinderkrankheiten** (fig.): *teething troubles; growing pains*

Das neue Geschäft leidet noch an gewissen Kinderkrankheiten, die jedoch bald überwunden sein werden.
*The new business is still suffering from certain teething troubles (growing pains), which will, however, soon be overcome.*

**kinderleicht** sein: *to be child's play; to be as easy as ABC ( to be as easy as falling off a log); to be as easy as pie (colloq.)*

Die Lösung dieser Rechenaufgabe ist doch kinderleicht (ein Kinderspiel; läßt sich doch spielend machen).
*The solution of this sum is child's play (as easy as ABC; as easy as falling off a log; as easy as pie).*

die **Kinderschuhe** ausgetreten haben (fig.): *to be out of the nursery ( out of kindergarten); to be out of one's napkins (colloq.)*

Die junge Schauspielerin ist erst 15 Jahre alt und hat kaum die Kinderschuhe ausgetreten.
*The young actress is only fifteen years old and hardly out of the nursery ( out of kindergarten; out of her napkins).*

noch in den **Kinderschuhen** stecken (fig.): *to be still in the nursery; still to go to kindergarten; to be still in one's napkins (colloq.)*

Diese jungen Mädchen besuchen jeden Ball, obwohl sie eigentlich noch in den Kinderschuhen stecken.

*These young girls go to every dance although they are really still in the nursery (still go to kindergarten; are really still in their napkins).*

ein **Kinderspiel** sein (fig.): cf. **kinderleicht** sein

eine gute **Kinderstube** genießen (fig.): *to enjoy a good upbringing; to be well brought-up (well-bred)*

Man merkt an dem ganzen Benehmen dieses Studenten, daß er eine gute Kinderstube genossen hat.
*One can see by this student's whole behaviour that he has enjoyed a good upbringing (has been well brought-up; is well-bred).*

von **Kindesbeinen** an: *from one's infancy; since one was a toddler (colloq.)*

Von Kindesbeinen an habe ich viel Sport getrieben.
*From my infancy (Since I was a toddler) I have always gone in for a lot of sport.*

ein richtiger **Kindskopf** sein (fig.): *to be a proper (a regular) baby.* Cf. auch: ein **Grünschnabel** sein

Trotz ihrer 16 Jahre ist Emma noch ein richtiger Kindskopf.
*In spite of being sixteen, Emma is still a proper (regular) baby.*

**Kinkerlitzchen** (fam.): *trash; fripperies (colloq.)*

Mach' voran mit deiner Arbeit und halte dich nicht mit Kinkerlitzchen auf!
*Get on with your work and don't waste your time on trash (fripperies)!*

auf der **Kippe** stehen (fig.): *it is touch-and-go with s.b. (s.th.); to hang in the balance; to hang by a thread; to be on the verge of collapse*

Seit den letzten Wahlen steht die Regierung auf der Kippe.
*Since the last election it has been touch-and-go with the government (the government has been hanging in the balance [by a thread]; has been on the verge of collapse).*

einen **kippen** (fam.): cf. (sich) einen hinter die **Binde** gießen

die **Kirche** im Dorf lassen (fig.): *to keep within bounds; to draw the line somewhere*

Deine Wünsche kann ich leider nicht alle erfüllen. Wir müssen doch die Kirche im Dorf lassen.
*I am afraid I cannot fulfil all your wishes. We must keep within bounds (must draw the line somewhere).*

kein (großes) **Kirchenlicht** sein (fig.): cf. das **Pulver** nicht erfunden haben

arm wie eine **Kirchenmaus** sein: *to be as poor as a church-mouse (as Job; as a beggar)*

Dieser Bauer, dem alle Scheunen und Viehställe abgebrannt sind, ist arm wie eine Kirchenmaus (wie Hiob; bettelarm) geworden.
*That farmer, whose barns and cattle-sheds have all been burnt down, has become as poor as a church-mouse (as Job; as a beggar).*

**Kirchturmpolitik:** *parish-pump politics; parochial attitudes*

Mit Kirchturmpolitik kann man heute nichts mehr erreichen.
*One can no longer achieve anything today with parish-pump politics (parochial attitudes).*

Mit ihm ist nicht gut **Kirschen** essen (fig.): *He is an awkward (a tricky [difficult]) person to get on with; He is an awkward (a tricky [difficult]) customer*

Ich weiß schon lange, daß mit diesem launischen Kerl nicht gut Kirschen essen ist.
*I have known for a long time that that moody fellow is an awkward (a tricky [difficult]) person to get on with (an awkward [a tricky; difficult] customer).*

eine alte **Kiste** (fig. u. fam.): cf. ein **Klapperkasten**

**Kisten** und Kasten vollhaben: *to have one's pockets well filled (well lined); to have one's nest well feathered; to have one's coffers well filled*

Manche Leute können nie genug verdienen, wenn sie auch Kisten und Kasten vollhaben.
*Some people can never earn enough, even when they have their pockets well filled (well lined; their nest well feathered; their coffers well filled).*

die (ganze) **Kiste** schmeißen (fam.): cf. den (ganzen) **Laden** schmeißen

eine schwierige **Kiste** sein (fam.): *to be a tough (tricky) job (proposition); to be a poser (a pretty problem); to be a hard nut to crack*

Es wird eine schwierige Kiste (harte Nuß) sein, dein altes Fahrrad zu reparieren.
*It will be a tough (tricky) job (proposition; a poser; a pretty problem; It will be a hard nut to crack) to repair your old bicycle.*

**Kitsch** sein (fam.): *to be rubbish (trash); to be tripe (sl.)*

Dieser neue Film ist der reinste Kitsch.
*This new film is utter rubbish (trash; tripe).*

der ganze **Kitt** (fam.): cf. der ganze **Kram**

ins **Kittchen** kommen (fam.): cf. in den **Kasten** kommen

etwas **kitten** (fig.): *to heal (to patch up) s. th.*

Der Riß zwischen den beiden Freunden ist noch nicht sehr tief. Er läßt sich noch kitten (leimen).
*The rift between the two friends is not yet very deep. It can still be healed (patched up).*

eine **kitz(e)lige** Angelegenheit sein: *to be a ticklish affair*

Überlassen wir es anderen, diese kitz(e)lige Angelegenheit zu regeln.
*Let's leave it to others to settle this ticklish affair.*

ein **Klacks** sein (fam.): cf. eine **Lappalie** sein

viel **Klamauk** um (von) etwas machen (fam.): cf. viel **Wind** um (von) etwas machen

(alte) **Klamotten** (fam.): *(old) togs (colloq.); old rags (colloq.)*
Ich habe alle meine (alten) Klamotten an arme Leute verschenkt.
*I have given all my (old) togs (all my old rags) away to poor people.*

in die **Klappe** gehen (fam.): cf. in die **Falle** gehen b)

eine freche **Klappe** haben (fam.): cf. ein loses **Maul** haben

die **Klappe** halten (fam.): *to hold one's tongue; to keep one's mouth shut; to shut up (colloq.); to shut one's trap (sl.); to pipe down (sl.)*
Seine geschwätzige Frau kann nie die Klappe (den Rand) halten (ist eine [richtige] Quasselstrippe).
*His talkative wife can never hold her tongue (can never keep her mouth shut; can never shut up [shut her trap; pipe down]).*

zum **Klappen** kommen **(klappen)** (fig.): *to come off; to click*
Ich werde mein Bestes tun, Sie dieses Jahr zu besuchen. Hoffentlich wird es zum Klappen kommen (wird es klappen).
*I shall do my best to visit you this year. I hope it will come off (click).*

**klapperdürr** sein: cf. nur noch **Haut** und Knochen sein

sich **klapp(e)rig** fühlen: *to feel shaky (rocky); to feel rickety (colloq.)*
Nach meiner langen Krankheit fühle ich mich noch immer etwas klapp(e)rig.
*I still feel a bit shaky (rocky; rickety) after my long illness.*

ein **Klapperkasten** (fam.): *a ramshackle (rickety) old thing (colloq.); a crate (colloq.)*
Wir wollen ein neues Auto kaufen, da unser alter Klapperkasten (unsere alte Kiste) zu viel (an) Reparaturen kostet.
*We are going to buy a new car, because our ramshackle (rickety) old thing (old crate) costs too much in repairs.*

**Klappern** gehört zum Handwerk (Sprichw.): *The noise is part of the business*
In diesem Stadtteil ist es sehr laut, weil sich dort viele Betriebe befinden. Da ist aber nichts zu machen: Klappern gehört nun mal zum Handwerk.
*It is very noisy in this part of the city because there are a lot of factories there. But there's nothing to be done about it; the noise is just part of the business.*

einen **Klaps** bekommen (fam.): a) *to get a slap (a smack);* b) *to go crazy (mad); to go bats (berserk) (colloq.); to go off one's rocker (sl.)*
a) Mutter sagte zu meinem Schwesterchen: „Wenn du jetzt nicht brav bist, bekommst du einen Klaps."

b) Ihr Bruder ist sonst sehr vernünftig, aber gestern bekam er einen Klaps und versuchte, Selbstmord zu begehen.

*a) Mother said to my little sister: "If you don't behave yourself, you'll get a slap (a smack)."*

*b) Her brother is usually very sane but yesterday he went crazy (bats; berserk; off the rocker) and tried to commit suicide.*

einen **Klaps** haben (fam.): cf. nicht richtig im **Dachstübchen** sein

**klat(e)rig** sein (fam.): *to be grubby; to be scruffy (colloq.)*

Ihre Kinder sind nie sauber angezogen; sie sehen immer klat(e)rig aus.

*Her children are never cleanly dressed; they always look grubby (scruffy).*

**Klatsch** und Tratsch (fam.): *tittle-tattle; chit-chat; town-talk; gossip (gossiping)*

Wenn gewisse Leute mehr arbeiten würden, gäbe es nicht so viel (Klatsch und) Tratsch (Geschwätz; Getratsche; Gewäsch) auf der Welt.

*If certain people worked more, there would not be so much tittle-tattle (chit-chat; town-talk; gossip; gossiping) in the world.*

eine **Klatschbase** sein: *to be a scandalmonger (tale-bearer; prattler; gossip; chatterbox); to be a gas-bag (sl.)*

Meine Putzfrau ist eine schreckliche Klatschbase (Plaudertasche; Schwatzbase; ein schreckliches Klatschmaul [Waschweib]) und erzählt alles, was sie bei anderen Leuten hört.

*My charwoman is a terrible scandalmonger (tale-bearer; prattler; gossip; chatterbox; gas-bag) and tells everything she hears at other people's.*

ein **Klatschmaul** sein (fam.): cf. eine **Klatschbase** sein

**klatschnaß** sein: cf. bis auf die **Haut** durchnäßt sein

ein **Klatschnest:** *a scandal-shop*

Ich hätte nie gedacht, daß so eine große Stadt ein so entsetzliches Klatschnest ist.

*I should never have thought that such a large town was such a terrible scandal-shop.*

j.es **Klaue** kennen (fig. u. fam.): *to know s.b.'s fist.* Cf. auch: **Gekrakel**

Wenn ich seine Klaue nicht schon lange kennen würde, könnte ich seine Briefe nicht entziffern.

*If I had not known his fist for a long while, I could not decipher his letters.*

j.em in die **Klauen** geraten (fig. u. fam.): *to fall (to get) into s.b.'s clutches (hands); to get mixed up (involved) with s.b.*

Dein Bruder ist in die Klauen unlauterer Elemente geraten.

*Your brother has fallen (got) into the clutches of (hands of; has got mixed up [involved] with) unsavoury elements.*

**klauen** (fam.): *to pinch (to swipe; to nick) (sl.); to knock off (sl.); to whip (to lift) (sl.).* Cf. auch: etwas **mitgehen** heißen

Wer hat mir meinen Bleistift geklaut (gemopst; stibitzt; Wer hat meinen Bl. auf die Seite geschafft; Wer hat sich meinen Bl. unter den Nagel gerissen)?
*Who's pinched (swiped; nicked; knocked off; whipped; lifted) my pencil?*

j.em eine **kleben** (fam.): *to give s.b. a box on the ears; to fetch s.b. one (colloq.); to give s.b. a swipe (a clout) (colloq.); to give (to fetch) s.b. a fourpenny one (sl.)*

Da ich frech war, hat mir mein Vater eine geklebt (verpaßt; eine Backpfeife [Ohrfeige] gegeben; eine 'reingehauen ['runtergehauen]).
*Because I was cheeky, my father gave me a box on the ears (fetched me one; gave me a swipe [clout]; gave [fetched] me a fourpenny one).*

**klebenbleiben** (fig. u. fam.): cf. **sitzenbleiben** c)

bei j.em einen **Klecks** in den Akten haben (fig. u. fam.): cf. (bei j.em) schlecht **angeschrieben** sein

j.en (etwas) über den (grünen) **Klee** loben: cf. j.en (etwas) in den **Himmel** (er)heben

ein lustiges **Kleeblatt** (fig.): *a jolly (merry; happy) trio*

Unsere drei Stenotypistinnen bilden ein lustiges Kleeblatt.
*Our three shorthand-typists form a jolly (merry; happy) trio.*

nicht in den **Kleidern** hängenbleiben (fig.): *to leave its mark(s); not to leave one unscarred*

Mein Freund Wilhelm zog sich vor einem Jahr eine schwere Lungenentzündung zu und sieht jetzt noch schwächlich aus. So eine Krankheit bleibt eben nicht in den Kleidern hängen.
*A year ago my friend William caught pneumonia badly and still looks weak. An illness like that leaves its mark(s) (does not leave one unscarred).*

**Kleider** machen Leute (Sprichw.): *Clothes make the man (Fine feathers make fine birds) (prov.)*

Dieser gut angezogene junge Mann wird sicher in seinem Beruf viel Erfolg haben. Kleider machen Leute.
*That well-dressed young man is sure to be very successful in his profession. Clothes make the man (Fine feathers make fine birds).*

**klein** beigeben: *to retreat; to give in; to give way; to climb down*

Der Redner sprach so überzeugend, daß seine Gegner klein beigeben mußten.
*The speaker talked so convincingly that his opponents had to retreat (give in; give way; climb down).*

j.en **klein** und häßlich machen (fig.): cf. j.en **madig** machen

**klein** und häßlich (ganz klein) sein (fig.): *to look small; to hang one's head. Cf.*
auch: den **Kopf** hängen lassen

> Als der Lehrer sagte, wir hätten in unserm Diktat viele Fehler gemacht, waren
> wir klein und häßlich (ganz klein[laut]).
> *We looked small (hung our heads) when the teacher said that we had made a lot of*
> *mistakes in our dictation.*

**Kleinholz** von (aus) j.em machen (fig. u. fam.): cf. **Hackfleisch** aus j.em
machen

ein **Kleinigkeitskrämer** sein (fam.): *to be a hair-splitter; to be a small-minded*
*pedant; to be a fusspot (sl.)*

> Mit so einem Kleinigkeitskrämer (Haarspalter; Umstandskrämer) kann man
> nichts besprechen (Mit ihm kann man nichts besprechen, da er über einen Stroh-
> halm stolpert).
> *One cannot discuss anything with such a hair-splitter (small-minded pedant; fusspot).*

j.en **kleinkriegen** (fig.): cf. j.em den **Nacken** beugen

etwas **kleinkriegen**: *to make short work of s. th.; to get through s. th.*

> Das Geld, das er in der Lotterie gewonnen hat, wird er schon kleinkriegen.
> *He will make short work of the money (will soon get through the money) which he won*
> *in the lottery.*

sich nicht **kleinkriegen** lassen (fig.): *not to let o. s. be browbeaten; not to let s. th.*
*get one down (get the better of one) (colloq.); not to mope (colloq.)*

> Ein Optimist läßt sich durch Mißgeschicke nicht kleinkriegen.
> *An optimist does not let himself be browbeaten by misfortunes (does not let misfortunes*
> *get him down [get the better of him]; does not mope in the face of misfortunes).*

**kleinlaut** sein: cf. **klein** und häßlich sein

**Kleinvieh** macht auch Mist (Sprichw.): *Many a little makes a mickle (prov.);*
*Every little helps*

> Der Eintrittspreis bei diesem Zirkus ist niedrig, aber infolgedessen gehen viele
> Leute hin. Kleinvieh macht auch Mist (Viele Wenig machen ein Viel).
> *The price of admission at this circus is low, but as a result many people go to it. Many a*
> *little makes a mickle (Every little helps).*

in der **Klemme** sein (fig.): *to be in a tight corner (in a fix); to be in a spot (in*
*a hole; in the mire; in a jam; in a mess; in the cart; in a scrape; up a gum-tree; in*
*the soup; up against it) (colloq.)*

> Wenn ich binnen acht Tagen diese Rechnung nicht bezahlen kann, bin ich rich-
> tig in der Klemme (Patsche; auf dem Pfropfen; in der Tinte; in der Zwickmühle;
> im Dreck [Druck]).

*If I cannot pay this bill within a week, I shall be in a tight corner (in a proper fix [spot; hole; jam; mess; scrape; properly in the mire [soup; cart]; properly up a gum-tree; up against it).*

wie eine **Klette** an j.em hängen (haften): *to cling (to stick) to s.b. like a leech (like a limpet); to follow s.b. like his shadow.* Cf. auch: j.em auf **Schritt** und Tritt folgen

Dieser lästige Verkäufer hängt (haftet) an mir wie eine Klette (folgt mir wie ein Schatten).
*This annoying salesman clings (sticks) to me like a leech (limpet; follows me like my shadow).*

**Klimbim** (fam.): *fuss; hullabaloo (colloq.); pother (colloq.)*

Warum macht er immer soviel Klimbim? Kann er nicht bescheidener sein?
*Why does he always make such a fuss (hullabaloo; pother)? Can't he be more moderate?*

alles, was mir vor die **Klinge** kommt (fig.): *everything that comes my way (crosses my path)*

Wenn ich Hunger habe, esse ich alles, was mir vor die Klinge kommt.
*When I am hungry, I eat everything that comes my way (crosses my path).*

mit j.em die **Klingen** kreuzen (fig.): *to cross swords with s.b.; to challenge s.b.* Cf. auch: den **Kampf** mit j.em aufnehmen; mit j.em **Händel** haben

Ich liebe es, in einer Diskussion die Klingen (Degen) mit anderen Leuten zu kreuzen.
*I like crossing swords with (challenging) other people in discussion.*

eine gute **Klinge** schlagen (fig.): cf. beim Essen **einhauen**

j.en über die **Klinge** springen lassen: *to put s.b. to the sword; to put s.b. to death*

Der Tyrann ließ alle Gegner erbarmungslos über die Klinge springen.
*Mercilessly the tyrant put all his enemies to the sword (to death).*

**klipp** und klar sagen: *to say in so many words (in plain language [English]; without mincing matters; straight out; outright; point-blank).* Cf. auch: j.em etwas ins **Gesicht** sagen; j.em klaren (reinen) **Wein** einschenken

Ich sagte ihm klipp und klar (frank und frei; kurz und bündig), daß ich seine Ansicht nicht teile.
*I told him in so many words (in plain language; in plain English; without mincing matters; straight out; outright; point-blank) that I did not share his view.*

j.em über alle **Klippen** hinweghelfen (fig.): *to help s.b. over all his hurdles; to smooth s.b.'s path for him*

Im Notfall wird dir dein Gönner über alle Klippen hinweghelfen.
*In an emergency your patron will help you over all your hurdles (will smooth your path for you).*

an einer **Klippe** scheitern (fig.): *to run aground; to founder; to come unstuck (colloq.)*

Nachdem ihm bisher alles gut gelungen war, scheiterte er an dieser unerwarteten Klippe.
*Having previously succeeded well in everything, he ran aground (foundered; came unstuck) here unexpectedly.*

**klitschnaß** sein: cf. bis auf die **Haut** durchnäßt sein

**klönen** (fam.): *to have a chin-wag (colloq.); to have a natter (sl.)*

Wenn Sie uns wieder mal besuchen kommen, wollen wir etwas länger miteinander klönen.
*When you come to see us again, we'll have a rather longer chin-wag (natter) together.*

als ob er einen **Kloß** im Munde (Halse) hätte: *as though he had a plum (a hot potato) in his mouth*

Ein Amerikaner ist oft schwer zu verstehen. Er spricht, als ob er einen Kloß im Munde (Halse) hätte.
*An American is often hard to understand. He talks as though he had a plum (a hot potato) in his mouth.*

klar wie **Kloßbrühe** sein (fam.): cf. **sonnenklar** sein

sich einen **Klotz** ans Bein binden (fig.): *to hang a millstone round one's neck; to make things more difficult for o.s.*

Der Geschäftsmann wird bald einsehen müssen, daß er sich mit der Eröffnung dieser neuen Filiale nur einen Klotz ans Bein gebunden (er mit . . . einen Knüppel am Bein) hat.
*The shopkeeper will soon have to realise that by opening this new branch he has only hung a millstone round his neck (only made things more difficult for himself).*

Auf einen groben **Klotz** gehört ein grober Keil (Sprichw.): *You must meet (match) roughness with roughness*

Mit Höflichkeiten kommen Sie bei diesem unfeinen Mann nicht weiter. Auf einen groben Klotz gehört ein grober Keil (Auf einen Schelm anderthalben).
*You will not get anywhere with that crude man with courtesies. You must meet (match) roughness with roughness.*

schlafen wie ein **Klotz**: cf. schlafen wie ein **Murmeltier**

es klafft eine **Kluft** (fig.): *there is an unbridgeable (a yawning) gulf.* Cf. auch: Das **Tischtuch** ist zwischen uns zerschnitten

Zwischen diesen beiden Familien klafft eine unüberbrückbare Kluft.
*There is an unbridgeable (a yawning) gulf between these two families.*

eine **Kluft** überbrücken (fig.): *to bridge a gulf (a gap)*. Cf. auch: etwas ins **Lot** bringen

Die Außenminister versuchen, die Kluft zwischen ihren beiden Ländern zu überbrücken.
*The foreign ministers are trying to bridge the gulf (gap) between their two countries.*

sich in seine gute **Kluft** werfen (fam.): *to put on one's Sunday best (colloq.); to tog o.s. up (colloq.)*

Da wir heute abend eingeladen sind, muß ich mich noch in meine gute Kluft (in Gala) werfen.
*As we are invited out this evening, I must put on my Sunday best (tog myself up).*

nicht recht **klug** sein: cf. nicht richtig im **Dachstübchen** sein

aus etwas nicht **klug** werden: *not to be able to make head or tail (to make any sense) of s.th.; not to know what to make of s.th.; to be all at sea with s.th.*

Aus diesem unklaren Zeitungsbericht kann kein Mensch klug (gescheit; schlau) werden.
*Nobody can make head or tail (any sense) of (Nobody knows what to make of; Everybody is all at sea with) this vague newspaper report.*

Der **Klügere** gibt nach (Sprichw.): *Better bend than break (prov.); It is wiser to give way*

Es hat keinen Zweck, so halsstarrig zu sein. Der Klügere gibt nach.
*It is no good being so obstinate. Better bend than break (It is wiser to give way).*

j.en in **Klump(atsch)** schlagen (fam.): cf. j.en zu **Brei** schlagen

nichts zu **knabbern** haben: cf. am **Hungertuche** nagen

an etwas zu **knacken** haben (fig.): cf. an etwas zu **kauen** haben

einen **Knacks** bekommen (fig.): *to suffer a setback; to take a knock (colloq.)*

Infolge seiner beleidigenden Worte hat unsere Freundschaft einen Knacks bekommen.
*Our friendship suffered a setback (took a knock) as a result of his insulting words.*

(auf) **Knall** und Fall: cf. auf der **Stelle**

einen **Knall** haben (fam.): cf. nicht richtig im **Dachstübchen** sein

Der große **Knall** kommt (fig.): *The big bang comes (colloq.); The balloon goes up (colloq.)*

Schon lange hatte die Firma schlecht gewirtschaftet, und eines Tages kam der große Knall.
*The firm had been mismanaged for a long while, and one day the big bang came (the balloon went up).*

ein **Knalleffekt**: *a sensation*

Der Knalleffekt der Feierlichkeit war, daß sich die beiden Töchter des Gastgebers verlobten.
*The sensation at the party was that the host's two daughters got engaged.*

**knallrot** werden: *to turn (to go) as red as a beetroot (as a lobster); to turn (to go) crimson*

Als Karl meine Schwester sah, wurde er knallrot (feuerrot; krebsrot; puterrot; rot wie ein Truthahn; errötete er bis in die Haarspitzen [Haarwurzeln], bis über die Ohren).
*When he saw my sister, Charles turned (went) as red as a beetroot (lobster; turned [went] crimson).*

**knauserig** (ein **Knauser**) sein (fam.): *to be mean (hard-fisted; tight-fisted; stingy; mingy; niggardly).* Cf. auch: ein **Geizhals** sein

Sei doch nicht so knauserig (knickerig; so ein Knauser [Knicker]), sondern gib deinem Freund auch ein Stück Schokolade!
*Don't be so mean (hard-fisted; tight-fisted; stingy; mingy; niggardly), and give your friend a piece of chocolate too.*

**kneifen** (fig.): cf. einen **Rückzieher** machen

**knickerig** (ein **Knicker**) sein (fam.): cf. **knauserig** sein

etwas übers **Knie** brechen (fig.): *to make short work of s. th.; quickly to dispose of s. th.; quickly to get rid of s. th. (colloq.)*

Unglücklicherweise läßt sich dieses Problem nicht ohne weiteres übers Knie brechen.
*Unfortunately we cannot make short work of (cannot quickly dispose [get rid] of) this problem.*

in die **Knie** sinken: *to fall on one's knee*

Die Kammerjungfer sank vor der Königin in die Knie.
*The chambermaid fell on her knee before the queen.*

j.en in die **Knie** zwingen (fig.): *to force (to bring) s. b. to his knees*

Wir hielten uns für unbesiegbar, aber die zahlenmäßige Überlegenheit der Feinde zwang uns in die Knie.
*We considered ourselves invincible, but the numerical superiority of the enemy forced (brought) us to our knees.*

**kniefällig** (fig.): *on bended knee*

Der Dieb bat mich kniefällig um Verzeihung.
*The thief begged me for forgiveness on bended knee.*

**Knies(t)** haben (fam.): *to have a row; to have a tiff (colloq.).* Cf. auch: sich mit j.em in den **Haaren** liegen

> Das junge Ehepaar hat bereits miteinander Knies(t) gehabt.
> *The young couple have already had a row (tiff) with each other.*

den **Kniff** heraushaben: *to have got the knack (the hang) of s.th.*

> Lange haben wir vergebens versucht, Federball zu spielen, aber jetzt haben wir den Kniff (Bogen; Dreh) heraus (haben wir es im Griff).
> *For a long while we tried in vain to play badminton, but now we've got the knack (hang) of it.*

alle **Kniffe** kennen: cf. alle **Schliche** kennen

ein **Knirps** sein: *to be a Tom Thumb (a midget); to be pocket-sized (pint-sized) (colloq.); to be a tich (sl.)*

> Wie alt ist denn dieser Knirps (Däumling; Dreikäsehoch), der schon so schön sprechen kann?
> *How old is this Tom Thumb (midget; tich; pocket-sized [pint-sized] lad) who speaks so nicely?*

bis auf die **Knochen** abgemagert sein: cf. nur noch **Haut** und Knochen sein

wie Blei in den **Knochen** liegen: cf. wie **Blei** in den Gliedern liegen; j.em in den **Gliedern** liegen

deutsch bis in die **Knochen** sein: cf. **kerndeutsch** sein

bis auf die **Knochen** durchnäßt sein: cf. bis auf die **Haut** durchnäßt sein

j.en bis auf die **Knochen** durchschauen: *to see (right) through s.b.*

> Infolge seiner bisherigen Handlungen kann man diesen verächtlichen Menschen bis auf die Knochen durchschauen.
> *As a result of his earlier actions one can see (right) through this despicable person.*

j.em in die **Knochen** fahren: cf. j.em in die **Glieder** fahren

etwas in den **Knochen** haben (j.em in den Knochen stecken): *s.th. is in s.b.'s bones; s.th. is engrained in s.b.*

> Dieser alte Offizier hat noch (Diesem alten Offizier steckt noch) die militärische Disziplin in den Knochen.
> *Military discipline is still in that old officer's bones (still engrained in that old officer).*

**knochendürr** sein: cf. nur noch **Haut** und Knochen sein

die reinste **Knochenmühle** sein (fig. u. fam.): *to be like a sausage-factory (a madhouse) (colloq.)*

In dieser Apotheke ist viel zu tun. Der Eigentümer sagt, sie sei die reinste Knochenmühle (Tretmühle).
*There is a lot to do in this chemist's. The owner says it is like a sausage-factory (a madhouse).*

**knochentrocken** sein: *to be bone-dry (as dry as a bone)*

Bei diesem starken Wind ist die Wäsche sicher schon knochentrocken (rappeltrocken).
*With this strong wind the washing is sure to be bone-dry (as dry as a bone) by now.*

ein alter (altmodischer) **Knopp** sein (fam.): *to be an old buffer (old fogy [fogey]) (sl.)*

Wer ist denn dieser alte (altmodische) Knopp da drüben?
*Who's that old buffer (fogy [fogey]) over there?*

den Gordischen **Knoten** durchschlagen (zerhauen): *to cut the Gordian Knot*

Das Problem schien unlösbar, aber jetzt haben wir den Gordischen Knoten durchschlagen (zerhauen).
*The problem seemed insoluble, but now we have cut the Gordian Knot.*

**knüll** sein (fam.): cf. **sternhagelvoll** sein

einen **Knüppel** am Bein haben (fig.): cf. sich einen **Klotz** ans Bein binden

j.em einen **Knüppel** zwischen die Beine werfen (fig.): *to put a spoke in s.b.'s wheel; to trip s.b. up (colloq.).* Cf. auch: j.em ein **Bein** stellen

Die Oppositionsparteien haben der Regierung einen Knüppel zwischen die Beine geworfen (einen Riegel vorgeschoben), indem sie gegen den neuen Gesetzentwurf gestimmt haben.
*The opposition parties have put a spoke in the government's wheel (tripped the government up) by voting against the new bill.*

bei j.em liegt der **Knüppel** beim Hund (fig.): *It is (a case of) Hobson's choice; s.b. has no option (no alternative)*

Da wir kein Geld haben, können wir nicht nach Italien in die Ferien fahren. Der Knüppel liegt (eben bei uns) beim Hund.
*Since we have no money, we cannot go to Italy for our holidays. It's (a case of) Hobson's choice (We have no option [alternative]).*

**knüppeldick** (fam.): *with a heavy hand; with telling effect*

In den letzten Jahren hat das Schicksal meinen Freund knüppeldick getroffen.
*In the last few years fate has struck my friend with a heavy hand (with telling effect).*

etwas **knüppeldick** haben (fam.): cf. etwas bis **dahin** (stehen) haben

unter j.es **Knute** stehen (fig.): cf. unter j.es **Fuchtel** stehen

Viele **Köche** verderben den Brei (Sprichw.): *Too many cooks spoil the broth (prov.)*

Das Unternehmen ist gescheitert, weil jeder eine andere Meinung hatte. Viele Köche verderben den Brei.
*The enterprise failed because each person had a different opinion. Too many cooks spoil the broth.*

Hunger ist der beste **Koch** (Sprichw.): cf. **Hunger** ist der beste Koch

in j.em **kochen** (fig.): cf. j.es **Blut** wallen machen; vor **Wut** kochen

vor Wut **kochen** (fig.): cf. vor **Wut** kochen

aufgewärmter **Kohl** (fig.): *a re-hash; a hackneyed yarn; hashed-up stuff (colloq.)*

Wie oft willst du uns immer wieder diese alten Geschichten erzählen? Es ist ja doch nur aufgewärmter Kohl!
*How many more times are you going to tell us these old tales? They are nothing but a re-hash (hackneyed yarns; hashed-up stuff).*

j.es **Kohl** fettmachen (fig. u. fam.): *to set s.b. up nicely (colloq.); to feather s.b.'s nest*

Dieser Geländekauf ist ihm sehr willkommen. Er macht seinen Kohl schön fett.
*He is very satisfied with having bought that plot of land. It will set him up (feather his nest) nicely.*

den **Kohl** nicht fettmachen (fig. u. fam.): *It won't get (take) s.b. (very) far; S.b. won't get fat on that (colloq.)*

Eine so geringfügige Hilfe nützt uns nichts. Sie macht den Kohl nicht fett.
*Such trifling help is no use to us. It won't take us (very) far (We shan't get fat on that).*

Schöne Worte machen den **Kohl** nicht fett (Sprichw.): *Fine words butter no parsnips (prov.); You will not grow fat on compliments.* Cf. auch: j.en mit bloßen Worten **abspeisen;** Was kann ich mir dafür (schon) **kaufen!**

Ich weiß, daß der Chef dich gelobt hat, aber schöne Worte machen den Kohl nicht fett. Du solltest eine Gehaltserhöhung verlangen.
*I know that the boss praised you, but fine words butter no parsnips (you won't grow fat on compliments). You ought to ask for a rise.*

**Kohl** reden (fam.): cf. **Quatsch** reden

**kohlen** (fam.): *to try it on (colloq.)*

Sag' mir offen die Wahrheit und kohle (flunkere) nicht!
*Tell me the truth frankly and don't try it on.*

feurige **Kohlen** auf j.es Haupt sammeln (fig.): *to heap coals of fire on s.b.'s head*

Wer Schlechtes mit Gutem vergilt, sammelt feurige Kohlen auf des Übeltäters Haupt.
*He who returns good for evil heaps coals of fire on the wrongdoer's head.*

wie auf (heißen [glühenden]) **Kohlen** sitzen: *to sit like a cat on hot bricks; to be on pins and needles; to be all of a dither (colloq.)*

Es war schon 8 Uhr, und Wilhelm saß wie auf (heißen [glühenden]) Kohlen (wie auf Nadeln), denn er hatte versprochen, (bis) um 7 (schon) zu Hause zu sein.
*It was eight o'clock already, and William was sitting like a cat on hot bricks (was on pins and needles; was all of a dither) because he had promised to be home by seven.*

**kohl(pech)rabenschwarz** sein: a) (von Personen): cf. schwarz wie ein **Mohr(enkind)**; b) (von Sachen): *to be as black as pitch (as ink; as jet); to be pitch-black (jet-black); to be as black as sin (colloq.)*

Die Nacht draußen war kohl(pech)rabenschwarz (stockdunkel; stockfinster).
*The night outside was as black as pitch (ink; jet; sin; was pitch-black [jet-black]).*

einen **Koller** bekommen (fam.): cf. aus der **Haut** fahren

**Komödie** spielen (fig.): cf. **Theater** spielen

ein wandelndes (wahres) **Konversationslexikon** sein (fig.): *to be a walking encyclopaedia (a mine of information)*

Dieser Gelehrte ist ein wandelndes (wahres) Konversationslexikon.
*This scholar is a walking encyclopaedia (a mine of information).*

j.en aus dem **Konzept** bringen: cf. Aktivformen zu: sich aus dem **Konzept** bringen lassen

sich aus dem **Konzept** bringen lassen (aus dem Konzept kommen): *to be put out (put off); to be put off one's stroke; to be put (thrown) out of one's stride (out of joint; out of step; out of gear)*

Der junge Redner ließ sich durch einige Zwischenrufe aus dem Konzept (Geleise; Text) bringen (kam durch einige Zw. aus dem Konzept [Geleise; Text]).
*The young speaker was put out (put off [his stroke]; put [thrown] out of his stride [out of joint; out of step; out of gear]) by a few interruptions.*

Man wird dir nicht gleich den **Kopf** abreißen (Es wird dich nicht gleich den Kopf kosten): *They won't bite you (colloq.); They won't bite (cut) your head off (colloq.)*

Du kannst ruhig mit den Leuten im Finanzministerium sprechen. Man wird dir nicht gleich den Kopf abreißen (Es wird dich nicht gleich den Kopf kosten).
*You can talk to the people in the income-tax office all right. They won't bite you (bite [cut] your head off).*

sich an die **Köpfe** kriegen (fig. u. fam.): cf. sich in die **Haare** geraten

eins (etwas) auf den **Kopf** bekommen (kriegen) (fig. u. fam.): cf. eine **Abreibung** kriegen

seinen **Kopf** aufsetzen (fig.): *to be pig-headed; to be as obstinate (stubborn) as a mule.* Cf. auch: störrisch wie ein **Esel** sein

> Ich versuchte, ihn anzureden, er aber setzte seinen Kopf auf und wollte nichts mit mir zu tun haben.
> *I tried to talk to him but he was pig-headed (as obstinate [stubborn] as a mule) and would not have anything to do with me.*

aus dem **Kopf**: *out of one's head; by heart*

> Manches schöne Gedicht kann ich noch heute aus dem Kopf hersagen.
> *I can still recite a number of beautiful poems out of my head (by heart) today.*

Was man nicht im **Kopfe** hat, muß man in den Beinen haben (Sprichw.): *If your head lets you down, you must use your feet*

> Karl hatte seine Schulbücher vergessen und mußte schnell wieder nach Hause laufen. Was man nicht im Kopfe hat, muß man in den Beinen haben.
> *Charles had forgotten his school-books and had to run home again quickly. If your head lets you down, you must use your feet.*

auf seinem **Kopf** bestehen (fig.): *to want to have (to insist on having) one's own way; to dig in one's heels*

> Mein Bruder ließ sich von mir nicht beeinflussen, sondern bestand auf seinem Kopf (setzte seinen Kopf durch) und weigerte sich, mit nach Hause zu kommen.
> *My brother did not let me influence him but wanted to have (insisted on having) his own way (but dug his heels in) and refused to come home with me.*

Der **Kopf** brummt mir (fig.): *My head is in a whirl (a daze); My head is buzzing (going round and round; spinning).* Cf. auch: Mir ist ganz **dumm** im Kopf; **rammdösig** werden

> Als ich nach der langen mündlichen Prüfung aufstand, brummte (rauchte) mir der Kopf (Schädel; schwamm es mir vor den Augen).
> *When I got up from the long oral examination my head was in a whirl (a daze; my head was buzzing [going round and round; spinning]).*

seinen **Kopf** durchsetzen (fig.): cf. auf seinem **Kopf** bestehen

nicht j.es **Kopf** entsprungen sein: cf. nicht j.es **Hirn** entsprungen sein

von **Kopf** bis Fuß: *from head to foot; from top (tip) to toe*

> Die Flüchtlinge wurden durch die Wohltätigkeitsvereine von Kopf bis Fuß (vom Scheitel bis zur Sohle [Zehe]; vom Wirbel bis zur Zehe) neu eingekleidet.
> *The refugees were re-clothed by the welfare organisations from head to foot (from top [tip] to toe).*

nicht auf den **Kopf** gefallen sein (fig. u. fam.): *to be no fool; to know what's what; to be up to scratch (to snuff) (colloq.).* Cf. auch: es faustdick hinter den **Ohren** haben; wissen, wo **Barthel** den Most holt

Ich weiß ganz genau, was du denkst. Ich bin doch nicht auf den Kopf gefallen.
*I know just exactly what you're thinking. I'm no fool (I know what's what; I'm up to scratch [to snuff]).*

sich etwas durch den **Kopf** gehen lassen: *to think s. th. over; to turn s. th. over in one's mind; to put on one's thinking-cap about s. th.; to chew s. th. over (colloq.).* Cf. auch: eine **Nacht** über etwas schlafen

Laß dir meinen Vorschlag durch den Kopf gehen und ruf' mich morgen früh an.
*Think over my suggestion (Turn over my suggestion in your mind; Put on your thinking-cap about my suggestion; Chew my suggestion over) and ring me up tomorrow morning.*

sein Geld auf den **Kopf** schlagen (hauen) (fam.): cf. auf großem **Fuße** leben

wie vor den **Kopf** geschlagen (gestoßen) sein: *to be stunned (dazed; stupefied; benumbed; taken aback; dumbfounded)*

Als wir diese Nachricht in der Zeitung lasen, waren wir wie vor den Kopf geschlagen (gestoßen).
*When we read this news in the paper, we were stunned (dazed; stupefied; benumbed; taken aback; dumbfounded).*

mit seinem **Kopf** für etwas haften: *to pledge one's life for s. th.*

Der Minister haftet mit seinem Kopf dafür, daß sein Personal völlig ehrlich ist.
*The minister pledges his life that his staff is entirely honest.*

den **Kopf** hängenlassen (fig.): *to lose heart; to look blue (colloq.); to have a hang-dog look (colloq.); to look (to be) down in the mouth (colloq.).* Cf. auch: **klein** und häßlich sein

Da das Mädchen ihn schlecht behandelt hatte, war Fred sehr deprimiert und ließ den Kopf hängen.
*As the girl had treated him badly, Fred was very depressed and lost heart (looked blue; had a hang-dog look; looked [was] down in the mouth).*

ein heller (fähiger) **Kopf** sein: *to be a bright chap (fellow); to be a brainy chap (fellow) (colloq.)*

Da Wilhelm ein heller (fähiger) Kopf ist (Köpfchen hat; helle ist), kann man ihn auf diesem wichtigen Posten gut gebrauchen.
*Since William is a bright (brainy) chap (fellow), we can do with him in this important position.*

im **Kopf** herumgehen: *to go (to run) through s. b.'s head; to haunt s. b.*

Der neue Schlager geht mir schon seit Tagen im Kopf herum.
*The new hit-tune has been going (running) through my head (has been haunting me) for days.*

**Kopf** hoch!: *Chin up!; Cheer up!*
Kopf hoch! Du wirst vielleicht nächstes Jahr ins Ausland fahren können.
*Chin up! (Cheer up!) Perhaps you will be able to go abroad next year.*

den **Kopf** hochtragen (fig.): *to hold (to carry) one's head high (aloft)*
Seit seiner Wahl zum Abgeordneten trägt Heinrich den Kopf hoch.
*Since his election as a deputy Henry has held (carried) his head high (aloft).*

Es will (geht) mir nicht in den **Kopf**: *I cannot get hold of (grasp) the idea; It will not dawn on me; It will not sink in (colloq.); It will not register (colloq.)*
Es will (geht) mir nicht in den Kopf, daß ich den Unfall verschuldet haben soll.
*I cannot get hold of (grasp) the idea (It will not dawn on me [sink in; register]) that I am supposed to be responsible for the accident.*

sich einen klaren **Kopf** verschaffen: *to blow away the cobwebs; to get one's head (mind) clear*
Ich muß eine Zeitlang in der frischen Luft spazierengehen, um mir einen klaren Kopf zu verschaffen.
*I must go for a walk in the fresh air for a while to blow away the cobwebs (to get my head [mind] clear).*

j.em auf den **Kopf** kommen (fig. u. fam.): cf. j.en **abkanzeln**

**Kopf** an Kopf: cf. gedrängt wie die **Heringe**

um **Kopf** und Kragen gehen: cf. es geht um j.es **Hals**

**Kopf** und Kragen riskieren: *to risk one's neck (one's all)*
Die Verschwörer wußten, daß sie Kopf und Kragen riskierten.
*The conspirators knew that they were risking their necks (their all).*

j.en einen **Kopf** kürzer machen (fam.): *to chop s. b.'s block off (sl.)*
Während der meisten Revolutionen werden viele Menschen einen Kopf kürzer gemacht.
*During most revolutions many people get their blocks chopped off.*

j.em ein Loch (Löcher) in den **Kopf** fragen (fig.): cf. j.em ein **Loch** (Löcher) in den Kopf fragen

Nägel mit **Köpfen** machen (fig.): cf. **Nägel** mit Köpfen machen

den **Kopf** obenbehalten (fig.): *to keep one's head (one's presence of mind)*
Die Rettungsmannschaft behielt den Kopf oben und konnte alle Schiffbrüchigen retten.
*The rescue-team kept their heads (presence of mind) and were able to rescue all the shipwrecked people.*

Der **Kopf** raucht mir (fig.): cf. Der **Kopf** brummt mir

j.em etwas (glatt) vor den **Kopf** sagen: cf. j.em etwas (glatt) vor die **Platte** sagen

den **Kopf** in den Sand stecken (fig.): *to bury one's head in the sand; to blind o.s.; to shut one's eyes.* Cf. auch: die **Augen** vor etwas verschließen

> In dieser Situation nützt es nichts, den Kopf in den Sand zu stecken (Vogelstraußpolitik zu machen [zu treiben]).
> *In this situation it is no use burying one's head in the sand (blinding oneself; shutting one's eyes).*

sich etwas aus dem **Kopf** schlagen: *to get (to put) s.th. out of (to dismiss s.th. from) one's mind (head); to give s.th. up; to have to forget s.th.*

> Wir haben es uns aus dem Kopf geschlagen, dieses Jahr ein Auto zu kaufen.
> *We have got (put) the idea out of (dismissed the idea from) our minds (have given up the idea) to buy (have had to forget about buying) a car this year.*

den **Kopf** aus der Schlinge ziehen (fig.): cf. sich aus der **Schlinge** ziehen

bis über den **Kopf** in Schulden stecken: cf. bis über die **Ohren** in Schulden stecken

den **Kopf** über etwas schütteln: *to shake one's head at (over) s.th.*

> Über sein leichtsinniges Benehmen kann man nur den Kopf schütteln.
> *One can only shake one's head at (over) his reckless behaviour.*

sich etwas in den **Kopf** setzen: *to have a bee in one's bonnet; to take s.th. into one's head; to set one's mind (heart) on s.th.*

> Mein älterer Bruder hat es sich in den Kopf gesetzt, Landschaftsgärtner zu werden, und wir können ihn nicht davon abbringen.
> *My elder brother has a bee in his bonnet about becoming (has taken it into his head to become; has set his mind [heart] on becoming) a landscape-gardener, and we cannot dissuade him.*

Soviel **Köpfe**, soviel Sinne (Sprichw.): *There are as many minds as men (So many men, so many minds)*

> Der Ausschuß konnte zu keinem Entschluß kommen, weil die Mitglieder sich nicht einigen konnten. Soviel Köpfe, soviel Sinne.
> *The committee could not reach any decision because the members were not able to agree. There were as many minds as men (So many men, so many minds).*

nicht wissen, wo einem der **Kopf** steht (fig.): *not to know where (which way) to turn; to be at one's wit's end; not to know whether one is coming or going (whether* *one is standing on one's head or one's heels)*. Cf. auch: mit seiner **Kunst** zu (am) Ende sein

Ich habe in letzter Zeit so viele Aufträge bekommen, daß ich nicht weiß, wo mir der Kopf steht.
*I have received so many orders recently that I don't know where (which way) to turn (whether I am coming or going [standing on my head or my heels]; ... recently that I am at my wit's end).*

j.em zu (in den) **Kopf** steigen (fig.): *to go to (to turn) s.b.'s head; to give s.b. a swollen head*

Der große Beifall ist diesem Geiger zu (in den) Kopf gestiegen.
*The great applause has gone to (has turned) this violinist's head (has given this violinist a swollen head).*

alles auf den **Kopf** stellen (fig.): *to turn everything upside-down (inside-out; topsy-turvy).* Cf. auch: etwas **durchstöbern**

Wenn meine Mutter im Frühjahr Hausputz hält, stellt sie alles (die ganze Bude) auf den Kopf (kehrt sie das Oberste zu unterst [das Unterste zu oberst]).
*When my mother does the spring-cleaning, she turns everything upside-down (inside-out; topsy-turvy).*

j.en mit dem **Kopf** auf etwas stoßen (fig.): j.en mit der **Nase** auf etwas stoßen

j.en vor den **Kopf** stoßen (fig.): *to put s.b. off; to nark s.b. (colloq.); to get s.b.'s goat (colloq.).* Cf. auch: bei j.em **anecken**

Durch seine unfreundliche Art hat dein Bruder schon viele Menschen vor den Kopf gestoßen.
*Your brother has put many people off (has narked many people; has got many people's goat) by his unfriendly manner.*

j.em den **Kopf** verdrehen (fig.): *to turn s.b.'s head; to knock s.b. off his balance (colloq.)*

Durch sein gutes Aussehen hat dieser junge Mann manchem Mädchen den Kopf verdreht.
*That young man has turned many a girl's head (knocked many a girl off her balance) by his good looks.*

den **Kopf** verlieren (fig.): *to lose one's head (one's wits; one's nerve); to panic; to get in a flap (sl.).* Cf. auch: **kopflos** sein

Das Mädchen verlor in der Angst den Kopf und fing an zu schreien.
*In her fear the girl lost her head (her wits; her nerve; the girl panicked [got into a flap]) and began to scream.*

nicht den **Kopf** verlieren (fig.): *to keep one's head (one's nerve); to keep one's wits about one; to keep a level (cool) head.* Cf. auch: den **Kopf** obenbehalten und die Negativformen der Ausdrücke unter: den **Kopf** verlieren

Der General ermahnte seine Soldaten, auch im Unglück nicht den Kopf zu verlieren.
*The general urged his soldiers to keep their heads (nerve; to keep their wits about them; to keep a level [cool] head) even in misfortune.*

viel im **Kopf** haben (fig.): *to have a great deal on one's mind (a great deal to think about)*

Wir dürfen ihn mit unserer Unterhaltung nicht stören, da er augenblicklich viel im Kopf hat.
*We mustn't disturb him with our conversation because he has a great deal on his mind (a great deal to think about) at the moment.*

j.em über den **Kopf** wachsen (fig.): *to get out of hand; to become too much for s.b.; to get on top of s.b.; to get the better of s.b.; to submerge (to drown) s.b.*

Ich kann mir im Augenblick keine Mittagsruhe gönnen, da die Arbeit mir über den Kopf zu wachsen droht.
*At the moment I cannot afford an afternoon nap, because the work threatens to get out of hand (to become too much for me; to get on top of me; to get the better of me; to submerge [to drown] me).*

mit dem **Kopf** durch die Wand wollen (gegen die Wand rennen) (fig.): *to knock (to beat; to run) one's head against a wall (a brick wall)*

Manchmal muß man auf seine liebsten Wünsche verzichten. Es nützt nichts, mit dem Kopf durch die Wand zu wollen (gegen die Wand zu rennen).
*Sometimes one has to give up one's dearest desires. It is no use knocking (beating; running) one's head against a wall (a brick wall).*

j.em den **Kopf** warmmachen (fig.): cf. j.em die **Hölle** heißmachen

j.em den **Kopf** waschen (fig. u. fam.): cf. j.en **abkanzeln**

den **Kopf** über Wasser halten (fig.): *to keep one's head above water; to break even; to make ends meet*

Bei seiner großen Familie hat es unser Schuster schwer, den Kopf (od.: sich) über Wasser zu halten und nicht in Schulden zu geraten.
*With his large family our cobbler finds it difficult to keep his head above water (to break even; to make ends meet) and not get into debt.*

sich den **Kopf** zerbrechen (zermartern) (fig.): *to rack (to cudgel) one's brains.* Cf. auch: j.em **Kopfzerbrechen** machen

Fred zerbricht (zermartert) sich den Kopf (das Hirn; Es ist für Fred ein Rätselraten), wo er diese wichtige Quittung hingelegt haben kann.
*Fred is racking (cudgelling) his brains as to where he could have put that important receipt.*

j.em den **Kopf** zurechtsetzen (fig.): cf. j.em (die) **Flötentöne** beibringen. Cf. auch: j.en **abkanzeln**

298

j.em etwas auf den **Kopf** zusagen: cf. j.em etwas ins **Gesicht** sagen. Cf. auch: **klipp** und klar sagen

die **Köpfe** zusammenstecken (fig.): *to put our (your etc.) heads together; to get together; to go into a huddle (colloq.)*

Nachdem die Arbeiter die Köpfe zusammengesteckt hatten, brachten sie neue Pläne vor.
*After they had put their heads together (had got together; had gone into a huddle), the workers produced new plans.*

**Köpfchen** haben (fam.): cf. ein heller (fähiger) **Kopf** sein

**kopflos** sein (fig.): *to be at a loss (taken aback).* Cf. auch: wie vor den **Kopf** geschlagen sein

Die Nachricht kam so unerwartet, daß ich völlig kopflos war.
*The news came so unexpectedly that I was completely at a loss (taken aback).*

j.en **kopfscheu** machen: *to scare s.b. away (off); to make s.b. jittery (colloq.); to give s.b. the jitters (colloq.).* Cf. auch: j.en **rappelig** machen

Wenn du ihm so etwas sagst, machst du ihn kopfscheu.
*If you say that sort of thing to him, you will scare him away ([off]; make him jittery; you will give him the jitters).*

**kopfstehen** (fig.): a) *to be struck dumb; to be flabbergasted (colloq.); to gasp for breath (colloq.); to goggle (colloq.); to throw a fit (sl.);* b) *to be upside-down (topsy-turvy)*

a) Wenn ich Ihnen erzähle, was ich neulich erfahren habe, werden Sie kopfstehen.
b) Anläßlich des großen Festes stand das ganze Städtchen kopf.
*a) You will be struck dumb (flabbergasted; will gasp for breath; will goggle; will throw a fit) if I tell you what I learned recently.*
*b) On the occasion of the great celebration the little town was all upside-down (topsy-turvy).*

sich **kopfüber** in etwas stürzen (fig.): *to dive (to plunge) head first (head foremost; headlong) into s.th.*

Er hatte keine Zeit, sich mit mir zu unterhalten, sondern stürzte sich kopfüber in die Arbeit.
*He had no time to talk to me but dived (plunged) head first (head foremost; headlong) into his work.*

j.em **Kopfzerbrechen** machen: *It gives s.b. a headache; It makes s.b. rack (cudgel) his brains*

Mutter macht sich viel Kopfzerbrechen, wie sie mit ihrem Geld bis zum Monatsende auskommen soll.

*It gives mother a headache (makes mother rack [cudgel] her brains) how she is to manage
with her money until the end of the month.*

einen **Korb** bekommen (fig.): cf. die Passivform der Ausdrücke unter: j.em
einen **Korb** geben

j.em einen **Korb** geben (fig.): *to turn s.b. down; to throw s.b. over; to jilt s.b.;
to give s.b. his marching-orders (colloq.); to give s.b. the bird (colloq.); to chuck
s.b. up (sl.)*

Mein Bruder will nicht mehr heiraten, nachdem man ihm zweimal einen Korb
gegeben hat.
*My brother doesn't want to marry any more after having been turned down (thrown over;
jilted; given his marching-orders [the bird]; chucked up) twice.*

j.en (scharf) aufs **Korn** nehmen (fig.): cf. ein scharfes **Auge** auf j.en haben

kein **Körnchen:** cf. nicht die **Bohne**

am ganzen **Körper** zittern: cf. zittern wie **Espenlaub**

auf seine **Kosten** kommen (fig.): *to get one's money's worth; to have one's fill; to
be catered for*

Es wurden so viele verschiedene Stücke im Konzert gespielt, daß jeder auf seine
Kosten gekommen ist.
*So many different pieces were played at the concert that everybody got his money's worth
(had his fill; was catered for).*

j.en in den **Kot** ziehen (fig. u. fam.): cf. j.en durch (in) den **Dreck** ziehen

ein **Kotzmittel** sein (fig. u. vulg.): cf. ein **Brechmittel** sein

wegen einer Sache **Krach** machen (schlagen): *to kick up a row (rumpus;
shindy) about s.th. (colloq.); to cut up rough (colloq.); to kick up a stink about
s.th. (sl.); to raise merry hell about s.th. (sl.).* Cf. auch: aus der **Haut** fahren

Als der Angestellte wieder einmal zu spät ins Büro kam, hat der Chef tüchtig
Krach (Radau; Spektakel) gemacht ([geschlagen]; randaliert; hat der Chef einen
Tanz aufgeführt).
*When the clerk arrived late at the office again, the boss kicked up a proper row (rumpus;
shindy; stink; raised merry hell; cut up rough).*

keine **Kraft** in den Knochen haben: cf. kein **Mark** in den Knochen haben

ein **Kraftmeier** sein (fam.): *to be a barbarian; to be a ruffian (colloq.)*

Ich begreife nicht, wie diese feine Frau so einen Kraftmeier heiraten konnte.
*I cannot understand how that refined woman could marry such a barbarian (ruffian).*

Es geht einem an den **Kragen** (fig.): cf. Es geht um j.es **Hals**

j.em an den **Kragen** gehen (fig.): cf. j.em an die **Kehle** fahren

j.en beim **Kragen** nehmen (packen) (fig.): cf. j.en beim **Kanthaken** fassen (packen)

Das ist nicht meine **Kragenweite** (fig. u. fam.): *That's not my cup of tea (colloq.); That's not my idea of fun (colloq.)*

> Du kannst nachts um zwei Uhr zu Bett gehen, wenn du willst. Das ist aber nicht meine Kragenweite; ich brauche viel Schlaf.
> *You can go to bed at two in the morning if you like, but that's not my cup of tea (not my idea of fun). I need a lot of sleep.*

Eine **Krähe** hackt der anderen nicht die Augen aus (Sprichw.): *Like does not destroy like (prov.); Rogues stick together*

> Man kann nicht erwarten, daß ein Verbrecher seine Mithelfer verrät. Eine Krähe hackt der anderen nicht die Augen aus.
> *One cannot expect a criminal to give his accomplices away. Like does not destroy like (Rogues stick together).*

in **Krähwinkel** wohnen (fig.): cf. in **Buxtehude** wohnen

der ganze **Kram** (fam.): *the whole bag of tricks (colloq.); the whole set-out (colloq.); the whole shoot (colloq.); the whole caboodle (sl.)*

> Was machst du nur mit solchen alten Sachen? Wirf doch den ganzen Kram (Kitt; Schlamassel; Zim[me]t; Zinnober) fort!
> *What can you do with old things like those? Throw the whole bag of tricks (the whole set-out [shoot; caboodle] away!*

j.em nicht in den **Kram** (hinein)passen (fam.): *not to suit s.b.'s book; not to fit in with s.b.'s arrangements*

> Daß du morgen kommen willst, paßt mir gar nicht in den Kram.
> *It does not suit my book (fit in with my arrangements) at all that you want to come tomorrow.*

eine **Krämerseele** sein (haben): *to have a petty (small) mind; to be small-minded*

> Es fehlt diesem Menschen jede Großzügigkeit. Er ist (hat) eine wahre Krämerseele.
> *That person lacks all broad-mindedness. He has a really petty (small) mind (is really small-minded).*

einen **Krammel** im Hals haben: *to have a frog in one's throat (colloq.)*

> Unser Lehrer mußte heute flüstern, weil er einen Krammel im Hals hat.
> *Our master had to whisper today because he had a frog in his throat.*

(ein) **Krampf** (fig. u. fam.): *trash; rubbish; tripe (sl.)*

Auf einer Kirmes kaufen wir nichts, da dort doch alles Krampf (Mist) ist.
*We never buy anything at a fair, because everything there is trash (rubbish; tripe).*

sich **krampfhaft** bemühen: *to try with might and main; to try for all one is worth; to strive tooth and nail*

Karl bemüht sich krampfhaft, Klassenerster zu werden.
*Charles is trying with might and main (for all he is worth; is striving tooth and nail) to become top of the class.*

sich **kranklachen:** cf. sich **totlachen**

sich die **Kränke** an den Hals ärgern (fam.): cf. sich **grün** und blau (schwarz) ärgern

die **Kränke** kriegen (fam.): cf. sich **grün** und blau (schwarz) ärgern

eine **Kratzbürste (kratzbürstig)** sein (fam.): *to be cantankerous (cross-grained); to be crusty (grumpy; waspish) (colloq.)*

Meine Schwester hat keine Freundinnen, weil sie (so) eine Kratzbürste (so kratzbürstig) ist.
*My sister has no friends because she is so cantankerous (cross-grained; crusty; grumpy; waspish).*

Dagegen ist kein **Kraut** gewachsen: *There is no counter (no answer) to that*
Gegen den Tod ist kein Kraut gewachsen.
*There is no counter (answer) to death.*

wie **Kraut** und Rüben durcheinanderliegen: *to be higgledy-piggledy (topsy-turvy); to be at sixes and sevens; to be all over the place (colloq.)*

Räumt Eure Spielsachen auf! In Euerm Zimmer liegt alles wie Kraut und Rüben (alles kunterbunt; kreuz und quer) durcheinander.
*Clear up your toys! Your room is all higgledy-piggledy (topsy-turvy; at sixes and sevens; all over the place).*

ins **Kraut** schießen (fig.): *to rise (to grow; to increase) out of all proportion (all keeping; by leaps and bounds); to get out of hand; (nur plur.) to spring up like mushrooms.* Cf. auch: wie (die) **Pilze** aus der Erde schießen

Seit dem Krieg ist die Zahl der politischen Parteien ins Kraut geschossen.
*Since the war the number of political parties has risen (grown; increased) by leaps and bounds (out of all proportion [all keeping]; has got out of hand; Since the war political parties have sprung up like mushrooms).*

**Krawall** machen: cf. einen **Heidenlärm** machen

den **Krebsgang** gehen (fig.): *to advance backwards; to take a step backwards; to go the wrong way; to take one step forward and two steps backward*

Wenn die Regierung diese Maßnahmen durchführt, so wird das nichts als Ärger und Enttäuschung mit sich bringen. Man würde (nur) den Krebsgang gehen.
*If the government carries out these measures it will cause nothing but annoyance and disappointment. It will be advancing backwards (taking a step backwards; going the wrong way; taking one step forward and two steps backward).*

**krebsrot** (rot wie ein [gesottener] **Krebs**) werden: cf. **knallrot** werden

ein **Krebsschaden** (fig.): *a canker*

Die neuen Maßnahmen werden sich bald zu einem Krebsschaden für unsere Wirtschaft entwickeln.
*The new measures will soon develop into a canker in our economy.*

tief in der **Kreide** stehen (sitzen) (fig.): cf. bis über den **Kopf** in Schulden stecken

weiß wie **Kreide (kreidebleich; kreideweiß)** sein: cf. weiß wie die **Wand** sein

sich im **Kreise** drehen: cf. sich in einem **circulus vitiosus** bewegen

**Krethi** und Plethi: cf. **Hinz** und Kunz

drei **Kreuze** hinter j.em (her)machen (fig.): *to be glad to see the back of s.b.; to say good riddance to s.b.*

Wenn unsere unangenehme Tante wieder abgereist ist, machen wir alle drei Kreuze hinter ihr her.
*When our unpleasant aunt has left, we shall all be glad to see the back of her (we shall all say good riddance to her).*

übers **Kreuz** dumm sein: cf. dumm wie **Bohnenstroh** sein

aufs **Kreuz** fallen (fig. u. fam.): cf. wie aus den **Wolken** (ge)fallen

zu **Kreuze** kriechen (fig.): *to eat humble pie; to eat dirt; to sing small; to go cap in hand; to climb down (colloq.).* Cf. auch: **klein** beigeben

Der freche Hausierer mußte zu Kreuze kriechen und meine Mutter um Verzeihung bitten.
*The impertinent hawker was made to eat humble pie (eat dirt; sing small; go cap in hand; climb down) and apologise to my mother.*

es ist ein **Kreuz** mit j.em (fig.): *s.b. is a thorn in one's flesh; it is a plague (vexation; worry) with s.b.; s.b. is one's cross*

Es ist ein Kreuz mit Wilhelm. Er fällt in seinen Prüfungen immer durch, obwohl ich ihm helfe.
*William is a thorn in my flesh (It is a plague [vexation; worry] with William; William is my cross). He always fails his examinations, although I help him.*

**kreuz** und quer: a) *criss-cross; zig-zag;* b) cf. wie **Kraut** und Rüben durch-einanderliegen

Die Expedition ging kreuz und quer durch Afrika.
*The expedition went criss-cross (zig-zag) through Africa.*

sein **Kreuz** tragen (auf sich nehmen) (fig.): *to bear (to shoulder; to take up) one's cross (burden)*

Auch dieser reiche Mann muß sein Kreuz (Bündel; Päckchen) tragen (auf sich nehmen), denn seine Frau macht ihm das Leben schwer.
*That rich man, too, has his cross (burden) to bear (to shoulder; to take up), for his wife makes life difficult for him.*

ein **Kreuzfeuer:** *a cross-fire*

Zwischen den einzelnen Rednern entwickelte sich ein wahres Kreuzfeuer.
*A real cross-fire developed between the various speakers.*

**kreuzfidel** sein: *to be as happy as a sand-boy (as a king; as the day is long); to be as cheerful as a cricket; to be cock-a-hoop (colloq.).* Cf. auch: ein lustiger **Vogel** sein

Ich bin froh, wenn mein Bruder uns besucht, denn er ist immer kreuzfidel (quietschfidel; quietschvergnügt; seelenvergnügt; ein munterer Buchfink; munter wie ein Eichhörnchen).
*I am glad when my brother visits us, for he is always as happy as a sand-boy (as a king; as the day is long; as cheerful as a cricket; cock-a-hoop).*

**kreuzlahm** sein: *to be as stiff as a poker (as a ramrod; as a board); to be properly knocked up (sl.)*

Nach der vielen Arbeit von gestern bin ich heute ganz kreuzlahm.
*After all that work yesterday I'm as stiff as a poker (as a ramrod; as a board; I'm properly knocked up) today.*

**kreuzunglücklich** sein: *to be broken-hearted (heartbroken; [terribly] down-hearted); to be as miserable as sin (colloq.); to be down in the mouth (sl.)*

Meine Schwester war kreuzunglücklich (todunglücklich), weil die neue Kaffee-kanne auf den Boden gefallen war.
*My sister was broken-hearted (heartbroken; [terribly] downhearted; as miserable as sin; down in the mouth) because the new coffee-pot had fallen on to the floor.*

einen **Kreuzzug** für etwas unternehmen (fig.): *to crusade (to campaign) for s. th.*

Ich bin nicht bereit, für solche Ideen einen Kreuzzug zu unternehmen.
*I am not prepared to crusade (to campaign) for such ideas.*

**kribbelig** werden (fam.): *to get fidgety; to begin to get the fidgets (colloq.)*
Das Theaterstück war zu lang, und die Zuschauer wurden kribbelig.
*The play was too long, and the audience got fidgety (began to get the fidgets).*

vor j.em **kriechen** (fig.): cf. vor j.em auf dem **Bauche** rutschen

das **Kriegsbeil** begraben (fig.): *to bury the hatchet; to sheathe the sword*
Nach jahrelanger Feindschaft haben die beiden Nachbarvölker endlich das Kriegsbeil begraben (den Krieg [zwischen sich] aus der Welt geschafft). Jetzt leben sie friedlich nebeneinander.
*After years of hostility the two neighbouring peoples have finally buried the hatchet (sheathed the sword). Now they are living peacefully side by side.*

auf **Kriegsfuß** mit j.em stehen (leben) (fig.): cf. sich mit j.em in den **Haaren** liegen

eine **Krise** glücklich überwinden: *to have turned the corner; to have rounded the bend; to be over the worst; to be out of the wood*
Mein Vater hat jetzt die Krise glücklich überwunden und dürfte bald aus dem Krankenhaus entlassen werden.
*My father has now turned the corner (rounded the bend; is now over the worst; is now out of the wood) and ought soon to be discharged from hospital.*

**kristallklar** sein: cf. **sonnenklar** sein

unter aller **Kritik** sein: *to be beneath contempt (beyond words; unspeakable)*
Sein Benehmen vor den anderen Kindern war einfach unter aller Kritik (unterm Hund [unter allem Hund]; unter aller Kanone).
*His behaviour in front of the other children was simply beneath contempt (beyond words; unspeakable).*

**Krokodilstränen** vergießen (fig.): *to shed (to weep) crocodile tears*
Sein Kummer ist nicht echt. Er vergießt nur Krokodilstränen.
*His sorrow is not real. He is only shedding (weeping) crocodile tears.*

Das setzt allem die **Krone** auf (fig.): cf. Das ist doch die **Höhe!**

Was ist ihm in die **Krone** gefahren? (fig. u. fam.): *What's up with him? (colloq.); What's got into him? (colloq.); What's bitten him? (sl.)*
Was ist dir in die Krone gefahren? Du bist in letzter Zeit so mürrisch.
*What's up with you? (What's got into you? What's bitten you?) You have been so moody recently.*

einen in der **Krone** haben (fig. u. fam.): cf. zu tief in den **Becher** geguckt haben

die **Krone** der Schöpfung: *the pride of creation; the acme (the pink) of perfection; the cat's whiskers (sl.)*

> Die eingebildete Schauspielerin hält sich offenbar für die Krone der Schöpfung.
> *The conceited actress obviously considers herself to be the pride of creation (the acme [pink] of perfection; the cat's whiskers).*

die **Krönung** (fig.): *the crowning touch (moment); the climax (culmination; highlight)*

> Die Krönung (Der Glanzpunkt) des Festes war ein großartiges Feuerwerk.
> *The crowning touch (moment) in (the climax [culmination; highlight] of) the celebration was a magnificent firework-display.*

ein **Krösus** sein: cf. **Geld** wie Heu haben

ein paar **Kröten** (fig. u. fam.): *a few coppers (pence)*

> In seiner schlimmen geldlichen Lage ist ihm mit ein paar Kröten nicht geholfen.
> *In his serious financial situation a few coppers (pence) are no help to him.*

**krötig** werden (eine **Kröte** sein) (fig. u. fam.): *to turn nasty (colloq.); to cut up rough (colloq.)*

> Wenn man zu meiner Schwester etwas sagt, das ihr nicht paßt, kann sie leicht krötig (biestig) werden (eine Kröte sein).
> *If you say something to my sister that she doesn't like, she can easily turn nasty (cut up rough).*

Das kann doch ein Blinder mit dem **Krückstock** fühlen: cf. Das kann doch ein **Blinder** sehen (mit dem Krückstock fühlen)

Der **Krug** geht so lange zu Wasser, bis er bricht (Sprichw.): *It is the last straw that breaks the camel's back (prov.); It is easy to overdo it; I (you, etc.) may go too far*

> Alle seine Handlungen sind sehr bedenklich. Ich fürchte, daß er eines Tages mit den Gesetzen in Konflikt kommt. Der Krug geht so lange zu Wasser, bis er bricht.
> *All his actions are very dubious. I fear that he will come into conflict with the law some day. It is the last straw that breaks the camel's back (It is easy to overdo it; He may go too far).*

eine freche **Kruke** sein (fig. u. fam.): cf. ein freches **Stück** sein

**krumme** Dinge drehen (fam.): *to be mixed up (involved) in crooked business; to get up to underhand tricks*

Bereits als Schuljunge hat er krumme Dinge gedreht.
*Even as a schoolboy he was mixed up (involved) in crooked business (got up to underhand
tricks).*

j.en **krumm** und lahm schlagen: cf. j.en **grün** und blau schlagen

**krumme** Touren lieben (fam.): cf. die krummen **Wege** lieben

Früh **krümmt** sich, was ein Häkchen werden will (Sprichw.): *A crooked
nature soon shows itself; Once a rogue, always a rogue*

Schon aus der Jugendzeit des Verbrechers konnte man ersehen, was einmal
aus ihm werden würde. Früh krümmt sich, was ein Häkchen werden will.
*One could already see from the criminal's youth what kind of man he would become. A
crooked nature soon shows itself (Once a rogue, always a rogue).*

sich **krümmen** und winden (fig.): cf. sich winden wie ein **Aal**

etwas **krummnehmen** (fam.): *to take s.th. amiss (ill; in bad part); it gets
s.b.'s goat (colloq.); it sticks in s.b.'s gizzard (sl.)*

Er sieht böse aus. Was hat er denn nur krummgenommen?
*He looks angry. What has he taken amiss (ill; in bad part) now? (What has got his
goat now? What's stuck in his gizzard now?)*

**Kübel** der Verleumdung über j.en ausschütten: *to heap (to pour) slanders on
s.b.; to smear s.b.*

Man hat Kübel der Verleumdung über sie ausgeschüttet.
*People have heaped (poured) slanders on her (have smeared her).*

in Teufels **Küche** kommen (fig.): cf. sich in die **Nesseln** setzen

**Küchenlatein:** *dog-Latin*

Dieser halbgebildete Mann versucht, uns mit seinem Küchenlatein zu imponieren.
*This half-educated man is trying to impress us with his dog-Latin.*

Ja, **Kuchen!** (fam.): cf. Ja, **Puste** (Pustekuchen)!

ein **Kücken** sein (fig.): *to be a fledgeling (a chicken)*. Cf. auch: noch in
den **Kinderschuhen** stecken

Was? Du willst schon einen Ball mitmachen und bist noch ein Kücken!
*What! You want to go to a dance, although you're still a fledgeling (chicken)?*

Hol' dich der **Kuckuck!** (Scher' dich [Geh'] zum Kuckuck!): cf. Scher'
dich zum Henker!

Hol's der **Kuckuck!**: cf. Hol's der **Teufel!**

in **Kuckucks** Namen: cf. in **Gottes** Namen

weiß der **Kuckuck**: cf. Das wissen die **Götter**

zum **Kuckuck** noch mal!: cf. in **Gottes** Namen

sich ein **Kuckucksei** ins Nest legen (fig.): *to bring a cuckoo into the nest*

> Mit der Adoptierung eines Waisenkindes hat sich das Ehepaar ein Kuckucksei ins Nest gelegt; denn das Kind zeigt schlechte Gewohnheiten.
> *By adopting an orphan the couple have brought a cuckoo into the nest, for the child is showing bad habits.*

ein **Kuddelmuddel** (fam.): cf. ein **Wirrwarr**

sich (vor Lachen) **kugeln** (fig. u. fam.): cf. sich **totlachen**

zum **Kugeln** sein (fig. u. fam.): cf. zum **Piepen** sein

**kugelrund** sein: *to be as plump as a partridge (as round as a barrel).* Cf. auch: **Fett** ansetzen

> Du siehst gut aus. In den letzten zwei Jahren bist du kugelrund (dick wie ein Bierfaß [eine Biertonne]; wie ein Mops) geworden.
> *You look fine. In the last two years you have become as plump as a partridge (as round as a barrel).*

dastehen wie die **Kuh** vorm (neuen) Scheunentor: *the wind is taken (right) out of s.b.'s sails; to look blank; to stand there cluelessly (colloq.)*

> Vor dem Theater befand sich (hing) ein Schild „Geschlossen". Wir standen da wie die Kuh vorm (neuen) Scheunentor (wie der Ochs vorm Berge).
> *In front of the theatre was the notice "Closed". The wind was taken (right) out of our sails (We looked blank; We stood there cluelessly).*

eine blöde (dumme) **Kuh** sein (fig. u. fam.): cf. eine blöde (dumme) **Gans** sein

**Kuhaugen** machen (fam.): cf. **Stielaugen** machen

ein **Kuhdorf** (fig. u. fam.): cf. ein **Kaff**

**Kuhhandel** (fig. u. fam.): *jiggery-pokery (colloq.); wangling (colloq.); hugger-mugger (colloq.)*

> In der Innenpolitik dieses Landes treiben die Parteien viel Kuhhandel.
> *In the home affairs of this country the parties do a lot of jiggery-pokery (wangling; hugger-mugger).*

Das geht auf keine **Kuhhaut**! (fam.): cf. Das ist (doch) die **Höhe**!

j.en **kühllassen** (fig.): cf. j.en **kaltlassen**

arbeiten (schaffen) wie ein **Kuli**: cf. arbeiten (schaffen) wie ein **Pferd**

hinter die **Kulissen** gucken (fig.): *to peep (to have a peep [a look] behind the scenes [curtain]; to go backstage*

> Seine Familie erscheint sehr glücklich; wenn man jedoch hinter die Kulissen guckt (einen Blick hinter die K. tut), bekommt man einen ganz anderen Eindruck.
> *His family appears very happy, but when one peeps (has a peep [a look]) behind the scenes (curtain; goes backstage), one gets a quite different impression.*

nicht von (der) **Kultur** beleckt sein: *to be unsullied (untouched) by civilisation; s.b.'s mind is virgin soil*

> Der neue Wirt tut sehr fein, ist aber in Wirklichkeit wenig von (der) Kultur beleckt.
> *The new landlord pretends to be very refined but in reality he is almost unsullied (untouched) by civilisation (his mind is almost virgin soil).*

j.em den **Kümmel** reiben (fig. u. fam.): cf. j.en **abkanzeln;** j.em eine **Standpauke** halten

ein übler **Kunde** sein (fig.): *to be an ugly (unpleasant) customer; to be a bad egg (colloq.)*

> Es ist nicht ratsam, sich mit diesem üblen Kunden (Vertreter) einzulassen.
> *It is not advisable to have any dealings with that ugly (unpleasant) customer (bad egg).*

mit seiner **Kunst** zu (am) Ende sein (fig.): *to be at the end of one's tether (one's resources); to be at one's wit's end.* Cf. auch: nicht wissen, wo einem der **Kopf** steht; nicht **aus** noch ein wissen

> Ich habe alles versucht, um diese Klingel zu reparieren, aber jetzt bin ich mit meiner Kunst (meinem Latein; meinem Verstand; meiner Weisheit) zu (am) Ende.
> *I have tried everything to mend this bell, but now I am at the end of my tether (my resources; at my wit's end).*

Das ist keine **Kunst!**: *There's nothing to it (in it); Any fool can do that (colloq.)*

> Hier über den Rhein schwimmen? Das ist doch keine Kunst. Er ist ja gar nicht breit.
> *Swim across the Rhine here? There's nothing to (in) it (Any fool can do that). It's not wide.*

eine **Kunstpause** machen (fig.): *to have a break; to have a breather (colloq.).*
Cf. auch: eine **Atempause; ausspannen; bremsen**

> Du hast jetzt drei Stunden angestrengt im Garten gearbeitet. Nun mach' eine Kunstpause (Nun schalte ab) und ruh' dich mal aus.
> *You have been working strenuously in the garden for three hours. Have a break (breather) now and rest.*

**Kunststück!** (fam.): *So I should think! (colloq.); I should think so too! (colloq.); About time too! (colloq.)*

Du weißt jetzt also, wie man dieses Problem löst? Na, Kunststück! Das wissen die anderen schon lange.
*So you now know how to solve this problem. So I should think! (I should think so too! About time too!) The others have known for a long time.*

**kunterbunt** durcheinanderliegen: cf. wie **Kraut** und Rüben durcheinanderliegen

mein alter Freund und **Kupferstecher**: cf. mein alter **Freund** und Kupferstecher

j.en in die **Kur** nehmen (fig.): *to take s.b. in hand; to put s.b. through his paces; to get to work on s.b. (colloq.)*

Da mein Bruder schwach in Mathematik ist, habe ich ihn jetzt in die Kur genommen und studiere täglich mit ihm.
*As my brother is weak in mathematics, I am taking him in hand (am putting him through his paces; am getting to work on him) and studying with him every day.*

einen neuen **Kurs** einschlagen (fig.): cf. das **Steuer** herumwerfen

die **Kurve** kriegen (fig. u. fam.): *to take the plunge; to make the grade (colloq.)*

Der alte Junggeselle hat nun doch noch die Kurve (den Dreh) gekriegt und vorige Woche geheiratet.
*The old bachelor took the plunge (made the grade) at last and got married last week.*

**kurz** angebunden sein (fig.): cf. kurz **angebunden** sein

**kurz** und bündig sagen: cf. **klipp** und klar sagen

**kurz** und gut **(kurzum)**: cf. mit éinem **Wort**

etwas **kurz** und klein schlagen: *to smash (to break) s.th. to pieces (bits); to smash s.th. to smithereens (sl.)*

Der zornige Junge hat seinen neuen Tennisschläger kurz und klein geschlagen, weil sein Gegner den ersten Satz gewonnen hatte.
*The angry boy smashed (broke) his new tennis racquet to pieces (bits; smashed ... to smithereens) because his opponent had won the first set.*

zu **kurz** kommen: *to go short; to come (to get) off badly*

Mit seinem Nachtisch ist unser jüngster Sohn leider zu kurz gekommen.
*Our youngest son unfortunately went short (came [got] off badly) with his dessert.*

über **kurz** oder lang: *sooner or later; some time or other*

Über kurz oder lang wird dieser Schwindel doch entdeckt werden.
*Sooner or later (Some time or other) that swindle must be discovered.*

den **kürzeren** ziehen (fig.): *to come off second-best; to get the worst of it; to go to the wall*

Beim Schachspielen mit meinem Bruder ziehe ich regelmäßig den kürzeren.
*I regularly come off second-best (get the worst of it; go to the wall) when I play chess with my brother.*

sich **kurzfassen**: *to cut the cackle and come to the horses; to come to the point (at once); to cut it short*

Da ich weiß, daß Ihre Zeit kostbar ist, will ich mich kurzfassen.
*As I know that your time is valuable, I will cut the cackle and come to the horses (come to the point [at once]; cut it short).*

j.en **kurzhalten**: cf. j.em den **Brotkorb** höher hängen

**kurzsichtig** handeln: *to act short-sightedly*

Wenn du das tätest, würdest du sehr kurzsichtig handeln.
*If you did that, you would be acting very short-sightedly.*

**kurztreten** (fig.): cf. **bremsen**


# L

ein langer **Laban** sein (fam.): cf. lang wie eine **Bohnenstange** sein

Daß ich nicht **lache**! (fam.): *Don't make me laugh (sl.); Come off it! (sl.)*

Bei deinen Kenntnissen hast du Angst vor dem Examen? Daß ich nicht lache! (Mach' keine Witze!)
*With your knowledge you're afraid of the examination? Don't make me laugh (Come off it!).*

Du kannst **lachen**!: *Good for you! Bully for you! (colloq.)*

Dein Vater hat dir ein neues Auto gekauft? Du kannst lachen!
*Your father has bought you a new car? Good for you! (Bully for you!)*

sich krank (krumm) **lachen**: cf. sich **totlachen**

sich vor **Lachen** kugeln (ausschütten; biegen; schütteln; wälzen): cf. sich **totlachen**

nichts zu **lachen** haben (fig.): *not to have anything to laugh about; It's hard lines on s.b. (colloq.); It's no joke for s.b. (colloq.); It's tough on s.b. (sl.)*

Die junge Witwe hat nichts zu lachen. Sie muß sich und ihre drei Kinder allein ernähren.

*The young widow has nothing to laugh about (It's hard lines [tough] on [no joke for] the young widow). She has herself and her three children to support by herself.*

vor **Lachen** platzen (bersten): cf. sich **totlachen**

Dir wird das **Lachen** noch vergehen!: *Your laughter will turn to tears; You will find it is no laughing-matter; You'll laugh on the other side of your face (colloq.)*

Wenn ich deinem Vater das erzähle, wird dir das Lachen noch vergehen.
*When I tell your father about that, your laughter will turn to tears (you'll find it is no laughing-matter; you'll laugh on the other side of your face).*

Wer zuletzt **lacht,** lacht am besten (Sprichw.): *He who laughs last, laughs longest (prov.); s. b. will have the last laugh*

Ihr habt mich jetzt geschlagen, aber ich werde mich rächen. Wer zuletzt lacht, lacht am besten.
*You've beaten me now but I shall have my revenge. He who laughs last, laughs longest (I shall have the last laugh).*

die **Lacher** auf seiner Seite haben: *to have the laugh on one's side; the laugh is with s. b.*

Bei seinen witzigen Bemerkungen über die Regierung hatte der Redner die Lacher auf seiner Seite.
*In his witty remarks about the government the speaker had the laugh on his side (the laugh was with the speaker).*

etwas ins **Lächerliche** ziehen: *to ridicule s. th.; to poke fun at s. th.; to make fun of s. th.; to turn s. th. into a laughing-matter*

Ich will ihm nichts von meinen Plänen erzählen, weil er alles ins Lächerliche zieht.
*I'm not going to tell him anything of my plans because he ridicules (pokes fun at; makes fun of) everything (turns everything into a laughing-matter).*

der **Lackierte** sein (fam.): *to be the dunce; to be the muggins (colloq.); to be the mug (goon) (sl.); to be Joe Soap (sl.)*

Da du deine Entscheidung so lange hinausgezögert hast, bist du jetzt der Lackierte, weil ein anderer dir zuvorgekommen ist.
*Since you have delayed your decision so long, you're now the dunce (muggins; mug; goon; you're now Joe Soap), because somebody else has forestalled you.*

den (ganzen) **Laden** schmeißen (fam.): *to cope with (to run) the (whole) thing (business); to run the (whole) show (colloq.)*

Da sein Chef erkrankt war, mußte er den (ganzen) Laden (die ganze Kiste [Sache]) schmeißen.
*As his boss was ill, he had to cope with (run) the (whole) thing (show; business).*

ein **Ladenhüter** sein (fig.): *to be a flop (colloq.); to be a dead loss (colloq.)*

Der Buchhändler merkte bald, daß der neue Roman ein Ladenhüter sein würde.
*The bookseller soon noticed that the new novel was going to be a flop (dead loss).*

ein eingebildeter **Laffe** sein (fam.): cf. ein eingebildeter **Affe** sein

die **Lage** peilen (fig.): cf. einen **Fühler** ausstrecken

in gleich übler **Lage** sein: cf. in éinem **Boot** sitzen

ins feindliche **Lager** übergehen (fig.): *to cross into the enemy camp; to go over to the enemy; to change (one's) colours; to transfer one's allegiance to the other side*

Das Wahlergebnis zeigte, daß viele bisherige Wähler dieser Partei ins feindliche Lager übergegangen waren.
*The election result showed that many who had formerly voted for this party had crossed into the enemy camp (had gone over to the enemy; had changed [their] colours; had transferred their allegiance to the other side).*

**lahm** wie eine Ente (eine lahme Ente) sein: *to be as lame as a duck (as slow as a snail)*

Sei doch energischer! Du bist lahm wie eine Ente (eine lahme Ente; ein lahmes [krankes] Huhn).
*Be more energetic. You're as lame as a duck (as slow as a snail).*

ein blutiger **Laie** sein: *to be the veriest tyro (layman)*

In technischen Dingen bin ich ein blutiger Laie.
*In technical matters I am the veriest tyro (layman).*

weiß wie ein **Laken** sein: cf. weiß wie die **Wand** sein

aussehen wie ein **Lamm,** das zur Schlachtbank geführt wird: *to look like a lamb that is being led to the slaughter*

Als sie zum Examen ging, sah sie aus wie ein Lamm, das zur Schlachtbank geführt wird.
*When she went into the examination she looked like a lamb that was being led to the slaughter.*

**lammfromm** (sanft wie ein **Lamm**) sein: *to be as meek (gentle) as a lamb*

Dein Bruder sieht lammfromm (sanft wie ein Lamm) aus, ist es aber gar nicht.
*Your brother looks as meek (gentle) as a lamb, but he isn't at all.*

eine **Lammsgeduld** entwickeln: *to show (to acquire; to have) the patience of Job; to be long-suffering*

Ein Vater muß oft eine Lammsgeduld (Engelsgeduld) mit seinen Kindern entwickeln.
*A father often has to show (to acquire; to have) the patience of Job (to be long-suffering) with his children.*

**Lampenfieber** haben: *to have stage-fright; to have butterflies in one's stomach*

Die junge Schauspielerin hatte offenbar Lampenfieber, und der Schweiß stand ihr auf der Stirn.
*The young actress obviously had stage-fright (butterflies in her stomach), and her forehead was covered in perspiration.*

Viele Jahre sind ins **Land** gegangen: *A great deal of water has flowed under the bridge*

Seit meinen Studententagen sind nun schon viele Jahre ins Land gegangen (ist schon viel Wasser den Rhein [usw.] hinuntergeflossen).
*A great deal of water has flowed under the bridge since my student-days.*

das Gelobte **Land**: *the Promised Land*

Viele Europäer betrachten die Schweiz als das Gelobte Land.
*Many Europeans regard Switzerland as the Promised Land.*

das **Land**, wo Milch und Honig fließt: *a land flowing with milk and honey*

Er hat ein ideales Bild von Amerika. Für ihn ist es das Land, wo Milch und Honig fließt.
*He has an idealistic picture of America. For him it is a land flowing with milk and honey.*

wieder **Land** sehen (fig.): *to near dry land (again); to see (to get to) the end of the tunnel; to see daylight (again)*

Nach dieser glücklichen Lösung meiner schwierigen Probleme sehe ich nun endlich wieder Land.
*After having happily solved these difficult problems I am now nearing dry land ([again]; I can now see the end [am now getting to the end] of the tunnel; I can now see daylight [again]).*

sich j.en an **Land** ziehen (fig. u. fam.): *to hook s.b. (colloq.); to catch s.b. (colloq.); to land s.b. (colloq.)*

Dieses Mädchen ist aus armen Verhältnissen, hat sich aber einen reichen Mann an Land gezogen (geangelt).
*This girl comes from a poor home but has hooked (caught; landed) a rich husband.*

bei j.em mit etwas nicht **landen** können (fig.): *not to get anywhere with s.b. by s.th.; not to get anything out of s.b. by s.th.; not to make any impression on s.b. with s.th.; not to get any change out of s.b. by s.th. (colloq.)*

Mit solchen Unverschämtheiten kann er bei mir nicht landen.
*He will not get anywhere with me (get anything [any change] out of me) by (make any impression on me with) such impertinences.*

eine **Landratte** (fig.): *a land-lubber*

Wilhelm ist eine ausgesprochene Landratte und scheut jede Seereise.
*William is a real land-lubber and avoids any sea-voyage.*

fluchen wie ein **Landsknecht**: *to swear like a trooper (like a lord; like a sergeant-major)*

Unser Schuldiener kann sehr zornig werden und flucht dann wie ein Landsknecht (Bierkutscher; Droschkenkutscher; Fuhrknecht; Marktweib; schimpft dann wie ein Rohrspatz).
*Our school caretaker can get very angry, and then he swears like a trooper (lord; sergeant-major).*

etwas **lang** und breit erzählen: *to expatiate on s.th.; to launch out on a description of s.th.; to make a long story of s.th.; to tell of s.th. in a long-winded (long-drawn-out) manner.* Cf. auch: etwas lang (weit) **ausspinnen**

Vater hat uns seine Kriegserlebnisse lang und breit (groß und breit; langatmig; langstielig) erzählt.
*Father expatiated to us on his war-experiences (launched out on a description of [made a long story of] his war-experiences to us; told us of his war-experiences in a long-winded [long-drawn-out] manner).*

Wer **lang** hat, läßt lang hängen (Sprichw.): *He who has a lot can do a lot*

Seine wohlhabende Familie kann sich solche Feste leisten. Wer lang hat, läßt lang hängen.
*His well-to-do family can afford such celebrations. He who has a lot can do a lot.*

nicht mehr **lange** mitmachen (fam.): *to be on one's last legs (colloq.); to be coming up to the last fence (colloq.); not to last much longer (colloq.)*

Der alte Bibliothekar sieht in letzter Zeit sehr elend aus. Er wird wohl nicht mehr lange mitmachen.
*The old librarian has been looking very poorly recently. I reckon he's on his last legs (he's coming up to the last fence; I don't reckon he'll last much longer).*

Was **lange** währt, wird endlich gut (Sprichw.): cf. Was lange **währt,** wird endlich gut

sich in die **Länge** ziehen: *to drag on; to be long-drawn-out*

Die politischen Verhandlungen zogen sich in die Länge und dauerten über zwei Jahre.
*The political negotiations dragged on (were long-drawn-out) and lasted over two years.*

etwas **langatmig** erzählen: cf. etwas **lang** und breit erzählen

**längelang** (der **Länge** lang) hinfallen (hinschlagen): *to fall full-length; to measure one's length (on the ground)*

Bei unserm Spaziergang durch den Wald stolperte mein Schwager über eine Baumwurzel und fiel (schlug) längelang (der Länge lang) hin.
*On our walk through the wood my brother-in-law tripped over the root of a tree and fell full-length (measured his length [on the ground]).*

ein **Langfinger** sein: cf. lange **Finger** machen

Nur **langsam!**: *Take your time!; Take it easy!; Steady!; Steady on!*

> Nur langsam! (Nur [Immer] mit der Ruhe! Nur sachte!) Wir haben noch eine halbe Stunde Zeit, bis der Zug abfährt.
> *Take your time! (Take it easy!; Steady!; Steady on!) We've still got half-an-hour before the train leaves.*

**langsam** aber sicher: *slowly but surely*

> Langsam aber sicher näherte er sich dem Gipfel des Berges.
> *Slowly but surely he approached the summit of the mountain.*

**langsamtreten** (fig.): cf. **bremsen**

etwas **langstielig** erzählen: cf. etwas **lang** und breit erzählen

eine **Lanze** für j.en brechen (einlegen) (fig.): *to take up cudgels for (on behalf of) s.b.; to strike a blow for s.b.; to throw in one's weight on s.b.'s side.* Cf. auch: ein gutes **Wort** für j.en einlegen

> Wenn Sie eine Lanze für Ihren Neffen brechen ([einlegen]; Wenn Sie sich für Ihren Neffen ins Mittel legen [für ... in die Schranken treten]), wird er den Posten sicher(lich) bekommen.
> *If you take up cudgels for (on behalf of) your nephew (strike a blow for your nephew; throw in your weight on your nephew's side), he will certainly get the job.*

eine **Lappalie** sein: *to be neither here nor there; to be nothing to write home about (colloq.); to be a (mere) flea-bite (sl.)*

> Rege dich wegen der zerbrochenen Brille nicht so auf. Es ist doch (nur) eine Lappalie (ein Klacks; du kannst sie leicht reparieren lassen.
> *Don't get so agitated about your broken glasses. It's neither here nor there (nothing to write home about; a [mere] flea-bite); you can easily get them repaired.*

sich um **Lappalien** streiten: cf. sich um des **Kaisers** Bart streiten

j.em durch die **Lappen** gehen (fig. u. fam.): *to slip from s.b.'s grasp (through s.b.'s fingers)*

> Wie ärgerlich, daß uns diese günstige Gelegenheit durch die Lappen gegangen ist.
> *How annoying that that favourable opportunity has slipped from our grasp (through our fingers).*

blinder **Lärm**: cf. blinder **Alarm**

blinden **Lärm** schlagen: cf. blinden **Alarm** schlagen

viel **Lärm** um nichts machen: *to make much ado (to make a fuss) about nothing; to raise a storm in a tea-cup; to kick up a fuss (row) about nothing (colloq.)*

Ich bin vom Fahrrad gestürzt, aber es ist nichts passiert. Ihr macht viel Lärm um nichts (einen Sturm im Wasserglas).
*I fell off my bicycle, but no harm has been done. You are making much ado (a fuss) about nothing (raising a storm in a tea-cup; kicking up a fuss [row] about nothing).*

Das muß man ihm **lassen:** *You must grant (give; allow) him that; Give the devil his due (colloq.)*

In der Schule zählt Georg nicht zu den besten Schülern, aber Geige spielen kann er vortrefflich. Das muß man ihm (Das muß ihm der Neid) lassen. (Alles, was recht ist).
*In school George is not reckoned to be among the best pupils, but he can play the violin excellently, you must grant (give; allow) him that (. . . excellently. Give the devil his due).*

j.em zur **Last** fallen: *to be a burden (hindrance) to s.b.; to be a millstone round s.b.'s neck; to put s.b. out; to impose (o.s.) upon s.b.*

Ich bin nur zwei Tage bei meinem Freund in München geblieben, da ich ihm nicht zur Last fallen wollte.
*I only stayed two days at my friend's in Munich because I did not want to be a burden (hindrance) to him (be a millstone round his neck; put him out; impose [myself] upon him).*

j.em eine **Last** vom Herzen nehmen: *to take a load (a weight) off s.b.'s mind (shoulders)*

Durch die Nachricht, daß mein Vater gut in Amerika angekommen sei, ist mir eine Last vom Herzen genommen.
*With the news that my father has arrived safely in America a load (weight) has been taken off my mind (shoulders).*

j.em etwas zur **Last** legen: *to lay s.th. at s.b.'s door; to put s.th. on s.b.'s shoulders*

Der Diebstahl wurde einem Arbeiter der Firma zur Last gelegt (in die Schuhe geschoben).
*The theft was laid at the door of (put on the shoulders of) one of the firm's workers.*

sich eine **Last** von der Seele wälzen: *to get a load off one's mind (shoulders); to get it off one's chest (out of one's system) (colloq.)*

Ich muß dem Chef sagen, was passiert ist, und mir diese Last von der Seele wälzen (reden).
*I must tell the boss what has happened, and get this load off my mind (shoulders; get it off my chest; get it out of my system).*

ein **Lästermaul** sein: *to be a scandal-monger*

Unsere Putzfrau ist ein Lästermaul. Sie erzählt unwahre Geschichten über anständige Leute.
*Our charwoman is a scandal-monger. She tells untrue stories about respectable people.*

mit seinem **Latein** zu (am) Ende sein (fig.): cf. mit seiner **Kunst** zu (am) Ende sein

Geh' mir aus der **Laterne!** (fam.): *Get out of the (my) light (the daylight)! (colloq.)*

Geh' mir (doch) aus der Laterne! Glaubst du, du seiest (bist) durchsichtig?
*Get out of the (my) light (the daylight)! Do you think you're transparent?*

etwas mit der **Laterne** suchen (fig.): *to hunt high and low for s.th.; to go on all fours (on one's hands and knees) to look for s.th. (colloq.)*

Handwerker, die auf telefonischen Anruf sofort kommen, muß man heute mit der Laterne suchen.
*Today one has to hunt high and low for (to go on all fours [on one's hands and knees] to look for) workmen who come immediately they are rung up.*

j.em mit dem **Laternenpfahl** winken (fig.): cf. einen **Wink** mit dem Zaunpfahl geben

eine lange **Latte** sein (fig.): cf. lang wie eine **Bohnenstange** sein

Fertig ist die **Laube!** (fig.): *The whole thing (business) is over (done)*

Nun brauche ich von meinem Aufsatz nur noch die letzten zwei Seiten zu schreiben, und fertig ist die Laube!
*I now only need to write the last two pages of my essay and the whole thing (business) will be over (done).*

auf der **Lauer** liegen (fig.): *to lurk round the corner*

Bei dem heutigen riesigen Straßenverkehr liegt der Tod ständig auf der Lauer.
*With the enormous amount of traffic on the roads today death lurks round every corner.*

seinen Gefühlen freien **Lauf** lassen: *to give vent to one's feelings; to give one's feelings free rein; to let one's feelings run riot; to let o.s. go (colloq.); to let off steam (colloq.)*

Als er erfuhr, daß sein Antrag abgelehnt sei, ließ er seinen Gefühlen freien Lauf (machte er seinen Gefühlen Luft; ließ er seinen Gefühlen die Zügel schießen) und schimpfte auf die Behörden.
*When he learnt that his application had been rejected, he gave vent to his feelings (gave his feelings free rein; let his feelings run riot; let himself go; let off steam) and cursed the authorities.*

am **laufenden** Band (fig.): cf. am laufenden **Band**

auf dem **laufenden** sein: *to be (to keep) up to date (up with the times; abreast of the times); to be on the ball (colloq.); to be in the know (colloq.)*

Eine gute Zeitung muß immer auf dem laufenden sein (mit der Zeit gehen).

*A good paper always has to be (to keep) up to date (up with the times; abreast of the times; on the ball; in the know).*

sich wie ein **Lauffeuer** verbreiten: cf. sich wie der **Blitz** (blitzschnell) verbreiten

j.em den **Laufpaß** geben: *to give s.b. the push (colloq.); to send s.b. packing (colloq.); to give s.b. the bird (sl.)*

Der Angestellte wollte Geld von mir, aber ich habe ihm den Laufpaß gegeben (ihn sich packen heißen).
*The clerk wanted money from me but I gave him the push (bird; sent him packing).*

Ihm ist eine **Laus** über die Leber gelaufen (fig. u. fam.): *Something has rubbed him up the wrong way; He has got out of bed the wrong side; He's got the needle (sl.).* Cf. auch: mit dem linken **Fuß** zuerst aufstehen

Der Metzger ist heute in schlechter Laune. Ihm muß eine Laus über die Leber gelaufen sein.
*The butcher is in a bad mood today. Something must have rubbed him up the wrong way (He must have got out of bed the wrong side; He's got the needle).*

sich eine **Laus** in den Pelz setzen (fig.): *to let o.s. in for something (for it) (colloq.); to saddle o.s. with something (colloq.); to let o.s. in for a packet (sl.)*

Unlängst habe ich meinem Sohn ein Fahrrad versprochen. Da habe ich mir eine Laus in den Pelz gesetzt, denn er erinnert mich jetzt ständig daran.
*Recently I promised my son a bicycle. I have let myself in for something (for it; for a packet; have saddled myself with something) there, because he is continually reminding me about it.*

angeben wie ein Sack **Läuse** (fam.): cf. **angeben**

sich **lausig** machen (fam.): cf. **aufmucken**

etwas **läuten** hören (fig.): *to hear a buzz (colloq.); a little bird tells me (you etc.) (colloq.).* Cf. auch: j.em zu **Ohren** kommen

Ich habe etwas (davon) läuten hören, daß die ganze Familie meines Freundes auswandern will, aber zu mir hat er nichts gesagt.
*I have heard a buzz (A little bird has told me) that my friend's entire family is going to emigrate, but he hasn't said anything to me.*

**lauthals** über etwas lachen: *to laugh out loud at s.th.; to guffaw at s.th. (colloq.).* Cf. auch: sich **totlachen**

Über so eine dumme Bemerkung kann man nur lauthals lachen.
*One can only laugh out loud (guffaw) at such a stupid remark.*

wie das blühende **Leben** aussehen: *to look the (very) picture of health; to look as fit as a fiddle; to look in the pink (colloq.)*

Nach seinen Ferien in der Schweiz sah mein Bruder wie das blühende Leben aus.
*After his holidays in Switzerland my brother looked the (very) picture of health (as fit as a fiddle; in the pink).*

**Leben** in die Bude bringen (fam.): *to make things hum; to shake (to ginger) things up (a bit) (colloq.)*

Wenn Karl bei uns zu Besuch kommt, bringt er immer Leben in die Bude.
*When Charles visits us, he always makes things hum (shakes [gingers] things up [a bit]).*

Das hätte ich im **Leben** nicht gedacht: *Little did I expect (think) that; I should never in my life have expected (thought) that; That would not have occurred to me in a month of Sundays (colloq.)*

Daß mein Vater die Fahrerprüfung noch machen würde, hätte ich im Leben nicht gedacht.
*Little did I expect (think; I should never in my life have expected [thought]; It would not have occurred to me in a month of Sundays) that my father would pass the driving test.*

sein **Leben** fristen: *to keep body and soul together; to scrape a living*

Die Flüchtlinge mußten sich in ihrer neuen Heimat sofort Arbeit suchen, um ihr Leben fristen zu können.
*The refugees had to look for work at once in their new home in order to keep body and soul together (in order to scrape a living).*

aus dem **Leben** gegriffen: *taken from (real) life*

Wir mögen nur Filme, deren Stoff aus dem wirklichen Leben gegriffen ist.
*We only like films whose subjects are taken from real life.*

etwas für sein **Leben** gern tun: *to be able to do s. th. until the cows come home; to be mad on (about) s. th. (colloq.); to be crazy on (about) s. th. (sl.).* Cf. auch: einen **Narren** an j.em (etwas) gefressen haben

Austern essen wir für unser Leben gern.
*We can eat oysters until the cows come home (We're mad [crazy] on [about] oysters).*

ein gottgefälliges **Leben** führen: *to walk with God; to live one's life in God; to live a life pleasing to God*

Deine Großmutter hat stets ein gottgefälliges Leben geführt.
*Your grandmother always walked with God (lived her life in God; lived a life pleasing to God).*

j.em das **Leben** zur Hölle machen: *to make s. b.'s life hell (a hell on earth); to make s. b.'s life not worth living.* Cf. auch: j.em das **Leben** sauer machen

Die zänkische Frau machte ihrem Mann das Leben zur Hölle.
*The quarrelsome woman made her husband's life hell (a hell on earth; not worth living).*

320

**leben** und leben lassen: *to live and let live*

Leben und leben lassen ist die Parole meines Onkels. Er lebt selbst gut und gönnt den anderen auch ein gutes Leben.
*Live and let live is my uncle's motto. He lives well himself and allows others to do the same.*

in des **Lebens** Mai stehen: *to be in the springtime of life (the prime [the flower; the heyday] of youth)*

Ich möchte noch einmal jung sein und in des Lebens Mai stehen.
*I should like to be young and in the springtime of life (the prime [flower; heyday] of youth) again.*

das nackte **Leben** retten: *to escape with what one stands up in*

Bei dem Brand konnten die Hausbewohner nur das nackte Leben retten.
*The occupants of the house were only able to escape from the fire with what they stood up in.*

sich das **Leben** nehmen: *to take one's (own) life*

In der Verzweiflung nahm sich der arme Mann das Leben (legte . . . Hand an sich; tat sich . . . ein Leid an).
*The poor man took his (own) life in despair.*

ein neues **Leben** anfangen: cf. einen neuen **Menschen** anziehen. Cf. auch: den alten **Adam** ausziehen

j.em das **Leben** sauer machen: *to make life a burden (a drudgery; to make life miserable) for s.b.* Cf. auch: j.em das **Leben** zur Hölle machen

Du solltest ihm das Leben nicht mit so viel Arbeit sauer machen.
*You ought not to make life a burden (a drudgery; miserable) for him with so much work.*

sein **Leben** in die Schanze schlagen (fig.): *to risk (to hazard) one's life (neck)*

Im letzten Krieg mußten Millionen von Soldaten bei der Erfüllung ihrer Pflicht ihr Leben in die Schanze schlagen (aufs Spiel setzen).
*In the last war millions of soldiers had to risk (hazard) their lives (necks) in the execution of their duty.*

sich durchs **Leben** schlagen: *to struggle (to plod; to hobble) along; to fight one's way through life.* Cf. auch: sich **durchschlagen**

Früher mußten sich die Arbeiter mühsam durchs Leben schlagen, aber jetzt ist alles viel leichter.
*Formerly the workers had to struggle (plod; hobble) along laboriously (to fight their way through life), but now everything is much easier.*

sein **Leben** aufs Spiel setzen: cf. sein **Leben** in die Schanze schlagen

nicht zum **Leben** und nicht zum Sterben reichen (zum Leben zu wenig, zum Sterben zu viel sein): *to be not enough to keep body and soul together.* Cf. auch: nicht **hin** und nicht her reichen

Seine kleine Pension reicht nicht zum Leben und nicht zum Sterben (ist zum Leben zu wenig, zum Sterben zu viel).
*His small pension is not enough to keep body and soul together.*

auf **Leben** und Tod: cf. ein Kampf bis auf den **Tod** (auf Leben und Tod)

j.em den **Lebensfaden** abschneiden (fig.): *to be (to mean; to spell) the end for s.b.; to throttle s.b.; to squeeze the life out of s.b.; to cut s.b.'s life short; to deal a death-blow to s.b.*

Ein großes Kaufhaus schneidet dem Einzelhändler oft den Lebensfaden ab (bläst ... das Lebenslicht aus), da der kleine Mann seine Ware nicht so billig verkaufen kann.
*A big store is often (often means [spells]) the end for the private trader (often throttles [squeezes the life out of] the private trader; often cuts short the private trader's life; often deals the private trader a death-blow), for the little man cannot sell his goods so cheaply.*

die **Lebensgeister** heben: *to raise one's spirits; to put new heart (spirit) into s.b.; to cheer s.b. up; to buck s.b. up (colloq.)*

Laßt uns ein Glas Wein trinken. Das wird die Lebensgeister heben.
*Let's drink a glass of wine. That will raise our spirits (put new heart [spirit] into us; cheer [buck] us up).*

ein **Lebenskünstler** sein: *to be a master in the art of living; to be a bon vivant*

Was ihm auch passiert, mein Bruder genießt das Leben. Er ist ein wahrer Lebenskünstler.
*Whatever happens to him, my brother enjoys life. He is a real master in the art of living (a real bon vivant).*

j.em das **Lebenslicht** ausblasen: cf. j.em den **Lebensfaden** abschneiden

j.es **Lebenslicht** erlischt: *s.b. passes away (passes over); s.b. is gathered unto (joins) his fathers*

Großvater ist schwer erkrankt, und der Arzt meint, daß sein Lebenslicht bald erloschen sein wird (daß er bald zu seinen Vätern versammelt werden wird; das Zeitliche segnen wird; nicht mehr lange mitmachen wird).
*Grandfather is seriously ill, and the doctor thinks that he will soon pass away (over; will soon be gathered unto his fathers; will soon join his fathers).*

Ihm ist eine Laus über die **Leber** gelaufen (fig. u. fam.): cf. Ihm ist eine **Laus** über die Leber gelaufen

frei (frisch) von der **Leber** (weg) reden: cf. kein **Blatt** vor den Mund nehmen

die gekränkte **Leberwurst** spielen (fam.): *to act (to behave) like a bear with a sore tail; to sulk in a corner*

Daß meine Schwester Marie so schnell beleidigt ist und die gekränkte Leberwurst (Bratwurst) spielt (im Schmollwinkel sitzt), finde ich gar nicht schön.
*I don't like it at all that my sister Mary is so quickly offended and acts (behaves) like a bear with a sore tail (sulks in a corner).*

ein **Leckerbissen** sein: *to be a tit-bit (a dainty; a treat)*

Eis mit Schlagsahne ist für manchen ein besonderer Leckerbissen.
*Ice with whipped cream is a special tit-bit (dainty; treat) for many people.*

ein **Leckermaul** sein: *to have a sweet tooth*

Dieses Kind möchte am liebsten nur Süßigkeiten essen. Es ist ein wahres Leckermaul ([Zuckermäulchen]; eine wahre Naschkatze).
*That child would like to eat nothing but sweets. He has a very sweet tooth.*

j.em das **Leder** gerben (fig.): cf. j.em das **Fell** gerben

zäh wie **Leder** sein: *to be as tough as leather (as old boots)*

Kellner, dieses Fleisch kann man nicht essen. Es ist zäh wie Leder (ist mordszäh).
*Waiter, this meat is uneatable. It is as tough as leather (old boots).*

**leer** (bei etwas) ausgehen: *to go (to come) away empty-handed; not to get anything out of s. th.*

Ich spiele in keiner Lotterie mehr, da ich doch jedes Mal leer dabei ausgehe (dabei in den Mond [in die Röhre] gucke).
*I am not going to go in for any more sweepstakes, because every time I go (come) away empty-handed (because I never get anything out of them).*

(teures) **Lehrgeld** zahlen müssen (fig.): *to have to pay by experience; to have to learn the hard way*

Wer seinen Beruf wechselt, muß zumeist (teures) Lehrgeld zahlen, bis er alles beherrscht.
*A person who changes his occupation generally has to pay by experience (to learn the hard way) until he has mastered everything.*

j.em vom **Leibe** bleiben (fig.): *to keep (to stay) away from s. b.; to keep clear of s. b.*

Bleibe mir in Zukunft mit deinen Ratschlägen vom Leibe (Halse)!
*Keep (Stay) away from me (Keep clear of me) in future with your advice.*

etwas am eigenen **Leibe** erfahren: *to experience (to feel) s. th. for o. s.; to have a taste of s. th. for o. s.*

Dieser einst so reiche Kaufmann hat jetzt am eigenen Leibe erfahren, was Armut heißt.
*That shopkeeper, who was once so rich, has now experienced (felt) for himself what poverty is (has now had a taste of poverty for himself).*

j.em wie auf den **Leib** geschrieben sein: *to be made to measure for s.b.; to be almost as though it had been written for s.b.; s.b. is made for the part*

> Der Hauptdarsteller in diesem Theaterstück hat wunderbar gespielt. Die Rolle ist ihm wie auf den Leib geschrieben.
> *The principal actor in this play acted wonderfully. The part is made to measure for him (It is almost as though the part had been written for him; He is made for the part).*

gut bei **Leibe** sein (fam.): *to be well covered; to be of Falstaffian proportions*

> Mein reicher Onkel Karl ist gut bei Leibe (gut im Futter).
> *My rich uncle Charles is well covered (of Falstaffian proportions).*

sich j.en vom **Leibe** halten (fig.): *to keep s.b. at arm's length (at a distance; away; off).* Cf. auch: j.em eine Person (etwas) vom **Halse** halten

> Ich halte mir diesen Agenten schon lange vom Leibe, da er nur seine eigenen Interessen im Sinne hat.
> *I have kept that agent at arm's length (at a distance; away; off) for a long time, because he only has his own interests in mind.*

kein Hemd auf dem **Leibe** haben (fig.): cf. keinen roten **Heller** besitzen

**Leib** und Leben: *life and limb*

> Wer in einer Dynamitfabrik arbeitet, wird gut bezahlt; denn er bringt täglich Leib und Leben in Gefahr.
> *A man working in a dynamite factory is well paid, for every day he risks life and limb.*

j.em auf den **Leib** (zu Leibe) rücken (fig.): *to come to grips with s.b.; to join issue with s.b.; to tackle (to get at; to press) s.b.*

> Wenn du deinem Schuldner nicht auf den Leib ([zu Leibe]; auf die Pelle; auf den Pelz) rückst, wird er dir dein Geld niemals zurückgeben.
> *Unless you come to grips (join issue) with (tackle; get at; press) that debtor, he will never give you your money back.*

mit **Leib** und Seele: *with heart and soul; with all one's might (one's heart); with might and main.* Cf. auch: etwas für sein **Leben** gern tun

> Mein Neffe spielt mit Leib und Seele Tennis, jedoch ohne großen Erfolg.
> *My nephew plays tennis with heart and soul (with all his might [heart]; with might and main), but without much success.*

**Leib** und Seele zusammenhalten: *to keep body and soul together*

> Gut gefrühstückt (Ein gutes Frühstück) hält Leib und Seele zusammen.
> *A good breakfast keeps body and soul together.*

seinem **Leibe** kein Stiefvater sein (fam.): cf. seinem Leibe kein **Stiefvater** sein

am ganzen **Leibe** zittern: cf. zittern wie **Espenlaub**

aus **Leibeskräften** lachen: cf. aus vollem **Halse** lachen

ein **Leibgericht** (eine **Leibspeise**): *favourite dish; pet dish*
> Mein Leibgericht (Meine Leibspeise) sind Forellen mit ausgelassener Butter.
> *My favourite (pet) dish is trout with melted butter.*

laufen (rennen), als wenn der **Leibhaftige** hinter einem her ist: cf. laufen wie ein **Besenbinder**

seinen **Leibriemen** enger schnallen (fig.): cf. seinen **Riemen** enger schnallen

wie er **leibt** und lebt: *to be the very (the living) image (the very spit; the spitting image) of s.b.*
> Das Porträt war ausgezeichnet. Es war unser Professor, wie er leibt und lebt.
> *The portrait was excellent. It was the very (the living) image (the very spit; the spitting image) of our professor.*

über **Leichen** gehen (fig.): *to stop (to stick) at nothing; to ride rough-shod over s.b.; to trample s.b. (s.th.) underfoot*
> Heinrich ist so ehrgeizig, daß er über Leichen gehen und selbst seine Freunde ausnützen würde.
> *Henry is so ambitious that he would stop (stick) at nothing and even take advantage of his friends (that he would even ride rough-shod over his friends; even trample his friends underfoot).*

nur über j.es **Leiche**: *only over s.b.'s dead body*
> Nur über meine Leiche nimmst du mir dieses Geld ab!
> *Only over my dead body will you take this money from me!*

eine **Leichenbittermiene** machen: cf. ein **Gesicht** machen wie sieben Tage Regenwetter

**leichenblaß** sein: cf. weiß wie die **Wand** sein

**leichter** gesagt als getan: *easier said than done*
> Ich möchte ein größeres Haus kaufen, aber das ist leichter gesagt als getan.
> *I should like to buy a larger house, but that's easier said than done.*

ein Bruder **Leichtfuß** sein (fam.): cf. eine leichte **Fliege** sein

sich ein **Leid** antun: cf. sich das **Leben** nehmen

sein **Leid** in sich fressen: *to fret and pine; to brood on one's sorrows; to be sorry for o.s.*
> Es hat keinen Zweck, herumzusitzen und sein Leid in sich zu fressen.
> *There is no point in sitting around and fretting and pining (and brooding on one's sorrows; and being sorry for oneself).*

**Leidensgefährten** sein: *to be fellow-sufferers*
In dieser Prüfung sind wir Leidensgefährten.
*In this examination we are fellow-sufferers.*

immer die alte **Leier** anstimmen (fig.): cf. ständig (immer) auf einem Thema **herumreiten**

immer die gleiche (alte) **Leier** sein (fig.): *to be always the same old story (song; yarn; thing; refrain; saw)*

Es ist immer die gleiche (alte) Leier (das gleiche [alte] Lied; die gleiche [alte] Litanei [Walze]): heute macht man Versprechungen, morgen vergißt man sie. *It is always the same old story (song; yarn; thing; refrain; saw). One makes promises today and forgets them tomorrow.*

j.en auf den **Leim** führen (locken) (fig.): *to swindle s.b.; to pull the wool over s.b.'s eyes; to take s.b. in; to take s.b. for a ride (colloq.); to diddle s.b. (colloq.); to do s.b. down (colloq.); to do s.b. in the eye (colloq.); to do s.b. (sl.).* Cf. auch: j.em das **Fell** über die Ohren ziehen

Ich habe gleich gemerkt, daß dieser Hausierer mich auf den Leim führen (leimen; anführen; beschummeln; beschuppen; einseifen; lackmeiern; über den Löffel barbieren; übers Ohr hauen; prellen; 'reinlegen) wollte. *I saw at once that that canvasser was out to swindle me (pull the wool over my eyes; take me in; take me for a ride; diddle me; do me down; do me in the eye; do me).*

auf den **Leim** gehen (sich auf den Leim führen (locken) lassen; sich **leimen** lassen) (fig.): cf. **anbeißen** und Passivformen zu: j.en auf den **Leim** führen (locken)

aus dem **Leim** gehen: a) *to fall (to come) apart; to come away; to come loose;* b) (fam.) cf. aufgehen wie ein **Hefekloß**

Der Rahmen dieses Ölgemäldes ist leider aus dem Leim gegangen. *The frame of this oil painting has unfortunately fallen (come) apart (come away [loose]).*

etwas **leimen** (fig.): cf. etwas **kitten**

j.en **leimen** (fig. u. fam.): cf. j.en auf den **Leim** führen

ein **Leisetreter** sein (fig.): *to be a sneak (creeper) (colloq.); to be a pussyfoot (sl.)*

Auf diesen Leisetreter (Duckmäuser) soll man nicht hören, denn er ist unehrlich. *You must not listen to that sneak (creeper; pussyfoot); he is dishonest.*

alles über éinen **Leisten** schlagen (fig.): *to measure everything with the same yardstick (by the same standards); (neg.) to have to treat each on his (its etc.) merits*

Ein Richter muß jeden Fall individuell behandeln. Er kann nicht alles über éinen Leisten schlagen (über éinen Kamm scheren).
*A judge has to treat each case individually. He cannot measure everything with the same yardstick (by the same standards; he has to treat each on its merits).*

ein **Leitfaden** (fig.): *a guide; a sketch*
Sein Buch ist kein ausführliches Werk, sondern nur ein Leitfaden.
*His book is not a detailed work but only a guide (sketch).*

eine lange **Leitung** haben (fam.): cf. schwer von **Kapee** sein

j.em eine **Lektion** erteilen: cf. j.en **abkanzeln;** j.em eine **Standpauke** halten

eine **Leseratte** sein (fam.): cf. ein **Bücherwurm** sein

zu guter **Letzt:** *to round it off; on top of it all; to cap it all*
Mein Freund hat viel Unglück in seinem Leben gehabt. Zu guter Letzt ließ sich seine Frau von ihm scheiden.
*My friend has had a great deal of unhappiness in his life. To round it off (On top of it all; To cap it all) his wife divorced him.*

sein **Letztes** hergeben: *to give (to do) one's utmost; to exert o.s. to the utmost; to make a supreme effort; no sacrifice (effort) is too great for s.b.*
Bei der Sportveranstaltung gaben alle Teilnehmer ihr Letztes her, um den Sieg zu erringen.
*At the sports meeting all the competitors gave (did) their utmost (exerted themselves to the utmost; made a supreme effort) to win (No sacrifice [effort] was too great for all the competitors at the sports meeting in their efforts to win).*

geschiedene **Leute** sein: *It's good-bye to our (your etc.) friendship; Our (Your etc.) friendship is at an end (is over); to have fallen out; not to be on speaking terms*
Seitdem er mich so beleidigt hat, sind wir geschiedene Leute.
*It's been good-bye to our friendship (Our friendship has been at an end [over]; We have fallen out with each other; We have not been on speaking terms) since he offended me like that.*

in aller **Leute** Mund sein: cf. in aller **Munde** sein

unter die **Leute** kommen: a) (von Personen) *to mix (with other people); to get around (colloq.);* b) (von Sachen) *to get about (around); to become public; to be noised abroad*
a) Er fühlt sich daheim am glücklichsten und kommt wenig unter die Leute (Menschen).
b) Wir wollen mit niemandem über unsere Verlobung sprechen. Sie soll nicht vorzeitig unter die Leute (die Menschen) kommen.
*a) He feels happiest at home and does not mix much (with other people) (and does not get around much).*

*b) We are not going to talk about our engagement to anybody. It must not get about (around; become public; be noised abroad) too early.*

ein **Leuteschinder** sein: *to be a slave-driver (a hard task-master)*

Für diese Firma möchte ich niemals arbeiten; der Chef ist ein wahrer Leuteschinder.
*I should never like to work for that firm; the boss is a real slave-driver (a really hard task-master).*

j.em die **Leviten** lesen (fig.): cf. j.en **abkanzeln;** j.em eine **Standpauke** halten

j.em geht ein **Licht** auf (fig.): *it dawns on s. b.; s. b. sees the light (sees daylight; wakes up); s. b. tumbles to the fact (colloq.).* Cf. auch: Der **Groschen** ist gefallen

Dem Mädchen ist ein Licht (eine Stallaterne; sind die Augen) aufgegangen (. . . ist es gedämmert), daß der junge Mann es nicht ernst mit ihm meint.
*It has dawned on the girl (The girl has woken up [has tumbled] to the fact), that the young man is not serious about her; The girl has seen the light [seen daylight]: the young man is not serious about her).*

j.em ein **Licht** aufstecken (fig.): *to open s.b.'s eyes; to set s.b. right*

Über den wahren Charakter dieses Menschen will ich dir jetzt ein Licht aufstecken.
*I will now open your eyes to (set you right about) that person's true character.*

bei **Lichte** besehen (betrachtet) (fig.): *on closer inspection (examination); on reflection; when I (you etc.) come to look at it*

Die Beschaffung der nötigen Werkzeuge schien uns zunächst ganz einfach zu sein, aber bei Lichte besehen (betrachtet), stellte sie sich als recht schwierig heraus.
*At first it seemed to us quite simple to obtain the necessary tools, but on closer inspection (examination; on reflection; but when we came to look at it,) it turned out to be extremely difficult.*

sich im besten **Lichte** zeigen (fig.): cf. sich in ein gutes **Licht** setzen

etwas ans **Licht** bringen (fig.): cf. etwas an den **Tag** bringen

**Licht** in etwas bringen (fig.): *to shed (to throw) light on s.th.*

Auf Grund seiner Nachforschungen konnte der Detektiv etwas Licht in die mysteriöse Angelegenheit bringen (Licht auf . . . werfen).
*On the basis of his investigations the detective was able to shed (throw) some light on the mysterious affair.*

etwas in ein falsches **Licht** setzen (rücken) (fig.): *to portray s.th. in a false light; to put a false (a wrong) complexion (slant) on s.th.*

Die Zeitungen haben den Prozeß in ein falsches Licht gesetzt (gerückt).
*The papers have portrayed the trial in a false light (have put a false [wrong] complexion [slant] on the trial).*

kein großes **Licht** sein (fig. u. fam.): cf. das **Pulver** nicht erfunden haben

sich in ein gutes **Licht** setzen (fig.): *to show (to put) o.s. in a good light; to show one's good points; to show o.s. to one's best (the best) advantage; to make a good impression*

> Georg versteht es, sich bei seinen Lehrern in ein gutes Licht zu setzen (im besten Lichte zu zeigen).
> *George knows how to show (put) himself in a good light with (to show his good points to; to show himself to his [the] best advantage to; to make a good impression on) his teachers.*

in keinem guten **Licht** erscheinen (fig.): *to appear in a bad light; not to appear in a good light; to create a bad impression; not to create a good impression*

> Du wirst in keinem guten Licht erscheinen, wenn du dich nicht höflicher benimmst.
> *You will appear in a bad light (won't appear in a good light; will create a bad impression; will not create a good impression) if you don't behave more politely.*

etwas in (ein) helles **Licht** rücken (setzen) (fig.): *to bring s.th. into the limelight (into the open)*

> Wir hätten von der Ausstellung nichts gewußt, wenn die Zeitungen sie nicht in (ein) helles Licht gerückt (gesetzt) hätten.
> *We should not have known anything about the exhibition if the papers had not brought it into the limelight (the open).*

j.en hinters **Licht** führen (fig.): *to pull the wool over s.b.'s eyes; to throw dust in s.b.'s eyes; to lead s.b. up the garden path.* Cf. auch: j.en auf den **Leim** führen; j.em **Wind** vormachen

> Mein Sohn versuchte, mich hinters Licht zu führen (mir Sand in die Augen zu streuen), indem er erklärte, es gebe keine Schulzeugnisse mehr.
> *My son tried to pull the wool over my eyes (throw dust in my eyes; lead me up the garden path) by maintaining that there were no more school-reports.*

ans **Licht** kommen (fig.): cf. an den **Tag** kommen

sein **Licht** leuchten lassen (fig.): *to blow one's own trumpet; to let one's light shine before men; to sing one's own praises*

> Der junge Student prahlt mit seinen Kenntnissen und läßt gern sein Licht leuchten (singt gern sein eigenes Lob).
> *The young student boasts about his knowledge and likes to blow his own trumpet (to let his light shine before men; to sing his own praises).*

etwas ins rechte **Licht** rücken (setzen) (fig.): *to see s.th. in its true light (its true colours)*

> Jetzt verstehe ich die ganze Sachlage und kann seine Motive ins rechte Licht rücken (setzen).
> *Now I understand the whole situation and am able to see his motives in their true light (colours).*

sich ins rechte **Licht** rücken (setzen) (fig.): *to get on the right side of s.b.* Cf. auch: sich in ein gutes **Licht** setzen

> Dieser Beamte versteht es, sich bei seinen Vorgesetzten ins rechte Licht zu rücken (setzen).
> *That official knows how to get on the right side of his superiors.*

etwas in rosigem **Licht** betrachten (fig.): *to take a rosy (a bright) view of s.th.; to look on the bright side of things.* Cf. auch: alles durch eine rosarote (rosige) **Brille** betrachten

> Der Bräutigam ist optimistisch und betrachtet seine Zukunft in rosigem Licht.
> *The bridegroom is optimistic and takes a rosy (bright) view of his future (and is looking on the bright side of things).*

sein **Licht** unter einen (den) Scheffel stellen (fig.): *to hide one's light under a bushel*

> Du brauchst dein Licht nicht unter einen (den) Scheffel zu stellen, denn auf diesem Gebiet bist du Fachmann.
> *You don't need to hide your light under a bushel, for you are an expert in this field.*

das **Licht** scheuen: *to avoid the public eye (gaze); to shun publicity; to hide one's head*

> Verbrecher scheuen das Licht.
> *Criminals avoid the public eye (gaze; shun publicity; hide their heads).*

ein schlechtes (schiefes) **Licht** auf j.en (etwas) werfen (fig.): *to show (to put) s.b. (s.th.) in a bad light; to cast aspersions on s.b. (s.th.)*

> Bisher hatte ich eine sehr hohe Meinung von ihm, jetzt aber haben Ihre Bemerkungen ein schlechtes (schiefes) Licht auf seinen Charakter geworfen.
> *Formerly I had a very high opinion of him, but your remarks have now shown (put) him in a bad light (have now cast aspersions on his character).*

j.em im **Lichte** stehen (fig.): *to be in s.b.'s way; to block (to bar) s.b.'s path (way)*

> Karl kann in seinem Beruf schlecht weiterkommen, weil ihm ältere Kollegen im Lichte (Wege) stehen (den Weg versperren).
> *It is hard for Charles to get on in his profession because senior colleagues are in his way (are blocking [barring] his path [way]).*

das **Licht** der Welt erblicken: *to see the light of day; to come into the world*

Beethoven hat am 16. Dezember 1770 das Licht der Welt erblickt (ist am ...
zur Welt gekommen).
*Beethoven saw the light of day (came into the world) on December 16, 1770.*

**Licht** auf etwas werfen (fig.): cf. **Licht** in etwas bringen

ein **Lichtblick**: *a ray (gleam) of hope (of light)*

Endlich ein Lichtblick in dieser traurigen Zeit!
*A ray (gleam) of hope (light) at last in these sad times.*

j.en vor **Liebe** fressen können (fam.): cf. Sie ist zum **Anbeißen**

Die **Liebe** geht durch den Magen (Sprichw.): *The way to a man's heart is
through his stomach*

Meine Mutter kocht für meinen Vater immer gut; denn sie weiß, daß die Liebe
durch den Magen geht.
*My mother always cooks well for my father, for she knows that the way to a man's heart
is through his stomach.*

Alte **Liebe** rostet nicht (Sprichw.): *An old flame never dies (prov.)*

Dieser alte Junggeselle hat jetzt seine Jugendfreundin geheiratet. Alte Liebe
rostet nicht.
*This old bachelor has now married the girl friend of his youth. An old flame never dies.*

Eine **Liebe** ist der anderen wert (Sprichw.): *One good turn deserves another
(prov.)*

Voriges Jahr hat mir mein Bruder finanziell geholfen. Jetzt bin ich in der Lage,
ihm zu helfen. Eine Liebe ist der anderen wert.
*Last year my brother helped me financially. Now I am in a position to help him. One
good turn deserves another.*

mit etwas **liebäugeln**: *to have set one's heart on s.th.; to covet s.th.* Cf. auch:
j.es **Herz** hängt an etwas

Endlich hatte mein Sohn so viel Geld zusammen, um sich das teure Buch, mit
dem er schon lange geliebäugelt hatte, kaufen zu können.
*At last my son had enough money together to be able to buy the expensive book which he
had set his heart on (coveted) so long.*

**Liebedienerei**: cf. **Augendienerei**

j.en **liebhaben** können (fam.): cf. j.em den **Buckel** herunterrutschen können; Scher' dich zum **Henker**!

das Ende vom **Lied** sein (fig.): cf. das **Ende** vom Lied sein

immer das gleiche (alte) **Lied** sein (fig.): cf. immer die gleiche (alte) **Leier** sein immer das gleiche (alte) **Lied** singen (fig.): cf. (ständig, immer) auf einem Thema **herumreiten**

Davon kann ich ein **Lied** singen (fig.): *I know all about that; I could sing a song (tell you a thing or two) about that; I could write a novel about that (colloq.)*

> Es tut mir leid, daß Sie so sehr unter Rheuma zu leiden haben. Davon kann auch ich ein Lied singen.
> *I am sorry that you suffer so much from rheumatism. I know all about that (I could sing a song [tell you a thing or two; write a novel] about that) as well.*

ein **Lineal** verschluckt haben (fig.): cf. einen **Besenstiel** verschluckt haben

in vorderster **Linie** stehen (fig.): *to be in the front rank; to be on the highest level (on the top rung)*

> Dieser ehemalige Universitätsprofessor steht heute als Politiker in vorderster Linie (Front).
> *This former university professor is today in the front rank (on the highest level [the top rung]) as a politician.*

mit dem **linken** Bein (Fuß) zuerst aufstehen (fig.): cf. mit dem linken **Fuß** zuerst aufstehen

j.en **links** liegenlassen (fig.): cf. j.en kalt (kühl) **abrutschen** lassen

etwas **links** liegenlassen (fig.): *to turn one's back on s.th.; to put s.th. on one side; to give s.th. the go-by (colloq.); to drop s.th. (colloq.)*

> Du hast in der Schule viel zu tun und solltest das Fußballspiel eine Zeitlang links liegenlassen.
> *You have a lot to do at school and ought to turn your back on football (put football on one side; give football the go-by; drop football) for a while.*

etwas über die **Lippen** bringen: cf. etwas im **Munde** führen

sich j.em auf die **Lippen** drängen: *to rise (to come) to one's lips*

> Ein Ausdruck des Zorns drängte sich mir auf die Lippen, als ich sah, wie ungezogen sich der Junge benahm.
> *An angry remark rose (came) to my lips when I saw how rudely the boy was behaving.*

an j.es **Lippen** hängen (fig.): *to hang on s.b.'s words (s.b.'s every word); to follow s.b.'s every word*

> Alle Schüler hängen an den Lippen (am Mund) dieses freundlichen Lehrers.
> *All the pupils hang on this friendly teacher's words (every word; follow this friendly teacher's every word).*

Zwischen **Lipp'** und Kelchesrand schwebt der dunklen Mächte Hand (Sprichw.): *There's many a slip 'twixt the cup and the lip (prov.)*

Seine Aussichten sind gut, aber er hat den neuen Posten noch nicht. Zwischen Lipp' und Kelchesrand schwebt der dunklen Mächte Hand.
*His prospects are good but he has not got the new job yet. There's many a slip 'twixt the cup and the lip.*

eine **Lippe** riskieren (fam.): *to speak out; to trail one's coat; to stick one's neck out (sl.)*

Als Fachmann konnte er auf der Tagung eine Lippe riskieren und offen seine Meinung sagen.
*As an expert he was able to speak out (to trail his coat; to stick his neck out) at the meeting and give his opinion openly.*

j.em auf den **Lippen** schweben: *s.th. is on the tip of s.b.'s tongue; s.b. has s.th. on the tip of his tongue*

Der Name dieses Filmstars schwebt mir auf den Lippen (auf der Zunge; Ich habe den Namen . . . auf der Zunge), aber ich komme nicht darauf.
*The name of that film-star is on the tip of my tongue (I have the name . . . on the tip of my tongue) but I can't recall it.*

ein **Lippenbekenntnis:** *lip-service*

Wir halten seine Zustimmung zu unserm Parteiprogramm für ein bloßes Lippenbekenntnis.
*We regard his agreement with our party-programme as mere lip-service.*

mit **List** und Tücke: *by low cunning; by means of wiles and ruses*

Mit List und Tücke ist es dem Gauner gelungen, viele harmlose Menschen zu betrügen.
*By low cunning (By means of wiles and ruses) the rogue succeeded in swindling many innocent people.*

eine schwarze **Liste:** *a black list*

Seine Firma steht auf der schwarzen Liste, weil sie ihre Rechnungen nicht pünktlich bezahlt.
*His firm is on the black list because it does not pay its bills promptly.*

immer die gleiche (alte) **Litanei** sein (fig.): cf. immer die gleiche (alte) **Leier** sein

sein eigenes **Lob** singen: cf. sein **Licht** leuchten lassen

ein **Loblied** auf j.en (etwas) singen (fig.): cf. j.en (etwas) in den **Himmel** (er)heben

Das **lobe** ich mir: *I'm glad (pleased) to see it; That's what I like to see*

Aus deinem Zeugnis ersehe ich, daß du ein tüchtiger Schüler geworden bist. Das lobe ich mir.
*I observe from your report that you have become a hard-working pupil. I'm glad (pleased) to see it (That's what I like to see).*

éin **Loch** aufmachen (aufreißen), um ein anderes zuzustopfen (fig.): *to rob Peter to pay Paul*

> Wie soll das weitergehen? Du leihst dir Geld, um deine alten Rechnungen zu bezahlen. Man darf nicht éin Loch aufmachen (aufreißen), um ein anderes zuzustopfen. (Man darf nicht den Teufel mit Beelzebub austreiben.)
> *How can this go on? You are borrowing money to pay your old debts. You can't rob Peter to pay Paul.*

sich ein **Loch** (Löcher) in den Bauch beißen (fam.): cf. vor **Wut** kochen

j.em ein **Loch** (Löcher) in den Bauch fragen (fam.): cf. j.em ein **Loch** (Löcher) in den Kopf fragen

sich ein **Loch** in den Bauch lachen (fam.): cf. sich **totlachen**

j.em éin **Loch** (Löcher) in den Bauch reden (fam.): *to talk one's head off; to talk until one is blue in the face; to talk o.s. hoarse; to talk the hind leg off a donkey (colloq.); to talk o.s. stupid (silly) (colloq.).* Cf. auch: das **Blaue** vom Himmel herunterreden; sich den **Mund** fusselig reden

> Wenn mein Bruder jemanden von irgendetwas überzeugen will, redet er ihm ein Loch (Löcher) in den Bauch (redet er ihn dumm und dämlich; ihn dusselig; ihn tot und lebendig).
> *When my brother wants to convince somebody of something, he talks his head off (talks himself hoarse [stupid; silly]; talks until he is blue in the face; talks the hind leg off a donkey).*

ein **Loch** in den Geldbeutel fressen (in die Kasse reißen) (fig.): *to burn a hole in s.b.'s pocket; to make a hole in s.b.'s purse; to take a toll of s.b.'s funds.* Cf. auch: einer Sache stark **zusetzen**

> Meine dreiwöchige Sommerreise mit der ganzen Familie hat ein gehöriges Loch in meinen Geldbeutel gefressen (in meine Kasse gerissen).
> *My three weeks' summer holiday with the whole family has burnt a pretty big hole in my pocket (made a pretty big hole in my purse; taken a pretty big toll of my funds).*

ins **Loch** kommen (fam.): cf. in den **Kasten** kommen

j.em ein **Loch** (Löcher) in den Kopf fragen (fam.): *to drive s.b. mad with one's questions; to drive s.b. crazy (dotty) with one's questions (colloq.)*

> Mein ältester Enkel(sohn) ist sehr ermüdend. Er fragt mir täglich ein Loch (Löcher) in den Kopf (Bauch).
> *My oldest grandson is very tiring. Every day he drives me mad (crazy; dotty) with his questions.*

**Löcher** in die Luft gucken: cf. **Maulaffen** feilhalten

auf dem letzten **Loch** pfeifen (fig.): *to be on one's last legs; to be at the end of one's tether; to be at one's wit's end*

> Seine Familie pfeift auf dem letzten Loch. Jede Woche kommt der Gerichts-vollzieher zu ihr.
> *His family is on its last legs (at the end of its tether; at its wit's end). The bailiff goes there every week.*

saufen wie ein **Loch** (fam.): *to drink like a fish; to guzzle (to swizzle) like a fish (sl.)*

> In den letzten Jahren säuft sein Bruder wie ein Loch (Faß).
> *In recent years his brother has been drinking (guzzling; swizzling) like a fish.*

**Löcher** in die Wand (Wände) stieren (fam.): cf. **Maulaffen** feilhalten

Aus welchem **Loch** pfeift der Wind? (fig.): *Which way is the wind blowing?*

> Bevor ich diese Aktien kaufe, will ich wissen, aus welchem Loch der Wind pfeift.
> *Before I buy these shares, I want to know which way the wind is blowing.*

etwas ein **Loch** zurückstecken (fig.): cf. etwas einen **Pflock** zurückstecken

nicht **lockerlassen** (fig.): *not to give up (give way; let up); to stick at it (colloq.).* Cf. auch: nicht **wanken** und nicht weichen

> Wir werden nicht lockerlassen, bis der ganze Vorfall aufgeklärt ist.
> *We shall not give up (give way; let up; We shall stick at it) until the whole incident is cleared up.*

eine Geldsumme **lockermachen** (fam.): *to fork (to dig; to fish) out a sum of money (colloq.).* Cf. auch: etwas **springen** lassen

> Mach' doch mal fünf Mark locker und setz' sie auf dieses Pferd!
> *Fork (Dig; Fish) out five marks and put it on this horse.*

j.en über den **Löffel** barbieren (fig. u. fam.): cf. j.en auf den **Leim** führen

die Weisheit nicht mit **Löffeln** gegessen haben (fam.): cf. die **Weisheit** nicht mit Löffeln gegessen haben

mit einem goldenen **Löffel** auf die Welt gekommen sein (fig.): cf. ein **Glückskind** sein

sich etwas hinter die **Löffel** schreiben (fig. u. fam.): *to write s.th. on one's mental tablet (colloq.); to get s.th. into one's (thick) head (colloq.)*

> Du mußt deutlicher sprechen (reden). Schreib' dir das doch endlich hinter die Löffel (Ohren)!
> *You must speak more distinctly. Write that on your mental tablet (Get that into your [thick] head)!*

seinen **Lohn** bekommen (fig.): *to get one's deserts; to get what one deserves*

Dieser Gauner ist jetzt verhaftet worden und wird zweifellos seinen Lohn bekommen.
*That rogue has now been arrested and will without doubt get his deserts (what he deserves).*

sich **lohnen:** cf. sich **rentieren**

sich auf seinen **Lorbeeren** ausruhen (fig.): *to rest on one's laurels*

Nach einer glänzenden Karriere kann sich der berühmte Schauspieler jetzt auf seinen Lorbeeren ausruhen.
*After a brilliant career the famous actor can now rest on his laurels.*

seine ersten **Lorbeeren** ernten (fig.): *to win (to gain) one's first laurels.* Cf. auch: sich die **Sporen** verdienen

Schon in seinen jungen Jahren hat dieser Dramatiker seine ersten Lorbeeren geerntet.
*This dramatist won (gained) his first laurels in his early years.*

das große **Los** ziehen: a) (Wettbewerb usw.) *to win first prize;* b) (fig.) *to pick (to back) a winner (colloq.)*

a) Sein Kollege hat in der Lotterie das große Los gezogen.
b) Mein Bruder hat mit seiner Frau das große Los gezogen (in den Glückstopf gegriffen), denn sie ist hübsch und tüchtig.
*a) His colleague has won first prize in the lottery.*
*b) My brother has picked (backed) a winner in his wife, for she is pretty and hardworking.*

einer Sache **los** und ledig sein: *to be rid of s.th.; to be through with s.th.; to have seen the back of s.th.; s.th. is over and done with*

Vorige Woche habe ich im Fußball-Toto mehrere tausend Mark gewonnen. Jetzt bin ich meiner Sorgen los und ledig.
*Last week I won several thousand marks on the football-pools. Now I am rid of (through with; have seen the back of) my troubles (Now my troubles are over and done with).*

nichts **los** (fam.): *nothing on (nothing happening)*

Laß' uns weiterfahren. In diesem Städtchen ist nichts los.
*Let's drive on. There's nothing on (happening) in this little town.*

j.en **loseisen** (fam.): *to wrench (to prise; to drag) s.b. away*

Du wirst Schwierigkeiten haben, deinen Freund auf ein paar Stunden von seinem Geschäft loszueisen.
*You will have difficulty in wrenching (prising; dragging) your friend away from his business for a few hours.*

etwas **loshaben** (fam.): cf. gut **bestellt** sein

**losschießen (loslegen)** (fam.): *to fire away (colloq.); to shoot (sl.)*

Du willst mir etwas sagen; also schieß' (leg') los!
*You want to tell me something. Well, fire away! (Well, shoot!)*

etwas ins **Lot** bringen (fig.): *to mend matters; to patch things up; to smooth things over.* Cf. auch: eine **Kluft** überbrücken

Die Schwester hofft, ihre beiden feindlichen Brüder aussöhnen zu können und so alles ins Lot zu bringen.
*The sister hopes to be able to reconcile her two antagonistic brothers and thus mend matters (patch things [everything] up; smooth things [everything] over).*

Davon gehen hundert auf ein **Lot** (fig.): *They are ten a penny; There are plenty more where he (you etc.) came from (colloq.)*

Er ist nur ein ganz mittelmäßiger Maler. Von ihm gehen hundert auf ein Lot.
*He is only a very mediocre painter. Ones like him are ten a penny (There are plenty more where he came from).*

im **Lot** sein (fig.): cf. auf der **Höhe** sein

brüllen wie ein **Löwe:** *to roar like a lion (like a bear); to bellow like a bull*

Wenn mein Onkel in Zorn gerät, brüllt er wie ein Löwe (Stier).
*When my uncle gets angry, he roars like a lion (a bear; bellows like a bull).*

Man soll den schlafenden **Löwen** nicht wecken (Sprichw.): *Let sleeping dogs lie (prov.); Let well alone (prov.)*

Laß' von diesem umstrittenen Thema ab. Man soll den schlafenden Löwen nicht wecken.
*Leave that disputed subject alone. Let sleeping dogs lie (Let well alone).*

**Luchsaugen** haben (**luchsäugig**) sein: cf. **Augen** wie ein Luchs haben

eine **Lücke** ausfüllen (fig.): *to fill a gap; to supply (to fulfil) a need*

Sein neues Buch wird eine lang empfundene Lücke in der Geschichte der Musik ausfüllen.
*His new book will fill a long-felt gap (will supply [fulfil] a long-felt need) in the history of music.*

eine **Lücke** hinterlassen (fig.): *to leave a gap*

Der Tod dieses bekannten Gelehrten wird eine große Lücke in der Anglistik hinterlassen.
*The death of this well-known scholar will leave a big gap in English studies.*

in die **Lücke** springen (fig.): cf. in die **Bresche** springen

ein **Lückenbüßer** sein: *to be a stop-gap (a make-shift; a stand-in)*

Da der große Schauspieler plötzlich erkrankt war, mußte ein anderer seine Rolle übernehmen. Es war aber nur ein Lückenbüßer.

*As the great actor had suddenly been taken ill, somebody else had to take over his part, but he was only a stop-gap (make-shift; stand-in).*

ein kleines **Luder** sein (fam.): cf. ein kleines **Aas** sein

Hier herrscht dicke **Luft** (fig. u. fam.): *Things are (The atmosphere is) getting unpleasant here; Things are (The atmosphere is) getting hot around here (colloq.)*

Als ich ins Zimmer kam, merkte ich, daß dort dicke Luft herrschte, und ich ging gleich wieder fort.

*When I came into the room, I noticed that things were (the atmosphere was) getting unpleasant (hot) and I left again at once.*

seinen Gefühlen **Luft** machen: cf. seinen Gefühlen freien **Lauf** lassen

aus der **Luft** gegriffen sein (fig.): *to be arrant rubbish; to be a cock-and-bull story; to be a complete fiction (fabrication); to be a figment of the imagination.* Cf. auch: ein **Ammenmärchen** erzählen; **Quatsch** sein

Der Zeitungsbericht von dem Tod des Präsidenten war völlig aus der Luft gegriffen.

*The newspaper report of the president's death was arrant rubbish (a pure cock-and-bull story; a complete fiction [fabrication]; purely a figment of the imagination).*

in die **Luft** gehen (fig.): cf. aus der **Haut** fahren

nicht von der **Luft** und von der Liebe leben können: *not to be able to live on air (on air-pie)*

Leider läßt es mein Gehalt noch nicht zu, daß wir heiraten. Wir können doch nicht von der Luft und von der Liebe leben.

*I am afraid that my salary does not yet allow us to get married. We cannot live on air (on air-pie).*

in der **Luft** liegen (fig.): *to be in the air; to be in the offing*

In diesem Lande herrschen schwere Zeiten. Eine Revolution scheint in der Luft zu liegen.

*Hard times are prevailing in this country. There seems to be a revolution in the air (in the offing).*

Die **Luft** ist rein (fig.): *The coast is clear*

Sobald die Luft rein war, schlichen (sich) die Einbrecher ins Haus.
*As soon as the coast was clear, the burglars crept into the house.*

die **Luft** reinigen (fig.): *to clear the air (the atmosphere)*

Die streitenden Parteien sollten ihre Meinungen offen aussprechen. Das wird wahrscheinlich die Luft reinigen.

*The conflicting parties ought to express their opinions openly. That will probably clear the air (the atmosphere).*

**Luft** schaffen (fig.): *to give o.s. room to breathe (to move); to clear the deck*

Ich will meine vielen alten Briefe sortieren, um etwas Luft zu schaffen.
*I am going to sort my many old letters, so as to give myself (some) room to breathe (to move; so as to clear the deck a bit).*

**Luft** schnappen: *to get a breath of (fresh) air*

Ich bin aus dem rauchigen Zimmer gegangen, um Luft zu schnappen.
*I went out of the smoky room to get a breath of (fresh) air.*

in der **Luft** schweben (hängen) (fig.): *to hang (to be) in the air; to be in the balance; to hang fire*

Wir wollten dieses Jahr nach England fahren, aber unsere Pläne schweben (hängen) noch immer in der Luft (sind noch immer in der Schwebe).
*We wanted to go to England this year but our plans are still (hanging) in the air (are still in the balance; are still hanging fire).*

j.en an die (frische) **Luft** setzen (befördern): cf. j.en auf die **Straße** setzen; j.en vor die **Tür** setzen

völlig **Luft** für j.en sein (fig.): *to be absolutely nothing to s.b.; to be a person (matter) of supreme indifference to s.b.; not to exist for s.b.; not to care two hoots (two straws; a rap; a fig; a hang; a damn) about s.b. (s.th.) (colloq.); not to give two hoots (two straws; a rap; a fig; a hang; a damn) for s.b. (s.th.) (colloq.)*

Du irrst dich, wenn du glaubst, ich interessiere mich für diese Frau. Im Gegenteil, sie ist für mich völlig Luft (ist mir völlig Wurst [schnuppe; piepe]).
*You are mistaken if you think that I'm interested in that woman. On the contrary, she is absolutely nothing (a person of supreme indifference) to me (doesn't exist for me; I don't care two hoots [two straws; a rap; a fig; a hang; a damn] about her; I don't give two hoots [two straws; a rap; a fig; a hang; a damn] for her).*

in der **Luftlinie**: *as the crow flies*

Diese beiden Städte sind in der Luftlinie etwa 200 Kilometer voneinander entfernt.
*These two towns are about 200 kilometres apart as the crow flies.*

**Luftschlösser** bauen (fig.): *to build castles in the air; to build card-castles*

Wilhelm träumt ständig von großen Erfolgen. Ich fürchte, daß er Luftschlösser baut.
*William is continually dreaming about great successes. I fear that he is building castles in the air (card-castles).*

**Lug** und Trug sein: *to be a pack (a tissue) of lies; to be a cock-and-bull story* *(a trumped-up tale)*. Cf. auch: ein **Ammenmärchen** erzählen; **erstunken** und erlogen; aus der **Luft** gegriffen sein

> Seine Behauptungen waren nichts als (lauter) Lug und Trug (als ein Lügengewebe).
> *His claims were nothing but a pack (a tissue) of lies (a cock-and-bull story; a trumped-up tale).*

**lügen** wie gedruckt: cf. lügen, daß sich die **Balken** biegen

**Lügen** haben kurze Beine (Sprichw.): cf. Lügen haben kurze **Beine**

eine faustdicke **Lüge:** cf. eine **faustdicke** Lüge

j.en **Lügen** strafen: *to give the lie to s.b.'s story; to show s.b.'s story up*

> Was der Angeklagte behauptete, war alles unwahr, und die Zeugen konnten ihn Lügen strafen.
> *What the accused claimed was all untrue, and the witnesses were able to give the lie to his story (to show his story up).*

ein **Lügengewebe** sein: cf. **Lug** und Trug sein

ein langer **Lulatsch** sein (fam.): cf. lang wie eine **Bohnenstange** sein

sich **lümmeln** (fam.): cf. sich **fläzen**

sich nicht **lumpen** lassen (fam.): *to spare no expense; to loosen one's purse-strings.* Cf. auch: eine Geldsumme **lockermachen**

> Mein Vater ließ sich nicht lumpen und bestellte ein teueres Essen für uns.
> *My father spared no expense (loosened his purse-strings) and ordered an expensive meal for us.*

eine gute **Lunge** haben: *to have a good pair of lungs*

> Dieser Redner hat eine gute Lunge. Selbst in der hintersten Reihe klingt seine Stimme laut.
> *That speaker has a good pair of lungs. His voice sounds loud even in the back row.*

sich die **Lunge** aus dem Leibe schreien (fig.): *to shout o.s. hoarse; to shout (to scream) one's head off (colloq.)*

> Obwohl sich die Mutter die Lunge aus dem Leibe (die Kehle aus dem Hals) schrie, wollte ihr kleiner Sohn nicht nach Hause kommen.
> *Although the mother shouted (screamed) her head off (shouted herself hoarse), her small son would not come home.*

seine **Lunge** schonen: *to save one's breath*

> Behalte deine Meinung für dich und schone deine Lunge (spare deinen Atem).
> *Keep your opinion to yourself and save your breath.*

**Lunte** riechen (fig.): cf. den **Braten** riechen

etwas unter die **Lupe** nehmen (fig.): *to look into s.th.; to examine s.th. with a fine tooth-comb; to scrutinise s.th.*

Diese neue Theorie muß streng unter die Lupe genommen werden.
*One must look closely into (closely scrutinise) this new theory (examine this new theory with a fine tooth-comb).*

Es ist nicht alles (Das Leben ist nicht) eitel **Lust** und Freude (Sprichw.): *Life is not all beer and skittles (fun and games) (prov.)*

Manchmal muß man auch ernst sein. Es ist nicht alles (Das Leben ist nicht) eitel Lust und Freude.
*Sometimes one has to be serious, too. Life is not all beer and skittles (fun and games).*

etwas mit **Lust** und Liebe tun: *to do s.th. (to go at s.th.) with a will (with heart and soul); to put one's heart into s.th.; to throw o.s. into s.th. with relish (delight).*
Cf. auch: mit **Leib** und Seele

Wenn man etwas mit Lust und Liebe tut, so ist die Arbeit schnell fertig.
*If one does (goes at) something with a will (with heart and soul; If one puts one's heart into something; throws oneself into something with relish [delight]), the work is quickly done.*


# M


j.en in der **Mache** haben (fam.): *to take s.b. in hand; to get to work on s.b. (to work on s.b.) (colloq.); to have a go at s.b. (sl.)*

Karl ist jetzt vernünftig geworden, weil alle seine Freunde ihn tüchtig in der Mache gehabt haben.
*Charles has now become reasonable because all his friends have taken him in hand (have got to work [have worked] on him; have had a go at him).*

etwas in der **Mache** haben (fam.): *to have s.th. on the stocks; to have s.th. going; to have s.th. in hand*

Ich bin gegenwärtig sehr beschäftigt, weil ich mehrere Arbeiten in der Mache habe.
*I am very busy at present, as I have several pieces of work on the stocks (going; in hand).*

**Mache** sein (fam.): *to be humbug (make-believe; sham); to be kidding (sl.)*

Vieles von dem, was die Parteien vor einer Wahl versprechen, ist reine Mache.
*Much of what the parties promise before an election is pure humbug (make-believe; sham; kidding).*

ein **Machtwort** sprechen: *to put one's foot down; to lay down the law*

Die Kinder machen so einen Krach, daß ich mal (zu ihnen) hineingehen und ein Machtwort sprechen muß.
*The children are making such a row that I must go in and put my foot down (and lay down the law).*

## Mädchen für alles sein: *to be a maid-of-all-work*

Die junge Elisabeth wird von der ganzen Familie ausgenutzt. Sie ist wirklich Mädchen für alles.
*Young Elizabeth is taken advantage of by the whole family. She is a real maid-of-all-work.*

### ein spätes Mädchen sein: *to be an old maid*

Meiner Schwester graut (es) vor dem Gedanken, ein spätes Mädchen zu werden.
*My sister dreads the thought of becoming an old maid.*

### kalt wie eine Made sein (fam.): *to be as cold as ice (as marble; as a fish)*

Du hast eine schlechte Blutzirkulation. Du fühlst dich heute wieder kalt wie eine Made an.
*You have a bad circulation. You feel as cold as ice (as marble; as a fish) again today.*

### sich (wohl)fühlen wie die Made im Speck: *to be as happy as a pig in mud (as a fish in water); to feel in clover; to feel on top of the world*

Seitdem er diese neue Stellung hat, fühlt sich mein Schwager (wohl) wie die Made im Speck (wie ein Fisch im Wasser; wie ein Pascha; wie der Vogel im Hanfsamen).
*Since he got that new position my brother-in-law feels as happy as a pig in mud (as a fish in water; feels in clover; feels on top of the world).*

### j.en madig machen (fam.): *to take s.b. down a peg; to dress s.b. down.* Cf. auch: j.en abkanzeln

Als wir uns mit unseren sportlichen Leistungen brüsten wollten, hat unser Lehrer uns kritisiert und regelrecht madig (klein und häßlich) gemacht.
*When we were about to boast of our sporting achievements our teacher criticised us and really took us down a peg (dressed us down).*

### Der Magen dreht sich mir um: *It turns my stomach over; My stomach turns over; It makes me (feel) sick*

Wenn ich an Lebertran nur denke, dreht sich mir der Magen um.
*It turns my stomach over (My stomach turns over; It makes me [feel] sick) just to think of cod-liver oil.*

### etwas liegt j.em (schwer) im Magen (fig.): *it upsets s.b.; it preys on s.b.'s mind; it has got s.b. worried (colloq.)*

Mehrere Schüler sehen bedrückt aus. Die kommende Prüfung liegt ihnen wohl (schwer) im Magen.
*Several pupils are looking depressed. The coming examination is probably upsetting them (preying on their minds; has probably got them worried).*

Wer zuerst kommt, **mahlt** zuerst (Sprichw.): *First come, first served (prov.);*
*The early bird catches the worm (prov.)*. Cf. auch: Morgenstunde hat **Gold**
im Munde

Wenn wir gute Plätze haben wollen, müssen wir rechtzeitig an der Kasse sein.
Wer zuerst kommt, mahlt zuerst.
*If we want to get good seats, we must be at the box-office in good time. First come, first*
*served (The early bird catches the worm).*

wie einst im **Mai** (fig.): *as in one's heyday; as in the heyday of one's youth; as in*
*one's salad days (colloq.)*

Die alten Herren waren so fröhlich wie einst im Mai.
*The old men were as merry as in their heyday (the heyday of their youth; their salad days).*

Nur einmal blüht im Jahr der **Mai** (Sprichw.): Es ist nicht alle **Tage**
Sonntag

Schulden haben (machen) wie ein **Major**: cf. bis über die **Ohren** in Schulden
stecken

an j.em (etwas) **mäkeln** (fam.): cf. über etwas **meckern**

**Makulatur** reden (fam.): cf. **Quatsch** reden

zum **Malen** schön sein: cf. **bildschön** sein

etwas an den **Mann** bringen (fig.): *to find a market (a sale) for s.th.; to dispose*
*(to get rid) of s.th.*

Wenn ich auch im Augenblick diese Perlenkette nicht verkaufen kann, so
hoffe ich doch, sie in der Weihnachtszeit an den Mann zu bringen.
*Even if I cannot sell this pearl necklace at the moment, I still hope to find a market (a*
*sale) for it (to dispose [get rid] of it) at Christmas time.*

ein **Mann** der Feder sein: *to be a man of letters*

Kein Mann der Feder würde für diese Zeitschrift schreiben.
*No man of letters would write for this periodical.*

seinen **Mann** finden (fig.): *to find (to meet) one's match (one's equal; one's*
*master)*. Cf. auch: an den **Rechten** kommen

Der bekannte deutsche Schachspieler hat endlich seinen Mann (Meister) ge-
funden. Er wurde von einem russischen Spieler besiegt.
*The famous German chess-player has at last found (met) his match (equal; master).*
*He has been beaten by a Russian player.*

ein gemachter **Mann** sein (fig.): *to be a made man; to be made (colloq.)*

Durch diese Erfindung ist Karl ein gemachter Mann geworden.
*With this invention Charles is a made man (is made).*

**Manns** genug sein: *to be man enough*

Ich brauche keine Hilfe. Ich bin Manns genug, um selbst meine Arbeit zu machen.
*I need no help. I am man enough to do my own work.*

ein geschlagener (gebrochener) **Mann** sein: *to be ruined (a ruined man); to be finished; to be a broken man; to be done for (colloq.)*

Der Bankdirektor hat sein ganzes Geld auf der Spielbank verspielt und ist jetzt ein geschlagener (gebrochener) Mann.
*The bank director has gambled away all his money at the casino and is now ruined (a ruined [broken] man; is now finished [done for]).*

**Mann** Gottes! (fam.): cf. in **Gottes** Namen!

. . . **Mann** hoch: *(all) . . . of us (them); the . . . of us (them); . . . of us (them); all told; . . . strong*

Wir gingen sechs Mann hoch ins Kino, um die Premiere des Films zu sehen.
*We went to the cinema, (all) six of us (the six of us; six of us, all told; six strong), to see the premiere of the film.*

alle **Mann** hoch: *the (whole) lot of us (you etc.); every man-jack (of us; of you etc.)*

Morgen früh fahren wir alle Mann hoch nach Frankfurt.
*The (whole) lot of us are (Every man-jack [of us] is) going to Frankfurt tomorrow morning.*

ein Mädchen an den **Mann** bringen: cf. j.en unter die **Haube** bringen

mit **Mann** und Maus untergehen: *to sink (to go down) with the loss of all on board (of every living soul); to sink (to go down) with all hands (on board)*

Das Schiff stieß auf einen Eisberg und ging mit Mann und Maus unter.
*The ship struck an iceberg and sank (went down) with the loss of all on board (every living soul; with all hands [on board]).*

den starken **Mann** markieren (fam.): *to act big (colloq.); to act (to play) the big white chief (colloq.); to act (to play) the big shot (sl.)*

Für diese komplizierte Arbeit bist du viel zu unerfahren. Du machst dich lächerlich, wenn du den starken Mann markierst.
*You are far too inexperienced for this complicated work. You make yourself ridiculous by acting big (by acting [playing] the big white chief [the big shot]).*

seinen **Mann** stehen (stellen) (fig.): *to stand fast; to stand up to it like a man; to stand one's ground; to hold one's own; to pull one's weight*

Im letzten Kriege hat sich die Zivilbevölkerung dieses Landes tapfer verhalten und ihren Mann gestanden (gestellt).

*In the last war the civilian population of this country behaved bravely and stood fast (stood up to it like a man; stood its ground; held its own; pulled its weight).*

der **Mann** auf der Straße: *the man in the street*

> Der Mann auf der Straße versteht nichts von solchen technischen Einzelheiten.
> *The man in the street does not understand anything about such technical details.*

der **Mann** des Tages sein: cf. der **Held** des Tages sein

ein **Mann** des Todes sein: *to be doomed to death; to be a dead man (colloq.); to be a dead 'un (sl.); to be a goner (sl.); to have had it (sl.).* Cf. auch: j.es **Tage** sind gezählt

> Wenn du diesen Draht anrührst, bist du (ein Mann; ein Kind) des Todes (ein Todeskandidat; sitzt dir der Tod im Nacken).
> *If you touch this wire, you will be a dead man (a dead 'un; a goner; you've had it).*

den wilden **Mann** spielen: *to behave like a savage (a madman); to go berserk*

> Als die Polizei den Betrunkenen auf die Wache bringen wollte, spielte er den wilden Mann und versuchte fortzulaufen.
> *When the police wanted to take the drunken man to the police-station, he behaved like a savage (a madman; he went berserk) and tried to run away.*

Ein **Mann,** ein Wort (Sprichw.): *A man's word is his bond (prov.)*

> Als Ehrenmänner brauchen wir nichts Schriftliches. Ein Mann, ein Wort.
> *As honourable men we do not need anything in writing. A man's word is his bond.*

ein **Mann** von Wort sein: *to be a man of one's word; to be as good as one's word*

> Wir können uns auf diesen Autohändler verlassen. Er ist ein Mann von Wort.
> *We can depend on this car-dealer. He is a man of his word (as good as his word).*

schwer(e) **Manschetten** vor j.em (etwas) haben (fig. u. fam.): *to be in a (blue) funk (a panic) about s.th. (colloq.); to be in a flap about s.th. (sl.).* Cf. auch: eine **Heidenangst** haben

> Ich habe keine Angst vor dem Examen, aber einige meiner Freunde haben schwer(e) Manschetten vor ihm.
> *I am not afraid of the examination, but some of my friends are in a (blue) funk (a panic; a flap) about it.*

etwas mit dem **Mantel** der Liebe zudecken (den Mantel christlicher Nächstenliebe über etwas breiten): *to hush s.th. up; to keep s.th. quiet; to draw a veil over s.th.*

> Es war ein geringfügiger Fehler, und wir beschlossen, ihn mit dem Mantel der Liebe zuzudecken (den Mantel christlicher Nächstenliebe darüber [über ihn] zu breiten).
> *It was a trivial mistake, and we decided to hush it up (to keep it quiet; to draw a veil over it).*

den **Mantel** nach dem Wind hängen (fig.): *to set (to trim) one's sails (to sail)
according to the wind; to swim with the tide; to go with the crowd*

> Dieser Abgeordnete hängt den Mantel (dreht die Fahne; dreht sich) nach dem
> Wind (schwimmt mit dem Strom; ist wetterwendisch). Jetzt hat er schon wieder
> die Partei gewechselt.
> *This deputy sets (trims) his sails (This deputy sails) according to the wind (swims with
> the tide; goes with the crowd): he has now changed parties again.*

einer Sache ein **Mäntelchen** umhängen (fig.): *to give a false colouring to s. th.;
to put a false construction on s. th.; to camouflage s. th.; to cover s. th. up*

> Er war offenbar schuldig, versuchte jedoch, seinen schändlichen Taten ein
> Mäntelchen umzuhängen.
> *He was obviously guilty, but he tried to give a false colouring to (put a false construction
> on; camouflage; cover up) his shameful deeds.*

**mären** (fam.): cf. **bummeln** b)

j.em durch **Mark** und Bein gehen: *to pierce (to cut; to sting) s. b. to the quick.*
Cf. auch: j.em in die **Glieder** fahren

> Die Untreue ihres Verlobten ging meiner Kusine durch Mark und Bein (traf . . .
> bis ins Mark [an der Wurzel]; versetzte . . . einen Dolchstoß [einen Stich (ins
> Herz)]; tat . . . in der Seele weh).
> *The unfaithfulness of her fiancé pierced (cut; stung) my cousin to the quick.*

kein **Mark** in den Knochen haben: *to be worn out; not to be up to it; to be as
weak as a kitten*

> Ich kann diese schweren Steine in meinem Alter nicht heben; denn ich habe
> kein Mark (keine Kraft) in den Knochen mehr.
> *I cannot lift these heavy stones at my age; I am worn out (as weak as a kitten) now (am
> no longer up to it).*

j.en bis ins **Mark** treffen (fig.): cf. j.em durch **Mark** und Bein gehen

eine komische **Marke** sein (fam.): cf. ein komischer **Kauz** sein

eine schöne (nette) **Marke** sein (fam.): *to be a fine (nice) one (colloq.)*

> Du bist mir eine schöne (nette) Marke! Du leihst dir mein Fahrrad (aus) und
> bringst es mir in diesem schmutzigen Zustand zurück.
> *You're a fine (nice) one! You borrow my bicycle and bring it back to me in this dirty state.*

seine Haut zu **Markte** tragen (fig.): cf. seine **Haut** zu Markte tragen

fluchen (schimpfen) wie ein **Marktweib**: cf. fluchen wie ein **Landsknecht**

kalt wie **Marmor** sein: cf. **eiskalt** sein

j.em den **Marsch** blasen (fig. u. fam.): cf. j.en **abkanzeln** blau wie ein **Märzveilchen** sein (fam.): cf. **sternhagelvoll** sein

Das ist die **Masche**! (fam.): *That's just the job (the thing)! (colloq.)*

Dieser Vorschlag ist die Masche (eine Wolke; eine Wucht)! Wir werden ihn sofort befolgen.
*That suggestion is just the job (thing). We shall adopt it at once.*

eine (dicke) **Maschine** sein (fig. u. fam.): cf. ein **Schlachtroß** sein

die **Maske** abwerfen (fig.): *to throw off one's mask (one's disguise); to come out in one's true colours; to give the game (the show) away*

Als wir sagten, daß wir nichts kaufen wollten, warf der Hausierer die Maske ab und wurde unverschämt.
*When we said that we did not want to buy anything, the hawker threw off his mask (disguise; came out in his true colours; gave the game [show] away) and became impudent.*

j.em die **Maske** vom Gesicht reißen (fig.): *to unmask s.b.; to show s.b. up (in his real [true] colours).* Cf. auch: j.en **entlarven**

Diesem unehrlichen Menschen hat man jetzt glücklicherweise die Maske vom Gesicht gerissen.
*Fortunately that dishonest person has now been unmasked (been shown up [in his real (true) colours]).*

sein gerüttelt **Maß** haben (fig.): *to have one's fill; to have more than enough (to do); to have one's plate full.* Cf. auch: alle **Hände** voll zu tun haben

Im Augenblick kann ich mir keine Ferien erlauben, da ich mein gerüttelt Maß an Arbeit habe.
*At the moment I cannot allow myself a holiday, because I have my fill of work (more than enough work [to do]; my plate full).*

Das **Maß** ist voll (fig.): cf. Das ist doch die **Höhe**!

das **Maß** vollmachen (zum Überlaufen bringen) (fig.): *to be the last straw; to put the lid on it (colloq.); to be the giddy limit (sl.).* Cf. auch: Das ist doch die **Höhe**!

Ich habe ihm schon mein Auto geliehen. Daß er jetzt auch noch Geld haben will, macht das Maß voll (bringt das Maß zum Überlaufen).
*I have already lent him my car. It is the last straw (puts the lid on it; is the giddy limit) that he now wants money as well.*

ohne **Maß** und Ziel: *out of all proportion; to excess; to overdo s.th.*

Er wird nicht lange leben, denn er arbeitet ohne Maß und Ziel.
*He won't live long, for he is working out of all proportion (to excess; he is overdoing his work).*

mit zweierlei **Maß** messen (fig.): *to judge by (to apply) a double standard*

347

Ein Lehrer muß alle Schüler gleich behandeln. Er darf nicht mit zweierlei Maß messen.
*A teacher must treat all pupils alike. He must not judge by (must not apply) a double standard.*

den **Maßstab** für j.en (etwas) abgeben (fig.): *to set the standard (to lay down a standard) for s. b. (s. th.); to provide a model for s. b. (s. th.)*

Das Verhalten des Ministers gibt den Maßstab für das seiner Untergebenen ab.
*The minister's conduct sets the standard (lays down a standard; provides a model) for that of his juniors.*

**Mattscheibe** haben (fam.): *s. b.'s mind is a blank*

Du kannst diese einfache Frage nicht beantworten? Du hast heute wohl Mattscheibe?
*You can't answer this simple question? I suppose your mind is a blank today.*

**Mätzchen** machen (fam.): *to play about; to play the fool; to lark about (colloq.); to ass about (sl.).* Cf. auch: **Possen** reißen

Sitz' still auf deinem Stuhl und mach' nicht solche Mätzchen; sonst kippt der Stuhl um.
*Sit still on your chair and don't play (lark; ass) about (play the fool) like that, otherwise the chair will tip over.*

**mau** sein (fam.): cf. **mies** sein

das **Maul** nicht auftun (fam.): cf. den **Mund** nicht auftun

ein böses (loses) **Maul** haben (fam.): *to have a sharp (vitriolic) tongue*

Diese Frau hat ein böses (loses) Maul (einen losen Mund; eine freche Klappe; eine böse [lose; scharfe; spitze] Zunge). Für niemanden hat sie ein gutes Wort.
*That woman has a sharp (vitriolic) tongue. She has not got a good word for anybody.*

j.em das **Maul** stopfen (fig. u. fam.): *to cut s. b. short; to silence (to muzzle) s. b.; to shut s. b. up (sl.)*

Als der Kerl frech zu mir wurde, habe ich ihm das Maul (den Mund; den Schnabel) gestopft (verboten; bin ich ihm über den Mund gefahren) und (habe ihm) mit einer Anzeige wegen Beleidigung gedroht.
*When the fellow became impertinent to me, I cut him short (silenced [muzzled] him; shut him up) and threatened to report him for insulting behaviour.*

sich das **Maul** verbrennen (fig. u. fam.): cf. sich den **Mund** verbrennen

ein schiefes **Maul** ziehen **(maulen)** (fam.): cf. ein schiefes **Gesicht** machen

**Maulaffen** feilhalten (fam.): *to stand there gaping (goggling); to stand there with one's mouth open; to stand and stare.* Cf. auch: j.en **anglotzen**

Mach' dich an deine Arbeit und halte nicht Maulaffen feil (gucke nicht Löcher in die Luft; stiere nicht Löcher in die Wand).
*Get on with your work and don't stand there gaping (goggling; with your mouth open; stand and stare).*

ein **Maulheld** sein (fam.): *to be a braggart (a big talker); to be a swank (colloq.); to talk big (colloq.); to have a loud mouth (colloq.).* Cf. auch: den **Mund** vollnehmen; **angeben**

Seinen Worten folgen keine Taten. Er ist ein bloßer Maulheld (Prahlhans; ein bloßes Großmaul).
*His words are not followed by deeds. He is just a braggart (big talker; He just talks big; just has a loud mouth).*

ein böses (loses) **Maulwerk** haben (fam.): cf. ein böses (loses) **Maul** haben

Davon beißt keine **Maus** einen Faden ab (fig.): *There's nothing you can say about that; You can't get away from that (colloq.)*

Es besteht kein Zweifel, daß er daran schuld ist. Davon beißt keine Maus einen Faden ab.
*There is no doubt that it is his fault. There's nothing you can say about that (You can't get away from that).*

Das trägt die **Maus** auf dem Schwanze weg (fig.): cf. Das trägt die **Katze** auf dem Schwanze weg

**mäuschenstill** sein: a) (von Menschen) *to be as quiet as a mouse;* b) (unpers.) *to be so quiet that one can hear a pin drop (that one can hear one's heart beat)*

a) Ihr müßt (mucks)mäuschenstill sein, wenn ich euch eine Geschichte erzählen soll.
b) Es war (mucks)mäuschenstill in dem Konzertsaal (Man hätte in ... eine Stecknadel zur Erde fallen hören).
*a) You must be as quiet as mice if you want me to tell you a story.*
*b) It was so quiet in the concert-hall that one could have heard a pin drop (could hear one's heart beat).*

sich in ein **Mauseloch** verkriechen (mögen): *to like the ground to (open and) swallow one up; to like to crawl into a corner; to like to hide in a corner; to wish that the heavens would fall*

Sie hätte sich vor Scham am liebsten in ein Mauseloch verkrochen ([verkriechen mögen]; Sie hätte vor ... gewünscht, daß sie die Erde [der Erdboden] verschlingen möchte; Sie wäre vor ... in den Erdboden versunken [Sie hätte vor ...versinken mögen]).
*She would have liked the ground to (open and) swallow her up for shame (She would have liked to crawl into [to hide in] a corner for shame; She wished that the heavens would fall for shame).*

**mausetot** sein: *to be as dead as a door-nail (as mutton); to be stone-dead*

Ich schoß, und der Habicht fiel mausetot zu Boden.
*I fired, and the hawk fell to the ground, as dead as a door-nail (as mutton; stone-dead).*

sich **mausig** machen (fam.): *to preen o.s.; to give o.s. airs; to crow (colloq.).* Cf. auch: **angeben;** sich spreizen wie ein **Truthahn**

Hans hat keinen Grund, sich wegen seiner guten Übersetzung mausig zu machen, da sein Vater ihm dabei (bei ihr) geholfen hat.
*Jack has no reason to preen himself on (to give himself airs [to crow] about) his good translation, because his father helped him with it.*

ein **Meckerer** sein (fam.): *to be a fault-finder (a grouser); to be a nagger (colloq.); to be a drip (sl.)*

Er ist kein Kritiker, sondern ein kleinlicher Meckerer (Kritikaster; Nörgelfritze).
*He is not a critic but a petty fault-finder (grouser; nagger; a drip).*

über etwas **meckern** (fam.): *to find fault with s.th.; to grouse (to carp) at s.th.; to nag about s.th. (colloq.); to drip (to beef) at s.th. (sl.)*

Fritz meckert ständig über das (mäkelt ständig an dem), was andere tun.
*Fred is always finding fault with (grousing [carping; dripping; beefing] at; nagging about) what others do.*

schlafen wie ein **Mehlsack:** cf. schlafen wie ein **Murmeltier**

nach **mehr** schmecken: *to make one ask for (want) more; to whet one's appetite for more*

Dieser Kuchen ist ja wunderbar. Er schmeckt nach mehr.
*This cake is wonderful. It makes one ask for (want) more (whets one's appetite for more).*

**Meier** heißen (wollen), wenn ... (fam.): cf. sich **hängen** lassen a)

Das riecht man drei **Meilen** gegen den Wind (fam.): *You can smell it a mile off (colloq.)*

Du warst schon wieder an der Parfümflasche! Das riecht man ja drei Meilen gegen den Wind.
*You've been at the scent-bottle again. One can smell it a mile off.*

**meilenweit** von etwas entfernt sein (fig.): *to be miles away from s.th.*

Von wahrer Künstlerschaft ist dieser Maler meilenweit entfernt.
*This painter is miles away from being a real artist.*

**mein** und dein verwechseln (fig.): *to be a pilferer (a filcher); to mistake other people's property for one's own*

Die Polizei fand in der Wohnung des Arbeiters ein ganzes Lager gestohlener Waren vor. Jahrelang hatte er mein und dein verwechselt.

*In the workman's house the police found a whole store of stolen goods. He had been a pilferer (filcher; had mistaken other people's property for his own) for years.*

j.em die **Meinung** sagen: cf. j.en **abkanzeln**

seinen **Meister** finden (fig.): cf. seinen **Mann** finden

Es ist noch kein **Meister** vom Himmel gefallen (Sprichw.): *No-one is born a master*

Du mußt eifrig studieren, denn es ist noch kein Meister vom Himmel gefallen. *You must study hard; no-one is born a master.*

Übung macht den **Meister** (Sprichw.): *Practice makes perfect (prov.)*
Wenn du übst, wirst du dieses Klavierstück richtig spielen können. *If you practise, you will be able to play this piano-piece properly. Practice makes perfect.*

nichts zu **melden** haben (fig. u. fam.): *to count for nothing; to have no say (in things)*
Mein Bruder tut, als wenn er in seiner Firma eine wichtige Person sei, aber in Wirklichkeit hat er nichts zu melden (zu sagen). *My brother acts as if he were an important person in his firm, but in reality he counts for nothing (he has no say [in things]).*

eine **Memme** sein: cf. ein **Muttersöhnchen** sein

sich in alles (ein)**mengen**: cf. sich in alles (ein)**mischen**

**Mensch** (Meier)! (fam.): cf. in **Gottes** Namen!

nur (noch) ein halber **Mensch** sein (fig.): *not to be oneself; not to be up to the mark; to be only a shadow of one's former self*
Seit dem Tode ihres Töchterchens ist Anna nur (noch) ein halber Mensch (ein Schatten ihrer selbst). *Anna has not been herself (has not been up to the mark; has only been a shadow of her former self) since the death of her little daughter.*

unter die **Menschen** kommen: cf. unter die **Leute** kommen

Kein **Mensch** muß müssen: *There is no such thing (word) as must*
Ihr könnt ins Kino gehen, wenn Ihr wollt; ich bleibe zu Hause. Kein Mensch muß müssen. *You can go to the cinema if you want to; I shall stay at home. There is no such thing (word) as must.*

einen neuen **Menschen** anziehen: *to turn over a new leaf; to put on a new front*
Nach diesem Erlebnis hat er einen neuen Menschen (Adam) angezogen und ist jetzt die Freundlichkeit selber.

*He has turned over a new leaf (has put on a new front) since that experience and is now kindness itself.*

das **Menschenmögliche** tun: *to do all that is humanly possible; to do one's level best (one's utmost)*

Die Ärzte taten das Menschenmögliche, um der jungen Frau das Leben zu retten.
*The doctors did all that was humanly possible (their level best; their utmost) to save the young woman's life.*

keine **Menschenseele**: *not a (living) soul*

Es war schon spät, und wir trafen keine (Menschen)seele (keinen Schwanz; kein Schwein) mehr auf der Straße.
*It was very late and we did not meet a (living) soul in the street.*

**Menschenskind!** (fam.): cf. in **Gottes** Namen

**meschugge** sein (fam.): cf. nicht richtig im **Dachstübchen** sein

ein Kampf bis aufs **Messer**: cf. ein Kampf bis in den **Tod**

j.em das **Messer** an die Kehle setzen (fig.): cf. j.em die **Pistole** auf die Brust setzen

j.en ans **Messer** liefern: *to send (to lead) s. b. to his doom; to leave s. b. to his fate*

Der Mörder konnte nunmehr verhaftet und ans Messer geliefert werden.
*The murderer was then able to be arrested and sent (led) to his doom (left to his fate).*

Auf diesem **Messer** kann man nach Rom reiten: *This knife won't cut butter*

Hoffentlich kommt bald ein Scherenschleifer (Messerschleifer). Auf unsern Messern kann man nach Rom reiten.
*I hope a knife-grinder will come soon. Our knives won't cut butter.*

auf des **Messers** Schneide stehen (fig.): *to be on a razor's-edge; to be in the balance; to be touch-and-go; to be delicately (finely) poised*

Ein endgültiger Entschluß ist noch nicht gefaßt worden. Es steht alles noch auf des Messers Schneide.
*A final decision has not yet been made. Everything is still on a razor's-edge (in the balance; touch-and-go; delicately [finely] poised).*

**messerscharf** denken: *s. b.'s thoughts are clear-cut (are as sharp as a knife)*

Ein Gelehrter sollte messerscharf denken und folgern.
*A scholar's thoughts and conclusions should be clear-cut (as sharp as a knife).*

alt wie **Methusalem** sein: *to be as old as Methuselah (as Noah; as the hills)*

Dieser Rentner muß alt wie Methusalem (steinalt; uralt) sein (im biblischen Alter stehen).
*This pensioner must be as old as Methuselah (as Noah; as the hills).*

einen **Metzgersgang** tun (fig.): *to go on a fool's errand (on a wild goose chase)*

Das war mal wieder ein Metzgersgang. Ich habe niemanden zu Hause ange-troffen.
*That was another fool's errand (wild goose chase). I found nobody at home.*

der **Mief** (fam.): *the fug (colloq.)*

Ich riß die Fenster weit auf, weil ich den Mief in dem Zimmer nicht ertragen konnte.
*I threw the windows wide open because I could not bear the fug in the room.*

**Miene** machen (fig.): *to look like doing s. th.*

Die Kohlenpreise sind gestiegen, und die Eisenindustrie macht Miene, gleich-falls Preissteigerungen vorzunehmen.
*Coal prices have risen, and the iron and steel industry looks like making price-increases in its turn.*

gute **Miene** zum bösen Spiel machen (fig.): *to make the best of a bad job; to grin and bear it*

Zu spät merkte ich, daß mein Geld für die Reise nicht reichen würde, und ich mußte einfach gute Miene zum bösen Spiel machen.
*I noticed too late that my money would not suffice for the journey but I just had to make the best of a bad job (to grin and bear it).*

ohne eine **Miene** zu verziehen: *without turning a hair; without batting an eyelid; without moving a muscle*

Meine Schwester nahm die bittere Arznei, ohne eine Miene zu verziehen (ohne mit der Wimper zu zucken).
*My sister took the bitter medicine without turning a hair (batting an eyelid; moving a muscle).*

**mies** sein (fam.): *to be rotten (tough) (colloq.)*

Daß unser bester Spieler heute nicht mitspielen kann, ist mies (mau).
*It's rotten (tough) that our best player can't play today.*

ein **Miesepeter** sein (fam.): *to be a (an old) misery (colloq.); to be a drip (sl.)*

Mit diesem Miesepeter ist nichts anzufangen.
*You can't do anything with that (old) misery (with that drip).*

ein **Miesmacher** sein: *to be a prophet of gloom; to be an old misery (colloq.)*

Dein Onkel ist ein richtiger Miesmacher. Er ist mit nichts zufrieden.
*Your uncle is a real prophet of gloom (a real old misery). He is never satisfied with anything.*

eine Haut wie **Milch** und Blut haben: *to have a schoolgirl complexion; to have a skin (complexion) like satin (like velvet)*. Cf. auch: weich wie **Samt** sein

Dieses Mädchen hat schönes Haar und eine Haut wie Milch und Blut.
*This girl has beautiful hair and a schoolgirl complexion (a skin [complexion] like satin [velvet]).*

ein **Milchgesicht**: cf. ein **Grünschnabel**

**mimosenhaft** empfindlich sein: *to be as touchy as a gunpowder fuse; to be like a cat on hot bricks*
Deine Schwester ist sehr nervös und mimosenhaft empfindlich.
*Your sister is very nervous and as touchy as a gunpowder fuse (like a cat on hot bricks).*

alle **Minen** springen lassen (fig.): cf. alle **Hebel** in Bewegung setzen

in letzter **Minute**: cf. in zwölfter **Stunde**

Wie du **mir,** so ich dir (Sprichw.): *Tit for tat (prov.); Sauce for the goose is sauce for the gander (prov.).* Cf. auch: **Gleiches** mit Gleichem vergelten
Wenn du mich so behandelst, brauchst du dich nicht zu wundern, von mir auf ähnliche Weise behandelt zu werden. Wie du mir, so ich dir.
*If you treat me like that, you can't be surprised to be treated by me in a similar way. Tit for tat (Sauce for the goose is sauce for the gander).*

**mir** nichts dir nichts: *as bold as brass; as cool as a cucumber; just like that*
Was fällt dir denn ein? Du kannst doch nicht mir nichts dir nichts in unsern Garten kommen und mein Fahrrad nehmen.
*What do you think you're doing? You can't come into our garden as bold as brass (as cool as a cucumber; just like that) and take my bicycle.*

sich in alles (ein)**mischen**: *to meddle (to interfere) in everything; to stick (to poke) one's nose into everything (colloq.).* Cf. auch: ein neugieriger **Patron** sein; etwas **durchschnüffeln**
Karl will alles wissen und mischt (mengt) sich in alles ([ein]; steckt seine Nase in alles [in jeden Dreck]).
*Charles wants to know everything, and meddles (interferes) in (sticks [pokes] his nose into) everything.*

ein **Mischmasch** (fam.): *a jumble; a hotch-potch (colloq.)*
Du solltest lernen, klar und logisch zu denken. Dein Aufsatz ist ja der reinste Mischmasch (das reinste Sammelsurium).
*You ought to learn to think clearly and logically. Your essay is a proper jumble (hotch-potch).*

nicht auf j.es **Mist** gewachsen sein (fig. u. fam.): cf. nicht j.es **Hirn** entsprungen sein

**Mist** reden (fig. u. fam.): cf. **Quatsch** reden

**Mist** sein (fig. u. fam.): cf. **Krampf** sein

ein **Mistfink** sein (fam.): cf. ein **Schmierfink** sein

etwas **mitgehen** heißen (fig.): *to walk off with s. th.; to lift (to pinch) s. th. (colloq.); to knock s. th. off (sl.).* Cf. auch: **klauen**

Als ich im Restaurant meinen Mantel wieder anziehen wollte, entdeckte ich, daß ein anderer ihn hatte mitgehen heißen.
*When I wanted to put on my coat again in the restaurant, I discovered that someone else had walked off with it (had lifted [pinched] it; had knocked it off).*

ein **Mitgiftjäger**: *a fortune-hunter*

Daß dieser Mitgiftjäger ein reiches Mädchen heiraten würde, war vorauszusehen.
*It was to be foreseen that that fortune-hunter would marry a rich girl.*

nicht mehr lange **mitmachen** (fam.): cf. j.es **Lebenslicht** erlischt

j.en **mitnehmen** (fig.): *to leave s. b. like a limp rag (colloq.); to take it out of s. b. (colloq.); to knock s. b. up (sl.)*

Diese letzte Grippe hat mich sehr mitgenommen (geschlaucht).
*This last bout of influenza has left me like a limp rag (taken a lot out of me; knocked me up a lot).*

j.em übel **mitspielen** (fig.): *to be hard on s. b.; to deal s. b. a heavy blow; to take a heavy toll of s. b.*

Der Krieg hat auch der Zivilbevölkerung übel mitgespielt.
*The war was hard on (took a heavy toll of) the civilian population (dealt the civilian population a heavy blow) as well.*

Ab durch die **Mitte!** (fam.): *Be off (Away) with you!; Out you go!; Clear out!; Hop (Beat) it! (sl.).* Cf. auch: **abhauen**

Als der Lehrling erneut um Urlaub bat, erwiderte sein Meister barsch: Ab durch die Mitte!
*When the apprentice asked again for leave, his master retorted roughly: Be off (Away) with you! (Out you go!; Clear out!; Hop [Beat] it!)*

die goldene **Mitte (Mittelstraße**; der goldene **Mittelweg**): *the golden mean; the happy medium; the middle course*

Nicht zu viel und nicht zu wenig, sondern immer die goldene Mitte (Mittelstraße; den goldenen Mittelweg) wählen: das ist meine Absicht.
*Not too much and not too little, but always choose the golden mean (the happy medium; the middle course) – that is my aim.*

alle **Mittel** anwenden (gebrauchen): cf. alle **Hebel** in Bewegung setzen sich für j.en ins **Mittel** legen: cf. eine **Lanze** für j.en brechen (einlegen)

**Mittel** und Wege suchen: *to look for (to cast around for) ways and means*
Ich suche Mittel und Wege, um im Sommer nach Amerika zu fahren.
*I am looking (casting around) for ways and means of going to America in the summer.*

einen **Mohren** weißwaschen (fig.): *to wash a blackamoor white; to whitewash
a chimney*
Sie unterstützen diesen schlechten Menschen und loben ihn? Sie wollen doch
nicht einen Mohren weißwaschen?
*You support this bad person and praise him? Surely you don't want to wash a blackamoor
white (to whitewash a chimney)?*

schwarz wie ein **Mohr(enkind)** sein: *to be as black as pitch (as night; as a
nigger; as soot; as coal); to be pitch-black (jet-black)*
Fritz hatte im Schlamm gespielt und kam schwarz wie ein Mohr(enkind)
([Rabe; wie die Nacht]; kam [kohlpech]rabenschwarz; kam mit Dreck und
Speck) nach Hause.
*Fred had been playing in the mud and came home as black as pitch (night; a nigger; soot;
coal; came home pitch-black [jet-black]).*

den **Mond** anbellen (fig.): *to bark at the moon; to lash the waves; to beat the air.*
Cf. auch: gegen **Windmühlen** kämpfen
Als einfacher Arbeiter kannst du über die großen Industriellen schimpfen, wie
du willst. Du bellst ja doch nur den Mond an.
*As an ordinary worker, you can curse the great industrialists as you like. You are only
barking at the moon (lashing the waves; beating the air).*

nach dem **Monde** gehen (fig. u. fam.): *to go by fits and starts; to go in jerks*
Meine Uhr ist nicht zuverlässig. Sie geht nach dem Mond.
*My clock is not reliable. It goes by fits and starts (in jerks).*

in den **Mond** gucken (fig. u. fam.): cf. **leer** ausgehen

hinter dem **Mond** sein (leben) (fig. u. fam.): cf. auf dem **Mond** leben

auf dem **Mond** leben (fig. u. fam.): *to have been living on the moon (in a dream)*
Wenn du glaubst, du könntest für 500 Mark ein gutes Auto kaufen, so lebst du
auf (hinter) dem Mond (kommst du aus dem Mustopf).
*If you think you can buy a good car for 500 marks, you must have been living on the moon
(in a dream).*

j.em im **Mondschein** begegnen können (fig. u. fam.): cf. j.em den **Buckel**
herunterrutschen können; Scher' dich zum **Henker**!

**Moneten** haben (fam.): cf. (gut) bei **Kasse** sein; **Geld** wie Heu haben

sich ein **Monogramm** in den Bauch beißen (fam.): cf. vor **Wut** kochen blauen **Montag** machen (fam.): *to take the extra day off*

Da zwischen dem Sonntag und dem morgigen Feiertag nur ein Arbeitstag liegt, machen viele Arbeiter heute blauen Montag.

*As there is only one working-day between the Sunday and the holiday tomorrow, many workers are taking the extra day off today.*

**Moos** haben (fam.): cf. (gut) bei **Kasse** sein; **Geld** wie Heu haben

dick wie ein **Mops** sein (fam.): cf. **kugelrund** sein

sich freuen wie ein **Mops** (fam.): cf. sich **diebisch** freuen

**mopsen** (fam.): cf. **klauen**

sich **mopsen** (fam.): *to mope around (colloq.); to feel fed up (colloq.); to feel browned-off (cheesed-off) (sl.).* Cf. auch: sich zu **Tode** langweilen

Da wir in den Ferien nicht verreist sind, habe ich mich zu Hause sehr gemopst.

*As we did not go away in the holidays, I moped around (felt properly fed up [browned-off; cheesed-off]) at home.*

j.em eine **Moralpauke, -predigt** halten: cf. j.em eine **Standpauke** halten

**Mord** und Totschlag geben: *to be a set-to; to end in bloodshed; to be a carve-up (sl.).* Cf. auch: **handgreiflich** werden

In der politischen Kundgebung wurden einige Leute sehr aufgeregt, und es gab beinahe Mord und Totschlag.

*In the political meeting a few people became very excited, and there was almost a set-to (a carve-up; it almost ended in bloodshed).*

aus seinem Herzen keine **Mördergrube** machen (fig.): cf. aus seinem **Herzen** keine Mördergrube machen

eine **Mordsangst** haben (fam.): cf. eine **Heidenangst** haben

ein **Mordserfolg** sein (fam.): *to be a howling (raging) success (colloq.)*

Die Neuinszenierung des Theaterstückes war ein Mordserfolg.

*The new production of the play was a howling (raging) success.*

**mordshäßlich** sein: *to be as ugly as sin*

Else ist gut und freundlich, aber leider auch mordshäßlich (grundhäßlich; potthäßlich; häßlich wie die Nacht [Sünde]).

*Elsie is kind and friendly but unfortunately as ugly as sin as well.*

einen **Mordshunger (Mordsappetit)** haben: *to be as hungry as a hunter (as a wolf; as a horse; as a hawk)*

Ich habe einen Mordshunger (Mordsappetit; Bärenhunger; Heißhunger; Wolfshunger; bin hungrig wie ein Bär [Wolf]). Hoffentlich gibt es etwas Gutes zu essen.
*I'm as hungry as a hunter (wolf; horse; hawk). I hope there's something good to eat.*

ein **Mordskerl** sein (fam.): cf. ein **Allerweltskerl** sein

**mordslangweilig** sein: *to be deadly dull (as dull as ditch-water); to be a crashing bore (colloq.)*

Es wundert mich, daß du diesem Redner zuhören kannst. Ich finde ihn mordslangweilig (Er ist ein langweiliger Peter; ein Tränentier).
*I am surprised that you can listen to that speaker. I find him deadly dull (as dull as ditch-water; a crashing bore).*

sich einen **Mordsspaß (Mordsulk)** leisten: *to cut a proper caper (colloq.); to have a proper frolic (colloq.); to get up to a proper skylark (colloq.)*

Anläßlich seines Geburtstages haben wir uns einen Mordsspaß (Mordsulk; Hauptspaß) geleistet. Wir erschienen bei ihm in toller Verkleidung.
*On the occasion of his birthday we cut a proper caper (had a proper frolic; got up to a proper skylark). We appeared at his house in mad disguises.*

j.em (einen) **Mordsspaß** machen: *to make s.b. as pleased as Punch (as happy as a sandboy); to give s.b. a (real) kick (colloq.); to delight s.b. no end (colloq.)*

Der Besuch des Zoos hat mir (einen) Mordsspaß gemacht.
*The visit to the zoo made me as pleased as Punch (as happy as a sandboy; gave me a [real] kick; delighted me no end).*

**mordswütend** werden: *to see red; to raise Cain; to get into a towering rage; to blaze up; to go up in smoke (colloq.); to get into a wax (colloq.); to blow one's top (colloq.); to raise merry hell (sl.).* Cf. auch: aus der **Haut** fahren; in **Harnisch** geraten; vor **Wut** kochen

Als er mir sagte, er habe meine Uhr hinfallen lassen, wurde ich mordswütend (bitterböse).
*When he told me that he had dropped my watch, I saw red (raised Cain; got into a towering rage; blazed up; went up in smoke; got into a wax; blew my top; raised merry hell).*

**mordszäh** sein: cf. zäh wie **Leder** sein

j.en **Mores** lehren (fam.): cf. j.em (die) **Flötentöne** beibringen; j.en **abkanzeln**

**Morgenstunde** hat Gold im Munde (Sprichw.): cf. Morgenstunde hat **Gold** im Munde

eine (komische; seltsame) **Motte** sein (fig. u. fam.): cf. ein komischer **Kauz** sein

Ich denke, ich kriege die **Motten!** (fig. u. fam.): cf. Ich denke, mich laust der **Affe!**

aus der **Mottenkiste** stammen (fig. u. fam.): *to smell of moth-balls (colloq.)*

Der Film, den wir gestern gesehen haben, war sehr alt. Er stammt wohl aus der Mottenkiste.
*The film that we saw yesterday was very old. It smelt of moth-balls.*

aus einer **Mücke** einen Elefanten machen (fig.): *to make a mountain out of a mole-hill*

Warum übertreiben und aus einer Mücke einen Elefanten machen?
*Why exaggerate and make a mountain out of a mole-hill?*

seine **Mucken** haben (fam.): *to have one's moods; to be temperamental*

Mein Feuerzeug hat ewig seine Mucken und zwingt mich zur Benutzung von Streichhölzern.
*My lighter is always having its moods (is always temperamental) and forcing me to use matches.*

keinen **Mucks** sagen (fam.): *not to open one's mouth; not to make a squeak (colloq.)*

Normalerweise redet Heinrich sehr viel, aber heute sagt er keinen Mucks (nicht piep; schweigt er sich tot; läßt er keinen Ton verlauten).
*Normally Henry talks a great deal but today he won't open his mouth (make a squeak).*

**mucksmäuschenstill** sein (fam.): cf. **mäuschenstill** sein

mit **Mühe** und Not: cf. mit **Ach** und Krach

Gottes **Mühlen** mahlen langsam, mahlen aber trefflich fein (Sprichw.): *God's mills (The wheels of fate) grind slow but sure (prov.)*

Endlich sind nach vielen Monaten die Übeltäter verhaftet worden. Gottes Mühlen mahlen langsam, mahlen aber trefflich fein.
*At last, after many months, the miscreants have been arrested. God's mills (The wheels of fate) grind slow but sure.*

j.em wie ein **Mühl(en)rad** im Kopf herumgehen: *to buzz around in s.b.'s head; to pound through s.b.'s head; to turn over and over in s.b.'s head*

Diese beunruhigenden Gedanken gehen mir wie ein Mühl(en)rad im Kopf herum.
*These alarming thoughts are buzzing around in (pounding through; turning over and over in) my head.*

**Mumm** in den Knochen haben (fam.): *to have grit (colloq.); to have guts (sl.)*

Wer Polizist werden will, muß Mumm (Murr) in den Knochen haben.
*Anybody who wants to become a policeman must have grit (guts).*

nicht wagen, **mumm** zu sagen (fam.): cf. den **Mund** nicht auftun

**Mumpitz** reden (fam.): cf. **Quatsch** reden

sich etwas vom **Munde** absparen: *to go short of food; to go without food; to stint o.s. of food*

> Der arme Student mußte sich Geld vom Munde absparen, um sich die nötigen Lehrbücher zu kaufen.
> *The poor student had to go short of food (to go without food; to stint himself of food) in order to buy the necessary text-books.*

in aller (Leute) **Mund** sein (im Munde der Leute sein): a) *to be the talk of the town;* b) (nur von Sachen auch) *to be on everybody's lips (in everybody's mouth)*

> a) Durch ihr ausgelassenes Benehmen ist diese junge Schauspielerin in aller (Leute) Mund (im Munde der Leute; ins Gerede gekommen).
> b) Die Uraufführung dieses englischen Theaterstückes ist in aller (Leute) Mund (im Munde der Leute; bildet [ist] das Stadtgespräch).
> *a) By her abandoned behaviour this young actress has become the talk of the town.*
> *b) The premiere of that English play is the talk of the town (is on everybody's lips [in everybody's mouth]).*

den **Mund** auftun (fig.): *to speak up (for o.s.); to speak out*

> Du hättest den Mund auftun sollen, wenn du so dringend einen neuen Mantel nötig hattest.
> *You ought to have spoken up ([for yourself]; to have spoken out) if you needed a new coat so badly.*

den **Mund** nicht auftun (fig.): *not to say boo to a goose (colloq.)*

> Karl ist sehr scheu; er wagt nicht, den Mund (das Maul) aufzutun (mumm zu sagen).
> *Charles is very shy; he wouldn't say boo to a goose.*

kein Blatt vor den **Mund** nehmen (fig.): cf. kein **Blatt** vor den Mund nehmen

j.em über den **Mund** fahren (fig.): cf. j.em das **Maul** stopfen

sich Fransen an den **Mund** reden (fig. u. fam.): cf. sich den **Mund** fusselig reden

etwas im **Munde** führen: *to let s.th. pass (cross) one's lips; to let fall s.th.*

> Ich verbiete es euch, solche unanständigen Wörter im Munde zu führen (in den Mund zu nehmen; über die Lippen [Zunge] zu bringen).
> *I forbid you to let such indecent words pass (cross) your lips (to let fall such indecent words).*

sich den **Mund** fusselig reden (fig. u. fam.): *to talk o.s. blue in the face; to talk* *until one is blue in the face; to talk o.s. stupid (silly) (colloq.). Cf.* auch: j.em ein **Loch** (Löcher) in den Bauch reden

Ich habe mir den Mund fusselig (Fransen an den Mund) geredet, daß er sich bei dieser Kälte wärmer anziehen soll. Nun ist er erkältet und muß ins Bett.
*I talked myself blue in the face (talked until I was blue in the face; talked myself stupid [silly]) telling him to put on warmer clothes in this cold weather. Now he has a chill and has got to go to bed.*

nicht auf den **Mund** gefallen sein (fig.): *not (never) to be at a loss for an answer; to know all the answers; to have a ready tongue (in one's head); to be always ready with an answer; to give as good as one gets*

Der Redner war nicht auf den Mund (aufs Maul) gefallen (war schlagfertig). Auf jeden Zwischenruf aus der Versammlung wußte er sofort eine treffende Antwort.
*The speaker was not (never) at a loss for an answer (knew all the answers; had a ready tongue [in his head]; was always ready with an answer; gave as good as he got). For every interjection in the meeting he had a telling reply.*

den **Mund** halten: *to hold one's tongue (one's peace); to keep one's mouth shut; to keep one's trap (one's big mouth) shut (sl.); to shut (to dry) up (sl.)*

Du sollst den Mund (Schnabel) halten, wenn man nicht mit dir redet.
*Hold your tongue (peace; Keep your [big] mouth [your trap] shut; Shut [Dry] up) if you are not being spoken to.*

an j.es **Mund** hängen (fig.): cf. an j.es **Lippen** hängen

j.em etwas (Worte) in den **Mund** legen: a) *to put s.th. into s.b.'s head; to put s.b. up to s.th. (colloq.);* b) *to put words into s.b.'s mouth*

a) Auf eine solche Entschuldigung wäre er von sich aus nie gekommen. Ein anderer muß sie ihm in den Mund gelegt haben.
b) Ich habe es nicht gern, wenn man mir Worte in den Mund legt, die ich nie geäußert habe.
*a) He would never have thought of such an apology of his own accord. Somebody else must have put it into his head (put him up to it).*
*b) I do not like it when people put words into my mouth which I have never uttered.*

einen losen **Mund** haben: cf. ein loses **Maul** haben

**Mund** und Nase aufsperren: cf. mit offenem **Munde** dasitzen (dastehen)

etwas in den **Mund** nehmen (fig.): cf. etwas im **Munde** führen

mit offenem **Munde** dasitzen (dastehen): *to sit (to stand) open-mouthed; to sit (to stand) gaping*

Im Kasperletheater saßen alle Kinder mit offenem Munde da (sperrten alle Kinder Mund und Nase auf).

*At the Punch-and-Judy show all the children were sitting with open mouths (were sitting gaping).*

j.em nach dem **Munde** reden (fig.): *to talk up to s.b.*

Dieser Schmeichler redet den Leuten nur nach dem Munde.
*That flatterer only talks up to people.*

reinen **Mund** halten: *to keep s.th. quiet; to keep s.th. dark (colloq.); to keep s.th. under one's hat (up one's sleeve) (colloq.); to keep mum (colloq.)*

Was ich dir soeben anvertraut habe, muß geheim bleiben. Halte also bitte reinen Mund.
*What I have just confided to you must remain secret, so please keep it quiet (dark; under your hat; up your sleeve; keep mum).*

den **Mund** aufreißen wie ein Scheunentor: *to gape like a crater; to gape like a drain (sl.)*

Wenn er gähnt, reißt dieser schlecht erzogene Mensch den Mund (so weit) wie ein Scheunentor auf.
*When he yawns, that rude man gapes like a crater (drain).*

j.em den **Mund** stopfen (fig.): cf. j.em das **Maul** stopfen

j.em den **Mund** verbieten (fig.): cf. j.em das **Maul** stopfen

sich den **Mund** verbrennen (fig.): *to burn one's fingers; to get into hot water (colloq.).* Cf. auch: sich die **Finger** verbrennen

Laß die Nachbarn tun, was sie wollen. Wenn du etwas sagst, kannst du dir leicht den Mund (das Maul; den Schnabel; die Zunge) verbrennen.
*Let the neighbours do what they like. If you say anything, you may easily burn your fingers (get into hot water).*

den **Mund** vollnehmen (fig.): *to brag; to talk big (colloq.); to shoot a line (sl.).* Cf. auch: ein **Maulheld** sein; **angeben**

Nimm nur nicht den Mund so voll. Was du da vorhast, geht entschieden über deine Kräfte.
*Don't brag (talk so big; shoot such a line). What you intend to do is definitely beyond your powers.*

mit dem **Munde** vorneweg sein (fam.): *to put one's spoke (one's oar) in (colloq.)*

Kinder sollten warten, bis sie gefragt werden, und nicht immer mit dem Munde vorneweg sein.
*Children ought to wait until they are asked, and not always put their spoke (oar) in.*

j.em den **Mund** wässerig machen (fig.): *to make s.b.'s mouth water; to whet s.b.'s appetite*

Mit seinen Schilderungen von England hat uns mein Freund den Mund wässerig gemacht. Nächstes Jahr werden wir auch hinfahren.
*My friend made our mouths water (whetted our appetite) with his descriptions of England. Next year we shall go there too.*

j.em die Worte im **Munde** (her)umdrehen (fig.): cf. j.em die **Worte** im Munde (her)umdrehen

j.em das Wort aus dem **Munde** nehmen (fig.): cf. j.em das **Wort** aus dem Munde nehmen

**mundfaul** sein: *to be tongue-tied*

Unser Lehrer kann es nicht vertragen, wenn wir mundfaul sind und nur mit ja oder nein antworten.
*Our master cannot stand it when we are tongue-tied and only answer yes or no.*

j.em etwas **mundgerecht** machen (fig.): *to talk s.b. into s.th.; to make s.th. palatable (attractive) to s.b.*

Ich habe nur deshalb so gehandelt, weil er mir den Gedanken (daran) mundgerecht (schmackhaft) gemacht hatte.
*I only acted like that because he had talked me into the idea (had made the idea palatable [attractive] to me).*

j.en (etwas) **mundtot** machen: *to silence s.b. (s.th.); to stifle s.b. (s.th.); to squash s.b. (s.th.) (colloq.); to gag s.b. (colloq.)*

Es ist der Regierung nicht gelungen, die Gegner dieses neuen Gesetzes mundtot zu machen.
*The government has not succeeded in silencing (stifling; squashing; gagging) the opponents of this new law.*

ein böses (loses) **Mundwerk** haben (fam.): cf. ein böses (loses) **Maul** haben

ein gutes (geöltes) **Mundwerk** haben (fam.): *to have a good flow of words; to have a glib tongue; to have the gift of the gab (colloq.).* Cf. auch: nicht auf den **Mund** gefallen sein

Die Verkäufer auf dem Jahrmarkt müssen ein gutes (geöltes) Mundwerk haben, wenn sie ihre Waren verkaufen wollen.
*The traders at the fair have to have a good flow of words (a glib tongue; the gift of the gab) if they want to sell their wares.*

etwas für bare **Münze** nehmen (fig.): *to take s.th. at its face value; to take s.th. as it stands.* Cf. auch: etwas für's **Evangelium** nehmen

Es ist vielleicht ein Fehler von mir, daß ich alles, was ein anderer sagt, für bare Münze nehme.
*It is perhaps a mistake of mine to take at its face value (as it stands) everything that somebody else says.*

j.em etwas mit gleicher **Münze** heimzahlen (fig.): cf. **Gleiches** mit Gleichem vergelten

mit klingender **Münze** bezahlen: *to pay on the nail (on the dot)*

Wir pflegen, mit klingender Münze zu bezahlen, weil wir keine Schulden machen wollen.
*We are accustomed to pay on the nail (on the dot) because we do not want to get into debt.*

**murksen** (fam.): *to muck (to mess) about (sl.)*

Du murkst schon seit einer Stunde an deinen Rechenaufgaben (herum). Sie sind doch ganz einfach.
*You have been mucking (messing) about with your sums for an hour. They're really quite simple.*

schlafen wie ein **Murmeltier**: *to sleep like a log (a top; a dormouse)*

Wir wollen ihn nicht wecken, da er wie ein Murmeltier (Klotz; Ratz; [Mehl]sack) schläft.
*We won't wake him, because he is sleeping like a log (top; dormouse).*

**Murr** in den Knochen haben (fam.): cf. **Mumm** in den Knochen haben

j.en ins **Mus** hacken (fig. u. fam.): cf. **Hackfleisch** aus j.em machen

j.en zu **Mus** quetschen (fig. u. fam.): *to squash s.b. to a jelly; to squeeze the breath (the life) out of s.b.*

Bei (In) der Ausstellung herrscht ein so großes Gedränge, daß man fast zu Mus gequetscht wird.
*There is such a great crowd at the exhibition that one is almost squashed to a jelly (almost has the breath [life] squeezed out of one).*

aus dem **Mustopf** kommen (fig. u. fam.): cf. auf dem **Monde** leben

**Müßiggang** ist aller Laster Anfang (Sprichw.): *Idleness (only) breeds evil (vice)*

Du solltest etwas Nützliches in deiner Freizeit tun. Müßiggang ist aller Laster Anfang.
*You ought to do something useful in your spare time. Idleness (only) breeds evil (vice).*

nach berühmtem **Muster**: *in my (your etc.) usual way; as usual*

Wir wollten am Abend musizieren, aber Heinrich hatte nach berühmtem Muster die Noten vergessen.
*In the evening we wanted to play something, but Henry, in his usual way, had forgotten the music (Henry had forgotten the music as usual).*

an j.em sein **Mütchen** kühlen: *to vent (to work off) one's rage on s.b.; to take it out of s.b. (sl.).* Cf. auch: der **Blitzableiter** sein

Auch wenn du dich über irgendjemanden geärgert hast, ist es nicht recht, daß du dein Mütchen an mir kühlen (deine Wut . . . auslassen) willst.
*Even if you are annoyed at somebody, it isn't right for you to want to vent (to work off) your rage on me (to take it out of me).*

Dem **Mutigen** gehört die Welt (Sprichw.): *Fortune favours the brave (prov.)*

Wir bewundern deine Unternehmungslust und Kühnheit. Dem Mutigen gehört die Welt.
*We admire your initiative and boldness. Fortune favours the brave.*

bei **Mutter** Grün schlafen: *to sleep in the open air; to sleep under the stars (the sky); to sleep next to Mother Nature*

Die Hotels waren alle besetzt, und wir mußten bei Mutter Grün schlafen.
*The hotels were all full, and we had to sleep in the open air (under the stars [sky]; next to Mother Nature).*

Vorsicht ist die **Mutter** der Weisheit (Sprichw.): *Discretion is the better part of valour (prov.)*

Bei diesen glatten Straßen fahre ich lieber etwas langsamer. Vorsicht ist die Mutter der Weisheit.
*With these slippery roads I prefer to drive rather more slowly. Discretion is the better part of valour.*

ein **Mutterkind** sein (fig.): cf. ein **Muttersöhnchen** sein

etwas mit der **Muttermilch** einsaugen (fig.): *to have s. th. in the cradle*

Seine Liebe zur Musik hat dieser bekannte Pianist bereits mit der Muttermilch eingesogen.
*That famous pianist already had his love of music in the cradle.*

**mutterseelenallein** sein: *to be all by o. s. (all alone); to be on one's Jack Jones (sl.)*

Unser Onkel hat Tage, wo er mutterseelenallein sein will.
*Our uncle has days when he wants to be all by himself (all alone; on his Jack Jones).*

ein **Muttersöhnchen** sein (fig.): *to be tied to one's mother's apron-strings (colloq.); to be a molly-coddle (a milksop) (colloq.); to be a sissy (sl.)*

Franz wurde von seinen Klassenkameraden ausgelacht, weil er ein Muttersöhnchen (Mutterkind; eine Flasche [Memme]; ein Schlappschwanz [Waschlappen]) war (an Mutters Schürzenband hing) und nicht mit ihnen spielen wollte.
*Frank was laughed at by his classmates because he was tied to his mother's apron-strings (was a molly-coddle; milksop; sissy) and would not play with them.*

einen üblen **Nachgeschmack** hinterlassen (fig.): *to leave a nasty taste in one's mouth*

> Sein schlechtes Benehmen verdarb unsern ganzen Abend und hinterließ einen üblen Nachgeschmack.
> *His bad behaviour spoiled our whole evening and left a nasty taste in our mouths.*

etwas **nachkäuen** (fam.): *to churn out s. th. (colloq.); to dish out (to dish up) s. th. (sl.).* Cf. auch: aufgewärmter **Kohl**

> Dieser Journalist ist kein origineller Geist. Er käut nur nach, was andere schon vor ihm gesagt haben.
> *That journalist is not an original mind. He only churns out (dishes out [up]) what others have already said before him.*

das **Nachsehen** haben: *only to be able to look on; only to be able to stand and watch; to be left out in the cold (colloq.)*

> Ernst hat den Preis gewonnen, und seine Kameraden haben das Nachsehen (Zugucken).
> *Ernest has won the prize, and his companions can only look on (stand and watch; are left out in the cold).*

j.em **nachsteigen** (fig. u. fam.): *to chase s. b. (colloq.); to be after s. b. (colloq.); to have one's eye on s. b. (colloq.).* Cf. auch: ein **Auge** auf j.en werfen

> Dein Bruder steigt meiner Schwester nach, wie ich höre.
> *Your brother is chasing (is after; has his eye on) my sister, I hear.*

j.em **Nacht** vor den Augen werden: cf. j.em schwarz vor den **Augen** werden

über **Nacht:** cf. mit éinem **Schlage**

über **Nacht** erscheinen: *to appear (to shoot up) overnight.* Cf. auch: wie (die) **Pilze** aus der Erde schießen

> Dieses neue Geschäft ist einfach über Nacht erschienen.
> *This new shop has simply appeared (shot up) overnight.*

Dann gute **Nacht!** (fig. u. fam.): *Then it's all up (all over) (colloq.); Then we shall have to shut up shop (colloq.)*

> Wenn wir unsere Konkurrenten nicht bald ausschalten können, dann gute Nacht!
> *If we cannot soon eliminate our competitors, then it's all up (over; we shall have to shut up shop).*

häßlich wie die **Nacht** sein: cf. **mordshäßlich** sein

bei **Nacht** und Nebel: *at dead of night; in the middle of the night; in the small hours*

Nach diesem Skandal hat der Bankier die Stadt bei Nacht und Nebel verlassen.
*After this scandal the banker left the town at dead of night (in the middle of the night; in the small hours).*

sich die **Nacht** um die Ohren schlagen (fig.): cf. die **Nacht** zum Tage machen

eine **Nacht** über etwas schlafen: *to sleep on s. th.*

Ich möchte (mich) lieber nicht jetzt entscheiden, sondern über der Sache eine Nacht schlafen (die Sache beschlafen).
*I do not want to decide now but would rather sleep on the matter.*

schwarz wie die **Nacht**: cf. schwarz wie ein **Mohr(enkind)** sein

die **Nacht** zum Tage machen: *to turn night into day*

Ich gehe lieber um 11 Uhr zu Bett. Ich will die Nacht nicht zum Tage machen (will mir nicht die Nacht um die Ohren schlagen; will kein Nachtschwärmer sein).
*I prefer to go to bed at eleven o'clock. I don't want to turn night into day.*

aussehen wie eine **Nachteule** (fam.): cf. wie eine **Vogelscheuche** aussehen

eine **Nachteule** sein (fig.): *to be a night-bird (a nocturnal animal) (colloq.)*

Dieser Gelehrte arbeitet bis tief in die Nacht hinein; er ist eine wahre Nachteule.
*That scholar works well on into the night; he is a real night-bird (nocturnal animal).*

singen wie eine **Nachtigall**: *to sing like a nightingale (a lark)*

Else hat eine schöne Stimme. Sie singt wie eine Nachtigall.
*Elsie has a lovely voice. She sings like a nightingale (lark).*

**Nachtigall,** ich hör' dir trapsen! (fig. u. fam.): *Aha, I know what this is about! (colloq.)*

Da ich weiß, daß mein Nachbar nur zu mir kommt, wenn er Geld haben will, sagte ich mir bei seinem Erscheinen: Nachtigall, ich hör' dir trapsen!
*As I know that my neighbour only comes to me when he wants money, I said to myself when he appeared: Aha, I know what this is about!*

ein **Nachtschwärmer** sein (fig.): cf. die **Nacht** zum Tage machen

**nachzotteln** (fam.): *to dawdle (to drag; to trail) along*

Wenn unsere Familie spazierengeht, zottelt mein jüngster Bruder immer hinter uns nach (drein).
*When our family goes for a walk, my youngest brother always dawdles (drags; trails) along behind us.*

j.em den **Nacken** beugen (fig.): *to subjugate s.b.; to keep s.b. in shackles (in subjugation); to bend s.b. to one's will.* Cf. auch: j.en in die **Knie** zwingen

Ein Diktator versteht es, seinen Gegnern den Nacken zu beugen (seine Gegner kleinzukriegen).
*A dictator knows how to subjugate his enemies (to keep his enemies in shackles [in subjugation]; to bend his enemies to his will).*

j.em im **Nacken** sitzen (fig.): *to stand over s.b.; to prod s.b. (colloq.); to ginger s.b. up (sl.)*

Unser Gärtner arbeitet sehr langsam. Ich muß ihm ständig im Nacken sitzen (muß ständig hinter ihm hersein), damit seine Arbeit vorangeht.
*Our gardener works very slowly. I continually have to stand over him (prod him; ginger him up) to make him get on with his work.*

j.em den **Nacken** steifen (fig.): cf. j.em den **Rücken** stärken

den **Nacken** steifhalten (fig.): *to keep a stiff upper lip; to keep one's pecker up (colloq.)*

Halte den Nacken (die Ohren) steif und laß dich von ihm nicht einschüchtern!
*Keep a stiff upper lip (Keep your pecker up) and do not be intimidated by him.*

der Tod sitzt j.em im **Nacken** (fig.): *Death is just round the corner; Death threatens s.b.'s every step*

Die Arbeiter in einer Dynamitfabrik haben einen gefährlichen Beruf. Der Tod sitzt ihnen ewig (ständig) im Nacken.
*Workers in a dynamite factory have a dangerous occupation. Death is just round the corner (Death threatens their every step).*

**Nackenschläge** bekommen (fig.): *to suffer a reverse (a setback; a series of reverses [blows]).* Cf. auch: an **Boden** verlieren

Bei den letzten Wahlen hat unsere Partei heftige Nackenschläge bekommen (Rückschläge erlitten).
*Our party suffered a serious reverse (setback; series of reverses [blows]) at the last election.*

**nackte** Tatsachen: *bare facts*

Das sind die nackten Tatsachen. Deren Interpretation muß ich Ihnen überlassen.
*Those are the bare facts. Their interpretation I must leave to you.*

ein **Nacktfrosch (Nackedei)** sein (fam.): cf. **splitternackt** sein

Keine **Nadel** konnte zur Erde fallen: cf. gedrängt wie die **Heringe** sitzen

wie auf **Nadeln** sitzen: cf. wie auf (heißen; glühenden) **Kohlen** sitzen

wie eine **Nadel** suchen: cf. wie eine **Stecknadel** suchen gegen j.en **Nadelstiche** austeilen (fig.): *to make pin-pricks (digs) at s.b.; to dig one's claws into s.b. (colloq.)*

Tante Emma ist eine gehässige Person. Sie teilt gegen jedermann Nadelstiche aus.
*Aunt Emma is a spiteful person. She makes pin-pricks (digs) at (digs her claws into) everybody.*

einen Beruf an den **Nagel** hängen (fig.): *to throw (give) up a profession*

Aus gesundheitlichen Gründen mußte mein Vater seinen Beruf an den Nagel hängen.
*For reasons of health my father had to throw (give) up his profession.*

etwas brennt j.em auf den **Nägeln** (fig.): *s.b. is itching (aching; burning) to deal with s.th.; s.th. is a burning issue to s.b.*

Dieses Problem brennt jedem politisch denkenden Menschen auf den Nägeln.
*Every politically-minded person is itching (aching; burning) to deal with this problem (This problem is a burning issue to every politically-minded person).*

den **Nagel** auf den Kopf treffen (fig.): *to hit the nail on the head; to strike home*

Seine Kritik an der neuen Oper hat den Nagel auf den Kopf getroffen.
*His criticism of the new opera has hit the nail on the head (has struck home).*

**Nägel** mit Köpfen machen (fig.): *to barb one's darts; to use live ammunition (colloq.)*

Unsere bisherigen Versuche waren zaghaft und sind gescheitert. Jetzt müssen wir Nägel mit Köpfen machen.
*Our earlier attempts were hesitant and failed. Now we must barb our darts (use live ammunition).*

sich etwas unter den **Nagel** reißen (fig. u. fam.): cf. **klauen**

ein **Nagel** zu j.es Sarge sein (fig.): *to be a nail in (to drive a [another] nail into) s.b.'s coffin*

Dieser Junge bringt mich mit seinen dummen Fragen in (zur) Verzweiflung. Er ist ein Nagel zu meinem Sarge.
*This boy drives me to desperation with his stupid questions. He is a nail in (is driving a [another] nail into) my coffin.*

**nagelneu** sein: *to be brand-new*

Mein Bruder sah in seinem (niegel)nagelneuen Anzug sehr flott aus.
*My brother looked very smart in his brand-new suit.*

j.em etwas **nahelegen** (fig.): *to urge s.b. to do s.th.; to bring s.th. home to s.b.; to impress s.th. on s.b.; to rub s.th. into s.b. (colloq.)*

Dem Minister wurde nahegelegt, von seinem Posten zurückzutreten.
*The minister was urged to resign (It was brought home to [impressed on; rubbed into] the minister that he should resign).*

aus dem **Nähkästchen** erzählen (plaudern) *(*fig.): *to indulge in tittle-tattle*

Wenn unsere Damen nachmittags zusammenkommen, erzählen (plaudern) sie gern aus dem Nähkästchen.
*When our ladies meet together in the afternoon, they like to indulge in tittle-tattle.*

aus den **Nähten** platzen: *to burst at the seams*

Du bist in letzter Zeit so dick geworden, daß deine Anzüge drohen, aus den Nähten zu platzen.
*You have become so fat recently that your suits are threatening to burst at the seams.*

Mein **Name** ist Hase (, ich weiß von nichts) (fam.): *How should I know ?; Search me ! (sl.)*

Wer hat denn meinen neuen Füllfederhalter mitgenommen? – Mein Name ist Hase (, ich weiß von nichts).
*Who's taken my new fountain-pen? – How should I know? (Search me!)*

sich einen **Namen** machen: *to make a name (reputation) for o.s.; to make one's mark*

Durch seine neuen Baumethoden hat sich dieser Architekt einen Namen gemacht.
*That architect has made a name (reputation) for himself (made his mark) with his new building methods.*

eine Sache beim rechten **Namen** nennen: cf. das **Kind** beim rechten Namen nennen

einen **Narren** an j.em (an etwas) gefressen haben (fam.): *to be mad about s.b. (s.th.); to be crazy about s.b. (s.th.) (sl.); to be sold (gone) on s.b. (s.th.) (sl.); to have fallen for s.b. (s.th.) (sl.); to have a crush on s.b. (s.th.) (sl.)*

Herr Müller hat einen Narren (Affen) an diesem Mädchen gefressen und will es zur Alleinerbin machen.
*Mr Müller is mad (crazy) about (sold [gone] on; has fallen for; has a crush on) this girl, and wants to make her his sole heir.*

j.en zum **Narren** haben (halten): cf. j.en zum **besten** haben

(Ein) **Narrenwitz** ist bald zu (hat bald ein) Ende (Sprichw.): *A fool's bolt is soon shot (prov.)*

Du brauchst dich über sein dummes Verhalten nicht aufzuregen. (Ein) Narrenwitz ist bald zu (hat bald ein) Ende.
*You don't need to worry about his stupid conduct. A fool's bolt is soon shot.*

eine **Naschkatze** (ein Naschkätzchen) sein: cf. ein **Leckermaul** sein

mit langer **Nase** abziehen (fig.): *to go away with a long face*

> Die Wohnung war schon vermietet, und wir mußten mit langer Nase abziehen.
> *The flat was already let, and we had to go away with long faces.*

es j.em an der **Nase (Nasenspitze)** ansehen: *to see it written all over s.b.'s face*

> Ich sah es meinem Bruder an der Nase (Nasenspitze) an, daß er uns beschwindelt hatte.
> *I saw it written all over my brother's face that he had swindled us.*

sich die **Nase** begießen (fam.): cf. (sich) einen hinter die **Binde** gießen

j.em etwas auf die **Nase** binden (fig. u. fam.): *to pour s.th. out to s.b.; to let on about s.th. to s.b. (colloq.); to spill the beans to s.b. (sl.)*

> Natürlich werde ich dieser schwatzhaften Person unser Geheimnis nicht auf die Nase binden.
> *Naturally I shall not pour out our secret (let on about our secret; spill the beans) to that talkative person.*

in der **Nase** bohren (fam.): cf. die **Daumen** drehen

seine **Nase** in die Bücher stecken (fig.): *to stick to one's books; to keep one's nose to the grindstone*

> Du solltest lieber deine Nase in die Bücher stecken als jeden Abend ins Kino (zu) gehen.
> *You ought rather to stick to your books (to keep your nose to the grindstone) than go to the cinema every evening.*

sich an seine eigene **Nase** fassen (packen) (fig.): *to remember the mote in one's own eye; to put one's own house in order first*

> Solche Fehler, wie sie in diesem Brief stehen, machst du auch. Faß (Pack') dich an deine eigene Nase (Kehr' vor deiner eigenen Tür)!
> *You, too, make the sort of mistakes that are in this letter. Remember the mote in your own eye (Put your own house in order first).*

eine feine (gute) **Nase** für etwas haben (fig.): *to have a flair (an instinct; an eye) for s.th.*

> Mancher Sammler hat eine feine (gute) Nase (einen feinen [guten] Riecher) für alte Briefmarken, die von großem Wert sind.
> *Certain collectors have a flair (an instinct; an eye) for old stamps which are of great value.*

j.em auf der **Nase** geschrieben stehen (fig.): cf. j.em auf der **Stirn** geschrieben stehen j.en vor die **Nase** gesetzt bekommen (fig.): *to have s.b. pushed in front of one; to have s.b. plonked in front of one (colloq.)*

Ich hatte Anspruch auf einen höheren Posten, aber jetzt habe ich jemanden anders vor die Nase gesetzt bekommen (hat man mir jemanden anders vor die Nase gesetzt).
*I was entitled to a higher position, but now I've had somebody else pushed (plonked) in front of me.*

j.en an der **Nase** herumführen (j.en **nasführen**) (fig.): *to lead s.b. by the nose; to lead s.b. up the garden path; to push (to kick) s.b. around (colloq.); to give s.b. the run-around (colloq.)*

Schon seit Jahren führt mich dieses Mädchen an der Nase herum (nasführt mich dieses Mädchen).
*This girl has been leading me by the nose (leading me up the garden path; pushing[kicking] me around; giving me the run-around) for years.*

j.em auf der **Nase** herumtanzen (fig.): *to make a fool of s.b.; to knead s.b. like dough; to dance on s.b.'s chest (colloq.)*

Dieser Mann erträgt alles. Du kannst ihm, wenn du willst, auf der Nase herumtanzen.
*That man tolerates everything. You can make a fool of him (knead him like dough; dance on his chest) if you want to.*

sich nicht auf der **Nase** herumtanzen lassen (fig.): *not to be made a fool of; not to stand (put up with) any nonsense (cheek).* Cf. auch: sich nicht an den **Wimpern** klimpern lassen

Passen Sie nur auf! Ich lasse mir nicht auf der Nase herumtanzen.
*Just you watch out. I'm not going to be made a fool of (not going to stand [put up with] any nonsense [cheek]).*

die **Nase** hochtragen (fig.): *to give o.s. (to put on) airs; to be stuck-up (colloq.); to stick one's nose in the air (colloq.).* Cf. auch: **hochnäsig** sein

Nach diesem Vorfall hat er wahrhaftig keinen Grund, die Nase hochzutragen.
*After this incident he really has no cause to give himself (to put on) airs (to be stuck-up; to stick his nose in the air).*

auf der **Nase** liegen (fig. u. fam.): *to be laid up; to be on one's back (colloq.)*

Karls Gesundheit ist nicht die beste. Er liegt oft auf der Nase.
*Charles' health is not of the best. He is often laid up (on his back).*

vor j.es **Nase** liegen: *to be under (in front of) s.b.'s nose*

Wir mußten lachen. Vater suchte seine Brille, und sie lag gerade vor seiner Nase.
*We had to laugh. Father was looking for his glasses, and they were right under (in front of) his nose.*

j.em eine lange **Nase** machen (fam.): *to cock a snook at s.b. (colloq.); to put one's fingers to one's nose at s.b. (colloq.)*

> Der ungezogene Junge machte dem Polizisten eine lange Nase und lief davon.
> *The rude boy cocked a snook (put his fingers to his nose) at the policeman and ran away.*

der **Nase** nachgehen: *to follow one's nose*

> Sie brauchen nur immer der Nase nachzugehen, wenn Sie zum Rathaus wollen.
> *You only need to follow your nose if you want to get to the town-hall.*

j.em etwas unter die **Nase** reiben (fig. u. fam.): cf. j.em etwas aufs **Butterbrot** schmieren

die richtige **Nase** für etwas haben (fig.): *s.b.'s instinct (intuition) is right; to scent what is going to happen; to diagnose s. th. correctly*

> Ihr werdet jetzt doch wohl einsehen, daß ich in dieser Angelegenheit die richtige Nase (den richtigen Riecher) gehabt habe.
> *Now I hope that you will see that my instinct (intuition) was right (that I scented what was going to happen) in this matter (that I diagnosed this matter correctly).*

über j.en (etwas) die **Nase** rümpfen: *to turn up one's nose at s.b. (s.th.); to stick one's nose in the air at s.b. (s.th.) (colloq.)*

> Viele ältere Leute rümpfen über die heutige Jugend die Nase.
> *Many older people turn up their noses (stick their noses in the air) at present-day youth.*

nicht weiter als seine **Nase** sehen (fig.): *not to see further than (the end of) one's nose*

> Er ist bestimmt nicht fähig, das Geschäft (weiter) zu entwickeln; denn er kann nicht weiter als seine Nase sehen.
> *He is definitely not capable of developing the business, because he cannot see further than (the end of) his nose.*

seine **Nase** in alles (hinein)stecken (fig.): cf. sich in alles (ein)**mischen**

j.em in der **Nase** stecken (fig. u. fam.): cf. auf etwas **erpicht** sein

j.en mit der **Nase** auf etwas stoßen (fig.): *to rub s.th. in (colloq.); to hammer (to din) s.th. in to s.b. (colloq.)*

> Er hätte die Schulden schon lange abzahlen sollen, aber ich mußte ihn mit der Nase (mit dem Kopf) darauf stoßen.
> *He ought to have paid off the debts long ago, but I had to rub it in (to hammer [din] it in to him).*

j.em die Tür vor der **Nase** zuschlagen: cf. j.em die **Tür** vor der Nase zuschlagen

die **Nase** (von etwas) (gestrichen) vollhaben (fig. u. fam.): cf. etwas bis **dahin** (stehen) haben

j.em vor der **Nase** wegfahren: *to drive off right in front of s.b. (before s.b.'s
very eyes)*

> Ich wollte eben in den Bus einsteigen, als er mir gerade vor der Nase wegfuhr.
> *I was just about to get into the bus when it drove off right in front of me (before my very
> eyes).*

j.em etwas aus der **Nase** ziehen (fig. u. fam.): cf. j.em etwas **abknöpfen**

alle **nas(e)lang** (fig. u. fam.): *time and again; time after time; times out of
number; all the confounded time (sl.)*

> Es ärgert mich, daß er mich alle nas(e)lang mit seinen dummen Fragen stört.
> *It annoys me that he worries me time and again (time after time; times out of number; all
> the confounded time) with his stupid questions.*

ein **Naseweis** sein (fam.): cf. ein **Grünschnabel** sein

bei j.em **nassauern** (fam.): *to sponge on s.b. (colloq.)*

> Wilhelm lädt sich oft bei uns zum Essen ein, da er gern nassauert.
> *William often invites himself to dinner with us, because he likes sponging.*

Das geht mir wider die **Natur**: cf. j.em gegen den **Strich** gehen

j.em zur zweiten **Natur** werden: *to become second nature (a matter of course) to
s.b.*

> Es ist mir zur zweiten Natur geworden, morgens früh aufzustehen.
> *It has become second nature (a matter of course) to me to get up early in the morning.*

in **Nebel** gehüllt sein (fig.): *to be shrouded in mist*

> Die Zukunft dieses Planes ist noch in Nebel gehüllt.
> *The future of this plan is still shrouded in mist.*

**nebenbeigehen** (fig. u. fam.): *to go astray; to stray (to waver) from the straight and
narrow path*

> Unser Nachbar ist seiner Frau nicht treu; er geht nebenbei (fremd).
> *Our neighbour is not faithful to his wife; he goes astray (strays [wavers] from the straight
> and narrow path).*

der **Neid** der Besitzlosen: *the envy of the have-nots; a case of sour grapes.* Cf.
auch: die **Trauben** hängen einem zu hoch

> Man behauptet, daß mein neues Haus zu klein sei. Es ist aber nur der Neid der
> Besitzlosen.
> *People claim that my new house is too small, but it is only the envy of the have-nots (only
> a case of sour grapes).*

vor **Neid** blaß werden (vor Neid bersten): *to go green (to burst) with envy;
to be eaten up (consumed) with envy*

Meine Kollegen wurden blaß (barsten; platzten; vergingen) vor Neid, als der
Chef meine Leistungen lobte.
*My colleagues went green (burst; were eaten up [consumed]) with envy when the boss
praised my achievements.*

Das muß ihm der **Neid** lassen: cf. Das muß man ihm **lassen**

ein **Neidhammel** sein (fig. u. fam.): *to be a dog in the manger; to be a kill-joy
(a spoilsport)*. Cf. auch: ein **Spielverderber** sein

Warum bist du so ein Neidhammel, bloß weil ich diese kleine Erbschaft gemacht habe?
*Why are you such a dog in the manger (kill-joy; spoilsport) just because I've come into
this little inheritance?*

den Becher bis zur **Neige** leeren (fig.): cf. den **Becher** bis zur Neige leeren

auf die (zur) **Neige** gehen: *to be getting (running) low; to go downhill; to give out*

Mehr Wein dürfen wir heute nicht trinken, da unser Vorrat auf die (zur) Neige geht.
*We must not drink any more wine today because our stock is getting (running) low (is
going downhill; is giving out).*

**Nepperei** sein (fam.): cf. **Halsabschneiderei** sein

j.em auf die **Nerven** gehen (fallen): *to get on s.b.'s nerves; to get s.b. down
(colloq.); to get under s.b.'s skin (colloq.); to give s.b. the needle (sl.)*. Cf. auch:
j.en bis aufs **Blut** peinigen

Der ewige Lärm in unserm Hause geht (fällt) mir allmählich auf die Nerven
(geht mir an [auf] die Nieren; fällt mir auf den Wecker).
*The eternal noise in our house is gradually getting on my nerves (getting me down; getting
under my skin; gives me the needle).*

Du hast (aber) **Nerven**! (fam.): *You've got a nerve! (colloq.); You're a cool one
(cool customer)! (colloq.)*. Cf. auch: (Aber) sonst geht's dir **gut**?

Meine wertvolle Geige soll ich dir schenken? Du hast (aber) Nerven!
*You want me to give you my precious violin? You've got a nerve (You're a cool one [cus-
tomer])!*

ein **Nervenbündel** sein (fig.): *to be a bundle of nerves; to be a nervous wreck*

Seit seinen Erlebnissen im Kriege ist mein Sohn ein wahres Nervenbündel.
*Since his experiences in the war my son has been a real bundle of nerves (a real nervous
wreck).*

eine **Nervensäge** sein (fig.): *to be a drag (a strain) on one's nerves; to be nerve-
racking*

Unsere alte Tante ist eine wahre Nervensäge für uns.
*Our old aunt is a real drag (strain) on our nerves (is terribly nerve-racking).*

sich in die **Nesseln** setzen (fig.): *to get into hot water; to get into a scrape (colloq.); to catch (to cop) a packet (sl.)*

Mit deiner unüberlegten Frage hast du dich (ordentlich) in die (Brenn-)Nesseln gesetzt (bist [hast] du ins Fettnäpfchen getreten; bist du [ordentlich] in die Patsche geraten; bist du in Teufels Küche gekommen).
*You've got into proper hot water (into a proper scrape; You've caught [copped] a proper packet) as a result of your rash question.*

sich sein (eigenes) **Nest** bauen (fig.): *to build o.s. a (little) nest*

Nach der Hochzeit wollen wir uns auf dem Lande unser (eigenes) Nest bauen.
*After the wedding we are going to build ourselves a (little) nest in the country.*

das eigene **Nest** beschmutzen (fig.): *to foul one's own nest*

Schäme dich, so von deinen Verwandten zu sprechen. Man beschmutzt doch nicht das eigene Nest.
*Shame on you for speaking about your relations like that! One doesn't foul one's own nest.*

das **Nest** leer finden (aufs leere Nest kommen) (fig.): *to find that the bird has flown.* Cf. auch: Der **Vogel** ist ausgeflogen

Die Polizei erschien zu spät und fand das Nest leer (kam aufs leere Nest).
*The police appeared too late and found that the bird had flown.*

Das sind ja **nette** Sachen! (fam. u. iron.): *I've been hearing some pretty things (stories)! (colloq.)*

Das sind ja nette Sachen, die ich da über dich höre.
*I've been hearing some pretty things (stories) about you!*

seine **Netze** überall auswerfen (fig.): *to cast one's net far and wide*

Er hat seine Netze überall ausgeworfen, um einen passenden Mann für seine Tochter zu finden.
*He has cast his net far and wide in order to find a suitable husband for his daughter.*

ins **Netz** gehen (fig.): cf. in die **Falle** gehen a)

auf **neunundneunzig** sein (fam.) cf. **geladen** sein

nach **nichts** aussehen: *to look as dull as ditch-water (colloq.); to look like nothing on earth (colloq.); to be no great shakes (colloq.); to be nothing to write home about (colloq.)*

Ihr Schaufenster sieht nach nichts aus. Sie sollten sich einen Fensterdekorateur nehmen.
*Your shop-window looks as dull as ditch-water (like nothing on earth; is no great shakes; is nothing to write home about). You ought to engage a window-dresser.*

376

für **nichts** und wieder nichts: *for no reason at all; with no cause whatever*

Dein Freund ist sehr zänkisch und fängt für nichts und wieder nichts Streit an.
*Your friend is very quarrelsome and starts arguments for no reason at all (with no cause whatever; to no purpose at all).*

Von **nichts** kommt nichts (Sprichw.): a) *You cannot build on air; You must have something to start with;* b) cf. Ohne **Fleiß** kein Preis

Seine Firma hat zu wenig Kapital, um sich zu vergrößern. Von nichts kommt nichts.
*His firm has too little capital to expand. You cannot build on air (You must have something to start with).*

vor dem **Nichts** stehen: *to be faced with ruin; ruin is staring s.b. in the face; to find o.s. standing on the edge of the cliff (the precipice)*

Er hatte alle seine Ersparnisse bereits ausgegeben, und als er nun auch noch seinen Posten verlor, stand er vor dem Nichts.
*He had already spent all his savings, and when he lost his job as well, he was faced with ruin (ruin was staring him in the face; he found himself standing on the edge of the cliff [precipice]).*

**Nichts** für ungut!: *No offence (meant)!; No harm meant!; No hard feelings!*

Ich habe nur meine persönliche Meinung geäußert. Nichts für ungut! Ich wollte Sie nicht kränken.
*I only expressed my personal opinion. No offence (meant; No harm meant; No hard feelings)! I did not want to hurt you.*

ein **Nichtsnutz** sein: *to be a good-for-nothing (a wastrel; a ne'er-do-well)*

Niemand kann begreifen, warum dieses Mädchen so einen Nichtsnutz (Schlot; Tunichtgut; Taugenichts) geheiratet hat.
*Nobody can understand why this girl has married such a good-for-nothing (wastrel; ne'er-do-well).*

ein **Nickerchen** machen (fam.): *to have (to take) a nap (forty winks); to have a snooze (doze) (colloq.)*

Nach dem Mittagessen machen viele alte Leute ein Nickerchen (legen sich . . . aufs Ohr).
*After lunch many old people have (take) a nap (forty winks; have a snooze [doze]).*

**nie** und nimmer(mehr): *never as long as I (you etc.) live; never in my (your etc.) life*

Nie und nimmer(mehr) werde ich mich mit so einem kleinen Gehalt begnügen.
*Never as long as I live (Never in my life) will I content myself with such a small salary.*

**niedergeschlagen** sein: *to be depressed; to be in the doldrums; to be down in the dumps (down in the mouth) (colloq.)*

Ernst hatte gerade erfahren, daß er die Prüfung nicht bestanden hatte, und war infolgedessen sehr niedergeschlagen.

*Ernest had just learned that he had not passed the examination, and he was consequently very depressed (very much in the doldrums [down in the dumps; down in the mouth]).*

etwas **niedriger** hängen (fig.): *to expose s.th.; to brand s.th.; to bring s.th. into the open; to hold s.th. up to public gaze.* Cf. auch: an den **Pranger** stellen

Eine so anstößige Gesinnung sollte niedriger gehängt werden.
*Such an objectionable attitude ought to be exposed (branded; brought into the open; held up to public gaze).*

**niegelnagelneu** sein: cf. **nagelneu** sein

j.em an (auf) die **Nieren** gehen: cf. j.en auf die **Nerven** gehen

was nicht **niet- und nagelfest** ist: *what is not nailed (screwed) down; what is not a fixture*

Die Einbrecher haben alles, was nicht niet- und nagelfest war, mitgenommen.
*The burglars have taken everything that was not nailed (screwed) down (that was not a fixture).*

am **Nimmermehrstag (Nimmerleinstag):** *on the Day of Judgement; when pigs fly (colloq.)*

Wie ich ihn kenne, wird er mir mein Geld erst am Nimmermehrstag (Nimmerleinstag) zurückgeben.
*If I know him, he'll give me back my money on the Day of Judgement (when pigs fly).*

ein **Nimmersatt** sein: cf. ein **Freßsack** sein

**noch und noch** haben: *to have plenty; to have heaps (lots and lots) (colloq.).* Cf. auch: in **Hülle** und Fülle

Die Ernte aus unserm Garten war sehr gut. Wir haben Obst und Gemüse noch und noch.
*Our garden crops were very good. We have plenty (heaps; lots and lots) of fruit and vegetables.*

ein **Nörgelfritz(e)** sein (fam.): cf. ein **Meckerer** sein

**Not** bricht Eisen (Sprichw.): cf. **Not** kennt kein Gebot

**Not** macht erfinderisch (Sprichw.): *Necessity is the mother of invention (prov.)*

Man weiß nie, was man leisten kann, bis man (zu etwas) gezwungen wird. Not macht erfinderisch.
*One never knows what one can do till one is forced. Necessity is the mother of invention.*

**Not** kennt kein Gebot (Sprichw.): *Needs must when the devil drives (prov.); Necessity knows no law (prov.)*

Man muß oft etwas tun, das einem unangenehm ist. Aber Not kennt kein Gebot (Not bricht Eisen).

*One often has to do something that is unpleasant for one. But needs must when the devil drives (necessity knows no law).*

mit knapper **Not**: cf. mit **Ach** und Krach

seine liebe **Not** haben: cf. alle **Hände** voll zu tun haben

Es ist **Not** am Mann: *people are in short supply; there is a dearth (shortage) of people*

Mit Lehrkräften ist zur Zeit Not am Mann, und viele alte (Lehrer) müssen wieder eingestellt werden.
*Teachers are in short supply (There is a dearth [shortage] of teachers) at the present time, and many old ones are having to be re-engaged.*

wenn **Not** am Mann ist: *if it comes (if the worst comes) to the worst; if it comes to the push; as a last resort*

Wenn Not am Mann ist, müssen auch hohe Beamte bei ganz alltäglichen Aufgaben mithelfen.
*If the worst comes to the worst (If it comes to the worst [the push]; As a last resort) even high civil servants must help with quite everyday jobs.*

In der **Not** frißt der Teufel Fliegen (Sprichw.): cf. In der Not frißt der **Teufel** Fliegen

in **Not** und Tod: *to the (bitter) end; in all weathers*

Die beiden Freunde standen in Not und Tod zusammen.
*The two friends stayed together to the (bitter) end (in all weathers).*

aus der **Not** eine Tugend machen: *to make a virtue out of necessity*

Unser Biervorrat reichte nicht aus. Wir mußten also aus der Not eine Tugend machen und setzten unsern Gästen unsern guten Wein vor.
*Our supply of beer did not go round, so we had to make a virtue out of necessity and serve our guests with our good wine.*

zur **Not**: cf. wenn alle **Stränge** reißen

nach **Noten** (fam.): cf. nach **Strich** und Faden

Du hast es **nötig,** ... (fam.): *to do s. th. is just what you need (colloq.); It's just like you to do s. th. (colloq.).* Cf. auch: Das sieht ihm **ähnlich!**

Herr Braun hat es gerade nötig, sich als den großen Spender aufzuspielen. Jeder weiß, daß er in Wirklichkeit sehr geizig ist.
*To play the great philanthropist is just what Mr Brown needs (It's just like Mr Brown to play ...). Everyone knows that in reality he is very mean.*

einen **Notpfennig** zurücklegen: cf. etwas auf die hohe **Kante** legen

im **Nu**: cf. im **Handumdrehen**

eine komische **Nudel** sein (fam.): cf. ein komischer **Kauz** sein

**null** und nichtig sein: *to be null and void*

> Durch die neue Gesetzgebung sind viele frühere Gesetze null und nichtig geworden.
> *As a result of the new legislation many old laws have become null and void.*

eine **Null** sein (fig.): *to be a nonentity; to be an also-ran (colloq.)*

> Wilhelm ist, verglichen mit seinem Schwager, völlig unbedeutend. Er ist (ihm gegenüber) eine Null (der reinste Waisenknabe).
> *William is completely insignificant compared with his brother-in-law. He is a nonentity (an also-ran).*

auf **Numero** Sicher gehen (fig.): *to play safe (for safety); to keep on the safe side; to cover one's tracks*

> Dein Freund ist sehr vorsichtig und wagt nicht viel. Er geht auf Numero Sicher.
> *Your friend is very cautious and does not risk much. He plays safe (for safety; keeps on the safe side; covers his tracks).*

eine große **Nummer** sein (fig. u. fam.): cf. eine große **Kanone** sein

eine gute **Nummer** bei j.em haben (fam.): cf. bei j.em gut **angeschrieben** sein

auf **Nummer** Sicher sein (fig.): cf. hinter **Schloß** und Riegel sitzen

**nun** und nimmermehr: cf. **nie** und nimmer(mehr)

eine harte **Nuß** sein (fig.): cf. eine schwierige **Kiste** sein

zu **Nutz** und Frommen . . .: *for the benefit of . . .; in the interests of*

> Zu Nutz und Frommen aller Ferienreisenden muß offen zugegeben werden, daß der Aufenthalt in diesem Land sehr teuer ist.
> *For the benefit (In the interests) of all holiday travellers it must be frankly admitted that it is very expensive to stay in this country.*


# O


Und **ob!** (fam.): *I should say! (sl.); Not half! (sl.); Rather! (sl.)*

> Hat es dir in Italien gefallen? – Und ob! (Und wie!)
> *Did you like it in Italy? – I should say! (Not half! Rather!)*

die **Oberhand** gewinnen (fig.): *to get the upper hand (whip-hand); to be top dog (colloq.)*

Wir sind gespannt, welche Partei bei den nächsten Wahlen die Oberhand gewinnen (Oberwasser bekommen) wird.
*We wonder which party will get the upper hand (whip-hand; will be top dog) at the next election.*

das **Oberste** zu unterst kehren: cf. alles auf den **Kopf** stellen

nicht richtig im **Oberstübchen** sein (fam.): cf. nicht richtig im **Dachstübchen** sein

**Oberwasser** haben (bekommen) (fig.): cf. die **Oberhand** gewinnen

ein **Ochse** sein (fig. u. fam.): cf. ein **Rindvieh** sein

dastehen wie der **Ochs(e)** vorm Berge: cf. dastehen wie die **Kuh** vorm Scheunentor

den **Ochsen** hinter den Pflug spannen (fig.): cf. das **Pferd** beim Schwanze aufzäumen

Der **Ochse** stößt sich nur einmal am Scheunentor (Sprichw.): cf. (Ein) gebranntes **Kind** scheut das Feuer

**ochsen** (fam.): cf. **büffeln**

**öde** werden (fig. u. fam.): cf. **mordswütend** werden

Jetzt ist der **Ofen** aus! (fig. u. fam.): *That's the end; I (You etc.) have had enough of it (colloq.); I (You etc.) am fed up with it (colloq.).* Cf. auch: Das ist doch die **Höhe**!

Du willst also schon wieder Geld von mir? Nein, jetzt ist der Ofen aus!
*So you want money from me again? No, that's the end (I've had enough of it; I'm fed up with it)!*

ein **Ofenhocker** sein: cf. ein **Stubenhocker** sein

**offen** und ehrlich sein: *to be open and above-board*

In allem, was er tut, ist dein Bruder offen und ehrlich.
*In everything he does your brother is open and above-board.*

in die **Öffentlichkeit** flüchten: *to rush into print*

Du mußt deiner Sache sicher sein, bevor du in die Öffentlichkeit flüchtest.
*You must be sure of your case before you rush into print.*

nicht **ohne** sein (fam.): a) (von Sachen) *to be to the point; to have something to be said for it; not to be sneezed (laughed) at (colloq.);* b) (von Menschen) *to be not so tame (harmless) as one looks; to be pretty hot (sl.)*

a) Sein neuer Vorschlag ist gar nicht so ohne.

b) Seine Schwester sieht schüchtern aus, ist aber in Wirklichkeit gar nicht so ohne.

a) *His new suggestion is very much to the point (has a great deal to be said for it; is not to be sneezed [laughed] at).*

b) *His sister looks shy, but in fact she's not as tame (harmless) as she looks (she's pretty hot).*

die **Ohren** aufmachen (fig.): cf. die **Ohren** spitzen

bis über die **Ohren** erröten: cf. **knallrot** werden

es faustdick hinter den **Ohren** haben (fig. u. fam.): cf. mit allen **Hunden** gehetzt sein

feine **Ohren** haben (fig.): *not to be hard of hearing; to be quick on the uptake; to have sharp ears*

Ich begriff natürlich sofort, wem der Vorwurf galt. Ich habe feine Ohren!
*I understood at once, of course, whom the rebuke was meant for. I'm not hard of hearing (I'm quick on the uptake; I've got sharp ears).*

ganz **Ohr** sein: *to be all ears*

Als mein Onkel zu erzählen begann, waren wir ganz Ohr.
*When my uncle began to tell a story, we were all ears.*

nur mit halbem **Ohr** zuhören: *to listen with half an ear; to half-listen*

Würden Sie die Frage bitte wiederholen? Ich habe nur mit halbem Ohr zugehört.
*Would you please repeat the question? I was only listening with half an ear (only half-listening).*

die **Ohren** hängen lassen (fig. u. fam.): *to look crestfallen (downcast); to look down in the mouth (colloq.); to look blue (colloq.)*

Über sein Mißgeschick ist Ernst niedergeschlagen und läßt die Ohren hängen.
*Ernest is depressed by his misfortune and looks crestfallen (downcast; down in the mouth; blue).*

j.en übers **Ohr** hauen (fig. u. fam.): cf. j.en auf den **Leim** führen (j.en leimen)

zum einen **Ohr** hinein- und zum anderen hinausgehen; *to go in at one ear and out at the other; to go straight through*

Kurt wird nie etwas lernen. Alles, was man ihm sagt, geht zum einen Ohr hinein und zum anderen hinaus.
*Curt will never learn anything. Everything one tells him goes in at one ear and out at the other (goes straight through).*

etwas noch in den **Ohren** haben (fig.): *s. th. is still ringing in s. b.'s ears*

Wir haben diese prahlerische Rede noch in den Ohren.
*That boastful speech is still ringing in our ears.*

j.em klingen die **Ohren**: *s. b.'s ears tingle (burn)*

Dir müssen gestern abend die Ohren ordentlich geklungen haben, da du im Mittelpunkt unserer Unterhaltung gestanden hast.
*Your ears must have been really tingling (burning) yesterday evening, for you were the centre of our conversation.*

j.em zu **Ohren** kommen: *to come to (to reach) s. b.'s ears; to come to s. b.'s hearing (s. b.'s notice); to hear something to the effect*

Uns ist zu Ohren gekommen, daß die Tagung auf Mittwoch verschoben werden soll.
*It has come to (reached) our ears (come to our hearing [notice]; We have heard something to the effect) that the meeting is to be postponed until Wednesday.*

sich hinter den **Ohren** kratzen: *to scratch one's head*

Der Schaffner konnte mir keine richtige Auskunft geben, sondern kratzte sich nur hinter den Ohren.
*The ticket-collector could not give me any proper information, and only scratched his head.*

sich aufs **Ohr** legen: cf. ein **Nickerchen** machen

j.em sein **Ohr** (ein williges Ohr) leihen (fig.): *to lend s. b. one's ear (a willing ear)*

Unser Arbeitgeber leiht den Sorgen seiner Angestellten sein Ohr (ein williges Ohr).
*Our employer lends his ear (a willing ear) to his employees' troubles.*

j.em in den **Ohren** liegen (fig.): *to nag at (to pester) s. b.; to clamour; to get at s. b. (colloq.)*

Ich habe jetzt ein Klavier gekauft. Monatelang lag mir die ganze Familie mit diesem Wunsch in den Ohren.
*I have now bought a piano. For months the whole family had been nagging at me (pestering me; getting at me; clamouring for me) to grant this request).*

j.em etwas links und rechts um die **Ohren** hauen (fam.): *to hit s. b. over the head with s. th.; to rub s. b.'s nose in s. th. (colloq.)*

Dieses beschmutzte Buch sollte ich dir eigentlich links und rechts um die Ohren hauen.
*I really ought to hit you over the head with (rub your nose in) this dirty book.*

sich die Nacht um die **Ohren** schlagen (fig.): cf. die **Nacht** zum Tage machen

tauben **Ohren** predigen (fig.): *to talk to deaf ears; to talk to a brick wall (to the wind) (colloq.)*

> Immer vergißt er, was ich ihm zu tun befehle. Ich predige einfach tauben Ohren (leeren Wänden).
> *He always forgets what I order him to do. I am simply talking to deaf ears (to a brick wall; to the wind).*

sich etwas hinter die **Ohren** schreiben (fig. u. fam.): cf. sich etwas hinter die **Löffel** schreiben

bis über die **Ohren** in Schulden stecken: *to be up to one's eyes in debt; to be heavily in the red*

> Der Besitzer dieser Fabrik steckt schon seit Ostern bis über die Ohren (bis über den Kopf; bis an den Hals) in Schulden (steht . . . tief in der Kreide; hat schon . . . Schulden wie ein Major; mehr Schulden als Haare auf dem Kopfe; ist schon . . . haushoch verschuldet; Dem Besitzer . . . steht . . . das Wasser bis an den Hals [bis an die Kehle]).
> *The owner of that factory has been up to his eyes in debt (heavily in the red) since Easter.*

die **Ohren** spitzen: *to prick up one's ears; to sit up and take notice*

> Als mein Sohn etwas von einem Fahrrad hörte, spitzte er die Ohren (machte er . . . auf).
> *When my son heard something about a bicycle, he pricked up his ears (sat up and took notice).*

die **Ohren** steifhalten (fig.): cf. den **Nacken** steifhalten

auf diesem **Ohre** taub sein (nicht hören) (fig.): *to be deaf in that ear; that is s.b.'s blind spot; to turn a deaf ear (a blind eye) to s. th.*

> Wir wollten einen Fernsehapparat haben, aber Vater ist auf diesem Ohre taub (hört nicht auf diesem Ohre [will auf diesem Ohre nicht hören]).
> *We wanted to have a television set, but father is deaf in that ear (but that is father's blind spot; but father has turned a deaf ear [a blind eye] to our request).*

noch nicht trocken hinter den **Ohren** sein (fig. u. fam.): cf. ein **Grünschnabel** sein

sich bis über die **Ohren** in j.en verlieben: *to fall head over heels in love with s.b.; to fall for s.b. (colloq.).* Cf. auch: in j.en **verschossen** sein

> Mein Freund hat sich bis über die Ohren in meine Schwester verliebt.
> *My friend has fallen head over heels in love with (has fallen for) my sister.*

viel um die **Ohren** haben (fig.): *to be up to one's eyes in work; to have a lot on one's plate (colloq.).* Cf. auch: alle **Hände** voll zu tun haben

Leider kann ich morgen nicht mitkommen, da ich im Augenblick viel um die Ohren habe.
*I am afraid that I cannot come with you tomorrow, because at the moment I am up to my eyes in work (have a lot on my plate).*

Wände haben **Ohren**: cf. **Wände** haben Ohren

j.em eine **Ohrfeige** geben: cf. j.em eine **kleben**

wie ein **Ohrwürmchen** sein: cf. um den kleinen **Finger** zu wickeln sein

**Öl** ins Feuer gießen (fig.): *to pour oil on (to add fuel to; to fan) the flames; to pour oil on the fire*

Die Frau versuchte, den Streit zwischen den beiden Männern zu beenden, aber in Wirklichkeit goß sie nur Öl ins Feuer.
*The woman tried to end the quarrel between the two men, but in fact she only poured oil on (added fuel to; fanned) the flames (poured oil on the fire).*

**Öl** auf die Wogen gießen (fig.): *to pour oil on (the) troubled waters*

Die Arbeiter waren über ihre niedrigen Löhne empört, aber das Versprechen einer Erhöhung im Herbst hat Öl auf die Wogen gegossen (hat die Wogen geglättet).
*The workers were indignant at their low wages, but the promise of a rise in the autumn poured oil on (the) troubled waters.*

aus **Olims** Zeiten sein (stammen): cf. **Anno** Tobak

der **Olymp** (im Theater): *the gods (colloq.)*

Da wir unsere Plätze nicht vorbestellt hatten, mußten wir auf dem Olymp sitzen.
*As we had not reserved our seats, we had to sit in the gods.*

j.em (einer Sache) zum **Opfer** fallen: *to fall victim to s.b. (s.th.)*

Seine ganze Familie ist der Grippeepidemie zum Opfer gefallen.
*His whole family has fallen victim to the influenza epidemic.*

fehl am **Ort** sein: cf. fehl am **Platze** sein

an **Ort** und Stelle: cf. auf der **Stelle**

an **Ort** und Stelle sein: *to be on the spot (on the scene)*

Fünf Minuten nach dem Unfall war die Polizei schon an Ort und Stelle.
*Five minutes after the accident the police were on the spot (scene).*

frech wie **Oskar** sein (fam.): cf. ein **Frechdachs** sein

# P

**Pack** (fam.): *rabble (colloq.); riff-raff (colloq.); ragtag and bobtail (colloq.); a mob (colloq.); a crew (colloq.)*

Mit solchem Pack (Gesindel) solltest du dich überhaupt nicht abgeben.
*You shouldn't concern yourself with such rabble (riff-raff; ragtag and bobtail; such a mob [crew]).*

sein **Päckchen** tragen (fig.): cf. sein **Kreuz** tragen (auf sich nehmen)

etwas **packen** (fam.): cf. etwas **schaffen**

j.en sich **packen** heißen (fam.): cf. j.em den **Laufpaß** geben

der **Packesel** sein (fig.): *to be a beast of burden*

Muß ich denn immer der Packesel (beladen wie ein Esel) sein und die Koffer tragen?
*Must I always be a beast of burden and carry the cases?*

au **pair**: cf. **schlicht** um schlicht

j.en auf die **Palme** bringen (fig. u. fam.): cf. j.en in **Harnisch** bringen

die **Palme** des Sieges erringen: cf. die **Siegespalme** erringen

etwas auf sein **Panier** schreiben (fig.): *to inscribe s.th. on one's banner (shield); to put s.th. out as one's motto*

Der fromme Wohltäter hat auf sein Panier geschrieben, allen Armen zu helfen.
*The pious philanthropist has inscribed it on his banner (shield; has put it out as his motto) that he will help all poor people.*

den **Pantoffel** schwingen (fig. u. fam.): cf. die **Hosen** anhaben

unter dem **Pantoffel** stehen (ein **Pantoffelheld** sein) (fam.): cf. ein **Ehekrüppel** sein

stur wie ein **Panzer** sein (fam.): *to hold on like grim death; to be as determined as a bulldog*

Wenn mein Freund sich etwas vorgenommen hat, läßt er sich durch nichts von seinem Ziel abbringen. Er ist stur wie ein Panzer.
*When my friend has decided on something, he lets nothing deter him from his purpose. He holds on like grim death (is as determined as a bulldog).*

ein **Papagei** sein (fig.): *to be a parrot; to be a copy-cat (colloq.)*

Johann hat keine eigene Meinung. Er ist nichts als (ist nur) ein Papagei.
*John has no opinion of his own. He is nothing but a parrot (copy-cat).*

etwas zu **Papier** bringen: *to get (to put) s.th. down in writing; to put (to get) s.th. on paper*

Es wäre besser gewesen, wenn der Redner seine Ansprache vollständig zu Papier gebracht hätte.
*It would have been better if the speaker had got (put) his talk down completely in writing (had put [got] his talk completely on paper).*

nur auf dem **Papier** stehen: *to exist only on paper*

Die neue Regierung hat alle Gesetze annulliert, die seit Jahren nicht mehr beachtet wurden und nur noch auf dem Papier standen.
*The new government has annulled all the laws which had not been observed for years and existed only on paper.*

nicht von **Pappe** sein (fig. u. fam.): a) *to be no rubbish (trash; cheap imitation) (colloq.); to be the real thing (colloq.); to be the real McCoy (sl.);* b) cf. sich **gewaschen** haben

Der Verlobungsring meiner Schwester ist nicht von Pappe.
*My sister's engagement ring is no rubbish (trash; cheap imitation; is the real thing; the real McCoy).*

**Pappelwasser** getrunken haben (fam.): cf. reden wie ein **Buch**

seine **Pappenheimer** kennen (fig.): *to know one's man (men); to know whom one is dealing with*

Nur diese beiden Jungen können einen solchen Unfug angerichtet haben. Ich kenne meine Pappenheimer.
*These are the only two boys who can have caused such mischief. I know my men (know whom I am dealing with).*

etwas für einen **Pappenstiel** kaufen (verkaufen) (fam.): cf. etwas für ein **Butterbrot** kaufen (verkaufen)

kein **Pappenstiel** sein (fam.): *to be quite a bit (colloq.); not to be chickenfeed (colloq.)*

3000 Mark hast du für dieses gebrauchte Auto bezahlt? Das ist doch wirklich kein Pappenstiel (Katzendreck).
*You paid 3000 marks for that second-hand car? That's certainly quite a bit (not chickenfeed).*

keinen **Pappenstiel** wert sein (fam.): cf. keinen (roten) **Heller** wert sein

päpstlicher als der **Papst** sein: *to be more royalist than the king*

Tu' nicht mehr, als die Vorschriften es verlangen. Du brauchst doch nicht päpstlicher zu sein als der Papst.
*Don't do any more than the regulations require. You don't need to be more royalist than the king.*

den **Papst** zum Vetter haben (fig.): *to be in with (to know) the right people; to have good contacts (connections)*

Karl erreicht alles, weil er den Papst zum Vetter hat.
*Charles gets everything because he is in with (knows) the right people (has good contacts [connections]).*

j.em in die **Parade** fahren (fig.): *to parry (to counter) the blow; to counter*

Als ich diese Äußerung tat, fuhr mir mein Bekannter in die Parade und behauptete das Gegenteil.
*When I made that remark, my friend parried (countered) the blow (countered) and declared the opposite.*

es mit beiden **Parteien** halten: *to run with the hare and hunt with the hounds; to have it both ways*

Wenn du zu mir halten willst, mußt du meinen Gegner aufgeben. Du kannst es nicht mit beiden Parteien halten.
*If you want to stay with me, you must give up my rival. You cannot run with the hare and hunt with the hounds (cannot have it both ways).*

die **Partie** aufgeben (fig.): cf. den **Kampf** aufgeben

sich wie ein **Pascha** fühlen: cf. sich wohlfühlen wie die **Made** im Speck

Da haben wir die **Pastete!** (fam.): cf. eine schöne (nette) **Bescherung** sein

ein frecher **Patron** sein: cf. ein **Frechdachs** sein

ein neugieriger **Patron** sein: *to be a Nosey Parker (a busy-body) (colloq.); to be nosey (colloq.).* Cf. auch: sich in alles (ein)**mischen**

Mein Vetter ist ein neugieriger Patron. Er will immer wissen, wo ich hingehe.
*My cousin is a Nosey Parker (busy-body; is nosey). He always wants to know where I am going.*

in die **Patsche** geraten (fig. u. fam.): cf. sich in die **Nesseln** setzen

j.em aus der **Patsche** helfen (fig. u. fam.): *to help s.b. out of a tight corner (spot; out of a hole)*

Durch (die) Sammlung eines namhaften Geldbetrages haben wir unserm Kollegen aus der Patsche geholfen.
*By collecting a considerable sum of money we helped our colleague out of a tight corner (spot; out of a hole).*

in der **Patsche** sitzen (stecken) (fig. u. fam.): cf. in der **Klemme** sein (sitzen)

**patschnaß** sein (fam.): cf. bis auf die **Haut** durchnäßt sein einen auf die **Pauke** hauen (fig. u. fam.): *to paint the town red (colloq.); to set the town alight (colloq.); to let it rip (sl.)*

Wenn wir unsere Gehaltsnachzahlung bekommen, wollen wir anständig einen auf die Pauke hauen.
*When we get our arrears of salary, we're really going to paint the town red (set the town alight; let it rip).*

mit **Pauken** und Trompeten (fig.): *resoundingly; in fine style; with flags flying; with drums beating and trumpets sounding*

Es war vorauszusehen, daß dieser faule Student mit Pauken und Trompeten durchs Examen fallen würde.
*It was to be foreseen that that lazy student would fail his examination resoundingly (in fine style; with flags flying; with drums beating and trumpets sounding).*

**Pech** haben: *to be out of luck; to have rotten (tough) luck (colloq.); to have an unlucky (a tough) break (colloq.)*

Unser Tennisklub hat dieses Jahr Pech gehabt. Wir haben die meisten Spiele verloren.
*Our tennis club has been out of luck (has had rotten [tough] luck; has had an unlucky [tough] break) this year. We have lost most of our matches.*

wie **Pech** und Schwefel zusammenhalten, -kleben: cf. **Busenfreunde** sein

**pech(kohlraben)schwarz** sein: cf. **kohl(pech)rabenschwarz** sein

eine **Pechsträhne** haben: *to strike a bad (rough) patch*

Im Augenblick habe ich eine Pechsträhne, denn seit Wochen gelingt mir nichts mehr.
*I have struck a bad (rough) patch at the moment. For weeks nothing I have done has succeeded.*

ein **Pechvogel** sein (fig. u. fam.): *to be an unlucky dog (devil) (colloq.)*

Du bist wirklich ein Pechvogel (Unglücksrabe; Unglückswurm). Gestern hast du deine Uhr verloren, und heute zerbrichst du deine Brille.
*You really are an unlucky dog (devil). Yesterday you lost your watch and today you have broken your glasses.*

den **Pegasus** besteigen: *to break into verse*

Bei der Hochzeitsfeier hielt ich eine kurze (Prosa-)Rede, und dann bestieg ich (anschließend) den Pegasus.
*At the wedding reception I made a short speech and then broke into verse.*

die Lage **peilen** (fig.): cf. einen **Fühler** ausstrecken

j.em auf die **Pelle** rücken (fig. u. fam.): cf. j.em auf den **Leib** (zu Leibe) rücken j.em auf der **Pelle** sitzen (fig. u. fam.): a) *to sit on top of s.b.;* cf. auch: gedrängt wie die **Heringe** sitzen; b) *to pester (to plague; to harass) s.b.; to be on s.b.'s heels; to get at s.b. (sl.)*

    a) Der Raum war so eng, daß wir uns gegenseitig auf der Pelle saßen.

    b) Obwohl mein Freund weiß, daß ich viel Arbeit habe, sitzt er mir immer auf der Pelle und hält mich auf.

    *a) The space was so limited that we were sitting on top of each other.*

    *b) Although my friend knows that I have a lot of work, he is always pestering (plaguing; harassing; getting at) me (is always on my heels) and holding me up.*

j.em auf den **Pelz** rücken (fig. u. fam.): cf. j.em auf den **Leib** (zu Leibe) rücken

**pennen** (fam.): *to keep one's head down (sl.)*

    Da ich heute zu lange gepennt hatte, bin ich zu spät in die Schule gekommen.

    *As I kept my head down too long today, I was late for school.*

Du wirst keine **Perle** aus der Krone verlieren (Dir wird keine Perle aus der Krone fallen) (fig.): cf. Du wirst keinen **Stein** aus der Krone verlieren (Dir wird kein Stein aus der Krone fallen)

**Perlen** vor die Säue werfen (fig. u. fam.): *to cast pearls before swine*

    Ungebildeten Menschen (Theater)karten für eine klassische Tragödie zu schenken, bedeutet (heißt) Perlen vor die Säue werfen.

    *To give uneducated people tickets for a classical tragedy is to cast pearls before swine.*

eine wahre **Perle** sein (fig.): *to be a real gem (jewel; pearl; treasure)*

    Unser neues Dienstmädchen ist eine wahre Perle (ein Engel).

    *Our new maid is a real gem (jewel; pearl; treasure).*

j.en (etwas) fürchten wie die **Pest:** *to fear s.b. (s.th.) like the Day of Judgement; to stand in fear and trembling of s.b. (s.th.)*

    Unser Chef ist sehr streng und rücksichtslos. Wir fürchten ihn alle wie die Pest.

    *Our boss is very strict and inconsiderate. We all fear him like the Day of Judgement (stand in fear and trembling of him).*

j.en (etwas) hassen wie die **Pest:** *to hate s.b. (s.th.) like poison*

    Spinat kann ich einfach nicht essen. Ich hasse ihn wie die Pest.

    *I just can't eat spinach. I hate it like poison.*

j.en (etwas) meiden (fliehen) wie die **Pest:** *to avoid s.b. (s.th.) like the plague*

    Seit dieser Krankheit muß ich das kalte Baden wie die Pest meiden (fliehen).

    *Since that illness I have had to avoid cold baths like the plague.*

stinken wie die **Pest** (fam.): *to stink to high heaven (colloq.); to stink like hell (sl.)*

    In der Nähe dieser chemischen Fabrik stinkt es wie die Pest.

    *It stinks to high heaven (stinks like hell) near this chemical works.*

eine **Pestbeule** aufstechen (fig.): cf. eine **Eiterbeule** aufstechen

ein langweiliger **Peter** sein (fam.): cf. **mordslangweilig** sein

als ob dir die **Petersilie** verhagelt sei: *as though the bottom had dropped out of your life; as though your house had been burned down*

> Was ist denn passiert? Du siehst ja aus, als ob dir die Petersilie verhagelt sei.
> *What has happened? You look as though the bottom had dropped out of your life (as though your house had been burned down).*

etwas in **petto** haben: *to have (to keep) s.th. up one's sleeve*

> Wir merkten bald, daß die Eltern etwas Besonderes planten. Sie verrieten uns jedoch nicht, was sie in petto hatten.
> *We soon noticed that our parents were planning something special. However, they did not reveal to us what they had (were keeping) up their sleeves.*

**petzen** (fam.): *to let on (colloq.); to sneak (sl.); to blab (sl.).* Cf. auch: j.en **verpetzen**

> Der Lehrer hätte das nie entdeckt, wenn Kurt nicht gepetzt hätte.
> *The teacher would have never found that out if Curt had not let on (sneaked; blabbed).*

ausgetretene **Pfade** wandeln (fig.): *to follow (to keep to) the beaten track; to stick in the rut; to be in a groove*

> Es fehlt der Geschäftsführung dieser Firma an Originalität und Initiative. Sie wandelt nur ausgetretene Pfade.
> *The management of this firm lacks originality and initiative. It only follows (keeps to) the beaten track (sticks in the rut; It is in a groove).*

j.em ein **Pfahl** im Fleische sein (fig.): cf. j.em ein **Dorn** im Auge sein

in seinen vier **Pfählen** (fig.): cf. in seinen vier **Wänden**

ein paar **Pfähle** zurückstecken (fig.): cf. einen **Pflock** zurückstecken

aufgehen wie ein **Pfannkuchen** (fam.): cf. aufgehen wie ein **Hefekloß**

platt (flach) wie ein **Pfannkuchen** sein: cf. platt wie 'ne **Flunder** sein

stolz wie ein **Pfau** sein (sich spreizen wie ein Pfau): cf. stolz wie ein **Spanier** sein; sich spreizen wie ein **Truthahn**

j.en dahin wünschen, wo der **Pfeffer** wächst: *to wish s.b. at the bottom of the sea (colloq.); to call s.b. all the names under the sun (colloq.); to wish s.b. in hell (sl.)*

> Emma kommt immer zu unmöglichen Zeiten zu Besuch. Manchmal könnten wir sie dahin wünschen, wo der Pfeffer wächst.
> *Emma always visits us at impossible times. Sometimes we could wish her at the bottom of the sea (call her all the names under the sun; wish her in hell).*

nach j.es **Pfeife** tanzen (fig.): *to dance to s.b.'s tune; to play s.b.'s game; to play second fiddle to s.b.*

Ich sehe nicht ein, warum ich immer nach deiner Pfeife (Flöte; Geige) tanzen soll.
*I don't see why I should always dance to your tune (play your game; play second fiddle to you).*

auf etwas **pfeifen** (fig. u. fam.): *not to care two hoots (pins) about s.th. (colloq.); You can keep s.th. (colloq.); not to care a tinker's cuss for s.th. (sl.); You can stick s.th. on the wall (up your jumper) (sl.)*

Auf solche Vergnügungen kann ich gern verzichten. Ich pfeife auf sie.
*I can well do without such pleasures. I do not care two hoots (pins) about (a tinker's cuss for) them (You can keep them [stick them on the wall; stick them up your jumper]).*

j.em etwas **pfeifen** (fig. u. fam.): cf. j.em etwas **blasen**

wie ein **Pfeil (pfeilgeschwind)** davonschießen: *to fly away (to shoot off) like an arrow from a bow (as swift as an arrow; like lightning)*

Ernst schoß wie ein Pfeil (pfeilgeschwind) davon und erreichte als erster das Ziel.
*Ernest flew away (shot off) like an arrow from the bow (as swift as an arrow; like lightning) and reached the winning-post first.*

seine **Pfeile** verschossen haben (fig.): cf. sein **Pulver** verschossen haben

nicht für einen **Pfennig** etwas haben: *not to have a scrap (shred; glimmer; an iota) of s.th.; not to have a ha'porth (penn'orth) of s.th. (sl.)*

Mein Freund hat nicht für einen Pfennig (Sechser) Unternehmungsgeist, so daß ich mir um seine Zukunft Sorge mache.
*My friend hasn't a scrap (shred; glimmer; an iota; a ha'porth; penn'orth) of initiative, so that I am worried about his future.*

platt wie ein **Pfennig** sein: cf. platt wie 'ne **Flunder** sein

auf den **Pfennig** sehen (mit dem Pfennig rechnen; auf den Pfennig spukken): *to count (to watch) one's pennies (every penny)*

Wer nur ein geringes Einkommen hat, muß auf den Pfennig sehen (mit dem Pfennig rechnen; auf den Pfennig spucken; jeden Pfennig [dreimal] umdrehen).
*Anyone who has only a small income has to count (to watch) his pennies (every penny).*

Wer den **Pfennig** nicht ehrt, ist des Talers nicht wert (Sprichw.): *Take care of the pence, and the pounds will take care of themselves (prov.)*

Solche kleinen Ausgaben machen viel aus. Du solltest sparsamer sein; denn wer den Pfennig nicht ehrt, ist des Talers nicht wert.
*Small expenses like that make a lot of difference. You ought to be more economical. Take care of the pence, and the pounds will take care of themselves.*

jeden **Pfennig** (dreimal) umdrehen: cf. auf den **Pfennig** sehen

ein **Pfennigfuchser** sein: cf. ein **Geizhals** (Geizkragen) sein

arbeiten wie ein **Pferd**: *to work like a nigger (Trojan; horse; to work like mad (colloq.).* Cf. auch: sich **totarbeiten** (totschuften)

> Du mußt arbeiten wie ein Pferd (Kuli; Wilder; dich abrackern [abschinden; abschuften]), wenn du das ganze Holz kleinhacken willst.
> *You will have to work like a nigger (Trojan; horse; like mad) if you want to chop up all that wood.*

alles auf éin **Pferd** setzen (fig.): cf. alles auf éine **Karte** setzen

aufs falsche **Pferd** setzen (fig.): *to back (to gamble on) the wrong horse; to call the wrong trumps*

> In Wirklichkeit war das Mädchen gar nicht reich. Ihr Verlobter hatte aufs falsche Pferd (auf die falsche Karte) gesetzt.
> *In reality the girl was not rich at all. Her fiancé had backed (gambled on) the wrong horse (called the wrong trumps).*

Das hält (ja) kein **Pferd** aus!: *That is more than flesh and blood can bear (stand); That is beyond human endurance*

> Jetzt marschieren wir schon vier Stunden und immer bergauf. Das hält (ja) kein Pferd aus.
> *We have now been walking for four hours, and always uphill. That is more than flesh and blood can bear (That is beyond human endurance).*

das **Pferd** beim Schwanze aufzäumen (fig.): *to put the cart before the horse*

> Sie haben den Fußboden poliert, bevor Sie die Zimmerdecke gestrichen haben. Das nenne ich, das Pferd beim Schwanze aufzäumen (den Ochsen hinter den Pflug spannen).
> *You have polished the floor before painting the ceiling. That's what I call putting the cart before the horse.*

sich aufs hohe **Pferd** setzen (fig.): cf. sich aufs hohe **Roß** setzen

auf dem hohen **Pferde** sitzen (fig.): cf. auf dem hohen **Rosse** sitzen

mit j.em **Pferde** stehlen können (fig. u. fam.): *s. b. is game for anything (colloq.); to be able to rob the Bank of England with s. b. (colloq.)*

> Erich ist ein ganz verwegener Bursche. Mit ihm kann man Pferde stehlen.
> *Eric is a most reckless fellow. He is game for anything (You could rob the Bank of England with him).*

Man kann ein **Pferd** zur Tränke führen, aber nicht zum Saufen zwingen (Sprichw.): *You can lead (take) a horse to the water, but you can't make him drink (prov.)*

Ich muß zum Zahnarzt gehen, lasse mir aber diesen Zahn nicht ziehen. Man kann ein Pferd zur Tränke führen, aber nicht zum Saufen zwingen.
*I must go to the dentist's, but I won't let him pull this tooth out. You can lead (take) a horse to the water, but you can't make him drink.*

Mich bringen keine zehn **Pferde** dazu (fig. u. fam.): *(A team of) wild horses would not drag me to it (would not make me do it)*

Mich bringen keine zehn Pferde dazu, einem Stierkampf zuzusehen.
*(A team of) wild horses would not drag me to watch (would not make me watch) a bull-fight.*

eine **Pferdearbeit** sein: cf. eine **Hundearbeit** sein

den **Pferdefuß** zeigen (fig.): cf. sein wahres **Gesicht** zeigen

eine **Pferdekur** (durch)machen: *to take drastic action; to use drastic (radical) remedies*

Wegen der Grippe hätte ich im Bett bleiben sollen, ich habe aber eine Pferdekur (Roßkur) (durch)gemacht, weil ich am nächsten Tage in Urlaub fahren wollte.
*I should have stayed in bed with my influenza, but I took drastic action (used drastic [radical] remedies) because I wanted to go on leave the next day.*

keinen **Pfifferling** wert sein: cf. keinen (roten) **Heller** wert sein

geputzt (geschmückt) wie ein **Pfingstochse** sein (fam.): *to be dressed up to the nines; to be dressed up (dolled up; got up) to kill (sl.)*

Schau' dir mal das Mädchen drüben an. Es ist (ja) geputzt (geschmückt) wie ein Pfingstochse (ordentlich aufgetakelt).
*Just look at that girl over there. She's certainly dressed up to the nines (dressed [dolled; got] up to kill).*

ein heißes **Pflaster** sein (fig.): *to be hot (a hot spot) (colloq.)*

Die Diebesbande hat sich verflüchtigt (davongemacht), da ihr unsere Stadt ein zu heißes Pflaster geworden war.
*The gang of thieves has fled, because our town had become too hot (too hot a spot) for them.*

ein **Pflaster** (**Pflästerchen**) auf die Wunde sein (fig.): *to be a crumb of comfort; to be the sugar on the pill*

Ich bekam zum Geburtstag das erhoffte Fahrrad nicht, aber Vater versprach es mir für das nächste Jahr. Das war wenigstens ein Pflaster (Pflästerchen) auf die Wunde.
*I did not get the bicycle for my birthday that I had hoped for, but father promised it to me for next year. That was at least a crumb of comfort (That was the sugar on the pill).*

**pflaumenweich** sein (fig.): *to have no punch (no fire; no drive); to have no go (colloq.); to be as flabby as a jellyfish (colloq.)*

Bei seinem Mangel an Unternehmungsgeist wird Karl es nie zu etwas bringen. Er ist (zu) pflaumenweich.
*With his lack of initiative Charles will never get anywhere. He has no punch (no fire; no drive; no go; He is as flabby as a jellyfish).*

etwas einen **Pflock** (ein paar Pflöcke) zurückstecken (fig.): *to cut (to whittle; to pare) s.th. down; to cut back s.th.; to take s.th. down a peg*
Soviel Geld kann ich dir einfach nicht mehr geben. Du mußt deine Ansprüche einen Pflock (ein paar Pflöcke [Pfähle]; ein Loch) zurückstecken.
*I simply can't give you as much money as that any longer. You must cut (whittle; pare) down (cut back) your demands (take your demands down a peg).*

j.em eins auf die **Pfoten** geben (fam.): *to rap s.b.'s knuckles; to give s.b. a rap over the knuckles*
Als die Mutter ihre kleine Tochter beim Naschen ertappte, gab sie ihr eins auf die Pfoten.
*When the mother caught her little daughter eating sweets, she rapped her knuckles (gave her a rap over the knuckles).*

auf dem **Pfropfen** sitzen (fam.): cf. in der **Klemme** sein (sitzen)

**pfropfenvoll** sein: *to be crammed (full); to be full to overflowing; to be chock-full*
Bei der Vorlesung des bekannten Professors war der Saal pfropfenvoll (gepfropft [brechend; gerammelt] voll).
*The hall was crammed (crammed full; full to overflowing; chock-full) for the famous professor's lecture.*

mit seinem **Pfunde** wuchern (fig.): *to make the most of one's talents; to put one's talents to the most profitable use*
Jeder(mann) begreift, daß ein Maler mit seinem Pfunde wuchern und demjenigen seine Bilder verkaufen muß, der am meisten bezahlen kann.
*Everyone understands that a painter wants to make the most of his talents (to put his talents to the most profitable use) and sell his pictures to the man who can pay the most.*

ein **pfundiger** Kerl (Mensch) sein (fam.): cf. ein **Allerweltskerl** sein

ein **Pfundsessen** (fam.): *a good feed (colloq.); a slap-up meal (sl.); a tuck-in (sl.)*
Das Pfundsessen nach diesem langen Spaziergang war gerade das, was ich wollte.
*The good feed (slap-up meal; tuck-in) after that long walk was just what I wanted.*

ein **Pfundskerl** sein (fam.): cf. ein **Allerweltskerl** sein

**Phrasen** dreschen (fam.): *to mouth platitudes; to make pedestrian remarks*
Bei der freien Diskussion, die sich an den Vortrag anschloß, wurden viele Phrasen gedroschen, und es kam nichts bei ihr heraus.

*During the open discussion which followed the talk many platitudes were mouthed (many pedestrian remarks were made), and nothing came out of it.*

nicht **piep** sagen (fam.): cf. keinen **Mucks** sagen

j.em **piepe** sein (fam.): cf. völlig **Luft** für j.en sein

es **piept** bei j.em (fam.): cf. nicht richtig im **Dachstübchen** sein

zum **Piepen** sein (fam.): *to be a scream (colloq.); to be a yell (sl.)*

Das Lustspiel, das ich gestern sah, war wirklich zum Piepen (Brüllen; Kugeln; Lachen, Schießen; Schreien; Totlachen; Wälzen).
*The comedy I saw yesterday was really a scream (yell).*

einen **Piepmatz** haben (fig. u. fam.): cf. nicht richtig im **Dachstübchen** sein

j.en **piesacken** (fam.): cf. j.en **drangsalieren**

einen **Pik** (eine **Pike**) auf j.en haben: *to have (to bear) a grudge (a spite) against s.b.; to have a down on s.b. (colloq.); to have it in for s.b. (sl.)*

Ich weiß nicht, warum unser Lehrer einen Pik (eine Pike) auf mich hat (mich auf dem Strich [Zug] hat).
*I don't know why our master has (bears) a grudge (spite) against me (has a down on me; has it in for me).*

von der **Pike** auf dienen (fig.): *to start at the bottom (at the foot; on the bottom rung) of the ladder; to rise from the ranks; to work one's way up through the ranks*

Jeder Handwerksmeister muß von der Pike auf dienen und als Lehrling anfangen.
*Every master-craftsman has to start at the bottom (foot; on the bottom rung) of the ladder (has to rise from [to work his way up through] the ranks) and begin as an apprentice.*

**pikfein** angezogen sein: cf. **geschniegelt** und gebügelt (gestriegelt) sein

die bittere **Pille** schlucken (fig.): *to swallow a bitter pill; to take a hard knock*

Wir mußten die bittere Pille schlucken (in den sauren Apfel beißen) und unser Haus verkaufen.
*It was a bitter pill for us to swallow (a hard knock for us to take) when we had to sell our house.*

eine bittere **Pille** sein (fig.): *to be a bitter pill (a hard [heavy] blow)*

Die Erhöhung der Postgebühren ist eine bittere Pille (ein harter Schlag) für jedermann.
*The raising of postal charges is a bitter pill (hard [heavy] blow) for everybody.*

die bittere **Pille** versüßen (fig.): *to gild (to sugar) the pill*

Der Chirurg hielt eine Operation für nötig, bezeichnete sie jedoch als eine Kleinigkeit. Offenbar wollte er mir die bittere Pille versüßen.
*The surgeon considered an operation necessary but termed it a triviality. Obviously he wanted to gild (sugar) the pill for me.*

wie (die) **Pilze** aus der Erde schießen: *to shoot up (to spring up) like mushrooms; to shoot up (to spring up) overnight*

In unserer Stadt sind nach dem Kriege die Häuser wie (die) Pilze (Spargel) aus der Erde geschossen.
*In our town houses have shot up (sprung up) like mushrooms (overnight) since the war.*

**pimp(e)lig** sein (fam.): *to snivel (colloq.)*

Du mußt dich abhärten und nicht so pimp(e)lig sein.
*You must toughen yourself and not snivel so much.*

**Pinke(pinke)** haben (fam.): cf. (gut) bei **Kasse** sein; **Geld** wie Heu haben

j.em die **Pistole** auf die Brust setzen (fig.): *to hold (to put) a pistol to s.b.'s head; to hold a knife at s.b.'s throat; to hold s.b. at the point of the sword*

Mit ihrem Streik wollten die Eisenbahnarbeiter der Regierung die Pistole (den Dolch) auf die Brust (das Messer an die Kehle) setzen.
*The railway workers wanted to hold (put) a pistol to the government's head (to hold a knife at the government's throat; to hold the government at the point of the sword) by striking.*

wie aus der **Pistole** geschossen: *like a shot (out of a gun); in a flash; like lightning*

Der Student konnte im mündlichen Examen alle Fragen wie aus der Pistole geschossen beantworten.
*In the oral examination the student was able to answer all the questions like a shot ([out of a gun]; in a flash; like lightning).*

**pitschnaß** sein (fam.): cf. bis auf die **Haut** durchnäßt sein

eine **Plackerei** sein: *to be a grind (a fag) (colloq.)*

Es wäre eine furchtbare Plackerei (Schinderei), wenn ich diese Wand noch einmal anstreichen müßte.
*It would be a terrible grind (fag) if I had to paint this wall again.*

auf dem **Plan** stehen: *to be on the cards (on the programme)*

Es steht leider nicht auf dem Plan, daß ich dieses Jahr nach Venedig fahre.
*Unfortunately it's not on the cards (programme) this year that I shall go to Venice.*

auf den **Plan** treten: *to appear on the scene; to turn up; to come forward*

Immer wieder tritt man mit neuen Vorschlägen für eine Verbesserung des Unterrichtssystems auf den Plan.

*Time and again people appear on the scene (turn up; come forward) with proposals for improving the educational system.*

flach (platt) wie ein **Plättbrett** sein (fam.): cf. platt wie 'ne **Flunder** sein

j.em etwas (glatt) vor die **Platte** sagen (fam.): *to blurt s.th. out to s.b.; to come straight out with s.th. (colloq.).* Cf. auch: **klipp** und klar sagen

In meiner Empörung habe ich dem Mann meine Meinung glatt vor die Platte (den Kopf) gesagt.
*In my indignation I blurted out my opinion to the man (I came straight out with my opinion).*

fehl am **Platze** sein: *to be out of place*

Ihr Wutausbruch ist unverständlich und vollkommen fehl am Platze (Orte).
*Your angry outburst is incomprehensible and completely out of place.*

einen **Platz** an der Sonne erringen (fig.): *to gain a place in the sun*

Diese außereuropäischen Länder wollen selbständig werden und einen Platz an der Sonne erringen.
*These non-European countries want to become independent and gain a place in the sun.*

die **Platze** kriegen (fam.): cf. vor **Wut** kochen

eine **Plaudertasche** sein (fam.): cf. eine **Klatschbase** sein

**pleite** gehen (machen) (fam.): *to go bankrupt; to go broke (colloq.); to go smash (bust; phut) (sl.)*

Seine Firma ist voriges Jahr pleite gegangen (hat . . . pleite gemacht).
*His firm went bankrupt (broke; smash; bust; phut) last year.*

eine völlige **Pleite** sein (fam.): *to be a complete flop (fizzle; washout) (colloq.); to be a dead loss (sl.)*

Wegen des schlechten Wetters war der Karneval eine völlige Pleite.
*Because of the bad weather the carnival was a complete flop (fizzle; washout; dead loss).*

Der **Pleitegeier** geht um (fam.): *There has been a spate (an epidemic) of bankruptcies; Everybody is going broke (bust) (sl.)*

In dieser Gegend geht der Pleitegeier um. Viele Fabriken haben in den letzten Wochen den Betrieb eingestellt.
*There has been a spate (an epidemic) of bankruptcies (Everybody is going broke [bust] in this district). Many factories have gone out of production in the last few weeks.*

gedrängt wie die **Pökelheringe** sitzen: cf. gedrängt wie die **Heringe** sitzen

Noch ist **Polen** nicht verloren (fig.): *While there's life there's hope; The day is not yet lost; It's not all up yet (colloq.)*

Im Augenblick sieht die Lage schlecht aus, aber noch ist Polen nicht verloren.
*At the moment the situation looks bad, but while there's life there's hope (the day is not yet lost; it's not all up yet).*

ein **Polizeispitzel** sein: *to be a copper's nark (colloq.); to be a squealer (sl.)*
Dieser Mann sieht verdächtig aus. Ich vermute, daß er ein Polizeispitzel ist.
*That man looks suspicious. I suspect that he's a copper's nark (a squealer).*

**polizeiwidrig** dumm sein (fam.): *to be too stupid for words; to be as dumb as they make them (sl.).* Cf. auch: dumm wie **Bohnenstroh** sein
Thomas wurde als einziger nicht in die nächste Klasse versetzt. Er ist (auch) wirklich polizeiwidrig dumm.
*Thomas was the only one not to be moved up into the next class. He really is too stupid for words (as dumb as they make them).*

Es herrscht **polnische** Wirtschaft (fig. u. fam.): cf. ein **Schweinestall** sein

**pomadig** sein (fam.): *to be a slow-coach (a stick-in-the-mud) (colloq.).* Cf. auch: **lahm** wie eine Ente sein
Ich möchte meinen Neffen manchmal schütteln, weil er so pomadig ist.
*Sometimes I should like to shake my nephew because he's such a slow-coach (stick-in-the-mud).*

von **Pontius** zu Pilatus laufen (fig.): *to go from pillar to post*
Ich bin von Pontius zu Pilatus gelaufen, um dieses Ersatzteil für mein Fahrrad zu kaufen.
*I went from pillar to post to buy this spare part for my bicycle.*

viel **Porzellan** zerschlagen (fig.): cf. **Flurschaden** anrichten

in **Posemuckel** wohnen (fig. u. fam.): cf. in **Buxtehude** wohnen

sich in **Positur** setzen: *to put on an air; to strike an attitude*
Der erste Geiger dieses Orchesters setzt sich ordentlich in Positur, bevor er zu spielen anfängt.
*The leader of this orchestra certainly puts on an air (strikes an attitude) before he starts to play.*

**Possen** reißen: *to play the fool (the clown; the buffoon)*
Fritz kann nie ernst sein. Er muß immer Possen reißen.
*Fred can never be serious. He always has to play the fool (clown; buffoon).*

auf dem **Posten** sein (fig.): cf. auf der **Höhe** sein

auf verlorenem **Posten** kämpfen (fig.): *to fight a losing battle; to defend a lost cause*

Er muß einsehen, daß er seine Meinung niemals durchsetzen kann. Er kämpft auf verlorenem Posten.

*He must realise that he can never make his opinion prevail. He is fighting a losing battle (defending a lost cause).*

einen **Posttag** zu spät **(post festum)** kommen (fig.): *to be behindhand; to be (a bit) behind the times (colloq.)*

Sie kommen mit Ihrem Vorschlag einen Posttag zu spät (post festum). Es ist alles schon festgelegt.

*You are behindhand ([a bit] behind the times) with your suggestion. Everything is already settled.*

**Potemkinsche** Dörfer vorspiegeln (fig.): cf. einen **Türken** bauen

**potthäßlich** sein (fam.): cf. **mordshäßlich** sein

ein **Poussierstengel** sein (fam.): *to be a flirt; to be a gadabout (colloq.); to be fast (colloq.); to be hot (sl.)*

Seine Schwester ist ein wahrer Poussierstengel. Man sieht sie jeden Tag mit jungen Männern.

*His sister is a real flirt (gadabout; is pretty fast [hot]). Every day one sees her with young men.*

ein **Prahlhans** sein: cf. ein **Maulheld** sein

ein alter **Praktikus** sein: *to be an old hand (old stager; experienced campaigner)*

Mir brauchen Sie keine Ratschläge zu erteilen. Ich bin in meinem Beruf ein alter Praktikus (Hase).

*You don't need to give me any advice. I'm an old hand (stager; experienced campaigner) in my job.*

j.en (etwas) an den **Pranger** stellen (fig.): *to pillory s.b. (s.th.); to show (to hold) up s.th.*

In seiner Predigt hat der Pfarrer die unmoralischen Sitten der Zeit an den Pranger gestellt (angeprangert).

*In his sermon the minister pilloried (showed [held] up) the immoral habits of the time.*

auf dem **Präsentierteller** sitzen (fig.): cf. im **Rampenlicht** sein (stehen)

j.em etwas **predigen** (fig.): cf. j.em etwas **vorpredigen**

die Stimme eines **Predigers** in der Wüste sein (fig.): *to be a voice crying in the wilderness*

Niemand hat auf die Vorschläge des Redners gehört. Es war die Stimme eines Predigers in der Wüste.

*No one listened to the speaker's suggestions. He was a voice crying in the wilderness.*

ein gepfefferter **Preis** sein: *to be a steep (stiff; high) price; to be a hefty price (colloq.)*

Ich kann dieses Gemälde nicht kaufen, weil der Händler so einen gepfefferten (happigen) Preis verlangt.
*I cannot buy that painting because the dealer is asking such a steep (stiff; high; hefty) price.*

um jeden **Preis**: *at all costs; whatever I (you etc.) do*

Wir müssen um jeden Preis (auf jeden Fall) verhindern, daß so etwas nochmals geschieht.
*At all costs (Whatever we do) we must prevent anything like that from happening again.*

der **Prellbock** sein (fig.): *to act as a buffer (as a go-between; as a cushion)*

Mein kleiner Bruder hat schon wieder eine Fensterscheibe eingeschlagen. Ich muß wieder der Prellbock sein und versuchen, die Eltern zu beschwichtigen.
*My little brother has broken a window-pane again. I must act as a buffer (go-between; cushion) again and try to placate our parents.*

j.en **prellen** (fam.): cf. j.en auf den **Leim** führen (leimen)

**prima** sein (fam.): cf. **erstklassig** sein

eingehen wie eine **Primel** (fam.): *slowly to fade (to wither) away*

Seit dem Tode ihres Mannes ist die alte Frau sehr bekümmert und unglücklich. Sie wird wohl eingehen wie eine Primel.
*Since her husband's death the old woman has been very worried and unhappy. I suppose she will slowly fade (wither) away.*

**Primus** (der Klasse) sein: *to be top of the class (form)*

Leider werde ich (wohl) niemals Primus (der Klasse) sein.
*I'm afraid I shall never be top of the class (form).*

auf einem **Prinzip** herumreiten (ein Prinzip zu Tode reiten): *to ride (to drive; to flog) a principle to death; to stick to one's old ideas (colloq.)*

Dieser Minister reitet auf seinen alten Prinzipien herum (reitet seine alten Prinzipien zu Tode) und will von neuen Ideen nichts wissen.
*This minister rides (drives; flogs) his old principles to death (sticks to his old ideas) and will not listen to new ideas (new ones).*

ein **Prinzipienreiter** sein: *to be a stickler for principles*

Ein Prinzipienreiter erkennt Ausnahmefälle nicht an.
*A stickler for principles admits no exceptions.*

die **Probe** aufs Exempel machen: *to put it to the test*

Bei Wärme dehnen sich die Körper aus. Machen wir doch die Probe aufs Exempel! (Stellen wir's doch [einmal] auf die Probe!)
*Bodies expand when heated. Let us put it to the test.*

etwas auf die **Probe** stellen: cf. die **Probe** aufs Exempel machen

**Probieren** geht über Studieren (Sprichw.): *The proof of the pudding is in the eating (prov.)*

> Theoretisch mag das wohl stimmen, ich möchte aber sehen, wie es in der Praxis aussieht. Probieren geht über Studieren (Beim Setzen wird sich's zeigen [weisen]).
> *That may be right theoretically, but I should like to see what it looks like in practice. The proof of the pudding is in the eating.*

Der **Prophet** gilt nichts in seinem Vaterland (Sprichw.): *No man is a prophet in his own country (prov.)*

> Seltsamerweise hat dieser Denker nur im Ausland Einfluß ausgeübt. Der Prophet gilt nichts in seinem Vaterland.
> *Strangely enough, this thinker has only been influential abroad. No man is a prophet in his own country.*

ein **Protz** sein: *to be a braggart (a Gascon); to be a loud-mouthed person (colloq.)*

> Viele Neureiche pflegen, mit ihrem Geld zu prahlen. Niemand kann solche Protze leiden.
> *Many newly-rich are in the habit of boasting about their money. No one can bear such braggarts (Gascons; loud-mouthed people).*

mit j.em (etwas) kurzen **Prozeß** machen (fig.): *to give s.b. short shrift; to make short work of s.b. (s.th.) (colloq.)*

> Mein Vater hat mit dem Bettler kurzen Prozeß (nicht viel Umstände) gemacht und ihn fortgeschickt (hat den Bettler ohne Umschweife fortgeschickt).
> *My father gave the beggar short shrift (made short work of the beggar) and sent him away.*

der **Prügelknabe** sein: cf. der **Sündenbock** sein

wie ein begossener **Pudel** davonschleichen: *to creep away with one's tail between one's legs (colloq.); to slink off like a whipped cur (colloq.)*

> Der Chef schrie den Angestellten zornig an, der dann wie ein begossener Pudel (dann mit eingezogenem Schwanz) davonschlich.
> *The boss shouted angrily at the employee, who crept away with his tail between his legs (who slunk off like a whipped cur).*

des **Pudels** Kern: cf. mit éinem **Wort**

**pudelnaß** sein (fam.): cf. bis auf die **Haut** durchnäßt sein

j.em den **Puls** fühlen (fig.): cf. bei j.em einen **Fühler** ausstrecken

das **Pulver** nicht erfunden haben (fig.): *to be no great light (not a shining light); s.b. won't set the Thames on fire (colloq.); to be no great shakes (not much cop) (sl.)*

Der junge Mann hat das Pulver nicht erfunden (ist kein Geistesheld [kein Kirchenlicht; kein großes Licht]). Sein Brief an mich ist ungewandt und voller Fehler.
*The young man is no great light (not a shining light; no great shakes; not much cop; won't set the Thames on fire). His letter to me was clumsy and full of mistakes.*

keinen Schuß **Pulver** wert sein: cf. keinen **Schuß** Pulver wert sein

sein **Pulver** verschossen haben (fig.): *to have shot one's bolt.* Cf. auch: mit seiner **Kunst** zu (am) Ende sein

Ich habe mein Pulver (meine Pfeile) verschossen und kann mit meinem Gegner nicht mehr konkurrieren.
*I have shot my bolt and cannot compete with my rival any more.*

wie auf einem **Pulverfaß** sitzen: *to be sitting (living) on the top of (on the edge of) a volcano (on a charge of dynamite; on a powder-barrel)*

Bis die Bevölkerung die beruhigende Nachricht vom Scheitern der Revolution bekam, saß sie wie auf einem Pulverfaß (lebte sie auf einem Vulkan).
*Until the population received the reassuring news of the failure of the revolution, they were sitting (living) on the top of (on the edge of) a volcano (on a charge of dynamite; on a powder-barrel).*

ein **Pummel(chen)** sein (fam.): *to be a tubby little thing (colloq.).* Cf. auch: **kugelrund** sein

Die kleine Elsbeth ist ein wahrer Pummel (ein wahres Pummelchen).
*Little Betty is a really tubby little thing.*

etwas auf **Pump** kaufen **(pumpen)** (fam.): *to buy s.th. on tick (colloq.).* Cf. auch: etwas **abstottern**

In diesem Geschäft kann ich immer auf Pump kaufen (pumpen).
*I can always buy on tick in this shop.*

sich etwas von j.em **pumpen** (fam.): *to touch (to tap) s.b. for s.th. (colloq.)*

Gestern habe ich mir von meinem Vater hundert Mark gepumpt.
*I touched (tapped) my father for a hundred marks yesterday.*

ein dunkler **Punkt** (fig.): *an obscure point*

Im allgemeinen ist jetzt alles klar, aber dieser eine dunkle Punkt muß noch geklärt werden.
*In general everything is now clear, but this one obscure point is still to be cleared up.*

ohne **Punkt** und Komma reden (fig.): *to gabble (to prattle) on and on*

Diese geschwätzige alte Frau redet stundenlang ohne Punkt und Komma (ist eine richtige Quasselstrippe).
*This garrulous old woman gabbles (prattles) on and on for hours.*

einen **Punkt** machen (fig.): *to call a halt; to put a stop to it.* Cf. auch: **bremsen**

> Wir haben in der letzten Woche zuviel Geld ausgegeben und müssen jetzt einen Punkt machen.
> *We spent too much money last week and must now call a halt (put a stop to it).*

der springende **Punkt** (fig.): *the salient point (crucial point); the real issue (crucial issue); the crux of the matter*

> Wir wollen ein Haus bauen, aber der springende Punkt ist, daß wir nicht genug Geld haben.
> *We want to build a house, but the salient (crucial) point (the real [crucial] issue; the crux of the matter) is that we have not enough money.*

an einen toten **Punkt** gelangen (fig.): *to reach deadlock (to come to a deadlock); to reach stalemate; to come to a standstill*

> Die Verhandlungen sind an einen toten Punkt gelangt. Hoffentlich werden bald weitere Fortschritte gemacht.
> *The negotiations have reached (come to a) deadlock (reached stalemate; come to a standstill). It is to be hoped that further progress will soon be made.*

ein wunder **Punkt** (fig.): *a sore (tender; sensitive) spot (point)*

> Rede nicht von seiner Entlassung. Es ist sein wunder Punkt (seine wunde Stelle; Du berührst seine empfindliche Saite).
> *Don't talk about his dismissal. It's a sore (tender; sensitive) spot (point) with him.*

Und damit **Punktum!**: cf. Und damit **basta!**

wie eine **Puppenstube** aussehen: *to be in apple-pie order; to look like a doll's-house.* Cf. **blitzblank** (blitzsauber)

> Diese Hausfrau ist sehr ordentlich. Ihr Wohnzimmer sieht wie eine Puppenstube aus.
> *This housewife is very tidy. Her living-room is in apple-pie order (looks like a doll's-house).*

Mir geht die **Puste** aus (fam.): *It takes my breath away; I am flabbergasted (speechless); I am knocked sideways (colloq.)*

> Mir ging die Puste aus, als ich eine so hohe Arztrechnung bezahlen mußte.
> *It took my breath away (I was flabbergasted [speechless; knocked sideways]) when I had to pay such a heavy doctor's bill.*

Ja, **Puste (Pustekuchen)!** (fam.): cf. Keine (Nicht die) **Spur!**

j.em etwas **pusten** (fig. u. fam.): cf. j.em etwas **blasen**

eine dumme **Pute** sein (fig. u. fam.): cf. eine dumme **Gans** sein

eine eingebildete **Pute** sein (fig. u. fam.): *to be as vain as a peacock; to be stuck-up (colloq.); to be toffee-nosed (colloq.).* Cf. auch: **hochnäsig** sein

Dieses Mädchen ist eine eingebildete Pute. Es ging (an uns) vorbei, als würde es uns nicht kennen.
*That girl is as vain as a peacock (is stuck-up [toffee-nosed]). She passed by as if she did not know us.*

**puterrot** werden: cf. **knallrot** werden

vom **Putzteufel** besessen sein (fam.): *to be a slave to the dustpan (colloq.)*
Eine Hausfrau soll für Sauberkeit in ihrem Haushalt sorgen, darf aber nicht vom Putzteufel besessen sein.
*A housewife must see that her household is clean, but she must not be a slave to the dustpan.*


# Q

**Quadratlatschen** (fam.): cf. **Elbkähne**

die **Quadratur** des Kreises (Zirkels) suchen: *to try to square the circle*
Das ist eine unmögliche Aufgabe. Es hat keinen Zweck, die Quadratur des Kreises (Zirkels) zu suchen.
*That is an impossible task. There is no point in trying to square the circle.*

**Quark** reden (fam.): cf. **Quatsch** reden

eine **Quasselstrippe** (fam.): a) (geschwätziger Mensch) cf. die **Klappe** halten; ohne **Punkt** und Komma reden; b) (Telefon) *a blower (sl.)*
b) Ich schaffe mir bald eine Quasselstrippe an.
*b) I'm going to get the blower soon.*

**Quatsch** reden (fam.): *to talk nonsense (rubbish); to talk fiddlesticks (poppycock; balderdash) (colloq.); to talk eyewash (piffle; bosh) (sl.)*
Rede doch keinen Quatsch (Quark; Kappes; Kohl; Mist; Mumpitz; Stuß; keine Makulatur; kein Blech; kein dummes Zeug [zusammen]; Rede doch nicht kariert). Ich weiß, daß du meinen Bleistift in deiner Tasche hast.
*Don't talk nonsense (rubbish; fiddlesticks; poppycock; balderdash; eyewash; piffle; bosh)! I know that you've got my pencil in your pocket.*

**Quatsch** sein (fam.): *to be nonsense* (usw. wie unter „**Quatsch** reden")

**Quecksilber** im Leibe haben (fig.): *to have St. Vitus' Dance; to have the fidgets (colloq.)*
Ihr Kind hat wirklich Quecksilber im Leibe (eine Spirale im Hintern; ist ein richtiger Zappelphilipp). Es kann nie ruhig sitzen.
*Your child really has got St. Vitus' Dance (the fidgets). It can never sit still.*

etwas aus anderer (dritter) **Quelle** erfahren: cf. etwas von anderer (dritter) **Seite** erfahren

etwas aus erster **Quelle** haben (fig.): *to have s.th. at first hand; to have s.th. from the source (fountain-head); to have s.th. straight from the horse's mouth; to have s.th. hot (straight) from the press*
> Ich kann für die Richtigkeit dieser Nachricht bürgen. Ich habe sie aus erster Quelle (Hand).
> *I can vouch for the correctness of this news. I have it at first hand (from the source [fountain-head]; straight from the horse's mouth; hot [straight] from the press).*

an die **Quelle** gehen (fig.): *to go to the source (fountain-head)*
> Wer die Wahrheit wissen will, muß unmittelbar an die Quelle gehen.
> *Anyone who wants to know the truth must go directly to the source (fountain-head).*

etwas aus guter **Quelle** haben (wissen) (fig.): *to have (to hear) s.th. from a reliable (good) source*
> Ich glaube nur noch das, was ich aus guter Quelle habe (weiß).
> *I only believe what I have (hear) from a reliable (good) source.*

an der **Quelle** sitzen (fig.): *to be at the source* (usw. wie unter „an die **Quelle** gehen")

j.em in die **Quere** kommen: a) (wörtl.) *to get in s.b.'s way; to bump into s.b.;* b) (fig.) cf. j.em einen **Strich** durch die Rechnung machen
> a) Sei doch vorsichtiger (achtsamer)! Du kommst mir mit deinem Besen ständig in die Quere.
> *a) Do be more careful! You're continually getting in my way (bumping into me) with your broom.*

**quietschfidel (quietschvergnügt)** sein (fam.): cf. **kreuzfidel** sein

mit j.em **quitt** sein (fam.): a) *to be finished with s.b.; to be through with s.b. (colloq.);* b) *to be quits (square).* Cf. auch: **Wurst** wider Wurst
> a) Seit diesem Vorfall bin ich mit ihm quitt.
> b) Wilhelm hat mir die zwanzig Mark zurückgegeben, und nun sind wir quitt.
> *a) Since that incident I am finished (through) with him.*
> *b) William has given me back the twenty marks, and now we are quits (square).*

**quittengelb** aussehen: *to be as yellow as a lemon*
> Du mußt zum Arzt gehen. Du siehst quittengelb (zitronengelb; gelb wie eine Zitrone) aus.
> *You must go to the doctor. You are as yellow as a lemon.*

stehlen wie ein **Rabe**: a) (von einem Mann) *to be a thieving magpie;*
b) (von einer Frau) cf. eine diebische **Elster** sein

   a) Dieser Arbeiter ist fristlos entlassen worden. Monatelang natte er in der
   Fabrik wie ein Rabe gestohlen.
   *a) That workman has been summarily dismissed. He had been behaving like a thieving*
   *magpie in the factory for months.*

eine Stimme wie ein **Rabe** haben: *to have a voice like a crow; to caw like a crow*
   Die Tochter des Apothekers ist ganz hübsch, hat aber eine Stimme wie ein
   Rabe.
   *The chemist's daughter is quite pretty, but she has a voice like a crow (she caws like a*
   *crow).*

ein weißer **Rabe** sein (fig.): *to be a rare bird (a rara avis)*
   Ein Maler, der noch nach der Natur malt, ist heute ein weißer Rabe unter den
   Künstlern.
   *A painter who still paints from nature is a rare bird (rara avis) today.*

ein **Rabenaas** sein (fam.): *to be a rotter (colloq.); to be a swine (sl.)*
   Dieses Rabenaas hat mir mein Fahrrad gestohlen.
   *That rotter (swine) has stolen my bicycle.*

**rabenschwarz** sein: cf. **kohl(pech)rabenschwarz** sein

j.em Geld in den **Rachen** werfen (fig.): *to throw good money after bad; to pour*
*money down the drain (the sink) (colloq.)*
   Seine Neffen sind sehr verschwenderisch. Da er ihnen schon viel Geld gegeben hat, hat er keine Lust, ihnen weiteres Geld in den Rachen zu werfen.
   *His nephews are very wasteful. As he has already given them a lot of money, he does not*
   *feel like throwing good money after bad (pouring money down the drain [sink]).*

ein **Racker** sein (fam.): *to be a handful (a tartar) (colloq.).* Cf. auch: ein
kleines **Aas** sein
   Ellen ist schon jetzt ein richtiger Racker. Ich bin gespannt, wie sie sich weiter-
   entwickeln wird.
   *Ellen is already a proper handful (tartar). I wonder how she will develop.*

das fünfte **Rad** am Wagen sein (fig.): *to be odd man out; to be de trop*
   Ich lasse Euch allein(e). Ich wäre sonst (doch) nur das fünfte Rad am Wagen.
   *I'll leave you alone. Otherwise I'd only be odd man out (de trop).*

bei j.em ist ein **Rad** locker (los) (fig. u. fam.): cf. nicht richtig im **Dachstüb-**
**chen** sein

unter die **Räder** geraten (kommen) (fig. u. fam.): *to go to the dogs; to go wrong; to go off the rails; to come to grief; to go to pieces; to err (to stray) from the straight and narrow path.* Cf. auch: auf die abschüssige **Bahn** geraten

> Der junge Graf geriet (kam) leider unter dem Einfluß dieser Männer schnell unter die Räder (unter den Schlitten).
> *Unfortunately the young Count quickly went to the dogs (went wrong; went off the rails; came to grief; went to pieces; erred [strayed] from the straight and narrow path) under the influence of those men.*

**Radau** machen: cf. **Krach** machen

den **Rahm** abschöpfen (fig.): *to skim off the cream; to skim the milk; to have (to take) first pick; to take the pick of the bunch*

> Beim Verkauf der Bücher des Gelehrten schöpften die großen Bibliotheken den Rahm ab (klaubten ... die besten [größten] Rosinen aus dem Kuchen) und erwarben die wertvollsten Werke.
> *At the sale of the scholar's books the big libraries skimmed off the cream (skimmed the milk; had [took] first pick; took the pick of the bunch) and acquired the most valuable works.*

aus dem **Rahmen** fallen (fig.): *not to fit into the picture; to be out of place*

> Dieser eingebildete Kerl fällt unter solchen bescheidenen Menschen völlig aus dem Rahmen.
> *That conceited fellow does not fit into the picture at all with (is completely out of place) among such modest people.*

**rammdösig** werden (fam.): *to become all fuddled (in one's head) (colloq.).* Cf. auch: Der **Kopf** brummt mir

> Durch diese ganze Aufregung bin ich ganz rammdösig geworden.
> *As a result of all this excitement I've become all fuddled (in my head).*

im **Rampenlicht** stehen: *to be in the limelight; to be in the public gaze.* Cf. auch: im **Blickpunkt** stehen

> Ich hätte keine Angst, vor der Königin im Rampenlicht zu stehen (auf dem Präsentierteller zu sitzen).
> *I would not be afraid to be in the limelight (the public gaze) in the presence of the Queen.*

außer **Rand** und Band sein: cf. aus dem **Häuschen** sein

am **Rande** des Grabes stehen (fig.): cf. in den letzten **Zügen** liegen

den **Rand** halten (fam.): cf. die **Klappe** halten

mit etwas zu **Rande** kommen: *to cope with s. th.; to manage s. th.; to get on top of s. th.; to get the measure of s. th.* Cf. auch: mit etwas zu **Stuhle** kommen

Mit diesem Problem kann ich einfach nicht zu Rande kommen.
*I simply can't cope with (manage; get on top of; get the measure of) this problem.*

am **Rande** des Verderbens stehen: *to be on the verge of ruin*

Infolge seines Umganges mit solchen Leuten steht mein Freund Richard jetzt am Rande des Verderbens.
*As a result of his association with such people my friend Richard is on the verge of ruin.*

etwas am **Rande** vermerken (fig.): *to observe (to mention) in passing; to observe (to mention) s.th. as an aside*

Ich will nur am Rande vermerken, daß mir dieser Mann schon lange verdächtig war.
*I just wish to observe (mention) in passing (as an aside) that that man had appeared suspicious to me for a long while.*

am **Rande** vermerkt (bemerkt): *incidentally; by the way*

Heute kommt Heinrich wieder zu spät. Am Rande vermerkt (bemerkt): das tut er immer.
*Henry's late again today. He always is, incidentally (by the way).*

Das versteht sich am **Rande**: *It goes without saying; One can take it for granted*

Daß diese beiden Leute nicht zusammengehören, versteht sich am Rande.
*It goes without saying (One can take it for granted) that these two people don't belong together.*

**randalieren**: cf. **Krach** machen

j.em (einer Sache) den **Rang** ablaufen: *to outstrip s.b. (s.th.); to get the better of s.b. (s.th.); to be one up on s.b. (s.th.) (colloq.)*

Im Außenhandel ist Ihr Land sehr zurückgeblieben. Andere Länder haben ihm schon längst den Rang abgelaufen.
*In the export trade your country is very backward. Other countries outstripped it (got the better of it) long ago (have long been one up on it).*

j.em (einer Sache) den **Rang** streitig machen: *to vie with s.b. (s.th.); to challenge s.b. (s.th.); to assail s.b.'s (s.th.'s) position; to hold a candle to s.b.*

Dieser Tennisspieler ist ohne Zweifel der beste im Land. Niemand kann ihm den Rang streitig machen.
*This tennis-player is without doubt the best in the country. No one can vie with him (can challenge him; can assail his position; can hold a candle to him).*

ersten **Ranges**: cf. wie er im **Buche** steht

j.es **Ränke** durchschauen: cf. j.es **Spiel** durchschauen

**Ränke** schmieden: *to hatch a plot; to work up a conspiracy*

Ich bin gar nicht damit einverstanden, daß gegen deinen Onkel Ränke geschmiedet werden.
*I am not at all in agreement with hatching a plot (working up a conspiracy) against your
uncle.*

einen **Rappel** haben (fam.): cf. nicht richtig im **Dachstübchen** sein

j.en **rappelig** machen (fam.): *to put s.b. on edge; to make s.b. jittery (colloq.)*
Dieser ewige Lärm macht mich ganz rappelig (itterig).
*This eternal noise puts me quite on edge (makes me quite jittery).*

**rappeltrocken** sein: cf. **knochentrocken** sein

einen **Raptus** haben (fam.): cf. nicht richtig im **Dachstübchen** sein

sich **rar** machen: *to make o.s. scarce; to be a rare bird (colloq.); to be out of circulation (colloq.)*
Früher haben wir dich öfters gesehen. Warum machst du dich in letzter Zeit so
rar?
*We used to see you a lot. Why have you been making yourself scarce (been such a rare
bird; been out of circulation) recently?*

der grüne **Rasen** deckt j.en: cf. zur ewigen **Ruhe** eingehen

ohne **Rast** und Ruhe arbeiten: *to work without pause; to work without let-up
(colloq.); to keep one's nose to the grindstone (colloq.)*
Ein Forscher arbeitet ohne Rast und Ruhe, weil er glaubt, eine Mission erfüllen
zu müssen.
*A researcher works without pause (let-up; keeps his nose to the grindstone) because he
believes that he has a mission to fulfil.*

mit sich zu **Rate** gehen: *to take stock; to take counsel with o.s.; to think things
over; to do some heart-searching*
Vater mußte mit sich zu Rate gehen, ehe er entscheiden konnte, ob er seinem
armen Freund helfen könne oder nicht.
*Father had to take stock (take counsel with himself; think things over; do some heart-
searching) before he could decide whether he could help his poor friend or not.*

Da ist guter **Rat** teuer: *That's a tough (hard) nut to crack (colloq.); That's a
pretty problem (colloq.); That's a poser (colloq.).* Cf. auch: eine schwierige **Kiste** sein
Wie kannst du jetzt nach dem plötzlichen Tode deiner Eltern dein Studium
noch zu Ende führen? Da ist guter Rat teuer.
*How, after your parents' sudden death, can you now finish your studies? That's a tough
(hard) nut to crack (That's a pretty problem; That's a poser).*

j.em mit **Rat** und Tat beistehen: *to lend s.b. (many) a helping hand; to stand at s.b.'s elbow*

> Der deutsche Konsul stand uns während unseres Aufenthaltes in diesem Lande mit Rat und Tat bei.
> *During our stay in that country the German Consul lent us (many) a helping hand (stood at our elbow).*

Zeit bringt **Rat** (Sprichw.): cf. Kommt **Zeit,** kommt Rat

eine eiserne **Ration**: *iron rations*

> Die Mitglieder der Expedition führten alle eine eiserne Ration mit sich.
> *The members of the expedition all carried iron rations with them.*

ein **Rätsel** aufgeben (fig.): *to set a poser; to give s.b. s.th. to think about; to pose a problem (difficulty); to set a brain-teaser (colloq.)*

> Die Form der neuen Gesetze ist kompliziert und gibt uns manches Rätsel auf.
> *The form of the new laws is complicated and sets us many a poser (brain-teaser; gives us a lot to think about; poses many a problem [difficulty]).*

vor einem **Rätsel** stehen: *to be baffled; to be at a loss; to be foxed (colloq.)*

> Ich stehe vor einem Rätsel: ich habe einfach keine Ahnung, wem ich dieses Buch geliehen habe.
> *I am baffled (at a loss; foxed). I have simply no idea to whom I lent that book.*

ein **Rätselraten** sein (fig.): cf. sich den **Kopf** zerbrechen (zermartern)

Die **Ratten** verlassen das sinkende Schiff (fig.): *The rats are leaving the sinking ship; They are leaving me (you etc.) to stew in my (your etc.) own juice (to boil in my [your etc.] own oil)*

> Jeder weiß, daß diese Firma bald bankrott machen wird, und viele Angestellten haben bereits gekündigt. Die Ratten verlassen das sinkende Schiff.
> *Everybody knows that this firm will soon go bankrupt, and many employees have already given notice. The rats are leaving the sinking ship (They are leaving it to stew in its own juice [to boil in its own oil]).*

ein **Rattenschwanz** von (fam.): *a procession (trail) of; a (whole) heap (pile) of (colloq.)*

> Ich bezahle meine Schulden immer sofort, weil ich einen Rattenschwanz von unbezahlten Rechnungen nicht ausstehen kann.
> *I always pay my debts at once, because I cannot stand a procession (trail; a [whole] heap [pile]) of unpaid bills.*

schlafen wie ein **Ratz**: cf. schlafen wie ein **Murmeltier**

mit etwas **Raubbau** treiben: *to play fast and loose (to play havoc) with s.th.; to ruin s.th.; to wear s.th. out*

Schränke das Rauchen ein; du treibst Raubbau (Schindluder) mit deiner Gesundheit.
*Cut down your smoking. You are playing fast and loose (havoc) with (are ruining; are
wearing out) your health.*

eine **Räubergeschichte** erzählen (fig.): cf. ein **Ammenmärchen** erzählen

in **Rauch** aufgehen (fig.): cf. ausgehen wie das **Hornberger** Schießen

Kein **Rauch** ohne Feuer (Sprichw.): cf. Kein Rauch ohne **Feuer**

**rauchen** wie ein Schlot: cf. rauchen wie ein **Schlot**

etwas in den **Rauchfang** schreiben (fig.): cf. etwas in den **Schornstein**
schreiben

Ein **räudiges** Schaf steckt die ganze Herde an (Sprichw.): cf. Ein räudiges **Schaf** steckt die ganze Herde an

einen **raufkommen**: *to rise in s.b.'s estimation; to move up one (colloq.)*
Daß du mir dieses Buch, das ich schon lange lesen wollte, zu meinem Geburtstag schenkst, finde ich großartig. Du kommst einen rauf!
*I think it's fine that you have given me that book for my birthday which I have been wanting
to read for a long while. You have risen in my estimation (You've moved up one).*

ein **Rauhbein** sein (fam.): *to be a rough (crude) customer; to be a rough (crude)
type (colloq.); to be a roughneck (colloq.).* Cf. auch: **rauhbeinig** werden
Dieser Händler ist sehr unhöflich. Es macht keinen Spaß, bei so einem Rauhbein (ungehobelten [ungeschliffenen] Menschen) einzukaufen.
*That shopkeeper is very impolite. There is no pleasure in buying from a rough (crude)
customer (type; a roughneck) like that.*

**rauhbeinig** werden (fam.): *to cut up rough (colloq.); to turn up (turn out) nasty
(colloq.).* Cf. auch: ein **Rauhbein** sein
Jener Arbeiter kann sehr rauhbeinig werden, besonders wenn er getrunken hat.
*That workman can cut up very rough (turn up [out] very nasty), especially when he has
been drinking.*

die **rauhe** Wirklichkeit: *the cruel (stark) reality; the hard facts*
Solche Träume werden dich nur irreführen. Du mußt dich an die rauhe Wirklichkeit gewöhnen.
*Such dreams will only mislead you. You must accustom yourself to the cruel (stark) reality
(the hard facts).*

j.em **Raupen** in den Kopf setzen (fig.): cf. j.em **Flausen** in den Kopf setzen

einen **Rausch** haben: cf. einen **Schwips** haben

ein **rauschendes** Fest: *a lavish party; a rip-roaring party (colloq.)*

In der Villa des Millionärs wird manches rauschende Fest gefeiert.
*Many lavish (rip-roaring) parties are held in the millionaire's villa.*

j.en **'rauspauken** (fam.): *to get s.b. off (colloq.); to save s.b.'s bacon (colloq.)*

Er wurde der Unterschlagung beschuldigt, aber sein Rechtsanwalt hat ihn
'rausgepaukt.
*He was accused of embezzlement but his counsel got him off (saved his bacon).*

mit etwas **rechnen** (fig.): *to count (to bank) on s.th.*

Dieser Erfolg war nicht unerwartet. Ich hatte damit (mit ihm) gerechnet (darauf
gebaut; mich darauf gespitzt).
*This success was not unexpected. I had counted (banked) on it.*

eine alte **Rechnung** begleichen (fig.): *to pay off (to wipe off; to settle) an old
score; to settle an old account*

Glauben Sie nur nicht, daß ich Ihre beleidigenden Worte vergessen habe. Wir
haben noch eine alte Rechnung zu begleichen.
*Don't think that I've forgotten your insulting words. We've still got to pay off (wipe
off; settle) an old score (to settle an old account).*

auf eigene **Rechnung** geschehen (fig.): *to be at s.b.'s own risk (peril); to
be on s.b.'s own head*

Wenn Sie diese gefährliche Reise doch unternehmen, so geschieht es auf Ihre
eigene Rechnung.
*If you still undertake this dangerous journey, then it's at your own risk (peril; on your
own head).*

eine gepfefferte **Rechnung:** *a stiff (steep; hefty) bill.* Cf. auch: ein gepfefferter **Preis**

Mit so einer gepfefferten (gesalzenen) Rechnung für meinen neuen Anzug hatte
ich nicht gerechnet.
*I had not reckoned with such a stiff (steep; hefty) bill for my new suit.*

auf seine **Rechnung** kommen: *to obtain (to show) a return (a profit); to re-
coup one's outlay; to cover o.s.*

Unsere intensive Geschäftswerbung ist nicht umsonst gewesen. Wir sind durch
sie durchaus auf unsere Rechnung gekommen.
*Our intensive advertising has not been in vain. We have obtained (shown) a good return
(profit; have recouped our outlay; have covered ourselves) as a result of it.*

einer Sache **Rechnung** tragen (fig.): *to take s.th. into account (into consideration); to allow for s.th.*

Das Gericht hat dem bisherigen guten Benehmen des Angeklagten Rechnung
getragen.

*The court took the previous good behaviour of the accused into account (consideration; allowed for the previous good behaviour of the accused).*

die **Rechnung** ohne den Wirt machen (fig.): *to reckon without one's host; to work in the dark*

> Wenn du dieses Grundstück kaufen willst, so erkundige dich zunächst nach den Bedingungen. Sonst machst du die Rechnung ohne den Wirt.
> *If you want to buy that plot of land, inquire first about the conditions, otherwise you will be reckoning without your host (working in the dark).*

Alles, was **recht** ist: cf. Das muß man ihm **lassen**

**recht** und billig sein: *to be fair and just; to be right (fair; proper); to be the proper thing*

> Es ist nur recht und billig, daß du deinen Eltern finanziell (aus)helfen solltest.
> *It is only fair and just (only right [fair; proper]) that you should help (It is the proper thing for you to help) your parents out financially.*

Was dem einen **recht** ist, ist dem anderen billig (Sprichw.): *Sauce for the goose is sauce for the gander (prov.)*

> Wenn ich nicht schwimmen gehen darf, so sollte es meine Schwester auch nicht (dürfen). Was dem einen recht ist, ist dem anderen billig.
> *If I mustn't go swimming, my sister ought not to either. Sauce for the goose is sauce for the gander.*

**recht** und schlecht: cf. **schlecht** und recht

das **Recht** mit Füßen treten (fig.): *to trample justice underfoot*

> Wer das Recht mit Füßen tritt, wird bald zur Rechenschaft gezogen.
> *He who tramples justice underfoot will quickly be called to account.*

Du bist mir der **Rechte**! (fam.): *A fine one (A fine fellow) you are! (colloq.); You're a fine one (fellow)! (colloq.)*

> Gestern warst du mit dem Plan einverstanden, aber heute paßt er dir nicht mehr. Du bist mir der Rechte (Richtige)!
> *Yesterday you agreed to the plan but today it doesn't suit you any more. A fine one (fellow) you are! (You're a fine one [fellow]!)*

Das geschieht dir ganz **recht!**: cf. Da hast du dein **Fett!**

an den **Rechten** kommen: *to meet one's match (equal; master); to meet one's Waterloo; to bite off more than one can chew (colloq.)*

> Walter glaubte, er könne jeden beim Schachspielen schlagen, aber bei mir ist er an den Rechten gekommen (hat er seinen Mann [Meister] gefunden). Ich habe ihn binnen kurzer Zeit geschlagen.
> *Walter thought he could beat everybody at chess, but with me he met his match (equal; master; his Waterloo; with me he bit off more than he could chew). I beat him in a short time.*

nach dem **Rechten** sehen: *to keep an eye (a watch) on things; to look after things*

Sie müssen mal nach dem Rechten sehen, wenn Ihr neues Haus rechtzeitig fertig werden soll.
*You must keep an eye (a watch) on things (look after things) if your new house is to be finished in time.*

j.em **Rede** und Antwort stehen: *to account (to answer) to s.b.; to give s.b. an account*

Ich bin jederzeit bereit, Ihnen über meine Motive Rede und Antwort zu stehen.
*I am ready at any time to account (answer) to you for my motives (to give you an account of my motives).*

j.en zur **Rede** stellen: cf. j.en ins **Gebet** nehmen

nicht der **Rede** wert sein: *to be not worth mentioning (talking about); to be nothing to speak of*

Ich habe mir den Fuß verstaucht, aber die Schmerzen sind nicht der Rede wert.
*I have sprained my foot, but the pain is not worth mentioning (talking about; is nothing to speak of).*

mit sich **reden** lassen (fig.): *one can talk to s.b.; to be approachable*

Unser Chef ist ein vernünftiger Mann, der mit sich reden läßt.
*Our boss is a reasonable man to whom one can talk (a reasonable and approachable man).*

**Reden** ist Silber, Schweigen ist Gold (Sprichw.): cf. Reden ist **Silber, Schweigen ist Gold**

j.en **reell** bedienen: *to give s.b. (good) value for (his) money; to give s.b. his money's worth*

Es sollte das Bestreben eines jeden Kaufmannes sein, seine Kundschaft reell zu bedienen.
*It should be the aim of every shopkeeper to give his customers (good) value for (their) money (to give his customers their money's worth).*

ein altes (dummes) **Reff** sein (fam.): *to be an old hag (colloq.)*

Das alte (dumme) Reff wollte mir wegen meines Verhaltens Vorwürfe machen.
*The old hag was going to blame me for my behaviour.*

Keine **Regel** ohne Ausnahme (Sprichw.): *There is an exception to every rule (prov.)*

In diesem Land ist der Sommer sonst heiß, aber dieses Jahr ist er kühl und regnerisch. Keine Regel ohne Ausnahme.
*The summer is usually hot in this country but this year it is cold and wet. There is an exception to every rule.*

Die Ausnahme bestätigt die **Regel** (Sprichw.): *The exception proves the rule (prov.)*

Aus der Tatsache, daß nur ein Eisenbahnwagen schmutzig war, konnte man ersehen, daß alle Wagen sauber sein sollten. Die Ausnahme bestätigt die Regel.
*As a result of the fact that only one railway coach was dirty, one could see that all the coaches were supposed to be clean. The exception proves the rule.*

nach allen **Regeln** der Kunst (fig.): *with a vengeance; in the strongest sense of the word; by any standards.* Cf. auch: wie er im **Buche** steht

Hier gibt es keine Entschuldigung. Es war ein Betrug nach allen Regeln der Kunst.
*There is no excuse for this. It was a trick with a vengeance ( , in the strongest sense of the word; by any standards).*

Sich **regen** bringt Segen (Sprichw.): cf. Hilf dir selbst, so hilft dir **Gott**

Auf **Regen** folgt Sonnenschein (Sprichw.): *Sunshine follows the rain (prov.); Every cloud has a silver lining (prov.)*

Ihre Lage wird nicht immer so traurig bleiben. Auf Regen folgt Sonnenschein.
*Your position will not always be so sad. Sunshine follows the rain (Every cloud has a silver lining).*

vom **Regen** in die Traufe kommen (fig.): *to fall out of the frying-pan into the fire; to go from bad to worse*

Wir sind vom Regen in die Traufe gekommen, da unsere neuen Nachbarn ja noch unangenehmer als ihre Vorgänger sind.
*We have fallen out of the frying-pan into the fire (We have gone from bad to worse), since our new neighbours are even more unpleasant than their predecessors.*

gespannt wie ein **Regenschirm** sein (fam.): *to be on tenterhooks; to be all worked (keyed) up (colloq.)*

Karl war gespannt wie ein Regenschirm (Flitzebogen), ob er die Prüfung bestanden habe oder nicht.
*Charles was on tenterhooks (all worked [keyed] up) about whether he had passed the examination or not.*

das **Regiment** führen (fig.): cf. die **Hosen** anhaben

in höheren **Regionen** schweben (fig.): *to be in the clouds; to have one's head in the clouds; to be in another world*

Dieser Sprachforscher lebt nur für seine Arbeit und schwebt ständig in höheren Regionen (ist . . . in einer anderen Welt).
*This philologist lives only for his work and is perpetually in the clouds (perpetually has his head in the clouds; is perpetually in another world).*

416

alle **Register** ziehen (fig.): *to pull out all the stops.* Cf. auch: alle **Hebel** in Bewegung setzen

Sie müssen alle Register ziehen, wenn Sie diesen wichtigen Posten bekommen wollen.
*You must pull out all the stops if you want to get that important job.*

rauh wie ein **Reibeisen** sein: *to be as rough as a nutmeg-grater (as emery-paper)*

Meine Hände sind durch meine Arbeit rauh wie ein Reibeisen geworden.
*My hands have become as rough as a nutmeg-grater (as emery-paper) with my work.*

im **Reichtum** schwimmen (fig.): cf. **Geld** wie Heu haben

Was schnell **reift,** fällt bald ab (Sprichw.): *Soon ripe, soon rotten (prov.)*

Mit zehn Jahren war Wilhelm außerordentlich gescheit, er hat aber alles schnell wieder vergessen. Was schnell reift, fällt bald ab.
*At ten William was exceptionally clever, but he quickly forgot everything. Soon ripe, soon rotten.*

den **Reigen** eröffnen (fig.): *to set the ball rolling; to start things off; to kick off (colloq.)*

Bei der Prüfung mußte ich den Reigen eröffnen. Ich wurde als erster gefragt.
*At the examination I had to set the ball rolling (to start things off; to kick off). I was the first to be questioned.*

in **Reih'** und Glied antreten: *to line up; to get into line;* (außerdem nur militär.) *to fall in*

Die Soldaten waren in Reih' und Glied angetreten, als der Oberst erschien.
*The soldiers were lined up (had got into line; were fallen in) when the colonel appeared.*

Die **Reihen** lichten sich: *The ranks are thinning out (are getting thin)*

Der erste Weltkrieg liegt schon weit zurück. Die Reihen der Teilnehmer an ihm haben sich bereits stark gelichtet.
*The first World War was a long while ago. The ranks of those who took part in it have already greatly thinned out (are already [getting] very thin).*

aus der **Reihe** tanzen (fig.): *to break away; to go off on one's own; to stray from the fold (colloq.); to step out of the ranks*

Alle Mitglieder unserer Familie sind Beamte. Jetzt tanzt mein Sohn aus der Reihe und will Maler werden.
*The members of our family are all civil servants. Now my son has broken away (has gone off on his own; has strayed from the fold; has stepped out of the ranks) and wants to become a painter.*

sich keinen **Reim** aus etwas machen können (fig.): cf. sich keinen **Vers** aus etwas machen können

etwas ins **reine** bringen: *to straighten (to iron) s. th. out; to settle s. th.; to clear s. th. up; to get s. th. straight (colloq.)*. Cf. auch: sich **ausbügeln**.

> Bevor wir weiter verhandeln, wollen wir zuerst diese Angelegenheit ins reine bringen.
> *Before we negotiate further, let us first straighten (iron) out (clear up; settle) this matter (get this matter straight).*

mit j.em ins **reine** kommen: *to come to an understanding with s. b.; to make a working arrangement with s. b.; to come to terms with s. b.*

> Mein Kollege ist nicht sehr sympathisch, aber ich versuche, mit ihm ins reine zu kommen.
> *My colleague is not very likeable, but I try to come to an understanding (to make a working arrangement; come to terms) with him.*

j.em eine ’**reinhauen** (fam.): cf. j.em eine **kleben**

j.en ’**reinlegen**: cf. j.en auf den **Leim** führen (leimen)

sich **reinwaschen** (fam.): *to clear o. s.; to put o. s. in the clear (colloq.)*

> Vergebens versuchte der Beschuldigte, sich von dem Vorwurf reinzuwaschen.
> *The accused tried in vain to clear himself of (to put himself in the clear with) the charge.*

**Reisefieber** haben: *to have travel-nerves; to have travel-jitters (colloq.)*

> Morgen fahren wir nach Italien. Hast du schon Reisefieber?
> *Tomorrow we're going to Italy. Have you got travel-nerves (travel-jitters)?*

**Reißaus** nehmen: cf. **Fersengeld** geben

**reißend** abgehen: cf. abgehen wie die warmen **Semmeln**

**Reklame** für etwas machen: *to make propaganda for s. th.; to boost s. th. up (colloq.); to plug s. th. (sl.)*

> Für die verschiedenen Seifenpulver wird in den Zeitungen viel Reklame gemacht (die [Werbe]trommel gerührt).
> *A great deal of propaganda is made in the papers for the various soap-powders (The various soap-powders are greatly boosted up [are plugged] in the papers).*

j.en **rempeln** (fam.): *to charge s. b.; to barge s. b. (colloq.)*

> Dieser Fußballspieler spielt sehr roh; er rempelt, wo er nur kann.
> *That footballer plays very roughly; he charges (barges) whenever he can.*

das **Rennen** aufgeben (fig.): cf. den **Kampf** aufgeben

das **Rennen** machen (fig.): *to make the running; to set the pace; to lead the field*

> Von den zahlreichen Bewerbern um diesen Posten macht mein Schwager das Rennen.

*Of the many applicants for this job my brother-in-law is making the running (setting the pace; leading the field).*

## sich **rentieren**: *to pay*

Es würde sich sicher rentieren (lohnen; verlohnen; auszahlen), hier einen Gasthof zu errichten (zu bauen).
*It would certainly pay to build an inn here.*

## aus seiner **Reserve** heraustreten: *to come out of one's shell; to let one's hair down (colloq.)*

Warum ist Alma so scheu und zurückhaltend? Sie sollte einmal etwas aus ihrer Reserve heraustreten.
*Why is Alma so shy and reserved? She ought to come out of her shell (let down her hair) a bit.*

## mit **Respekt** zu sagen: cf. mit **Verlaub** zu sagen

## j.em (einer Sache) den **Rest** geben: a) (von Menschen und Sachen) *to give s.b. (s.th.) the coup de grâce; to deal s.b. (s.th.) a knock-out blow (a death-blow); to finish (to polish) s.b. (s.th.) off (colloq.); to be the last straw for s.b. (s. th.);* b) (nur von Menschen) *to cook s.b.'s goose (sl.)*

a) Der Frost des vergangenen Winters hat meinem schönen Apfelbaum den Rest gegeben.

b) Diese Lungenentzündung hat meinem alten Vater den Rest gegeben (Durch diese L. hat sich mein alter V. den Rest geholt).

*a) Last winter's frost gave my beautiful apple-tree the coup de grâce (dealt ... a knock-out blow [a death-blow]; finished [polished] ... off; was the last straw for ...).*

*b) That pneumonia gave my old father the coup de grâce (usw. wie unter a); cooked my father's goose).*

## Der **Rest** ist für die Gottlosen: *The dogs can have the rest; The rest is for the dogs (for anyone who wants it)*

Das Essen war so reichlich, daß wir Gemüse und Kartoffeln übrigließen. Der Rest war für die Gottlosen.
*There was so much food that we left some vegetables and potatoes. The dogs could have the rest (The rest was for the dogs [for anyone who wanted it]).*

## sich den **Rest** holen: cf. j.em (einer Sache) den **Rest** geben a) und b)

## j.en **restlos** schlagen: *to beat s.b. all ends up; to beat s.b. hollow; to wipe the floor with s.b. (sl.)*

Franz war ein weit besserer Spieler und hat mich restlos geschlagen.
*Frank was a far better player and beat me all ends up (hollow; wiped the floor with me).*

## eine **Retourkutsche** (fig.): *a come-back; repartee*

Ich hatte meiner Schwester oft gesagt, sie solle nicht immer so laut sprechen. Jetzt sagte sie heute zu mir: Sprich doch leiser! – Das war nur eine Retourkutsche.
*I had often told my sister not to talk so loudly. Then today she said to me: Talk more softly! – That was only a come-back (only repartee).*

sich nicht zu **retten** wissen (fig.): cf. nicht **aus** noch ein wissen

ein **Rettungsanker** sein (fig.): *to act as a sheet-anchor; to act as a saviour; to act as a friend in need*

> Als der Student kein Geld mehr hatte, half ihm sein guter Onkel aus seiner unglücklichen Lage und war sein Rettungsanker.
> *When the student had no money left, his kind uncle helped him out of his unhappy situation and acted as his sheet-anchor (saviour; friend in need).*

sich **revanchieren**: *to pay s. b. back; to do the same by s. b.; to return the compliment*

> Schneiders machen uns oft Geschenke. Hoffentlich können wir uns bald einmal revanchieren.
> *The Schneiders often give us presents. I hope we shall soon be able to pay them back (do the same by them; return the compliment).*

ein **Revolverblatt** sein (fam.): cf. ein **Käseblatt** sein

ein **Rhinozeros** sein (fig. u. fam.): cf. ein **Rindvieh** sein

Du bist mir der **Richtige!**: cf. Du bist mir der **Rechte!**

j.en (etwas) nicht **riechen** können (fig. u. fam.): *not to be able to stand (to stick) s. b. (s. th.) (the sight of s. b. (s. th.) (colloq.); s. b. (s. th.) puts one's back up (colloq.)*

> Der Beamte am Postschalter ist sehr unfreundlich. Niemand kann ihn riechen (ausstehen; besehen; besichtigen; verknusen; verputzen).
> *The official at the post-office counter is very unfriendly. No one can stand (stick) him (the sight of him; He puts everybody's back up).*

den richtigen **Riecher** für etwas haben (fig. u. fam.): cf. die richtige **Nase** für etwas haben

j.em einen **Riegel** vorschieben (fig.): cf. j.em einen **Knüppel** zwischen die Beine werfen

einer Sache einen **Riegel** vorschieben (fig.): *to put a stop (an end) to s. th.; to wipe s. th. out; to knock s. th. on the head (colloq.)*

> Den kleinen Betrügereien mancher dieser Fabrikarbeiter muß ein Riegel vorgeschoben werden.
> *The little deceptions of certain of these factory workers must be put a stop (an end) to (must be wiped out; must be knocked on the head).*

sich am **Riemen** reißen (fig. u. fam.): cf. sich **zusammennehmen**

seinen **Riemen** enger schnallen (fig. u. fam.): *to tighten one's belt; to cut one's coat according to one's cloth; to draw in one's horns.* Cf. auch: sich nach der **Decke** strecken

> Wenn die Gehälter mit den steigenden Preisen nicht Schritt halten, muß man sparsam sein und seinen (Leib)riemen (Gürtel) enger schnallen.
> *If salaries do not keep pace with rising prices, one must live economically and tighten one's belt (cut one's coat according to one's cloth; draw in one's horns).*

nach Adam **Riese**: cf. nach **Adam** Riese

eine Stimme zum **Rindfleischessen** haben (fam.): cf. eine Stimme wie ein **Rabe** haben

ein **Rindvieh** sein (fig. u. fam.): *to be a blockhead (dolt; bonehead; donkey; numskull; goon; fathead) (colloq.)*

> Ich hätte nie gedacht, daß Karl so ein Rindvieh (Däm[e]lack; Dummkopf; Dussel; Esel; Hornochse; Hornvieh; Rhinozeros; Roß; Schaf[skopf]) ist (so dumm ist, daß er brummt; vor Dummheit brummt).
> *I should never have thought that Charles was such a blockhead (dolt; bonehead; donkey; numskull; goon; fathead).*

nichts Ordentliches in den **Rippen** haben (fam.): cf. nur noch **Haut** und Knochen sein

Ich kann es mir doch nicht aus den **Rippen** schneiden (fam.): *I can't produce it out of a hat (colloq.); I can't make it from air (colloq.)*

> Wie soll ich denn eure Wünsche erfüllen? Ich kann mir das viele Geld doch nicht aus den Rippen schneiden.
> *How can I fulfil your requests? I can't produce all that money out of a hat (make all that money from air).*

j.em einen **Rippenstoß** geben (versetzen) (fig.): *to jog s. b.'s memory; to give s. b. a reminder*

> Wenn Ernst mir die zweihundert Mark nicht bald zurückgibt, werde ich ihm einen kleinen Rippenstoß geben (versetzen) müssen.
> *If Ernest does not give me back the two hundred marks soon, I shall have to jog his memory a bit (to give him a gentle reminder).*

sich ein rot(es) **Röckelchen** verdienen (fig. u. fam.): cf. sich lieb **Kind** machen

sich an j.es **Rockschöße (-zipfel)** hängen (fig.): *to hold on to (to cling to) s. b.'s coat-tails (apron-strings)*

Kurt sollte selbständiger werden und sich nicht immer an meine Rockschöße (-zipfel) hängen.
*Curt ought to be more independent and not always hold on (cling) to my coat-tails (apron-strings).*

ein schwankes **Rohr** sein (fig.): *not to know one's own mind; to be like a reed before the wind*

Bald stimmt er für diese Partei, bald für jene. Er ist ein schwankendes Rohr.
*Sometimes he votes for this party, sometimes for that. He does not know his own mind (He is like a reed before the wind).*

in die **Röhre** gucken (fig. u. fam.): cf. **leer** (bei etwas) ausgehen

schimpfen wie ein **Rohrspatz** (fam.): cf. fluchen wie ein **Landsknecht**

aus der **Rolle** fallen (fig.): *to act out of character; to forget o.s.; to kick over the traces*

Wie konnte er nur so aus der Rolle fallen, wo er doch sonst so ruhig ist?
*How could he act so out of character (How could he kick over the traces [forget himself] like that), when he is normally so quiet?*

eine armselige **Rolle** spielen (fig.): cf. eine traurige **Figur** spielen

die erste **Rolle** spielen (fig.): cf. die erste **Geige** spielen

eine große **Rolle** spielen (fig.): *to play a great part (an important rôle)*

Das Wort „Demokratie" spielt in der Politik eine große Rolle.
*The word democracy plays a great part (an important rôle) in politics.*

keine **Rolle** spielen (fig.): *to be no object; to be of no consequence; not to matter two hoots (two pins; a jot; a scrap) (colloq.); not to matter a tinker's cuss (sl.)*

Bei meinem Onkel spielt das Geld überhaupt keine Rolle.
*Money is no object at all (is of no consequence at all) to my uncle (does not matter two hoots [two pins; a jot; a scrap; a tinker's cuss] to my uncle).*

in **Rom** gewesen sein, ohne den Papst gesehen zu haben (fig.): *It is like having been to London without seeing the Queen*

Du bist in Köln gewesen und hast den Dom nicht besichtigt? Dann warst du in Rom, ohne den Papst gesehen zu haben.
*You were in Cologne and did not visit the cathedral? That is like having been to London without seeing the Queen.*

**Rom** ist nicht an éinem Tag erbaut (worden) (Sprichw.): *Rome was not built in a day (prov.)*

Die Lösung des Problems läßt sich nicht sofort finden. Rom ist nicht an éinem Tag erbaut (worden).
*The solution to the problem cannot be found at once. Rome was not built in a day.*

422

Viele *(Alle)* Wege führen nach **Rom** (Sprichw.): *All roads lead to Rome (prov.)*

> Ihr Ziel läßt sich auf verschiedene Weise erreichen. Viele (Alle) Wege führen nach Rom.
> *Your goal can be reached in various ways. All roads lead to Rome.*

einen ganzen **Roman** erzählen (fig.): *to tell a whole rigmarole (colloq.)*

> Der Dieb wollte sich herausreden und erzählte mir einen ganzen Roman.
> *The thief wanted to talk his way out, and told me a whole rigmarole.*

Keine **Rose** ohne Dornen (Sprichw.): *There is no rose without a thorn (prov.); Everything has its dark side*

> Sogar ein Millionär hat seine Sorgen. Keine Rose ohne Dornen.
> *Even the millionaire has his troubles. There is no rose without a thorn (Everything has its dark side).*

nicht auf **Rosen** gebettet sein (fig.): *Life is not a bed of roses (a piece of cake) for s.b.; not to be lying on a bed of roses; not to have a cushy time (sl.); Life is not all beer and skittles for s.b. (sl.)*

> Seine Eltern sind beide gestorben, und er ist keineswegs auf Rosen gebettet (sein Leben ist kein Zuckerlecken).
> *His parents are both dead, and life is not a bed of roses (a piece of cake) for him (he is not lying on a bed of roses [not having a cushy time]; life is not all beer and skittles for him).*

große **Rosinen** im Kopf haben (fig. u. fam.): *to have high-flown ideas (notions) in one's head; to be full of high-falutin' ideas (colloq.); to have been bitten by a big bug (sl.)*

> Mein älterer Bruder hat große Rosinen im Kopf. Er will Musik studieren und ein großer Pianist werden.
> *My elder brother has high-flown ideas (notions) in his head (is full of high-falutin' ideas; has been bitten by a big bug). He wants to study music and become a great pianist.*

sich die besten (größten) **Rosinen** aus dem Kuchen klauben (fig.): cf. den **Rahm** abschöpfen

ein (dummes) **Roß** sein (fig. u. fam.): cf. ein **Rindvieh** sein

sich aufs hohe **Roß** setzen (auf dem hohen Rosse sitzen) (fig.): *to mount (to get on) one's high horse; to ride the high horse.* Cf. auch: sich **mausig** machen

> Der eingebildete Schauspieler setzte sich aufs hohe Roß (Pferd; saß auf dem hohen Rosse [auf hohem Pferde]) und lehnte jede Kritik ab.
> *The conceited actor mounted (got on) his high horse (rode the high horse) and rejected all criticisms.*

eine **Roßkur** (durch)machen: cf. eine **Pferdekur** (durch)machen etwas **rot** anstreichen (fig.): cf. etwas rot im **Kalender** anstreichen

Heute **rot,** morgen tot (Sprichw.): *Here today and gone tomorrow (prov.)*

Dieser verhältnismäßig junge Bankier ist ganz plötzlich gestorben, obwohl ihm gesundheitlich gar nichts fehlte. Heute rot, morgen tot.
*That comparatively young banker has died quite suddenly, though there was nothing at all wrong with him. Here today and gone tomorrow.*

sich wie ein **roter** Faden hindurchziehen: cf. sich wie ein roter **Faden** hindurchziehen

Der **Rubel** rollt (fig.): *The akkers are rolling in; The coffers are filling up*

Zu dieser Jahreszeit hat unsere Firma viele Kunden zu bedienen. Der Rubel rollt.
*At this time of year our firm has a great number of customers to deal with. The akkers are rolling in (The coffers are filling up).*

sich einen **Ruck** geben (fig.): *to take the plunge; to take the bit between one's teeth; to pluck up courage; to screw one's courage to the sticking-place; to galvanise o.s. into action; to pull o.s. together*

Bei diesem kalten Wetter möchte ich (eigentlich) lieber drinnen bleiben, ich muß mir aber einen Ruck (meinem Herzen einen Ruck [Stoß]) geben und in den Garten gehen, um den Zaun zu reparieren.
*In this cold weather I would rather stay indoors, but I must take the plunge (pluck up courage; screw my courage to the sticking-place; galvanise myself into action; take the bit between my teeth; pull myself together) and go into the garden to mend the fence.*

einen breiten **Rücken** haben (fig.): cf. einen breiten **Buckel** haben
sich den **Rücken** decken (fig.): *to cover o.s.*

Glücklicherweise hatten sich die Eigentümer unseres Schiffes gegen solche Schäden den Rücken gedeckt.
*Fortunately the owners of our ship had covered themselves against such damage.*

(fast) auf den **Rücken** fallen: cf. aufs **Kreuz** fallen
j.em in den **Rücken** fallen (fig.): *to attack s.b. from behind (from [in] the rear); to stab s.b. in the back; to double-cross s.b. (colloq.)*

Ich dachte, man könnte sich auf ihn verlassen, er ist uns jedoch in den Rücken gefallen.
*I thought we could depend on him, but he has attacked us from behind (from [in] the rear; stabbed us in the back; double-crossed us).*

sich den **Rücken** freihalten (fig.): *to keep the distance; to preserve the gap; to hold one's own*

Durch ihre neuen Siege hält sich unsere Fußballmannschaft gegenüber den in der Tabelle folgenden Vereinen den Rücken frei.
*By their recent victories our football team are keeping the distance (preserving the gap) between them and (are holding their own against) the clubs below them in the table.*

j.em (einer Sache) den **Rücken** kehren (fig.): *to turn one's back on s.b. (s.th.);*
*to give s.b. (s.th.) the go-by (colloq.).* Cf. auch: j.en kalt **abrutschen** lassen

Seit seinem Erfolg im Ausland hat Erich seinen früheren Freunden den Rücken
gekehrt.
*Since his success abroad Eric has turned his back on his former friends (given his former*
*friends the go-by).*

j.em heiß und kalt über den **Rücken** laufen: cf. j.en **heiß** und kalt überlaufen

j.em den **Rücken** stärken (eine **Rückenstärkung** sein) (fig.): *to give s.b.*
*moral support; to back s.b. up; to strengthen (to stiffen) s.b.; to buck s.b. up*
*(colloq.)*

Das Verständnis seitens aller Kollegen hat mir für meinen Kampf mit der Be-
hörde den Rücken gestärkt (den Nacken gesteift; ist mir ... eine Rückenstärkung).
*The understanding on the part of all my colleagues has given me moral support (has*
*strengthened [stiffened] me; has backed [bucked] me up) for my struggle with the authori-*
*ties.*

kein **Rückgrat** haben (fig.): *to have no backbone; to have no guts (colloq.)*

Da Karl kein Rückgrat hat, ist er trotz seiner Begabung im Leben nicht voran-
gekommen.
*Since Charles has no backbone (guts), he has not got on in life, in spite of his gifts.*

**Rückschläge** erleiden: cf. **Nackenschläge** bekommen

einen **Rückzieher** machen (fig.): *to retreat; to withdraw; to climb down (colloq.)*

Als wir ihm mit einer Klage bei Gericht drohten, machte er einen Rückzieher
(kniff er).
*When we threatened him with court action, he retreated (withdrew; climbed down).*

das **Ruder** fest in der Hand haben (fig.): cf. das **Heft** in der Hand haben;
fest im **Sattel** sitzen

ans **Ruder** kommen (fig.): *to take over; to take charge; to take the reins; to take*
*the wheel; to take over the ship; to take control of the ship; to come to power*

In diesem Land sind jetzt neue Männer ans Ruder gekommen (haben ...
die Zügel in die Hand genommen; das Heft [Staatsruder] ergriffen).
*In that country new men have now taken over (taken charge; taken the reins; taken*
*the wheel; taken over the ship; taken control of the ship; come to power).*

lange am **Ruder** gewesen sein (fig.): *to have been a long while at the helm; to*
*have held the reins for a long while; to have had a long innings*

Als Ministerpräsident ist Gladstone lange am Ruder gewesen.
*Gladstone was a long while at the helm (held the reins for a long while; had a long innings) as Prime Minister.*

**j.em einen (schweren) Rüffel erteilen** (fam.): cf. j.en **abkanzeln**

**j.en zur letzten Ruhe bestatten (betten):** *to lay s.b. to rest; to bear s.b. to his last resting-place*

Vorigen Dienstag ist sein alter Großvater zur letzten Ruhe bestattet (gebettet) worden.
*Last Tuesday his old grandfather was laid to rest (borne to his last resting-place).*

**Ruhe ist die erste Bürgerpflicht** (Sprichw.): *A citizen's first duty is to keep the peace (prov.)*

Man darf seinem Zorn nicht sofort Ausdruck verleihen. Denn Ruhe ist die erste Bürgerpflicht.
*One must not display one's anger immediately, for a citizen's first duty is to keep the peace.*

**zur ewigen Ruhe eingehen:** *to go to one's last resting-place (to one's haven of rest)*

Jetzt ist die alte Frau endlich zur ewigen Ruhe eingegangen (Jetzt endlich deckt der grüne Rasen diese alte Frau).
*Now at last the old woman has gone to her last resting-place (to her haven of rest).*

**j.en in Ruhe lassen:** *to leave s.b. in peace; to leave s.b. alone*

Ich wünschte, du würdest mich jetzt in Ruhe (Frieden) lassen.
*I wish you would leave me in peace (alone) now.*

**Nur (Immer) mit der Ruhe!:** cf. Nur **langsam!**

**Ein gutes Gewissen ist ein sanftes Ruhekissen** (Sprichw.): *A clear conscience is a soft pillow (prov.); He who has a clear conscience sleeps well*

Warum sollte ich mich aufregen? Ich habe mir nichts vorzuwerfen. Ein gutes Gewissen ist ein sanftes Ruhekissen.
*Why should I worry? I have nothing to blame myself for. A clear conscience is a soft pillow (He who has a clear conscience sleeps well).*

**sich nicht mit Ruhm bedecken** (fam.: bekleckern): *not to cover o.s. with glory; not to come off particularly well; not to make history; not to shine*

Bei der Prüfung habe ich mich leider nicht mit Ruhm bedeckt (bekleckert; Die Prüfung war kein Ruhmesblatt für mich).
*I am afraid I did not cover myself with glory (did not come off particularly well; did not make history; did not shine) at the examination.*

**kein Ruhmesblatt für j.en sein:** cf. sich nicht mit **Ruhm** bedecken

den **Rummel** kennen (fam.): *to know the ins and outs of s.th. (colloq.); to know the ropes (colloq.); to be in the know (colloq.); to know one's stuff (sl.); to be up to snuff (sl.); There are no flies on s.b. (sl.).* Cf. auch: vom **Bau** sein; alle **Schliche** kennen

Über Autoreparaturen brauchst du mir nichts zu erzählen. Ich kenne den Rummel.
*You don't need to tell me anything about car repairs. I know the ins and outs of them (I know the ropes; I'm in the know [up to snuff]; I know my stuff; There are no flies on me).*

etwas mit **Rumpf** und Stumpf ausrotten (fig.): cf. etwas mit **Stumpf** und Stiel ausrotten

eine **Runde** ausgeben: *to stand a round of drinks*

Wir waren im Kegelklub bei bester Stimmung, und da ich Geburtstag hatte, habe ich eine Runde ausgegeben.
*We were in the best of spirits at the skittle-club, and as it was my birthday, I stood a round of drinks.*

die **Runde** machen (fig.): *to go the rounds; to circulate*

Sie haben auch schon von diesem Gerücht gehört? Es macht offenbar die Runde.
*So you've heard this rumour as well? It's apparently going the rounds (circulating).*

j.en (etwas) **rundweg** ablehnen: *to turn s.b. (s.th.) down point-blank (flat); to reject s.th. out of hand*

Sein armseliges Angebot habe ich rundweg (glatt; schlankweg) abgelehnt.
*I turned his miserable offer down point-blank (flat; rejected ... out of hand).*

j.em eine '**runterhauen** (fam.): cf. j.em eine **kleben**

j.en **rupfen** (fig. u. fam.): *to fleece (to pluck) s.b. (colloq.); to rook s.b. (colloq.); to sting s.b. (sl.)*

In diesem Geschäft hat man mich ordentlich gerupft.
*I was properly fleeced (plucked; rooked; stung) in that shop.*

aussehen wie in **Russisch-Polen**: cf. ein **Schweinestall** sein

sich eine **Rute** aufbinden (fig.): *to make a rod for one's own back*

Mit diesem Hund haben wir uns eine Rute aufgebunden. Er ist sehr ungehorsam.
*We have made a rod for our own backs with this dog. He is very disobedient.*

Wer die **Rute** spart, verzieht das Kind (Sprichw.): *Spare the rod and spoil the child (prov.)*

Sie müssen strenger mit Ihrem Sohn sein. Wer die Rute spart, verzieht das Kind.
*You must be stricter with your son. Spare the rod and spoil the child.*

an etwas ist nicht zu **rütteln** und zu schütteln (fig.): *s.th. has been settled once and for all; s.th. is quite unshakable; s.th. is as definite as anything can be; s.th. is as firm as a rock (as the Rock of Gibraltar)*

> Das ist nun einmal der genaue Wortlaut des Gesetzes. An ihm ist nicht zu rütteln und zu schütteln (zu drehen und zu deuteln).
> *That is the exact wording of the law. It has been settled once and for all (is quite unshakable; is as definite as anything can be; is as firm as a rock [as the Rock of Gibraltar]).*

## S

mit dem **Säbel** rasseln (fig.): *to rattle the sabre; to brandish (to shake) one's fist*

> Es steckt nichts hinter seinen Drohungen. Er rasselt nur mit dem Säbel.
> *There is nothing behind his threats. He is only rattling the sabre (only brandishing [shaking] his fist).*

bei der **Sache** bleiben: *to keep (to stick) to the point*

> Es wäre ratsam für uns, bei der Sache zu bleiben.
> *It would be advisable for us to keep (to stick) to the point.*

bei der **Sache** sein: cf. mit dem **Herzen** dabei sein

mit j.em gemeinsame **Sache** machen: *to throw in one's lot with s.b.; to make common cause with s.b.; to decide to sink or swim together; to join forces (to join up) with s.b.*

> Die beiden Parteien teilen ungefähr dieselben Ansichten und haben jetzt gemeinsame Sache gemacht.
> *The two parties share roughly the same views and have now thrown in their lot with each other (made common cause with each other; decided to sink or swim together; joined forces; joined up with each other).*

seine **Sache** gut machen: *to acquit o.s. well; to get on all right; to make a success of s.th.; to make a good job of s.th. (colloq.)*

> Meine Arbeit wurde gelobt, und der Lehrer sagte, ich hätte meine Sache gut gemacht (verstanden).
> *My work was praised, and the master said that I had acquitted myself well (had got on all right; had made a success [a good job] of it).*

zur **Sache** kommen: *to come to the point; to get down to s.th. (to business); to cut the cackle and come to the horses (colloq.); to get down to brass tacks (colloq.)*

Wir sitzen schon seit einer Stunde da. Lassen Sie uns endlich einmal zur Sache kommen.
*We have been sitting here for an hour now. Let's come to the point (get down to it [to business; to brass tacks]; cut the cackle and come to the horses).*

Was sind das für **Sachen**!: *What a business! (colloq.); What a thing to do! (colloq.)*

Du hast dein Brüderchen so ins Gesicht geschlagen, daß es Nasenbluten bekommen hat. Was sind das (bloß) für Sachen!
*You hit your little brother so hard in the face that it made his nose bleed. What a business! (What a thing to do!)*

Das tut nichts zur **Sache**: *That is of no relevance; That makes no difference; That has nothing to do with it; That is beside the point*

Im Examen werden gute Sprachkenntnisse verlangt. Ob man im Ausland war oder nicht, tut nichts zur Sache.
*For the examination a good knowledge of languages is required. Whether one has been abroad or not is of no relevance (makes no difference; has nothing to do with it; is beside the point).*

unverrichteter **Sache** abziehen (fortgehen): cf. unverrichteter **Dinge** abziehen (fortgehen)

seine **Sache** verstehen: cf. seine **Sache** gut machen

von keiner **Sachkenntnis** getrübt sein (iron.): *not to suffer from (not to be burdened with) any expert knowledge*

Dieser Bericht liest sich ganz schön, ist jedoch von keiner Sachkenntnis getrübt.
*This account reads quite well, but it does not suffer from (is not burdened with) any expert knowledge.*

(Nur) **sachte**!: cf. Nur **langsam**!

in **Sack** und Asche Buße tun (trauern): *to cover o.s. in sackcloth and ashes; to hang one's head in shame*

Wir haben es wirklich nicht böse gemeint. Wir tun in Sack und Asche Buße (Wir trauern in Sack und Asche) und bitten um Verzeihung.
*We really did not mean to be unkind. We cover ourselves in sackcloth and ashes (hang our heads in shame) and ask your forgiveness.*

Den **Sack** schlägt man, den Esel meint man (Sprichw.): *to blame one person and mean another; to pursue the shadow*

Der Chef sagte, er sei mit meiner Arbeit nicht zufrieden, aber in Wirklichkeit dachte er dabei an den Prokuristen. Den Sack schlägt man, den Esel meint man.
*The boss said that he was not satisfied with my work, but in fact he was thinking of the chief clerk. He blamed one person and meant another (He was pursuing the shadow).*

lieber einen **Sack** Flöhe hüten (fam.): *to prefer to keep an elephant (in one's back garden) (colloq.)*

> Ich kann verstehen, daß Sie mit Ihren drei hübschen Töchtern Ihre Sorgen haben. Ich möchte lieber (einen Sack) Flöhe hüten.
> *I can understand that you have your troubles with your three pretty daughters. I would rather keep an elephant (in my back garden).*

tief in den **Sack** greifen (fam.): cf. tief in die **Tasche** greifen

angeben wie ein **Sack** Läuse (fam.): cf. **angeben**

sich in seinen eigenen **Sack** lügen (fam.): *to dupe (to blind) o.s.; to pull the wool over one's eyes; to kid o.s. (colloq.)*

> Du lügst dir nur in deinen eigenen Sack, wenn du meinst, das Grundstück billig erworben zu haben.
> *You are only duping (blinding; kidding) yourself (pulling the wool over your eyes) if you think that you have acquired that plot of land cheaply.*

mit **Sack** und Pack: cf. mit **Kind** und Kegel

schlafen wie ein **Sack**: cf. schlafen wie ein **Murmeltier**

j.en in den **Sack** stecken (fig. u. fam.): cf. j.en in die **Tasche** stecken

in eine **Sackgasse** geraten (fig.): *to run up against a brick wall; to get into a dead-end; to get stuck; to run into an impasse; to get bogged down; to reach deadlock*

> Da die Verhandlungen in eine Sackgasse geraten waren, wurde die Tagung abgebrochen.
> *Since the negotiations had run up against a brick wall (had got into a dead-end; had got stuck; had run into an impasse; had got bogged down; had reached deadlock), the meeting was broken off.*

tief in den **Säckel** greifen: cf. tief in die **Tasche** greifen

Was der Mensch **säet,** das wird er ernten (Sprichw.): *As ye sow, so shall ye reap (prov.).* Cf. auch: die **Suppe** auslöffeln, die man sich eingebrockt hat

> Wer zeitlebens geizig gewesen ist, kann in der Not nicht mit Großmut rechnen. Was der Mensch säet, das wird er ernten (Man muß auslöffeln, was man sich eingebrockt hat; Wie man in den Wald hineinruft, so schallt es zurück).
> *Whoever has been mean during his lifetime cannot count on generosity in time of need. As ye sow, so shall ye reap.*

ohne **Saft** und Kraft sein (fig.): *to have no life in it; to be anaemic (insipid; uninspired)*

> Wir waren von dem Sänger enttäuscht. Sein Vortrag war ganz ohne Saft und Kraft.

*We were disappointed in the singer. His performance had no life in it at all (was utterly anaemic [insipid; uninspired]).*

j.en in seinem eigenen **Saft** schmoren lassen (fig.): *to let s.b. stew (to leave s.b. to stew) in his own juice; to leave s.b. to face the music (colloq.); to let s.b. carry the can (back) (sl.)*

Ich hatte ihn schon oft vor einem solchen Schritt gewarnt, er hat aber nie auf mich gehört. Jetzt kann ich ihn nur in seinem eigenen Saft (Fett) schmoren lassen.
*I often warned him against such a step but he never listened to me. Now I can only let him stew (leave him to stew) in his own juice (leave him to face the music; let him carry the can [back]).*

Was Sie nicht **sagen!** (fam.): *Well, well!; What are you talking about?; You don't say! (colloq.)*

Ich soll diesen Herrn beleidigt haben? Was Sie nicht sagen! Ich kenne ihn überhaupt nicht.
*I am supposed to have offended this gentleman? Well, well! (What are you talking about? You don't say!) I don't even know him.*

nichts zu **sagen** haben (fig.): cf. nichts zu **melden** haben

**sage** und schreibe: *believe it or not; would you believe it; literally*

Die Skulptur war ungewöhnlich billig. Ich habe sage und schreibe nur zweihundert Mark für sie bezahlt.
*The sculpture was extraordinarily cheap. Believe it or not (Would you believe it), I only paid two hundred marks for it (I paid literally only two hundred marks for it).*

eine **Saite** bei j.em (in j.es Herzen) anschlagen (fig.): *to strike (to touch) a sympathetic cord in s.b. (in s.b.'s heart)*

Wenn man diese Seite bei ihm (in seinem Herzen) anschlägt, wird er sehr hilfsbereit.
*If one strikes (touches) this sympathetic cord in him (in his heart), he will be very helpful.*

andere **Saiten** aufziehen (fig.): *to change one's tune; to take a different line*

Wenn du weiterhin in der Schule so faul bist, werde ich andere Saiten aufziehen müssen.
*If you continue to be so lazy at school, I shall have to change my tune (to take a different line).*

die empfindliche **Saite** berühren (fig.): cf. ein wunder **Punkt** sein

Da haben wir den **Salat!** (fam.): cf. Da haben wir die **Bescherung!**

einen langen **Salm** machen: cf. wie die **Katze** um den heißen Brei gehen

bei j.em noch et was im **Salz** liegen haben (fig.): cf. ein **Hühnchen** mit j.em
zu rupfen haben

(wie) zur **Salzsäule** erstarrt sein: *to stand rooted to the spot; to stand there petri-*
*fied; to be shaken rigid (sl.)*

> Wir waren wie zur Salzsäule erstarrt (standen wie angewurzelt [behext; ver-
> donnert; versteinert] da), als wir erfuhren, daß das Flugzeug abgestürzt war.
> *We stood rooted to the spot (stood there petrified; were shaken rigid) when we learned*
> *that the plane had crashed.*

ein **Sammelsurium** sein: cf. ein **Mischmasch** sein

in **Samt** und Seide: *in silks and satins; in one's Sunday best.* Cf. auch: **geschnie-**
**gelt** und gebügelt (gestriegelt) sein

> Eine Dame, die ständig in Samt und Seide herumläuft, wird schwerlich eine
> tüchtige Hausfrau sein.
> *A lady who continually walks around in silks and satins (in her Sunday best) will hardly*
> *be an efficient housewife.*

weich wie **Samt (samtweich)** sein: *to be as soft as velvet (as silk; as down; as*
*a feather); to be silky*

> Mutters Haut ist weich wie Samt (wie Seide; samtweich; seidenweich). Fühl'
> nur mal.
> *Mother's skin is as soft as velvet (as silk; as down; as a feather; is [so] silky). Just feel it.*

j.en mit **Samthandschuhen** anfassen (fig.): cf. j.en mit **Glacéhandschuhen**
anfassen

**samt** und sonders: *the whole lot; one and all; each and every one; the whole shoot*
*(pack; bunch; crew) (colloq.)*

> Wir wollen mit dieser Familie nichts mehr zu tun haben, denn sie ist samt und
> sonders grob und unehrlich.
> *We are not going to have anything more to do with that family, because they are rude and*
> *dishonest, one and all (each and every one; the whole lot [shoot; pack; bunch; crew]).*

j.em **Sand** in die Augen streuen (fig.): cf. j.en hinters **Licht** führen

auf **Sand** gebaut sein (fig.): *to be built on sand*

> Das neue Unternehmen mußte scheitern, da es von vornherein auf Sand ge-
> baut war.
> *The new enterprise was bound to fail, because it had been built on sand from the beginning.*

wie **Sand** am Meer sein: *to be legion; to be as thick as hail; to be like wasps*
*round a honey-pot; to be like the sands on the sea-shore.* Cf. auch: in **Hülle** und
Fülle

Die Menschen vor dem Eingang zum Fußballstadion waren (so zahlreich) wie Sand am Meer.
*The people in front of the entrance to the football stadium were legion (as thick as hail; like wasps round a honey-pot; like the sands on the sea-shore).*

im **Sande** verlaufen (fig.): cf. ausgehen wie das **Hornberger** Schießen

**sanft** und selig schlafen: *to sleep peacefully (soundly).* Cf. auch: schlafen wie ein **Murmeltier**

Ausnahmsweise habe ich heute Nacht sanft und selig geschlafen.
*Last night I slept peacefully (soundly) for a change.*

mit **Sang** und Klang: *with (brass) bands playing*

Trotz der Hitze zogen wir mit Sang und Klang zum Stadttor hinaus.
*In spite of the heat we marched out of the town-gate with (brass) bands playing.*

ohne **Sang** und Klang (sang- und klanglos): *unwept, unhonoured and unsung*

Dieser einst so mächtige Politiker ist vorige Woche ohne Sang und Klang (sang- und klanglos) beerdigt worden.
*That politician, once so powerful, was buried last week unwept, unhonoured and unsung.*

etwas **satt** haben: cf. etwas bis **dahin** (stehen) haben

sich an j.em (etwas) nicht **satt** sehen können: *not to be able to take one's eyes off s.b. (s.th.) (to tear one's eyes away from s.b. [s.th.]); never to be able to have one's fill of s.b. (s.th.) (colloq.)*

An einem schönen Filmstar können sich die Männer nicht satt sehen.
*The men cannot take their eyes off (tear their eyes away from; can never get their fill of) a beautiful film-star.*

in allen **Sätteln** gerecht sein (fig.): *to be able to put (to turn) one's hand to anything; to be an all-round man.* Cf. auch: **Hans** (Dampf) in allen Gassen sein

Dieser vielseitige Bursche ist in allen Sätteln gerecht.
*That versatile fellow can put (turn) his hand to anything (is an all-round man).*

j.en in den **Sattel** heben (fig.): *to give s.b. a leg up; to help s.b. to get on; to lend s.b. a helping hand.* Cf. auch: j.em auf die **Beine** helfen

Wir haben alles getan, um diesen begabten Menschen in den Sattel zu heben.
*We have done everything to give this gifted person a leg up (to help ... to get on; to lend ... a helping hand).*

fest im **Sattel** sitzen (fig.): *to be firmly in the saddle; to have the reins firmly in one's hand; to have a firm grip on things; to be well in command (to be master) of the situation; to have things under one's thumb.* Cf. auch: alle **Fäden** in der Hand haben; das **Heft** in der Hand haben

Die Regierung braucht die Angriffe der Opposition nicht zu fürchten. Sie sitzt fest im Sattel (hat die Zügel fest in der Hand; ist Herr der Lage).
*The government need not fear the opposition's attacks. It is firmly in the saddle (has the reins firmly in its hands; has a firm grip on things; is well in command [is master] of the situation; has things well under its thumb).*

**sattelfest** sein (fig.): *to be sure of o.s. (of one's ground); to be well up; to be on top.* Cf. auch: gut **bestellt** sein; **kapitelfest** sein

Wer ein Examen gut bestehen will, muß in allen Fächern sattelfest sein.
*Anyone who wants to pass an examination has to be sure of himself (of his ground) in all subjects (has to be well up in all subjects; has to be on top of all subjects).*

bluten wie eine **Sau** (fam.): cf. bluten wie ein **Schwein**

**saudumm** sein (fam.): cf. dumm wie **Bohnenstroh** sein

Es stößt j.em **sauer** auf (fig. u. fam.): *It gets s.b.'s goat (colloq.); It leaves a nasty taste in s.b.'s mouth (colloq.); It gives s.b. the needle (sl.)*

Es stößt Paul sauer auf, daß man ihn so ungerecht behandelt.
*It gets Paul's goat (leaves a nasty taste in Paul's mouth; gives Paul the needle) to be treated so unfairly.*

**sauer** auf etwas reagieren (fig. u. fam.): *to take s.th. amiss; to cut up rough (colloq.); to take a poor view (a dim view) of s.th. (colloq.)*

Unser Onkel ist sehr gut zu uns. Wenn wir ihn jedoch um Geld bitten, reagiert er sauer und schlägt es uns ab.
*Our uncle is very kind to us, but if we ask him for money, he takes it amiss (cuts up rough; takes a poor view [dim view] of it) and turns us down.*

einem **sauer** werden: *to put a strain on s.b.; to become trying; to take it out of s.b. (colloq.)*

Bei großer Hitze wird uns allen das Arbeiten sauer.
*In great heat work puts a strain on all of us (becomes trying to [takes it out of] all of us).*

es sich **sauer** werden lassen: die Reflexivformen der Ausdrücke unter: einem **sauer** werden

Wie kommt **Saul** unter die Propheten? (fig.): *Where did that black sheep come from?*

Ihr habt, wie wir sehen, einen Bergarbeiter in eurer Juristenfamilie. Wie kommt Saul unter die Propheten?
*We see you have a miner in your family of lawyers. Where did that black sheep come from?*

aus einem **Saulus** ein Paulus werden (fig.): *to make a volte-face (a change of front).* Cf. auch: **umsatteln**

434

Du kannst dir Schallplatten mit Tanzmusik kaufen, wenn du willst. Ich aber bleibe bei der klassischen Musik. Aus einem Saulus wird kein Paulus.
*You can buy records of dance-music if you want to, but I am sticking to classical music. I am not going to make a volte-face (a change of front).*

**saure** Arbeit und wenig Lohn: *to get all the kicks and none of the ha'pence*
Ein Polizist hat keine beneidenswerte Arbeit. Saure Arbeit und wenig Lohn.
*A policeman has not got an enviable job. He gets all the kicks and none of the ha'pence.*

die **Sauregurkenzeit:** *a slack period; the off-season*
Der August ist bei uns die Sauregurkenzeit, in der wir nicht viel verkaufen.
*August is for us a slack period (the off-season) when we do not sell much.*

in **Saus** und Braus leben: *to go gay; to have a good time; to live in the lap of luxury; to paint the town red (colloq.); to wallow in luxury (colloq.); to have high jinks (colloq.).* Cf. auch: leben wie ein **Fürst**
Wenn dein Vetter weiterhin so in Saus und Braus lebt, wird er bald ein ruinierter Mann sein.
*If your cousin continues to go gay (have a good time; live in the lap of luxury; paint the town red; wallow in luxury; have high jinks) like that, he will soon be a ruined man.*

den **Saustall** ausmisten (fig. u. fam.): cf. den **Stall** ausmisten

ein **Saustall** sein (fig. u. fam.): cf. ein **Schweinestall** sein

ein **Sauwetter** sein (fam.): cf. ein **Hundewetter** sein

j.em einen **Schabernack** spielen: *to play a practical joke (a prank) on s.b.*
Wir wollten unserm Lehrer einen Schabernack (Streich) spielen (ein Schnippchen schlagen), indem wir die Kreide versteckten; er ist jedoch zu früh ins Klassenzimmer gekommen.
*We wanted to play a practical joke (a prank) on our master by hiding the chalk but he came into the classroom too soon.*

j.en (etwas) in **Schach** halten (fig.): *to hold (to keep) s.b. (s.th.) in check; to curb (to check) s.b. (s.th.); to put s.b. (s.th.) in his (its) (proper) place*
Solche wilden Jungens sollten von ihren Eltern in Schach gehalten (in die Schranken [zurück]gewiesen) werden.
*Wild boys like those ought to be held (kept) in check (curbed; checked; put in their [proper] place) by their parents.*

eine **Schachfigur** sein (fig.): cf. ein **Strohmann** sein

**schachmatt** sein (fig.): cf. **absein**

j.en **schachmatt** setzen (fig.): *to checkmate s.b.; to stymie s.b. (colloq.); to bunker s.b. (colloq.); to do for s.b. (sl.)*

Durch die Intrigen seiner Konkurrenten wurde der junge Ingenieur schachmatt gesetzt und verlor alle seine Aufträge.
*As a result of his competitors' intrigues the young engineer was checkmated (stymied;
bunkered; done for) and lost all his orders.*

ein geschickter **Schachzug** (fig.): *a shrewd (clever; cunning) move*

Der Vorschlag einer solchen Konferenz war ein geschickter Schachzug des
Ministerpräsidenten.
*It was a shrewd (clever; cunning) move on the part of the prime minister to propose such
a conference.*

eine alte **Schachtel** sein (fig. u. fam.): *to be an old maid; to be an old girl (old
miss) (colloq.)*

Obwohl sie schon eine alte Schachtel (Scharteke; Schraube) ist, denkt sie immer
noch ans Heiraten.
*Although she is an old maid (girl; miss), she still thinks of getting married.*

der **Schädel** brummt j.em (fam.): cf. der **Kopf** brummt j.em

Durch **Schaden** wird man klug (Sprichw.): *One lives and learns (prov.); One
learns by one's mistakes.* Cf. auch: (Ein) gebranntes **Kind** scheut das Feuer

Mir wurde das Fahrrad gestohlen, weil ich es nicht abgeschlossen hatte. Durch
Schaden wird man klug.
*My bicycle was stolen because I had not locked it. One lives and learns (One learns by
one's mistakes).*

Wer den **Schaden** hat, braucht für den Spott nicht zu sorgen (Sprichw.):
*Insult is sure to be added to injury*

Seine Kameraden lachten ihn aus, weil er den Bus verpaßt hatte und darum
zu spät in die Schule kam. Wer den Schaden hat, braucht für den Spott nicht zu
sorgen.
*His friends laughed at him because he had missed the bus and arrived late at school.
Insult is sure to be added to injury.*

die **Schafe** von den Böcken sondern (fig.): cf. die **Böcke** von den Schafen
sondern

ein dummes **Schaf** sein (fig. u. fam.): cf. eine dumme **Gans** sein;
ein **Rindvieh** sein

Ein räudiges **Schaf** steckt die ganze Herde an (Sprichw.): *One infects the
others; One sets the others off*

Wir haben unsern Kindern streng verboten, mit diesem ungezogenen Jungen
zu spielen. Denn ein räudiges Schaf steckt die ganze Herde an.
*We have strictly forbidden our children to play with that rude boy; one infects the others
(sets the others off).*

das schwarze **Schaf** sein (fig.): *to be the black sheep; to be the bad egg (colloq.)*

Mein Bruder Karl ist das schwarze Schaf in der Familie. Er macht ständig Schulden.
*My brother Charles is the black sheep (bad egg) of the family. He is perpetually getting into debt.*

sein **Schäfchen** scheren (fig.): cf. sein **Schäfchen** ins trockene bringen

sein **Schäfchen** ins trockene bringen (fig.): *to feather one's own nest; to line one's own pocket; to make a nest-egg for o.s.; to look after number one (colloq.).* Cf. auch: einen guten **Schnitt** bei etwas machen

Die meisten Kaufleute sind in erster Linie darauf bedacht, ihr Schäfchen ins trockene zu bringen (ihr Schäfchen zu scheren; sich gesund zu machen [stoßen]).
*Most business-men are primarily concerned with feathering their own nests (lining their own pockets; making a nest-egg for themselves; looking after number one).*

etwas **schaffen** (fam.): *to make s.th. (colloq.)*

Unser Bus fährt schon in 10 Minuten. Hoffentlich schaffen (packen) wir es noch.
*Our bus leaves in ten minutes. I hope we make it.*

j.em viel (schwer) zu **schaffen** machen: *to give (to cause) s.b. a lot of trouble; to worry (to trouble) s.b. a great deal*

In den letzten Jahren macht mir mein Asthma viel (schwer) zu schaffen.
*In the last few years my asthma has been giving (causing) me a lot of trouble (has been worrying [troubling] me a great deal).*

die **Schale** seines Zornes über j.en ausgießen (fig.): *to pour out the vials of one's wrath on s.b.; to unload one's anger (wrath) on s.b.*

Der Geistliche hat die Schale seines Zornes über die schlechten Elemente in der Gemeinde ausgegossen.
*The priest poured out the vials of his wrath (unloaded his anger [wrath]) on the evil elements in the parish.*

den **Schalk** im Nacken haben (fig.): *to have the devil in one; to be an imp (a scamp)*

Trotz seines unschuldigen Aussehens hat dein Töchterchen wirklich den Schalk (Schelm) im Nacken (den Teufel im Leibe).
*In spite of her innocent appearance your little daughter has really got the devil in her (is really an imp [a scamp]).*

**Schall** und Rauch sein (fig.): *to be full of sound and fury; to be (but) vain pomp*

Alles Irdische ist nur Schall und Rauch.
*All earthly things are full of sound and fury (are [but] vain pomp).*

(frei) **schalten** und walten: cf. sein eigener **Herr** sein

j.en (frei) **schalten** und walten lassen: *to give s.b. carte blanche; to give s.b. a free hand; to give s.b. a blank cheque; to give s.b. plenty of rope (colloq.)*

> Zu meinem Stellvertreter habe ich volles Vertrauen. Ich lasse ihn (frei) schalten und walten.
> *I have complete confidence in my deputy. I give him carte blanche (a free hand; a blank cheque; plenty of rope).*

ein Pferd zu **Schanden** reiten: *to ride a horse into the ground; to ride a horse to its knees (to death)*

> Der rücksichtslose Reiter hat sein armes Pferd zu Schanden geritten.
> *The reckless rider has ridden his poor horse into the ground (to death; to its knees).*

zu jeder **Schandtat** bereit sein (fig.): *always to be ready for a prank (for devilry); always to be ready for a lark (for a bit of fun) (colloq.)*

> Meine Klassenkameraden machen jeden Unfug mit. Sie sind zu jeder Schandtat bereit.
> *My classmates like to share in any mischief. They are always ready for a prank (for devilry; for a lark; for a bit of fun).*

sein Leben in die **Schanze** schlagen (fig.): cf. sein **Leben** in die Schanze schlagen

**scharf** auf etwas sein (fam.): cf. auf etwas **erpicht** sein

die **Scharte** auswetzen (fig.): *to make amends; to make up for s.th.; to purge one's offence*

> Da mein letztes Schulzeugnis schlecht war, bin ich diesmal sehr fleißig gewesen. Ich hoffe, dadurch die Scharte ausgewetzt zu haben.
> *As my last school report was bad, I have been very hard-working this time. In this way I hope that I have made amends (made up for it; purged my offence).*

eine alte **Scharteke** sein (fam.): cf. eine alte **Schachtel** sein

j.em wie ein **Schatten** folgen: cf. wie eine **Klette** an j.em hängen

nur ein **Schatten** seiner selbst sein (fig.): cf. nur ein halber **Mensch** sein

nicht über seinen **Schatten** springen können (fig.): cf. nicht aus seiner **Haut** herauskönnen

j.en (etwas) in den **Schatten** stellen (fig.): *to put s.b. (s.th.) in the shade; to push s.b. (s.th.) into the background; to overshadow s.b. (s.th.); to eclipse s.b. (s.th.); to dwarf s.b.; to be head and shoulders above s.b. (s.th.).* Cf. auch: j.em **haushoch** überlegen sein

Unser neuer Arzt stellt alle seine Vorgänger in den Schatten (drückt ... an die Wand; drängt ... in den Hintergrund).
*Our new doctor puts all his predecessors in the shade (pushes ... into the background; overshadows [eclipses; dwarfs; is head and shoulders above] all his predecessors).*

die **Schattenseite** (fig.): cf. die **Kehrseite** der Medaille

die **Schattenseite** des Lebens (fig.): *the gloomy (dark) side of life*

Jeder hat Enttäuschungen erlebt und die Schattenseite des Lebens kennengelernt.
*Everyone has experienced disappointments and known the gloomy (dark) side of life.*

etwas zur **Schau** tragen: *to parade s. th.; to show off s. th.; to swank about s. th. (colloq.)*

Mancher eingebildete Kaufmann trägt seinen Reichtum gern zur Schau.
*Certain conceited business-men like to parade their wealth (to show off [to swank about] their wealth).*

eine **Schauergeschichte**: *a blood-and-thunder story (a spine-chiller) (colloq.)*

Du schläfst nachts so unruhig, weil du abends Schauergeschichten liest.
*You sleep so restlessly at night because you read blood-and-thunder stories (spine-chillers) in the evenings.*

eine **Schaukelpolitik** treiben: *to pursue a fickle (vacillating; unstable; hot-and-cold) policy*

Dieser Staat treibt seit längerer Zeit eine gefährliche Schaukelpolitik.
*For a considerable time this state has been pursuing a dangerously fickle (vacillating; unstable) policy (a dangerous hot-and-cold policy).*

ein **Schaumschläger** sein (fig.): *to be a windbag (a swashbuckler) (colloq.); to be a gas-bag (sl.)*

Mein Kollege ist nur ein Schaumschläger. Man kann sich auf seine Angaben nicht verlassen.
*My colleague is only a windbag (swashbuckler; gas-bag). One cannot rely on his statements.*

**Schaumschlägerei** (fig.): *patter; blether (swashbuckling; tub-thumping) (colloq.); gas (jaw; gabble) (sl.)*

Wir wünschen feste Angebote und keine Schaumschlägerei.
*We want firm offers and not just patter (blether; swashbuckling; tub-thumping; gas; jaw; gabble).*

ein **Schauspiel** für Götter sein: cf. ein **Anblick** für Götter sein

j.en **scheel** ansehen: cf. j.en über die **Achsel** ansehen

sich eine **Scheibe** von j.em (etwas) abschneiden können (fig. u. fam.): *to be* *able to learn (to pick up) a thing or two from s.b. (s.th.); to be able to pick up a tip or two from s.b.; to be able to take a leaf out of s.b.'s book*

Dieser Techniker ist sehr geschickt. Du könntest dir eine Scheibe von ihm abschneiden.
*This technician is very clever. You could learn (pick up) a thing or two (pick up a tip or two) from him (take a leaf out of his book).*

eine **Scheidewand** aufrichten (fig.): cf. einen **Trennungsstrich** ziehen

am **Scheidewege** stehen (fig.): *to be at the cross-roads (at the parting of the ways)*

Meine ältere Schwester steht jetzt am Scheidewege, ob sie Philologie oder Medizin studieren soll.
*My elder sister is now at the cross-roads (the parting of the ways): should she study literature or medicine.*

den **Schein** wahren: *to keep up (to preserve) appearances*

Du mußt deinen alten Lehrer manchmal besuchen, und wenn auch nur, um den Schein zu wahren.
*You must visit your old teacher sometimes, even if it is only a matter of keeping up (preserving) appearances.*

vom **Scheitel** bis zur Sohle (Zehe): cf. von **Kopf** bis Fuß

der Katze die **Schelle** umhängen (fig.): cf. der **Katze** die Schelle umhängen

Auf einen **Schelm** anderthalben (Sprichw.): cf. Auf einen groben **Klotz** gehört ein grober Keil

den **Schelm** im Nacken haben (fig.): cf. den **Schalk** im Nacken haben

Da steht **Schelm** wider Schelm: *The one is as big a rogue as the other*

Die beiden Männer, die miteinander streiten, sind verlogen und unehrlich. Da steht Schelm wider Schelm.
*The two men who are arguing with each other are deceitful and dishonest. The one is as big a rogue as the other.*

nach **Schema F** gehen (fig.): *to run in a groove; to be in its proper place; to go according to plan (to the book); to go off pat (colloq.)*

Mein Onkel hat sein Tagewerk genau eingeteilt. Bei ihm muß alles nach Schema F gehen.
*My uncle has strictly divided up his day's work. With him everything has to run in a groove (to be in its proper place; to go according to plan [to the book]; to go off pat).*

j.em **Scherereien** machen: *to lead s.b. a dance; to be a headache to s.b.; to give s.b. the run-around (colloq.)*

Ernst war ein böses Kind und hat mir den ganzen Tag (über) viel Scherereien gemacht.
*Ernest has been a bad child and led me a pretty dance (been a real headache to me; given me the run-around) all day.*

sein **Scherflein** beitragen: *to contribute one's mite; to do one's bit*

Wenn jeder sein Scherflein beiträgt, kann diese Sammlung zur Unterstützung der Armen ein voller Erfolg werden.
*If everybody contributes his mite (does his bit), this collection for the support of the poor can be a complete success.*

**Scherz** beiseite: *joking apart (aside); no kidding (sl.); on the level (sl.)*

Du willst als alter Junggeselle jetzt noch heiraten? Scherz (Spaß) beiseite, wie alt bist du denn eigentlich?
*You still want to marry, you old bachelor? Joking apart (aside; No kidding; On the level), how old are you really?*

j.en **scheuchen** (fig. u. fam.): cf. j.en **drangsalieren**

**Scheuklappen** vor den Augen haben (mit Scheuklappen herumlaufen) (fig.): *to have blinkers on; to be blind to reality*

Wer den Ernst des Problems nicht erkennt, hat Scheuklappen vor den Augen (läuft mit Scheuklappen herum).
*Anyone who does not recognise the seriousness of the problem has blinkers on (is blind to reality).*

Alte **Scheunen** brennen lichterloh (Sprichw.): *(There's) no fool like an old fool (prov.)*

Trotz ihrer 50 Jahre hat sich Tante Emilie in den Dorfschullehrer verliebt. Alte Scheunen brennen lichterloh (Alter schützt vor Torheit nicht).
*In spite of being fifty, Aunt Emily has fallen in love with the village schoolmaster. (There's) no fool like an old fool.*

essen (fressen) wie ein **Scheunendrescher** (fam.): *to eat like a horse (like a lumberjack); to tuck in like an army (colloq.); to stuff o.s. like a pig (sl.).* Cf. auch: ein **Freßsack** sein

Wir staunen über deinen riesigen Appetit. Du ißt (frißt) ja wie ein Scheunendrescher (Werwolf).
*We are amazed at your huge appetite. You eat like a horse (lumberjack; tuck in like an army; stuff yourself like a pig).*

sich **schibbelig** lachen (fam.): cf. sich **totlachen**

**Schick** haben: cf. **Chic** haben

j.es **Schicksal** ist besiegelt: *s.b.'s fate (doom) is sealed; s.b.'s goose is cooked (colloq.); s.b. has had his chips (sl.)*

Der Fischhändler hat bankrott gemacht. Sein Schicksal ist besiegelt.
*The fishmonger has gone bankrupt. His fate (doom) is sealed (His goose is cooked; He has had his chips).*

sein **Schicksal** schmieden: *to carve one's own destiny; to make one's own future; to be the architect of one's own fortune*. Cf. auch: Jeder ist seines Glückes **Schmied**

> In der neuen Heimat mußte jeder Flüchtling eine geeignete Beschäftigung suchen und sein Schicksal (Glück) schmieden (seines Glückes Schmied sein).
> *In his new home every refugee had to look for suitable employment and carve his own destiny (make his own future; be the architect of his own fortune).*

j.en **schief** ansehen: cf. j.en über die **Achsel** ansehen

**schief** gewickelt sein (fig. u. fam.): cf. auf dem **Holzwege** sein

**schiefgehen:** *to go awry (astray); not to come off; not to work out; to turn out badly; to be a flop (colloq.); to fizzle out (colloq.)*

> Meine Bemühungen, ihm einen guten Posten zu beschaffen, sind leider schiefgegangen (verquer gegangen; sind mir leider verhagelt).
> *I am afraid that my efforts to get him a good job have gone awry (astray; have not come off [worked out]; have turned out badly; have been a flop; have fizzled out).*

sich **schieflachen** (fam.): cf. sich **totlachen**

**schielen** wie ein Brummer ('ne Brumme) (fam.): *to be boss-eyed (colloq.); to have one eye in the pot and the other up the chimney (colloq.)*

> Sieh mal diesen unglücklichen Mann an. Er schielt ja wie ein Brummer ('ne Brumme; sieht mit dem linken Auge in die rechte Westentasche).
> *Look at this unfortunate man. He is boss-eyed (He has one eye in the pot and the other up the chimney).*

ausgehen wie das Hornberger **Schießen**: cf. ausgehen wie das **Hornberger** Schießen

zum **Schießen** sein (fam.): cf. zum **Piepen** sein

aufpassen wie ein **Schießhund**: *to have one's wits about one; to watch like a hawk; to keep one's eyes skinned*

> In manchem Gasthof muß man aufpassen wie ein Schießhund, damit man nicht beschwindelt wird.
> *In certain inns one must have one's wits about one (watch like a hawk; keep one's eyes skinned) to see that one is not swindled.*

das **Schiff** der Wüste: *the ship of the desert*

> Das Kamel wird mit Recht das Schiff der Wüste genannt.
> *The camel is appropriately called the ship of the desert.*

**Schiffbruch** erleiden (fig.): *to founder; to end up on the rocks; to come to grief; to break down*

Daß dieses zweifelhafte Unternehmen bald Schiffbruch erleiden würde, war vorauszusehen.
*It was to be foreseen that this doubtful enterprise would soon founder (end up on the rocks; come to grief; break down).*

mit allen **Schikanen** (fig. u. fam.): *with all the trimmings (the extras; the frills); with all the fancy stuff (sl.)*

Die heutigen Passagierflugzeuge sind luxuriös ausgestattet und mit allen Schikanen versehen.
*The passenger aeroplanes of today are luxuriously appointed and provided with all the trimmings (extras; frills; fancy stuff).*

j.en **schikanieren**: cf. j.en **drangsalieren**

j.en auf den **Schild** (er)heben (fig.): *to bring s.b. to the forefront (to the fore); to put s.b. on a pedestal*

Dieselben Parteien, die diesen Minister auf den Schild gehoben (erhoben) hatten, haben ihn jetzt gestürzt.
*The same parties which brought this minister to the forefront (fore; which put ... on a pedestal) have now caused his downfall.*

etwas im **Schilde** führen (fig.): *to play a deep game; to hatch s.th.; to have designs; to have s.th. up one's sleeve*

Ich bin gespannt, was dieser Mann gegen mich im Schilde führt (gegen mich ausheckt).
*I wonder what deep game that man is playing against me (what that man is hatching against me; what designs that man has on me; what that man has up his sleeve against me).*

nichts Gutes im **Schilde** führen (fig.): *to be up to no good; to be up to mischief; to be up to something shady*

Wir erwischten den Unbekannten, als er (sich) um unser Haus schlich. Offenbar führte er nichts Gutes im Schilde.
*We caught the stranger creeping round our house. He was obviously up to no good (to mischief; to something shady).*

seinen **Schild** rein (blank) erhalten (fig.): *to keep one's record (slate; hands) clean; to keep one's honour untarnished; to have no blot on one's escutcheon*

Trotz der schlechten Verhältnisse habe ich bisher meinen Schild rein (blank) erhalten.
*Despite the bad conditions I have kept my record (slate; hands) clean (kept my honour untarnished; I have no blot on my escutcheon) up to now.*

ein **Schildbürgerstreich** sein: *It reminds one of the wise men of Gotham; to be a bright thing to do (colloq.)*

Zuerst wurde die Straße gepflastert und dann wieder aufgerissen, um ein Kabel zu legen. Das war ein wahrer Schildbürgerstreich (Schwabenstreich).
*First the road was paved and then torn up again for a cable to be laid. That reminds one of the wise men of Gotham (That was a bright thing to do).*

j.em wie einem kranken **Schimmel** zureden: *to talk to s.b. as if he were a wounded (a sick) chicken*

> Wir mußten meinem Bruder wie einem kranken Schimmel zureden, das Examen noch einmal zu versuchen.
> *We had to talk to my brother as if he were a wounded (sick) chicken to persuade him to attempt the examination again.*

keinen (blassen) **Schimmer** haben (fig.): cf. keine (blasse) **Ahnung** haben

j.en mit **Schimpf** und Schande entlassen: *to dismiss s.b. with dishonour (with ignominy; in disgrace)*

> Der Kassierer wurde wegen Unterschlagung mit Schimpf und Schande entlassen.
> *The cashier was dismissed with dishonour (ignominy; in disgrace) for embezzlement.*

eine **Schimpfkanonade** loslassen: *to pour out a torrent of abuse; to let off a volley of revilement; to curse s.b. with bell, book and candle (colloq.)*

> Als der Ehemann erst nach Mitternacht nach Hause zurückkam, ließ die Ehefrau eine Schimpfkanonade los.
> *When the husband did not return home until after midnight, the wife poured out a torrent of abuse (let off a volley of revilement at him; cursed him with bell, book and candle).*

Eindruck **schinden** (fam.): cf. **Eindruck** schinden

eine (furchtbare) **Schinderei** sein (fam.): cf. eine (furchtbare) **Plackerei** sein

mit etwas **Schindluder** treiben (fam.): cf. mit seinen Kräften **aasen;** mit etwas **Raubbau** treiben

mit j.em **Schindluder** treiben (fam.): *to play an underhand game with s.b.; to play fast and loose with s.b.; to play a dirty trick on s.b. (colloq.); to do the dirty on s.b. (sl.)*

> Vor zwei Jahren hat eben dieser Mann versucht, auch mit mir Schindluder zu treiben.
> *This very man tried to play an underhand game with me (to play a dirty trick on me; to play fast and loose with me; to do the dirty on me) two years ago.*

j.en auf die **Schippe (Schüppe)** nehmen (fig. u. fam.): cf. j.en auf den **Arm** nehmen

**Schlachtenbummler** (fig.): *fans; supporters*

Die auswärtige Mannschaft hatte viele Schlachtenbummler mitgebracht.
*The visiting team had brought a lot of fans (supporters) with them.*

ein **Schlachtroß** sein (fig. u. fam.): *to be a tank (a Colossus; a handful)*

Während sein Vater ein schmächtiger Mann ist, ist seine Mutter ein wahres Schlachtroß (eine richtige Maschine).
*Whereas his father is a slight man, his mother is a real tank (Colossus; handful).*

seinen ewigen (letzten) **Schlaf** schlafen (fig.): *to sleep one's last sleep; to lie at rest*

Beethoven schläft seinen ewigen (letzten) Schlaf in Wien.
*Beethoven is sleeping his last sleep (lies at rest) in Vienna.*

den **Schlaf** des Gerechten schlafen: *to sleep the sleep of the just*

Nach einem anstrengenden Tag schlief ich den Schlaf des Gerechten.
*After a strenuous day I slept the sleep of the just.*

etwas im **Schlaf** hersagen können: *to be able to recite s. th. in one's sleep*

Der Schauspieler kennt seine Rolle so gut, daß er sie im Schlaf (an den Fingern) hersagen kann.
*The actor knows his part so well that he can recite it in his sleep.*

etwas im **Schlaf** tun können (fig.): *to be able to do s. th. in one's sleep; to be able to do s. th. blindfold; to be able to do s. th. standing on one's head (colloq.)*

Ich bin so ans Bügeln gewöhnt, daß ich es im Schlaf (am Schnürchen) tun könnte.
*I am so used to ironing that I could do it in my sleep (do it blindfold; do it standing on my head).*

j.en am (beim) **Schlafittchen** nehmen (fam.): cf. j.en beim **Kanthaken** fassen (packen)

eine **Schlafmütze** sein (fig. u. fam.): *to be a sleepy-head (a lazybones); to be a stick-in-the-mud (colloq.)*

Wenn Fritz weiterhin eine solche Schlafmütze bleibt, wird er es im Leben zu nichts bringen.
*If Fred goes on being such a sleepy-head (lazybones; stick-in-the-mud), he will not get anywhere in life.*

mit éinem **Schlage:** *in an instant; in a flash; in the twinkling of an eye; with a single stroke; overnight*

Dieser ausgezeichnete Roman hat den jungen Autor mit éinem Schlage (über Nacht) bekannt gemacht.
*This excellent novel made its young author famous in an instant (in a flash; in the twinkling of an eye; with a single stroke; overnight).*

445

wie vom **Schlag** gerührt (getroffen) sein: cf. wie vom **Blitz** getroffen sein

(wie) ein **Schlag** ins Gesicht sein (fig.): *to be (like) a slap in the face; to be like a douche of cold water.* Cf. auch: wie eine kalte **Dusche** wirken

> Die ungerechte Kritik war für den Sänger (wie) ein Schlag ins Gesicht (Kontor; wie ein Keulenschlag).
> *The unjust criticism was (like) a slap in the face (like a douche of cold water) to the singer.*

vom gleichen **Schlage** sein: *to be of a piece* (nur plural. zu gebrauchen); *to be cast in the same mould;* (meistens im schlechten Sinne) *to be tarred with the same brush*

> Diese beiden Brüder sind keineswegs vom gleichen Schlage (können sich keineswegs die Hand reichen).
> *These two brothers are by no means of a piece (cast in the same mould; tarred with the same brush).*

ein harter **Schlag** für j.en sein: cf. eine bittere **Pille** sein

ein **Schlag** ins Kontor sein (fig. u. fam.): cf. (wie) ein **Schlag** ins Gesicht sein

j.en rührt (trifft) der **Schlag** (fig.): cf. wie vom **Blitze** getroffen sein

**Schlag** auf Schlag (fig.): *one on top of the other; one after another; in quick (rapid) succession; pell-mell*

> Nach dem Erdbeben folgten die Unglücksnachrichten Schlag auf Schlag.
> *After the earthquake reports of the disaster followed one on top of the other (one after another; in quick [rapid] succession; pell-mell).*

keinen **Schlag** tun (arbeiten) (fam.): *not to do a stroke (of work); not to stir (to lift) a finger*

> Wir litten unter der abnormen Hitze und konnten keinen Schlag (keinen Streich [Strich]) tun (arbeiten) (keine Hand rühren).
> *We suffered from the abnormal heat and could not do a stroke (of work; could not stir [lift] a finger).*

j.em einen **Schlag** versetzen (fig.): *to be a set-back for s.b.; to set s.b. back; to be a blow to s.b.; to deal s.b. a blow*

> Der plötzliche Rückgang seines Geschäftes hat dem Metzger einen heftigen Schlag (Stoß) versetzt.
> *The sudden decline in his business has been a serious set-back for (blow to) the butcher (has set the butcher back a lot; has dealt the butcher a serious blow).*

ein **Schlag** ins Wasser sein (fig.): *to be a fiasco; to misfire; to be a flop (a wash-out) (colloq.).* Cf. auch: **Fiasko** machen

446

Unsere Protestkundgebung verfehlte ihre Wirkung. Sie war ein Schlag ins Wasser.
*Our protest meeting failed in its effect. It was a fiasco (flop; wash-out; it misfired).*

Da **schlag'** einer lang hin! (fam.): *What do you think of that? (colloq.); Would you believe it! (colloq.); What do you say to that? (colloq).* Cf. auch: **Sieh** mal einer an!

Mein zweijähriger Sohn hat sämtliche Blumen abgerissen. Da schlag' einer lang hin!
*My two-year-old son has broken off all the flowers. What do you think of that? (Would you believe it! What do you say to that?)*

**schlagfertig** sein: cf. nicht auf den **Mund** gefallen sein

**Schlagseite** haben (fig. u. fam.): cf. zu tief in den **Becher** geguckt haben

der ganze **Schlamassel** (fam.): cf. der ganze **Kram**

eine **Schlampe (schlampig)** sein (fam.): *to be a slattern (a slatternly [slovenly] woman); to be a scruffy woman (a slut) (sl.)*

Deine Wirtin scheint eine Schlampe (schlampig) zu sein. An deiner Stelle würde ich ausziehen.
*Your landlady seems to be a slattern (a slatternly [slovenly; scruffy] woman; a slut). In your place I would move out.*

falsch wie eine **Schlange** sein: cf. falsch wie eine **Katze** sein

**Schlange** stehen: *to queue (up); to wait (to stand) in a queue*

Im Krieg mußten wir vor allen Geschäften Schlange stehen.
*In the war we had to queue ([up]; wait [stand] in a queue) at all the shops.*

in **Schlangenlinie** gehen (fahren): *to zig-zag; to career*

Der Betrunkene fuhr in Schlangenlinie (zickzack; im Zickzack) auf seinem Fahrrad über die Straße.
*The drunken man zig-zagged (careered) across the road on his bicycle.*

**schlank** wie eine Tanne sein: cf. schlank wie eine **Tanne** sein

j.en (etwas) **schlankweg** ablehnen: cf. j.en (etwas) **rundweg** ablehnen

**schlappmachen** (fam.): *to pass out; to drop in one's tracks; to crumple up (colloq.)*

Nach dem langen Wettlauf machten einige Läufer einfach schlapp.
*After the long race some of the runners simply passed out (dropped in their tracks; crumpled up).*

ein **Schlappschwanz** sein (fig. u. fam.): cf. ein **Muttersöhnchen** sein

ein **Schlaraffenleben** führen: *to live in clover; to live a life of idle luxury*

In den nächsten Ferien wollen wir nach Italien fahren und ein Schlaraffenleben führen.
*For our next holidays we want to go to Italy and live in clover (live a life of idle luxury).*

aus etwas nicht **schlau** werden (fam.): cf. aus etwas nicht **klug** werden

ein **Schlauberger (Schlaumeier)** sein: *to be a smart Alec (colloq.); to be a crafty devil (an artful dodger) (colloq.); to be a sly old bird (fox) (colloq.)*

Mein Freund Heinrich, der Schlauberger (Schlaumeier), hat (so)gleich festgestellt, daß wir privat viel billiger leben könnten als im Hotel.
*My friend Henry, the smart Alec (crafty devil; artful dodger; sly old bird [fox]), discovered at once that we could live much more cheaply in private rooms than in a hotel.*

j.en **schlauchen** (fam.): cf. j.en **mitnehmen**

bei j.em **schlecht** angeschrieben sein: cf. bei j.em gut (schlecht) **angeschrieben** sein

**schlecht** und recht: *as best one can; by hook or by crook*

Seine arme Familie muß sich schlecht und recht (recht und schlecht) durchs Leben schlagen.
*His poor family has to struggle through life as best it can (by hook or by crook).*

j.en **schlechtmachen**: *to tell tales (stories) about s.b. (out of school); to run s.b. down; to paint s.b. black*

Was hast du davon, wenn du mich auf diese Weise schlechtmachst?
*What do you get out of telling tales (stories) about me (running me down; painting me black) in this way?*

den **Schleier** lüften (fig.): *to lift (to draw aside) the veil; to unveil the secret; to let the secret out*

Die Sache wurde lange geheimgehalten, aber endlich wurde der Schleier gelüftet und die Wahrheit bekanntgemacht.
*The matter was kept secret for a long while but finally the veil was lifted (drawn aside; the secret was unveiled [was let out]) and the truth made known.*

den gleichen (alten) **Schlendrian** weitergehen: *to muddle along in the same old way; to follow the same old pattern; to jog along in the same old rut (groove)*

Der Regierungswechsel hat nichts geändert. Es geht alles den gleichen (alten) Schlendrian (Trott) weiter (Es wird weiter gewurstelt).
*The change of government has not altered anything. Everything is muddling along in the same old way (following the same old pattern; jogging along in the same old rut [groove]).*

j.en ins **Schlepptau** nehmen (fig.): *to take s.b. in tow; to take s.b. under one's wing; to catch s.b. up in one's wake.* Cf. auch: j.en unter seine **Fittiche** nehmen

Da Heinrich keine Initiative besitzt, läßt er sich von anderen ins Schlepptau nehmen.
*As Henry possesses no initiative, he lets himself be taken in tow by others (taken under other people's wings; caught up in other people's wake).*

die **Schleusen** des Himmels: *the floodgates of heaven*

Die Schleusen des Himmels öffneten sich, und es regnete unaufhörlich.
*The floodgates of heaven opened and it rained incessantly.*

alle **Schliche** kennen: *to know the ins and outs; to know all the tricks (of the trade) (colloq.); to know all the dodges (wheezes) (sl.).* Cf. auch: mit allen **Hunden** gehetzt sein

Wer an der Börse spekulieren will, muß alle Schliche (Kniffe) kennen.
*Anyone who wants to speculate on the Stock Exchange must know the ins and outs (all the tricks [of the trade]; all the dodges [wheezes]).*

hinter j.es **Schliche** kommen (j.em auf die Schliche kommen): *to see through s.b.'s (little) game; to get what s.b. is up to (colloq.); to see through s.b.'s racket (sl.); to cotton on to s.b. (sl.); to be wise to s.b.'s game (racket) (sl.)*

Die Bank ist jetzt hinter die Schliche (Sprünge) dieses Kaufmanns (diesem Kaufmann auf die Schliche [Sprünge]) gekommen.
*The bank has now seen through (is now wise to) that business-man's (little) game (racket; has now got what that business-man is up to; has now cottoned on to that business-man).*

**schlicht** um schlicht: *au pair; on an exchange basis*

Für Schulkinder erfolgt ein Aufenthalt im Ausland am besten schlicht um schlicht (au pair).
*A stay abroad for schoolchildren is best arranged au pair (on an exchange basis).*

j.em **Schliff** beibringen (fig.): *to rub the edges off s.b.; to lick s.b. into shape (colloq.); to give s.b. a bit of polish (colloq.)*

Da der junge Mann vom Lande stammt, müssen wir ihm zunächst noch Schliff beibringen.
*As the young man comes from the country, we must first rub the edges off him (lick him into shape; give him a bit of polish).*

den letzten **Schliff** geben (fig.): cf. die letzte **Feile** anlegen

in die **Schlinge** gehen (fig.): cf. in die **Falle** gehen a)

sich aus der **Schlinge** ziehen (fig.): *to save one's skin (one's neck); to wriggle out of the noose; to get out of a tight spot*

Der Gauner hat es bisher verstanden, sich immer wieder aus der Schlinge zu ziehen.
*Up to now the rogue has always known how to save his skin (neck; to wriggle out of the noose; to get out of a tight spot).*

j.em auf den **Schlips** treten (fig. u. fam.): *to get s.b.'s goat (colloq.); to rub s.b. up the wrong way (colloq.); to put s.b.'s back up (colloq.); to put s.b.'s monkey up (sl.)*

> Warum bist du so verärgert? Hat dir jemand auf den Schlips (Schwanz) getreten (Fühlst du dich auf den Schlips [Schwanz] getreten)?
> *Why are you so annoyed? Has somebody got your goat (rubbed you up the wrong way; put your back [monkey] up)?*

unter den **Schlitten** geraten (fig. u. fam.): cf. unter die **Räder** geraten

mit j.em **schlittenfahren** (fig. u. fam.): cf. j.en **drangsalieren**

ein **Schloß** vor dem Mund haben (fig.): *to be muzzled; to be tongue-tied*

> Man möchte meinen, er hätte ein Schloß vor dem Mund, weil er nichts sagt.
> *One would think he was muzzled (tongue-tied) since he does not say anything.*

j.en hinter **Schloß** und Riegel setzen: cf. j.en **dingfest** machen

hinter **Schloß** und Riegel sitzen: *to be behind bars; to be under lock and key; to be taken care of; to be in jug (quod; clink) (colloq.).* Cf. auch: in den **Kasten** kommen.

> Die Bevölkerung war beruhigt, als der Verbrecher endlich hinter Schloß und Riegel (schwedischen Gardinen; im Kasten) saß (auf Nummer Sicher war; brummen mußte).
> *The population was relieved when the criminal was behind bars (under lock and key; was taken care of; was in jug [quod; clink]) at last.*

heulen wie ein **Schloßhund**: *to cry one's eyes out; to wail like a siren (colloq.); to howl like a babe in arms (colloq.)*

> Der Junge heulte wie ein Schloßhund (Kettenhund; heulte zum Steinerweichen), weil er seinen Ball verloren hatte.
> *The boy was crying his eyes out (wailing like a siren; howling like a babe in arms) because he had lost his ball.*

rauchen wie ein **Schlot**: *to smoke like a chimney*

> Schon seit seiner Jugend raucht unser Chef wie ein Schlot (Schornstein).
> *Our boss has been smoking like a chimney since his youth.*

ein **Schlot** sein (fig. u. fam.): cf. ein **Nichtsnutz** sein

etwas **schlucken** (fig.): a) *to swallow s.th. up; to absorb s.th.;* b) *to bear the brunt of s.th.; to go through (to put up with) the hardship of s.th.*

> a) Dieser große Konzern hat kürzlich mehrere kleine Betriebe geschluckt.
> b) An den teueren Zeiten haben vor allem die Rentner zu schlucken.
> *a) This large combine recently swallowed up (absorbed) several small works.*
> *b) It is above all the pensioners who have to bear the brunt of (have to go through [to put up with] the hardship of) expensive times.*

ein armer **Schlucker** sein (fig. u. fam.): cf. ein armer **Haufen** sein

Und damit **Schluß**!: cf. Und damit **basta**!

den **Schlußpunkt** hinter etwas setzen (fig.): cf. den **Schlußstrich** unter etwas ziehen

den **Schlußstrich** unter etwas ziehen (fig.): *to call (to put) an end to s.th.; to wipe s.th. out; to draw the pen through s.th.; to wipe the slate clean; to let bygones be bygones; to skip s.th. (colloq.).* Cf. auch: etwas **ad acta** legen

> Wir haben einen Schlußstrich unter unsern alten Streit gezogen (einen Schlußpunkt hinter . . . gesetzt) und uns ausgesöhnt.
> *We have called (put) an end to (wiped out; drawn the pen through; skipped) our old quarrel (have wiped the slate clean; have let bygones be bygones) and become reconciled.*

j.em etwas **schmackhaft** machen (fig.): cf. j.em etwas **mundgerecht** machen

bei j.em ist **Schmalhans** Küchenmeister (fig.): *s. b. is on short commons (short rations)*

> In jeder armen Familie ist begreiflicherweise Schmalhans Küchenmeister.
> *Every poor family is, of course, on short commons (rations).*

bei j.em **schmarotzen**: cf. bei j.em **nassauern**

nicht nach ihm und nicht nach ihr **schmecken** (fig. u. fam.): *to taste like nothing on earth (colloq.);* (nur von Eßwaren) *to taste like old rope (sl.);* (nur von Getränken) *to taste like dish-water (sl.)*

> Diesen faden Käse darfst du nicht wieder kaufen. Er schmeckt nicht nach ihm und nicht nach ihr.
> *You must not buy this insipid cheese again. It tastes like nothing on earth (like old rope).*

eine Sache **schmeißen** (fam.): cf. den ganzen **Laden** schmeißen

ein **Schmetterling** sein (fig.): cf. eine leichte **Fliege** sein

einen **schmettern** (fam.): cf. einen hinter die **Binde** gießen

seines Glückes **Schmied** sein: cf. sein **Schicksal** schmieden

Jeder ist seines Glückes **Schmied** (Sprichw.): *Every man is the architect of his own fortune (prov.).* Cf. auch: sein **Schicksal** schmieden

> Wer es zu Ansehen bringen will, muß fleißig und tüchtig sein. Jeder ist seines Glückes Schmied.
> *A man who wants to acquire esteem must be hard-working and efficient. Every man is the architect of his own fortune.*

vor die rechte **Schmiede** gehen (fig.): *to address o.s. to the proper quarter; to go to the right shop (colloq.)*

Ich bin nicht zuständig für solche Sachen. Sie sollten gleich vor die rechte Schmiede gehen.
*I am not responsible for such matters. You ought to address yourself to the proper quarter (to go to the right shop).*

**Schmiere** stehen (fam.): *to keep a look-out (watch-out); to keep cave (colloq.)*

Einer von uns muß Schmiere stehen, damit wir nicht erwischt werden.
*One of us must keep a look-out (watch-out; keep cave) so that we are not caught.*

j.en **schmieren** (fig. u. fam.): *to grease s.b.'s palm; to cross s.b.'s palm (with silver); to buy s.b. (colloq.); to get round s.b. (colloq.)*

Man sollte nie versuchen, einen Zollbeamten zu schmieren (einem Zollbeamten Schmiergelder zu bezahlen).
*One should never try to grease a Customs officer's palm (to cross a Customs officer's palm [with silver]; to buy [to get round] a Customs officer).*

Wer gut **schmiert,** der gut fährt (Sprichw.): *He who pays the piper, calls the tune (prov.)*

Wenn man Geld hat, kann man alles erreichen. Wer gut schmiert, der gut fährt.
*If one has money, one can achieve anything. He who pays the piper, calls the tune.*

ein **Schmierfink** sein (fam.): *to be a grubby urchin (colloq.); to be a mucky pup (sl.)*

Man sieht (es) seinen Schulbüchern an, daß er ein Schmierfink (Dreckspatz; Mistfink; Schmutzfink; eine Miestbiene) ist.
*One can see from his school-books that he is a grubby urchin (a mucky pup).*

j.em **Schmiergelder** bezahlen: cf. j.en **schmieren**

**Schmiß** haben (**schmissig** sein) (fam.): *to go with a swing; to have a lilt*

Dieser neue Schlager hat Schmiß (ist wirklich schmissig).
*This new hit-tune does go with a swing (have a lilt).*

im **Schmollwinkel** sitzen: cf. die gekränkte **Leberwurst** spielen

ein **Schmuckkästchen** sein (fig.): *to be as pretty as a picture; to be a (perfect) picture*

Dein neues Haus ist wirklich ein Schmuckkästchen.
*Your new house really is as pretty as a picture (is a [perfect] picture).*

j.en (etwas) in den **Schmutz** ziehen (fig.): cf. j.en (etwas) in den **Dreck** ziehen

ein **Schmutzfink** sein: cf. ein **Schmierfink** sein

reden, wie einem der **Schnabel** gewachsen ist (fig. u. fam.): *to be plain-spoken; not to mince matters; to speak one's mind.* Cf. auch: kein **Blatt** vor den Mund nehmen; **klipp** und klar sagen

Unsere Lehrer haben uns aufgefordert, so zu reden, wie uns der Schnabel gewachsen ist.
*Our teachers have instructed us to be plain-spoken (not to mince matters; to speak our minds).*

den **Schnabel** halten (fig. u. fam.): cf. den **Mund** halten

j.em den **Schnabel** stopfen (fig. u. fam.): cf. j.em das **Maul** stopfen

sich den **Schnabel** verbrennen (fig. u. fam.): cf. sich den **Mund** verbrennen

eine **Schnapsidee** sein (fam.): cf. eine **Kateridee** sein

wie eine **Schnecke** kriechen: *to crawl like a snail.* Cf. auch: im **Schneckentempo**

Wir belustigten uns über die Kleinbahn, die wie eine Schnecke den Berg hinaufkroch.
*We were amused by the miniature railway, which crawled up the mountain like a snail.*

j.en zur **Schnecke** machen (fig. u. fam.): *to make s.b. feel small; to take it out of s.b. (colloq.).* Cf. auch: j.en mit **Füßen** treten; j.en **abkanzeln**; j.en **anschnauzen**

Mit seinen Beschuldigungen hat er mich völlig zur Schnecke gemacht.
*He made me feel very small (really took it out of me) with his accusations.*

im **Schneckentempo**: *at a snail's-pace*

Wenn die Arbeiter in solchem Schneckentempo weiterarbeiten, werden wir erst im nächsten Jahre in unser neues Haus einziehen können.
*If the workmen go on working at such a snail's-pace, we shall not be able to move into our new house until next year.*

wie der **Schnee** an der Sonne schmelzen: *to disappear like an ice-cream in the sun.* Cf. auch: wie **Butter** an der Sonne schmelzen

Unsere Vorräte an Lebensmitteln sind wie der Schnee an der Sonne geschmolzen.
*Our food supplies have disappeared like an ice-cream in the sun.*

sich freuen wie ein **Schneekönig**: cf. sich **diebisch** freuen

**schneeweiß** sein: *to be snow-white (as white as snow)*

Das Mädchen trug ein schneeweißes (blütenweißes) Kleid.
*The girl was wearing a snow-white dress (a dress as white as snow).*

keinen **Schneid** haben: *to have no grit (gumption) (colloq.); to have no guts (sl.).*
Cf. auch: die **Zivilcourage**

Mein Vetter wird es im Leben nicht weit bringen. Er hat einfach keinen Schneid.
*My cousin will not get far in life. He has simply no grit (gumption; guts).*

auf des Messers **Schneide** stehen (fig.): cf. auf des **Messers** Schneide stehen

j.en **schneiden** (fig.): *to cut s.b.; to cold-shoulder s.b.; to give s.b. the cold-shoulder.* Cf. auch: j.en kalt (kühl) **abrutschen** lassen

Als ich meinen groben Nachbarn auf der Straße traf, habe ich ihn einfach geschnitten.
*When I met my rude neighbour in the street, I simply cut (cold-shouldered) him (gave him the cold-shoulder).*

frieren wie ein **Schneider**: *to be perished (with cold); to be as cold as a brass monkey (sl.)*

Als ich bei dem kalten Wetter nach Hause kam, fror ich wie ein Schneider.
*When I got home in that cold weather I was perished ([with cold]; I was as cold as a brass monkey).*

leicht wie ein **Schneider** sein: cf. **federleicht** sein

j.em ein **Schnippchen** schlagen: *to get the better of s.b.; to hoodwink s.b.; to pull a fast one on s.b. (sl.).* Cf. auch: j.em einen **Schabernack** spielen

Der Vater hatte Rolands Fahrrad versteckt, aber der Sohn hat ihm ein Schnippchen geschlagen (einen Streich gespielt) und ist trotzdem weggefahren.
*Roland's father had hidden his bicycle, but the son got the better of him (hoodwinked him; pulled a fast one on him) and still rode off.*

einen guten **Schnitt** (seinen Schnitt) bei etwas machen (fig.): *to turn over (to make) a nice profit on s.th.; to make a pretty penny on s.th.; to get a good rake-off (cut) from s.th. (colloq.); to make a nice bit out of s.th. (colloq.)* Cf. auch: sein **Schäfchen** ins trockene bringen

Bei diesem Tausch habe ich einen guten Schnitt (meinen Schnitt) gemacht.
*I turned over (made) a nice profit (made a pretty penny) on (got a good rake-off [cut] from; made a nice bit out of) this exchange.*

einen **Schnitzer** machen: cf. einen **Bock** schießen

j.em **schnuppe** sein (fam.): cf. völlig **Luft** für j.en sein

über die **Schnur** hauen (fig.): cf. über die **Stränge** hauen

wie am **Schnürchen** gehen: *to go off smoothly; to go like clockwork; s.b. has s.th. at one's finger-tips; s.b. has s.th. taped (colloq.); s.b. has s.th. off pat (colloq.)*

In unserer Fabrik ist die Verwaltung sehr tüchtig, und alles geht wie am Schnürchen (wie geölt [geschmiert]).
*In our factory the management is very efficient and everything goes off smoothly (like clockwork; and has everything at its finger-tips; has everything taped; has everything off pat).*

etwas am **Schnürchen** tun können (fig. u. fam.): cf. etwas im **Schlaf** tun können

**schnurstracks** zu j.em (etwas) gehen: *to go post-haste to s.b. (s.th.); to make a bee-line (a rush) for s.b. (s.th.)*
Um sich zu beschweren, ging er schnurstracks zu seinem Chef.
*He went post-haste to (made a bee-line [a rush] for) his boss in order to protest.*

die heimische **Scholle**: *one's native land (soil)*
Dieser Dichter hat immer wieder die heimische Scholle besungen.
*This poet has sung time and again of his native land (soil).*

an der (heimischen) **Scholle** kleben (fig.): *to cling to one's native soil*
Du solltest auch mal ins Ausland fahren, anstatt so eng an der (heimischen) Scholle zu kleben.
*You too ought to go abroad, instead of clinging so closely to your native soil.*

zu **schön,** um wahr zu sein: *too good to be true*
Was du mir da erzählst, ist zu schön, um wahr zu sein.
*What you are telling me is too good to be true.*

die Gelegenheit beim **Schopf** ergreifen (fassen, packen) (fig.): cf. die **Gelegenheit** beim Schopf ergreifen (fassen, packen)

sein Geld zum **Schornstein** hinausjagen (fig. u. fam.): cf. auf großem **Fuße** leben

rauchen wie ein **Schornstein**: cf. rauchen wie ein **Schlot**

etwas in den **Schornstein** schreiben (fig.): *to write s.th. off; to say good-bye to s.th.; to whistle for s.th. (colloq.)*
Dieser Geschäftsmann hat bankrott gemacht, und wir werden das ihm geliehene Geld wohl in den Schornstein (Kamin; Rauchfang) schreiben müssen.
*That business-man has gone bankrupt, and we shall probably have to write off (say good-bye to; whistle for) the money we lent him.*

j.em (wie ein reifer Apfel [eine reife Frucht]) in den **Schoß** fallen (fig.): *to fall into s.b.'s waiting hands (empty hands); to land in s.b.'s lap*
Die Regierung war zu schwach geworden, und die politische Führung des Landes ist der Opposition (wie ein reifer Apfel [eine reife Frucht]) in den Schoß gefallen.

*The government had become too weak, and the political leadership of the country fell into the waiting (empty) hands of the opposition (landed in the lap of the opposition).*

Kein Unglück ist so groß, es trägt ein Glück im **Schoß** (Sprichw.): *It's an ill wind that blows nobody any good (prov.); It's a long lane that has no turning (prov.)*

Auch schlechte Zeiten können Gutes mit sich bringen. Kein Unglück ist so groß, es trägt ein Glück im Schoß.
*Even bad times can bring some good. It's an ill wind that blows nobody any good (a long lane that has no turning).*

noch im **Schoße** der Götter ruhen (fig.): *still to rest (to lie) in the lap of the gods*

Wie sich die Zusammenarbeit der Nationen entwickeln wird, ruht noch im Schoße der Götter (ist noch in den Sternen geschrieben; steht noch in den Sternen).
*How cooperation between nations will develop still rests (lies) in the lap of the gods.*

j.en in die **Schranken** fordern (fig.): cf. j.em den **Fehdehandschuh** hinwerfen

j.en (etwas) in **Schranken** halten (fig.): *to keep s.b. (s.th.) within bounds (limits)*

Die Veranstalter haben versichert, daß sie das Tanzvergnügen in den gebührlichen Schranken halten werden.
*The organisers have given an assurance that they will keep the dance within the limits (bounds) of respectability.*

für j.en in die **Schranken** treten (fig.): cf. eine **Lanze** für j.en brechen (einlegen)

j.en in die **Schranken** (zurück)weisen (fig.): cf. j.en in **Schach** halten

eine alte **Schraube** sein (fig. u. fam.): cf. eine alte **Schachtel** sein

eine **Schraube** ohne Ende sein (fig.): *to be an endless tale (an endless spiral); to be like an endless belt.* Cf. auch: sich in einem **circulus vitiosus** bewegen

Die Lohnerhöhungen infolge der Preissteigerungen scheinen eine Schraube ohne Ende zu sein.
*Wage increases as a result of rising prices seem to be an endless tale (spiral; like an endless belt).*

eine **Schraube** los (locker) haben (fig. u. fam.): cf. nicht richtig im **Dachstübchen** sein

mit dem **Schrecken** davonkommen: *to get off (to escape) with a fright (a scare)*

Vergangenen Sonntag hatten wir einen Autounfall. Wir sind jedoch mit dem Schrecken davongekommen.
*Last Sunday we had a car accident, but we got off (escaped) with a fright (scare).*

der **Schreck(en)** fährt j.em in die Glieder: cf. wie vom **Blitz** getroffen sein

der letzte **Schrei** sein (fig.): *to be the last word; to be the dernier cri; to be the latest craze (colloq.)*

Dies hier ist der letzte Schrei in Damenschirmen.
*This is the last word (dernier cri; latest craze) in ladies' umbrellas.*

zum **Schreien** sein (fam.): cf. zum **Piepen** sein

eine **schreiende** Ungerechtigkeit: *a glaring injustice; a crying scandal*

Die Entlassung des tüchtigen Arbeiters war eine schreiende Ungerechtigkeit.
*The dismissal of the efficient workman was a glaring injustice (crying scandal).*

Vom Erhabenen zum Lächerlichen ist nur ein **Schritt** (Sprichw.): *It is only a step from the sublime to the ridiculous*

Das Publikum brach in lautes Gelächter aus, als der Schauspieler, der den König spielte, ausrutschte und hinfiel. Vom Erhabenen zum Lächerlichen ist nur ein Schritt.
*The audience burst out laughing when the actor who was playing the part of the king slipped and fell. It is only a step from the sublime to the ridiculous.*

mit j.em (etwas) **Schritt** halten (fig.): *to keep pace (to keep up) with s.b. (s.th.); to keep abreast of s.b. (s.th.)*

Wir müssen mit der Entwicklung der Physik Schritt halten.
*We must keep pace (keep up) with (keep abreast of) developments in physics.*

j.em drei **Schritt** vom Leibe bleiben (fig.): *to keep one's distance (from s.b.); to keep at arm's length (from s.b.); to keep away from s.b.*

Ich sagte ihm, er solle mir mit seinen unverschämten Forderungen drei Schritt vom Leibe bleiben.
*I told him to keep his distance (at arm's length; away) (from me) with his impertinent demands.*

einen guten **Schritt** am Leibe haben: *to have a good pair of legs (on one)*

Sie können den Weg in einer Viertelstunde zurücklegen, da Sie einen guten Schritt am Leibe haben.
*You can cover the distance in a quarter of an hour, for you've got a good pair of legs (on you).*

sich j.en drei **Schritt** vom Leibe halten (fig.): *to keep s.b. at arm's length (at a distance); to give s.b. a wide berth*

457

Sie sollten sich diesen unangenehmen Menschen drei Schritt vom Leibe halten.
*You ought to keep that unpleasant person at arm's length (at a distance; to give . . . a wide berth).*

**Schritt** für Schritt: *step by step; bit by bit*

Die Lebensverhältnisse dieser Leute haben wir Schritt für Schritt verbessert.
*We have improved the living conditions of these people step by step (bit by bit).*

j.em auf **Schritt** und Tritt folgen: *to follow (to dog) s.b.'s every footstep (every movement); to shadow s.b.*

Mehrere Detektive folgten dem Verdächtigen auf Schritt und Tritt (beschatteten den Verdächtigen).
*Several detectives followed (dogged) the suspect's every footstep (movement; shadowed the suspect).*

**Schritte** unternehmen (fig.): *to take steps; to make moves; to take action*

Mein Freund hat mir versprochen, in dieser Angelegenheit alle nötigen Schritte zu unternehmen.
*My friend has promised me to take all the necessary steps (action; make all the necessary moves) in this matter.*

ein **Schritt** nach vorn (vorwärts) (fig.): *a step forward; a move (a step) in the right direction*

Unsere Handlung halte ich für einen Schritt nach vorn (vorwärts).
*I consider our action to be a step forward (a move [step] in the right direction).*

etwas einen **Schritt** weiterbringen (fig.): *to bring (to take) s.th. a step forwards; to take s.th. a stage further*

Wir haben unsere Vorbereitungen für das Fest einen guten Schritt weitergebracht.
*We have brought (taken) our preparations for the celebration a considerable step forwards (have taken . . . a considerable stage further).*

j.en **schröpfen** (fig.): cf. j.em das **Fell** über die Ohren ziehen

von altem (echtem) **Schrot** und Korn sein (fig.): *to be of the old school (old guard); to be a sterling . . .; to be worth one's weight in gold; to be of sterling worth; to be a top-notch . . . (colloq.).* Cf. auch: sich nicht mit **Gold** aufwiegen lassen

Der General war ein Offizier von altem (echtem) Schrot und Korn (stammte noch aus der alten Schule).
*The general was an officer of the old school (guard; a sterling [top-notch] officer; an officer worth his weight in gold; an officer of sterling worth).*

**schuften** (fam.): cf. arbeiten wie ein **Pferd;** sich **totarbeiten** (totschuften)

458

wissen, wo einen der **Schuh** drückt (fig.): *to know where the shoe pinches; to know where the trouble lies*

> Ich weiß nicht, wo meinen Nachbarn der Schuh drückt.
> *I don't know where my neighbour's shoe pinches (where my neighbour's trouble lies).*

j.em etwas in die **Schuhe** schieben (fig.): cf. j.em etwas zur **Last** legen

j.en wie einen **Schuhputzer** behandeln: *to treat s.b. like dirt (like a dog [a cur])*

> Kein Angestellter kann unsern Chef leiden, weil er jeden wie einen Schuhputzer (wie Dreck) behandelt.
> *No employee can stand our boss, because he treats everyone like dirt (like a dog [cur]).*

nicht wert sein, j.em die **Schuhriemen** zu lösen (fig.): *to be not good enough (not worthy; not fit) to do up s.b.'s bootlaces (to clean s.b.'s shoes)*

> Trotz seiner Hochnäsigkeit ist er nicht wert, seinem Vater die Schuhriemen zu lösen.
> *In spite of his haughtiness he is not good enough (worthy; fit) to do up his father's bootlaces (to clean his father's shoes).*

sich die **Schuhsohlen** nach etwas ablaufen: cf. sich die **Füße** nach etwas ablaufen

mehr **Schulden** als Haare auf dem Kopfe haben: cf. bis über die **Ohren** in Schulden stecken

**Schulden** haben wie ein Major: cf. bis über die **Ohren** in Schulden stecken

j.em nichts **schuldig** bleiben (fig.): *to give as good as one gets; not to be at a loss for an answer; to give s.b. tit for tat (colloq.).* Cf. auch: **Gleiches** mit Gleichem vergelten; nicht auf den **Mund** gefallen sein

> Mein Gegner griff mich heftig an, ich bin ihm jedoch nichts schuldig geblieben.
> *My opponent attacked me violently, but I gave as good as I got (was not at a loss for an answer; gave him tit for tat).*

(noch) aus der alten **Schule** stammen (fig.): cf. von altem (echtem) **Schrot** und Korn sein

bei j.em in die **Schule** gehen (fig.): *s.b. can teach me (you etc.) a thing or two; to learn (to pick up) a thing or two from s.b.*

> Du solltest hören, wie schön mein Bruder Klavier spielt. Du könntest bei ihm in die Schule gehen.
> *You ought to hear how nicely my brother plays the piano. He could teach you a thing or two (You could learn [pick up] a thing or two from him).*

durch eine harte **Schule** gehen (eine harte Schule durchmachen) (fig.): *to learn things the hard way; to go through the mill (colloq.); to rough it (sl.)*

> Es schadet einem jungen Manne nichts, wenn er durch eine harte Schule gehen (eine harte Schule durchmachen) muß.
> *It does a young man no harm to have to learn things the hard way (to go through the mill; to rough it).*

**Schule** machen: *to set the fashion; to attract disciples; to catch on (colloq.)*

> Der neue Malstil hat in ganz Europa rasch Schule gemacht.
> *The new style of painting quickly set the fashion (attracted disciples; caught on) in the whole of Europe.*

aus der **Schule** plaudern (fig.): *to tell tales out of school; to shoot one's mouth off (sl.)*

> Wir wollten diese Nachricht für uns behalten. Jemand muß aber aus der Schule geplaudert haben.
> *We wanted to keep that news to ourselves, but somebody must have been telling tales out of school (shooting his mouth off).*

die **Schule** schwänzen: cf. **schwänzen**

sich sein **Schulgeld** zurückzahlen lassen: *to ask for one's money (fees) back*

> Wenn er so einfache Dinge nicht gelernt hat, kann er sich sein Schulgeld zurückzahlen lassen.
> *If he has not learnt simple things like that, he might as well ask for his money (fees) back.*

j.en über die **Schulter** ansehen (fig.): cf. j.en über die **Achsel** ansehen

j.em die kalte **Schulter** zeigen (fig.): cf. j.en kalt (kühl) **abrutschen** lassen

etwas auf die leichte **Schulter** nehmen (fig.): cf. etwas auf die leichte **Achsel** nehmen

**Schulter** an Schulter: *shoulder to shoulder*

> In diesem Regiment haben viele Studenten Schulter an Schulter mit Arbeitern gekämpft.
> *Many students fought shoulder to shoulder with workers in this regiment.*

**schummeln** (fam.): *to diddle people (colloq.); to fiddle (sl.)*

> Beim Herausgeben des Geldes schummelt die Frau des Metzgers oft.
> *The butcher's wife often diddles people (fiddles) when she gives them their change.*

j.en auf die **Schüppe** (Schippe) nehmen (fig. u. fam.): cf. j.en auf den **Arm** nehmen

j.em wie **Schuppen** von den Augen fallen: *the scales fall from s.b.'s eyes; the veil drops from s.b.'s eyes; s.b.'s eyes are opened (to the truth)*

Als ich meinem Vetter erzählte, wie hoffnungslos die Zukunft aussehe, fiel es ihm wie Schuppen von den Augen.
*When I told my cousin how hopeless the future looked, the scales fell from his eyes (the veil dropped from his eyes; his eyes were opened [to the truth]).*

j.en **schurigeln**: cf. j.en **drangsalieren**

an Mutters **Schürzenband** hängen (fig.): cf. ein **Muttersöhnchen** sein

ein **Schürzenjäger** sein (fig.): cf. ein **Herzensdieb** sein

j.em einen **Schuß** vor den Bug setzen (fig.): cf. j.em einen vor den **Bug** feuern

gut in (im) **Schuß** sein: a) (von Menschen) cf. auf der **Höhe** sein; b) (von Sachen) *to be running well; to be in full swing (in top gear)*
    b) Nach einigen Schwierigkeiten ist das Geschäft jetzt wieder gut in (im) Schuß.
    *b) After a few difficulties the business is now running well again (is now in full swing [in top gear] again).*

in **Schuß** kommen: cf. in **Fluß** kommen

j.em vor den **Schuß** kommen (fig.): *to come across s.b.; to run (to bump) into s.b. (colloq.)*
    Ich dachte eben an Heinrich, als er mir gerade vor den Schuß kam und mir seine Hilfe anbot.
    *I was just thinking about Henry when he came across me (ran [bumped] into me) and offered me his help.*

keinen **Schuß** Pulver wert sein (fig.): *to be worse than useless; not to be worth twopence (tuppence; a fig; two pins) (colloq.)*. Cf. auch: keinen (roten) **Heller** wert sein
    Seit meiner Krankheit bin ich keinen Schuß Pulver mehr wert.
    *Since my illness I haven't been worth twopence (tuppence; a fig; two pins; I have been worse than useless).*

weit vom **Schuß** sein (fig.): *to be (well) out of harm's way (out of range)*
    Vor dem Krieg fuhr er nach Südamerika und war infolgedessen während dieser schweren Jahre weit vom Schuß.
    *Before the war he went to South America and was consequently (well) out of harm's way (out of range) during those difficult years.*

zu weit vom **Schuß** sein (fig.): *to be too far from the scene (of events); to be too far out of range*
    Wir sind in Europa zu weit vom Schuß, um die Lage im Fernen Osten richtig beurteilen zu können.
    *In Europe we are too far from the scene ([of events]; too far out of range) to be able to judge correctly the situation in the Far East.*

**Schuster,** bleib bei deinem Leisten! (Sprichw.): *The cobbler must stick to his last (Cobbler, stick to your last) (prov.)*

Er kümmert sich um Dinge, die er nicht versteht. Man möchte ihm zurufen: Schuster, bleib bei deinem Leisten!
*He concerns himself with things that he does not understand. One feels like shouting to him that the cobbler must stick to his last (. . . him, Cobbler, stick to your last).*

auf **Schusters** Rappen reiten (fig.): *to go on Shanks's pony (mare)*

Wilhelm reitet öfters auf Schusters Rappen in sein Geschäft, weil ihm die frische Luft guttut.
*William often goes to his office on Shanks's pony (mare) because the fresh air does him good.*

etwas in **Schutt** und Asche legen: *to sack s. th.; to raze s. th. to the ground; to reduce s. th. to a mass (heap; pile) of ruins (rubble)*

Die Soldaten legten das Städtchen in Schutt und Asche.
*The soldiers sacked the little town (razed . . . to the ground; reduced . . . to a mass [heap; pile] of ruins [rubble]).*

in **Schutt** und Asche liegen: *to be a mass (heap; pile) of ruins (rubble; debris)*

Nach dem Erdbeben lagen viele Dörfer in Schutt und Asche.
*After the earthquake many villages were a mass (heap; pile) of ruins (rubble; debris).*

ein **Schwabenstreich** sein: cf. ein **Schildbürgerstreich** sein

eine **Schwäche** für j.en (etwas) haben: *to have a weakness for s. b. (s. th.); to have a soft spot for s. b. (s. th.) (colloq.).* Cf. auch: etwas für j.en (etwas) **übrig** haben

Ich habe eine Schwäche für diese Pralinen.
*I have a weakness (soft spot) for these chocolates.*

Eine **Schwalbe** macht noch keinen Sommer (Sprichw.): *One swallow does not make a summer (It takes more than one swallow to make a summer) (prov.)*

Diesen einen Aufsatz hast du gut gemacht, aber éine Schwalbe macht noch keinen Sommer.
*You have done this one essay well, but one swallow does not make a summer (it takes more than one swallow to make a summer).*

**Schwamm** drüber! (fam.): *Rub (Scrub) it out! (colloq.); (Let's) forget it! (colloq.); (Let's) Skip it! (sl.).* Cf. auch: den **Schlußstrich** unter etwas ziehen

Sprechen wir nicht mehr über diese leidige Angelegenheit. Schwamm (Streusand) drüber (Strich drunter)!
*Let us say no more about this painful affair. Rub (Scrub) it out ([Let's] forget it; [Let's] Skip it)!*

j.es **Schwanengesang** sein (fig.): *to be s.b.'s swan-song*

Das letzte Werk eines Komponisten oder Dichters nennt man seinen Schwanen-gesang.
*One calls a composer's or poet's last work his swan-song.*

mit etwas **schwanger** gehen (fig. u. fam.): *to conceive s.th.; to turn s.th. over in one's mind; to chew s.th. over (colloq.)*

Wir gehen mit dem Gedanken schwanger, eine Garage an unser Haus zu bauen.
*We have conceived the idea (are turning over in our minds [are chewing over] the idea) of building a garage on to our house.*

den **Schwanz** einziehen (fig. u. fam.): *to draw in one's horns; to put one's tail between one's legs (colloq.); to climb down (colloq.).* Cf. auch: die **Hörner** ein-ziehen

Als ich ihm seine häßliche Bemerkung vorwarf, zog er den Schwanz ein und nahm sie zurück.
*When I reproached him for his spiteful remark, he drew in his horns (put his tail between his legs; climbed down) and took it back.*

kein **Schwanz** (fig. u. fam.): cf. keine **Menschenseele**

j.em auf den **Schwanz** treten (fig. u. fam.): cf. j.em auf den **Schlips** treten

**schwänzen:** *to play truant (from school); to cut school*

Dein Bruder ist bestraft worden, weil er mehrmals (die Schule) geschwänzt hat.
*Your brother has been punished because he has played truant ([from school]; cut school) several times.*

arbeiten, bis einem die **Schwarte** knackt (kracht) (fig. u. fam.): *to work until one's back breaks.* Cf. auch: arbeiten wie ein **Pferd;** sich **totarbeiten** (tot-schuften)

Bei diesem Lehrer müssen wir arbeiten, bis uns die Schwarte knackt (kracht).
*With this teacher we have to work until our backs break.*

**schwarz** angeschrieben sein (fig.): cf. bei j.em gut (schlecht) **angeschrieben** sein

sich **schwarz** ärgern (fig.): cf. sich **grün** und blau ärgern

**schwarzen** Gedanken nachhängen: cf. schwarzen **Gedanken** nachhängen

sich alles **schwarz** ausmalen (fig.): *to take a gloomy (black) view of things; to look on the black side of everything*

Ich weiß nicht, warum du so pessimistisch bist und dir alles schwarz ausmalst.
*I do not know why you are so pessimistic and take such a gloomy (black) view of things (and look on the black side of everything).*

mit etwas sieht es **schwarz** aus (fig.): *to look black ([bleak]; things [prospects]*
*look black [bleak]) for s.th.; to look grim (things look grim) for s.th. (colloq.)*

Mit der Weinernte sieht es dieses Jahr schwarz aus.
*It looks (Things [Prospects] look) black (grim; bleak) for the wine-harvest this year.*

**schwarz** wie ein Rabe sein: cf. schwarz wie ein **Mohr(enkind)** sein

das **schwarze** Schaf sein (fig.): cf. das schwarze **Schaf** sein

**schwarz** sehen (fig.): *to foresee a dark (a grim) future; to find the outlook dismal*
*(grim; bleak)*

Ich sehe schwarz für diese Organisation, wenn sie nicht mehr Kapital bekommt.
*I foresee a dark (grim) future (I find the outlook dismal [grim; bleak]) for this organi-*
*sation if it does not get more capital.*

einen **schwarzen** Tag haben (fig.): *to have a black day (an off-day)*

In der Schule hatte ich heute einen schwarzen Tag. Ich habe viele Fehler gemacht.
*I had a black day (an off-day) in school today. I made a lot of mistakes.*

ein **schwarzer** Tag sein (fig.): *to be a black (black-letter; sad; sorry) day*

Heute war für unsere Außenpolitik ein schwarzer Tag.
*Today was a black (black-letter; sad; sorry) day for our foreign policy.*

warten, bis man **schwarz** wird (fig.): *to wait until one is blue in the face; to*
*kick (to cool) one's heels till Domesday (colloq.)*

Ich habe jetzt keine Zeit für diesen lästigen Menschen. Er kann (mag) warten,
bis er schwarz wird.
*I have no time for that annoying person now. He can wait until he's blue in the face*
*(He can kick [cool] his heels till Domesday).*

**schwarz** auf weiß: *in black and white; in writing*

Wenn Sie es mir nicht glauben wollen, (so) kann ich es Ihnen schwarz auf weiß
beweisen. Hier ist das betreffende Schriftstück.
*If you won't believe me, I can prove it to you in black and white (in writing). Here is the*
*document concerned.*

aus **schwarz** weiß machen (fig.): *to call black white; to turn black into white;*
*to turn things upside-down*

Du darfst die Tatsachen nicht verdrehen und nicht aus schwarz weiß machen.
*You must not twist the facts and call black white (turn black into white; turn things*
*upside-down).*

j.em nicht das **Schwarze** unter dem Nagel gönnen (fig.): *to grudge s.b. every*
*little thing; hardly to let s.b. breathe*

464

Meine Schwester ist neidisch; sie gönnt mir nicht das Schwarze unter dem Nagel.
*My sister is jealous; she grudges me every little thing (she hardly lets me breathe).*

ins **Schwarze** treffen (fig.): *to score a bull; to hit the bull's-eye (the mark).* Cf. auch: den **Nagel** auf den Kopf treffen

Diese kritische Bemerkung des Redners traf ins Schwarze und löste lauten Beifall aus.
*That critical remark of the speaker's scored a bull (hit the bull's-eye [mark]) and produced loud applause.*

**Schwarzarbeit** tun (**schwarzarbeiten**): *to work unofficially; to work contrary to the rules; to handle "black" work; to be a blackleg*

Die Gewerkschaften haben es allen Arbeitern verboten, Schwarzarbeit zu tun (schwarz zu arbeiten).
*The trade unions have forbidden all workers to work unofficially (contrary to the rules; to handle "black" work; to be blacklegs).*

eine **Schwatzbase** sein (fam.): cf. eine **Klatschbase** sein

in der **Schwebe** sein (fig.): cf. in der **Luft** schweben

eine **Schwefelbande** (fam.): *a gang (mob) of ruffians (hooligans; rowdies)*

Diese (kleine) Schwefelbande macht sich ein Vergnügen daraus, die Erwachsenen zu belästigen.
*This gang (mob) of ruffians (hooligans; rowdies) delights in annoying adults.*

**Schweigen** ist auch eine Antwort (Wer schweigt, stimmt zu) (Sprichw.): *Silence means consent (prov.)*

Mein Vater hat nichts gesagt, ich nehme jedoch an, daß er einverstanden ist. Schweigen ist auch eine Antwort (Wer schweigt, stimmt zu).
*My father did not say anything but I presume that he is agreeable. Silence means consent.*

sich in **Schweigen** hüllen: cf. sich in **Stillschweigen** hüllen

ein armes **Schwein** sein (fig. u. fam.): cf. ein armer **Haufen** sein

bluten wie ein **Schwein** (fam.): *to bleed like a stuck pig (sl.)*

Karl hatte sich in den Finger geschnitten und blutete wie ein Schwein (eine Sau).
*Charles had cut his finger and was bleeding like a stuck pig.*

**Schwein** haben (fam.): *to be in luck; to have (to be) a bit (a stroke) of luck; to have (to be) a lucky break (colloq.)*

Du hast wirklich Schwein (Dusel) gehabt, daß du deine Brieftasche wiedergefunden hast.
*You really were in luck (had a bit [stroke] of luck [a lucky break]; It really was a bit [stroke] of luck [a lucky break] for you) to find your wallet again.*

kein **Schwein** (fam.): cf. keine **Menschenseele**

j.em den **Schwein(e)hund** blasen (fam.): cf. j.en **abkanzeln**

der innere **Schwein(e)hund** (fam.): *the beast within one*

Jeder muß sich bemühen, den inneren Schwein(e)hund zu überwinden.
*Everyone must strive to overcome the beast within him.*

ein **Schwein(e)hund** sein (fam.): *to be a rotten dog (colloq.); to be a swine (a rotter; a lousy tyke) (sl.)*

Gib mir meine Uhr zurück, du Schwein(e)hund!
*Give me my watch back, you rotten dog (swine; rotter; lousy tyke).*

eine **Schweinerei** sein (fam.): *to be a rotten (a dirty) business (trick) (colloq.)*

Es war eine richtige Schweinerei, daß dieser ehrenwerte Mann so verleumdet wurde.
*It was a really rotten (dirty) business (trick) that that honest man was slandered in this way.*

ein **Schweinestall** sein (fam.): *to be a pig-sty (bear-garden) (colloq.); to look like nothing on earth (colloq.); to be a shambles (sl.)*

Warum bist du so unordentlich? Dein Zimmer ist ein richtiger Schweinestall (Saustall; In deinem Zimmer herrscht polnische Wirtschaft; sieht es aus wie bei den Hottentotten [wie in Russisch-Polen]).
*Why are you so untidy? Your room is a proper pig-sty (bear-garden; shambles; looks like nothing on earth).*

ein **Schweinewetter** sein (fam.): cf. ein **Hundewetter** sein

im **Schweiße** seines Angesichts: *by the sweat of one's brow*

Die meisten Menschen müssen sich das tägliche Brot im Schweiße ihres Angesichts verdienen.
*Most people have to earn their daily bread by the sweat of their brows.*

die Früchte seines **Schweißes** (fig.): *the fruits of one's labours*

Bei meinem Besuch zeigte mir der Bildhauer die Früchte seines Schweißes.
*During my visit the sculptor showed me the fruits of his labours.*

viel **Schweiß** kosten (fig.): *to cost a great deal of sweat; to be a real grind (a real sweat) for s.b. (colloq.)*

Unsere neue Brücke hat die Ingenieure viel Schweiß gekostet.
*Our new bridge cost the engineers a great deal of sweat (was a real grind [sweat] for the engineers).*

j.em nicht wieder über die **Schwelle** kommen dürfen: *not to cross s.b.'s threshold (enter s.b.'s house) again*

Dieser unehrliche Verkäufer darf uns nicht wieder über die Schwelle kommen.
*That dishonest salesman shall not cross our threshold (enter our house) again.*

an der Schwelle des Todes stehen: cf. am **Rande** des Grabes stehen

ein **Schwerenöter** sein: cf. ein **Herzensdieb** sein

eine **Schwergeburt** sein (fig. u. fam.): cf. eine **Herkulesarbeit** sein

den **Schwerpunkt** auf etwas legen (fig.): cf. den **Hauptakzent** auf etwas legen

das **Schwert** in die Scheide stecken (fig.): cf. die **Streitaxt** begraben

ein zweischneidiges **Schwert** sein (fig.): *to be a two-edged (double-edged) sword*
Wir bezahlen lieber alles in bar, denn der Ratenkauf ist ein zweischneidiges Schwert.
*We prefer to pay cash for everything, for paying by instalments is a two-edged (double-edged) sword.*

ins **Schwimmen** geraten (fig.): *to become blurred (hazy)*
Die ehemals festen Grundsätze dieser Partei sind neuerdings etwas ins Schwimmen geraten.
*This party's principles, formerly clear, have recently become somewhat blurred (hazy).*

der ganze **Schwindel** (fig. u. fam.): cf. der ganze **Kram**

den **Schwindel** kennen (fig. u. fam.): *to know that trick (ruse; ploy); to know that racket (sl.)*
Dein Kleid ist nicht so schön, wie es im Inserat angepriesen war. Den Schwindel kenne ich (schon).
*Your dress is not as nice as it is made out in the advertisement. I know that trick (ruse; ploy; racket).*

sich die **Schwindsucht** an den Hals ärgern (fam.): cf. sich **grün** und blau ärgern

einen **Schwips** haben (fam.): *to be tipsy (tight; tiddly; half-seas-over) (colloq.).*
Cf. auch: zu tief in den **Becher** geguckt haben; **sternhagelvoll** sein
Bei der Geburtstagsfeier hatte ich nach einiger Zeit einen ordentlichen Schwips (einen [schweren] Affen; schwer geladen; einen über den Eichstrich getrunken; einen sitzen [stecken]; hatte ich mir ... einen angekümmelt [angezwitschert]; war ich ... beschwipst [selig]).
*After a while I was properly tipsy (tight; tiddly; was half-seas-over) at the birthday party.*

j.en in **Schwung** bringen (fig.): *to spur (to galvanise) s.b. into action; to prod s.b.; to ginger (to buck) s.b. up (colloq.)*

Der Vater hat seinen faulen Sohn in Schwung gebracht und läßt ihn unter seiner Aufsicht arbeiten.
*The father spurred (galvanised) his lazy son into action (prodded his lazy son; gingered [bucked] his lazy son up) and made him work under his supervision.*

in **Schwung** kommen (fig.): cf. in **Fluß** kommen

**Schwung** hinter etwas machen (fig.): **Zuck** hinter etwas machen

nicht für einen **Sechser**: cf. nicht für einen **Pfennig**

seine **Seele** aushauchen: cf. den **Geist** aufgeben

j.em etwas auf die **Seele** binden (fig.): cf. j.em etwas zu **Gemüte** führen

j.em schwer auf der **Seele** brennen (fig.): cf. j.em wie ein **Alp** auf der Seele liegen

j.em schwer auf die **Seele** fallen (fig.): *to go through one's mind (head) in a flash; to flash through s.b.'s mind*

Im Auto fiel mir plötzlich schwer auf die Seele (aufs Herz), daß ich die Haustür nicht abgeschlossen hatte.
*In the car it went through my mind (head) in a flash (it flashed through my mind) that I had not locked the front door.*

umherirren wie die **Seele** im Fegefeuer: *to wander about (like a man [woman etc.]) in a daze*

Seitdem der Chauffeur diesen Verkehrsunfall verursacht hat, irrt er wie die Seele im Fegefeuer umher.
*Ever since the chauffeur caused that car accident, he has been wandering about (like a man) in a daze.*

zwei **Seelen** und éin Gedanke: *two minds with but a single thought*

Zu meinem Geburtstag haben mir Wilhelm und Georg beide dasselbe Buch geschenkt. Zwei Seelen und éin Gedanke!
*For my birthday William and George both gave me the same book. Two minds with but a single thought.*

keine **Seele**: cf. keine **Menschenseele**

sich eine Last von der **Seele** wälzen: cf. sich eine **Last** von der Seele wälzen

eine **Seele** von einem Menschen sein: *to be a dear soul; to be one in a million; to be one of the best*

Meine Tante ist eine Seele von einem Menschen.
*My aunt is a dear soul (one in a million; one of the best).*

sich etwas von der **Seele** reden: cf. sich eine **Last** von der Seele wälzen

Nun hat die liebe **Seele** Ruh'!: *Now we shall have some peace (at last) (colloq.)*
Heinrich hat jetzt von seinen Eltern den lang ersehnten Fußball bekommen.
Nun hat die liebe Seele Ruh'!
*Henry has now had from his parents the football which he had wished for so long. Now*
*we shall have some peace (at last).*

j.em aus der **Seele** sprechen: *to express s.b.'s heartfelt convictions;to speak (to*
*go) to s.b.'s heart*
Alles, was der Bischof sagte, war den Zuhörern aus der Seele (aus dem Herzen)
gesprochen.
*Everything the bishop said expressed the listeners' heartfelt convictions (spoke [went] to the*
*listeners' hearts).*

einem in der **Seele** wehtun: cf. einem durch **Mark** und Bein gehen

**seelenvergnügt** sein: cf. **kreuzfidel** sein

**Seemannsgarn** spinnen (fig.): cf. ein **Garn** spinnen

die **Segel** streichen (fig.): cf. die **Waffen** strecken

mit vollen **Segeln** (fig.): *full speed ahead; full tilt; full pelt; with might and*
*main; hell for leather (colloq.)*
Nach den Ferien sind Lehrer und Schüler mit vollen Segeln wieder an die
Arbeit gegangen.
*After the holidays teachers and pupils went full speed ahead with (full tilt [pelt]; with*
*might and main; hell for leather at) their work again.*

kein reiner **Segen** sein (fig.): *not to be an unmixed (an unadulterated) blessing*
Die Fortschritte der Physik sind leider kein reiner Segen.
*Progress in physics is unfortunately not an unmixed (unadulterated) blessing.*

ein wahrer **Segen** sein (fig.): cf. eine **Gottesgabe** sein

sich **sehen** lassen können: *to be worth seeing (watching; looking at)*
Unser Tennisklub kann sich sehen lassen. Er hat bereits viele Spiele gewonnen.
*Our tennis club is worth seeing (watching; looking at). It has already won many matches.*

keine **Seide** bei etwas spinnen (fig.): *not to make s.th. pay; there is no money in*
*s.th.; not to grow fat on s.th. (colloq.)*
An deiner Stelle würde ich dein Papiergeschäft verkaufen. Denn bei ihm kannst
du keine Seide spinnen.
*In your place I would sell your paper-shop. You won't make it pay (There is no money in*
*it; You won't grow fat on it).*

469

weich wie **Seide (seidenweich)** sein: cf. weich wie **Samt** (samtweich) sein

an einem **Seidenfaden** hängen (fig.): cf. an einem seidenen (dünnen) **Faden** hängen

die **Seifenblase** zum Platzen bringen (fig.): *to prick the bladder; to explode s.th.; to blow s.th. up.* Cf. auch: eine **Eiterbeule** aufstechen

> Der Regierung ist es gelungen, die Seifenblase zum Platzen zu bringen und die Hohlheit der Verschwörung aufzudecken.
> *The government has succeeded in pricking the bladder and exposing the hollowness of the plot (has succeeded in exploding the plot [blowing the plot up]).*

jedem das **Seine** lassen: *To each his own.* Cf. auch: **Ehre,** wem Ehre gebührt

> Du kannst vielleicht besser schwimmen, aber Ernst ist der bessere Tennisspieler. Man muß jedem das Seine lassen.
> *Perhaps you can swim better, but Ernest is the better tennis-player. To each his own.*

j.en von der **Seite** ansehen: cf. j.en über die **Achsel** ansehen

j.en auf seine **Seite** bringen (fig.): *to win s.b. over (to one's side); to get s.b. into one's camp*

> Dieser Mann ist sehr einflußreich. Ich muß versuchen, ihn auf meine Seite zu bringen.
> *That man is very influential. I must try to win him over ([to my side]; to get him into my camp).*

etwas von anderer (dritter) **Seite** erfahren: *to learn of s.th. from another quarter (source; from a third party)*

> Seine Verlobung habe ich nicht von ihm selbst, sondern von anderer (dritter) Seite (aus anderer [dritter] Quelle) erfahren.
> *I did not learn of his engagement from him personally but from another quarter (source; from a third party).*

alles von der guten **Seite** ansehen: *to look on everything from the bright side; to look on the bright side of everything*

> Heinrich ist ein unverbesserlicher Optimist und sieht alles von der guten Seite an.
> *Henry is an incurable optimist and looks on everything from the bright side (looks on the bright side of everything).*

auch seine guten **Seiten** haben (fig.): *to have one's (good) points too*

> Der Winter hat auch seine guten Seiten. Er härtet uns ab.
> *Winter has its (good) points too. It toughens us.*

etwas auf die **Seite** legen: cf. etwas auf die hohe **Kante** legen

einer Sache eine neue **Seite** abgewinnen (fig.): *to see the other side of s.th.; to see s.th. in a different light; to get another line (angle) on s.th. (colloq.)*

Früher war mir diese Fahrt lästig, jetzt aber habe ich ihr eine neue Seite abgewonnen und freue mich über die Abwechslung.
*Formerly this journey was tiresome, but now I see the other side of it (see it in a different light; have got another line [angle] on it) and enjoy the change.*

j.en auf die **Seite** schaffen (fig.): cf. j.en um die **Ecke** bringen

etwas auf die **Seite** schaffen (fig.): cf. etwas **klauen**

j.en an seiner schwachen **Seite** angreifen (fig.): *to touch s.b.'s weak spot; to catch s.b. on the wrong foot; to attack s.b. on his weak front.* Cf. auch: ein wunder **Punkt** sein

Wenn Sie von den Gefahren des Zigarettenrauchens sprechen, so greifen Sie mich (da) an meiner schwachen Seite an.
*By talking of the dangers of smoking cigarettes, you touch my weak spot (catch me on the wrong foot; attack me on my weak front).*

j.em zur **Seite** springen (fig.): *to come to s.b.'s aid (assistance); to back s.b. up.* Cf. auch: sich auf j.es **Seite** stellen

Ich danke Ihnen, daß Sie mir zur Seite gesprungen sind.
*Thank you for coming to my aid (assistance; for backing me up).*

sich auf j.es **Seite** stellen (fig.): *to take sides with s.b.; to side with s.b.; to range o.s. on s.b.'s side; to take s.b.'s part.* Cf. auch: j.em zur **Seite** springen

Ich war der Meinung, daß Eva in dieser Sache recht hatte, und ich habe mich gleich auf ihre Seite gestellt.
*I was of the opinion that Eva was right in this matter, and I at once took sides with her (sided with her; ranged myself on her side; took her part).*

j.en (etwas) einem Menschen (einer Sache) an die **Seite** stellen (fig.): *to put (to range) s.b. (s.th.) alongside s.b. (s.th.); to name (to mention) s.b. (s.th.) in the same breath as s.b. (s.th.)*

Sein Roman ist zwar gut, aber man kann ihn den klassischen Werken kaum an die Seite stellen.
*His novel is admittedly good, but one can hardly put (range) it alongside (name [mention] it in the same breath as) classical works.*

seine zwei **Seiten** haben (fig.): *to have two sides (aspects).* Cf. auch: ein zweischneidiges **Schwert** sein

Sein mutiger Schritt hat leider seine zwei Seiten. Denn er trägt auch eine Gefahr in sich.
*His courageous step unfortunately has two sides (aspects), for it also involves danger.*

ein **Seitenhieb** sein (fig.): *to be a blow (a thrust; a tilt); to be a dig (colloq.); s. th. is aimed at s. b. (s. th.); s. b. is getting at s. b. (s. th.) (colloq.)*

Diese ironische Bemerkung war ein deutlicher Seitenhieb (Stich) auf die Opposition.

*That ironical remark was an obvious blow (thrust; tilt; dig) at the opposition (was obviously getting [aimed] at the opposition).*

Wer's glaubt, wird **selig**! (fam.): cf. Das kannst du deiner **Großmutter** erzählen

**selig** sein (fig. u. fam.): cf. einen **Schwips** haben

abgehen wie warme **Semmeln:** *to sell (to go) like hot cakes*

Die Karten für diese Aufführung gehen ab wie warme Semmeln (wie beim Bäcker die Semmeln; gehen reißend ab).

*The tickets for this performance are selling (going) like hot cakes.*

seinen **Senf** dazugeben (fig. u. fam.): *to put (to stick) one's oar in; to put one's spoke in; to chip in (colloq.); to chime in (colloq.)*

Mußt du denn bei jeder Unterhaltung deinen Senf dazugeben?

*Must you put (stick) your oar into (put your spoke into; chip into; chime in) every conversation?*

einen langen **Senf** machen (fam.): cf. wie die **Katze** um den heißen Brei gehen

einen langen **Sermon** machen (fam.): cf. wie die **Katze** um den heißen Brei gehen

Beim **Setzen** wird sich's zeigen (weisen) (fig.): cf. **Probieren** geht über Studieren

mit tödlicher **Sicherheit:** *as sure as fate; dead certain; as sure as eggs is eggs (sl.)*

Mit tödlicher Sicherheit (Todsicher; Sicher wie das Amen in der Kirche; So sicher, wie zweimal zwei vier ist,) werden wir das Wettspiel gewinnen.

*We shall win the competition as sure as fate (as sure as eggs is eggs; We are dead certain to win the competition).*

sich in **Sicherheit** wiegen: *to lull o.s. into a false sense of security*

Die Polizei konnte den Mörder, der sich in Sicherheit gewiegt hatte, gestern abend verhaften.

*Yesterday evening the police were able to arrest the murderer, who had lulled himself into a false sense of security.*

auf lange **Sicht:** *in the long run; in the last analysis; on the long view*

Auf lange Sicht (Auf die Dauer) muß eine solche Politik scheitern.

*In the long run (In the last analysis; On the long view) such a policy must fail.*

ein Gedächtnis wie ein **Sieb** haben: *to have a head like a sieve (like a colander)*

Dreimal habe ich Karl daran erinnert, mir eine neue Zahnbürste zu kaufen, aber er vergißt es immer (wieder). Er hat ein Gedächtnis wie ein Sieb.
*Three times I have reminded Charles to buy me a new toothbrush, but he always forgets to. He has a head like a sieve (colander).*

Personen (z. B. Prüflinge) **sieben** (fig.): cf. die **Böcke** von den Schafen sondern

eine böse **Sieben** sein (fig. u. fam.): cf. eine alte **Hexe** sein

**Siebenmeilenstiefel**: *seven-league boots*

Wenn du diese Strecke in einer Stunde zurücklegen willst, mußt du Siebenmeilenstiefel anziehen.
*If you want to cover that distance in an hour, you will have to put seven-league boots on.*

seine **Siebensachen** (zusammen)packen (fam.): *to pack (to get) one's things together; to gather up one's stuff (colloq.).* Cf. auch: sein **Bündel** schnüren

Da es mir in der Pension nicht gefiel, packte ich meine Siebensachen (Brocken) (zusammen) und zog aus.
*As I did not like it in the boarding-house, I packed (got) my things together (gathered up my stuff) and moved out.*

seine **Siebensachen** verlieren (fam.): cf. **Hab** und Gut verlieren

(ein Gefühl) zur **Siedehitze** (bis zum **Siedepunkt**) steigern: *to raise a feeling to boiling-point; to bring a feeling to a white heat (to a head)*

Die bissige Bemerkung des Ministers steigerte die Wut der Opposition zur Siedehitze (bis zum Siedepunkt).
*The minister's caustic comment raised the opposition's anger to boiling-point (brought . . . to a white heat [a head]).*

j.en auf den **Siedepunkt** bringen (fig.): cf. j.en zur **Weißglut** bringen

den **Sieg** an seine Fahnen heften (fig.): *to win (to carry) the day; to emerge victorious*

Obwohl der Feldherr viele Siege an seine Fahnen heftete, verlor er schließlich doch den Krieg.
*Although the commander won (carried) the day (emerged victorious) on many occasions, he finally lost the war.*

unter dem **Siegel** der Verschwiegenheit: *under the pledge (seal) of silence (secrecy); within these four walls; between you and me and the gatepost (colloq.)*

Was ich Ihnen hier anvertraue, geschieht unter dem Siegel der Verschwiegenheit.
*What I am confiding to you here is done under the pledge (seal) of silence (secrecy; must remain within these four walls; is between you and me and the gatepost).*

die **Siegespalme** erringen: *to carry off (to win) the palm of victory (the laurels)*
Wer hat bei diesem Wettlauf die Siegespalme (die Palme des Sieges) errungen?
*Who carried off (won) the palm of victory (the laurels) in that race?*

**Sieh** mal einer an! (fam.): *Well, well!; Just imagine!; Would you believe it!
(colloq.); You don't say! (colloq.)*
Das hast du wirklich allein(e) gemacht? Sieh mal einer an!
*You really did do that by yourself? Well, well! (Just imagine!; Would you believe it!;
You don't say!)*

So **siehst** du aus! (fam.): cf. Mach' keine **Späße!**

in den **Sielen** sterben (fig.): *to die in harness; to die with one's boots on*
Mein Onkel hat bis zum Ende seines Lebens noch gearbeitet. Er ist in den
Sielen gestorben.
*My uncle worked right till the end of his life. He died in harness (with his boots on).*

Reden ist **Silber,** Schweigen ist Gold (Sprichw.): *Least said, soonest mended
(prov.); The less said, the better*
Über diesen unangenehmen Zwischenfall wollen wir nichts mehr sagen. Reden
ist Silber, Schweigen ist Gold.
*Let us say no more about this unpleasant incident. Least said, soonest mended (The less
said, the better).*

Ein **Silberstreifen** zeichnet sich am Horizonte ab (fig.): *There is a gleam
(ray) of light (hope) on the horizon.* Cf. auch: Auch das **Schlimmste** hat ein
Ende
Der Politiker behauptete in seiner Rede, daß sich ein Silberstreifen am Hori-
zonte abzeichne.
*The politician claimed in his speech that there was a gleam [ray] of light on the horizon.*

gleichen **Sinnes** sein: *to be of one mind (of like mind; of one opinion)*
So verschieden wir auch sonst denken, hier sind wir gleichen Sinnes.
*However differently we think in other matters, we are of one mind (of like mind; of one
opinion) in this.*

sich etwas aus dem **Sinn** schlagen: *to get (to put) s.th. out of one's mind
(head); to dismiss s.th. from one's mind (thoughts)*
Diesen unmöglichen Plan solltest du dir endlich aus dem Sinn (Kopf) schlagen.
*You ought to get (to put) this impossible plan out of your mind (head; to dismiss this
impossible plan from your mind [thoughts]).*

bei **Sinnen** sein (seine fünf Sinne beisammen haben): *to be in one's right
mind; to have one's wits about one*

Bist du denn bei Sinnen (Hast du denn deine fünf Sinne beisammen), so etwas Unwahres zu behaupten?
*Are you in your right mind (Have you got your wits about you), telling such an untruth?*

keinen **Sinn** und Verstand haben: *there is no point (sense); there is nothing to be gained; there is neither rhyme nor reason*

Es hat keinen Sinn und Verstand (keinen Wert [Zweck]), diesen mächtigen Mann anzugreifen.
*There is no point (sense) in (nothing to be gained by; neither rhyme nor reason in) attacking this powerful man.*

seine fünf **Sinne** zusammennehmen: *to summon one's wits; to take hold of o.s.; to pull o.s. together (colloq.); to buck o.s. up (sl.)*

Diese leichte Rechenaufgabe wirst du doch wohl ausrechnen können. Nimm deine fünf Sinne zusammen!
*Surely you will be able to work out this easy sum. Summon your wits! (Take hold of yourself!; Pull yourself together!; Buck yourself up!)*

**Sinnen** und Trachten: cf. **Dichten** und Trachten

**sinnlos** betrunken sein: cf. **sternhagelvoll** sein

mit der ganzen **Sippe**: cf. mit **Kind** und Kegel

eine **Sisyphusarbeit** (fig.): *a Sisyphean task.* Cf. auch: eine **Herkulesarbeit** sein

Ich gebe den Versuch auf, den Motor unseres Autos selbst zu reparieren. Es ist tatsächlich eine Sisyphusarbeit.
*I am giving up the attempt to repair the engine of our car myself. It is a real Sisyphean task.*

einen **sitzen** haben (fam.): cf. einen **Schwips** haben

etwas auf sich **sitzen** lassen (fam.): cf. etwas **einstecken** müssen

**sitzenbleiben** (fig.): a) (unverheiratet) *to remain (to be left) an old maid; to remain a wallflower; to be left on the shelf (colloq.);* b) (auf etwas) *to be left with s. th.; to be saddled (lumbered) with s. th. (colloq.);* c) (Schule) *not to move up; to stay down*

a) Eine so arrogante Person wird nie einen Mann bekommen, sondern sitzenbleiben.
b) Dieser Buchhändler hat unglücklich eingekauft und ist auf manchen Büchern, die niemand haben will, sitzengeblieben.
c) Es war vorauszusehen, daß dein fauler Bruder sitzenbleiben (klebenbleiben) würde.

*a) Such an arrogant person will never find a husband; she will remain (be left) an old maid (remain a wallflower; be left on the shelf).*
*b) This bookseller has made some unfortunate purchases and been left (saddled; lumbered) with certain books which nobody wants.*
*c) It was to be foreseen that your lazy brother would not move up (would stay down).*

j.en **sitzenlassen** (fig.): cf. j.en im **Stich** lassen

kein **Sitzfleisch** haben (fam.): *to have no perseverance; not to peg away (to stick) at s. th. (colloq.); not to keep one's nose to the grindstone (colloq.)*

> Für eine Tätigkeit, die stundenlange Schreibtischarbeit verlangt, hast du kein Sitzfleisch.
> *You have no perseverance for (You do not peg away [stick] at) a job (You do not keep your nose to the grindstone when it is a case of a job) which requires hours of desk-work.*

sich auf die **Socken** machen (fam.): *to get along (colloq.); to get a move on (colloq.); to look slippy (sharp) (sl.)*

> Mein Zug fährt in einer halben Stunde; ich muß mich auf die Socken (Sprünge; Strümpfe) machen.
> *My train leaves in half an hour. I must (be getting) along (must [be getting] a move on; must look slippy [sharp]).*

von den **Socken** sein (fam.): cf. wie aus den **Wolken** fallen

ein **Sonderling** sein: cf. ein komischer **Kauz** sein

nicht wert sein, daß einen die **Sonne** bescheint: *not fit to be on God's earth; not fit to be alive*

> Dieser Gauner ist nicht wert, daß ihn die Sonne bescheint.
> *This scoundrel is not fit to be on God's earth (to be alive).*

**Sonne** im Herzen haben (fig.): *to radiate happiness; to be a radiant personality*

> Meine Schwester ist immer fröhlich. Sie hat Sonne im Herzen.
> *My sister is always merry. She radiates happiness (is a radiant personality).*

**sonnenklar** sein: *to be as clear as daylight (as crystal); to be as plain as a pikestaff; to go without saying; to stand to reason; to be as plain as the nose on one's face (colloq.)*

> Es ist doch sonnenklar (klar wie Kloßbrühe; kristallklar; Es liegt auf der Hand; Es läßt sich an den [an allen] zehn Fingern abzählen), daß man ohne die nötigen Sprachkenntnisse die diplomatische Laufbahn nicht einschlagen kann.
> *It is as clear as daylight (crystal; as plain as a pikestaff; as plain as the nose on one's face; It goes without saying; It stands to reason) that one cannot embark on a diplomatic career without the necessary knowledge of languages.*

j.es **Sonnenschein** sein (fig.): *to be the life and soul of s. th.; to be s. b.'s delight*

> Meine jüngste Schwester ist der Sonnenschein unserer ganzen Familie.
> *My youngest sister is the life and soul (the delight) of our whole family.*

Es ist nicht alle Tage **Sonntag** (Sprichw.): cf. Es ist nicht alle **Tage** Sonntag
der **Sonntagnachmittagausgehanzug** (fam.): *one's Sunday best (colloq.).*
Cf. auch: **geschniegelt** und gebügelt (gestriegelt) sein

Morgen ist Feiertag. Laß dir deinen Sonntagnachmittagausgehanzug ausbürsten und aufbügeln.
*It's a holiday tomorrow. Have your Sunday best brushed and ironed.*

ein **Sonntagsjäger** sein: *to be a week-end sportsman*

Georg kann unmöglich ein Reh geschossen haben. Er ist ja doch nur ein Sonntagsjäger.
*George cannot possibly have shot a deer. He is only a week-end sportsman.*

etwas in die **Sonntagskehle** bekommen (fig.): cf. etwas in die falsche **Kehle** bekommen

ein **Sonntagskind** sein: cf. ein **Glückskind** sein

es geht (mit) j.em **soso**: *things are so-so (are middling) with s.b. (colloq.)*

Diesem (Mit diesem) Geschäftsmann geht es nur soso (lala).
*Things are only so-so (middling) with this shopkeeper.*

einen **Span** haben (fam.): cf. nicht richtig im **Dachstübchen** sein

Es gibt **Späne** (fam.): *The sparks (The fur) will fly (colloq.); Things will become hot (colloq.)*

Die Aufregung der Anwesenden steigerte sich derart, daß es Späne gab.
*The agitation of those present rose to such a pitch that the sparks (fur) flew (that things became hot).*

Wo gehobelt wird, da fallen **Späne** (Sprichw.): cf. Wo **gehobelt** wird, da fallen Späne

stolz wie ein **Spanier** sein: *to be as proud as a peacock; to be puffed up with pride; to plume o.s.; to give o.s. airs.* Cf. auch: sich spreizen wie ein **Truthahn**

Nach bestandenem Examen war mein Vetter stolz wie ein Spanier (Pfau).
*After having passed his examination my cousin was as proud as a peacock (was puffed up with pride; gave himself airs; My cousin plumed himself on having passed his examination).*

wie **Spargel** aus der Erde schießen: cf. wie (die) **Pilze** aus der Erde schießen

einen **Sparren** haben (fam.): cf. nicht richtig im **Dachstübchen** sein

**Spaß** beiseite: cf. **Scherz** beiseite

über den **Spaß** gehen: cf. über die **Hutschnur** gehen

Mach' keine **Späße!**: *None of your jokes! (colloq.); Are you joking (kidding)? (colloq.); That's what you think! (colloq.); Some hope! (colloq.)*

Du willst, daß ich dir ein neues Fahrrad kaufe, weil dir das alte nicht mehr gefällt? Mach' keine Späße (So siehst du aus)!
*You want me to buy you a new bicycle because you don't like the old one any more? None of your jokes! (Are you joking [kidding]?; That's what you think!; Some hope!)*

Damit ist nicht zu **spaßen**: *It is no joke; It is not to be taken (treated) lightly; It is not to be treated as a joke*

Mit dieser Entzündung ist nicht zu spaßen. Du solltest gleich zum Arzt gehen.
*This inflammation is no joke (is not to be taken [treated] lightly; is not to be treated as a joke). You ought to go to the doctor at once.*

ein **Spaßvogel** sein (fam.): *to be a wag (wit; comic; Merry Andrew; clown)*

In Gesellschaft meines Vetters amüsieren wir uns herrlich, denn er ist ein richtiger Spaßvogel.
*We enjoy ourselves wonderfully in my cousin's company; he is a real wag (wit; comic; Merry Andrew; clown).*

essen wie ein **Spatz**: *to peck (to nibble) at one's food*

Wenn er weiterhin nur wie ein Spatz ißt, wird er nicht kräftig werden.
*If he only goes on pecking (nibbling) at his food, he will not grow strong.*

Das pfeifen die **Spatzen** von den Dächern (fig.): *It is being shouted from the house-tops; It is being spread (being noised) abroad; It is the talk of the town; It is in everyone's mouth; Even the little birds know it; It is old hat (colloq.)*

Was du mir da erzählst, ist schon längst bekannt. Die Spatzen pfeifen es (schon) von den Dächern.
*What you are telling me has been known for a long time. It is being shouted from the house-tops (being spread [noised] abroad; It is the talk of the town [in everyone's mouth]; Even the little birds know it; It is old hat).*

ein **Spatzengehirn** haben (fig.): *to have the brains of a mouse; to be a pin-head (sl.)*

Bei seinem Spatzengehirn sollte er keine höhere Schule besuchen.
*He has the brains of a mouse (He is a pin-head) and ought not to go to secondary school.*

den **Speck** riechen (fig.): cf. den **Braten** riechen

glänzen wie eine **Speckschwarte**: *to shine like a mirror; to be as shiny as a bald pate (colloq.)*

Diesen alten Anzug kannst du nicht mehr anziehen, denn er glänzt wie eine Speckschwarte.
*You can't wear that old suit any more; it shines like a mirror (is as shiny as a bald pate).*

**Spektakel** machen: cf. **Krach** machen

Ein **Sperling** in der Hand ist besser als eine Taube auf dem Dache (Sprichw.): *A bird in the hand is worth two in the bush (prov.); Half a loaf is better than no bread (prov.)*

Wir wollen uns lieber mit diesem kleinen Gewinn begnügen, als uns einem großen Risiko aussetzen. Ein Sperling in der Hand ist besser als eine Taube auf dem Dache.
*We would rather content ourselves with this small profit than expose ourselves to a big risk. A bird in the hand is worth two in the bush (Half a loaf is better than no bread).*

eine **Sphinx** sein (fig.): *to be a Sphinx; to be an enigma*

Seine Frau wird uns ewig eine Sphinx sein.
*His wife will always be a Sphinx (an enigma) to us.*

einen **Spicker** benutzen (fam.): *to use a crib (colloq.)*

Ich konnte den lateinischen Text nicht verstehen und habe deshalb einen Spicker benutzt.
*I could not understand the Latin text and therefore used a crib.*

Das kannst du dir hinter den **Spiegel** stecken! (fam.): *Put that in your pipe and smoke it! (colloq.); So there! (colloq.)*

Durch dein unüberlegtes Verhalten hast du mich um den Erwerb dieses schönen Grundstücks gebracht. Das kannst du dir hinter den Spiegel stecken (Laß dir das gesagt sein)!
*By acting thoughtlessly you have prevented me from acquiring that fine plot of land, so put that in your pipe and smoke it (so there)!*

j.em den **Spiegel** vorhalten (fig.): *to hold up the mirror to s.b.*

Der Pfarrer hat seiner Gemeinde den Spiegel vorgehalten und ihr ihre Fehler aufgezeigt.
*The parson held up the mirror to his congregation and revealed to them their errors.*

**Spiegelfechterei** (fig.): *shadow-boxing; fencing; going through the motions*

Der Mann befaßte sich nicht mit den wirklichen Problemen. Seine Rede war nichts als Spiegelfechterei.
*The man did not deal with the real problems. His speech was nothing but shadow-boxing (fencing; going through the motions).*

**spiegelglatt** sein: *to be like a sheet of glass (as smooth as glass)*

Das Eis war spiegelglatt, und viele unerfahrene Schlittschuhläufer sind hingefallen.
*The ice was like a sheet of glass (as smooth as glass) and many inexperienced skaters fell over.*

ein abgekartetes **Spiel** sein (fig.): *to be a swindle; to be a put-up (rigged) job (a plant; a frame-up) (colloq.)*

Die Wahlergebnisse waren nicht echt. Es war ein abgekartetes Spiel (eine abgekartete Sache) der Regierungsparteien.
*The election results were not genuine. They were a swindle (a put-up job; a rigged job;
a plant; a frame-up) on the part of the government parties.*

Das **Spiel** ist aus (fig.)!: cf. Der **Bart** ist ab!

j.es **Spiel** durchschauen (fig.): *to see through (to fathom) s.b. (s.b.'s game;
s.b.'s tricks; s.b.'s design); to cotton on (to get wise) to s.b. (s.b.'s game; s.b.'s
tricks; s.b.'s design) (colloq.).* Cf. auch: etwas **spitzkriegen**

> Sein schmeichlerisches Benehmen ist nicht echt. Ich durchschaue schon längst
> sein Spiel (seine Ränke; Ich gucke [sehe] ihm schon längst in die Karten).
> *His flattering behaviour is not genuine. I saw through (fathomed; cottoned on to; got wise
> to) him (his game [tricks; design]) long ago.*

ein falsches (doppeltes) **Spiel** mit j.em treiben (fig.): *to cheat s.b.; to play a
double game with s.b.; to indulge in double-dealing with s.b.; to double-cross s.b.
(colloq.)*

> Der Diplomat versuchte, ein falsches (doppeltes) Spiel mit der ausländischen
> Regierung zu treiben.
> *The diplomat tried to cheat (to play a double game with; to indulge in double-dealing
> with; to double-cross) the foreign government.*

j.em freies **Spiel** lassen (fig.): cf. j.em freie **Hand** lassen

ein gefährliches (gewagtes) **Spiel** treiben (fig.): cf. mit dem **Feuer** spielen

bei j.em gewonnenes **Spiel** haben (fig.): *to win s.b. over; to have s.b. in the bag
(colloq.); to have s.b. eating out of one's hand (colloq.)*

> Der neue Geschichtslehrer hatte bei seinen Schülern sofort gewonnenes Spiel,
> indem er ihnen einige historische Anekdoten erzählte.
> *The new history master won his pupils over (had his pupils in the bag; had his pupils
> eating out of his hand) at once by telling them some historical anecdotes.*

seine Hand im **Spiel** haben (fig.): cf. seine **Finger** im Spiel haben

j.en aus dem **Spiel** lassen (fig.): *to leave s.b. out of it; to count s.b. out; to cut
s.b. out of it (colloq.)*

> Laßt mich aus dem Spiel, wenn Ihr solchen Unfug anstellen wollt.
> *Leave (Cut) me out of it (Count me out) if you're going to get up to such mischief.*

sein Leben aufs **Spiel** setzen (fig.): cf. sein Leben in die **Schanze** schlagen

mit j.em leichtes **Spiel** haben (fig.): *to have an easy time (of it) with s.b.; it is
a walk-over (is child's play) for s.b. with s.b. (colloq.).* Cf. auch: **kinderleicht**
sein

480

Der Betrüger hatte mit dem harmlosen alten Mann leichtes Spiel.
*The swindler had an easy time (of it) with the harmless old man (It was a walk-over [child's play] for the swindler with the harmless old man).*

mit im **Spiele** sein (fig.): *to be involved (present); to be at work; s.th. colours s.b.'s view (attitude)*

> Wir geben gern zu, daß etwas Mißtrauen bei uns mit im Spiele ist.
> *We willingly admit that a certain amount of mistrust is involved (present; at work) in our attitude (colours our view [attitude]).*

ein offenes **Spiel** spielen (fig.): cf. die **Karten** aufdecken

alles aufs **Spiel** setzen (fig.): *to stake (to bank; to risk) everything; to throw everything into the scales (into the attack); to go the whole hog (colloq.); to put one's shirt on s.th. (sl.)*

> Ich weiß, daß ich mich auf Ihre Auskünfte verlassen kann und bin bereit, in dieser Angelegenheit alles aufs Spiel zu setzen.
> *I know that I can rely on your information, and am prepared to stake (to bank; to risk) everything (to throw everything into the scales [attack]; to go the whole hog) in this matter (am prepared to put my shirt on this matter).*

auf dem **Spiele** stehen (fig.): *to be at stake*

> Tun Sie das nicht! Ihr Ruf steht auf dem Spiele.
> *Don't do that. Your reputation is at stake.*

sein **Spiel** mit j.em treiben (fig.): *to make sport with s.b.; to play (to trifle) with s.b.; to make a cat's-paw of s.b. (colloq.); to dangle s.b. on a string (colloq.); to play fast and loose with s.b. (colloq.)*

> Hüte dich vor Marie. Sie treibt nur ihr Spiel mit jungen Männern.
> *Beware of Mary. She only makes sport (plays; trifles; plays fast and loose) with young men (makes a cat's-paw of young men; dangles young men on a string).*

sein **Spiel** gut verbergen (fig.): cf. sich nicht in die **Karten** gucken lassen

j.em das **Spiel** verderben (fig.): *to·spoil (to ruin) s.b.'s prospects; to spoil the picture; to mess (to muck) up the situation for s.b. (colloq.)*

> Mit deiner Voreiligkeit hast du mir das Spiel verdorben.
> *You have spoilt (ruined) my prospects (spoilt the picture; messed [mucked] up the situation for me) by your impetuosity.*

das **Spiel** verloren geben (fig.): cf. den **Kampf** aufgeben

der **Spielball** sein (fig.): *to be the plaything (the toy; the puppet); to be the stooge (sl.)*

> Dieses kleine Land ist der Spielball der angrenzenden Großmächte geworden.
> *This little country has become the plaything (toy; puppet; stooge) of the neighbouring great powers.*

freien **Spielraum** gebrauchen (nötig haben) (fig.): cf. **Ellbogenfreiheit**

j.em (einer Sache) **Spielraum** lassen (fig.): *to give (to allow) scope (freedom; play; margin) to s.b. (s. th.)*

> Bei unserm Thema ist der Phantasie großer Spielraum gelassen worden.
> *A great deal of scope (freedom; play; A large margin) is given (allowed) to the imagination in our subject.*

die **Spielregeln** beachten (fig.): *to play the game (the man); to play fair; to keep to (to observe) the rules of the game*

> Man hofft, daß auch in der Weltpolitik die Spielregeln beachtet werden.
> *One hopes that even in world politics people will play the game (man; play fair; that the rules of the game will be generally kept to [observed]).*

vom **Spielteufel** besessen sein: *to be bitten by the gambling bug (colloq.)*

> Wer vom Spielteufel besessen ist, kann leicht sein ganzes Geld verlieren.
> *Anyone who has been bitten by the gambling bug can easily lose all his money.*

(ein) **Spielverderber** sein (fig.): *to be a spoil-sport; to be a kill-joy; to be a wet blanket (colloq.)*

> Mach' doch mit! Sei doch kein Spielverderber (Hemmschuh)!
> *Do play with us! Don't be such a spoil-sport (kill-joy; wet blanket).*

etwas **spielen** lassen (fig.): *to play on s. th.; to make the most of s. th.; to get s. th. to work*

> Wenn man in die diplomatische Laufbahn hinein will, muß man seine Beziehungen spielen lassen.
> *If one wants to go in for a diplomatic career, one has to play on (make the most of) one's contacts (to get one's contacts to work).*

etwas **spielend** tun (fig.): cf. **kinderleicht** sein

wie am **Spieße** schreien: *to scream (to yell) the place down (colloq.); to scream (to yell) like mad (colloq.); to scream (to yell) as if one were being roasted alive (colloq.); to scream (to yell) one's head off (colloq.); to cry blue murder (sl.)*

> Der Junge hatte sich schlimm in den Finger geschnitten und schrie wie am Spieße.
> *The boy had cut his finger badly and was screaming (yelling) the place down (yelling [screaming] like mad; screaming [yelling] as if he were being roasted alive; screaming [yelling] his head off; crying blue murder).*

den **Spieß** umdrehen (umkehren) (fig.): *to turn the tables (on s. b.); the boot is on the other foot; the laugh is on s. b.'s side; to get one's own back*

> Früher hat er immer besser gespielt als ich, aber jetzt habe ich den Spieß umgedreht (umgekehrt) und ihn vollständig geschlagen.

*Formerly he always played better than I but now I have turned the tables on him (got my own back) and beaten him completely (now the boot is on the other foot; the laugh is on my side) and I beat him completely.*

ein **Spießer (Spießbürger)** sein: *to be a Philistine*

Ein empfindsamer Mensch wird den Umgang mit Spießern (Spießbürgern) möglichst vermeiden.
*A sensitive person will avoid association with Philistines as far as possible.*

**Spießruten** laufen (fig.): *to run the gauntlet*

Die neugierige Menge stand zu beiden Seiten der Straße, und die Verhafteten mußten (an ihr vorbei) Spießruten laufen.
*The inquisitive crowd stood on both sides of the street, and the prisoners had to run the gauntlet (past them).*

**spindeldürr** sein: cf. nur noch **Haut** und Knochen sein

j.em **spinnefeind** sein: *to hate s. b. like poison; to hate s. b.'s guts (sl.)*

Infolge einiger Mißverständnisse sind sich diese beiden Nachbarn jetzt spinnefeind.
*As a result of a few misunderstandings these two neighbours now hate each other like poison (hate each other's guts).*

**spinnen** (fam.): cf. nicht richtig im **Dachstübchen** sein

eine **Spirale** im Hintern haben (fam.): cf. **Quecksilber** im Leibe haben

einen **Spitz** haben: cf. einen **Schwips** haben

einer Sache die **Spitze** abbrechen (fig.): *to take the sting out of s. th.; to blunt the edge of s. th.*

Der Bürgermeister hat es verstanden, jeder weiteren Kritik an seiner Politik die Spitze abzubrechen.
*The mayor knew how to take the sting out of (blunt the edge of) any further criticism of his policy.*

j.em (einer Sache) die **Spitze** bieten (fig.): *to meet (to face) s. b. (s. th.) head-on*

Wir sind fest entschlossen, den Angriffen unserer Feinde die Spitze zu bieten.
*We are firmly determined to meet (to face) our enemies' attacks head-on.*

sich an die **Spitze** stellen (fig.): *to take up (one's) position at the head; to take up pride of place; to appoint o. s. to lead*

Der junge Politiker hat sich an die Spitze der neuen Bewegung gestellt.
*The young politician has taken up (his) position (taken up pride of place) at the head of the new movement (has appointed himself to lead the new movement).*

etwas auf die **Spitze** treiben (fig.): *to carry s.th. to extremes; to let s.th. reach (to carry s.th. to the) breaking-point; to bring s.th. to a head*

Ihr solltet euren Streit nicht auf die Spitze (aufs Äußerste; zum Äußersten) treiben.
*You ought not to carry your quarrel to extremes (to let your quarrel reach [carry your quarrel to the] breaking-point; to bring your quarrel to a head).*

sich auf etwas **spitzen**: cf. mit etwas **rechnen**

**Spitzenreiter** sein (fig.): *to be top-dog (colloq.)*

Wir hoffen, daß unsere Fußballmannschaft dieses Jahr Spitzenreiter wird.
*We hope that our football team will be top-dog this year.*

etwas **spitzkriegen** (fam.): *to get wise to s.th. (colloq.); to cotton on to s.th. (colloq.); to tumble to s.th. (sl.).* Cf. auch: j.es **Spiel** durchschauen

Ich habe es längst spitzgekriegt, daß deine Schwester mich nicht leiden kann.
*I got wise (cottoned on; tumbled) to the fact long ago that your sister cannot bear me.*

einen **Spleen** haben (fam.): nicht richtig im **Dachstübchen** sein

**splitternackt** sein: *to be stark naked.* Cf. auch: im **Adamskostüm** sein

Bei dem schönen Sommerwetter spielten die Kinder splitternackt (fasernackt; als Nacktfrösche [Nackedeis]) im Garten.
*In the lovely summer weather the children were playing in the garden stark naked.*

sich die **Sporen** verdienen (fig.): *to win one's spurs; to serve one's apprenticeship.* Cf. auch: seine ersten **Lorbeeren** ernten

Auf welcher Bühne hat sich dieser Schauspieler die Sporen verdient?
*In which theatre did this actor win his spurs (serve his apprenticeship)?*

**spornstreichs**: cf. **schnurstracks**

**spottbillig** sein: *to be a gift; to be dirt-cheap (colloq.)*

Die neue Ausgabe dieses Buches ist zu dem Preis wirklich spottbillig (geradezu geschenkt).
*The new edition of this book is really a gift (dirt-cheap) at that price.*

jeder Beschreibung **spotten**: cf. jeder **Beschreibung** spotten

sitzen, wo die **Spötter** sitzen: cf. auf der **Bank** der Spötter sitzen

ein **Spottvogel** sein: cf. ein **Spaßvogel** sein

etwas zur **Sprache** bringen: *to bring (to put) s.th. up (to raise s.th.) (for discussion); to broach a subject*

484

In der nächsten Sitzung wollen wir dieses neue Thema zur Sprache bringen.
*In the next meeting we want to bring (put) up (to raise) this new subject ([for discussion]; to broach this new subject).*

Heraus mit der **Sprache!**: *Out with it!; Speak up!; Let's have it! (colloq.); Cough it up! (sl.)*

Wo bist du denn so lange gewesen? Heraus mit der Sprache!
*Where have you been all this time? Out with it! (Speak up!; Let's have it!; Cough it up!)*

nicht mit der **Sprache** herausrücken (herauswollen): cf. **herumdrucksen**

die **Spreu** vom Weizen sondern (fig.): cf. die **Böcke** von den Schafen sondern

zerstreut wie die **Spreu** im Winde: cf. in alle **Winde** zerstreut sein

etwas **springen** lassen (fig. u. fam.): *to fork out a bit (colloq.); to cough up a bit (colloq.); to open the coffers (colloq.); to show the colour of one's money (colloq.).* Cf. auch: eine Geldsumme **lockermachen**

Wir haben nur noch zwei Tage Ferien. Laß mal etwas springen.
*We've only got two days' holiday left. Fork out (Cough up) a bit (Open the coffers; Show the colour of your money).*

sein **Sprüchlein** hersagen (fig.): *to recite one's (little) piece*

Vor jeder Tür sagte der Bettler sein Sprüchlein her.
*The beggar recited his (little) piece at each door.*

auf dem **Sprunge** sein (fig.): *to be on the point; to be just about*

Ich bin eben auf dem Sprunge, ins Büro zu gehen, und kann jetzt keinen Besuch empfangen.
*I am just on the point of going (just about to go) to the office, and cannot receive visitors now.*

auf einen **Sprung** (fig.): *for a moment (minute; second); for a jiffy (colloq.)*

Gestern schaute ich bei meinem Vetter auf einen Sprung herein.
*Yesterday I looked in to see my cousin for a moment (minute; second; jiffy).*

j.em auf die **Sprünge** helfen (fig.): a) cf. j.em auf die **Beine** helfen; b) cf. j.em **Beine** machen

hinter j.es **Sprünge** kommen (j.em auf die Sprünge kommen) (fig.): cf. hinter j.es **Schliche** kommen (j.em auf die Schliche kommen)

sich auf die **Sprünge** machen (fig.): cf. sich auf die **Socken** machen

keine großen **Sprünge** machen können (fig.): *not to be able to go far; to keep within bounds; not to be able to set the Thames on fire (colloq.); not to be able to paint the town red (colloq.); not to be able to make much of a splash (sl.)*

Mit so einem kleinen Gehalt kann man keine großen Sprünge machen.
*You cannot go far (paint the town red) on (set the Thames on fire [make much of a splash] with) such a small salary (You have to keep within bounds with such a small salary).*

den **Sprung** ins Ungewisse tun (fig.): *to make a leap in the dark (a leap into the unknown)*

Karl will den Sprung ins Ungewisse tun und nach Brasilien auswandern.
*Charles wants to make a leap in the dark (into the unknown) and emigrate to Brazil.*

den **Sprung** wagen (fig.): *to take the plunge.* Cf. auch: die **Kurve** kriegen

Ich bin jetzt froh, daß ich den Sprung gewagt und das Examen gemacht habe.
*I am now glad that I took the plunge and sat the examination.*

**sprungbereit** sein (fig.): *to be ready at a moment's notice*

Du brauchst nur zu telefonieren. Ich bin jederzeit sprungbereit, zu dir zu kommen.
*You only need to phone me; I am ready at a moment's notice to come to you.*

ein **Sprungbrett** (fig.): *a springboard (a stepping-stone)*

Der junge Ingenieur betrachtet seine augenblickliche Stellung nur als (ein) Sprungbrett zu einem besseren Posten.
*The young engineer only regards his present job as a springboard (stepping-stone) to a better position.*

Da bleibt einem die **Spucke** weg! (fam.): cf. wie aus den **Wolken** (aus allen Wolken) gefallen

Mit Geduld und **Spucke** fängt man eine (manche) Mucke (Sprichw.): cf. Mit **Geduld** und Spucke fängt man eine Mucke

j.en von der **Spur** abbringen (fig.): *to throw (to put) s.b. off the scent (track)*

Eine falsche Aussage hatte die Polizei von der Spur abgebracht.
*A false statement had thrown (put) the police off the scent (track).*

j.em (einer Sache) auf der **Spur** sein (j.em [einer Sache] auf die Spur kommen) (fig.): *to be on the trail (scent; track) of s.b. (s.th.); to have got a line on s.b. (s.th.) (colloq.)*

Endlich ist man dem Meuchelmörder auf der Spur (auf die Spur gekommen).
*At last they are on the assassin's trail (scent; track; At last they have got a line on the assassin).*

j.en auf die **Spur** bringen (fig.): *to put (to set) s.b. on to the track (scent)*

Ein anonymer Brief hat mich auf die Spur des Einbrechers gebracht.
*An anonymous letter put (set) me on to the burglar's track (scent).*

auf der falschen **Spur** sein (fig.): *to be on the wrong track (scent); to be barking up the wrong tree (colloq.); to have got hold of the wrong end of the stick (colloq.).*
Cf. auch: auf dem **Holzwege** sein

Wenn Sie in mir den Verbrecher sehen, so sind Sie auf der falschen Spur.
*If you regard me as the criminal, then you are on the wrong track (scent; you are barking up the wrong tree; you have got hold of the wrong end of the stick).*

seine **Spuren** hinterlassen (fig.): *to leave one's marks (traces)*

Der letzte Weltkrieg wird auf Jahre hinaus seine Spuren hinterlassen.
*The last World War will leave its marks (traces) for years.*

Keine (Nicht die) **Spur**! (fig.): *Not a bit (of it)!; Not in the slightest!; Not on your life! (colloq.); That's what you think! (colloq.)*

Sie glauben, Ihr Sohn habe sich im Englischen wesentlich gebessert? Keine (Nicht die) Spur! (Ja, [Puste]kuchen!; Hat sich was!; Von wegen!)
*You think that your son has considerably improved in English? Not a bit (of it)! (Not in the slightest!; Not on your life!; That's what you think!)*

j.es **Spur** verlieren (fig.): *to lose track (trace; sight) of s.b.; to lose touch (contact) with s.b.*

Seitdem er ins Ausland verzogen ist, haben wir seine Spur (ihn aus den Augen [aus dem Gesichtskreis]) verloren.
*Since he moved abroad we have lost track (trace; sight) of him (lost touch [contact] with him).*

seine **Spuren** verwischen (fig.): *to cover one's tracks*

Der Bankräuber hat mit großer Geschicklichkeit seine Spuren verwischt.
*The bank robber has covered his tracks with great skill.*

in j.es **Spuren** wandeln (fig.): cf. in j.es **Fußstapfen** treten

seinen feinsten **Staat** tragen: *to wear one's best bib and tucker (colloq.); to wear one's Sunday best (colloq.).* Cf. auch: **Sonntagnachmittagausgehanzug; geschniegelt** und gebügelt sein

Die Gäste trugen ihren feinsten Staat.
*The guests were wearing their best bib and tucker (their Sunday best).*

mit etwas **Staat** machen: *to score (to be) a success with s.th.; to make (to score) a hit with s.th. (colloq.); to ring the bell with s.th. (colloq.); to hit it off with s.th. (colloq.)*

Mit deinem neuen Kleid wirst du sicher Staat machen.
*You are sure to score (to be) a success (to make [to score] a hit; to ring the bell; to hit it off) with your new dress.*

in vollem **Staate** erscheinen: *to appear in full regalia (in full ceremonial dress; in all one's glory)*

Zu der Jubiläumsfeier erschienen die Professoren und Studenten in vollem Staate (Wichs).

*At the anniversary celebrations the professors and students appeared in full regalia (in full ceremonial dress; in all their glory).*

das **Staatsruder** ergreifen (fig.): cf. ans **Ruder** kommen

über j.en den **Stab** brechen (fig.): *to pronounce (to pass) judgement on s.b.; to seal s.b.'s fate; to proclaim s.b.'s doom*

Jetzt hat die Gesellschaft den Stab über den Mörder gebrochen.

*Society has now pronounced (passed) judgement on the murderer (sealed the murderer's fate [proclaimed the murderer's doom]).*

Ein **Stachel** ist geblieben (fig.): *A thorn (A sting) remains; There is still a sting (a thorn) left; The quarrel still rankles*

Wenn Fritz sich auch mit Lydia ausgesöhnt hat, so ist doch nicht alles mehr (ganz) so wie früher. Ein Stachel ist geblieben.

*Even if Fred and Lydia are reconciled, all is still not quite the same as before. A thorn (sting) remains (There is still a sting [thorn] left; The quarrel still rankles).*

wider den **Stachel** löcken (fig.): *to kick against the pricks; to swim against the stream (current)*

Unter der Diktatur hat ein kleiner Personenkreis vergebens versucht, gegen den Stachel zu löcken (gegen den Strom zu schwimmen).

*Under the dictatorship a small circle of people tried in vain to kick against the pricks (to swim against the stream [current]).*

in **Stadt** und Land: *throughout the length and breadth of the country; up and down the country; far and wide; the world over; from pole to pole*

Dieser Archäologe ist in Stadt und Land (in der ganzen Welt) bekannt.

*This archaeologist is known the length and breadth of the country (up and down the country; far and wide; the world over; from pole to pole).*

**stadtbekannt** sein: *to be known far and wide*

Unser Schneider ist stadtbekannt (bekannt wie ein bunter Hund).
*Our tailor is known far and wide.*

das **Stadtgespräch** bilden (sein): cf. in aller (Leute) **Munde** sein b)

hart wie **Stahl** (**stahlhart**) sein: *to be as hard as iron (as nails)*

Es gibt Fälle, in denen auch ein gütiger Mensch hart wie Stahl (stahlhart) sein sollte.
*There are cases in which even a kind person must be as hard as iron (as nails).*

den **Stall** ausmisten (fig. u. fam.): *to clean the Augean stable(s); to clear up (to clean up) the mess (colloq.)*

Als der unordentliche Mieter auszog, hinterließ er viel Schmutz, und der Hausbesitzer mußte zunächst einmal den ganzen Stall (Saustall) ausmisten (den Augiasstall reinigen).
*When the untidy lodger moved out, he left a lot of dirt behind him, and the owner of the house first had to clean the Augean stable(s) (to clear [clean] up the mess).*

j.em geht eine **Stallaterne** auf (fam.): cf. j.em geht ein **Licht** auf

vom **Stamme** Nimm sein (fig. u. fam.): *to be a great one for accepting gifts (a great taker)*

Seine Schwiegertochter läßt sich gern beschenken. Sie ist überhaupt vom Stamme Nimm.
*His daughter-in-law likes getting presents. In fact she is a great one for accepting gifts (a great taker).*

einen schweren **Stand** haben (fig.): *to have a hard time of it; to have a tough job (colloq.); to have a rough passage (colloq.)*

Die Jungens in dieser Klasse sind schwer zu leiten, und der Lehrer hat oft einen schweren Stand mit ihnen.
*The boys in this class are difficult to control and the master often has a hard time of it (has a tough job; has a rough passage) with them.*

**standhaft** bleiben: *to stand firm; to put one's foot down; to dig one's heels (toes) in (colloq.)*

Ich rate dir, standhaft zu bleiben, wenn dein Freund dich wieder um Geld bitten sollte.
*I advise you to stand firm (to dig your heels [toes] in; to put your foot down) if your friend should ask you for money again.*

einer Sache **standhalten:** *to stand up to s. th.; to be equal to s. th.*

Die neugebaute Brücke hält jeder Belastung stand.
*The newly-built bridge will stand up (be equal) to any strain.*

j.em eine **Standpauke** halten (fam.): *to give s. b. a lecture.* Cf. auch: j.en **abkanzeln;** j.em gründlich **Bescheid** sagen

Der Lehrer hat mit Recht den schlechten Schülern eine Standpauke (Moralpauke, -predigt; Strafpredigt) gehalten (den Kümmel gerieben; eine Lektion erteilt; die Leviten [den Text] gelesen).
*The master rightly gave the bad pupils a lecture.*

j.em den **Standpunkt** klarmachen: cf. j.em gründlich **Bescheid** sagen

bei der **Stange** bleiben (fig.): *to rally round; to pull (all) together; to stick together (colloq.); to stick to one's post (colloq.)*

> Wir sollten bei der Stange bleiben und unserm Verein die Treue halten.
> *We should rally round ([all] pull together; stick together; stick to our posts) and keep faithful to our association.*

eine **Stange** Geld (Gold) kosten: *to cost a pretty penny; to cost pots of money (colloq.); to cost a mint of money (a tidy bit) (colloq.); to take plenty of dough (sl.)*

> Der Neubau eines Hauses kostet heutzutage eine Stange Geld ([Gold]; ein schönes Stück Geld [einen schönen Batzen Geld]).
> *To build a new house costs a pretty penny (pots [a mint] of money [a tidy bit]; takes plenty of dough) these days.*

j.em die **Stange** halten (fig.): *to stand up for s.b.; to stick up for s.b. (colloq.); to back s.b. up (colloq.).* Cf. auch: sich an j.es **Seite** stellen

> Da ich von Ihrer Unschuld überzeugt bin, werde ich Ihnen die Stange halten.
> *As I am convinced of your innocence, I shall stand (stick) up for you (back you up).*

j.en bei der **Stange** halten (fig.): *to get s.b. to rally round; to get s.b. to stick to his post (colloq.);* (nur plur.) *to get people to pull together;* (nur plur.) *to get people to stick together (colloq.)*

> Ich weiß nicht, ob wir unsere Parteimitglieder alle bei der Stange halten können.
> *I do not know whether we can get all our party members to rally round (to stick to their posts; to pull [to stick] together).*

etwas von der **Stange** kaufen (fam.): *to buy s.th. off the peg; to buy s.th. ready-made*

> Ob du es glaubst oder nicht: Ich habe diesen Anzug von der Stange gekauft.
> *Whether you believe it or not, I bought this suit off the peg (ready-made).*

eine lange **Stange** sein (fig. u. fam.): cf. lang wie eine **Bohnenstange** sein

**Staub** aufwirbeln (fig.): *to make (to cause) a stir (a flutter); to raise a dust (a rumpus) (colloq.)*

> Ihr interessanter Prozeß hat viel Staub aufgewirbelt.
> *Her interesting trial has made (caused) quite a stir (a flutter; has raised quite a dust [rumpus]).*

sich aus dem **Staube** machen (fam.): cf. **Fersengeld** geben

den **Staub** von den Füßen schütteln (fig.): *to shake the dust from one's feet*

> Mein Bruder hat sich entschlossen, den heimatlichen Staub von den Füßen zu schütteln und ins Ausland zu gehen.
> *My brother has resolved to shake the dust of his homeland from his feet and go abroad.*

zu **Staub** (und Asche) werden: *to turn to dust (and ashes); to return to the dust (the earth)*

Diese Generation ist längst zu Staub (und Asche) geworden.
*That generation has long since turned to dust (and ashes) (returned to the dust [the earth]).*

j.en (etwas) in den **Staub** ziehen (fig.): cf. j.en (etwas) in den **Dreck** ziehen

es j.em **stecken** (fam.): *to get one's own back (colloq.); to teach s.b. (colloq.); to show s.b. (colloq.); to learn s.b. (sl.)*

Karl hat mich bei meinen Verwandten verleumdet. Dem werde ich's stecken.
*Charles has slandered me to my relatives. I'll get my own back (I'll teach [show; learn] him).*

einen **stecken** haben (fam.): cf. einen **Schwips** haben

Dreck am **Stecken** haben (fig. u. fam.): *not to have a clean slate; to have a blot on one's escutcheon; not to be in the clear (colloq.)*

Alles deutet darauf hin, daß der Buchhalter unserer Firma Dreck am Stecken hat.
*Everything points to the fact that our firm's book-keeper has not got a clean slate (has a blot on his escutcheon; is not in the clear).*

Man hätte eine **Stecknadel** zur Erde fallen hören: cf. **mäuschenstill** sein

Keine **Stecknadel** konnte zur Erde fallen: cf. gedrängt wie die **Heringe** sitzen

j.en (etwas) wie eine **Stecknadel** suchen: *to search for s.b. (s.th.) high and low (in every nook and cranny; like the proverbial needle)*

Rolf sucht einen wichtigen Brief wie eine Stecknadel (Nadel) und kann ihn nirgends finden.
*Rolf is searching for an important letter high and low (in every nook and cranny; like the proverbial needle) and cannot find it anywhere.*

aus dem **Stegreif** reden (sprechen): *to talk impromptu (extempore; off the cuff); to extemporise*

Die Zuhörer haben es am liebsten, wenn der Vortragende aus dem Stegreif redet (spricht).
*The audience like it best when the speaker talks impromptu (extempore; off the cuff; when the speaker extemporises).*

etwas aus dem **Stegreif** sagen: *to say s.th. off-hand (on the spur of the moment)*

Lassen Sie mich einen Augenblick nachdenken, denn ich kann es Ihnen nicht aus dem Stegreif sagen.
*Let me reflect a moment; I can't tell you off-hand (on the spur of the moment).*

etwas zum **Stehen** bringen (fig.): *to bring s. th. to a halt; to check s. th.*

Der Gesundheitsbehörde ist es gelungen, die Epidemie zum Stehen zu bringen.
*The health authorities have succeeded in bringing the epidemic to a halt (in checking the epidemic).*

alles **stehen** und liegen lassen: *to leave everything just as it is; to drop everything; to put everything down*

Als ich erfuhr, daß mein Freund krank war, ließ ich alles stehen und liegen und eilte zu ihm.
*When I learned that my friend was ill, I left everything just as it was (dropped everything; put everything down) and hastened to him.*

Es **steht** und fällt mit . . . (fig.): *It stands or falls by . . .; It will be made or marred by . . .*

Der neue Staat steht und fällt mit seinem Ministerpräsidenten.
*The new state stands or falls (will be made or marred) by its prime minister.*

**steif** und fest behaupten: cf. **fest** und steif behaupten

j.em den **Steigbügel** halten (fig.): cf. j.en in den **Sattel** heben

keinen **Stein** auf dem anderen lassen: *not to leave a stone standing*

Die Soldaten ließen in der eroberten Stadt keinen Stein auf dem anderen.
*The soldiers did not leave a stone standing in the conquered city.*

ein **Stein** des Anstoßes (fig.): *a stumbling-block*

Ich habe Georg sehr gern, aber seine politischen Ansichten sind für mich ein Stein des Anstoßes.
*I like George very much but his political views are a stumbling-block for me.*

**Stein** und Bein frieren: *to freeze hard; to freeze solid; to be brass-monkey weather (sl.).* Cf. auch: eine **Hundekälte**

Zieh' dich warm an, weil es draußen Stein und Bein friert.
*Dress yourself warmly, for it is freezing hard (solid; is brass-monkey weather) outside.*

**Stein** und Bein schwören: *to swear by all that is holy (by all the saints [gods]); to call heaven to witness; to swear till one is black in the face (colloq.).* Cf. auch: **Himmel** und Erde zu Zeugen anrufen

Der Verhaftete schwor Stein und Bein, daß er nichts mit dem Raub zu tun habe.
*The prisoner swore by all that is holy (by all the saints [gods]; called heaven to witness; swore till he was black in the face) that he had nothing to do with the robbery.*

bei j.em einen **Stein** im Brett haben (fig.): cf. bei j.em gut **angeschrieben** sein

ein Herz von **Stein** haben (fig.): *to have a heart of stone; to be as hard as nails*

Dieser Apotheker behält sein ganzes Geld für sich. Er hat ein Herz von Stein (hat einen Stein, wo ein anderer sein Herz hat).
*This chemist keeps all his money for himself. He has a heart of stone (is as hard as nails).*

einen **Stein** haben, wo ein anderer sein Herz hat (fig.): cf. ein Herz von **Stein** haben

j.em fällt ein **Stein** vom Herzen (fig.): *it is (it takes) a load (a weight) off s.b.'s mind; s.b. breathes (freely) again; s.b. heaves a sigh of relief*

Meinem Vetter fiel ein Stein vom Herzen, als er erfuhr, daß er sein Examen bestanden hatte.
*It was (took) a load (weight) off my cousin's mind (My cousin breathed [freely] again; heaved a sigh of relief) when he learnt that he had passed his examination.*

Du wirst keinen **Stein** aus der Krone verlieren (Dir wird kein Stein aus der Krone fallen) (fig.): *You won't kill yourself (colloq.); It won't break your neck (colloq.)*

Du wirst keinen Stein (keine Perle) aus der Krone verlieren (Dir wird kein Stein [keine Perle] aus der Krone fallen), wenn du dich auch mit einfachen Leuten freundlich unterhältst.
*You won't kill yourself by having (It won't break your neck to have) a friendly conversation with simple folk as well.*

Wälzender **Stein** wird nicht moosig (Sprichw.): *A rolling stone gathers no moss (prov.)*

Wilhelm wechselt seine Tätigkeit viel zu oft und wird nie einen höheren Posten bekommen. Wälzender Stein wird nicht moosig.
*William changes his occupation far too often and will never get a senior post. A rolling stone gathers no moss.*

den **Stein** ins Rollen bringen (fig.): cf. etwas in **Gang** setzen (bringen)

j.em **Steine** in den Weg legen (fig.): cf. j.em ein **Bein** stellen

j.em **Steine** aus dem Weg räumen (fig.): *to remove the obstacles in (from) s.b.'s path; to clear the way for s.b.*

Der einflußreiche Vater konnte seinem Sohn alle Steine aus dem Weg räumen.
*The influential father was able to remove all the obstacles in (from) his son's path (to clear the way for his son).*

**steinalt** sein: cf. alt wie **Methusalem** sein

zum **Steinerweichen** heulen (fam.): cf. heulen wie ein **Schloßhund**

**steinhart** sein: a) (von Personen) *to be as hard as steel (stone; flint);* b) (von Sachen) *to be as hard as a rock (brick)*

a) Ein Geizhals ist steinhart und läßt sich durch kein menschliches Elend rühren.
b) Diese alten Brötchen kannst du nicht mehr essen. Sie sind steinhart.
*a) A miser is as hard as steel (stone; flint) and does not allow himself to be moved by human misery.*
*b) You cannot eat these old rolls any more. They are as hard as rocks (bricks).*

**steinreich** sein: cf. **Geld** wie Heu haben

auf der **Stelle**: *on the spot; there and then; that very moment*

Der Mantel war so schön, daß ich mich entschloß, ihn auf der Stelle (an Ort und Stelle; vom Fleck weg; stehenden Fußes; kurzer Hand [kurzerhand]; [auf] Knall und Fall) zu kaufen.
*The coat was so beautiful that I resolved to buy it on the spot (there and then; that very moment).*

nicht von der **Stelle** kommen (fig.): *to make no progress; to get no further; to get nowhere (colloq.)*

Nun sitzt er schon zwei Stunden an seiner Schularbeit und kommt nicht von der Stelle.
*He has been sitting at his homework for two hours now and made no progress (got no further; got nowhere).*

eine wunde **Stelle** sein (fig.): cf. ein wunder **Punkt** sein

zur **Stelle** sein: *to be on hand; to be on the spot (on the scene)*

Sie können sich darauf verlassen, daß ich pünktlich zur Stelle sein werde.
*You can rely on my being on hand (on the spot [scene]) punctually.*

einer Sache seinen **Stempel** aufdrücken (fig.): *to set one's seal (stamp) on s. th.; to leave one's imprint (mark) on s. th.*

Seine großartige Erfindung hat unserer ganzen Zeit ihren Stempel aufgedrückt.
*His wonderful invention has set its seal (stamp; left its imprint[mark]) on our whole age.*

den **Stempel** tragen (fig.): *to bear the mark (stamp)*

Die Werke unseres Autors tragen den Stempel großer Belesenheit.
*Our author's works bear the mark (stamp) of great scholarship.*

**stempeln** gehen (fam.): cf. auf der **Straße** liegen b)

vom **Stengel** fallen (fig. u. fam.): cf. wie aus den **Wolken** (ge)fallen

sich zum **Sterben** langweilen: cf. sich zu **Tode** langweilen

kein **Sterbenswörtchen** sagen: *not to breathe a word*

Bitte sagen Sie meinem Vater kein Sterbenswörtchen von meinen Plänen.
*Please do not breathe a word to my father about my plans.*

Sein **Stern** ist im Aufgehen (fig.): *His star is in the ascendant (is rising)*

Der junge Dichter hat seinen ersten Erfolg verzeichnet; sein Stern ist im Aufgehen.
*The young poet has registered his first success; his star is in the ascendant (is rising).*

unter einem glücklichen (günstigen; guten) **Stern** geboren sein: cf. ein **Glückskind** sein

unter keinem glücklichen (günstigen; guten) **Stern** stehen: *to be ill-fated (ill-starred); not to be in favour with the gods*

Seine Pläne stehen unter keinem glücklichen (günstigen; guten) Stern, denn er hat bisher niemanden gefunden, der bereit ist, sie zu unterstützen.
*His plans are ill-fated (ill-starred; not in favour with the gods), for up to now he has not found anyone who is prepared to support them.*

für j.en die **Sterne** vom Himmel holen (fig.): *to give s.b. the moon*

Für dieses Mädchen würde Hans die Sterne vom Himmel holen.
*Jack would give that girl the moon.*

Sein **Stern** ist im Sinken (fig.): *His star is on the wane (is waning; is setting)*

Man interessiert sich nicht mehr für diesen Schriftsteller. Sein Stern ist im Sinken.
*People are no longer interested in that writer. His star is on the wane (is waning; is setting).*

**sternhagelvoll** sein (fam.): *to be as drunk as a lord (colloq.); to be dead drunk (colloq.); to be tight (colloq.); to be blotto (pickled; plastered; sozzled; stinking) (sl.).* Cf. auch: einen **Schwips** haben; zu tief in den **Becher** geguckt haben

Ernst ist um Mitternacht sternhagelvoll (blau [wie ein Märzveilchen]; knüll; sinnlos betrunken; stinkbetrunken; voll wie eine [Strand]kanone [Strandhaubitze]) nach Hause gekommen.
*Ernest came home at midnight as drunk as a lord (dead drunk; tight; blotto; pickled; plastered; sozzled; stinking).*

das **Steuer** führen (in der Hand haben) (fig.): cf. das **Heft** in der Hand haben

das **Steuer** herumwerfen (fig.): *to take a new course; to follow a different road; to strike out in a new direction*

Die Regierung hat das Steuer herumgeworfen (einen neuen Kurs eingeschlagen) und wesentliche Neuerungen eingeführt.
*The government has taken a new course (is following a different road; has struck out in a new direction) and has introduced considerable innovations.*

**stibitzen** (fam.): cf. **klauen**

einen **Stich** ins Grüne haben (fam.): *to have a shady side (to one's character); to be a shady character; not to have kept always to the straight and narrow (path)*

Meide möglichst den Umgang mit dieser Frau. Sie hat einen Stich ins Grüne.
*Avoid any contact with that woman if possible. She has a shady side (to her character) (has a shady character; has not always kept to the straight and narrow [path]).*

einer Sache **Stich** halten: cf. **stichhaltig** sein

j.en im **Stich** lassen (fig.): *to leave s.b. in the lurch; to let s.b. down; to leave s.b. high and dry; to leave s.b. in the cart (colloq.); to leave s.b. holding the baby (sl.)*

Karl hat versprochen, mich abzuholen, aber jetzt hat er mich einfach im Stich gelassen ([in der Tinte] sitzen lassen).
*Charles promised to pick me up but now he has just left me in the lurch (let me down; left me high and dry; left me in the cart; left me holding the baby).*

ein **Stich** auf j.en sein (fig.): cf. ein **Seitenhieb** sein

j.em einen **Stich** (ins Herz) versetzen (fig.): cf. j.em durch **Mark** und Bein gehen

**stichhaltig** sein: *to hold water; to be watertight*

Deine Begründungen scheinen mir nicht stichhaltig zu sein (Stich zu halten).
*Your reasons do not appear to me to hold water (to be watertight).*

sich einen gehörigen **Stiebel (Stiefel)** einbilden (fam.): *to fancy o.s. (no end) (colloq.); to think no small beer of o.s. (colloq.).* Cf. auch: **angeben**

Heinrich bildet sich einen gehörigen Stiebel (Stiefel) ein, weil er einen reichen Onkel hat.
*Henry fancies himself ([no end]; thinks himself no small beer) because he has a rich uncle.*

einen guten **Stiebel (Stiefel)** vertragen können (fam.): *to be able to hold one's drink (colloq.); to be able to take one's pint (colloq.)*

Mein Vater ist an Alkohol gewöhnt und kann einen guten Stiebel (Stiefel) vertragen.
*My father is accustomed to alcohol and can hold his drink (take his pint).*

das **Stiefkind** sein (fig.): *to be a (the) Cinderella; to be left out in the cold (out of it) (colloq.); to be given the go-by (colloq.).* Cf. auch: (ein) **Aschenbrödel (Aschenputtel)** sein

Die Altersfürsorge ist offenbar für eure Regierung das Stiefkind.
*The care of the old folk is evidently a Cinderella to your government (has evidently been left out in the cold [left out of it]; given the go-by by your government).*

j.en (etwas) **stiefmütterlich** behandeln (fig.): *to play s.th. down; to leave s.b.* *(s.th.) out in the cold (out of it) (colloq.); to give s.b. (s.th.) the go-by (colloq.)*

Dieses Fach ist bisher auf den Universitäten stiefmütterlich behandelt worden. *This subject has up to now been played down (left out in the cold [out of it]; given the go-by) in the universities.*

seinem Leibe kein **Stiefvater** sein (fig. u. fam.): *not to stint one's appetites; not to deny the flesh*

Mein Onkel Heinrich lebt gut; er ist seinem Leibe kein Stiefvater. *My uncle Henry lives well; he does not stint his appetites (does not deny the flesh).*

**Stielaugen** machen (fam.): *to goggle; to (stand and) gape; to·stand open-mouthed.* Cf. auch: **Maulaffen** feilhalten

Als das siebzigjährige Ehepaar die Kirche verließ, machten alle Leute Stielaugen (Glotzaugen, Kuhaugen). *As the seventy-year-old couple left the church, all the people goggled ([stood and] gaped; stood open-mouthed).*

brüllen wie ein **Stier**: cf. brüllen wie ein **Löwe**

den **Stier** bei den Hörnern packen (fig.): cf. die **Gelegenheit** beim Schopfe fassen

wütend wie ein **Stier** sein: *to be as mad as a bull (as a wild boar); to be hopping mad (sl.).* Cf. auch: vor **Wut** kochen

Als Onkel die Plünderung seines Apfelbaums entdeckte, war er wütend wie ein Stier (Eber). *When uncle discovered that his apple-tree had been stripped, he was as mad as a bull (wild boar; hopping mad).*

**stiften** gehen (fam.): cf. **Fersengeld** geben

eine **Stilblüte**: *a slip of the pen; a bloomer (howler) (colloq.).* Cf. auch: eine **Kathederblüte**

Die Lektüre dieser Sammlung von Stilblüten macht uns großen Spaß. *We greatly enjoy reading that collection of slips of the pen (bloomers; howlers).*

die **Stille** vor dem Sturm (fig.): *the lull before the storm*

Im Augenblick ist alles ruhig, aber wir fürchten, daß es nur die Stille vor dem Sturm ist. *At the moment everything is quiet, but we fear that it is only the lull before the storm.*

sich in **Stillschweigen** hüllen: *to shroud o.s. in silence; to sit (to stand) there like a Sphinx*

Anstatt eine Antwort zu geben, hüllte sich der Beamte in (Still)schweigen. *Instead of giving a reply, the official shrouded himself in silence (sat there like a Sphinx).*

in gedrückter **Stimmung** sein: cf. **Trübsal** blasen

**stinkbetrunken** sein (fam.): cf. **sternhagelvoll** sein

**stinkfaul** sein (vor Faulheit stinken) (fam.): *to be bone lazy (bone idle); to be a lazybones (a lazy dog) (colloq.); to be as lazy as hell (sl.)*

> Da du das ganze Jahr stinkfaul (faul wie die Sünde) gewesen bist (vor Faulheit gestunken hast), hast du jetzt ein schlechtes Schulzeugnis bekommen.
> *Since you have been bone lazy (bone idle; a lazybones; a lazy dog; as lazy as hell) the whole year, you have now got a bad school-report.*

**stinkfrech** sein (fam.): cf. ein **Frechdachs** sein

**stinkreich** sein (fam.): cf. **Geld** wie Heu haben

eine **Stinkwut** haben (fam.): *to be in a towering rage (colloq.); to be in a proper wax (sl.).* Cf. auch: aus der **Haut** fahren; vor **Wut** platzen

> Vater hatte eine Stinkwut, weil die Arbeiter nicht gekommen waren.
> *Father was in a towering rage (a proper wax) because the workmen had not come.*

sich freuen wie ein **Stint** (fam.): cf. sich **diebisch** freuen

eine **Stippvisite** machen (fam.): *to pay a flying visit; to look in*

> Da ich es sehr eilig habe, kann ich bei dir nur eine Stippvisite machen.
> *As I am in a great hurry, I can only pay you a flying visit (look in on you).*

j.em (einer Sache) die **Stirn** bieten (fig.): *to face s.b. (s.th.); to face up to s.b. (s.th.); to show a bold front to s.b. (s.th.); to stand one's ground against s.b. (s.th.)*

> Wir werden jedem Angriff auf unsere Regierungsform die Stirn bieten.
> *We shall face (face up to; show a bold front to; stand our ground against) any attack on our form of government.*

j.em auf der **Stirn** geschrieben sein (fig.): *to be written on (all over) s.b.'s face.* Cf. auch: es j.em an der **Nase** (Nasenspitze) ansehen

> Sein schlechtes Gewissen steht Heinrich auf der Stirn (im Gesicht, auf der Nase) geschrieben.
> *Henry's bad conscience is written on (all over) his face.*

die **Stirn** haben (fig.): *to have the impudence (the affrontery; the audacity); to have the cheek (the nerve; the face) (colloq.)*

> Der Angeklagte hatte die Stirn (den Nerv), den Richter zu beschimpfen.
> *The accused had the impudence (affrontery; audacity; cheek; nerve; face) to insult the judge.*

dastehen wie ein **Stock**: *to stand there like a block of wood; to stand there like the Rock of Gibraltar (like a graven image) (colloq.)*

Steh' doch nicht wie ein Stock (stumm und steif) da! Gib mir doch Antwort! *Don't stand there like a block of wood (like a graven image; like the Rock of Gibraltar)! Answer me!*

über **Stock** und Stein: *up hill and down dale*

Mein kleiner Bruder wollte nicht zurückkommen, als ich ihn rief, und ich mußte über Stock und Stein hinter ihm herjagen. *My little brother would not come back when I called him and I had to chase him up hill and down dale.*

als ob (wenn) er einen **Stock** verschluckt hätte: cf. einen **Besenstiel** verschluckt haben

**stockblind** sein: *to be as blind as a bat (as a mole)*

Der alte Invalide muß auf der Straße geführt werden, weil er stockblind ist. *The old invalid has to be led along the road because he is as blind as a bat (a mole).*

**stockdumm** sein: cf. dumm wie **Bohnenstroh** sein

**stockdunkel**: cf. **kohl(pech)rabenschwarz** sein b); schwarz wie die **Nacht** sein

ein **Stockengländer (Stockpreuße** usw.) sein: *to be a Britisher (to be British; to be [a] Prussian) to the core (to the bone; to the backbone).* Cf. auch: **kerndeutsch** sein

Ich bin ein Stockengländer und werde mein Land immer verteidigen. *I am a Britisher (I am British) to the core (bone; backbone) and shall always defend my country.*

**stockfinster** sein: cf. **kohl(pech)rabenschwarz** sein b); schwarz wie die **Nacht** sein

**stocksteif** (steif wie ein **Stock)** sein: cf. einen **Besenstiel** verschluckt haben

**stocktaub** sein: *to be as deaf as a post; to be stone-deaf*

Sie müssen sehr laut sprechen, weil der alte Herr stocktaub ist. *You must talk very loudly, because the old gentleman is as deaf as a post (is stone-deaf).*

vor **Stolz** platzen (fig.): *to burst (to swell) with pride; to swagger around; to plume (to preen) o.s.* Cf. auch: stolz wie ein **Spanier** sein; sich spreizen wie ein **Truthahn**

499

Als mein Vetter den ersten Preis gewann, platzte er vor Stolz.
*When my cousin won first prize, he burst (swelled) with pride (he swaggered around; plumed [preened] himself).*

wie der **Storch** im Salat einher- (herum)stolzieren (fam.): cf. sich spreizen wie ein **Truthahn**

sich einen **Stoß** geben (fig.): cf. sich einen **Ruck** geben

j.em einen **Stoß** versetzen (fig.): cf. j.em einen **Schlag** versetzen

ein **Stoßgebet** zum Himmel schicken (fig.): *to offer (up) a quick prayer to Heaven*

> Laßt uns ein Stoßgebet zum Himmel schicken, daß wir morgen keine Arbeit in der Schule schreiben.
> *Let's offer (up) a quick prayer to Heaven that we shan't have to do an exercise in school tomorrow.*

j.em eine **Strafpredigt** halten (fig.): cf. j.em eine **Standpauke** halten

geladen (voll) wie eine **Strandkanone (Strandhaubitze)** sein (fam.): cf. **sternhagelvoll** sein

über die **Stränge** hauen (fig.): *to kick over the traces; to run riot; to get out of control (out of hand)*

> Dein leichtsinniger Bruder hat über die Stränge (Schnur) gehauen (ist über die Stränge geschlagen) und ist in (eine) schlechte Gesellschaft geraten.
> *Your frivolous brother has kicked over the traces (run riot; got out of control [hand]) and got into bad company.*

wenn alle **Stränge** reißen (fig.): *if it comes to the worst; if the worst comes to the worst; if all else fails; at a stretch; if needs be; if it comes to the push (colloq.); at a pinch (colloq.)*

> Im Augenblick gebrauche ich das Geld, das ich dir geliehen habe, nicht. Wenn alle Stränge (Stricke) reißen, (Zur Not) kannst du es mir in Raten zurückzahlen.
> *At the moment I do not need the money I lent you. If it comes to the worst (If the worst comes to the worst; If all else fails; At a stretch; If needs be; If it comes to the push; At a pinch), you can pay it back to me in instalments.*

über die **Stränge** schlagen (fig.): cf. über die **Stränge** hauen

an éinem (am gleichen) **Strang(e)** ziehen (fig.): *all to pull (to heave) together; to unite one's forces.* Cf. auch: mit j.em gemeinsame **Sache** machen

> Wenn wir alle in dieser Angelegenheit an éinem (am gleichen) Strang(e) ziehen, werden wir sicher erfolgreich sein.
> *If we all pull (heave) together (unite our forces) in this matter, we shall certainly be successful.*

j.en von der **Straße** auflesen (fig.): cf. j.en aus der **Gosse** auflesen

auf die **Straße** fliegen (fig.): cf. die Passivform der Ausdrücke unter: j.en auf die **Straße** setzen

auf der **Straße** liegen (fig.): a) (von Sachen) *to be waiting there to be picked up; to be lying in the gutter;* b) (von Personen) *to be on the streets (tramping the streets); to be on the dole*

a) Man sollte Auswanderer vor der Annahme warnen, in den USA liege das Geld auf der Straße.
b) Ich habe meine Stellung verloren und liege jetzt auf der Straße.
*a) One should warn emigrants against the notion that in the U.S.A. the money is waiting there to be picked up (is lying in the gutter).*
*b) I have lost my job and am on the streets (dole; tramping the streets).*

j.en auf die **Straße** setzen (fig.): *to get rid of s.b.; to sack s.b. (colloq.); to give s.b. the sack (the push) (colloq.); to give s.b. the order of the boot (colloq.); to kick (to boot) s.b. out (colloq.); to fire s.b. (colloq.); to tell s.b. to pack his bags (colloq.).* Cf. auch: j.en **ausbooten**

Alle unzuverlässigen Arbeiter wurden fristlos auf die Straße gesetzt (an die [frische] Luft gesetzt [befördert]; hat man ihr Bündel schnüren lassen).
*All the unreliable workers were summarily got rid of (sacked; given the order of the boot; kicked [booted] out; given the sack [push]; fired; told to pack their bags).*

das Geld auf die **Straße** werfen (fig.): cf das Geld zum **Fenster** hinauswerfen

auf der **Strecke** bleiben (fig.): *to fall by the wayside; to drop out*

Albert konnte den Marathonlauf nicht durchhalten. Er blieb schon nach wenigen Kilometern auf der Strecke.
*Albert could not last out the marathon race. He fell by the wayside (dropped out) after a few kilometres.*

j.en zur **Strecke** bringen (fig.): *to bring (to run) s.b. to earth (to ground); to bag s.b. (colloq.); to finish (to polish) s.b. off (colloq.)*

Gestern ist die langgesuchte Diebesbande von der Polizei zur Strecke gebracht worden.
*Yesterday the gang of thieves, hunted for a long time, was brought (run) to earth (ground; was bagged; was finished [polished] off) by the police.*

ein gemeiner **Streich**: cf. ein gemeines **Bubenstück**

j.em einen **Streich** spielen: cf. j.em einen **Schabernack** spielen; j.em ein **Schnippchen** schlagen

keinen **Streich** tun (fam.): cf. keinen **Schlag** tun

einen **Streit** vom Zaune brechen (fig.): *to pick a quarrel; to look for trouble; to be spoiling for a fight*

> Hans hat aus irgendeinem Grunde einen Streit vom Zaune gebrochen (Händel gesucht) und die Stimmung an unserm Tisch verdorben.
> *For some reason Jack picked a quarrel (was looking for trouble; was spoiling for a fight) and spoilt the atmosphere at our table.*

die **Streitaxt** begraben (fig.): *to bury the hatchet; to sheathe the sword; to let bygones be bygones.* Cf. auch: etwas **ad acta** legen

> Nach diesem Streit haben Vater und Sohn die Streitaxt begraben (das Schwert in die Scheide gesteckt).
> *After this quarrel father and son buried the hatchet (sheathed the sword; let bygones be bygones).*

ein **Streithammel** sein (fig. u. fam.): *to be a trouble-seeker (trouble-maker)*

> Unser Schreiner ist ein wahrer Streithammel, der sich mit jedermann zankt.
> *Our joiner is a real trouble-seeker (trouble-maker) and quarrels with everybody.*

**Streusand** drüber!: cf. **Schwamm** drüber!

**Strich** drunter!: cf. **Schwamm** drüber!

nach **Strich** und Faden (fig.): *through and through; right and left*

> Er sah ehrlich aus, aber in Wirklichkeit hat er uns nach Strich und Faden (nach Noten) beschwindelt.
> *He looked honest but in reality he swindled us through and through (right and left).*

auf den **Strich** gehen (fig. u. fam.): *to walk the streets*

> Dieses Mädchen geht abends oft auf den Strich.
> *That girl often walks the streets at night.*

j.em gegen den **Strich** gehen (fig.): *to go against the grain with s.b.; to offend s.b.'s principles (susceptibilities)*

> Es geht mir gegen den Strich (die Natur), von so einem armen Mann Geld anzunehmen.
> *It goes against the grain with me (It offends my principles [susceptibilities]) to accept money from such a poor man.*

j.en auf dem **Strich** haben (fig. u. fam.): cf. einen **Pik** (eine **Pike**) auf j.en haben

nur noch ein **Strich** sein (fig.): cf. nur noch **Haut** und Knochen sein

j.em einen **Strich** durch die Rechnung machen (fig.): *to upset the apple-cart; to spoil (to ruin; to frustrate) s.b.'s plans; to knock s.b.'s plans on the head (colloq.)*

Wir wollten vorigen Samstag (Sonnabend) aufs Land fahren, aber das schlechte Wetter hat uns leider einen Strich durch die Rechnung gemacht (ist uns leider in die Quere gekommen).
*We wanted to go into the country last Saturday, but the bad weather upset the apple-cart (spoilt [ruined; frustrated] our plans; knocked our plans on the head).*

keinen **Strich** tun (fig. u. fam.): cf. keinen **Schlag** tun

j.em einen **Strick** aus etwas drehen (fig.): *to trip s.b. up with s.th.; to use s.th. as a noose to put round s.b.'s neck; to use s.th. against s.b.*

Es ist niederträchtig, ihm aus seiner harmlosen Bemerkung einen Strick drehen zu wollen.
*It is despicable to want to trip him up with his own harmless remark (to use . . . as a noose to put round his neck; to use . . . against him).*

wenn alle **Stricke** reißen (fig.): cf. wenn alle **Stränge** reißen

j.en **striezen** (fam.): cf. j.en **drangsalieren**

j.en an der **Strippe** haben (fig. u. fam.): cf. j.en am **Gängelband** führen

leeres **Stroh** dreschen (fig.): *to beat the air; to flog dead horses*

In dieser politischen Versammlung wurde nur leeres Stroh gedroschen. Etwas Neues und Interessantes war nicht zu hören.
*In that political meeting people only beat the air (flogged dead horses). Nothing new or interesting was heard.*

**strohdumm** sein (**Stroh** im Kopfe haben): cf. dumm wie **Bohnenstroh** sein

ein **Strohfeuer** sein (fig.): *to be a passing fancy (whim; a short-lived passion); to be a flash in the pan*

Deine Liebe zu Elisabeth war offenbar nur ein Strohfeuer, denn Ihr seid bereits auseinandergegangen.
*Your love for Elizabeth was obviously only a passing fancy (whim; a short-lived passion; a flash in the pan), for you have already parted.*

nach einem **Strohhalm** greifen (sich an einen Strohhalm klammern) (fig.): *to catch (to clutch) at a straw; to cling to a straw*

Thomas ist wirklich in Not und wird nach jedem Strohhalm greifen (wird sich an jeden Strohhalm klammern).
*Thomas is in trouble and will catch (clutch) at any straw (cling to any straw).*

über einen **Strohhalm** stolpern (fig.): ein **Kleinigkeitskrämer** sein

ein **Strohmann** sein (fig.): *to be a go-between; to be a cat's paw (colloq.); to be a stooge (sl.)*

Der Industrielle schickte einen Strohmann (eine Schachfigur) vor, um diese Grundstücke zu erwerben.
*The industrialist sent out a go-between (cat's-paw; stooge) to acquire those plots of land.*

gegen den **Strom** schwimmen (fig.): cf. wider den **Stachel** löcken

mit dem **Strom** schwimmen (fig.): cf. den **Mantel** nach dem Wind hängen

in den **Strom** der Vergessenheit versinken (fig.): *to fall (to sink) into oblivion*

> Manche bekannte Persönlichkeit aus der ersten Hälfte dieses Jahrhunderts ist seitdem in den Strom der Vergessenheit versunken.
> *Many a personality well-known in the first half of this century has since fallen (sunk) into oblivion.*

in **Strömen** gießen (regnen): cf. **Bindfäden** regnen

etwas in den **Strumpf** stecken: cf. etwas auf die hohe **Kante** legen

sich auf die **Strümpfe** machen (fam.): cf. sich auf die **Socken** machen

ein **Stubengelehrter** sein: cf. ein **Bücherwurm** sein

ein **Stubenhocker** sein (fam.): *to be a stay-at-home; to be a stick-in-the-mud (colloq.)*

> Mit den Jahren ist mein Vetter ein richtiger Stubenhocker (Ofenhocker) geworden.
> *With the years my cousin has become a real stay-at-home (stick-in-the-mud).*

**Stubenweisheit:** *book-learning (book-knowledge)*

> Was dieser Autor schreibt, beruht nicht auf eigener Erfahrung des Lebens, sondern ist lauter Stubenweisheit.
> *What this author writes is not based on his own experience of life but is mere book-learning (book-knowledge).*

ein freches **Stück** sein (fam.): *to be a cheeky devil (colloq.)*

> Maria ist wirklich ein freches Stück (Aas; Besteck; Frauenzimmer; Weibsbild; eine freche Kruke [Type]).
> *Mary really is a cheeky devil.*

aus freien **Stücken** etwas tun: *to do s.th. of one's own accord (on one's own initiative; of one's own free will); to do s.th. off one's own bat (colloq.)*

> Wir brauchten ihn gar nicht zu drängen; er hat es aus freien Stücken getan.
> *We did not need to urge him at all; he did it of his own accord (on his own initiative; of his own free will; off his own bat).*

ein schönes **Stück** Geld kosten: cf. eine **Stange** Geld (Gold) kosten große **Stücke** auf j.en (etwas) halten (fig.): *to think a lot of s.b.; to hold s.b. in high esteem (in great respect); to think the world of s.b. (colloq.)*

> Dieser Physiker ist sehr gesucht, weil man große Stücke auf ihn hält.
> *This physicist is much sought-after, for people hold him in high esteem (in great respect; people think a lot [the world] of him).*

Das ist ein starkes **Stück**!: cf. Das ist doch die **Höhe**!

mit j.em (etwas) auf gleicher **Stufe** stehen (fig.): *to be on the same level as s.b. (s.th.); to be on a par with s.b. (s.th.)*

> Manche Bewohner dieses Landes stehen mit den primitivsten Völkern auf gleicher Stufe.
> *Certain inhabitants of this country are on the same level as (on a par with) the most primitive peoples.*

j.em den **Stuhl** unter dem Hintern (Hinterteil) wegziehen (fig. u. fam.): cf. j.em den **Boden** unter den Füßen wegziehen

mit etwas zu **Stuhle** kommen (fig. u. fam.): *to get somewhere with s.th. (colloq.); to make an impression on s.th. (colloq.)*. Cf. auch: mit etwas zu **Rande** kommen

> Mit dieser Arbeit ist der junge Wissenschaftler nie recht zu Stuhle gekommen.
> *The young scientist has never really got anywhere with (made any impression on) that work.*

j.em den **Stuhl** vor die Tür setzen (fig.): cf. j.en vor die **Tür** setzen

sich zwischen zwei **Stühle** setzen (fig.): *to fall between two stools*

> Wer sich nicht rechtzeitig entscheiden kann, läuft Gefahr, sich zwischen zwei Stühle zu setzen.
> *A person who cannot decide promptly runs the risk of falling between two stools.*

**stumm** und steif dastehen: cf. dastehen wie ein **Stock**

etwas mit **Stumpf** und Stiel ausrotten (fig.): *to root s.th. out; to remove (to extirpate; to eradicate) s.th. root and branch (by the roots); to get rid of s.th. lock, stock and barrel (hook, line and sinker)*

> Der Führer der neuen Partei versprach, alle Mißstände mit Stumpf und Stiel (mit Rumpf und Stumpf) auszurotten.
> *The leader of the new party promised to root out all abuses (to remove all abuses root and branch [by the roots]; to get rid of all abuses lock, stock and barrel [hook, line and sinker]).*

Seine **Stunde** hat geschlagen (ist gekommen): *His hour has come; His knell has sounded; His hour has struck*

Die Stunde des Mörders hat geschlagen (ist gekommen; Die Uhr . . . ist abgelaufen), und er wird hingerichtet.
*The murderer's hour has come (knell has sounded; hour has struck) and he is to be executed.*

in zwölfter **Stunde** (fig.): *at the eleventh hour; in the nick of time; at the last
moment*

> Der Patient wurde in zwölfter Stunde (in letzter Minute; kurz vor Toresschluß)
> durch eine Bluttransfusion gerettet.
> *The patient was saved at the eleventh hour (in the nick of time; at the last moment) by a
> blood transfusion.*

**Stunk** machen (fam.): *to stir up trouble; to kick up (to raise) a stink (sl.).* Cf.
auch: einen **Streit** vom Zaune brechen

> Dieser Arbeiter ist ein unerträglicher Mensch, der mit jedermann Stunk macht.
> *This worker is an intolerable person who stirs up trouble (kicks up [raises] a stink) with
> everybody.*

gegen etwas **Sturm** laufen (fig.): *to be up in arms at s.th.; to be in high dudgeon
at s.th. (colloq.)*

> Die Bevölkerung läuft gegen die neuen Preiserhöhungen Sturm.
> *The population is up in arms (in high dudgeon) at the new price increases.*

ein **Sturm** im Wasserglas (fig.): cf. viel **Lärm** um nichts machen

**Stuß** reden (fam.): cf. **Quatsch** reden

faul wie die **Sünde** sein: cf. **stinkfaul** sein

häßlich wie die **Sünde** sein: cf. **mordshäßlich** sein

eine **Sünde** und Schande sein: *to be a downright scandal (disgrace); to be a
crying (a howling) scandal (colloq.)*

> Es ist eine Sünde und Schande, wie sich die Leute auf diesem Karnevalsfest
> benommen haben.
> *The way the people behaved at that carnival was a downright scandal (disgrace; a crying
> [howling] scandal).*

ein **Sündenbabel (Sündenpfuhl)** (fig.): *a sink (a den) of iniquity*

> Dieser Vorort unserer Stadt gilt als ein Sündenbabel (Sündenpfuhl).
> *This suburb of our town is regarded as a sink (den) of iniquity.*

der **Sündenbock** sein (fig.): *to be the scapegoat (the whipping-boy)*

> Wenn irgendein Schaden in unserm Haus angerichtet wird, bin ich immer der
> Sündenbock (das Karnickel; der Prügelknabe).
> *When there is any damage done in our house, I am always the scapegoat (whipping-boy).*

ein hartgesottener **Sünder**: *a hardened (an incorrigible) sinner (criminal)*

Als hartgesottener Sünder kann er sich das Zigarettenrauchen nicht abgewöhnen.
*Being a hardened (an incorrigible) sinner (criminal), he cannot give up smoking cigarettes.*

die **Suppe** auslöffeln, die man sich eingebrockt hat (fig.): *to foot the bill; to take the rap (colloq.); to grin and bear it (colloq.); to stand the racket (sl.).* Cf. auch: Was der Mensch **säet,** das wird er ernten

Du hast auf uns nicht hören wollen. Nun mußt du die Suppe auslöffeln, die du dir eingebrockt hast.
*You did not want to listen to us. Now you must foot the bill (take the rap; grin and bear it; stand the racket).*

j.em eine schöne **Suppe** einbrocken (fig. u. fam.): *to let s.b. in for something (for a packet) (colloq.); to leave s.b. a packet (colloq.); to get s.b. into a pickle (colloq.)*

Du hast mir das Auto verkauft, und jetzt fährt es nicht. Da hast du mir eine schöne Suppe eingebrockt!
*You sold me the car and now it won't go. You've let me in for something (for a pretty packet; left me a pretty packet; got me into a pretty pickle) here.*

j.em die **Suppe** versalzen (in die Suppe spucken) (fig. u. fam.): *to spoil (to ruin) s.th. for s.b.; to spoil (to ruin) s.b.'s fun; to throw s.b. out of gear; to put s.b.'s nose out of joint (colloq.)*

Der Abend hatte mir großen Spaß gemacht, bis Hans erschien und mir die Suppe versalzte (in die Suppe spuckte; und mir ihn versalzte).
*I greatly enjoyed the evening until Jack appeared and spoilt (ruined) it for me (spoilt [ruined] my fun; threw me out of gear; put my nose out of joint).*

**Süßholz** raspeln (fig. u. fam.): *to whisper sweet nothings (colloq.)*

Meine Schwester kann junge Herren, die mit ihr nur Süßholz raspeln, nicht ausstehen.
*My sister cannot stand young men who only whisper sweet nothings to her.*

eine **Szene** machen (fig.): *to make a scene; to raise Cain*

Als Karl erst nach Mitternacht nach Hause kam, machte seine Mutter (ihm) eine Szene.
*When Charles did not come home until after midnight, his mother made a scene (raised Cain).*

etwas in **Szene** setzen (fig.): cf. **anzetteln**

starker **Tabak** sein (fig. u. fam.): cf. starker **Tobak** sein

Es ist noch nicht aller **Tage** Abend: *We have not yet heard the end of the matter*

> Die Protestkundgebung ist von der Regierung unterdrückt worden, aber die in Frage kommenden Ideen leben weiter. Es ist noch nicht aller Tage Abend.
> *The protest meeting has been suppressed by the government but the ideas in question will live on. We have not yet heard the end of the matter.*

Man soll den **Tag** nicht vor dem Abend loben (Sprichw.): *One must not count one's chickens before they are hatched (prov.)*

> Mein Schwager scheint die Operation gut überstanden zu haben. Indessen: Man soll den Tag nicht vor dem Abend loben.
> *My brother-in-law seems to have got over his operation all right. However, one must not count one's chickens before they are hatched.*

etwas an den **Tag** (ans **Tageslicht**) bringen (fig.): *to bring s.th. to light; to bring s.th. into the open (into the daylight)*

> Die Fälschung des Dokuments wurde glücklicherweise rechtzeitig an den Tag (ans Tageslicht; ans Licht) gebracht.
> *The forging of·the document was fortunately brought to light (into the open [daylight]) in time.*

j.es **Tage** sind gezählt: *s.b.'s days are numbered; to be a doomed man (woman etc.).* Cf. auch: ein **Mann** des Todes sein

> Unser Nachbar ist herzkrank, und seine Tage sind gezählt.
> *Our neighbour suffers with his heart, and his days are numbered (he is a doomed man).*

gute **Tage** haben: *to have a good time; to enjoy life; to make the most of life*

> Da mehrere Lehrer erkrankt sind, haben die Schüler gute Tage.
> *As several of the teachers are ill, the pupils are having a good time (are enjoying life; are making the most of life).*

keinen guten **Tag** haben: *to have an off-day; not to be in (good) form*

> Gestern war ich sehr müde und hatte keinen guten Tag (fühlte ich mich nicht in [guter] Form).
> *I was very tired yesterday and had an off-day (was not in [good] form).*

Jeder hat einmal seinen guten **Tag** (Sprichw.): *Every dog has its (his) day (prov.).* Cf. auch: Ein blindes **Huhn** findet auch ein Korn

> Heute waren die Lehrer sehr zufrieden mit mir. Jeder hat einmal seinen guten Tag.
> *Today the masters were very pleased with me. Every dog has its (his) day.*

sich einen guten **Tag** machen: *to have a good time for the day; to make a holiday of it; to take the day off*

> Nachdem wir unser Examen bestanden haben, wollen wir uns einen guten Tag machen und ins Gebirge fahren.
> *Having passed our examination, we are going to have a good time for the day (make a holiday of it; take the day off) and go into the mountains.*

am hellichten **Tage:** *in broad daylight*

> Das Eisenbahnunglück ereignete sich am hellichten Tage.
> *The train crash happened in broad daylight.*

in den **Tag** hineinleben: *to live for the moment (for the present)*

> Um die Zukunft kümmern wir uns nicht. Wir leben nur in den Tag hinein.
> *We are not worrying about the future. We are only living for the moment (for the present).*

in den **Tag** hineinreden: cf. ins **Blaue** hineinreden

den lieben, langen **Tag:** *the livelong day; morning, noon and night*

> Schularbeiten macht Wilhelm überhaupt nicht mehr. Den lieben, langen Tag spielt er auf der Straße.
> *William does not do any more homework at all. He plays in the street the livelong day (morning, noon and night).*

an den **Tag** (ans **Tageslicht**) kommen: *to come to light; to come (to leak) out*

> Dieser Schwindel wird früher oder später an den Tag (ans [Tages]licht) kommen (zutage treten).
> *This swindle will come to light (come [leak] out) sooner or later.*

viel reden, wenn der **Tag** lang ist (fam.): *to talk till the cows come home (colloq.)*

> Auf diesen Geschäftsmann ist kein Verlaß. Er redet viel, wenn der Tag lang ist.
> *There is no relying on this business-man. He will talk till the cows come home.*

verschieden sein wie **Tag** und Nacht: cf. **grundverschieden** sein

aussehen wie sieben (drei) **Tage** Regenwetter: cf. ein **Gesicht** machen wie sieben (drei) Tage Regenwetter

einen **Tag** im Kalender rot anstreichen: cf. etwas rot im **Kalender** anstreichen

einen schwarzen **Tag** haben: cf. einen **schwarzen** Tag haben

ein schwarzer **Tag** sein: cf. ein **schwarzer** Tag sein

Es ist nicht alle **Tage** Sonntag (Sprichw.): *Christmas comes but once a year (prov.)*

Du kannst nicht immer neue Spielzeuge bekommen. Es ist nicht alle Tage Sonntag (Nur einmal blüht im Jahr der Mai).
*You cannot always have new toys. Christmas comes but once a year.*

Nun wird's (aber) **Tag** (fam.): cf. Nun schlägt's **dreizehn!**

**tagaus,** tagein: *day in, day out*

Tagaus, tagein macht der alte Rentner einen langen Spaziergang.
*Day in, day out the old pensioner goes for a long walk.*

j.en aus dem **Takt** bringen (fig.): cf. die Aktivform der Ausdrücke unter: sich aus dem **Konzept** bringen lassen

aus dem **Takt** kommen (fig.): cf. sich aus dem **Konzept** bringen lassen

**taktfest** sein (fig. u. fam.): cf. auf der **Höhe** sein

viel **Tamtam** um etwas machen (fam.): cf. viel **Wind** um (von) etwas machen

schlank wie eine **Tanne** sein: *to be as slender as a wand (as a willow)*

Diese dicke alte Frau war als Mädchen schlank wie eine Tanne (gertenschlank).
*That fat old woman was as slender as a wand (willow) when she was a girl.*

einen **Tanz** aufführen (fig.): cf. **Krach** machen

**Tanz** ums Goldene Kalb (fig.): cf. das Goldene **Kalb** anbeten

etwas aufs **Tapet** bringen (fig.): *to bring s. th. up; to broach s. th.*

Wer hat denn dieses peinliche Thema aufs Tapet gebracht?
*Who brought up (broached) this embarrassing subject?*

wie von der **Tarantel** gestochen: *as though I (you etc.) had been stung by a bee (by a hornet); as though I (you etc.) had been bitten by an adder; as though I (you etc.) had sat in an ants' nest (colloq.)*

Wenn man etwas sagt, das ihm nicht paßt, wird er wütend, wie von der Tarantel gestochen.
*When one says something that he does not like, he becomes furious, as though he had been stung by a bee (a hornet; as though he had been bitten by an adder; as though he had sat in an ants' nest).*

etwas aus der eigenen **Tasche** bezahlen: *to pay for something out of one's own pocket*

Wir mußten das ganze Fest aus der eigenen Tasche bezahlen.
*We had to pay for the whole celebration out of our own pockets.*

tief in die **Tasche** greifen: *to dip deeply into one's pocket (one's purse); to fork out a lot of money (colloq.); to cough up a lot of money (sl.)*

Um das Studium seines Sohnes zu bezahlen, mußte der Vater tief in die Tasche (in den Sack [Säckel]) greifen.
*The father had to dip deeply into his pocket (purse; had to fork out [to cough up] a lot of money) to pay for his son's studies.*

j.en in der **Tasche** haben (fig.): *to have s.b. in one's pocket; to have s.b. where one wants him (colloq.); to have s.b. on ice (colloq.)*

Der Erfolg ist ihm sicher, weil er mehrere einflußreiche Persönlichkeiten in der Tasche hat.
*His success is assured because he has got several influential persons in his pocket (on ice; where he wants them).*

etwas in der **Tasche** haben (fig.): *to have s.th. in the bag (all lined up); It is in the bag that . . .; It is all lined up that . . .*

Mein Bruder hat seine Ernennung zum Bürgermeister in der Tasche.
*My brother has got his appointment for mayor in the bag (all lined up; It is in the bag [all lined up] that my brother will be appointed as mayor).*

j.em auf der **Tasche** liegen (fig.): *to be a drain on s.b.'s purse; to be a financial burden on s.b.; to live off s.b.*

Die meisten Studenten liegen ihren Eltern noch auf der Tasche.
*Most students are a drain on their parents' purses (are a financial burden on their parents; live off their parents).*

j.en in die **Tasche** stecken (fig.): *to knock s.b. into a cocked hat (colloq.); to knock spots off s.b. (colloq.); to beat s.b. hollow (colloq.); to beat s.b. into a frazzle (sl.).* Cf. auch: j.en in den **Schatten** stellen; j.em **haushoch** überlegen sein

Unser glänzender Architekt steckt alle hiesigen Kollegen in die Tasche (in den Sack).
*Our brilliant architect knocks all his colleagues here into a cocked hat (knocks spots off all his colleagues here; beats all his colleagues here hollow [into a frazzle]).*

wie ein **Taschenmesser** zusammenklappen: *to crumple up like a paper-bag*

Nach dem Zusammenstoß mit einem anderen Motorradfahrer klappte mein Vetter wie ein Taschenmesser zusammen (klappte mein Vetter um).
*After colliding with another motor-cyclist, my cousin crumpled up like a paper-bag.*

nicht alle **Tassen** im Schrank haben (fig. u. fam.): cf. nicht richtig im **Dachstübchen** sein

j.en auf frischer **Tat** ertappen (erwischen): *to catch (to take) s.b. red-handed (in the [very] act)*

Der Dieb wurde von den Hausbewohnern auf frischer Tat ertappt (erwischt).
*The thief was caught (taken) red-handed (in the [very] act) by the occupants of the house.*

sich in der **Tastatur** vergreifen (fig.): cf. sich im **Ton** vergreifen

vor **Tau** und Tag: cf. in aller **Herrgottsfrühe**

gegen etwas **taub** sein (sich taub gegen etwas stellen) (fig.): *to be deaf to s.th.; to turn a deaf ear to s.th.*

Gegen die wiederholten Bitten seines Sohnes um ein neues Fahrrad war der Vater taub (stellte sich der Vater taub).
*The father was deaf (turned a deaf ear) to his son's repeated requests for a new bicycle.*

Keiner ist so **taub** wie derjenige, welcher nicht hören will (Sprichw.): *None so deaf as he who will not listen (prov.)*

Oft hatten wir Wilhelm vergeblich zur Vorsicht ermahnt, und jetzt muß er die Folgen seines Leichtsinns tragen. Keiner ist so taub wie derjenige, welcher nicht hören will.
*We had often warned William in vain to be careful, and now he must bear the consequences of his recklessness. None so deaf as he who will not listen.*

Gebratene **Tauben** fliegen einem nicht ins Maul (Sprichw.): *It won't be handed to me (you etc.) on a plate (on a silver platter)*

Für das Examen müssen wir tüchtig arbeiten. Gebratene Tauben fliegen einem nicht ins Maul.
*We have got to work hard for our examination. It won't be handed to us on a plate (on a silver platter).*

sanft wie eine **Taube** sein: *to be as gentle as a dove (as a lamb).*
Cf. auch: **lammfromm** (sanft wie ein **Lamm**) sein

Vor diesem großen Schäferhund brauchst du keine Angst zu haben. Er ist sanft wie eine Taube.
*You do not need to be afraid of that big Alsatian. He is as gentle as a dove (lamb).*

wie in einem **Taubenschlag**: *like bees in a beehive*

In dem neuen Warenhaus geht es herein und heraus wie in einem Taubenschlag.
*People go in and out of the new store like bees in a beehive.*

etwas aus der **Taufe** heben (fig.): *to launch s.th.; to bring s.th. on to the market; to bring s.th. out of its case*

Auf der Industrieausstellung wurden mehrere neue Radiogeräte aus der Taufe gehoben.
*Several new radio sets were launched (brought on to the market; brought out of their cases) at the industrial exhibition.*

ein **Taugenichts** sein: cf. ein **Nichtsnutz** sein

ein **Tauziehen** (fig.): *a tug-of-war*

Der Kampf um den freien Ministerposten war ein wahres Tauziehen.
*The struggle for the vacant ministerial post was a real tug-of-war.*

Abwarten und **Tee** trinken! (fam.): *(Just) wait and see; (Just) sit back and wait*

Bis die Entscheidung gefallen ist, müssen wir uns in Geduld fassen. Abwarten und Tee trinken!
*We must be patient until the decision is made. (Just) wait and see ([Just] sit back and wait).*

über den großen **Teich** fahren (fig. u. fam.): *to cross the duck-pond (the water)*

Alljährlich fahren viele Deutsche über den großen Teich (über das große Wasser), um in Amerika ihr Glück zu versuchen.
*Every year many Germans cross the duck-pond (the water) to try their luck in America.*

das bessere **Teil** erwählen: *to choose (to follow; to take) the best course; to do the best thing*

Mein Freund behauptet, das bessere Teil erwählt zu haben, indem er Junggeselle geblieben sei.
*My friend maintains that he has chosen (followed; taken) the best course (done the best thing) by remaining a bachelor.*

sich sein **Teil** denken: *to have one's own thoughts (ideas); to think plenty (sl.)*

Als ich diese Prahlerei hörte, schwieg ich mich aus, aber ich dachte mir mein Teil.
*When I heard this boasting, I kept silent, but I had my own thoughts (ideas; I thought plenty).*

sein **Teil** (weg)haben: *to have got one's deserts (one's due); to have got what was coming to one (sl.)*

Ich hatte ihn vor dieser gefährlichen Skifahrt gewarnt. Jetzt hat er sein Teil (weg) und hat sich ein Bein gebrochen.
*I warned him about that dangerous ski-run. Now he has got his deserts (due) and broken a leg (Now he has got what was coming to him, and has broken a leg).*

j.en zum **Tempel** rausjagen (fig. u. fam.): cf. j.en vor die **Tür** setzen

j.em (j.en) **teuer** zu stehen kommen (fig.): *s.b. pays for s.th.; to cost s.b. dearly*

Diese Beleidigung wird Ihnen (Sie) teuer zu stehen kommen.
*You will pay for that insult (That insult will cost you dearly).*

ein armer **Teufel** sein (fig. u. fam.): cf. ein armer **Haufen** sein den **Teufel** mit Beelzebub austreiben (fig.): cf. ein **Loch** aufmachen, um ein anderes zuzustopfen

Da soll doch der **Teufel** dreinschlagen! (fam.): cf. Hol's der **Teufel**!

In der Not frißt der **Teufel** Fliegen (Sprichw.): *Beggars cannot be choosers (prov.)*

> Du solltest froh sein, überhaupt eine Anleihe bekommen zu haben, obwohl sie nicht so groß ist, wie du (sie) gewünscht hättest. In der Not frißt der Teufel Fliegen.
> *You ought to be glad to have received a loan at all, in spite of the fact that it is not as large as you would have wished. Beggars cannot be choosers.*

den **Teufel** nach etwas fragen (fig. u. fam.): cf. sich keinen **Deut** aus etwas machen

zum **Teufel** gehen (fig. u. fam.): a) *to go by the board; to be thrown to the winds; to go to blazes (colloq.)*; b) *to go to rack and ruin; to go to pieces; to go hang (colloq.); to go to the dogs (to the devil) (colloq.)*

> a) Infolge meiner Krankheit sind unsere Sommerpläne zum Teufel gegangen.
> b) Während meiner Abwesenheit ist der Garten einfach zum Teufel gegangen.
> *a) As a result of my illness our summer plans have gone by the board (have been thrown to the winds; have gone hang [to blazes]).*
> *b) During my absence the garden simply went to rack and ruin (went to pieces; went to the dogs [devil]).*

Der **Teufel** hat seine Hand im Spiel (fig.): *The devil has had a hand in it (has had his finger in the pie)*

> Man sollte sich von dieser bedenklichen Situation fernhalten. Der Teufel hat seine Hand im Spiel.
> *One ought to keep out of this dubious situation. The devil has had a hand in it (has had a finger in the pie).*

Hol's der **Teufel**! (fig. u. fam.): *Confound (Hang) it! (colloq.); Dash (Damn) it all! (colloq.); The devil (The deuce) take it! (colloq.)*

> Schon wieder jemand an der Tür. Hol's der Teufel (Henker; Kuckuck; Da soll doch der Teufel dreinschlagen)!
> *Somebody at the door again. Confound (Hang) it! (Dash [Damn] it!; The devil [deuce] take it!).*

j.en zum **Teufel** jagen (fig. u. fam.): cf. j.en einer Person vom **Hals** schaffen

ein kleiner **Teufel** sein (fig. u. fam.): cf. ein kleines **Aas** sein

in **Teufels** Küche kommen (fig. u. fam.): cf. sich in die **Nesseln** setzen den **Teufel** im Leibe haben (fig. u. fam.): cf. den **Schalk** im Nacken haben

der leibhaftige **Teufel** sein (fig. u. fam.): *to be the devil incarnate (the devil in person)*

> Sein Schwiegervater ist tatsächlich der leibhaftige Teufel.
> *His father-in-law really is the devil incarnate (the devil in person).*

Der **Teufel** ist los (fig. u. fam.): *Hell is (is let) loose; The fat is in the fire; Pandemonium breaks loose*

> Als mein Vater erfuhr, daß ich meine Uhr verloren hatte, war der Teufel (die Hölle) los.
> *When my father heard that I had lost my watch, hell was (was let) loose (the fat was in the fire; pandemonium broke loose).*

laufen, als ob man den **Teufel** im Nacken habe: cf. wie **verrückt** laufen

Wenn man den **Teufel** nennt, kommt er gerennt (Sprichw.): cf. Man soll den **Teufel** nicht an die Wand malen

j.en reitet der **Teufel** (fig.): *the devil has got into s.b. (has got hold of s.b.)*

> Plötzlich ritt ihn der Teufel (stach ihn der Hafer), und er fing an, seine ganzen Bücher fortzuwerfen.
> *Suddenly the devil got into him (got hold of him) and he started to throw all his books away.*

Scher' dich zum **Teufel!** (Hol' dich der Teufel!) (fig. u. fam.): cf. Scher' dich zum **Henker!**

Der **Teufel** ist nicht so schwarz, wie man ihn malt (Sprichw.): *The devil is not as black as he is painted (prov.)*

> Dieser Bursche ist zwar leichtsinnig, er hat jedoch auch seine gute Seite. Der Teufel ist nicht so schwarz, wie man ihn malt.
> *This fellow is certainly reckless but he has his good side too. The devil is not as black as he is painted.*

des **Teufels** sein wollen: cf. sich **hängen** lassen wollen

Man soll den **Teufel** nicht an die Wand malen (Sprichw.): *Sufficient unto the day is the evil thereof (prov.); Talk of the devil and he will appear (prov.)*

> Sprechen Sie doch nicht von der Möglichkeit eines neuen Krieges. Man soll den Teufel nicht an die Wand malen (Wenn man den Teufel nennt, kommt er gerennt).
> *Don't talk about the possibility of another war. Sufficient unto the day is the evil thereof (Talk of the devil and he will appear).*

den **Teufel** an die Wand malen (fig. u. fam.): cf. mit dem **Feuer** spielen; Man soll den **Teufel** nicht an die Wand malen

Weiß der **Teufel** (fig. u. fam.)!: cf. Das wissen die **Götter!**

wer (wo, wie usw.) zum **Teufel** (fam.): *who (where, how etc.) the devil (the deuce; the dickens) (colloq.)*

> Wer zum Teufel hat meine Pantoffeln fortgenommen?
> *Who the devil (deuce; dickens) has taken my slippers?*

j.en zum **Teufel** wünschen (fig. u. fam.): *to wish (to like to see) s.b. in hell (colloq.)*

> Jeder Schuldner möchte seine Gläubiger am liebsten zum Teufel wünschen.
> *Every debtor would wish (would like to see) his creditors in hell.*

Es müßte (schon) mit dem **Teufel** zugehen, wenn . . . (fam.): *It will be a freak of the devil if . . .*

> Es müßte (schon) mit dem Teufel zugehen, wenn ich den Posten nicht bekomme.
> *It will be a freak of the devil if I do not get the job.*

ein **Teufelskerl** sein (fam.): cf. ein **Allerweltskerl** sein

einen **Teufelslärm** machen (fig. u. fam.): cf. einen **Heidenlärm** machen

j.en aus dem **Text** bringen (aus dem Text kommen) (fig.): cf. j.en aus dem **Konzept** bringen (aus dem Konzept kommen)

j.em den **Text** lesen (fig.): cf. j.em eine **Standpauke** halten

bis zum **Tezett** (fig.): cf. etwas bis zum **Tz** kennen

(ein großes; viel) **Theater** um etwas machen (fig. u. fam.): cf. viel **Wind** um (von) etwas machen

das (reine) **Theater** (fig. u. fam.): cf. (ein) **Affentheater**

**Theater** spielen (fig. u. fam.): *to act; to put on an act (colloq.)*

> Er meint es nicht ernst, sondern spielt Theater (Komödie).
> *He does not mean it seriously but is only acting (putting on an act).*

ein ungläubiger **Thomas** sein (fig.): *to be a doubting Thomas*

> Neuen Erfindungen gegenüber ist mein Vater ein ungläubiger Thomas.
> *My father is a doubting Thomas where new inventions are concerned.*

**tief** blicken lassen (fig.): *to say a lot*

> Man sieht Anna und Jakob ständig zusammen. Das läßt tief blicken.
> *One perpetually sees Anne and James together. That says a lot.*

ein großes (hohes) **Tier** sein (fig. u. fam.): cf. eine große **Kanone** sein

toben wie ein wildes **Tier**: cf. **mordswütend** werden; wütend wie ein **Stier** sein

Jedem **Tierchen** sein Pläsierchen (Sprichw.): *To each his own (prov.); One takes one's choice*

> Meine Schwester geht gern ins Kino, ich selbst aber lese lieber Bücher. Jedem Tierchen sein Pläsierchen.
> *My sister likes to go to the cinema but I prefer myself to read books. To each his own (One takes one's choice).*

Du hast wohl **Tinte** getrunken (gesoffen) (fam.): cf. Aber sonst geht's dir **gut!**

klar wie dicke **Tinte** sein (fam.): *to be as clear as mud (colloq.)*

> Nach deiner Erklärung (Auslegung) ist mir die Lösung des Problems (so) klar wie dicke Tinte.
> *After your explanation the solution to the problem is as clear as mud to me.*

in der **Tinte** sitzen (fig. u. fam.): cf. in der **Klemme** sitzen

j.en (in der **Tinte**) sitzenlassen (fig. u. fam.): cf. j.en im **Stich** lassen

viel **Tinte** verspritzen (fig.): *to spill a lot of ink*

> Über die schlechte Straßenbeleuchtung in unserm Stadtviertel ist schon viel Tinte verspritzt worden, es hat aber nichts genützt.
> *A lot of ink has been spilt about the bad street-lighting in our part of the town, but it has not been any use.*

j.em einen **Tip** geben (fam.): *to give s.b. a lead; to give s.b. a tip (colloq.)*

> Ich wäre dir dankbar, wenn du mir in dieser Angelegenheit einen Tip geben könntest.
> *I should be grateful if you could give me a lead (tip) in this matter.*

nicht an j.en **tippen** können (fig. u. fam.): *not to match up to s.b.; not to be a patch on s.b. (colloq.); not to be able to hold a candle to s.b. (colloq.)*

> Dieser junge Maler kann nicht an die großen Meister tippen (kann den großen Meistern nicht das Wasser reichen).
> *This young painter does not match up to (is not a patch on; cannot hold a candle to) the great masters.*

**tipptopp** sein (fam.): *to be first-class; to be tip-top (colloq.); to be top-notch (colloq.).* Cf. auch: **erstklassig** sein

> In ihrer neuen Wohnung sieht alles tipptopp aus.
> *Everything looks first-class (tip-top; top-notch) in her new flat.*

unter den **Tisch** fallen (fig.): *to go by the board; to be dropped*

> Das letzte Musikstück fiel unter den Tisch, weil das Konzert schon zu lange gedauert hatte.
> *The last piece of music went by the board (was dropped), because the concert had already lasted too long.*

etwas unter den **Tisch** fallen lassen (fig.): *to shut one's eyes to s.th.; to turn a deaf ear (a blind eye) to s.th.; to drop s.th.* Cf. auch: gegen etwas **taub** sein

> Die vielen Verbesserungen, die ich vorschlug, hat er einfach unter den Tisch fallen lassen.
> *He simply shut his eyes (turned a deaf ear [a blind eye]) to (dropped) the many corrections which I suggested.*

etwas am grünen **Tisch** ausarbeiten (fig.): *to work s.th. out in (the atmosphere of) an office (in a back-room); to work s.th. out round a table*

> Man merkt diesen Bestimmungen an, daß sie am grünen Tisch ausgearbeitet worden sind.
> *One can see that these regulations have been worked out in (the atmosphere of) an office (in a back-room; round a table).*

reinen **Tisch** machen (fig.): cf. reine **Bahn** machen

j.en unter den **Tisch** trinken: *to drink s.b. under the table*

> Vergebens haben wir versucht, deinen Bruder unter den Tisch zu trinken.
> *We tried in vain to drink your brother under the table.*

weiß wie ein **Tischtuch** sein: cf. weiß wie die **Wand** sein

Das **Tischtuch** ist zwischen uns zerschnitten (fig.): *A gulf has opened up between us; We have fallen out (with each other); There is a breach between us.* Cf. auch: es klafft eine **Kluft**

> Seit diesem Zwischenfall ist das Tischtuch zwischen uns zerschnitten. Wir werden uns nie wiedersehen.
> *Since that incident a gulf has opened up between us (we have fallen out [with each other]; there is a breach between us). We shall never see one another again.*

von Anno **Tobak** sein (fam.): *the year dot*

> Sein Auto ist sehr alt. Es muß von Anno Tobak sein.
> *His car is very old. It must have been built in the year dot.*

starker **Tobak** sein (fig. u. fam.): *to be close to the bone (to the wind; to the knuckle) (colloq.); to be strong meat (colloq.)*

> Ich habe jene Gesellschaft von jungen Leuten verlassen. Was sie an Witzen erzählten, war mir zu starker Tobak (Tabak).
> *I have left that company of young people. The sort of jokes they told were too close to the bone (to the wind; to the knuckle; were too strong meat) for me.*

sich zu **Tode** ärgern: cf. sich **grün** und blau ärgern

Des einen **Tod** ist des anderen Brot (Sprichw.): cf. Wat den inen sin **Uhl,** is den annern sin Nachtigall

j.en zu **Tode** erschrecken: *to frighten s.b. to death; to frighten the life (the wits) out of s.b.; to scare the daylight out of s.b.; to put the fear of God into s.b.; to frighten s.b. stiff (colloq.)*

Die Explosion hat mich zu Tode erschreckt.
*The explosion frightened me to death (frightened the life [the wits] out of me; scared the daylight out of me; put the fear of God into me; frightened me stiff).*

zu **Tode** erschrocken sein: *to be frightened to death; to be dead with fright; to be frightened (scared) stiff (colloq.)*

Als wir die Nachricht in der Zeitung lasen, waren wir zu Tode erschrocken.
*When we read the news in the paper, we were frightened to death (were dead with fright; were frightened [scared] stiff).*

j.en in den **Tod** hassen: *to hate the sight of s.b.; not to be able to stand s.b. dead or alive; to hate s.b.'s guts (sl.)*

Diesen arroganten Menschen hasse ich in den Tod (kann ich in den Tod nicht leiden; Dieser arrogante Mensch ist mir in den Tod zuwider).
*I hate the sight of that arrogant person (cannot stand that arrogant person dead or alive; hate that arrogant person's guts).*

j.en zu **Tode** hetzen (fig.): *to drive (to work) s.b. to death*

Mancher Fabrikbesitzer hat früher sein Personal zu Tode gehetzt.
*Many a factory-owner used to drive (work) his staff to death.*

Ein Gedanke wird zu **Tode** gehetzt (fig.): *An idea is worked (done) to death; An idea becomes hackneyed (stale)*

Finden Sie nicht auch, daß dieser Gedanke allmählich zu Tode gehetzt worden ist?
*Don't you, too, find that this idea is gradually being worked (done) to death (becoming hackneyed [stale])?*

ein Kampf bis auf den **Tod** (auf Leben und Tod) sein: *to be a fight to the death (to the finish [end])*

Die beiden Gegner wollten nicht nachgeben. Es war ein Kampf bis auf den Tod (auf Leben und Tod; bis aufs Messer).
*Neither of the opponents would give way. It was a fight to the death (finish; end).*

sich zu **Tode** (sich **tödlich**) langweilen: *to be bored stiff; to be bored to death (to tears)*

Bei diesem Theaterstück haben wir uns zu Tode (tödlich; zum Sterben) ge-
langweilt.
*We were bored stiff (to death; to tears) by that play.*

auf den **Tod** daniederliegen: cf. in den letzten **Zügen** liegen

j.em sitzt der **Tod** im Nacken (fig.): cf. ein **Mann** des Todes sein

mit dem **Tode** ringen: cf. in den letzten **Zügen** liegen

sich zu **Tode** schämen: *to be thoroughly (properly) ashamed of o.s.; to hide one's*
*face (to bury one's head) in shame*

Ihr solltet Euch zu Tode schämen, daß Ihr den alten Mann so ausgelacht habt.
*You ought to be thoroughly (properly) ashamed of yourselves (to hide your faces [bury*
*your heads] in shame) for laughing at the old man like that.*

sich zu **Tode** schuften (fig. u. fam.): cf. sich **totarbeiten** (totschuften)

des **Todes** sein: cf. ein **Mann** des Todes sein

des **Todes** sein wollen: cf. sich **hängen** lassen wollen

sich über **Tod** und Teufel unterhalten (fig. u. fam.): *to talk about everything*
*under the sun*

Es war ein sehr anregender Abend, und wir haben uns über Tod und Teufel
unterhalten.
*It was a very stimulating evening and we talked about everything under the sun.*

j.em in den **Tod** zuwider sein (j.en in den **Tod** nicht leiden können): cf.
j.en in den **Tod** hassen

**todernst** sein: *to be deadly serious (in deadly earnest); to be as solemn as a judge*

Zuerst dachte ich, daß er spaßen wollte, er war aber todernst.
*At first I thought that he was being funny, but he was deadly serious (in deadly earnest;*
*as solemn as a judge).*

ein **Todeskandidat** sein (fig.): cf. ein **Mann** des Todes sein

j.em den **Todesstoß** versetzen (fig.): *to deal s.b. a mortal blow (a death-blow;*
*the final blow; the coup de grâce); to be the end (the death) of s.b. (colloq.)*

Deine traurige Nachricht wird deinem armen Onkel den Todesstoß versetzen.
*Your sad news will deal your poor uncle a mortal blow (a death-blow; the final blow; the*
*coup de grâce; will be the end [death] of your poor uncle).*

j.es **Todfeind** (j.em **todfeind**) sein: *to be s.b.'s deadly (mortal) enemy*

Es ist bekannt, daß diese beiden Ärzte Todfeinde (sich todfeind) sind.
*It is well-known that these two doctors are deadly (mortal) enemies.*

**todmüde** sein: cf. **hundemüde** sein

**todsicher:** cf. mit tödlicher **Sicherheit**

eine **todsichere** Sache sein: *to be a dead cert (certainty) (colloq.); to be a cinch (sl.)*

Daß du den Posten bekommen wirst, ist eine todsichere (bombensichere) Sache.
*It's a dead cert (certainty; a cinch) that you'll get the job.*

**todunglücklich** sein: cf. **kreuzunglücklich** sein

wie **toll** laufen: cf. wie **verrückt** laufen

ein **Tolpatsch** sein (fam.): *to be a blunderbuss (colloq.); to be a clumsy clot (sl.)*

Du bist auf den frisch eingesäten Rasen getreten, du Tolpatsch (Hans Tappinsmus).
*You have trodden on the freshly-sown lawn, you blunderbuss (clumsy clot).*

den **Ton** angeben (fig.): *to set the tone (the fashion; the pace); to call the tune*

Diese eingebildete Frau will überall den Ton angeben.
*This conceited woman wants to set the tone (fashion; pace; to call the tune) wherever she goes.*

einen **Ton** anschlagen (fig.): *to adopt a tone*

Was schlagen Sie da für einen unfreundlichen Ton an!
*What an unfriendly tone you are adopting!*

einen anderen **Ton** (eine andere **Tonart**) anschlagen (fig.): *to change one's tune; to sing a different tune; to take another line*

Zuerst hat Karl sich artig benommen, aber jetzt hat er einen anderen Ton (eine andere Tonart) angeschlagen und ist frech geworden.
*At first Charles behaved nicely, but now he has changed his tune (sings a different tune; has taken another line) and has become impertinent.*

zum guten **Ton** gehören: *to be good form; to be a mark (a sign) of good breeding; to be done (the done thing) (colloq.)*

Es gehört heutzutage zum guten Ton, daß junge Leute Musikstunden nehmen.
*Nowadays it is good form (a mark [sign] of good breeding; done; the done thing) for young people to have music lessons.*

Der **Ton** macht die Musik (Sprichw.): *It is not (so much) what you do, but the way that you do it (prov.)*

Warum können Sie mir Ihre Einwände nicht in höflicher Weise sagen, anstatt so unfreundlich zu sein? Der Ton macht die Musik.
*Why can't you tell me your objections in a polite manner, instead of being so unfriendly? It is not (so much) what you do, but the way that you do it.*

sich im **Ton** vergreifen (fig.): *to strike (to hit) the wrong note; to make a faux-pas; to make a bloomer (colloq.).* Cf. auch: einen **Bock** schießen

> Als du den berühmten Mann so anredetest, hast du dich im Ton (in der Tastatur) vergriffen.
> *When you addressed the famous man in that manner you struck (hit) the wrong note (made a faux-pas [bloomer]).*

keinen **Ton** verlauten lassen (fig. u. fam.): cf. keinen **Mucks** sagen

Hast du **Töne**? (fam.): *What do you say to that?; Can you beat that? (colloq.); Well, I'm blowed (jiggered)! (colloq.)*

> Hast du Töne (Worte)? Der Mann verlangt Entschädigung für Sachen, die ihm nie(mals) gehört haben.
> *What do you say to that? (Can you beat that?; Well, I'm blowed [jiggered]!) The man is demanding compensation for things that never belonged to him.*

große (dicke) **Töne** reden (fig. u. fam.): *to talk in grandiose terms; to talk big (colloq.); to shoot a line (colloq.); to shoot off one's mouth (sl.)*

> Auch andere haben große (dicke) Töne geredet, ohne etwas zu erreichen.
> *Others have talked in grandiose terms (have talked big; have shot a line; have shot off their mouths) as well without achieving anything.*

in den höchsten **Tönen** reden (fig.): *to talk in superlatives (in glowing terms)*

> Zeig' doch (lieber) mal, was du wirklich kannst, anstatt ständig in den höchsten Tönen über deine Fähigkeiten zu reden!
> *Show what you really can do, instead of perpetually talking in superlatives (in glowing terms) about your capabilities.*

Auf jeden **Topf** findet sich ein Deckel (Sprichw.): *There's a nut for every bolt (prov.)*

> Obwohl seine Schwester sehr häßlich ist, hat sie doch einen Mann gefunden. Auf jeden Topf findet sich ein Deckel.
> *Although his sister is very ugly, she has found a husband after all. There's a nut for every bolt.*

alles in éinen **Topf** werfen (fig.): *to mix (to muddle) everything up*

> Bei der Prüfung war der Kandidat so verwirrt, daß er alles in éinen Topf warf.
> *In the examination the candidate was so confused that he mixed (muddled) everything up.*

Gesprungene **Töpfe** halten am längsten (Sprichw.): *A creaking door hangs long on its hinges (Creaky doors last longest) (prov.)*

> Da sich meine kränkliche Großmutter sehr schont, wird sie wohl noch lange leben. Gesprungene Töpfe halten am längsten.
> *As my sick grandmother looks after herself well, she will probably live a long while yet. A creaking door hangs long on its hinges (Creaky doors last longest).*

kurz vor **Toresschluß** (fig.): cf. in zwölfter **Stunde**

Alter schützt vor **Torheit** nicht (Sprichw.): cf. Alte **Scheunen** brennen lichterloh

j.en **tot** und lebendig reden (fig. u. fam.): cf. j.em ein **Loch** (Löcher) in den Bauch reden

sich **totarbeiten** (fig. u. fam.): *to work (to slave) o.s. to death; to work one's fingers to the bone; to wear o.s. out; to work o.s. into the ground.* Cf. auch: arbeiten wie ein **Pferd**

> Dein Fleiß ist lobenswert; du brauchst dich aber nicht totzuarbeiten (totzuschuften; zu Tode zu schuften; abzurackern [abzuschinden; abzuschuften]).
> *Your industry is praiseworthy, but you don't need to work (slave) yourself to death (work yourself into the ground; work your fingers to the bone; wear yourself out).*

**totenblaß** (**totenbleich**) sein: cf. weiß wie die **Wand** sein

eine **Totengräbermiene** aufsetzen (fig.): cf. ein **Gesicht** machen wie sieben (drei) Tage Regenwetter

**totenstill** (eine **Totenstille**): *deathly silent (quiet); a deathly silence (deathly hush)*

> In unserer Klasse war es totenstill (herrschte [eine] Totenstille), als der Direktor eintrat.
> *Our class was deathly silent (quiet; There was a deathly silence [hush] in our class) when the headmaster entered.*

sich **totlachen** (fig. u. fam.): *to laugh till one cries; to laugh o.s. to death; to rock (to roar; to be convulsed) with laughter; to laugh like mad (colloq.); to laugh o.s. silly (colloq.); to burst (to hold) one's sides with laughter (colloq.)*

> Über diesen Witz haben wir uns totgelacht (krank-, krumm-, schibbelig, schiefgelacht; einen Ast [Bauch; Frack] gelacht; ein Loch in den Bauch gelacht; vor Lachen gebogen [ausgeschüttet; gekugelt; geschüttelt; gewälzt]; den Bauch vor Lachen gehalten [den Buckel vollgelacht]; haben wir zwerchfellerschütternd gelacht; sind wir vor Lachen geborsten [geplatzt]).
> *We laughed at that joke till we cried (We laughed ourselves to death [rocked (roared; were convulsed) with laughter; laughed like mad; laughed ourselves silly; burst (held) our sides with laughter] at that joke).*

zum **Totlachen** sein (fig.): cf. zum **Piepen** sein

sich **totschuften** (fam.): cf. sich **totarbeiten**

sich **totschweigen** (fam.): cf. keinen **Mucks** sagen

j.en auf **Touren** bringen (fig.): cf. j.en (etwas) in **Schwung** bringen

etwas in éiner **Tour** machen: *to do s.th. at a stretch (without a break; at one sitting; at one go; on end)*
  Wir haben vier Stunden lang in éiner Tour Skat gespielt.
  *We played skat for four hours at a stretch (without a break; at one sitting; at one go; on end).*

auf (hohe) **Touren** kommen (fig.): cf. in **Fluß** kommen

krumme **Touren** lieben (fam.): cf. die krummen **Wege** lieben

auf vollen **Touren** laufen (fig.): *to proceed apace; to go on (to proceed) at full pressure (at full speed; at full stretch)*
  Die Fahndung nach dem Bankräuber läuft auf vollen Touren.
  *The search for the bank robber is proceeding apace (is going on [proceeding] at full pressure [at full speed; at full stretch]).*

j.en in **Trab** bringen (fig.): cf. j.en in **Schwung** bringen

j.en in **Trab** halten (fig.): *to keep s.b. on the move (on the run); to keep s.b. extended; to keep s.b. on the go (colloq.)*
  In der letzten Zeit hatte er nicht viel freie Zeit, da verschiedene Aufgaben ihn ständig in Trab hielten.
  *He did not have much free time recently, because various tasks kept him continually on the move (run; go; kept him fully extended).*

etwas **tragisch** nehmen: cf. sich etwas zu **Herzen** nehmen

eine **Tragödie** sein (fig.): *to be a tragedy; to be tragic*
  Seine finanzielle Lage ist allmählich zu einer Tragödie geworden.
  *His financial position has gradually become a tragedy (become tragic).*

ein(e) **Trampel** (ein **Trampeltier**) sein (fam.): *to be a lumbering lout (colloq.); to be a clumsy clot (sl.)*
  Diese(s) Trampel (Dieses Trampeltier) von Dienstmädchen werden wir bald entlassen.
  *We shall soon sack this lumbering lout (clumsy clot) of a maid.*

**trampen** (fam.): cf. per **Anhalter** fahren

im **Tran** sein (fam.): a) cf. zu tief in den **Becher** geguckt haben; b) *to be in a daze (in a dream)*
  b) Durch Überanstrengung und Übermüdung war ich wie im Tran.
  *b) As a result of overstrain and over-tiredness I was in a daze (dream).*

j.em (einer Sache) keine **Träne** nachweinen (fig.): *not to shed any tears (not to cry one's eyes out) over s. th. (s. b.)*

Dem unangenehmen Nachbarn, der jetzt fortgezogen ist, weinen wir keine Träne nach.
*We shall not shed any tears (cry our eyes out) over that unpleasant neighbour who has now moved.*

in **Tränen** schwimmen (zerfließen; in Tränen gebadet [aufgelöst] sein): *s. b.'s eyes are swimming with tears; to cry one's eyes out; to be bathed in tears. Cf.* auch: sich die **Augen** ausweinen

Meine Schwester schwamm (zerfloß) in Tränen (war in Tränen gebadet [aufgelöst]), weil sie ihren Ring verloren hatte.
*My sister's eyes were swimming with tears (My sister was crying her eyes out [was bathed in tears]) because she had lost her ring.*

auf die **Tränendrüsen** drücken (fam.): *to make the tears roll (to set the tears rolling); to raise a lump in one's throat; to open up the waterworks (colloq.)*

Dieser sentimentale Film drückt wirklich auf die Tränendrüsen.
*This sentimental film really makes the tears roll (sets the tears rolling; raises a lump in one's throat; opens up the waterworks).*

ein **Tränentier** sein (fam.): cf. **mordslangweilig** sein; eine **Bummelliese** sein

eine **Transuse** (eine **Tranlampe**) sein (fig. u. fam.): cf. eine **Bummelliese** sein

(viel) **Trara** machen (fig. u. fam.): cf. (viel) **Brimborium** um etwas machen

**Tratsch** (fam.): cf. **Klatsch** und Tratsch

**Trau,** schau, wem!: *Stop, look and listen; Watch your step*

Bevor du dich in Geschäfte mit einem Unbekannten einläßt, solltest du dich genau nach ihm erkundigen. Trau, schau, wem!
*Before you enter into business with a stranger, you ought to make close enquiries about him. Stop, look and listen (Watch your step).*

Die **Trauben** hängen j.em zu hoch (Die Trauben sind j.em zu sauer): *It's a case of sour grapes*

Da du die Reise nach dem Süden nicht mitmachen kannst, behauptest du, es liege dir nichts an ihr. Die Trauben hängen dir zu hoch (sind dir zu sauer).
*As you cannot go with us on a trip to the Mediterranean, you claim that you attach no importance to it. It's a case of sour grapes.*

eine **Trauergestalt** (ein **Trauerkloß**) sein (fam.): *to be a picture of misery; to be a misery (a moper) (colloq.); to be a drip (sl.)*

Eine Trauergestalt (Einen Trauerkloß) wie dich können wir bei unserm Fest nicht gebrauchen.
*We can't do with a picture of misery (a misery; moper; drip) like you at our party.*

Der **Traum** ist aus (fig.): *The honeymoon is over*

Unsere Fußballmannschaft hatte anfangs die meisten Spiele gewonnen und hoffte, Meister zu werden; in letzter Zeit ist sie jedoch öfters geschlagen worden. Der Traum ist aus.
*Our football team won most of their games to start with and hoped to become champions, but recently they have often been beaten. The honeymoon is over.*

j.em nicht im **Traume** einfallen (an etwas nicht im Traum denken) (fig.): *s.b. would not dream of (doing) s.th.*

Es fällt mir nicht im Traume ein (Ich denke nicht im Traum daran), deinen Standpunkt zu verfechten.
*I would not dream of defending your point of view.*

**Träume** sind Schäume (Sprichw.): *All dreams evaporate*

Du hast also geträumt, du hättest in der Lotterie gewonnen? Träume sind Schäume.
*So you dreamt you had won something in the sweepstake? All dreams evaporate.*

etwas ins **Treffen** führen (fig.): cf. etwas ins **Gefecht** führen

eine **Treibhaushitze** sein: cf. eine **Bullenhitze** sein

einen **Trennungsstrich** ziehen (fig.): *to draw a (dividing) line; to distinguish*

Dieses Werk hat seine gute, aber auch seine schlechte Seite, und man muß einen klaren Trennungsstrich (eine klare Grenze) zwischen ihnen ziehen (eine Scheidewand ... aufrichten).
*This work has its good but also its bad side, and one must draw a firm (dividing) line (must distinguish sharply) between them.*

die **Treppe** hinauffallen (fig.): *to be kicked upstairs (colloq.)*

Durch diese Ernennung ist mein Neffe unverhofft die Treppe hinaufgefallen.
*By this appointment my nephew has unexpectedly been kicked upstairs.*

ein **Treppenwitz** der Geschichte (fig.): *a quirk (a freak) of history*

Daß dieses kleine Volk seinen viel größeren Nachbarn einmal besiegt hat, ist ein Treppenwitz der Geschichte.
*It is a quirk (freak) of history that this small nation once conquered its far larger neighbour.*

j.en **treten** (fig. u. fam.): *to get at (after) s.b. (colloq.); to chase s.b. up (sl.)*

Ohne Mahnung bezahlt Heinrich keine Rechnung. Man muß ihn wiederholt treten.

*Without a reminder Henry never pays a bill. One has to get at (after) him (chase him up) repeatedly.*

eine **Tretmühle** sein (fig.): cf. eine **Knochenmühle** sein

etwas auf **Treu** und Glauben hinnehmen: *to take s.th. in good faith; to take s.th. on trust; to treat s.th. as a gentlemen's agreement*

Ich wollte keinen schriftlichen Beweis von ihm verlangen, sondern habe seine Angabe einfach auf Treu und Glauben hingenommen.
*I did not want to ask for any written proof from him, but simply took his statement in good faith (on trust; treated his statement as a gentlemen's agreement).*

**treu** wie Gold sein: cf. treu wie **Gold** sein

zu **treuen** Händen übergeben: cf. zu treuen **Händen** übergeben

die **Triebfeder** sein (fig.): *to be the guiding light (the [driving] force; the power)*

Weißt du, wer die eigentliche Triebfeder bei diesem Unternehmen ist?
*Do you know who the real guiding light ([driving] force) is in (the real power is behind) this enterprise?*

eine dumme **Trine** sein (fam.): cf. eine dumme **Gans** sein

**Tritt** fassen (fig.): *to get off the mark; to make a start; to get into its stride*

Euer Fußballklub hat endlich Tritt gefaßt und seine ersten Spiele gewonnen.
*At last your football-club has got off the mark (made a start; got into its stride) and won its first games.*

noch nicht **trocken** hinter den Ohren sein (fig. u. fam.): cf. ein **Grünschnabel** sein

auf dem **trocknen** sitzen (fig.): cf. knapp bei **Kasse** sein

**Trödel(kram) (Trödelware):** *trash; rubbish*

An der Haustür wird einem zumeist Trödel(kram) (Trödelware) angeboten.
*It is generally trash (rubbish) that is offered for sale at the door.*

ein **Trödelfritze** sein (fam.): *to be a dawdler (slowcoach) (colloq.).* Cf. auch: **nachzotteln**

Nun beeile dich doch endlich, du (langweiliger) Trödelfritze (Bummelfritze)!
*Now do hurry up, you dawdler (slowcoach)!*

die **Trommel** rühren (fig.): cf. **Reklame** für etwas machen

eine **Tropenhitze (tropische** Hitze) sein: cf. eine **Bullenhitze** sein

Ein **Tropfen** genügt, um das Faß zum Überlaufen zu bringen (Sprichw.): *It's the last straw that breaks the camel's back (prov.)*

Er war schon sehr aufgeregt, und diese letzte Beleidigung war ihm zu viel. Ein Tropfen genügt, um das Faß zum Überlaufen zu bringen.
*He was already very agitated, and that last insult was too much for him. It's the last straw that breaks the camel's back.*

ein **Tropfen** auf einen heißen Stein sein (fig.): *to be a drop in the bucket (in the ocean); to be a flea-bite (colloq.)*

Verglichen mit seinen großen Schulden bedeutet der Geldbetrag, den du ihm leihen willst, nur einen Tropfen auf einen heißen Stein.
*Compared with his large debts, the sum of money that you want to lend him is only a drop in the bucket (ocean; is only a flea-bite).*

Steter **Tropfen** höhlt den Stein (Sprichw.): *Constant dripping wears away the stone (prov.)*

Sein übermäßiges Trinken hat seine Gesundheit völlig untergraben. Steter Tropfen höhlt den Stein.
*His excessive drinking has completely undermined his health. Constant dripping wears away the stone.*

nicht (recht) bei **Troste** sein (fam.): cf. nicht richtig im **Dachstübchen** sein

den gleichen (alten) **Trott** weitergehen (fig. u. fam.): cf. den gleichen (alten) **Schlendrian** weitergehen

im **trüben** fischen (fig.): *to fish in troubled waters*

Der Kassierer wurde als Betrüger entlarvt, nachdem er lange im trüben (in trüben Wassern) gefischt hatte.
*The cashier was unmasked as a swindler after having fished for a long time in troubled waters.*

**Trübsal** blasen (fam.): *to be downcast; to mope; to be down in the mouth (down in the dumps) (colloq.); to have the blues (colloq.)*

Anstatt Trübsal zu blasen (in gedrückter Stimmung zu sein), solltest du heitere Bücher lesen.
*You ought to read cheerful books instead of being downcast (moping; being down in the mouth [the dumps]; instead of having the blues) like that.*

alle **Trümpfe** in der Hand haben (fig.): cf. alle **Karten** in der Hand haben

noch einen **Trumpf** in der Hand haben (fig.): *still to have an ace (a trump card) up one's sleeve; still to have a card to play; still to have a bullet (a shot) in one's gun; still to have an arrow in one's quiver.* Cf. auch: noch ein **Eisen** im Feuer haben

Karl hat den Kampf mit seinen Gegnern noch nicht aufgegeben, denn er hat noch einen Trumpf in der Hand.

*Charles has not yet given up the struggle with his opponents, for he still has an ace (a trump card) up his sleeve (still has a card to play; still has a bullet [shot] in his gun [an arrow in his quiver]).*

**seinen höchsten Trumpf** ausspielen (fig.): *to play one's trump card*

Wenn ich meinen höchsten Trumpf ausspiele, wird mein Gegner zum Schweigen gebracht werden.
*When I play my trump card, my opponent will be silenced.*

**sich spreizen (blähen) wie ein Truthahn:** *to strut (to puff o.s. out) like a turkey-cock; to blow one's own trumpet.* Cf. auch: sich in die **Brust** werfen (sich brüsten); stolz wie ein **Spanier** sein; sich **mausig** machen

Der eingebildete Maler spreizt (bläht) sich wie ein Truthahn (Pfau; ist aufgeblasen; stolziert wie der Storch im Salat einher [herum]), seitdem er einen wichtigen Auftrag bekommen hat.
*The conceited painter has been strutting (puffing himself out) like a turkey-cock (has been blowing his own trumpet) since he received an important commission.*

**rot werden wie ein Truthahn:** cf. **knallrot** werden

**wirken wie das rote Tuch** (das rote Tuch für j.en sein) (fig.): *to be like a red rag to a bull; to make s.b. see red*

Diese unangenehme Person wirkt wie das rote Tuch auf uns (ist das rote Tuch für uns).
*For us that unpleasant person is like a red rag to a bull (That unpleasant person makes us see red).*

**aus der Not eine Tugend** machen: cf. aus der **Not** eine Tugend machen

ein **Tugendbold** sein: cf. ein **Ausbund** von Tugend sein

**j.es Tun** und Treiben (Tun und Lassen): *s.b.'s doings (affairs); s.b.'s goings-on (colloq.)*

Jedenfalls ist er ein großer Künstler. Sein sonstiges Tun und Treiben (Tun und Lassen) geht einen nichts an.
*Anyway he is a great artist. His other doings (affairs; goings-on) do not concern one.*

**Tünche** sein (fig. u. fam.): *to be sham (bogus; fake; on the surface); to be an act (colloq.); to be eyewash (sl.)*

Sie sieht harmlos und bescheiden aus, es ist aber alles Tünche bei ihr. In Wirklichkeit ist sie ganz anders.
*She looks harmless and modest, but it is all sham (bogus; fake; on the surface; eyewash; it is just an act). In reality she is quite different.*

ein **Tunichtgut** sein: cf. ein **Nichtsnutz** sein

das **Tüpfelchen** auf dem i sein (fig.): cf. die **Höhe** sein

j.en zwischen **Tür** und Angel sprechen (fig.): *to speak to s.b. in passing; to exchange a fleeting (passing) word with s.b.*

> Leider hatte dein Lehrer keine Zeit für mich, und ich konnte ihn nur zwischen Tür und Angel sprechen.
> *Unfortunately your master had no time for me and I could only speak to him in passing (only exchange a fleeting [passing] word with him).*

zwischen **Tür** und Angel stecken (fig.): *to be betwixt and between; to be (caught) in two minds; not to know which way to turn.* Cf. auch: in der **Klemme** sein

> Ich steckte (stak) zwischen Tür und Angel und wußte nicht, ob ich seinen Vorschlag annehmen sollte.
> *I was betwixt and between (was [caught] in two minds; did not know which way to turn) about accepting his suggestion.*

Gold öffnet jede **Tür** (Sprichw.): cf. **Gold** öffnet jede Tür

mit der **Tür** ins Haus fallen (fig. u. fam.): *to give the show away at once (colloq.); to go hell for leather at it (colloq.); to go (to charge) full tilt at it (colloq.)*

> Besonders taktvoll ist mein Nachbar nicht, denn er ist mir mit der Tür ins Haus gefallen und hat gleich (heraus)gesagt, daß er Geld von mir wolle.
> *My neighbour is not particularly tactful, for he gave the show away at once (went hell for leather at it; went [charged] full tilt at it) and said straight out that he wanted money from me.*

Jeder kehre vor seiner **Tür!** (Sprichw.): *Put your own house in order first (prov.).* Cf. auch: sich an seine eigene **Nase** fassen (packen)

> Man sollte von anderen Menschen nichts Schlechtes reden, sondern lieber an sich selbst Kritik üben. Jeder kehre vor seiner Tür.
> *One should not speak badly of other people but rather criticise oneself. Put your own house in order first.*

an alle **Türen** klopfen: *to call on everybody; to pass the hat round (colloq.)*

> Für diese verwitwete Mutter haben wir an alle Türen geklopft und viel Geld (für sie) erhalten.
> *We called on everybody (passed the hat round) for this widowed mother and received a lot of money for her.*

offene **Türen** einrennen (fig.): *to charge at an open door*

> Mit Ihrer angeblichen Neuerung rennen Sie nur offene Türen ein, denn sie ist schon längst bei uns eingeführt.
> *You are only charging at an open door with your supposed innovation, for it was introduced here long ago.*

die **Tür(en)** offenlassen (fig.): *to leave the door open*

Die Tür(en) zu weiteren Verhandlungen ist (sind) offengelassen worden (steht [stehen] offen).
*The door to further negotiations has been left open.*

j.en vor die **Tür** setzen (fig.): *to turn (to throw) s.b. out; to throw s.b. into the street; to show s.b. the door; to give s.b. the order of the boot (colloq.).* Cf. auch: j.en **achtkantig** hinauswerfen

Der Vater hat seinen ungezogenen Sohn (seinem . . . den Stuhl) vor die Tür (an die frische Luft) gesetzt (hat seinem . . . die Tür gewiesen; hat seinen . . . zum Tempel rausgejagt [zum Teufel gejagt]; hat seinem . . . gezeigt, wo der Zimmermann das Loch gelassen hat).
*The father turned (threw) his rude son out ([into the street]; showed . . . the door; gave . . . the order of the boot).*

vor der **Tür** stehen (fig.): *to be (close) at hand; to be just round the corner*

Die großen Ferien stehen vor der Tür, und wir wissen nicht, wohin fahren.
*The long vacation is (close) at hand (is just round the corner) and we do not know where to go.*

Die **Tür(en)** für etwas steht (stehen) offen (fig.): cf. die **Tür(en)** offenlassen

**Tür** und Tor öffnen (fig.): *to open the door; to leave the way open*

Nachdem dem Kaffeeschmuggel lange Zeit Tür und Tor geöffnet gewesen ist, wird die deutsch-belgische Grenze jetzt sehr streng überwacht.
*After the door had been open (After the way had been left open) for a long while for smuggling coffee, the Belgo-German frontier is now very closely guarded.*

vor verschlossene **Türen** kommen (fig.): *to run (to come) up against (to run into) a brick wall; to find all the doors closed*

Wenn man von den Leuten etwas haben will, kommt man oft vor verschlossene Türen.
*When one wants something from people, one often runs (comes) up against (runs into) a brick wall (often finds all the doors closed).*

j.em die **Tür** weisen (fig.): cf. j.en vor die **Tür** setzen

die **Tür(en)** zuschlagen (fig.): *to shut (to close) the door; to bar the way*

Auf dieser Konferenz ist die Tür (sind die Türen) zu weiteren Verhandlungen über diese Angelegenheit nicht zugeschlagen worden.
*At this conference the door to further negotiations on that matter has not been shut (closed; the way . . . has not been barred).*

j.em die **Tür** vor der Nase zuschlagen: *to slam (to shut) the door in s.b.'s face*

Als ich Sie besuchen wollte, schlug mir Ihre Hausangestellte die Tür vor der Nase zu.
*When I wanted to visit you, your maidservant slammed (shut) the door in my face.*

j.em einen **Türken** bauen (fig.): *to pull the wool over s.b.'s eyes; to put a false complexion on things*

Als der König die stark zerstörte Stadt besuchen wollte, wurden in Eile an den Straßen zur Verschönerung Bäume eingerammt und ihm so ein Türke gebaut (Potemkinsche Dörfer vorgespiegelt [vorgegaukelt]).
*When the king wanted to visit the badly-damaged city, trees were hurriedly put down along the streets in decoration so that the wool was pulled over his eyes (so that a false complexion was put on things).*

ein **Turm** sein (fig.): *to be a tower (pillar) of strength; to be a bulwark*

Dieser Spieler war ein Turm in der Abwehr.
*That player was a tower (pillar) of strength (a bulwark) in the defence.*

j.em **turmhoch** überlegen sein (j.en turmhoch überragen) (fig.): j.em **haushoch** überlegen sein

leben (sich lieben) wie die **Turteltauben**: *to live together like a pair of turtle-doves; to bill and coo like a pair of turtle-doves (colloq.)*

Heinrich und Margarete leben (lieben sich) wie die Turteltauben.
*Henry and Margaret live together (bill and coo) like a pair of turtle-doves.*

**Tüten** kleben (fam.): *to pick oakum.* Cf. auch: in den **Kasten** kommen

Der Verbrecher mußte fünf Jahre lang Tüten kleben.
*The criminal had to spend five years picking oakum.*

Kommt nicht in die **Tüte**! (fig. u. fam.): *Not on your life! (colloq.); Not on your Nellie! (sl.)*

Ich soll einen neuen Fernsehapparat kaufen? Kommt nicht in die Tüte!
*I'm to buy a new television set? Not on your life (on your Nellie)!*

nichts von **Tuten** und Blasen verstehen (fig. u. fam.): *not to know (to understand) the first thing about it; not to have the faintest idea about it (colloq.); not to have a clue (sl.).* Cf. auch: keine (blasse) **Ahnung** haben

In dieser Angelegenheit hätte ich meinen Bruder gern um Rat gefragt, aber er versteht nichts von Tuten und Blasen.
*I should have liked to ask my brother's advice in this matter, but he doesn't know (understand) the first thing (hasn't the faintest idea) about it (hasn't a clue).*

eine freche **Type** sein (fam.): cf. ein freches **Stück** sein

eine komische (närrische) **Type** sein (fam.): cf. ein komischer (närrischer) **Kauz** sein etwas bis zum **Tz** kennen (fam.): *to know s.th. down to the last letter; to know s.th. through and through; to know s.th. to a T (to perfection); to know s.th. inside out (colloq.); to have s.th. thoroughly taped (colloq.).* Cf. auch: etwas aus dem **FF** verstehen

Ein Schauspieler muß seine Rolle bis zum Tz (in- und auswendig) kennen.
*An actor must know his part down to the last letter (through and through; to a T; to perfection; inside out; must have his part thoroughly taped).*

# U

ein notwendiges **Übel** sein: *to be a necessary evil*

In der Stadt ist der Rauch von den vielen Schornsteinen ein notwendiges Übel.
*In towns the smoke from the many chimneys is a necessary evil.*

das **Übel** an der Wurzel packen (fig.): cf. die **Axt** an die Wurzel einer Sache legen

**übel** dran sein (fam.): cf. **arm** dran sein

j.em **übel** mitspielen (fig.): *to play a mean trick on s.b.; to do s.b. a bad turn; to play a rotten (a dirty) trick on s.b. (colloq.)*

Durch ihre Enthüllung meines Geheimnisses haben mir meine Kollegen übel mitgespielt.
*By disclosing my secret my colleagues have played a mean (rotten [dirty]) trick on me (have done me a bad turn).*

etwas **überbrücken** (fig.): *to bridge (to span) s.th.*

Die Kluft zwischen den beiden Nationen läßt sich nicht so leicht überbrücken.
*The gulf between the two nations cannot be bridged (spanned) so easily.*

j.en **überfahren** (fig. u. fam.): *to out-talk s.b.; to talk s.b. over*

Mit seiner Redegewandtheit fällt es diesem Geschäftsmann leicht, seine Käufer zu überfahren.
*With his loquacity that shopkeeper finds it easy to out-talk his customers (to talk his customers over).*

j.en **überflügeln** (fig.): *to outstrip (outflank; outshine) s.b.* Cf. auch: j.en in den **Schatten** stellen; j.en in die **Tasche** stecken

Wilhelm hat alle seine Klassenkameraden überflügelt.
*William has outstripped (outflanked; outshone) all his class-mates.*

etwas **überschatten** (fig.): *to overshadow s.th.; to put s.th. in the shadow*

Dieses große Ereignis überschattet alle übrigen Begebenheiten.
*This great event overshadows all other happenings (puts all other happenings in the shadow).*

**überschlau** sein (fam.): cf. das **Gras** wachsen hören

j.en **übertölpeln:** cf. j.en **übervorteilen**

j.en **übervorteilen:** *to get the better of s.b.; to steal a march on s.b.; to catch s.b. out (colloq.); to take s.b. in (colloq.); to pull a fast one on s.b. (sl.)*
Du mußt aufpassen, daß dieser schlaue Junge dich nicht übervorteilt (übertölpelt).
*You must take care that that cunning boy does not get the better of you (steal a march on you; catch you out; take you in; pull a fast one on you).*

etwas für j.en (für eine Sache) **übrig** haben (fam.): *to have a liking (a penchant) for s.b. (s.th.); to have a soft spot (in one's heart) for s.b. (s.th.).* Cf. auch: eine **Schwäche** für j.en (etwas) haben
Ich habe den Eindruck, daß du für meine Schwester etwas übrig hast.
*I have the impression that you have a liking (a penchant; a soft spot [in your heart]) for my sister.*

nichts für j.en (etwas) **übrig** haben (fam.): *to have no sympathy for s.b. (s.th.); to have no use (no time) for s.b. (s.th.)*
Für Sport hat mein Vater leider nichts übrig.
*I am afraid that my father has no sympathy (use [time]) for sport.*

**Übung** macht den Meister (Sprichw.): cf. Übung macht den **Meister**

sich ins **Uferlose** verlieren (fig.): *to ramble (to meander) on; to lose o.s. in a maze.* Cf. auch: den **Faden** verlieren
Anstatt sich auf sein Hauptthema zu konzentrieren, verlor sich der Redner ins Uferlose.
*Instead of concentrating on his main subject, the speaker rambled (meandered) on (lost himself in a maze).*

Wat den inen sin **Uhl,** is den annern sin Nachtigall (Sprichw.): *One man's loss is another man's gain (prov.)*
Mein Vater hat diesen wichtigen Posten bekommen, weil sein alter Vorgesetzter gestorben ist. Wat den inen sin Uhl, is den annern sin Nachtigall (Des einen Tod ist des anderen Brot).
*My father got this important job because his old boss died. One man's loss is another man's gain.*

Seine **Uhr** ist abgelaufen (fig.): Seine **Stunde** hat geschlagen

mit j.em (seinen) **Ulk** treiben: *to make fun of s.b.; to poke fun at s.b.* Cf. auch:
j.en auf den **Arm** nehmen

Es ist gefährlich, mit einem Höherstehenden (seinen) Ulk zu treiben.
*It is dangerous to make fun of (poke fun at) a superior.*

**um** sein (von der Zeit): *to be up (over)*

Nächste Woche sind unsere Schulferien leider schon um.
*Our school holidays are unfortunately up (over) next week.*

zum **Umfallen** müde sein: cf. **hundemüde** sein

j.en **umgarnen** (fig.): *to catch (to entangle) s.b. in one's net*

Elisabeth hat schon manchen Jüngling umgarnt (umstrickt).
*Elizabeth has already caught (entangled) many a youth in her net.*

j.en mit Liebreiz **umgaukeln** (fam.): *to overwhelm s.b. with charm; to lavish
one's charms on s.b.*

Anfangs umgaukelte Marie ihre zukünftigen Schwiegereltern mit Liebreiz.
*To start with Mary overwhelmed her future parents-in-law with charm (lavished her
charms on her . . .).*

**Umgekehrt** wird ein Schuh daraus (Umgekehrt ist auch was wert): *s.b. has
got hold of the wrong end of the stick (has got it all wrong; has got it the wrong way
round; has got it upside down)*

Die Zeitungen behaupten, die Lebensmittelpreise seien gesunken. Umgekehrt
wird ein Schuh daraus (Umgekehrt ist auch was wert): Sie sind in Wirklichkeit
wesentlich gestiegen.
*The papers claim that food prices have fallen. They have got hold of the wrong end of the
stick (have got it all wrong [the wrong way round; upside down]). They have in fact
risen appreciably.*

sich noch **umgucken** werden (fig. u. fam.): *to have the surprise (shock) of
one's life; to sit up and take notice (colloq.); to be staggered (stunned) (colloq.)*

Das Leben ist teuer geworden. Du wirst dich noch umgucken, wenn du mal
erst einen eigenen Haushalt führst.
*The cost of living is high. You will have the surprise (shock) of your life (You will sit up
and take notice; You will be staggered [stunned]) once you run your own household.*

**umkippen** (fig. u. fam.): *to pass out; to fold up (colloq.); to flake out (sl.)*

Die Hitze in dem überfüllten Saal war so groß, daß meine Schwester einfach
umkippte.
*The heat in the crowded hall was so great that my sister simply passed out (folded up;
flaked out).*

**umklappen** (fig. u. fam.): cf. wie ein **Taschenmesser** zusammenklappen j.en **umlegen** (fig. u. fam.): cf. j.en um die **Ecke** bringen

**umsatteln** (fig.): *to change horses; to swop horses (colloq.)*

Heinrich soll einen neuen Beruf ergriffen haben. Warum hat er denn umgesattelt?
*Henry is supposed to have taken up a new occupation. Why has he changed (swopped) horses?*

ohne **Umschweife**: *without beating about the bush.* Cf. auch: **klipp** und klar; j.em etwas ins **Gesicht** sagen; kurzen **Prozeß** machen

Die Wirtin hat ihrem Untermieter ohne Umschweife gesagt, daß er bis Ende des Monats ausziehen müsse.
*The landlady told her lodger without beating about the bush that he would have to move out by the end of the month.*

in anderen (gesegneten) **Umständen** sein: cf. guter **Hoffnung** sein

**Umstände** machen: cf. **Zores** machen

nicht viel **Umstände** machen: cf. nicht viel **Federlesen(s)** machen; kurzen **Prozeß** machen

ein **Umstandskrämer** sein (fam.): cf. ein **Kleinigkeitskrämer** sein

j.en **umstricken** (fig. u. fam.): cf. j.en **umgarnen**

**unbezahlbar** sein (fig.): *to be indispensable; to be worth one's weight in gold*

In Gesellschaft ist Karl einfach großartig; er ist wirklich unbezahlbar (Gold wert).
*In society Charles is simply wonderful. He really is indispensable (worth his weight in gold).*

**Undank** ist der Welt Lohn (Sprichw.): *The world pays with ingratitude*

Wie gut man es auch meinen mag, so werden doch die besten Absichten oft verkannt. Undank ist der Welt Lohn.
*However well-meaning one may be, the best intentions are (so) often misunderstood. The world pays with ingratitude.*

**ungehobelt** sein (fig.): cf. ein **Rauhbein** sein

**ungereimtes** Zeug sein: *s. th. has neither rhyme nor reason; s. th. does not add up (does not hang together); to make no sense*

Was du da erzählst, ist lauter ungereimtes Zeug (hat keinen Sinn und Verstand; hat weder Hand noch Fuß).
*What you are saying has neither rhyme nor reason (does not add up [hang together]; makes no sense).*

**ungeschliffen** sein (fig.): cf. ein **Rauhbein** sein

**ungeschminkt** reden (fig.): cf. kein **Blatt** vor den Mund nehmen

j.em die **ungeschminkte** Wahrheit sagen (fig.): cf. j.em die (ungeschminkte) **Wahrheit** sagen

**ungeschoren** davonkommen (fig.): *to escape (to get off) without a hair of one's head being harmed; to escape unscathed.* Cf. auch: j.em kein **Haar** krümmen

Der Einbrecher ist ungeschoren davongekommen.
*The burglar escaped (got off) without a hair of his head being harmed (escaped unscathed).*

Allzuviel ist **ungesund** (Sprichw.): *Enough is as good as a feast (is plenty) (prov.)*

Du mußt dich etwas mäßigen. Allzuviel ist ungesund.
*You must restrain yourself a bit. Enough is as good as a feast (is plenty).*

Ein **Unglück** kommt selten allein (Sprichw.): *It never rains but it pours (prov.); Troubles never come singly (prov.)*

Gleich nachdem sich Vater von einer Bronchitis erholt hatte, holte sich Mutter eine Erkältung. Éin Unglück kommt selten allein.
*Just as father had recovered from bronchitis, mother caught a chill. It never rains but it pours (Troubles never come singly).*

Kein **Unglück** ist so groß, es trägt ein Glück im Schoß (Sprichw.): cf. Kein Unglück ist so groß, es trägt ein Glück im **Schoß**

sich ins **Unglück** stürzen: *to land (o.s.) in trouble; to get (o.s.) into trouble; to bring ruin upon o.s.*

Durch seine Spielwut hat sich mein Bruder ins Unglück gestürzt.
*My brother has landed (himself) in trouble (got [himself] into trouble; has brought ruin upon himself) by his furious gambling.*

ein **Unglücksbote** sein: *to be a bringer of bad tidings*

Schon seit vier Tagen bringt uns der Briefträger nichts als schlechte Nachrichten. Er ist der reinste Unglücksbote.
*For four days now the postman has brought us nothing but bad news. He is a real bringer of bad tidings.*

ein **Unglücksprophet** sein: *to be a harbinger of bad fortune; to be a bird of ill omen*

Sprich nicht solche furchtbare Gedanken aus. Sei kein Unglücksprophet (keine Unke; Unke nicht so)!
*Do not utter such terrible thoughts. Do not be a harbinger of bad fortune (a bird of ill omen).*

ein **Unglücksrabe (Unglückswurm)** sein (fig.): cf. ein **Pechvogel** sein

nichts für **ungut**: cf. **nichts** für ungut

**unheilschwanger** aussehen (fig.): *to look black (grim; threatening)*
> Die politische Lage sieht wieder einmal unheilschwanger aus.
> *The political situation looks black (grim; threatening) again.*

eine **Unke** sein **(unken)** (fig. u. fam.): cf. ein **Unglücksprophet** sein

sich in (große) **Unkosten** stürzen: *to go to great expense; to dip deeply into one's pocket; to fork out a lot of money (colloq.); to saddle o.s. with a great outlay (colloq.)*
> Anläßlich der Vermählung ihrer Tochter hatten sich die Eltern in große Unkosten gestürzt.
> *The parents went to great expense (dipped deeply into their pockets; forked out a lot of money; saddled themselves with a great outlay) on the occasion of their daughter's wedding.*

**Unkraut** vergeht nicht (Sprichw.): *Ill weeds grow apace (prov.); The bad penny always turns up again (prov.)*
> Wie geht es dir denn? – O, mir geht's gut. Unkraut vergeht nicht.
> *How are you? – Oh, I'm all right. Ill weeds grow apace (The bad penny always turns up again).*

**Unrecht** Gut gedeihet nicht (Sprichw.): *Ill-gotten gains are cursed (bring no reward) (prov.)*
> Der Gauner, der auf unlautere Weise große Gewinne erzielt hatte, ist jetzt verhaftet worden. Unrecht Gut gedeihet nicht.
> *The rogue, who had made great profits in an underhand manner, has now been arrested. Ill-gotten gains are cursed (bring no reward).*

an den **Unrechten** kommen: cf. an die falsche **Adresse** kommen

die gekränkte **Unschuld** spielen: *to play (to act) the injured innocent*
> Obwohl Jakob die Äpfel doch gestohlen hatte, wollte er die gekränkte Unschuld spielen.
> *Although James really had stolen the apples, he tried to play (to act) the injured innocent.*

seine Hände in **Unschuld** waschen (fig.): *s.b.'s hands are clean (unsullied)*. Cf. auch: unschuldig wie ein neugeborenes **Kind** sein
> Mit dieser Protestkundgebung hatte ich nichts zu tun. Ich wasche meine Hände in Unschuld.
> *I had nothing to do with that protest-meeting. My hands are clean (unsullied).*

die **Unschuld** vom Lande sein: *to be a proper little innocent (a flower in the field)*

Unsere neue Hausangestellte ist die richtige Unschuld (Einfalt; das richtige Kätchen) vom Lande. Sie ist noch nicht einmal im Kino gewesen.
*Our new housemaid is a proper little innocent (a real flower in the field). She has never even been to the cinema.*

**unschuldig** wie ein neugeborenes Kind sein: cf. unschuldig wie ein neugeborenes **Kind** sein

den **Unschuldsengel** spielen: *to play the injured innocent; to put on an air of injured innocence*

Die gefährliche Agentin versuchte, vor Gericht den Unschuldsengel zu spielen.
*The dangerous woman-agent tried to play the injured innocent (to put on an air of injured innocence) in court.*

**unten** durch bei j.em sein (fam.): cf. **drunter** durch bei j.em sein

**unterderhand** etwas kaufen: cf. unter der **Hand** etwas kaufen

etwas **untergraben** (fig.): *to undermine s. th.*

Zu starker Alkohol- und Tabakgenuß untergräbt die Gesundheit.
*Excessive drinking and smoking undermines the health.*

sich nicht **unterkriegen** lassen (fig. u. fam.): *not to let s.b. (s.th.) get the better of one; not to let s.b. (s.th.) get one down (colloq.)*

Es ist schwer, sich von (bei) diesem kalten Wetter nicht unterkriegen zu lassen.
*It is difficult not to let this cold weather get the better of one (get one down).*

ein **Unterschied** sein wie Tag und Nacht: cf. **grundverschieden** sein

das **Unterste** zu oberst kehren: cf. alles auf den **Kopf** stellen

**Untreue** schlägt den eigenen Herrn (Sprichw.): *It is a case of the biter bit; The chickens have come home to roost*

Früher hat er mich betrogen, aber diesmal ist er selbst von einem anderen betrogen worden. Untreue schlägt den eigenen Herrn.
*He swindled me before but this time he has been swindled by somebody else. It is a case of the biter bit (The chickens have come home to roost).*

**unverblümt** reden (sprechen) (fig.): cf. kein **Blatt** vor den Mund nehmen

**üppig** werden (fig. u. fam.): cf. sich etwas **herausnehmen**

j.en **uzen**: cf. j.en auf den **Arm** nehmen

Der Wunsch ist **Vater** des Gedankens (Sprichw.): *The wish is father to the thought (prov.)*

Ich habe geträumt, ich hätte zehntausend Mark in der Lotterie gewonnen. Der Wunsch war Vater des Gedankens.
*I dreamt that I had won ten thousand marks in the sweepstake. The wish was father to the thought.*

zu seinen **Vätern** versammelt werden: cf. j.es **Lebenslicht** erlischt

j.en **veräppeln** (fam.): cf. j.en auf den **Arm** nehmen

sich etwas **verbauen** (fig.): *to wreck (to ruin) s. th.*

Durch seine unkluge Äußerung hat er sich seine Laufbahn verbaut.
*He has wrecked (ruined) his career by his unwise remark.*

seinen Ärger **verbeißen** (fig.): cf. seinen **Ärger** herunterschlucken (verbeißen)

sich in etwas **verbeißen** (fig.): *to be dead set on s. th.; to attach o. s. to s. th.; to be sold on s. th. (colloq.)*

Wilhelm hat sich nun einmal in diese absurde Idee verbissen (verrannt; ist . . . verbiestert; verbohrt).
*William is now dead set (sold) on (has now attached himself to) this absurd idea.*

in etwas **verbiestert** sein (fam.): cf. sich in etwas **verbeißen**

in etwas **verbohrt** sein (fam.): cf. sich in etwas **verbeißen**

**verboten** aussehen (fam.): cf. wie eine **Vogelscheuche** aussehen

etwas **verbrieft** und versiegelt haben (verbrieft und versiegelt sein) (fig.): *to have signed and sealed s. th.; to be signed and sealed*

Sie können sich auf mich verlassen. Ich habe den Vertrag verbrieft und versiegelt (Mein Vertrag ist verbrieft und versiegelt).
*You can rely on me. I have signed and sealed the contract (My contract is signed and sealed).*

dem **Verdienste** seine Krone (fig.): cf. **Ehre,** wem Ehre gebührt

wie **verdonnert** dastehen (fam.): cf. (wie) zur **Salzsäule** erstarrt sein

j.en **verdreschen** (fam.): cf. j.en **vermöbeln**

sich **verdrücken** (fam.): cf. **Fersengeld** geben; sich auf **französisch** empfehlen (sich) **verduften** (fig. u. fam.): cf. **abhauen; Fersengeld** geben; sich auf **französisch** empfehlen

in trautem **Verein:** *having a tête-à-tête; having a private session (colloq.); with our (your etc.) heads together (colloq.)*

> Das junge Pärchen sieht man oft in trautem Verein.
> *One often sees the young couple having a tête-à-tête (having a private session; with their heads together).*

ein **Vereinsmeier** sein (fam.): *to be a club-man; to be a club-type (colloq.)*

> Onkel Fritz ist ein richtiger Vereinsmeier. Jeden Abend geht er in den Kegelklub.
> *Uncle Fred is a real club-man (club-type). Every evening he goes to the skittle-club.*

sich **verfangen** (fig.): cf. sich **verstricken**

**Verflucht** (nochmal; Verflucht und zugenäht)! (fam.): *Damn (it all)! (colloq.); Damnation! (colloq.); Blast (it)! (sl.)*

> Verflucht (nochmal; Verflucht und zugenäht)! Wo habe ich nur meine Brieftasche hingelegt?
> *Damn ([it all]; Damnation; Blast [it])! Where have I put my wallet?*

sich in seine Bücher **vergraben** (fig.): *to bury o.s. (to immerse o.s.) in one's books*

> Unser Lehrer ist glücklich, wenn er sich in seine Bücher vergraben (vertiefen) kann.
> *Our teacher is happy when he can bury (immerse) himself in his books.*

etwas **verhackstücken** (fig. u. fam.): cf. etwas **vermurksen**

einer Sache **verhaftet** bleiben: *to cling (to hold) to s.th.; to be faithful to s.th.; to stick to s.th. (colloq.)*

> Dieser Künstler ist während seines ganzen Lebens der gleichen Kunstauffassung verhaftet geblieben.
> *During his whole life this artist has clung (held; stuck; been faithful) to the same view of art.*

**verhageln** (fig. u. fam.): cf. **schiefgehen**

wie **verhext** sein: *to be cursed; to be out of joint; to have an evil spell on it; there is a hoodoo on s.th.*

> Heute ist alles wie verhext. Ich kann weder meinen Füllfederhalter noch meinen Bleistift finden.
> *Everything is cursed (out of joint; has an evil spell on it; There is a hoodoo on everything) today. I cannot find either my pen or my pencil.*

j.en **verhohnepipeln** (fam.): cf. j.en auf den **Arm** nehmen

etwas **verhunzen** (fam.): cf. etwas **vermurksen**

sein Geld **verjuxen** (fam.): cf. sein Geld **verprassen**

etwas **verkloppen** (fam.): *to flog s. th. (sl.)*
> Um mir einen Tennisschläger kaufen zu können, habe ich meine alte Aktentasche verkloppt (verscheuert; versilbert).
> *I flogged my old brief-case to buy myself a new tennis-racquet.*

j.en **verkloppen** (fam.): cf. j.en **vermöbeln**

in j.en **verknallt** sein (fam.): cf. in j.en **verschossen** sein

j.en nicht **verknusen** können (fam.): cf. j.en nicht **riechen** können

j.en **verkohlen** (fam.): cf. j.em einen **Bären** aufbinden

etwas **verkorksen** (fam.): cf. etwas **vermurksen**

sich **verkrachen** (fam.): *to fall out; to have a row (colloq.)*
> Die beiden ehemaligen Freunde haben sich leider verkracht.
> *The two former friends have unfortunately fallen out (had a row).*

sich **verkrümeln** (fig. u. fam.): cf. sich auf **französisch** empfehlen

sein Geld **verläppern** (fam.): cf. sein Geld **verprassen**

mit **Verlaub** zu sagen: *with all (due) respect; if I may say so; saving your (his etc.) presence*
> Mein Chef ist wirklich, mit Verlaub (Respekt) zu sagen, ein rücksichtsloser Autofahrer.
> *With all (due) respect (If I may say so; Saving his presence), my boss really is a reckless driver.*

sich **verlohnen**: cf. sich **rentieren**

**verlottern (verludern)** (fam.): cf. auf die abschüssige (schiefe) **Bahn** geraten

sich einen **Verlust** ans Bein binden (fig. u. fam.): *to cut one's losses; to pour money down the drain (sl.)*
> Ich spiele jetzt nicht mehr in der Lotterie. Ich will mir nicht ständig einen Verlust ans Bein binden.
> *I am not going to gamble in the sweepstake any more. I don't want to keep on cutting my losses (pouring money down the drain).*

etwas **vermasseln** (fam.): cf. etwas **vermurksen**

j.en **vermöbeln** (fam.): *to give s.b. a good hiding (drubbing) (colloq.); to pitch into s.b. (sl.); to beat s.b. up (sl.)*

Als ich den Dieb erwischte, habe ich ihn ordentlich vermöbelt (durchgebleut; durchgewichst; verdroschen; verkloppt).
*When I caught the thief I gave him a good hiding (drubbing; I pitched into him [beat him up] properly).*

etwas **vermurksen** (fam.): *to mess (to muck) s.th. up (sl.); to make a mess (muck) of s.th. (sl.)*

Dieses Orchester hat die neue Symphonie schlimm vermurkst (verhackstückt; verhunzt; verkorkst; vermasselt; verpatzt; verpfuscht).
*That orchestra fairly messed (mucked) up the new symphony (made a proper mess [muck] of the new symphony).*

wie **vernagelt** sein (fig. u. fam.): cf. ein **Brett** vor dem Kopf haben

in j.en **vernarrt** sein: cf. in j.en **verschossen** sein

j.em eine **verpassen** (fig. u. fam.): cf. j.em eine **kleben**

etwas **verpatzen** (fam.): cf. etwas **vermurksen**

j.en **verpetzen** (fam.): *to give s.b. away; to sneak (to split) on s.b. (colloq.); to blow the gaff about s.b. (colloq.); to rat on s.b. (sl.).* Cf. auch: **petzen**

Weißt du, wer uns verpetzt (angepetzt; verpfiffen) hat?
*Do you know who gave us away (who sneaked [split; ratted] on us; who blew the gaff about us)?*

j.en **verpfeifen** (fam.): cf. j.en **verpetzen**

etwas **verpfuschen** (fam.): cf. etwas **vermurksen**

sein Geld **verprassen**: *to squander (to fritter away) one's money; to blue one's money (colloq.)*

Es ist unverantwortlich von ihm, so sein Geld zu verprassen (verjuxen; verläppern; verpulvern; verwichsen).
*It is irresponsible of him to squander (blue; fritter away) his money like that.*

sein Geld **verpulvern** (fam.): cf. sein Geld **verprassen**

j.en nicht **verputzen** können (fam.): cf. j.en nicht **riechen** können

etwas **verquatschen** (fam.): *to pervert s.th.; to garble s.th.; to give a false colouring to s.th.; to put a false complexion on s.th.*

Der Zeitungsbericht hat die Tatsachen völlig verquatscht.
*The newspaper report completely perverted (garbled; gave a completely false colouring to; put a completely false complexion on) the facts.*

j.em **verquer** gehen (fam.): cf. **schiefgehen**

in etwas **verrannt** sein (fig. u. fam.): cf. sich in etwas **verbeißen**

j.en (etwas) **verreißen** (fam.): cf. keinen guten **Faden** an j.em (etwas) lassen

wie **verrückt** (wie ein **Verrückter**) kämpfen: cf. wie ein **Berserker** kämpfen

wie **verrückt** (wie ein **Verrückter**) laufen (fam.): *to run like one possessed; to run like mad (colloq.); to run like a house on fire (colloq.).* Cf. auch: laufen wie ein **Besenbinder**

> Karl war zu spät aus dem Hause gegangen und mußte wie verrückt ([wie ein Verrückter]; wie besessen [irrsinnig; toll]; wie ein Irrer) laufen (mußte laufen, als ob er den Teufel im Nacken habe), um noch rechtzeitig an den (zum) Bahnhof zu kommen.
> *Charles was late leaving the house and had to run like one possessed (like mad; like a house on fire) to get to the station in time.*

sich keinen **Vers** aus etwas machen können (fig. u. fam.): *not to be able to make s.th. out (to make sense of s.th.); not to be able to make head or tail of s.th. (colloq.)*

> Dieses Buch ist soeben erschienen, doch in keiner Buchhandlung zu bekommen. Daraus kann ich mir keinen Vers (Reim) machen.
> *This book has just been published but it is not to be had in any bookseller's. I cannot make it out (make sense of it; make head or tail of it).*

**versacken** (fig. u. fam.): cf. auf die abschüssige (schiefe) **Bahn** geraten

j.em etwas **versalzen** (fig. u. fam.): cf. j.em die **Suppe** versalzen

**versauern** (fam.): *to vegetate; to go to seed (colloq.)*

> In diesem armseligen Dorf muß jeder früher oder später versauern.
> *In this miserable village everyone must vegetate (go to seed) sooner or later.*

**verscheuern** (fam.): cf. **verkloppen**

**verschlampen** (fam.): a) (von Personen) cf. auf die abschüssige (schiefe) **Bahn** geraten; b) (von Sachen) *to let s.th. go to rack and ruin; to let things slide*

Dieser Haushalt ist sehr unordentlich, weil die Frau alle Sachen verschlampt.
*This house is very untidy, because the wife lets everything go to rack and ruin (lets things slide).*

seine Absichten **verschleiern** (fig.): *to veil (to disguise; to hide; to conceal) one's intentions; to keep one's cards (well) hidden*

Ich weiß nicht, was dieser Mann will, denn er verschleiert seine wahren Absichten.
*I do not know what this man wants, because he veils (disguises; hides; conceals) his true intentions (keeps his cards [well] hidden).*

j.es Worte **verschlingen** (fig.): *to lap up s.b.'s words*

Wir haben die Worte des Redners geradezu verschlungen.
*We simply lapped up the speaker's words.*

in j.en **verschossen** sein (fig. u. fam.): *to be smitten with love for s.b.; to have fallen for s.b. (colloq.); to be soft on (gone on) s.b. (sl.).* Cf. auch: sich bis über die **Ohren** in j.en verlieben

Merkst du denn nicht, daß mein Bruder in deine Schwester verschossen (verknallt; vernarrt) ist?
*Can't you see that my brother is smitten with love (has fallen) for (is soft [gone] on) your sister?*

etwas **verschwitzen** (fig. u. fam.): *it goes out of s.b.'s head (mind)*

Ich sollte heute abend zu einem ehemaligen Schulkameraden kommen, habe es aber total verschwitzt.
*I was supposed to go to an old school-friend's this evening but it completely went out of my head (mind).*

ehe man sich's **versieht:** cf. im **Handumdrehen**

etwas **versilbern** (fig. u. fam.): cf. etwas **verkloppen**

mit seinem **Verstand** zu (am) Ende sein: cf. mit seiner **Kunst** zu Ende sein

Der **Verstand** bleibt einem stehen (steht einem still) (fig.): *It is beyond s.b.; S.b. cannot make it out; It beats s.b. (colloq.).* Cf. auch: sich keinen **Vers** aus etwas machen können

Zuerst hat man sein Gemälde abgelehnt, und nun hat es einen Ehrenplatz in der Galerie. Da bleibt mir der Verstand stehen (steht mir der Verstand still).
*First they rejected his painting and now it has a place of honour in the gallery. It is beyond me (I cannot make it out; It beats me).*

wie **versteinert** dastehen: cf. (wie) zur **Salzsäule** erstarrt sein

sich in etwas **verstricken** (fig.): *to get tied up (tangled up) in s.th.; to tie (to tangle) o.s. up in s.th.*

Der Angeklagte hat sich in Widersprüche verstrickt (verfangen; verwickelt).
*The accused got tied (tangled) up (tied [tangled] himself up) in contradictions.*

einen **Versuchsballon** steigen lassen (fig.): cf. einen **Fühler** ausstrecken

ein **Versuchskaninchen (-karnickel)** sein (fig. u. fam.): *to be a guinea-pig*
Der Arzt probiert eine neue Behandlungsmethode aus, und ich gehöre zu seinen Versuchskaninchen (-karnickeln).
*The doctor is trying out a new method of treatment and I am one of his guinea-pigs.*

in Gedanken **versunken** sein (fig.): *to be sunk (buried; lost) in thought*
Als wir eintraten, saß der alte Mann in Gedanken versunken in seinem Lehnstuhl.
*As we entered, the old man was sitting in his armchair, sunk (buried; lost) in thought.*

sich in seine Bücher **vertiefen** (fig.): cf. sich in seine Bücher **vergraben**

ein übler **Vertreter** sein (fig. u. fam.): cf. ein übler **Kunde** sein

etwas **vertuschen:** *to keep s. th. quiet; to hush s. th. up*
Ich habe vergebens versucht, das unangenehme Vorkommnis zu vertuschen.
*I tried in vain to keep the unpleasant event quiet (to hush up the unpleasant event).*

sein Geld **verwichsen** (fam.): cf. sein Geld **verprassen**

sich in etwas **verwickeln** (fig.): cf. sich in etwas **verstricken**

eine babylonische **Verwirrung** (fig.): *a Babel of tongues*
Unter den Delegierten der verschiedenen Länder herrschte eine babylonische Verwirrung.
*There was a Babel of tongues among the delegates from the different countries.*

**Vetternwirtschaft** (fig. u. fam.): *wire-pulling; backstairs influence; back-scratching (colloq.); the old school-tie (colloq.)*
Durch gute Beziehungen läßt sich natürlich viel erreichen. Ich bin aber grundsätzlich gegen jede Vetternwirtschaft.
*One can, of course, achieve a lot through good contacts, but I am in principle against any wire-pulling (backstairs influence; back-scratching; the old school-tie).*

eine **Viecherei** sein (fam.): cf. eine **Herkulesarbeit** sein

hausen (leben) wie das liebe **Vieh** (fam.): *to live like cattle (like animals)*
Nach dem letzten Kriege mußten viele Flüchtlinge hausen (leben) wie das liebe Vieh.
*After the last war many refugees were forced to live like cattle (animals).*

saufen wie das liebe **Vieh** (fam.): cf. saufen wie ein **Loch**

**j.en viehisch** behandeln: *to treat s.b. bestially (abominably; brutally); to treat s.b. like a dog (like a cur; like dirt)*

Der Aufseher soll die Gefangenen viehisch behandelt haben.
*The guard is said to have treated the prisoners bestially (abominably; brutally; like dogs; like curs; like dirt).*

**viel** auf j.en (etwas) geben: *to set great store by s.b. (s.th.); to attach great importance (value; weight) to s.th. (s.b.).* Cf. auch: großes **Gewicht** auf etwas legen

Ich gebe viel auf die Meinung meines Vetters.
*I set great store by (attach great importance [value; weight] to) my cousin's opinion.*

ein **Vielfraß** sein (fam.): cf. ein **Freßsack** sein

nicht bis **vier** zählen können (fig. u. fam.): cf. nicht bis **drei** zählen können

auf allen **vieren:** *on all fours*

Der Einbrecher kroch auf allen vieren um das Haus herum.
*The burglar crept round the house on all fours.*

alle **viere** von sich strecken (fam.): *to stretch out full length*

Ich war so furchtbar müde, daß ich mich in den Sessel warf und alle viere von mir streckte.
*I was so terribly tired that I threw myself into the armchair and stretched out full length.*

sich für j.en **vierteilen** lassen (fig.): cf. für j.en durchs **Feuer** gehen

eine **Visage** machen (fam.): cf. ein **Gesicht** machen wie sieben Tage Regenwetter; ein schiefes **Gesicht** machen

den **Vogel** abschießen (fig.): *to win the day; to bring home the bacon; to cap the lot (colloq.); to hit the jackpot (sl.).* Cf. auch: das **Rennen** machen

Georg hat in seiner Klasse den besten Aufsatz geschrieben. Ich habe gewußt, daß er den Vogel abschießen würde.
*George wrote the best essay in his class. I knew that he would win the day (bring home the bacon; cap the lot; hit the jackpot).*

Der **Vogel** ist ausgeflogen (ist fort) (fig.): *The bird has flown.* Cf. auch: das **Nest** leer finden; über alle **Berge** sein

Als man den Übeltäter in seiner Wohnung verhaften wollte, war der Vogel ausgeflogen (fort).
*When they wanted to arrest the offender in his house, the bird had flown.*

Friß, **Vogel,** oder stirb! (fig.): *It's do or die; It's sink or swim*

Du mußt dich jetzt entscheiden, ob du es tun willst oder nicht. Friß, Vogel, oder stirb! (Entweder – oder!)
*You must decide now whether you want to do it or not. It's do or die (sink or swim).*

einen **Vogel** haben (fig. u. fam.): cf. nicht richtig im **Dachstübchen** sein

sich wohlfühlen wie der **Vogel** im Hanfsamen: cf. sich wohlfühlen wie die **Made** im Speck

ein lockerer **Vogel** sein (fig. u. fam.): cf. eine leichte **Fliege** sein

ein lustiger **Vogel** sein (fig.): *to be a gay bird (gay dog) (colloq.); to be a cheerful chappie (colloq.); to be a bright spark (colloq.).* Cf. auch: **kreuzfidel** sein
> In seiner Gesellschaft langweilt man sich nicht. Er ist ein lustiger Vogel.
> *One is never bored in his company. He is a gay bird (dog; a cheerful chappie; a bright spark).*

aus der **Vogelperspektive (-schau)** gemacht: *a bird's-eye view*
> Diese Aufnahme von unserer Stadt ist aus der Vogelperspektive (-schau) gemacht worden.
> *This photograph of our town is a bird's-eye view.*

wie eine **Vogelscheuche** aussehen (fam.): *to look a fright (a sight) (colloq.); to look like a scarecrow (colloq.)*
> Deine alte Tante sieht aus wie eine richtige Vogelscheuche (eine Eule [Nachteule]; eine häßliche Ziege; sieht verboten) aus.
> *Your old aunt looks a proper fright (sight; like a proper scarecrow).*

**Vogelstraußpolitik** machen (treiben) (fig.): cf. den **Kopf** in den Sand stecken

j.en (etwas) nicht für **voll** ansehen (nehmen): *not to take s.b. (s.th.) seriously; not to pay any heed (attention) to s.b. (s.th.); not to give s.b. (s.th.) a thought; to take s.b. with a grain of salt.* Cf. auch: etwas cum **grano salis** nehmen
> Du solltest dich über diesen dummen Menschen nicht ärgern. Du mußt ihn nicht für voll ansehen (nehmen).
> *You ought not to get annoyed about that stupid person. You don't have to take him seriously (to pay any heed [attention] to him; to give him a thought; You must take him with a grain of salt).*

aus dem **vollen** schöpfen (fig.): *to draw on (to call on) unlimited resources; to have a full purse*
> Wer aus dem vollen schöpfen kann, braucht um die Zukunft keine Angst zu haben.
> *Anyone who can draw (call) on unlimited resources (who has a full purse) does not need to be anxious about the future.*

**vollgepfropft** sein: *to be packed tight; to be full to overflowing.* Cf. auch: **eingepfercht** sitzen; gedrängt wie die **Heringe** sitzen

Als wir in den Zug steigen wollten, waren alle Abteile schon vollgepfropft.
*When we wanted to get into the train, all the compartments were packed tight (were packed to overflowing).*

sich **vollaufen** lassen (fam.): cf. (sich) einen hinter die **Binde** gießen

**von wegen!** (fam.): cf. Ja, **Puste** (Pustekuchen)

der **Vorbote** sein (fig.): *to be the herald (harbinger); to herald*

Dein Schnupfen kann der Vorbote einer ernsthaften Erkrankung sein.
*Your cold may be the herald (harbinger) of (may herald) a serious illness.*

ein **Vorgeschmack** sein (fig.): *to be a foretaste (a taste of what is to come)*

Die Generalprobe des Lustspiels war für die Zuhörer ein angenehmer Vorgeschmack.
*The dress rehearsal of the comedy was a pleasant foretaste for the audience (a pleasant taste for the audience of what was to come).*

die **Vorhand** haben (fig.): *to have priority (precedence); to have (to get) first choice*

Bei allen Veranstaltungen haben frühere Abonnenten die Vorhand.
*For all performances former season-ticket holders have (get) priority (precedence; first choice).*

j.em die **Vorhand** lassen (fig.): *to give way to s.b.; to make way for s.b.; to leave the way open for s.b.*

Wenn du gern in diesen Film gehen möchtest, will ich auf meine Eintrittskarte verzichten und dir die Vorhand lassen (den Vorrang einräumen).
*If you would like to go to that film, I will give up my ticket and give way to (make way for; leave the way open for) you.*

j.em etwas **vorkauen** (fig. u. fam.): *to spoon-feed s.b. with s.th. (colloq.); to feed s.th. into s.b. (colloq.).* Cf. auch: j.em etwas **einbleuen**

Mein Neffe ist nicht sehr begabt. Man muß ihm alles vorkauen.
*My nephew is not very gifted; one has to spoon-feed him with everything (feed everything into him).*

sich j.en **vorknöpfen** (fig. u. fam.): *to button (to grab; to nab) s.b. (colloq.)*

Der Polizist hat sich den Rädelsführer vorgeknöpft, gerade als er seine Wohnung verließ.
*The policeman buttoned (grabbed; nabbed) the ringleader just as he was leaving his house.*

j.en von **vorn** und hinten betrügen: cf. j.en von **hinten** und von vorn betrügen

j.em etwas **vorpredigen** (fig. u. fam.): cf. j.em etwas **einbleuen** j.em den **Vorrang** einräumen: cf. j.em die **Vorhand** lassen

einer Sache **Vorschub** leisten: *to encourage s. th.; to give an impetus (a boost; a spur) to s. th.; to be a stimulus to s. th.*

Die unsicheren Jahre nach dem Krieg haben mancher unehrlichen Handlung Vorschub geleistet.
*The unsettled years after the war encouraged (gave an impetus [a boost; a spur] to; were a stimulus to) many dishonest actions.*

**Vorsicht** ist die Mutter der Weisheit (Sprichw.): cf. Vorsicht ist die **Mutter** der Weisheit

**vorsintflutlich:** *antediluvian.* Cf. auch: **altfränkisch** sein

In ihren alten Kleidern sieht meine Tante richtig vorsintflutlich aus.
*My aunt looks really antediluvian in her old clothes.*

einen **Vorsprung** vor j.em haben (fig.): *to have a start on s. b.; to have an advantage over s. b.*

Da Heinrich schon privat Englisch gelernt hatte, hatte er einen Vorsprung vor seinen Mitschülern.
*As Henry had already learnt English privately, he had a start on (an advantage over) his fellow-pupils.*

(nur) eine schwache **Vorstellung** von etwas haben: cf. (nur) eine schwache **Ahnung** von etwas haben

den **Vortritt** vor j.em haben: *to take (to have) precedence (priority) over s. b.* Cf. auch: j.em die **Vorhand** lassen

Der Präsident hat den Vortritt vor seinen Ministern.
*The president takes (has) precedence (priority) over his ministers.*

auf einem **Vulkan** leben (fig.): cf. wie auf einem **Pulverfaß** sitzen


# W


sich die **Waage** halten (fig.): *to balance each other; to cancel each other out*

Die Vorteile und die Nachteile unserer Wohnung halten sich die Waage.
*The advantages and the disadvantages of our flat balance each other (cancel each other out).*

etwas auf die **Waage** legen (fig.): cf. etwas auf die **Goldwaage** legen

in die **Waagschale** fallen (fig.): *to carry (considerable) weight; to tilt (to tip) the scales; to sway the balance*

Bei seiner Ernennung fiel ein langer Auslandsaufenthalt in die Waagschale.
*A long period abroad carried (considerable) weight (tilted [tipped] the scales; swayed the balance) in his appointment.*

etwas auf die **Waagschale** legen (fig.): cf. etwas auf die **Goldwaage** legen

etwas in die **Waagschale** werfen (fig.): *to throw s.th. into the scale; to bring s.th. into play (to the fore); to put one's weight behind s.th.*

Der Minister mußte bei der Durchbringung dieses Gesetzes seinen ganzen Einfluß in die Waagschale werfen.
*The minister had to throw all his influence into the scale (to bring all his influence into play [to the fore]) to get that law through (had to put all his weight behind getting that law through).*

j.en **wachrütteln** (fig.): *to shake (to ginger) s.b. up (colloq.); to prod s.b. (colloq.)*

Da Fritz sehr indolent ist, muß man ihn wachrütteln, damit er sich zum Handeln entschließt.
*Since Fred is very indolent, one has to shake (ginger) him up (prod him) in order to make him act.*

weich wie **Wachs** (wie weiches Wachs; **wachsweich**) sein: *to be like wax (like butter; like clay)*

Dieser gutmütige Vater gibt seinen Kindern in allem nach. Er ist weich wie Wachs (wie weiches Wachs; wachsweich) in ihren Händen.
*That goodnatured father gives way to his children in everything. He is like wax (butter; clay) in their hands.*

**wackelig** stehen (fig.): *to be shaky (rocky; rickety) (colloq.)*

Dieser Geschäftsmann scheint dem Bankrott nahe zu sein. Jedenfalls steht er (steht es mit ihm) sehr wackelig (knistert es [bei ihm] im Gebälk).
*This shop-keeper appears to be near bankruptcy. At all events his business is very shaky (rocky; rickety).*

j.en mit seinen eigenen **Waffen** schlagen (fig.): *to beat s.b. at his own game; to hoist s.b. with his own petard*

Der Redner der Oppositionspartei zitierte einige unkluge Äußerungen des Ministers und schlug ihn so mit seinen eigenen Waffen.
*The opposition speaker quoted a few of the minister's rash statements and so beat him at his own game (hoisted him with his own petard).*

**Waffen** gegen sich schmieden (fig.): cf. sich sein eigenes **Grab** graben

die **Waffen** strecken (fig.): *to lay down one's arms; to lower one's colours; to haul down (to strike) one's flag; to call the operation off*

Als er sah, daß er das Schachspiel verlieren würde, streckte er die Waffen (strich er die Flagge [Segel]) und gab auf.

*When he saw that he was going to lose the game of chess, he laid down his arms (lowered his colours; hauled down [struck] his flag; called the operation off) and gave up.*

sich nicht an den **Wagen** fahren lassen (fig.): *not to stand for s.th.; not to put up with s.th.; not to stick s.th. (colloq.)*

Dieser Mensch soll sich hüten mit seinen Drohungen. Denn ich lasse mir nicht an den Wagen fahren.

*That man had better look out with his threats. I am not going to stand for them (not going to put up with them; not going to stick them).*

Erst **wäge(n)**, dann wage(n) (Sprichw.): *Look before you leap (prov.)*

Du solltest dir genau überlegen, was du tust. Erst wäge(n), dann wage(n)!

*You ought to consider properly what you are doing. Look before you leap.*

Wer nichts **wagt,** der nichts gewinnt (Sprichw.): *Nothing venture, nothing gain (prov.)*

Wenn du weiterhin so zaghaft bleibst, wirst du nichts erreichen. Wer nichts wagt, der nichts gewinnt.

*If you go on being so hesitant, you will not achieve anything. Nothing venture, nothing gain.*

**waghalsig** (ein **Wagehals**) sein: *to be a daredevil*

Du mußt aufpassen, daß dieser waghalsige Kerl (dieser Wagehals) dich nicht in Gefahr bringt.

*You must take care that that daredevil does not lead you into danger.*

wie ein **Wahnsinniger** kämpfen: cf. kämpfen wie ein **Berserker**

Was lange **währt,** wird endlich gut (Sprichw.): *Good work takes time*

Viele Hindernisse waren zu überwinden, bis die neue Straße dem Verkehr übergeben werden konnte.

*There were many obstacles to overcome before the new road could be opened to traffic. Good work takes time.*

etwas nicht **wahrhaben** wollen: cf. etwas nicht **Wort** haben wollen

j.em die (reine; ungeschminkte) **Wahrheit** sagen: *to tell s.b. the plain, unvarnished truth; to tell s.b. a few home truths; to tell s.b. the facts of the case.* Cf. auch: j.em **heimleuchten;** j.em klaren **Wein** einschenken

Wenn er unverschämt werden sollte, werden wir ihm die (reine; ungeschminkte) Wahrheit sagen.

*If he should become impudent, we shall tell him the plain, unvarnished truth (a few home truths; the facts of the case).*

j.em gegenüber der reinste **Waisenknabe** sein (fig.): cf. eine **Null** sein

den **Wald** vor lauter Bäumen nicht sehen (fig.): *not to be able to see the wood for the trees*

> Durch die Beschäftigung mit Einzelfragen hat der junge Student das Hauptproblem gar nicht erkannt. Er hat den Wald vor lauter Bäumen nicht gesehen.
> *By concerning himself with individual questions the young student has not recognised the main problem at all. He cannot see the wood for the trees.*

Wie man in den **Wald** hineinruft, so schallt es zurück (Sprichw.): cf. Was der Mensch **säet,** das wird er ernten

husch, husch, die **Waldfee** machen (fig. u. fam.): cf. **fünf(e)** gerade sein lassen

immer die gleiche **Walze** sein (fig. u. fam.): cf. die gleiche (alte) **Leier** sein

zum **Wälzen** sein (fig. u. fam.): cf. zum **Piepen** sein

ein **Wälzer** (fam.): *a tome*

> Einen solchen Wälzer möchte ich nicht durcharbeiten müssen.
> *I should not like to have to work through such a tome.*

j.en an die **Wand** drücken (fig.): *to send (to drive) s.b. to the wall*

> Dieser ruchlose Mann hat alle seine Gegner an die Wand gedrückt.
> *This ruthless man has sent (driven) all his rivals to the wall.*

um die **Wände** (die **Wand**) hochzugehen (fam.): cf. um auf die **Bäume** zu klettern

**Wände** haben Ohren: *Walls have ears*

> Sprich bitte leiser! Wände haben Ohren!
> *Please talk more softly. Walls have ears.*

leeren **Wänden** predigen (fig.): cf. tauben **Ohren** predigen

in seinen vier **Wänden:** *within one's own four walls; on one's home ground (colloq.)*

> Mein Vater bleibt am liebsten in seinen vier Wänden (Pfählen).
> *My father likes best to stay within his own four walls (on his home ground).*

weiß wie die **Wand** sein: *to be as white as a sheet; to be deathly pale (as pale as a ghost [as death])*

> Heinrich kann doch nicht gesund sein. Er sieht weiß wie die Wand (wie ein Laken [Tischtuch]; leichenblaß; totenblaß [-bleich]; wie Kreide) aus (Er ist nur noch ein Geist).
> *Henry cannot be healthy. He looks as white as a sheet (deathly pale; as pale as a ghost [as death]).*

nicht **wanken** und nicht weichen (fig.): *not to budge (an inch); not to give way an inch*

> Mein Entschluß steht fest. Ich werde nicht wanken und nicht weichen (keinen Zoll breit nachgeben).
> *My decision is firm. I shall not budge ([an inch]; shall not give way an inch).*

sich den **Wanst** vollhauen (-schlagen) (fam.): cf. sich den **Bauch** vollschlagen

platt wie 'ne **Wanze** sein (fam.): cf. platt wie 'ne **Flunder** sein

Gute **Ware** lobt sich selber (Sprichw.): *Good wine needs no bush (prov.)*

> Was soll diese ganze Reklame? Gute Ware lobt sich selber.
> *What is the use of all this advertising? Good wine needs no bush.*

mit j.em nicht **warm** werden können (fig.): *not to be able to work up (to feel) any enthusiasm (warmth) for s.b.; not to feel drawn to s.b.; not to be able to warm to s.b.*

> Karl ist charakterlich so von mir verschieden, daß ich mit ihm nicht warm werden kann.
> *Charles is so different from me in character that I cannot work up (feel) any enthusiasm (warmth) for him (do not feel drawn to him; cannot warm to him).*

sich j.en **warmhalten** (fig.): *to keep in s.b.'s good books; to keep on the right side of s.b.; to keep (well) in with s.b.*

> Eine solche einflußreiche Persönlichkeit solltest du dir warmhalten, da sie dir noch nützlich sein kann.
> *You ought to keep in such an influential person's good books (on the right side of such an influential person; [well] in with such an influential person), for he may be useful to you.*

von hoher (der hohen) **Warte** aus (fig.): *from a lofty eminence; from lofty heights*

> Dieser Gelehrte betrachtet alle menschlichen Dinge von hoher (der hohen) Warte aus.
> *This scholar views all human matters from a lofty eminence (from lofty heights).*

Da kannst du lange **warten!** (fam.): *That's what you think! (colloq.); I wouldn't dream of it! (colloq.); Not on your life! (colloq.); You've got another think coming! (sl.)*

> Bildet er sich etwa ein, daß ich ihn zuerst grüßen werde? Da kann er lange warten!
> *Does he imagine that I am going to greet him first? That's what he thinks! (I wouldn't dream of it!; Not on your life!; He's got another think coming!)*

dumm aus der **Wäsche** gucken (fam.): *to look foolish; to pull a stupid face (colloq.); to look dumb (sl.)*

Als ich meinen Sohn fragte, wo sein Füllfederhalter hingekommen sei, hat er dumm aus der Wäsche geguckt.
*When I asked my son where his fountain-pen had got to, he looked foolish (dumb; pulled a stupid face).*

seine schmutzige **Wäsche** in der Öffentlichkeit (vor allen Leuten) waschen (fig.): *to wash one's dirty linen in public*

Wie konntest du vor Fremden so von deinen Familienangehörigen sprechen? Man soll doch nicht seine schmutzige Wäsche in der Öffentlichkeit (vor allen Leuten) waschen.
*How could you talk like that about members of your family in front of strangers! One must not wash one's dirty linen in public.*

ein **waschechter** Konservativer sein: *to be a dyed-in-the-wool conservative; to be a conservative to the backbone (to the core); to be a true-blue conservative.* Cf. auch: **kerndeutsch**; ein **Stockengländer** (usw.)

Mein Onkel ist ein waschechter Konservativer und wählt immer die Rechtsparteien.
*My uncle is a dyed-in-the-wool (true-blue) conservative (a conservative to the backbone [core]) and always votes for the parties of the Right.*

ein **Waschlappen** sein (fig. u. fam.): cf. ein **Muttersöhnchen** sein

ein altes **Waschweib** sein (fig. u. fam.): cf. eine **Klatschbase** sein

wie ein **Waschweib** tratschen (fam.): *to gossip like a washerwoman*

Meine Mutter kann es nicht vertragen, wenn wir jungen Mädchen wie die Waschweiber tratschen.
*My mother cannot stand us young girls gossiping like washerwomen.*

j.em (einer Sache) das **Wasser** abgraben (fig.): *to cut away the ground from beneath the feet of s.b. (s.th.); to steal s.b.'s (s.th.'s) thunder; to put s.b. (s.th.) out of a job*

Das neue Geschäft wird sicherlich den übrigen in der Umgegend das Wasser abgraben.
*The new shop will certainly cut the ground from beneath the feet of the others (will certainly steal the other's thunder) in the neighbourhood (will certainly put the others in the neigbourhood out of a job).*

(Das) **Wasser** hat keine Balken (Sprichw.): *There's nothing to walk on in the sea; Praise the sea but stay (keep) on land (prov.)*

Mein Freund fährt nicht gern mit dem Schiff, denn er behauptet: (Das) Wasser hat keine Balken.
*My friend does not like travelling by ship, for he says that there's nothing to walk on in the sea (says: Praise the sea but stay [keep] on land).*

bei **Wasser** und Brot sitzen: cf. in den **Kasten** kommen

übers große **Wasser** fahren: cf. über den großen **Teich** fahren

ins **Wasser** fallen (fig.): *to fall through; to come to naught (to nothing); to end in smoke*

> Wegen der Erkrankung der beiden Hauptdarsteller ist die Theateraufführung ins Wasser gefallen (zu Wasser [Essig] geworden; in die Binsen gegangen; im Eimer).
> *Because the two leading actors were indisposed, the performance fell through (came to naught [nothing]; ended in smoke).*

verschieden sein wie **Wasser** und Feuer: cf. **grundverschieden** sein

in trüben **Wassern** fischen (fig.): cf. im **trüben** fischen

Seitdem ist schon viel **Wasser** den Rhein (usw.) hinuntergeflossen: cf. Viele Jahre sind ins **Land** gegangen

Bis dahin fließt noch viel **Wasser** den Rhein (usw.) hinunter: *A lot of water will flow under the bridge before then*

> Bis die neue Straße gebaut ist, wird noch viel Wasser den Rhein (usw.) hinunterfließen.
> *A lot of water will flow under the bridge before the new road is built.*

nahe ans **Wasser** gebaut haben (fig.): *always to be turning on the waterworks; always to be opening the flood-gates*

> Meine Schwester hat nahe ans Wasser gebaut. Sie weint bei der geringsten Gelegenheit.
> *My sister is always turning on the waterworks (opening the flood-gates). She weeps on the most trivial occasions.*

mit allen **Wassern** gewaschen sein (fig.): cf. mit allen **Hunden** gehetzt sein

Das **Wasser** steht j.em bis an den Hals (bis an die Kehle) (fig.): cf. bis über die **Ohren** in Schulden stecken

sich über **Wasser** halten (fig.): cf. den **Kopf** über Wasser halten

auch nur mit **Wasser** kochen (fig.): *to be only human (only flesh and blood)*

> Glaube nur nicht, daß in anderen Familien alles immer in Ordnung ist. Dort wird auch nur mit Wasser gekocht.
> *Don't think that everything is always all right in other families. They are only human (flesh and blood) as well.*

**Wasser** auf j.es Mühle sein (fig.): *to be grist to s.b.'s mill; to be ammunition for s.b.; to give s.b. a boost (colloq.)*

Ich sagte ihm, ich würde genauso gehandelt haben wie er. Das war Wasser auf seine Mühle (Wind in sein Segel).
*I told him that I would have acted exactly as he had done. That was grist to his mill (ammunition for him; gave him a boost).*

Das **Wasser** läuft einem im Munde zusammen: *one's mouth waters*

Wenn ich an Karpfen denke, läuft mir das Wasser im Munde zusammen.
*My mouth waters when I think of carp.*

j.em nicht das **Wasser** reichen können (fig.): cf. nicht an j.en **tippen** können

von reinstem **Wasser** (fig.): cf. wie er im **Buche** steht
Stille **Wasser** sind (gründen) tief (Sprichw.): *Still waters run deep (prov.)*

Er sagt wenig, denkt aber viel. Stille Wasser sind (gründen) tief.
*He says little but thinks a lot. Still waters run deep.*

**Wasser** in den Wein der Begeisterung gießen (fig.): *to damp (to put a damper on) s.b.'s enthusiasm; to introduce a jarring note; to throw a spanner into the works*

Leider muß ich Wasser in den Wein deiner Begeisterung gießen (dir einen Dämpfer aufsetzen), denn das Gastspiel der berühmten Oper ist abgesagt worden.
*I am afraid I shall have to damp (put a damper on) your enthusiasm (to introduce a jarring note; to throw a spanner into the works), because the performance by the famous visiting opera-company has been cancelled.*

zu **Wasser** werden (fig.): cf. ins **Wasser** fallen

aussehen, als ob man kein **Wässerchen** trüben könnte (fig. u. fam.): *to look as if butter would not melt in one's mouth; to look a goody-goody (colloq.)*. Cf. auch: die **Unschuld** vom Lande sein

Alma sieht aus, als ob sie kein Wässerchen trüben könnte. In Wirklichkeit aber ist sie gar nicht so unschuldig.
*Alma looks as if butter would not melt in her mouth (looks a goody-goody), but in fact she is not so innocent at all.*

reden wie ein **Wasserfall** (fam.): cf. das **Blaue** vom Himmel herunterreden a); reden wie ein **Buch**

aussehen wie eine **Wasserleiche** (fam.): *to look washed out (colloq.); to look a wreck (colloq.); to look like death warmed up (sl.)*

Heinrich hatte am vorhergehenden Abend zu viel getrunken und sah am nächsten Morgen wie eine Wasserleiche (wie das Leiden Christi; wie Weißbier und Spucke) aus.
*Henry had drunk too much the previous night, and the next morning he looked washed out (looked a wreck; looked like death warmed up).*

wirken wie ein kalter **Wasserstrahl:** *to act like a cold douche (like a douche of cold water); to pull s.b. up (to stop s.b.) in his tracks*

> Deine unerwartete Mitteilung wirkte auf uns wie ein kalter Wasserstrahl (eine kalte Dusche).
> *Your unexpected information acted upon us like a cold douche (like a douche of cold water; pulled us up [stopped us] in our tracks).*

vom wilden **Waz** gebissen sein (fam.): cf. nicht richtig im **Dachstübchen** sein

j.em auf den **Wecker** fallen (fig. u. fam.): cf. j.em auf die **Nerven** fallen

j.em (einer Sache) den **Weg** bahnen (bereiten; ebnen) (fig.): *to pave the way for s.b. (s.th.); to prepare the ground for s.b. (s.th.); to tee s.th. up for s.b. (colloq.)*

> Mein Vater hatte mir bereits den Weg gebahnt (bereitet; geebnet; hatte bereits alles in die Wege geleitet), so daß ich die Stellung ohne weiteres bekam.
> *My father had already paved the way (prepared the ground) for me, so that I got the job without more ado. (My father had already teed the job up for me, so that I got it without more ado).*

sich einen **Weg** bahnen (fig.): *to carve out a path for o.s.; to cut a niche for o.s.; to make one's own way*

> Unter den heutigen Verhältnissen ist es schwierig, sich einen Weg zu bahnen.
> *Under present-day conditions it is hard to carve out a path (to cut a niche) for oneself (to make one's own way).*

auf dem besten **Wege** sein (fig.): *to be well on the way (road); to be on the highroad to success*

> Sein Sohn ist auf dem besten Wege, ein berühmter Jurist zu werden.
> *His son is well on the way (road) to becoming (is on the highroad to success as) a famous lawyer.*

etwas zu **Wege** bringen (fig.): *to bring s.th. off; to get s.th. through; to get s.th. done*

> Sie hat schon viel bei ihm erreicht; sie wird sicherlich auch das noch zu Wege bringen (noch deichseln; fingern; fummeln).
> *She has been very successful with him already, so she will be sure to bring this off (get this through [done]) as well.*

seine eigenen **Wege** gehen (fig.): *to go one's own way; to follow one's own path; to take one's own line*

> Dieser Wissenschaftler hält sich wenig an seine Vorgänger, sondern geht seine eigenen Wege.
> *This scientist does not follow his predecessors much but goes his own way (follows his own path; takes his own line).*

auf dem falschen **Wege** sein (fig.): cf. auf dem **Holzwege** sein

den **Weg** allen Fleisches gehen: *to go the way of all flesh*

Viele seiner Altersgenossen sind bereits den Weg allen Fleisches gegangen.
*Many of his contemporaries have already gone the way of all flesh.*

einen gangbaren **Weg** finden (fig.): *to find a viable (feasible; practicable) way*

Für die baldige Regelung unserer Angelegenheit haben wir jetzt einen gangbaren Weg zu finden.
*We have now got to find a viable (feasible; practicable) way of settling our matter.*

j.em (einer Sache) aus dem **Wege** gehen (fig.): *to keep out of s.b.'s (s.th.'s) way; to keep away from s.b. (s.th.); to fight shy of s.b. (s.th.); to keep (to steer) clear of s.b. (s.th.); to dodge s.b. (s.th.) (colloq.)*

Wilhelm geht mir schon seit Wochen aus dem Wege, weil er mir Geld schuldet.
*William has been keeping out of my way (keeping away from me; fighting shy of me; keeping [steering] clear of me; dodging me) for weeks, because he owes me money.*

seiner **Wege** gehen (fig.): *to go (on) one's way*

Ich gehe lieber meiner Wege, als daß ich mich in eine Streitigkeit einlasse.
*I would rather go (on) my way than get involved in a dispute.*

den geraden **Weg** gehen (fig.): *to follow (to keep to) the straight and narrow path*

Meine Tochter hat mir versprochen, in Zukunft den geraden Weg zu gehen.
*My daughter promised me to follow (keep to) the straight and narrow path in future.*

Damit hat es noch gute **Wege** (fig.): *That is still a long way off; There is still a long way to go (still plenty of time) before that.* Cf. auch: Bis dahin fließt noch viel **Wasser** den Rhein hinunter

Johann ist noch ein ganz junger Student. Bis zu seinem Examen hat es noch gute Wege (Weile).
*John is still a very young student. His examination is still a long way off (There is still a long way to go [still plenty of time] before his examination).*

j.em auf halbem **Wege** entgegenkommen (fig.): *to meet s.b. half-way; to split the difference; to strike a bargain with s.b.; to make (to do) a deal with s.b. (colloq.)*

Der Möbelhändler erklärte sich bereit, mir hinsichtlich des Preises auf halbem Wege entgegenzukommen.
*The furniture-dealer declared himself ready to meet me half-way (to split the difference; to strike a bargain with me; to make [to do] a deal with me) on the question of the price.*

auf halbem **Wege** stehenbleiben (fig.): *to stop half-way; in mid-career*

Bald werden wir unser Ziel erreichen; darum wollen wir nicht auf halbem Wege stehenbleiben.
*We shall soon reach our goal, so we don't want to stop half-way (in mid-career).*

j.em Hindernisse in den **Weg** legen (fig.): cf. j.em **Hindernisse** in den Weg legen

Der **Weg** zur Hölle ist mit guten Vorsätzen gepflastert (Sprichw.): *The way to hell is paved with good intentions (prov.)*

> Karl will Geld sparen, es gelingt ihm aber nicht. Der Weg zur Hölle ist mit guten Vorsätzen gepflastert.
> *Charles wants to save money but he never manages to. The way to hell is paved with good intentions.*

die krummen **Wege** lieben (fig.): *to follow (to get into) crooked paths (ways); to go crooked (colloq.)*

> Wer die krummen Wege (Touren) liebt, wird eines Tages mit dem Gericht zu tun haben (mit dem Gesetz in Konflikt geraten).
> *A person who follows (gets into) crooked paths ([ways]; who goes crooked) will one day come up against the law.*

j.em in (über) den **Weg** laufen: *to run into (across) s.b.; to chance across (to come across) s.b.; to bump into s.b. (colloq.)*

> Gestern bin ich einem alten Schulkameraden in (über) den Weg gelaufen.
> *Yesterday I ran (bumped) into ([across]; I chanced [came] across) an old schoolfriend.*

etwas in die **Wege** leiten (fig.): cf. j.em (einer Sache) den **Weg** bahnen

seinen **Weg** machen (fig.): *to make one's way in the world; to get on in the world; to make one's mark.* Cf. auch: es **weit** bringen

> Alle Kritiker sind davon überzeugt, daß der junge Pianist seinen Weg machen wird.
> *All the critics are convinced that the young pianist will make his way (will get on) in the world (will make his mark).*

neue **Wege** einschlagen (fig.): *to break new ground; to pioneer new (fresh) paths; to strike out in new directions*

> Die moderne Biologie hat neue Wege eingeschlagen.
> *Modern biology has broken new ground (pioneered new [fresh] paths; struck out in new directions).*

etwas aus dem **Wege** räumen (fig.): *to remove s.th.; to clear s.th. away; to get s.th. out of the way*

> Ich bin Ihnen sehr dankbar, daß Sie mir alle Schwierigkeiten aus dem Wege geräumt haben.
> *I am very grateful to you for having removed (cleared away) all my difficulties (got all my difficulties out of the way).*

j.en wieder auf den richtigen **Weg** bringen (fig.): *to put s.b. (s.b.'s feet) back on the right path ([road]; on the straight and narrow path); to set s.b. right again*

Dem Geistlichen ist es gelungen, den Verbrecher auf den richtigen Weg zu bringen.
*The clergyman has succeeded in putting the criminal (the criminal's feet) back on the right path ([road]; straight and narrow path; has succeeded in setting the criminal right again).*

Viele (Alle) **Wege** führen nach Rom (Sprichw.): cf. Viele (Alle) Wege führen nach **Rom**

j.em (einer Sache) im **Wege** stehen (fig.): cf. j.em (einer Sache) im **Lichte** stehen

sich selbst im **Wege** stehen (fig.): *to be one's own worst enemy; to queer one's own pitch*

Karl ist sehr begabt, aber faul und unzuverlässig. In dieser Hinsicht steht er sich selbst im Wege.
*Charles is very gifted, but lazy and unreliable. In this respect he is his own worst enemy (queers his own pitch).*

sich j.em in den **Weg** stellen (fig.): *to get in s.b.'s way; to bar s.b.'s way (path); to thwart s.b.*

Ein Tyrann vernichtet jeden, der sich ihm in den Weg stellt.
*A tyrant destroys everybody who gets in his way (who bars his way [path]; who thwarts him).*

j.em nicht über den **Weg** trauen (fig.): *not to trust s.b. further than one can see him; not to trust s.b. out of one's sight; not to trust s.b. an inch; not to trust s.b. further than one can throw him (colloq.)*

Einem unehrlichen Geschäftsmann ist nicht über den Weg zu trauen.
*One cannot trust a dishonest shopkeeper further than one can see (throw) him (cannot trust a dishonest shopkeeper out of one's sight [an inch]).*

den unteren **Weg** gehen (fig.): *to play second fiddle; to take a back seat; to knuckle under (colloq.); to sing small (colloq.)*

Als Angestellter mußt du den unteren Weg gehen und tun, was dir befohlen wird.
*As an employee you must play second fiddle (take a back seat; knuckle under; sing small) and do as you are told.*

j.em den **Weg** versperren (fig.): cf. j.em (einer Sache) im **Lichte** stehen

von **wegen!**: cf. Ja, **Puste** (Pustekuchen)

einen **weghaben** (fam.): cf. a) nicht richtig im **Dachstübchen** sein; b) einen **Schwips** haben ganz **wegsein** (fam.): cf. im siebenten **Himmel** sein

sich an j.en **wegwerfen** (fig.): *to throw o.s. at s.b.; to throw o.s. into s.b.'s arms.*
Cf. auch: sich j.em an den **Hals** werfen

Dieses Mädchen wirft sich an jeden jungen Mann weg.
*This girl throws herself at (into the arms of) every young man.*

mit **Weh** und Ach: cf. mit **Ach** und Krach

sich zur **Wehr** setzen (fig.): *to take up one's defence; to take up the challenge; to
take up cudgels on one's own behalf.* Cf. auch: sich seiner **Haut** wehren

Als der Architekt in der Tagespresse wegen seiner modernen Neubauten angegriffen wurde, hat er sich energisch zur Wehr gesetzt.
*When the architect was attacked in the daily press for his modern buildings, he vigorously
took up his own defence (took up the challenge; took up cudgels on his own behalf).*

ein freches **Weibsbild (-stück)** sein (fam.): cf. ein freches **Stück** sein

sich **weich** betten (weich gebettet sein) (fig.): *to have feathered one's (own)
nest very nicely; to be in clover; to be basking in the sunshine.* Cf. auch:
nicht auf **Rosen** gebettet sein

Durch seine Heirat mit einer reichen Frau hat sich mein Neffe weich gebettet
(ist mein Neffe jetzt weich gebettet).
*By marrying a rich woman my nephew has feathered his own nest very nicely (is now in
clover; is now basking in the sunshine).*

j.em **Weihrauch** streuen (fig.): *to laud (to praise; to extol) s.b. to the skies.*
Cf. auch: j.en (etw.) in den **Himmel** (er)heben

Ich verstehe nicht, warum man einem so unbedeutenden Menschen Weihrauch
streut (einen . . . beweihräuchert).
*I cannot understand why people laud (praise; extol) such an insignificant person to the
skies.*

Damit hat es noch gute **Weile:** cf. Damit hat es noch gute **Wege**

j.em klaren (reinen) **Wein** einschenken (fig.): *not to mince matters; to give
s.b. a piece of one's mind; to give it to s.b. straight from the shoulder (colloq.).* Cf.
auch: j.em die (ungeschminkte) **Wahrheit** sagen; **klipp** und klar sagen

Ich habe ihm klaren (reinen) Wein eingeschenkt und ihm gesagt, was ich von
seinem Benehmen halte.
*I did not mince matters but told him (gave him a piece of my mind [gave it to him straight
from the shoulder] and told him) what I thought of his behaviour.*

seine **Weisheit** für sich behalten: *to keep one's advice (one's opinion) to oneself;
to mind one's own business*

Ihre Vorschläge interessieren mich nicht. Behalten Sie Ihre Weisheit für sich. *Your suggestions do not interest me. Keep your advice (opinion) to yourself! (Mind your own business!)*

mit seiner **Weisheit** zu Ende sein: cf. mit seiner **Kunst** zu Ende sein

die **Weisheit** nicht mit Löffeln gegessen haben (fam.): *not to be a pillar of wisdom; not to be all that bright (colloq.); not to be such a bright spark (colloq.).* Cf. auch: das **Pulver** nicht erfunden haben

Jakob ist schon mit fünfzehn Jahren von der höheren Schule abgegangen. Er hat (ja auch) wirklich nicht die Weisheit mit Löffeln gegessen. *James left secondary school at fifteen. He was certainly not a pillar of wisdom (not all that bright; not such a bright spark).*

j.em etwas **weismachen**: cf. j.em einen **Bären** aufbinden

Was ich nicht **weiß**, macht mich nicht heiß (Sprichw.): *What the eye does not see, the heart does not grieve over (prov.)*

Solange ich diese Grausamkeit nicht selbst erlebe, kümmere ich mich nicht darum. Was ich nicht weiß, macht mich nicht heiß. *As long as I do not experience this cruelty for myself, I do not worry about it. What the eye does not see, the heart does not grieve over.*

aussehen wie **Weißbier** und Spucke (fam.): cf. aussehen wie eine **Wasserleiche**

sich bis zum **Weißbluten** verzehren (fig.): *to be bled white*

Im letzten Krieg hat sich unser Land bis zum Weißbluten verzehrt (ist unser Land bis aufs Blut ausgesaugt worden). *In the last war our country was bled white.*

j.en zur **Weißglut** bringen (fig.): *to make s.b. livid; to make s.b. boil; to make s.b. red-hot (colloq.)*

Mit bissigen Bemerkungen kann man ihn (bis) zur Weißglut (auf den Siedepunkt) bringen. *One can make him livid (boil; red-hot) with caustic remarks.*

**weit** und breit: *far and wide; for miles around*

Weit und breit war niemand zu sehen. *There was nobody to be seen far and wide (for miles around).*

es **weit** bringen (fig.): *to get on; to go (to come) a long way.* Cf. auch: seinen **Weg** machen

Dieser unternehmungslustige Mann hat es im Leben weit gebracht. *This enterprising man has got on (gone [come] a long way) in life.*

zu **weit** gehen (fig.): *to go too far; to overstep the mark; to overdo s.th.*

In deinen Forderungen bist du entschieden zu weit gegangen.
*You have definitely gone too far (overstepped the mark) in your demands (overdone your demands).*

mit j.em (etwas) nicht **weit** her sein (fig.): *to be nothing to write home about (colloq.); to be not up to much (not worth much) (colloq.); to be not much cop (sl.); to be no great shakes (sl.)*

Mit der Straßenbeleuchtung in unserer Stadt ist es nicht weit her.
*The street-lighting in our town is nothing to write home about (is not up to much [not worth much]; is not much cop; is no great shakes).*

**weitaus:** *far and away; by far*

Georg ist weitaus (bei weitem) der beste Spieler in unserm Tennisklub.
*George is far and away (by far) the best player in our tennis club.*

**weitblickend** (fig.): *far-sighted*

Was sagen Sie zu diesen weitblickenden Plänen?
*What do you say to these far-sighted plans?*

das **Weite** suchen: cf. **Fersengeld** geben

bei **weitem:** cf. **weitaus**

j.es **Weizen** blüht (fig.): *s.b.'s luck is in; s.b.'s ship has come in; fortune smiles on s.b.; the sun shines on s.b.*

Seitdem mein Konkurrent gestorben ist, blüht mein Weizen (lächelt mir das Glück).
*My luck has been in (My ship has come in; Fortune has smiled on me; The sun has shone on me) since my rival died.*

den **Weizen** von der Spreu sondern (fig.): cf. die **Böcke** von den Schafen sondern

alle **Welt:** *the whole world*

Alle Welt weiß, was geschehen ist, aber niemand spricht darüber.
*The whole world knows what has happened, but nobody speaks about it.*

nicht um alles in der **Welt** (nicht für die Welt): *not for the world; not for anything (on earth); not for all the tea in China; not if you paid me (colloq.); not for the life of me (colloq.)*. Cf. auch: **beileibe** nicht

Ich möchte nicht um alles in der Welt (nicht für die Welt) Junggeselle bleiben.
*I would not remain a bachelor for the world (for anything [on earth]; for all the tea in China; if you paid me; for the life of me).*

in einer anderen **Welt** sein (leben) (fig.): cf. in höheren **Regionen** schweben

die **Welt** aus den Angeln heben (fig.): *to shake the world to its foundations; to set the world aflame (afire); to turn the world upside-down*

> In seiner Jünglingszeit glaubt mancher, er könne die Welt aus den Angeln heben.
> *In his youth many a man thinks that he can shake the world to its foundations (set the world aflame [afire]; turn the world upside-down).*

nicht aus der **Welt** sein: *not to be out of the question; not to be such a remote possibility; not to be ruled out; to be on the cards*

> Daß dieser Witwer nochmals heiraten wird, ist nicht ganz aus der Welt (steht . . . außer Frage).
> *It is not completely out of the question (not such a remote possibility; cannot be ruled out; is quite on the cards) that that widower will marry again.*

am Ende der **Welt** (aus der Welt) wohnen: cf. in **Buxtehude** wohnen

in der ganzen **Welt:** cf. in **Stadt** und Land

ein Kind zur **Welt** bringen: *to give birth to a child*

> Meine Schwester ist sehr unglücklich, weil sie ein totes Kind zur Welt gebracht hat.
> *My sister is very unhappy because she has given birth to a still-born child.*

zur **Welt** kommen: cf. das **Licht** der Welt erblicken

nicht die **Welt** kosten (fig.): *not to cost the earth (world); not to cost all that much; not to ruin (to break) s.b. (colloq.)*

> Für die heißen Sommermonate solltest du dir einen Strohhut kaufen. Er kann ja nicht die Welt kosten (höllisch teuer sein).
> *You ought to buy yourself a straw hat for the hot summer months. It can't cost the earth (world; can't cost all that much; It won't ruin [break] you).*

ein Mann von **Welt (weltmännisch)** sein: *to be a man of the world; to be worldly-wise*

> Schon bei kurzer Unterhaltung merkt man ihm an, daß er ein Mann von Welt (sehr weltmännisch) ist.
> *Even in a short conversation with him one can see that he is a man of the world (very worldly-wise).*

Es gibt davon noch mehr auf der **Welt!:** *There's as good fish in the sea as ever came out of it (prov.); There are plenty more where that (that one) came from*

> Mein zuverlässiger Stellvertreter hat leider gekündigt, aber ich werde sicher noch einen guten anderen finden. Es gibt davon noch mehr auf der Welt.

*My reliable deputy has unfortunately given notice, but I am sure to find another good one. There's as good fish in the sea as ever came out of it (There are plenty more where that [one] came from).*

Dem Mutigen gehört die **Welt** (Sprichw.): *Fortune favours the brave (prov.).* Cf. auch: Wer nicht **wagt,** der nicht gewinnt

Dein unternehmungslustiger Junge wird sicherlich großen Erfolg haben. Dem Mutigen gehört die Welt.
*Your enterprising boy is sure to achieve great success. Fortune favours the brave.*

etwas aus der **Welt** schaffen (fig.): *to settle s. th.; to smooth s. th. over; to dispose of s. th.*

Den Rechtsanwälten der beiden Parteien ist es gelungen, die leidige Angelegenheit aus der Welt zu schaffen.
*The solicitors of the two parties succeeded in settling (disposing of) the embarrassing affair (in smoothing the embarrassing affair over).*

Da hört doch die **Weltgeschichte** auf! (fig. u. fam.): cf. Das ist doch die **Höhe!**

Viele **Wenig** machen ein Viel (Sprichw.): cf. **Kleinvieh** macht auch Mist

Wenn das **Wenn** und das Aber nicht wär'!: cf. Wenn das **Aber** nicht wär'!

nach vielem **Wenn** und Aber: *after a lot of ifs and buts; after a lot of humming and hawing (colloq.)*

Nach vielem Wenn und Aber (Hin und Her) hat die Stadtverwaltung den Bau eines Theaters genehmigt.
*After a lot of ifs and buts (humming and hawing) the town council approved the building of a theatre.*

Na, **wenn** schon!: *Well, what of it?; So what? (colloq.)*

Du hast deinen Ball verloren? Na, wenn schon! Du hast doch noch viele andere.
*You've lost your ball? Well, what of it? (So what?) You've got plenty more.*

**Wenn** schon, denn schon (fam.): *I (you etc.) must make it worth while; I (you etc.) must go the whole hog (colloq.); I (you etc.) must make a go of it (colloq.).* Cf. auch: Wer **A** sagt, muß auch B sagen

Für dieses Fest wollen wir möglichst viel Geld ausgeben. Wenn schon, denn schon!
*We are going to spend as much money as possible on this celebration. We must make it worth while (must go the whole hog; must make a go of it).*

die **Werbetrommel** rühren (fig.): cf. **Reklame** für etwas machen

Das **Werk** lobt den Meister (Sprichw.): *The work reveals (testifies to) the master*

Man sieht, daß dieses Bild von einem großen Künstler gemalt worden ist. Das Werk lobt den Meister.
*One can see that this picture was painted by a great artist. The work reveals (testifies to) the master.*

keinen **Wert** haben: cf. keinen **Sinn** und Verstand haben

großen **Wert** auf etwas legen: cf. großes **Gewicht** auf etwas legen

wie ein **Werwolf** essen (fressen): cf. essen (fressen) wie ein **Scheunendrescher**

viel **Wesens** von etwas machen: cf. viel **Wind** um (von) etwas machen

in ein **Wespennest** greifen (stechen) (fig.): *to put one's hand into a hornets' nest; to bring a hornets' nest about one's ears; to step into a clump of nettles.* Cf. auch: sich in die **Nesseln** setzen

Ich möchte Ihnen raten, sich nicht in diese Streitigkeit einzumischen. Sie würden nur in ein Wespennest greifen (stechen).
*I should advise you not to interfere in that dispute. You would only be putting your hand into a hornets' nest (only be bringing a hornets' nest about your ears; only be stepping into a clump of nettles).*

eine saubere (reine; weiße) **Weste** haben (fig. u. fam.): *to have a clean sheet (slate); not to have a blot on one's escutcheon; to have a spotless (immaculate) record*

Wir werden uns an diesem bedenklichen Unternehmen nicht beteiligen, weil wir eine saubere (reine; weiße) Weste behalten wollen.
*We shall not take part in this dubious enterprise because we want to keep a clean sheet (slate; do not want to have a blot on our escutcheon; want to keep a spotless [immaculate] record).*

j.em etwas unter die **Weste** schieben (fig. u. fam.): cf. j.em etwas aufs **Butterbrot** schmieren

j.en wie seine **Westentasche** kennen: cf. j.en **in-** und auswendig kennen

gut **Wetter** bei j.em machen (fig.): *to create a rosy atmosphere; to put s.b. in a good mood; to get on the right side of s.b.*

Deine Frau ist sehr verärgert; wenn du ihr aber einen Blumenstrauß mitbringst, wirst du gut Wetter bei ihr machen.
*Your wife is very annoyed, but if you take her a bunch of flowers, you will create a rosy atmosphere (will put her in a good mood; will get on her right side).*

vom schönen **Wetter** sprechen: *to talk about the weather*

Die Unterhaltung war sehr langweilig. Man sprach nur vom schönen Wetter.
*The conversation was very boring. People only talked about the weather.*

**wetterwendisch** sein (fig.): cf. den **Mantel** nach dem Wind hängen

ein **Wetterwinkel** sein (fig.): *to be a trouble-spot (trouble-area)*

Der Balkan ist oft ein Wetterwinkel der Geschichte gewesen.
*The Balkans have often been a trouble-spot (trouble-area) in history.*

**Wetterwolken** ziehen auf (fig.): *storm-clouds (dark clouds) are gathering*

Von Zeit zu Zeit ziehen Wetterwolken (Gewitterwolken) am politischen Himmel auf.
*From time to time storm-clouds (dark clouds) gather on the political horizon.*

etwas **wettmachen**: *to pay s.b. back for s.th.; to make s.th. good; to repay s.th.*

Den Gefallen, den er mir getan hat, habe ich längst wettgemacht.
*I paid him back for (made good; repaid) his favour to me long ago.*

in vollem **Wichs** erscheinen: cf. in vollem **Staat** erscheinen

kein **Wickelkind** mehr sein (fam.): *not to be a baby (a child) any more*

Du darfst mich nicht so behandeln. Ich bin doch kein Wickelkind mehr.
*You mustn't treat me like that. I'm not a baby (child) any more.*

Und **wie!**: cf. Und **ob!**

von der **Wiege** bis zur Bahre (bis zum Grabe): *from the cradle to the grave*

Von der Wiege bis zur Bahre (bis zum Grabe) hat dein Vater das Leben genossen.
*Your father enjoyed his life, from the cradle to the grave.*

flink wie ein **Wiesel** sein: *to be as lively as a cricket; to be as slippery as a weasel (as an eel); to be as nimble as a pickpocket*

Diesen Jungen wirst du niemals fangen. Er ist flink wie ein Wiesel.
*You will never catch that boy. He is as lively as a cricket (as slippery as a weasel [eel]; as nimble as a pickpocket).*

laufen wie ein **Wiesel**: cf. laufen wie ein **Besenbinder**

halb so **wild** sein (fam.): *not to be all that bad (serious); to be nothing to write home about (colloq.); to be nothing to get excited about (colloq.)*

Nun beruhige dich doch über den Schaden, den du angerichtet hast. Es ist ja halb so wild.
*Now do calm down about the damage you've caused. It's not all that bad (nothing to write home about; nothing to get excited about).*

arbeiten wie ein **Wilder**: cf. arbeiten wie ein **Pferd**

toben (sich gebärden) wie ein **Wilder**: *to rave like a madman (lunatic)*

Als Onkel Heinrich den Diebstahl bemerkte, tobte er (gebärdete er sich) wie ein Wilder.
*When Uncle Henry noticed the theft, he raved like a madman (lunatic).*

den dicken **Wilhelm** spielen (fam.): cf. **angeben**

Des Menschen **Wille** ist sein Himmelreich (Sprichw.): *A man's mind is his kingdom*

Mein Vetter will ein ganz armes Mädchen heiraten. Seine Eltern sind mit seinem Entschluß nicht einverstanden, aber des Menschen Wille ist sein Himmelreich.
*My cousin wants to marry a very poor girl. His parents do not agree with his decision, but a man's mind is his kingdom.*

Wo ein **Wille** ist, da ist auch ein Weg (Sprichw.): *Where there's a will, there's a way (prov.)*

Wir sind entschlossen, unsere Pläne durchzusetzen. Wo ein Wille ist, da ist auch ein Weg.
*We are determined to carry out our plans. Where there's a will, there's a way.*

Was du nicht **willst**, daß man dir tu', das füg' auch keinem andern zu (Sprichw.): *Do unto others as ye would they would do unto you (prov.); Love thy neighbour as thyself (prov.)*

Man soll im Leben zu niemandem ungerecht sein. Was du nicht willst, daß man dir tu', das füg' auch keinem andern zu.
*One must not be unjust to anybody in life. Do unto others as ye would they would do unto you (Love thy neighbour as thyself).*

von etwas **wimmeln**: *to swarm (to teem) with s.th.; to be riddled with s.th.; to be rotten with s.th. (colloq.); to be lousy (stiff) with s.b. (sl.)*

In den Sommermonaten wimmelt es in unserm schönen Städtchen von Touristen.
*In the summer months our lovely little town swarms (teems) with (is riddled [rotten; lousy; stiff] with) tourists.*

sich nicht an den **Wimpern** klimpern lassen (fig. u. fam.): *not to let o.s. be led by the nose; not to let o.s. be played about with (be mucked about) (colloq.); not to let o.s. be put upon (colloq.).* Cf. auch: sich nicht auf der **Nase** herumtanzen lassen

Ein so energischer Mann läßt sich nicht an den Wimpern klimpern.
*Such a vigorous man will not let himself be led by the nose (be played [mucked] about with; be put upon).*

ohne mit der **Wimper** zu zucken (fig.): cf. ohne eine **Miene** zu verziehen

von etwas **Wind** bekommen (fig.): *to get wind of s.th.; to get wise to s.th. (colloq.)*

Die Polizei hatte von dem geplanten Einbruch Wind bekommen und konnte die Übeltäter verhaften.
*The police had got wind of (got wise to) the burglary that had been planned, and were able to arrest the criminals.*

sich nach dem **Winde** drehen (fig.): cf. den **Mantel** nach dem Winde hängen

Jetzt pfeift der **Wind** aus einem anderen Loch (fig.): *Now the wind is blowing from another quarter; Now the boot is on the other foot*

Früher gab es keine Straßenverkehrsordnung. Jetzt aber pfeift der Wind aus einem anderen Loch, und jeder, der gegen die Vorschriften verstößt, wird bestraft.
*Formerly there were no traffic regulations, but now the wind is blowing from another quarter (now the boot is on the other foot), and anybody who breaks the rules is punished.*

viel **Wind** um (von) etwas machen (fig.): *to make a great song and dance about s.th. (colloq.); to make a great set-out (to-do) about s.th. (colloq.).* Cf. auch: etwas **aufbauschen**; (viel) **Brimborium** um etwas machen; (ein) großes **Getue** machen

Um diesen (Von diesem) ausländischen Film wird viel Wind (Aufhebens; Klamauk; Tamtam; Wesens; ein großes [viel] Theater) gemacht.
*There is a great song and dance (set-out; to-do) about this foreign film.*

sich den **Wind** um die Nase wehen (gehen) lassen (fig.): *to go out and have a look at the world*

Mein Vater will mich ins Ausland schicken, damit ich mir den Wind um die Nase wehen (gehen) lasse.
*My father wants to send me abroad so that I can go out and have a look at the world.*

Wer **Wind** säet, (der) wird Sturm ernten (Sprichw.): *He who sows a wind will reap a whirlwind (prov.)*

Wilhelm hat viele Bekannte verleumdet; doch jetzt hat man ihn angezeigt und seine Bestrafung verlangt. Wer Wind säet, (der) wird Sturm ernten.
*William slandered a great number of acquaintances but now he has been reported and his punishment demanded. He who sows a wind will reap a whirlwind.*

etwas in den **Wind** schlagen (fig.): *to throw s.th. to the (four) winds; to turn a deaf ear to s.th.; to make light of s.th.; to set s.th. at naught.* Cf. auch: gegen etwas **taub** sein

Ein trotziger Sohn schlägt jeden wohlgemeinten Rat seines Vaters in den Wind.
*An obstinate son throws all his father's well-meant advice to the (four) winds (turns a deaf ear to [makes light of; sets at naught] all his father's well-meant advice).*

**Wind** in j.es Segel sein (fig.): cf. **Wasser** auf j.es Mühle sein j.em den **Wind** aus den Segeln nehmen (fig.): *to take the wind out of s.b.'s sails; to rock s.b. on his heels; to knock s.b. back (colloq.)*

Die einfache, glaubwürdige Erklärung des Angeklagten hat mir den Wind aus den Segeln genommen.
*The accused's simple, credible explanation took the wind out of my sails (rocked me on my heels; knocked me back).*

mit dem **Wind** segeln (fig.): cf. den **Mantel** nach dem Wind hängen

in den **Wind** sprechen (fig.): cf. tauben **Ohren** predigen

in den **Wind** gesprochen sein (fig.): *to fall on deaf ears; to fall on stony ground; to be a waste of breath*

Alle Ermahnungen, das starke Rauchen zu unterlassen, sind bei ihm in den Wind gesprochen.
*All warnings to him to give up heavy smoking have fallen on deaf ears (on stony ground; have been a waste of breath).*

sich wie der **Wind** (mit **Windeseile**) verbreiten: cf. sich verbreiten wie ein **Lauffeuer**

j.em **Wind** vormachen (fig.): *to pull the wool over s.b.'s eyes; to hoodwink s.b.; to kid (to fool; to bamboozle) s.b. (colloq.).* Cf. auch: j.em einen **Türken** bauen

Mir können Sie keinen Wind (kein X für ein U; keinen blauen Dunst) vormachen. Ich bin über alles informiert.
*You can't pull the wool over my eyes (can't hoodwink [kid; fool; bamboozle] me). I am acquainted with everything.*

sehen (merken), woher der **Wind** weht (fig.): *to see which way the wind is blowing (where the wind lies); to see which way the current is flowing; to see in which direction things are moving (going); to see how the land lies (how the matter stands)*

Er hat mich ziemlich unfreundlich empfangen, und ich habe gleich gesehen (gemerkt), woher der Wind wehte (wie [wohin] der Hase lief; gewußt, was die Glocke geschlagen hatte).
*He received me in a rather unfriendly manner, and I saw at once which way the wind was blowing (where the wind lay; which way the current was flowing; in which direction things were moving [going]; how the land lay; how the matter stood).*

bei **Wind** und Wetter (Wind und Regen): *in all weathers; in wind and rain*

Bei Wind und Wetter (Regen) läßt er sein Auto nachts auf der Straße stehen.
*He leaves his car in the road at night in all weathers (in wind and rain).*

in alle **Winde** zerstreut sein (fig.): *to be scattered to the (four) winds (to the [four] corners of the earth)*

Meine Freunde aus der Kindheit sind jetzt in alle Winde zerstreut (zerstreut wie die Spreu im Winde).
*My childhood friends are now scattered to the (four) winds (the [four] corners of the earth).*

j.en **windelweich** schlagen (fam.): cf. j.en zu **Brei** schlagen

ein **Windhund** sein (fig. u. fam.): cf. eine leichte **Fliege** sein

gegen **Windmühlen** kämpfen (fig.): *to tilt at windmills*

Karl glaubte, viele Gegner zu haben, gegen die er vorgehen müsse. Er kämpfte jedoch nur gegen Windmühlen.
*Charles thought he had a lot of enemies to fight against, but he was only tilting at windmills.*

einen **Wink** verstehen (fig.): *to take a hint*

Ich verstand den Wink und ging sogleich fort.
*I took the hint and went away at once.*

j.em einen **Wink** mit dem Zaunpfahl geben (fig.): *to drop (to give) s.b. a broad hint*

Er hat mir einen Wink mit dem Zaunpfahl gegeben, daß er gern mein Nachfolger werden möchte.
*He dropped (gave) me a broad hint that he would like to become my successor.*

ein **Winkeladvokat** sein: *to be a pettifogger*

Für diesen Rechtsfall solltest du dir einen ordentlichen Rechtsanwalt nehmen und dich nicht mit irgendeinem Winkeladvokaten begnügen.
*For this case you ought to get a proper lawyer and not content yourself with some pettifogger.*

**Winkelzüge** *subterfuges; prevarications; dodges; a cock-and-bull story*

Laß diese Winkelzüge (Mach' mir keine Wippchen vor) und sag' mir die volle Wahrheit.
*Stop these subterfuges (prevarications; dodges; this cock-and-bull story) and tell me the whole truth.*

**Wippchen** (fam.): cf. **Winkelzüge**

vom **Wirbel** bis zur Zehe: cf. von **Kopf** bis Fuß

ein **Wirrkopf** sein: cf. ein **Faselhans** sein

ein **Wirrwarr**: *a jumble; a muddle; a Babel*

Nach der Rede des Bürgermeisters entstand ein großer Wirrwarr (Kuddelmuddel) der Meinungen.
*After the mayor's speech a great jumble (muddle; Babel) of opinions was heard.*

Es herrscht polnische **Wirtschaft** (fig.): cf. ein **Schweinestall** sein

j.em einen **Wischer** geben (fig. u. fam.): cf. j.em eins **auswischen**

nach bestem **Wissen** und Gewissen: *to the best of one's knowledge and belief*
Ich habe den Fragebogen nach bestem Wissen und Gewissen ausgefüllt.
*I filled in the questionnaire to the best of my knowledge and belief.*

nichts von j.em **wissen** wollen: *not to want (to have) anything to do with s.b.;*
*not to want (to have) any dealings with s.b.*
Ich will von Heinrich nichts mehr wissen, seitdem er versucht hat, mein Fahrrad zu stehlen.
*I don't want (to have) anything more to do with (any further dealings with) Henry since he tried to steal my bicycle.*

Verrat **wittern** (fig.): *to suspect treason (trickery); to smell a rat (colloq.)*
Wir hatten schon lange Verrat gewittert.
*We had suspected treason (trickery; had smelt a rat) for a long time.*

Mach' keine **Witze**! (fig. u. fam.): cf. Daß ich nicht **lache**!

I **wo**! (fam.): cf. I **bewahre**!

die **Wogen** glätten (fig.): cf. **Öl** auf die Wogen gießen

**wohl** oder übel: *willy-nilly; nolens volens; for better or for worse*
Da unser Mieter seit mehreren Monaten keine Miete gezahlt hatte, mußten wir ihm wohl oder übel kündigen.
*As our lodger had not paid the rent for several months, we had to give him notice willy-nilly (nolens volens; for better or for worse).*

das **Wohl** und Wehe: *the weal or woe*
Der Ministerpräsident war für das Wohl und Wehe der ganzen Nation verantwortlich.
*The prime minister was responsible for the weal or woe of the whole nation.*

sich in **Wohlgefallen** auflösen: cf. sich **ausbügeln**

**Wohltun** bringt Zinsen (Sprichw.): *One good turn deserves another (prov.)*
Ich konnte ihm neulich helfen, und jetzt ist er in der Lage, mir einen Gefallen zu tun. Wohltun bringt Zinsen.
*I was able to help him recently and now he is in a position to do me a favour. One good turn deserves another.*

hungrig wie ein **Wolf** sein (einen **Wolfshunger** haben): cf. einen **Mordshunger** haben

ein **Wolf** im Schafspelz sein (fig.): *to be a wolf in sheep's clothing; to be a fraud*

> Mein neuer Nachbar sieht mir verdächtig aus; er ist sicher ein Wolf im Schafspelz (ein falscher Fünfziger [Fuffziger]).
> *My new neighbour looks suspicious to me; he is sure to be a wolf in sheep's clothing (a fraud).*

Mit den **Wölfen** muß man heulen (Sprichw.): *When in Rome, do as the Romans do (prov.)*

> Sie müssen sich den hiesigen Verhältnissen anpassen. Mit den Wölfen muß man heulen.
> *You must adapt yourself to the conditions here. When in Rome, do as the Romans do.*

mit den **Wölfen** heulen (fig.): *to follow the crowd; to keep in step; to swim with the stream (current).* Cf. auch: den **Mantel** nach dem Wind hängen

> Es ist leichter, mit den Wölfen zu heulen als selbständig vorzugehen.
> *It is easier to follow the crowd (to keep in step; to swim with the stream [current]) than to proceed independently.*

Das ist 'ne **Wolke** (fig. u. fam.): cf. Das ist die **Masche!**

wie aus den **Wolken** (aus allen Wolken) gefallen (aus allen Wolken fallen): *to be thunderstruck (dumbfounded); to be flabbergasted (colloq.); to have the surprise of one's life (colloq.); You could have knocked me (him etc.) down with a feather (colloq.)*

> Als ich die Rechnung für die Reparaturen an meinem Auto las, war ich wie aus den Wolken (aus allen Wolken [Himmeln]) gefallen (fiel ich aus allen Wolken [fast aufs Kreuz; auf den Rücken; vom Stengel]; staunte ich Bauklötze; war ich von den Socken; blieb mir die Spucke weg).
> *When I read the bill for the repairs to my car, I was thunderstruck (dumbfounded; flabbergasted; I had the surprise of my life; you could have knocked me down with a feather).*

**Wolkenkuckucksheim:** *cloud-cuckoo-land; a fool's paradise*

> Viele Gelehrte sind weltfremd und leben in (einem) Wolkenkuckucksheim.
> *Many scholars are withdrawn from the world and live in cloud-cuckoo-land (in a fool's paradise).*

j.en in die **Wolle** bringen (fig. u. fam.): *to get s.b.'s goat (colloq.); to put s.b.'s back up (colloq.); to make s.b. ratty (colloq.); to put s.b.'s monkey up (colloq.)*

> Ich habe meine kleine Schwester geneckt und in die Wolle (in Harnisch; aus dem Häuschen) gebracht.
> *I teased my little sister and got her goat (put her back [monkey] up; made her ratty).*

in die **Wolle** geraten (fig. u. fam.): cf. in **Harnisch** geraten; aus der **Haut** fahren sich in die **Wolle** geraten (fig. u. fam.): cf. sich in die **Haare** geraten

j.em das **Wort** abschneiden (fig.): *to cut s.b. short.* Cf. auch: j.em ins **Wort** fallen

Ich verbitte es mir energisch, daß Sie mir so das Wort abschneiden.
*I strongly resent your cutting me short like that.*

j.en mit leeren **Worten** abspeisen (fig.): cf. j.en mit leeren Worten **abspeisen**

Ein **Wort** gab das andere: *One word led to another*

Bei der Diskussion gab ein Wort das andere, und man trennte sich schließlich in Unfrieden.
*In the discussion one word led to another and we finally parted in disagreement.*

ums **Wort** bitten: *to ask permission (leave) to speak; to try to catch the chairman's eye*

Viele Abgeordnete haben in dieser Sitzung ums Wort gebeten.
*Many deputies asked permission (leave) to speak (tried to catch the chairman's eye) during that session.*

mit éinem **Wort**: *in a word; What it boils down to is, that . . .; To cut a long story short; The long and short of it is, that . . .; (to put it) in a nutshell*

Ich bin mit verschiedenen Punkten dieses Vertrages nicht zufrieden. Mit éinem Wort (Kurz und gut; Kurzum; Des Pudels Kern): ich bin noch nicht bereit, ihn zu unterschreiben.
*I am not satisfied with various points in this contract. In a word (What it boils down to is, that; To cut a long story short; The long and short of it is, that; [To put it] In a nutshell), I am not yet prepared to sign it.*

ein gutes **Wort** für j.en einlegen: *to put in a (good) word for s.b.* Cf. auch: eine **Lanze** für j.en brechen (einlegen)

Da ich mich um diesen Posten beworben habe, wäre ich Ihnen dankbar, wenn Sie ein gutes Wort für mich einlegen würden.
*As I have applied for this post, I should be grateful if you would put in a (good) word for me.*

j.em das **Wort** entziehen: *to forbid s.b. to continue.* Cf. auch: j.em das **Wort** abschneiden

Der Vorsitzende sah sich gezwungen, dem Redner das Wort zu entziehen.
*The chairman found himself compelled to forbid the speaker to continue.*

das **Wort** ergreifen: *to make a speech; to take one's turn at (to mount) the rostrum; to take the floor; to hold forth (colloq.); to give tongue (colloq.)*

Am Grabe des Bürgermeisters werden mehrere Persönlichkeiten das Wort ergreifen.

*Several personalities are going to make a speech (to take their turn at [to mount] the rostrum; to take the floor; to hold forth; to give tongue) at the mayor's grave.*

**j.em das Wort erteilen**: *to call upon (to summon) s.b. to speak*

Bei der morgigen Tagung wird man mir sicherlich das Wort erteilen.
*I shall certainly be called upon (summoned) to speak at tomorrow's meeting.*

**j.em ins Wort fallen** (fig.): *to butt in; to chip in (colloq.); to put one's spoke in (colloq.).* Cf. auch: **j.em das Wort abschneiden**

Ich kann es nicht vertragen, wenn man mir ins Wort fällt und mich nicht ausreden läßt.
*I cannot stand it when people butt (chip) in (put their spoke in) and do not let me finish speaking.*

**allein das Wort führen**: *to do all the talking; to monopolise the conversation; to have all the say (colloq.).* Cf. auch: **die Hosen anhaben**; **das Zepter schwingen**

In diesem Haushalt führt die Frau allein das (große) Wort.
*In this household the wife does all the talking (has all the say; monopolises the conversation).*

**j.em sein (Ehren-)Wort geben**: *to give (to pledge) s.b. one's word (of honour; one's solemn word)*

Ich habe Vater mein (Ehren-)Wort (mein Wort zum Pfand) gegeben (habe . . . hoch und heilig versprochen), daß ich nicht mehr rauchen werde.
*I have given (pledged) father my word (of honour; my solemn word) not to smoke any more.*

**aufs Wort gehorchen**: *to obey s.b. to the letter; to obey s.b.'s every word*

Mein Sohn gehorcht mir aufs Wort.
*My son obeys me to the letter (obeys my every word).*

**j.em aufs Wort glauben**: *to take s.b. at his word; to take s.b.'s word for s.th.*

Sie können mir aufs Wort glauben (mich beim Wort nehmen), daß diese Ware ganz frisch ist.
*You can take me at my word (can take my word for it) that these goods are quite fresh.*

**das große Wort führen** (fig.): cf. **allein das Wort führen**

**j.em gute Worte geben**: *to talk nicely (to be nice) to s.b.; to soft-soap s.b. (sl.)*

Sie müssen ihm schon gute Worte geben, wenn Sie bei ihm etwas erreichen wollen.
*You will have to talk nicely (be nice) to him (to soft-soap him) if you want to get anywhere with him.*

**das Wort haben**: *to have the floor; to be at the rostrum; to have the attention of the house*

Ein Sprecher der Oppositionspartei hat jetzt das Wort.
*A spokesman for the opposition now has the floor (is now at the rostrum; now has the attention of the house).*

etwas nicht **Wort** haben wollen (fig.): *not to want to hear a word about s. th.*

Heinrich will es nicht Wort haben (wahrhaben), daß er bereits einmal verheiratet war.
*Henry will not hear a word about the fact that he has been married before.*

Das **Wort** bleibt mir im Halse (in der Kehle) stecken (fig.): *The words stick in my throat; The words choke me*

Ich wollte ihm mitteilen, daß sein Bruder verunglückt sei; aber das Wort blieb mir im Halse (in der Kehle) stecken.
*I wanted to tell him that his brother had had an accident, but the words stuck in my throat (choked me).*

sein **Wort** halten (fig.): *to keep (to stand by) one's word (one's promise); to be as good as one's word; not to go back on one's word; to stick to one's word (one's promise) (colloq.)*

Man kann sich auf meinen Bruder verlassen. Er hält stets sein Wort (steht immer zu seinem Wort).
*One can depend on my brother. He always keeps (stands by; sticks to) his word (promise; is always as good as his word; never goes back on his word).*

Hast du **Worte!** (fam.): cf. Hast du **Töne!**

Schöne **Worte** machen den Kohl nicht fett (Sprichw.): cf. Schöne Worte machen den **Kohl** nicht fett

zu **Wort(e)** kommen: *to get a hearing; to make o. s. heard; to get a word in (edgeways)*

Der Tumult in der Versammlung war so groß, daß der Redner nicht zu Wort(e) kommen konnte.
*The tumult in the meeting was so great that the speaker could not get a hearing (make himself heard; get a word in [edgeways]).*

das letzte **Wort** behalten: *to have the last word (the last say)*

In allen Diskussionen will mein Bruder das letzte Wort behalten.
*In all discussions my brother wants to have the last word (say).*

ein Mann von **Wort** sein: cf. ein **Mann** von Wort sein

kein **Wort** mitzureden haben (fig.): cf. nichts zu **bestellen** haben

j.em die **Worte** im Munde herumdrehen (j.em die Worte verdrehen) (fig.):
*to twist (to distort) s. b.'s words; to turn s. b.'s words upside-down*

So habe ich es nicht gemeint. Sie haben mir die Worte im Munde herumgedreht (mir die Worte verdreht).
*I did not mean it that way. You have twisted (distorted) my words (turned my words upside-down).*

j.em **Worte** in den Mund legen (fig.): cf. j.em etwas (Worte) in den **Mund** legen

j.em das **Wort** aus dem Munde nehmen (fig.): *to take the words out of s.b.'s mouth*

Ich wollte soeben das gleiche sagen. Sie haben mir das Wort aus dem Munde genommen.
*I was about to say the same thing. You took the words out of my mouth.*

j.en beim **Wort** nehmen (fig.): cf. j.em aufs **Wort** glauben; Das soll ein **Wort** sein!

j.em sein **Wort** zum Pfand geben: cf. j.em sein (Ehren-)**Wort** geben

j.em (einer Sache) das **Wort** reden (fig.): *to pronounce (to speak; to come out) in favour of s.b. (s.th.).* Cf. auch: für j.en (etwas) ein gutes **Wort** einlegen

Wir möchten einem Kompromiß aus beiden Ansichten das Wort reden.
*We would pronounce (speak; come out) in favour of a compromise between the two views.*

**Worte** sind leerer Schall (Sprichw.): *Words are but wind (prov.)*

Ich möchte Ihre Zusage schriftlich haben. Worte sind leerer Schall.
*I should like your consent in writing. Words are but wind.*

schöne **Worte** machen (fig.): *to be full of talk (colloq.)*

Man kann sich auf diesen Händler nie verlassen. Er macht nur schöne Worte und tut dann doch nicht, was er versprochen hat.
*One can never rely on this tradesman. He is only full of talk and does not do after all what he has promised.*

Das soll ein **Wort** sein! (fig.): *I'll take you at your word; I'll take that as a promise; That is a promise*

Du willst also nie wieder ein Tier quälen? Das soll ein Wort sein! (Ich nehme dich beim Wort!)
*So you'll never be cruel to an animal again? I'll take you at your word (I'll take that as a promise; That is a promise).*

zu seinem **Wort** stehen (fig.): cf. sein **Wort** halten

kein **Wort** über etwas verlieren: *to make no mention of s.th.; not to speak (to breathe) a word about s.th.*

Während des ganzen Abends wurde kein Wort über diesen peinlichen Vorfall verloren.
*No mention was made of (Not a word was spoken [breathed] about) that embarrassing incident the whole evening.*

kein wahres **Wort**: *not a word (grain; scrap; an atom; an iota) of truth*

An diesem Gerücht ist kein wahres Wort.
*There is not a word (grain; scrap; an atom; an iota) of truth in this rumour.*

j.en keines **Wortes** würdigen: *not to favour s.b. with a single word; not to utter a single word to s.b.; not to spare s.b. a single word*

Dieser hochnasige Mensch würdigte uns keines Wortes.
*That conceited person did not favour us with a single word (utter a single word to us; spare us a single word).*

**Wucherpreise** nehmen: cf. **Apothekerpreise** nehmen

Das ist 'ne **Wucht!** (fam.): cf. Das ist die **Masche!**

ein (politischer) **Wühler** sein: *to be a (political) agitator (trouble-maker)*

Ich weiß schon lange, daß dieser Gewerkschaftler ein (politischer) Wühler ist.
*I have known for a long time that that trade unionist is a (political) agitator (trouble-maker).*

alte **Wunden** aufreißen (fig.): cf. in der alten **Wunde** wühlen (bohren)

den Finger auf die **Wunde** legen (fig.): cf. den **Finger** auf die Wunde legen

in der alten **Wunde** wühlen (bohren) (fig.): *to reopen (to open up) an old wound (old sores)*

Du solltest von diesem Unglück nicht so viel reden. Du wühlst (bohrst) dadurch nur immer in einer alten Wunde (reißt dadurch nur alte Wunden auf).
*You ought not to talk so much about that accident. You are only reopening (opening up) an old wound (old sores).*

sein blaues **Wunder** erleben (fig. u. fam.): cf. etwas **erleben** können

**Wunder** tun (fig.): cf. **Berge** versetzen

**Wunder** wirken (fig.): *to work wonders (miracles; marvels)*

Meine ernste Ermahnung hat bei ihm Wunder gewirkt.
*My serious warning has worked wonders (miracles; marvels) with him.*

von j.em (einer Sache) **wunder(s)** was halten: *to think the world (earth) of s.b. (s.th.); to think no end of s.b. (s.th.) (colloq.)*

Von seinem neuen Chauffeur hält mein Vater wunder(s) was.
*My father thinks the world (earth; no end) of his new chauffeur.*

**wunder(s)** wer (was usw.) sein: *to be goodness knows who (what etc.); to be God knows who (what etc.) (colloq.)*

Der junge Angestellte glaubt, wunder(s) wer zu sein.
*The young clerk thinks he is goodness (God) knows who.*

Dein **Wunsch** ist mir Befehl: *Your wish is my command*

Wenn dir der Hut gefällt, so bekommst du ihn. Dein Wunsch ist mir Befehl.
*If you like the hat, you can have it. Your wish is my command.*

ein frommer **Wunsch** (fig.) *a pious hope; wishful thinking*

Einen Pelzmantel zu besitzen, ist für meine Mutter leider nur ein frommer Wunsch (nur Zukunftsmusik).
*To own a fur-coat is, I am afraid, only a pious hope (wishful thinking) on my mother's part.*

Der **Wunsch** ist Vater des Gedankens: cf. Der Wunsch ist **Vater** des Gedankens

Vom **Wünschen** ist noch keiner reich geworden (Sprichw.): *If wishes were horses, beggars would ride (prov.)*

Wenn ich mehr Geld hätte, würde ich mir ein Fahrrad kaufen. Aber vom Wünschen ist noch keiner reich geworden.
*If I had more money, I should buy myself a bicycle. But then, if wishes were horses, beggars would ride.*

**Würden** sind Bürden (Sprichw.): *Great honours bring great burdens*

Der Ministerpräsident kann sich selten Urlaub gönnen. Würden sind Bürden.
*The prime minister can rarely permit himself a vacation. Great honours bring great burdens.*

aus éinem **Wurf** sein (fig.): cf. aus éinem **Guß** sein

alles auf éinen **Wurf** setzen (fig.): cf. alles auf éine **Karte** setzen

einen guten **Wurf** tun (fig.): *to make (to score) a lucky hit; to strike a gold-mine; to pick a winner; to strike lucky; to hit the jackpot (colloq.)*

Mit seiner neuen Erfindung hat mein Schwager einen guten Wurf getan.
*My brother-in-law has made (scored) a lucky hit (struck a gold-mine; picked a winner; struck lucky; hit the jackpot) with his new invention.*

Die **Würfel** sind gefallen: *The die is cast*

Die Würfel sind gefallen, und wir können unsern Plan jetzt nicht mehr aufgeben.
*The die is cast, and we can no longer give up our plan now.*

Armes **Wurm (Würmchen)!** (fig. u. fam.): *Poor thing!; Poor (little) mite!; Poor kid! (colloq.)*

Das kleine Mädchen hat sich den Arm gebrochen. Armes Wurm (Würmchen; Ding)!
*The little girl has broken her arm. Poor thing! (Poor [little] mite!; Poor kid!)*

Da ist der **Wurm** drin (fig. u. fam.): *There is something rotten in it (colloq.)*

Sein Geschäft geht von Jahr zu Jahr schlechter. Da ist entschieden der Wurm drin.
*His business gets worse from year to year. There is definitely something rotten in it.*

Auch ein **Wurm** krümmt sich, wenn er getreten wird (Sprichw.): *Even a worm will turn (prov.)*

Ich hätte nie gedacht, daß dieser unbedeutende Angestellte sich beschweren würde. Aber auch ein Wurm krümmt sich, wenn er getreten wird.
*I should never have thought that that insignificant clerk would complain. But even a worm will turn.*

j.em die **Würmer** aus der Nase ziehen (fig. u. fam.): *to draw s.b. out; to worm (to squeeze) the information out of s.b. (colloq.); to pump s.b. for the information (colloq.)*

Karl wollte zuerst nichts verraten, ich habe ihm jedoch die Würmer aus der Nase gezogen.
*Charles did not want to give anything away at first, but I drew him out (wormed [squeezed] the information out of him; pumped him for the information).*

sich winden (krümmen) wie ein **Wurm**: cf. sich winden wie ein **Aal**

sich **wurmen** (es wurmt j.en) (fig. u. fam.): *to be nettled (riled); it nettles (riles) s.b.*

Ich habe mich gewurmt (Es hat mich gewurmt), daß ein jüngerer, weniger erfahrener Mann mein Vorgesetzter geworden (über mich gesetzt worden) ist.
*I was nettled (riled; It nettled [riled] me) that a younger, less experienced man was put above me.*

j.em eine besondere **Wurst** braten (fig. u. fam.): cf. j.em eine **Extrawurst** braten

Jetzt geht es um die **Wurst!** (fig. u. fam.): *Now's the time!; This is it! (colloq.); Now for it (colloq.); Here we go! (colloq.)*

Dies ist der entscheidende Augenblick. Jetzt geht es um die Wurst!
*This is the decisive moment. Now's the time! (This is it!; Now for it!; Here we go!)*

j.en in die **Wurst** hacken (fig. u. fam.): cf. **Hackfleisch** aus j.em machen

j.em **Wurst** sein (fam.): cf. völlig **Luft** für j.en sein mit der **Wurst** nach der Speckseite werfen (fig.): *to set a sprat to catch a mackerel*

> Kleinigkeiten können manchmal von großem Wert sein. Wilhelm hat gelernt, mit der Wurst nach der Speckseite zu werfen.
> *Trivialities can sometimes be of great value. William has learnt to set a sprat to catch a mackerel.*

**Wurst** wider Wurst! (fig. u. fam.): *Tit for tat; We're quits (even) (colloq.).*
Cf. auch: mit j.em **quitt** sein b)

> Gestern hast du mir bei meiner Schulaufgabe nicht geholfen. Darum will ich dir heute mein Fahrrad nicht leihen. Wurst wider Wurst!
> *Yesterday you wouldn't help me with my homework, so today I won't lend you my bicycle. Tit for tat (Now we're quits [even]).*

ein armes **Würstchen** sein (fig. u. fam.): cf. ein armer **Haufen** sein

mit der gleichen (alten) **Wurstelei** weitergehen (weiter **wursteln**) (fam.): cf. den gleichen (alten) **Schlendrian** weitergehen

ein **wurstiges** Benehmen (eine **Wurstigkeit**) (fam.): *a couldn't-care-less attitude (colloq.)*

> Heinrich ist sehr gleichgültig. Sein wurstiges Benehmen (Seine Wurstigkeit) gefällt uns gar nicht.
> *Henry is very indifferent. We do not like his couldn't-care-less attitude at all.*

In der Kürze liegt die **Würze** (Sprichw.): *Brevity is the soul of wit (prov.)*

> Die kurzen, klaren Ausführungen des Redners haben uns sehr imponiert. In der Kürze liegt die Würze.
> *The speaker's short, clear statements greatly impressed us. Brevity is the soul of wit.*

Geld ist die **Wurzel** allen Übels (Sprichw.): *Money (The love of money) is the root of all evil (prov.)*

> Sein Lotteriegewinn läßt ihn ein ausschweifendes Leben führen. Geld ist die Wurzel allen Übels.
> *His win in the lottery (sweepstake) has made him lead a dissolute life. Money (The love of money) is the root of all evil.*

j.en an der **Wurzel** treffen (fig.): cf. einem durch **Mark** und Bein gehen

j.en in die **Wüste** schicken (jagen) (fig.): *to sack s.b. (colloq.); to give s.b. the order of the boot (colloq.).* Cf. auch: j.en auf die **Straße** setzen; j.en **ausbooten**

> Bei dem Regierungswechsel wurden die meisten Minister in die Wüste geschickt ([gejagt]; wurden … abgesägt).
> *With the change of government most ministers were sacked (given the order of the boot).*

seine **Wut** an j.em auslassen: cf. an j.em sein **Mütchen** kühlen

eine blinde **Wut**: *a towering rage; a blind fury; a burning anger (rage; fury)*

Mich packte eine blinde Wut (ein heiliger Zorn), als ich die hohe Arztrechnung sah.
*I was seized by a towering rage (blind fury; burning anger [rage; fury]) when I saw the doctor's heavy bill.*

seine **Wut** in sich (hinein)fressen: *to swallow one's anger (rage); to put up with it (colloq.); to lump it (sl.)*

Meine Entlassung kam mir ungerecht vor, ich konnte aber nichts dagegen machen und mußte meine Wut in mich (hinein)fressen.
*My dismissal seemed unjust to me, but I could not do anything about it and had to swallow my anger (rage; had to put up with it; had to lump it).*

sich vor **Wut** nicht mehr kennen: cf. vor **Wut** kochen

vor **Wut** kochen (platzen; rasen; schäumen; schnauben): *to boil (to foam) with rage; to be livid (with rage); to go up in smoke (colloq.).* Cf. auch: eine blinde **Wut**

Ich kochte (platzte; raste; schäumte; schnaubte; kannte mich nicht mehr) vor Wut (kriegte die Platze; bekam zuviel; Mir lief die Galle über [platzte der Kragen]; Es kochte in mir; Ich biß mir ein Loch [Löcher; ein Monogramm] in den Bauch), als ich von dieser Unverschämtheit erfuhr.
*I boiled (foamed) with rage (I was livid [with rage]; went up in smoke) when I learned of this impertinence.*

# X

j.em ein **X** für ein U vormachen (fig.): cf. j.em **Wind** vormachen. Cf. auch: j.en hinters **Licht** führen

eine alte **Xanthippe** sein (fig.): cf. eine alte **Hexe** sein

**x-beliebig**: *whenever I (you etc.) like; any old . . . (colloq.)*

Nächste Woche bin ich immer zu Hause. Sie können mich zu jeder x-beliebigen Zeit besuchen.
*I shall be at home all next week. You can visit me whenever you like (at any old time).*

vor **x-Jahren**: *ages ago; in the year dot*

Diesen Rasierapparat habe ich mir schon vor x-Jahren gekauft.
*I bought that razor ages ago (in the year dot).*

**x-mal**: *any number of times; hundreds of times (colloq.); umpteen times (colloq.)*

Wir haben dir schon x-mal (zig-mal) gesagt, daß du früher aufstehen mußt.
*We have told you any number of times (hundreds of times; umpteen times) to get up earlier.*

nicht bis drei (vier) **zählen** können (fig. u. fam.): cf. nicht bis **drei** zählen können

sich die **Zähne** ausbeißen (fig.): *to wear o.s. out; to wear o.s. to pieces (to a shadow); to come to grief; to come a cropper (colloq.)*

An seinem energischen Widerstand hat sich schon mancher die Zähne ausgebissen.
*Many a person has worn himself out (worn himself to pieces [to a shadow]) against (has come to grief [has come a cropper] over) his vigorous resistance.*

bis an die **Zähne** bewaffnet sein: *to be armed to the teeth*

Die Bankräuber waren bis an die Zähne bewaffnet.
*The bank-robbers were armed to the teeth.*

einen **Zahn** drauflegen (fig. u. fam.): cf. die **Beine** in die Hand nehmen

j.em auf den **Zahn** fühlen (fig.): cf. bei j.em einen **Fühler** ausstrecken

die **Zähne** zeigen (fig.): *to bare (to show) one's teeth*

Karl ist normalerweise ein friedfertiger Mensch. Wenn er aber angegriffen wird, zeigt er die Zähne (Hörner).
*Charles is normally a peaceful person, but when he is attacked, he bares (shows) his teeth.*

der **Zahn** der Zeit (fig.): *the ravages (the passage) of time*

An diesem alten, verwitterten Turm kann man den Zahn der Zeit erkennen.
*One can see the ravages (passage) of time on this old, weather-beaten tower.*

j.em dén **Zahn** ziehen (fig.): *to scotch that (colloq.); to put paid to that (colloq.); to put the lid on that (colloq.); to knock that on the head (colloq.)*

Mein Neffe hatte gehofft, von mir etwas zu erben. Dén Zahn habe ich ihm aber gezogen.
*My nephew had hoped to inherit something from me, but I have scotched (put paid to; put the lid on) that (knocked that on the head).*

die **Zähne** zusammenbeißen (fig.): *to grit (to clench) one's teeth; to keep a stiff upper lip; to keep one's pecker up (colloq.)*

In schweren Zeiten muß man die Zähne zusammenbeißen.
*One has to grit (to clench) one's teeth (to keep a stiff upper lip; to keep one's pecker up) in difficult times.*

unter **Zähneklappern** (fam.): cf. mit (unter) **Heulen** und Zähneklappern

**zähneknirschend** (fig.): *gnashing one's teeth; with gnashing of teeth*

Ich war gezwungen, zähneknirschend mein Einverständnis zu geben.
*Gnashing my teeth (With gnashing of teeth) I was compelled to give my consent.*

auf dem **Zahnfleisch** gehen (fig. u. fam.): cf. **absein**; **hundemüde** sein

j.en nicht mit der **Zange** anfassen (mögen): cf. j.en nicht mit der **Feuerzange** anfassen

j.en in die **Zange** nehmen (fig.): *to give s.b. a shaking (colloq.); to put s.b. through it (colloq.); to give s.b. a pasting (sl.)*

Bei dem Fußballspiel nahmen die gegnerischen Stürmer unsere Hintermannschaft gehörig in die Zange.
*In the football match the opposing forwards gave our defence a proper shaking (put our defence through it properly; gave our defence a proper pasting).*

ein **Zankapfel** sein (fig.): *to be a bone of contention; to be a source of discord*

Ein unklares Testament wird leicht zum Zankapfel (zum Apfel der Zwietracht) der Erben.
*A vague will can easily become a bone of contention (a source of discord) among the inheritors.*

j.en **zappeln** lassen (fig.): *to let s.b. cool his heels; to keep s.b. hanging around (colloq.)*

Unsern faulen Klempner werde ich mit der Bezahlung (seiner Rechnung) zappeln lassen.
*I shall let our lazy plumber cool his heels before I pay him (shall keep our lazy plumber hanging about for his money).*

ein **Zappelphilipp** sein (fig. u. fam.): cf. **Quecksilber** im Leibe haben

**zartbesaitet** sein (fig.): *to be highly-strung*

Du mußt meine Schwester vorsichtig behandeln, da sie sehr zartbesaitet ist.
*You must treat my sister carefully, because she is very highly-strung.*

**Zaster** haben (fam.): cf. (gut) bei **Kasse** sein; **Geld** wie Heu haben

(ein) fauler **Zauber** (fig. u. fam.): *a fishy (shady) business (colloq.)*

Was er uns da erzählt hat, stimmt nicht. Es ist (ein) fauler Zauber.
*What he has told us is not right. It is a fishy (shady) business.*

j.en im **Zaume** halten (fig.): *to keep a tight rein (hold) on s.b.* Cf. auch: j.en in **Schach** halten

Es ist manchmal schwer, solche ausgelassenen Kinder im Zaume zu halten.
*It is sometimes hard to keep a tight rein (hold) on such unruly children.*

einen Streit vom **Zaune** brechen (fig.): cf. einen **Streit** vom Zaune brechen j.em mit dem **Zaunpfahl** winken (fig.): cf. j.em einen **Wink** mit dem Zaunpfahl geben

die **Zeche** bezahlen müssen (fig.): *to foot the bill; to stand (to take) the rap; to face the music; to stand the racket (colloq.); to carry the can (back) (sl.); to be left holding the baby (sl.)*

> Wie so oft, mußte der Unschuldige die Zeche bezahlen und den Tadel auf sich nehmen.
> *As so often, the innocent one had to foot the bill (stand [take] the rap; face the music; stand the racket; carry the can [back]; was left holding the baby) and (had to) take the blame himself.*

j.em auf die **Zehen** treten (fig.): cf. j.em auf den **Fuß** treten

Nicht der **Zehnte** weiß das: cf. Nicht der **Hundertste** weiß das

Es geschehen noch **Zeichen** und Wunder!: *Wonders will never cease!*

> Dieser sonst unzuverlässige Kunde hat diesmal pünktlich gezahlt. Es geschehen noch Zeichen und Wunder!
> *This usually unreliable customer has paid punctually this time. Wonders will never cease!*

eine **Zeichnung** machen (fig. u. fam.): *to dither (about) (colloq.); to hang around (colloq.); to dilly-dally (colloq.)*

> Da die Angelegenheit eilt, handle sofort. Mach' (doch) keine (lange) Zeichnung!
> *As the matter is urgent, act immediately. Don't dither ([about]; hang around; dilly-dally).*

zwischen den **Zeilen** lesen (fig.): *to read between the lines*

> Gewisse Schriftsteller bringen nicht ihre ganzen Gefühle offen zum Ausdruck. Man muß also in ihren Romanen zwischen den Zeilen lesen.
> *Certain writers do not openly express all their feelings, so one must read between the lines of their novels.*

j.em ein paar **Zeilen** schreiben: *to drop s.b. a line*

> Ich werde dir aus Athen ein paar Zeilen schreiben.
> *I shall drop you a line from Athens.*

ein lockerer **Zeisig** sein (fig. u. fam.): cf. eine leichte **Fliege** sein

seine **Zeit** abwarten: *to bide one's time; to wait one's opportunity (chance)*

> Es ist immer noch zu früh. Du mußt deine Zeit abwarten.
> *It is still too early. You must bide your time (wait your opportunity [chance]).*

für **Zeit** und Ewigkeit: *for good; for ever and a day*

> Meinen Rheumatismus muß ich leider für Zeit und Ewigkeit erdulden.
> *I am afraid I shall have to suffer my rheumatism for good (for ever and a day).*

mit der **Zeit** gehen: cf. auf dem **laufenden** sein

(Ach,) du liebe **Zeit**!: cf. (Ach) du liebe **Güte**!

Kommt **Zeit,** kommt Rat (Zeit bringt Rat) (Sprichw.): *Time will bring an answer; An answer will come in time*

Wir werden schon eine bessere Lösung der Angelegenheit finden. Kommt Zeit, kommt Rat (Zeit bringt Rat).
*We shall soon find a better solution to the question. Time will bring an answer (An answer will come in time).*

dem lieben Gott die **Zeit** stehlen (fig.): cf. die **Zeit** totschlagen

j.em die **Zeit** stehlen (rauben): *to take up (a lot of) s.b.'s time; to waste s.b.'s time*

Der Besuch solcher Kunden ist uns äußerst lästig, denn sie bleiben jedes Mal sehr lange und stehlen (rauben) uns die kostbare Zeit.
*Visits from such customers are extremely trying, because every time they stay a very long while and take up (a lot of) our valuable time (and waste our valuable time).*

die **Zeit** totschlagen (fig.): *to kill time; to while (to fritter; to idle) away the time*

Vater kann nie müßig herumsitzen und die Zeit totschlagen (dem lieben [Herr-] Gott den Tag [die Zeit] stehlen).
*Father can never sit around idly and kill time (while [fritter; idle] away the time).*

hinter der **Zeit** zurückbleiben: *to be behind the times; not to be up with (abreast of) the times*

Mein Großvater ist hinter der Zeit zurückgeblieben und kann viele neue Entwicklungen einfach nicht begreifen.
*My grandfather is behind the times (is not up with [abreast of]) the times and simply cannot grasp many modern developments.*

das **Zeitliche** segnen: cf. j.es **Lebenslicht** erlischt

seine **Zelte** abbrechen (fig.): *to break camp; to pack up; to shut up shop (colloq.); to up anchor (colloq.)*

Ich muß meine Zelte hier abbrechen, da ich in London einen neuen Posten bekommen habe.
*I must break camp (pack up; shut up shop; up anchor) here because I have got a new job in London.*

wie eine **Zentnerlast (zentnerschwer)** auf j.em lasten (liegen): cf. **bleischwer** auf j.em lasten

das **Zepter** schwingen (fig.): *to call the tune; to rule the roost; to lay down the law; to hold the whip-hand.* Cf. auch: die **Hosen** anhaben; allein das **Wort** führen

Wer schwingt in diesem Haushalt das Zepter?
*Who calls the tune (rules the roost; lays down the law; holds the whip-hand) in this household?*

j.en **zerfleischen** (fig.): *to tear s.b. to shreds (into tatters); to pull s.b. to pieces (shreds); to tear strips off s.b. (colloq.)*

Die beiden Redner haben sich in ihrer Wut gegenseitig zerfleischt.
*The two speakers tore each other to shreds (into tatters; pulled each other to pieces [shreds]; tore strips off each other) in their rage.*

etwas **zerpflücken** (fig.): cf. keinen guten **Faden** an j.em (etwas) lassen

sich nicht **zerreißen** können (fig. u. fam.): *not to be able to do everything at once; only to have one pair of hands (colloq.)*

Ich muß deinen Anzug reinigen und kann dir im Augenblick dein Abendessen noch nicht bringen. Ich kann mich doch nicht zerreißen (Ich kann doch nicht hexen).
*I must clean your suit and cannot bring you your supper at the moment. I can't do everything at once (I've only got one pair of hands).*

sich **zerren** (fig.): cf. sich **kabbeln**

**Zeter** und Mordio schreien (ein **Zetergeschrei** erheben): *to raise Cain; to scream the place down (colloq.); to cry (to yell) blue murder (sl.); to raise merry hell (sl.).* Cf. auch: einen **Heidenlärm** machen

Die von diesem Gauner Betrogenen schrieen Zeter und Mordio (erhoben ein Gezeter [Zetergeschrei]).
*Those who had been swindled by that rogue were raising Cain (screaming the place down; crying [yelling] blue murder; raising merry hell).*

dummes **Zeug** reden: cf. **Quatsch** reden

dummes **Zeug** sein: cf. **Quatsch** sein

j.em (etwas) am **Zeuge** flicken (fig.): *to find fault with s.b.; to carp (to cavil) at s.b.; to pick holes in s.b. (colloq.); to nag at s.b. (colloq.)*

Mein Vater hat mir immer (etwas) am Zeuge zu flicken.
*My father is always finding fault with me (carping [cavilling; nagging] at me; picking holes in me).*

das **Zeug** zu etwas (in sich) haben: *to have the makings of s.b.; to have the capacity to become s.b.; to have it in one to become s.b.*

Wir sind überzeugt, daß mein älterer Bruder das Zeug zu einem tüchtigen Arzt (in sich) hat.
*We are convinced that my elder brother has the makings of (has the capacity [has it in him] to become) an efficient doctor.*

was das **Zeug** hält (fig.): *for all one is worth; like mad (colloq.); like blazes (colloq.); like anything (colloq.); hell for leather (colloq.).* Cf. auch: wie **verrückt** laufen; laufen wie ein **Besenbinder**

> Um noch rechtzeitig die Schule zu erreichen, liefen wir, was das Zeug hielt.
> *In order to reach school in time, we ran for all we were worth (ran like mad [blazes; anything]; ran hell for leather).*

sich ins **Zeug** legen (fig.): *to put one's shoulder to the wheel; to keep one's nose to the grindstone; to put one's back into it; to set (to turn) to; to go at it with a will; to get down to it (to the job) (colloq.); to pound away (colloq.)*

> Um sein Examen zu bestehen, legte sich Wilhelm tüchtig ins Zeug (Geschirr) und arbeitete bis in die Nacht hinein.
> *In order to pass his examination, William put his shoulder to the wheel (kept his nose to the grindstone; put his back into it; went at it with a will; set [turned] to; got down to it [to the job]; pounded away) and worked late into the night.*

von etwas **Zeugnis** ablegen: *to bear witness to s.th.; to testify to s.th.; to be an earnest of s.th.*

> Diese Handlung legt Zeugnis von seinem ehrlichen Charakter ab.
> *This act bears witness (testifies) to (is an earnest of) his honest character.*

**zickzack** (im **Zickzack**) gehen (fahren): cf. in **Schlangenlinie** gehen (fahren)

eine alte **Ziege** sein (fig. u. fam.): *to be an old hag (colloq.)*

> Diese Lumpensammlerin ist eine alte Ziege (Eule).
> *That rag-and-bone woman is an old hag.*

eine dumme **Ziege** sein (fig. u. fam.): cf. eine dumme **Gans** sein

eine häßliche **Ziege** sein (fig. u. fam.): cf. wie eine **Vogelscheuche** aussehen

eine neugierige **Ziege** sein (fig. u. fam.): *to be a Nosey Parker (colloq.)*

> Die Nachbarin ärgert mich sehr, weil sie eine so neugierige Ziege ist.
> *The neighbour's wife annoys me very much because she is such a Nosey Parker.*

**ziegelrot**: *brick-red*

> Dieser Maler fällt durch seine ziegelrote Weste auf.
> *This painter attracts attention because of his brick-red waistcoat.*

bei j.em nicht **ziehen** (fig.): cf. j.en **kaltlassen**

über das **Ziel** (hinaus)schießen (fig.): *to overshoot (to overstep) the mark; to go too far; to overdo it*

In seinem Zeitungsartikel ist dieser Kritiker entschieden über das Ziel (hinaus)-geschossen.
*In his newspaper article this critic has definitely overshot (overstepped) the mark (gone too far; overdone it).*

zum **Ziel** kommen (fig.): *to reach (to arrive at; to come to) a decision; to make up one's mind; to clinch the matter*

Unterlassen wir diese endlose Diskussion und kommen wir doch zum Ziel.
*Let us stop this endless discussion and reach (arrive at; come to) a decision (make up our minds; clinch the matter).*

sich ein **Ziel** setzen (stecken) (fig.): *to aim at s. th.; to set o. s. a target (a task)*

Mein Bruder hat sich das Ziel gesetzt (gesteckt), Englisch binnen zwei Monaten zu lernen.
*My brother aims at learning English (has set himself the target [task] of learning English) within two months.*

die **Zielscheibe** des Spottes sein (fig.): *to be a laughing-stock; to be a butt of ridicule.* Cf. auch: sich zum **Gelächter** machen

Der kleine Junge ist oft die Zielscheibe des Spottes seiner Schulkameraden.
*The little boy is often the laughing-stock of (a butt of ridicule to) his schoolmates.*

eine **Zigarre** bekommen (fig. u. fam.): cf. eine **Abreibung** bekommen

**zig-mal** (fam.): cf. **x-mal**

ans **Zimmer** gefesselt sein (fig.): *to be confined to one's room (to bed)*

Georg hat eine ansteckende Krankheit und ist ans Zimmer gefesselt.
*George has an infectious disease and is confined to his room (to bed).*

das **Zimmer** hüten (fig.): *to keep to one's room; to stay in (to confine o. s. to) bed*

Es wäre ratsam, wenn du einige Tage das Zimmer hüten würdest.
*It would be advisable for you to keep to your room (to stay in [to confine yourself to] bed) for a few days.*

j.em zeigen, wo der **Zimmermann** das Loch gelassen hat (fam.): cf. j.en vor die **Tür** setzen

der ganze **Zim(me)t** (fig. u. fam.): cf. der ganze **Kram**

der ganze **Zinnober** (fig. u. fam.): cf. der ganze **Kram**

ohne den üblichen **Zinnober** (fig. u. fam.): *without the usual fuss; without the usual to-do (the usual set-out; the usual fireworks) (colloq.)*

Meine Eltern wollen ihre Silberhochzeit ohne den üblichen Zinnober begehen.
*My parents want to celebrate their silver-wedding without the usual fuss (to-do; set-out; fireworks).*

**Zinsen** bringen (fig.): *to pay dividends; to bring its reward; to bear fruit; to pay (off) (colloq.)*. Cf. auch: **Wohltun** bringt Zinsen

Sein Fleiß hat Zinsen gebracht, und er hat eine gute Stelle erhalten.
*His industry has paid dividends (brought its reward; borne fruit; paid [off]), and he has obtained a good position.*

j.em mit **Zinsen** heimzahlen (fig.): *to pay s.b. back with interest; to give s.b. as good as one gets (colloq.); to pay s.b. back and more besides (colloq.)*

Diesem Grobian will ich es mit Zinsen heimzahlen.
*I am going to pay that ruffian back with interest ([and more besides]; to give that ruffian as good as I got).*

das **Zipperlein** kriegen (fig. u. fam.): *to be enough to make one sick (colloq.); to be enough to give one the gripes (sl.)*. Cf. auch: sich **grün** und blau ärgern

Da kann man doch das Zipperlein (die Gicht [Kränke]) kriegen, wenn man sieht, wie diese Arbeiter herumsitzen und ihre Zeit vergeuden.
*It is enough to make you sick (to give you the gripes) to see these workmen sitting about wasting their time.*

j.en wie eine **Zitrone** auspressen: *to squeeze s.b. dry; to bleed s.b. white; to squeeze s.b. until the pips squeak (colloq.)*

Dieser Geldverleiher hat seine Kunden wie eine Zitrone ausgepreßt.
*This moneylender has squeezed his clients dry (bled his clients white; squeezed his clients until the pips squeak).*

wie eine **Zitrone** ausgepreßt sein: cf. **absein; hundemüde** sein

gelb wie eine **Zitrone (zitronengelb)** aussehen: cf. **quittengelb** aussehen

mit **Zittern** und Zagen: cf. mit (unter) **Heulen** und Zähneklappern

die **Zivilcourage:** *the strength (courage) of one's own convictions; the moral fibre; the guts (sl.)*

Mein Onkel besitzt die Zivilcourage, gegebenenfalls auch seinem Chef zu widersprechen.
*My uncle has the strength (courage) of his own convictions (has the moral fibre [the guts]) to contradict even his boss on occasions.*

keinen **Zoll** breit nachgeben (fig.): cf. nicht **wanken** und nicht weichen

ein alter **Zopf** sein (fig.): *to be an ancient (a hoary) relic; red tape*

In der Bürokratie gibt es noch so manchen alten Zopf, den man schleunigst beseitigen sollte.
*In a bureaucracy there are many ancient (hoary) relics (there is a great deal of red tape) that one should get rid of as quickly as possible.*

**Zores** machen (fam.): *to make a fuss; to make a set-out (a to-do) (colloq.)*

Wenn du unsertwegen keinen besonderen Zores (keine . . . Umstände) machst, werden wir gern zum Essen zu dir kommen.
*If you don't make a great fuss (set-out; to-do) on our account, we shall be pleased to come and have dinner with you.*

ein heiliger **Zorn:** cf. eine blinde **Wut**

**zotteln** (fam.): cf. **bummeln** b)

**Zuck** hinter etwas machen (fam.): *to put some gip into s. th. (colloq.); to shake (to ginger) s. th. up (colloq.); to get stuck into s. th. (sl.).* Cf. auch: **Dampf** hinter etwas machen

Machen Sie mal etwas Zuck (Schwung) dahinter, damit die Arbeit schneller fertig wird.
*Put some gip into it (Shake [Ginger] it up a bit; Get stuck into it) so that the job gets finished more quickly.*

kein **Zuckerlecken** sein (fig.): cf. nicht auf **Rosen** gebettet sein

ein **Zuckermäulchen** sein (fig. u. fam.): cf. ein **Leckermaul** sein

seine **Zuflucht** nehmen (fig.): *to take (to seek) refuge; to hide*

Als er in Schwierigkeiten geriet, nahm er zu dummen Ausreden seine Zuflucht.
*When he got into difficulties, he took (sought) refuge in (hid behind) stupid excuses.*

j.en auf dem **Zug** haben (fam.): cf. einen **Pik** (eine Pike) auf j.en haben

nicht zum **Zuge** kommen (fig.): *not to make a move*

Bisher ist diese politische Partei noch nicht zum Zuge gekommen.
*Up to now this political party has not made a move.*

in den letzten **Zügen** liegen: *to be on one's last legs; to be at (to be approaching) the end of one's days; to be at death's door; to have one foot in the grave; to be on the brink of the abyss*

Unser alter Pfarrer war schon lange krank und liegt jetzt in den letzten Zügen (auf den Tod danieder; steht jetzt am Rande des Grabes [an der Schwelle des Todes]; ringt jetzt mit dem Tode).
*Our old vicar has been ill for a long while and is now on his last legs (at [is now approaching] the end of his days; is now at death's door; now has one foot in the grave; is now on the brink of the abyss).*

**zugeknöpft** sein (fig.): *to be tight-lipped; to be buttoned-up (colloq.)*

Während Onkel viel spricht, ist Tante im Gegenteil sehr zugeknöpft (einsilbig).
*Whereas my uncle talks a lot, my aunt is by contrast very tight-lipped (buttoned-up).*

die **Zügel** straff anziehen (fig.): *to keep (to take) a tight hold (a firm grip) on s. th.; to rule with a rod of iron*

Man wird die Zügel straff anziehen müssen, wenn wieder Ordnung in den Betrieb kommen soll.
*They will have to keep (to take) a tight hold (firm grip) on things (to rule with a rod of iron) if order is to be restored in that works.*

die **Zügel** fest in der Hand haben (fig.): cf. das **Heft** in der Hand haben; fest im **Sattel** sitzen

die **Zügel** in die Hand nehmen (fig.): cf. ans **Ruder** kommen

die **Zügel** lockerlassen (fig.): *to slacken the reins; to let up*

Es war ein Fehler, daß wir unsern Kindern gegenüber die Zügel lockerließen.
*It was a mistake for us to slacken the reins (to let up) where our children were concerned.*

einem Gefühl die **Zügel** schießen lassen (fig.): cf. seinen Gefühlen freien **Lauf** lassen

auf etwas **zugeschnitten** sein (fig.): *to be geared (adjusted; trimmed) to s. th.; to be tailored to suit (to meet) s. th.*

Die neuen Regierungspläne sind vorwiegend auf das Militärische zugeschnitten.
*The government's new plans are geared (adjusted; trimmed) primarily to (are primarily tailored to suit [to meet]) military requirements.*

etwas **zugute** halten: *to take s. th. into account (into consideration); to make allowance(s) for s. th.*

Dem Angeklagten wurde seine Jugend zugute gehalten.
*The defendant's youth was taken into account (consideration; Allowance was made [Allowances were made] for the defendant's youth).*

j.em (einer Sache) **zugute** kommen: *to bring benefit to s. b. (s. th.); to be of benefit to s. b. (s. th.)*

Seine Spende wird den Waisenkindern unserer Stadt sehr zugute kommen.
*His donation will bring great benefit (be of great benefit) to the orphan children of our town.*

sich auf eine Sache etwas **zugute** tun: *to pride (to flatter) o. s.; to think a lot of o. s.; to think no end of o. s. (colloq.)*

Auf seine neue Erfindung tut sich der Ingenieur viel zugute.
*This engineer greatly prides (flatters) himself on (thinks a lot [no end] of himself for) his new invention.*

etwas auf sich **zukommen** lassen (fig.): *(just) to wait for things to happen; just to let things happen; (just) to sit back and wait*

Karl mangelt es an jeglicher Initiative. Er läßt alles auf sich zukommen.
*Charles lacks any kind of initiative. He (just) waits for things to happen (just lets things happen; [just] sits back and waits).*

**Zukunftsmusik** sein (fig.): cf. ein frommer **Wunsch** sein

wie **Zunder** brennen: *to catch fire like tinder (like straw)*

Das Mädchen kam dem Feuer zu nahe, und sofort brannte sein Kleid wie Zunder.
*The girl went too near to the fire, and her dress immediately caught fire like tinder (straw).*

Es sammelt sich **Zündstoff** an (fig.): *Feeling is rising (mounting); Passions are rising (mounting); S.b.'s temper is rising (mounting)*

Seit langem hatte sich Zündstoff unter der Bevölkerung angesammelt, der nun endlich zur Explosion kam.
*Feeling (Passions) had been rising (mounting) in the population (The temper of the population had been rising [mounting]) for a long time, and it (they) finally exploded.*

sich eher die **Zunge** abbeißen, als ...: *to prefer to die than ...; to prefer to have one's tongue cut out than ...*

Ich würde mir eher die Zunge abbeißen, als dieses Geheimnis zu verraten.
*I would rather die (rather have my tongue cut out) than give away this secret.*

eine böse (lose, scharfe, spitze) **Zunge** haben (fig.): cf. ein böses (loses) **Maul** haben

etwas nicht über die **Zunge** bringen: cf. etwas nicht über die **Lippen** bringen

eine feine **Zunge** haben (fig.): *to have a fine (delicate; discriminating) palate*

Ein guter Koch muß eine feine Zunge (einen feinen Gaumen) haben.
*A good cook must have a fine (delicate; discriminating) palate.*

etwas auf der **Zunge** haben (fig.): cf. j.em auf den **Lippen** schweben

die **Zunge** hängt j.em zum Halse heraus (fig.): *to be parched (with thirst); to be as dry as a limekiln*

Nach meiner anstrengenden Arbeit hing mir die Zunge zum Halse heraus, und ich trank rasch ein Glas Bier.
*After my strenuous work I was parched ([with thirst]; was as dry as a limekiln) and quickly drank a glass of beer.*

seine **Zunge** hüten (fig.): cf. seine **Zunge** im Zaume halten

j.em die **Zunge** lösen (fig.): *to loosen s.b.'s tongue; to make s.b. open up (colloq.)*

Der Sekt hatte meinem Vater die Zunge gelöst, und er erzählte viele drollige Geschichten aus seiner Studentenzeit.
*The champagne had loosened my father's tongue (had made my father open up), and he told many comic stories of his student days.*

j.em auf der **Zunge** schweben (fig.): cf. j.em auf den **Lippen** schweben

eine schwere **Zunge** haben (fig.): *to talk thickly*

Mein Neffe hatte eine schwere Zunge, weil er viel (Alkohol) getrunken hatte.
*My nephew talked thickly because he had been drinking a lot.*

sich die **Zunge** verbrennen (fig.): cf. sich den **Mund** verbrennen

seine **Zunge** im Zaume halten (fig.): *to keep (to hold) one's tongue in check; to curb (to control) one's tongue; to watch one's tongue (one's words); not to let one's tongue run away with one*

Als er solche beleidigenden Äußerungen hörte, fiel es Onkel Wilhelm schwer, seine Zunge im Zaume zu halten (seine Zunge zu hüten) und nicht grob zu antworten.
*When he heard such insulting remarks, Uncle William found it difficult to keep (to hold) his tongue in check (to curb [control; watch] his tongue; to watch his words; not to let his tongue run away with him) and (not) make a rude reply.*

das **Zünglein** an der Waage bilden (fig.): *(just) to tip (to sway) the scales (the balance); just to make that difference*

Ihre verhältnismäßig kleine Partei bildet bei vielen Abstimmungen das Zünglein an der Waage.
*Your relatively small party (just) tips (sways) the scales (the balance; just makes that difference) in many divisions.*

einem gut **zupaß** (zupasse) kommen: *to suit s.b. down to the ground; to suit s.b. to a T; to suit s.b. fine (admirably); to fit in well with s.b.; to serve s.b.'s purpose well*

Daß wir heute schulfrei haben, kommt mir gut zupaß (zupasse; zu statten). Jetzt kann ich mein Fahrrad reparieren.
*It suits me down to the ground (to a T; fine; admirably; fits in well with me; serves my purpose well) that we've got a holiday from school today. Now I can mend my bicycle.*

j.en **zurechtstauchen (zurechtstutzen)** (fig. u. fam.): cf. j.en **abkanzeln;** j.en **anschnauzen**

sich **zusammenbrauen** (fig.): *to brew up*

Der Himmel beginnt, sich rasch zu verdunkeln. Offenbar braut sich ein Gewitter zusammen.
*The sky is beginning to darken quickly. A storm is obviously brewing up.*

sich etwas **zusammenbrauen** (fig.): *to brew s.th. (up); to hatch s.th.; to concoct s.th.; to cook s.th. (up) (colloq.)*

Ich möchte wissen, was er sich in seinem Studierzimmer zusammenbraut.
*I should like to know what he is brewing ([up]; what he is hatching [concocting]; what he is cooking [up]) in his study.*

**zusammengepfercht** sitzen (fig.): cf. gedrängt wie die **Heringe** sitzen

sich **zusammenläppern** (fam.): *to mount up; to multiply*

Obwohl wir keine großen Anschaffungen gemacht haben, haben wir in diesem Monat viel Geld ausgegeben. Die vielen kleinen Ausgaben läppern sich eben zusammen.
*Although we have not made any large purchases, we have spent a lot of money this month. The many small expenses just mount up (multiply).*

sich **zusammennehmen**: *to take hold of o.s.; to take a grip on o.s.; to pull o.s. together*

Warum hast du solche Angst vor der Prüfung? Sei doch vernünftig und nimm (reiß) dich zusammen (reiß dich am Riemen).
*Why are you so afraid of the examination? Be sensible and take hold of (take a grip on) yourself (pull yourself together).*

etwas **zusammenpfuschen** (fam.): *to put (to throw) s.th. together; to shove (to slap) s.th. together (colloq.)*

Ich bin mit userm neuen Haus nicht zufrieden. Es ist sehr nachlässig zusammengepfuscht worden.
*I am not satisfied with our new house. It has been put (thrown; shoved; slapped) together very carelessly.*

sich etwas **zusammenreimen** (fig.): *to conjure s.th. up in one's mind; to figure s.th. out; to put two and two together*

Ich kann mir durchaus zusammenreimen, wie das Unglück passiert ist.
*I can conjure up perfectly in my mind (can figure out perfectly; can easily put two and two together about) how the accident happened.*

sich **zusammenreißen**: cf. sich **zusammennehmen**

j.em etwas **zuschanzen** (fam.): cf. j.em etwas **zuschustern**

j.em etwas **zuschustern** (fam.): *to shove (to push; to shovel) s.th. (off) on to s.b. (colloq.); s.b. gets landed (saddled) with s.th. (colloq.)*

Ihm wird immer die schwierigste Arbeit zugeschustert (zugeschanzt).
*The hardest work is always shoved (pushed; shovelled [off]) on to him (He always gets landed [saddled] with the hardest work).*

einer Sache stark **zusetzen**: *to take a heavy toll of s.th.; to make great inroads into s.th.; to make a hole in s.th.* Cf. auch: ein **Loch** in den Geldbeutel fressen

Die Reparaturen an meinem Auto haben meinem Bankkonto stark zugesetzt.
*The repairs to my car have taken a heavy toll of (made great inroads into; made a big hole in) my bank balance.*

einer Sache wacker **zusprechen**: cf. beim Essen tüchtig **einhauen**

einem gut **zustatten** kommen: cf. einem gut **zupaß** (zupasse) kommen

etwas **zutage** fördern: cf. etwas an den **Tag** (ans Tageslicht) bringen

**zutage** treten: cf. an den **Tag** (ans Tageslicht) kommen

**zuviel** bekommen (fig.): cf. vor **Wut** kochen (platzen; rasen; schäumen; schnauben)

etwas **zuwege** bringen: cf. etwas zu **Wege** bringen

Der **Zweck** heiligt die Mittel (Sprichw.): *The end justifies the means (prov.)*

Tierversuche scheinen grausam zu sein, dienen aber der Menschheit. Der Zweck heiligt die Mittel.
*Experiments on animals appear cruel, but they serve mankind. The end justifies the means.*

keinen **Zweck** haben: cf. keinen **Sinn** und Verstand haben

der **Zweck** der Übung sein (fig.): *to be the (whole) point; to be the purpose (object) of the exercise*

Bei jedem Spiel ist es der Zweck der Übung, den Gegner zu schlagen.
*In every game the (whole) point (the purpose [object] of the exercise) is to beat one's opponent.*

ohne **Zweck** und Ziel: *aimlessly; pointlessly; with no fixed purpose*

Das Leben ist sinnlos, wenn man ohne Zweck und Ziel dahinlebt.
*Life is meaningless if one lives on aimlessly (pointlessly; with no fixed purpose).*

aus lauter **Zweifeln** zusammengesetzt sein: *to hang fire; not to know one's own mind; to be a mass of doubts; to hum and haw (colloq.)*

Wenn man aus lauter Zweifeln zusammengesetzt ist, kommt man nicht weit.
*If one hangs fire (does not know one's own mind; is a mass of doubts; hums and haws), one will not get far.*

auf keinen grünen **Zweig** kommen (fig.): *not to get far; not to have a rosy future; not to make a success of things; not to make a go of things (colloq.); not to hit it off (colloq.)*

Ich befürchte, daß Eva und Kurt auf keinen grünen Zweig kommen werden.
*I fear that Eva and Curt will not get far (not have a rosy future; not make a success [a go] of things; not hit it off).*

sich etwas nicht **zweimal** sagen lassen: *not to need to be told twice; not to think twice about s. th.*

Als mein Vater sagte, ich solle mir von seinem Geld eine neue Armbanduhr kaufen, ließ ich es mir nicht zweimal sagen.
*When my father said that I should buy myself a new wrist-watch with his money, I did not need to be told twice (I did not think twice).*

so sicher sein, wie **zweimal** zwei vier ist: cf. mit tödlicher **Sicherheit**

ein **zweischneidiges** Schwert sein (fig.): cf. ein zweischneidiges **Schwert** sein

**zwerchfellerschütternd** lachen: cf. sich **totlachen**

in der **Zwickmühle** sitzen (fig.): cf. in der **Klemme** sein (sitzen)

j.en **zwiebeln** (fam.): cf. j.en **drangsalieren**

j.en bewegen **zwiespältige** Gefühle: *s. b. is torn by conflicting emotions*
Da mich zwiespältige Gefühle bewegen, kann ich mich nicht recht entscheiden.
*I cannot properly make up my mind, for I am torn by conflicting emotions.*

**Zwietracht** säen: *to sow discontent (discord); to stir up trouble*
Wilhelm scheint ein wahres Vergnügen darin zu finden, überall Zwietracht zu säen.
*William appears to take a real pleasure in sowing discontent (discord; in stirring up trouble) everywhere.*

an einem **Zwirnsfaden** hängen (fig.): cf. an einem seidenen **Faden** hängen

in **zwölfter** Stunde (fig.): cf. in zwölfter **Stunde**

KARL ENGEROFF / CICELY LOVELACE-KÄUFER

# An English-German Dictionary of Idioms

Idiomatic and Figurative English Expressions with German Translations

*313 Seiten, Linson (Hueber-Nr. 6217)*

Dieser Band vermittelt dem deutschen Benutzer eine klare Kenntnis von der Vielfalt der englischen Idiomatik, bietet aber andererseits Engländern, die Deutsch sprechen oder schreiben, die Möglichkeit, für die ihnen geläufigen Wendungen ihrer Muttersprache passende deutsche Übertragungen zu finden.

Für den Ausländer bildet die große Zahl von englischen Präpositionen bekanntlich besondere Schwierigkeiten. Diese machen, zusammen mit anderen grammatischen Eigenheiten der Wortverbindung, den einen Teil des idiomatischen Bereichs aus. Der andere besteht aus metaphorischen Wendungen, Sprichwörtern und Zitaten. Im Gegensatz zu anderen Sprachen nimmt das Englische die meisten seiner idiomatischen Ausdrücke aus dem Bereich des täglichen Lebens.

Die deutschen Übertragungen in diesem Wörterbuch stellen nicht nur korrekte Übersetzungen dar, sondern machen auch deutlich, auf welcher Sprachebene ein Wort oder ein Ausdruck angewandt wird. Darüber hinaus haben die Verfasser versucht, die Ausdrücke z. B. als slang, colloquial oder vulgär zu kennzeichnen. Das Werk enthält auch all jene Amerikanismen, die heute zum festen Bestand der englischen Sprache gehören.

Die Einteilung der Wörter nach grammatischen Kategorien und die phonetische Umschreibung von Wörtern, die zwar die gleiche Schreibweise haben, sich aber in der Bedeutung oder in der Aussprache unterscheiden, ist ebenfalls eine wertvolle Hilfe für den Benutzer.

,Jeder, der die Unerläßlichkeit einer gründlichen Kenntnis der Idiomatik und der idiomatischen Wendungen erkannt hat, wird für diese umfangreiche Sammlung dankbar sein.'

*Neusprachliche Mitteilungen*

MAX HUEBER VERLAG · MÜNCHEN

*Hans-Wilhelm Klein / Wolf Friederich*

# Englische Synonymik

4., völlig neu bearbeitete und erweiterte Auflage,
920 Seiten, Linson (Hueber-Nr. 2032)


*Armin Blass / Wolf Friederich*

# Englischer Wortschatz in Sachgruppen

141 Seiten, kart. (Hueber-Nr. 2077)


*John Leyton*

# Modern English Vocabulary
# in Narrative Form

244 Seiten, kart. (Hueber-Nr. 2084)


MAX HUEBER VERLAG · D–8045 ISMANING